Financial Markets and Institutions

Visit the Financial Markets and Institutions, fifth edition
Companion Website at **www.pearsoned.co.uk/howells** to find
valuable **student** learning material including:

- Multiple choice questions to test your learning
- Written answer questions providing the opportunity to answer longer questions
- Annotated links to valuable sites of interest on the web

WITHDRAWN

PEARSON
Education

We work with leading authors to develop the strongest
educational materials in business and finance, bringing
cutting-edge thinking and best learning practice to a
global market.

Under a range of well-known imprints, including
Financial Times Prentice Hall, we craft high quality print and
electronic publications which help readers to understand
and apply their content, whether studying or at work.

To find out more about the complete range of our
publishing, please visit us on the World Wide Web at:
www.pearsoned.co.uk

FINANCIAL MARKETS AND INSTITUTIONS

Fifth Edition

Peter Howells and Keith Bain

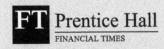

FT Prentice Hall
FINANCIAL TIMES

An imprint of **Pearson Education**

Harlow, England • London • New York • Boston • San Francisco • Toronto
Sydney • Tokyo • Singapore • Hong Kong • Seoul • Taipei • New Delhi
Cape Town • Madrid • Mexico City • Amsterdam • Munich • Paris • Milan

Pearson Education Limited
Edinburgh Gate
Harlow
Essex CM20 2JE
England

and Associated Companies throughout the world

Visit us on the World Wide Web at:
www.pearsoned.co.uk

First published under the Longman imprint 1990
Fifth edition published 2007

© Pearson Education Limited 2007

ISBN-13: 978-0-273-70919-0

British Library Cataloguing-in-Publication Data
A catalogue record for this book is available from the British Library

Library of Congress Cataloging-in-Publication Data
Howells, P.G.A., 1947–
    Financial markets and institutions / Peter Howells and Keith Bain. — 5th ed.
        p. cm.
    Includes bibliographical references and index.
    ISBN-13: 978-0-273-70919-0
    ISBN-10: 0-273-70919-4
    1. Financial institutions—Great Britain.   2. Finance—Great Britain.
I. Bain, K., 1942–   II. Title.

HG186.G7H68 2007
332.10941—dc22

                                                    2006051240

ARP impression 98

Typeset in 9.5/13pt Stone Serif by 35
Printed by bound by Ashford Colour Press, Gosport

The publisher's policy is to use paper manufactured from sustainable forests.

Contents

Preface to the fifth edition

The principal objective of this book is to help students make sense of the financial activity which these days is so prominently reported in the media. Making sense of anything requires some grasp of theory and principles. We have done what we can to minimise the use of theory, but because we want the book to be particularly useful to students on A-level and first degree courses, we have felt it necessary to explain some basic ideas in finance and economics. Much of this is in *Appendix 1: Portfolio theory*.

We try to 'make sense of' financial activity from the economist's perspective. Thus, we go to some lengths to show how financial activity has its origins in the real economy and in the need to lend and to borrow to enable real investment to take place. Similarly, when we talk about the shortcomings of financial markets and institutions, we are concerned with the effects that these shortcomings have on the functioning of the real economy. We have not produced a consumers' guide to financial products and services. Financial advisers, both actual and potential, should find much of interest here, but it is not a guide to financial products and services.

Because we want students to understand the events which they will come across, we have made frequent use of material from the *Financial Times* and from readily available statistical sources. We have gone to some pains to explain how to interpret the data from such sources. We hope this will encourage some students to update the evidence we have provided.

In preparing this latest edition, we have taken the opportunity to update figures and tables and to replace older with more recent illustrations. In response to readers' comments we have also added a new chapter on the malfunctioning of the financial system (Chapter 12) and we have restructured Chapter 6 in order to treat the pricing of bonds and equities separately.

PGAH
KB

Guided tour

Chapter Objectives – bullet points at the start of each chapter show what you can expect to learn from that chapter, and highlight the core coverage.

Boxes – provide different ways of illustrating and consolidating key points in the chapter. For example, Box 5.4 above provides information from the FT about selected instruments in the London money markets.

Key terms – provide clear definitions of key concepts in each chapter, highlighted in colour where first introduced.

Exercises – boxed in colour and interspersed throughout every chapter, providing an opportunity to practise the new calculations you will learn in each chapter. Answers to the exercises are provided at the end of each chapter.

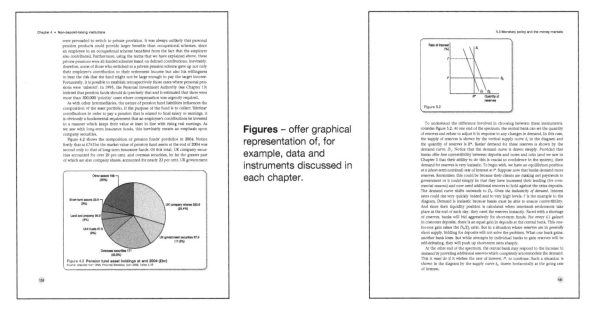

Figures – offer graphical representation of, for example, data and instruments discussed in each chapter.

Questions for discussion – at the end of each chapter are longer questions to ponder over and discuss amongst your peers in class. Answers for these can be found on the companion website.

Further reading – provides full details of sources to refer to for further information on the topics covered in the chapter.

Answers to exercises – provide answers to the boxed exercise in the chapter.

Acknowledgements

The publishers are grateful to the Financial Times Limited for permission to reprint the following material:

Box 4.3 Unit trust prices and yields, © *Financial Times*, 10/11 May 2003; Box 5.4 London money market rates, © *Financial Times*, 7 May 2003; Box 6.8 Fed's comments result in a tumble, © *Financial Times*, 10/11 May 2003; Box 6.9 Rally sends FTSE past . . . , © *Financial Times*, 7 May 2003; Box 6.10 UK Gilts – cash market, © *Financial Times*, 10/11 May 2003; Box 6.11 Food and drug retailers, © *Financial Times*, 7 May 2003; Box 7.6 UK interest rate cut surprises gilt traders, from FT.com, © *Financial Times*, 6 February 2003; Box 8.2 The market interpretation of news, © *Financial Times*, 7 February 2003; Box 9.2 Interest rate futures, © *Financial Times*, 19 March 2003.

We are grateful to the following for permission to reproduce copyright material:

Tables 2.1, 2.2 and 2.3 adapted from *Annual Accounts*, 2002 (Office of National Statistics 2002) Crown copyright material is reproduced with the permission of the Controller of HMSO and the Queen's Printer for Scotland; Tables 3.2, 3.3 and 3.5 adapted from *Monetary and Financial Statistics, January 2003* (Bank of England 2003) (all percentages are calculated by Pearson Education and not the Bank of England); Table 3.4 adapted from *Financial Statistics, December 2002* (Office of National Statistics 2002) Crown copyright material is reproduced with the permission of the Controller of HMSO and the Queen's Printer for Scotland; Figures 4.1, 4.2, 4.3 and 4.4 adapted from *Financial Statistics, February 2003* (Office of National Statistics 2003) Crown copyright material is reproduced with the permission of the Controller of HMSO and the Queen's Printer for Scotland; Tables 4.1, 6.1 and 6.2 adapted from *Financial Statistics, April 2003* (Office of National Statistics 2003) Crown copyright material is reproduced with the permission of the Controller of HMSO and the Queen's Printer for Scotland; Table 11.2 adapted from *UK Budget Report 2003* (HM Treasury at www.hm-treasury.gov.uk 2003) Crown copyright material is reproduced with the permission of the Controller of HMSO and the Queen's Printer for Scotland; Table 11.3 adapted from *Quarterly Bulletin* (Bank of England Winter 2001).

In some instances we have been unable to trace the owners of copyright material, and we would appreciate any information that would enable us to do so.

The authors would like to thank colleagues and students at the Universities of East London and the West of England who made numerous suggestions, spotted errors, criticised and encouraged. Our thanks go especially to Murray Glickman, Iris Biefang-Frisancho Mariscal and Derick Boyd.

Terms used in equations

B = monetary base

c = coupon rate

C = coupon payment

d = rate of discount

g = growth rate of earnings

i = nominal rate of interest

K = the actual return on an asset

$\hat{K}$ = the expected return on an asset

$\bar{K}$ = the required return on an asset

K_m = the rate of return on the 'whole market' portfolio or a whole market index fund

K_{rf} = the risk-free rate of return, usually equivalent to i and, in practice, normally the rate of interest on treasury bills or government bonds

M = the maturity value (of a bond or bill)

M_s = money stock

n = period to maturity

P = the purchase or market price (the price level, in the aggregate)

$\dot{P}$ = the rate of inflation

$\dot{P}^e$ = the expected rate of inflation

r = the real rate of interest

R = redemption value

σ = the standard deviation (of an asset's return)

σ^2 = the variance (of an asset's return)

y = yield

Supporting resources

Visit **www.pearsoned.co.uk/howells** to find valuable online resources

Companion Website for students
- Multiple choice questions to test your learning
- Written answer questions providing the opportunity to answer longer questions
- Annotated links to valuable sites of interest on the web

For instructors
- Instructor's Manual consisting of detailed outlines of each chapter's objectives, answers to the questions for discussion at the end of each chapter, notes on how to use weblinks and other resources
- Taking it further supplement containing notes and extra questions for each chapter, stretching the subject further and providing more advanced material

Also: The Companion Website provides the following features:

- Search tool to help locate specific items of content
- E-mail results and profile tools to send results of quizzes to instructors
- Online help and support to assist with website usage and troubleshooting

For more information please contact your local Pearson Education sales representative or visit **www.pearsoned.co.uk/howells**

CHAPTER 1

Introduction: the financial system

Objectives

What you will learn in this chapter:

- What are the components of a financial system
- What a financial system does
- The key features of financial intermediaries
- The key features of financial markets
- Who the users of the system are, and the benefits they receive

In this first chapter we want to find a preliminary answer to two questions. We want to know what is meant by the expression the 'financial system' and we want to know what such a system does.

For the purposes of this book, we shall define a financial system fairly narrowly, to consist of a set of markets, individuals and institutions which trade in those markets and the supervisory bodies responsible for their regulation. The end-users of the system are people and firms whose desire is to lend and to borrow.

Faced with a desire to lend or borrow, the end-users of most financial systems have a choice between three broad approaches. Firstly, they may decide to deal directly with one another, though this, as we shall see, is costly, risky, inefficient and, consequently, not very likely. More typically they may decide to use one or more of many organised markets. In these markets, lenders buy the liabilities issued by borrowers. If the liability is newly issued, the issuer receives funds directly from the lender. More frequently, however, a lender will buy an existing liability from another lender. In effect, this refinances the original loan, though the borrower is completely unaware of this 'secondary' transaction. The best-known markets are the stock exchanges in major financial centres such as London, New York and Tokyo. These and other markets are used by individuals as well as by financial and non-financial firms.

Alternatively, borrowers and lenders may decide to deal via institutions or 'intermediaries'. In this case lenders have an asset – a bank or building society deposit, or contributions to a life assurance or pension fund – which cannot be traded but can only be returned to the intermediary. Similarly, intermediaries create liabilities, typically in the form of loans, for borrowers. These too remain in the intermediaries'

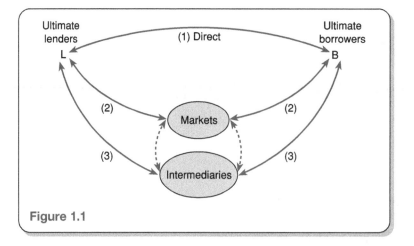

Figure 1.1

balance sheets until they are repaid. Intermediaries themselves will also make use of markets, issuing securities to finance some of their activities and buying shares and bonds as part of their asset portfolio. The choice between dealing directly, dealing through intermediaries and dealing through markets is summarised in Figure 1.1.

Helping funds to flow from lenders to borrowers is a characteristic of most components of the financial system. However, there are a number of other functions, each of which tends to be associated with a particular part of the system.

For example, the financial system usually provides a means of making payments. In most cases this is the responsibility of deposit-taking institutions (or a subset of them). Such institutions are usually members of a network (a 'clearing system') and accept instructions from their clients to make transfers of deposits to the accounts of other clients. Traditionally this was done by issuing a paper instruction (a 'cheque') but today it is done increasingly by electronic means.

We assume that most people are risk-averse. That is, they are prepared to make a payment (or sacrifice some income) in order to avoid uncertainty, especially if the uncertainty may mean the possibility of a serious loss. Among the non-deposit-taking institutions, this service is carried out by insurance companies. They allow people to choose the certainty of a slightly reduced current income (reduced by the premiums they pay) in exchange for avoiding a catastrophic loss of income (or wealth) if some accident should occur.

Pension funds, unit trusts and investment trusts all offer savers the opportunity to accumulate a diversified portfolio of financial assets, though each does it in a slightly different way. Pension funds, in particular, help people to accumulate wealth over a long period and then to exchange this for income to cover the (uncertain) period between retirement and death.

Lastly, it should always be remembered that while savers may be building up a portfolio of wealth by acquiring financial assets, they want to be able to rearrange that portfolio from time to time as they observe changes in the risk/return characteristics of the assets which they hold. If we use the phrase 'net acquisition' to describe the additional assets that a household is able to add to its portfolio each year, we must remember that total purchases of assets may be much larger because some assets already in the portfolio may have been sold as part of the portfolio adjustment process. A financial system must provide people with the means to make cheap and frequent adjustments to their portfolio of assets (and liabilities).

Box 1.1

A financial system

- channels funds from lenders to borrowers
- creates liquidity and money
- provides a payments mechanism
- provides financial services such as insurance and pensions
- offers portfolio adjustment facilities

Notice that this description of what a financial system *does* (which we have summarised in Box 1.1) is only one way of answering our second question. It is the answer that most economists would give because the activities on which it focuses are important to the functioning of the economy as a whole. Making borrowing and lending cheap and easy makes it easier for firms to invest and should, therefore, increase the rate of economic growth. An efficient payments system makes it easier to carry out transactions and encourages trade and exchange. The quantity of money in circulation, how wealthy people feel and the liquidity of their wealth are all potential influences upon the level of aggregate demand. We look at the connections between financial and real economic activity in more detail in Chapter 2.

But this is only one way of looking at what a financial system does. In the past thirty years, the UK has seen a dramatic increase in the size and complexity of its financial system. Within the categories that we list in Box 1.1 there is a much wider range of products and services than there was a generation ago. Consider the example of a mortgage loan taken out to buy the family home. Thirty years ago, such a loan would almost certainly have come from a building society. The borrower would probably have had to wait in a queue which he or she could join only after having saved for some period with the society. The loan would have been in sterling and the borrower would have paid a rate of interest which varied at short notice (broadly) with changes in the level of official interest rates imposed by the monetary authorities. The interest would have been paid monthly together with a small additional sum calculated to repay the loan over a scheduled period. In 2003, by contrast, such loans were instantly available from a range of institutions. They could be repaid by the method described above or they could be 'interest-only' mortgages in which the borrower pays only the interest but makes simultaneous payments into a long-term savings scheme (typically an endowment insurance policy) which is designed to repay the mortgage when the policy matures. The mortgage may have a rate of interest which can be fixed for long periods. The mortgage can even be arranged in a foreign currency if the borrower is convinced that a foreign interest rate will remain lower than the UK rate in future and that the pound is not going to fall in value against the foreign currency.

The point about all of this is the substantial increase in complexity that now attends the major financial decisions that most households have to make. If we assume that the relationship between financial 'consumers' and 'suppliers' is characterised by 'asymmetric information', then the increase in complexity puts consumers at an even bigger disadvantage when compared with suppliers. One consequence of this asymmetry has been a number of notable scandals where people have been sold products which were not suitable for their needs (for example, pension and endowment products). Another consequence has been the increase in the scope of financial regulation designed at least to limit the exploitation of this information advantage. A third has been the growth of a financial advice industry which one can see as allowing consumers to 'buy' additional protection for themselves by paying for information.

Seen from this consumerist perspective, Box 1.1 would look rather different. We would stress the categories of 'product' which the financial system provides. So we would focus upon 'protection products' (insurance), 'mortgage products', 'long-term savings products' (managed funds) and 'deposit products'. These, together with 'regulation' and 'advice', would be the chapter headings of this book. But, as we said above, our main interest lies with how the financial system grows out of and in return satisfies (to some degree at least) the needs of the real economy.

Thus, in this introductory chapter we shall look firstly at the institutions or intermediaries which make up part of the financial system. Then, in section 1.2, we turn our attention to financial markets (which make up another part). In section 1.3 we look at the end-users of the system and at some of the motives and principles underlying their behaviour. We can then appreciate some of the advantages that the end-users obtain from the financial system.

1.1 Financial institutions

1.1.1 Financial institutions as firms

Financial institutions are firms and their behaviour can be analysed in much the same way that economists analyse any other type of firm. Thus we can think of them as producing various forms of loans out of money which people are willing to lend.

Furthermore, we can assume that they are profit maximisers and that the profit arises from charging interest to borrowers at a rate which exceeds that paid to lenders. One characteristic of most financial firms (though this still does not make them anything special) is that they are large and therefore the profits are being maximised for shareholders rather than for 'entrepreneurs' who themselves own and manage the firms. Like any other firm, profits will be maximised at the point where total revenue minus total costs is at its greatest, that is where the marginal revenue accruing from an extra unit of output is just matched by the marginal cost of producing it. Also, quite conventionally, we can assume that the marginal cost of production is rising in the short term. Imagine, for simplicity, that a firm's output consists of loans and that the major variable input is the deposits which it can attract from members of the public who are able to save. Other things being equal, it will attract more deposits (than at present) with which to increase its production of loans only if it offers a higher rate of interest or better service (than at present). Whatever it does to get the extra deposit is likely to cost more than was involved in getting the previous marginal business.

Making the assumption that financial firms are profit maximisers, however, does not mean that we have to think of financial firms operating according to the model of perfect competition. Financial firms tend to be large and we shall see in section 1.1.3 that this is because economies of scale are very common in the production of financial products. This has inevitably led, and continues to lead, to situations where some financial business is dominated by a few, large organisations. In such cases we can observe many of the characteristics which oligopolistic theories of the firm would lead us to expect, for example, little apparent competition over prices but a great deal of effort going into marketing and product differentiation.

We can move even further away from the model of perfect competition and still stay on fairly familiar ground. We can drop the assumption of profit maximisation. There have been occasions in the recent past, particularly involving the major retail banks, when it has looked to outsiders as if decisions have been made to pursue other object- ives, at least in the short run. These other objectives might have been to increase market share at the expense of competitors, or to achieve a rate of growth (measured by the number of account holders) greater than that of their rivals. Obviously, this sort of behaviour is possible only if a certain level of profit has already been achieved and is reasonably secure, but it is quite different from rigorous profit maximisation. Even so, this still leaves the behaviour of financial firms looking very much like that of many other types of firm.

While it is important to bear in mind these similarities between financial and other types of firm, there is of course much that is distinctive about the business of financial firms: their products, and people's reasons for buying the products, are different from those of manufacturing and retail firms. For example, the decision to buy a financial 'product' often involves making a judgement about events which might develop quite a long way into the future. This is not necessary when buying goods for everyday consumption.

Furthermore, there are also significant differences between the products offered by financial firms. One distinction which is very commonly made, for example, lies between 'deposit-taking institutions' (DTIs) and 'non-deposit-taking institutions' (NDTIs). Deposit-taking institutions are organisations such as banks and building societies, whose liabilities (assets to lenders) are primarily deposits. These can be with- drawn at short (sometimes zero) notice and usually form part of the national money supply. Non-deposit-taking institutions are organisations such as life assurance com- panies whose liabilities are promises to pay funds to savers only in response to a specified event. Unless the specified event occurs, it is very difficult to withdraw these funds and there is usually a considerable financial penalty for savers who do so. Similarly, contributions to a pension fund cannot be easily withdrawn until the pension falls due for payment. We shall see in Chapters 3 and 4 that these differences in the ease with which savers can demand repayment have a major effect on what DTIs and NDTIs can do with the funds at their disposal.

The two types of intermediaries are shown in Box 1.2.

Box 1.2	Some deposit and non-deposit-taking intermediaries

Deposit takers	*Non-deposit takers*
Banks – Retail banks	Insurance companies
– Investment banks	Pension funds
– Overseas banks	Unit trusts
Building societies	Investment trusts

1.1.2 Financial institutions as 'intermediaries'

We now know that financial institutions take different forms and offer a wide range of products and services. Is there anything that they have in common? As a general rule, financial institutions are all engaged to some degree in what is called *intermediation*. Rather obviously 'intermediation' means acting as a go-between for two parties. The parties here are usually called lenders and borrowers or sometimes *surplus* sectors or units, and *deficit* sectors or units.

What general principles are involved in this 'going-between'? The first thing to say is that it involves more than just bringing the two parties together. One *could* imagine a firm which did only this. It would keep a register of people with money to lend and a register of people who wished to borrow. Every day, people would join and leave each register and the job of the firm would be to scan the lists continuously in order to match potential lenders whose desires matched those of potential borrowers. It would then charge a commission for introducing them to each other. With today's technology this would be quite easy and profitable, as many dating agencies and insurance brokers have discovered. This process, however, is not intermediation. If anything, it is best described as *broking*. When we use the term intermediation, the 'going-between' involves more than just introducing the parties to each other. Something else has to be provided.

As a general rule, what financial intermediaries do is:

to create assets for savers and liabilities for borrowers which are more attractive to each than would be the case if the parties had to deal with each other directly.

What this means is best understood if we consider an example. Take the case of a person wishing to borrow £140,000 to buy a house, intending to repay the loan over twenty years. Without the help of an intermediary, this person has to find someone with £140,000 to lend for this period and at a rate of interest which is mutually agreeable. The borrower might be successful. In that case, the lender has an asset (an interest-bearing loan) and the borrower has a liability (the obligation to pay interest and repay the loan). In practice, however, even if the would-be borrower employed a broker, it seems unlikely that the search would be successful. There are probably not many people willing to lend £140,000 to a comparative stranger, knowing that they cannot regain possession of the money for twenty years. Even if such a would-be saver were to be found, he would probably demand such a high rate of interest as compensation for the risk that no borrower would contemplate it.

> **Financial intermediary:** An organisation which borrows funds from lenders and lends them to borrowers on terms which are better for both parties than if they dealt directly with each other.

Suppose now that some form of financial intermediary like a building society were to emerge. This might operate (as societies do) by taking in large numbers of relatively small deposits on which the society itself pays interest. These could then be bundled together to make a smaller number of the large loans that people require for house purchase. Borrowers would then pay interest to the society. Obviously, this is beneficial to both parties – savers and borrowers. Savers can lend and earn interest on small sums, even though no one wishes to borrow small sums. Provided the society does not lend all the deposits but keeps some in reserve, individual savers know that they can get their deposit back at short notice. Because the conditions are so attractive to savers, the rate of interest charged to borrowers can be much lower than it otherwise would be.

If we persist with the idea of financial intermediaries as firms which, unlike brokers, *produce* something, then we may say that what they produce or create is *liquidity*. Precisely how it is that intermediaries can perform this function of creating more attractive assets and liabilities in safety (since it typically involves taking in short-term deposits and lending them on for longer periods) is something we shall discuss in more detail in the next section, after we have discussed some of the consequences of intermediation.

1.1.3 The creation of assets and liabilities

There are two general consequences of financial intermediation. The first is that there will exist more financial assets and liabilities than would be the case if the community were to rely upon direct lending. The case above makes this clear in Box 1.3. In the direct lending case, the saver acquires an asset of £140,000; the borrower incurs a liability of £140,000. Assets and liabilities each equal £140,000. If, however, an intermediary intervenes and takes in deposits of £140,000 which it then lends out, savers (depositors) have assets equal to £140,000 and the borrower has a liability equal to £140,000.

> **Asset:** Any piece of property, the ownership of which provides a flow of benefits over time.
>
> **Liability:** A debt owed to someone else.

Box 1.3 | **The creation of assets and liabilities**

(a) Direct lending

Lender			Borrower	
Liability	Asset		Liability	Asset
	140,000		140,000	
Total	140,000		140,000	

(b) Via an intermediary

Lender(s)		Intermediary		Borrower	
Liability	Asset	Liability	Asset	Liability	Asset
	40,000 ⎫				
	30,000 ⎟	140,000	140,000	140,000	
	25,000 ⎬				
	45,000 ⎭				
Total	140,000 (A)	140,000 (B)	140,000 (C)	140,000 (D)	
Total assets	(= A + C) = 280,000				
Total liabilities	(= B + D) = 280,000				

Superficially, things are as they were before. But notice, looking at the figures, that the intermediary itself has assets and liabilities. In accepting £140,000 as deposits from savers (their assets), it has simultaneously created for itself a liability (the need to pay interest and repay the deposit) of £140,000. Fortunately, on the other side of its balance sheet, it has created for itself an asset in the form of an interest-earning loan to the borrower. Total assets and liabilities in the community are now £280,000.

The second general consequence of the intervention of financial institutions is that lending and borrowing have become easier. It is now no longer necessary for savers to search out borrowers with matching needs. In this sense financial intermediaries have lowered the 'transaction costs' of lending and borrowing.

Neither will lenders have to demand such high rates of interest to compensate them for the risk and inconvenience involved in lending long term to unknown borrowers. In this sense financial intermediaries are taking on and managing the risk more effectively and cheaply than could ever be done by individuals. There are advantages to the borrower too. The borrower is saved the cost of search, and with savers willing to lend at modest interest rates, the cost of borrowing (even allowing for a margin for the intermediary) will be much lower than it would otherwise be. In the language of economics we can say that for any given rate of interest the equilibrium level of lending and borrowing will be greater in the presence of inter-mediation than it will be without it.

We shall return to these two fundamental consequences and to extensions of them many times.

So far, we have treated all financial institutions as essentially similar. For example, we said that financial institutions were much like any other sort of firm; we said that they act as 'intermediaries' whose function is to deal separately with borrowers and lenders, creating for each group liabilities and assets which are more attractive than would be the case if the two groups dealt directly with each other.

> **Liquidity:** The speed and convenience with which an asset can be converted into money for a certain value.

Creating assets which are attractive to lenders involves creating assets which are 'liquid'. A liquid asset is one which can be turned into money quickly, cheaply and for a known monetary value. Thus the achievement of a financial intermediary must be that lenders can recall their loan either more quickly or with a greater certainty of its capital value than would otherwise be the case. Notice that 'liquidity' has three dimensions: 'time' – the speed with which an asset can be exchanged for money; 'risk' – the possibility that the asset may have depreciated in value or that the issuer may have defaulted in some way on its terms (see Box 1.4); and 'cost' – the pecuniary and other sacrifices that have to be made in carrying out that exchange. However, intermediaries also have to supply the needs of borrowers in an attractive way. This includes making the loan available to the borrower for a certain period of time. How do intermediaries satisfy these apparently conflicting needs of lenders and borrowers?

Box 1.4 | **A selection of risks**

Default risk – the risk that a borrower fails to pay interest or to repay the principal at the date originally specified

Capital risk – the risk that an asset has a different value from what was expected when it is sold or matures

Income risk – the risk that the income from an asset is different from what was expected

Reinvestment risk – the risk that the rate of return available when funds from a maturing asset are reinvested in future is different from what was expected

---

Part of the answer is that intermediaries do it by *maturity transformation*. By this we mean that they accept deposits of a given maturity, i.e. deposits which are liable for repayment to lenders at a given date, and 'transform' them into loans of a quite different maturity. A good example is provided by building societies which accept deposits of a very short maturity. Indeed, some of these deposits are repayable on demand or 'at sight'. These deposits are then lent to house buyers who have the guaranteed use of the loan for up to twenty-five years.

The deposits that building societies hold, and the loans or 'advances' they have made, appear in the societies' balance sheet as liabilities and assets respectively. Of course, the societies have other assets and liabilities, but the balance sheet is dominated by deposits on the liabilities side and mortgage advances on the assets side.

Let us repeat: what we have just said in the case of building societies is typical of all financial intermediaries. Their services are attractive to lenders and borrowers alike, because they engage in maturity transformation. The degree of that transformation and of course the precise nature of the liabilities and assets involved will differ between institutions. Notice that we have used banks and building societies (i.e. deposit-taking institutions) to illustrate the process. This is because the process of intermediation is central to their activities. This is principally what they do. When we turn to NDTIs, however, intermediation itself becomes less central and more a by-product of their other activities. in the case of unit and investment trusts, for example, we shall see in sections 4.3 and 4.4 that we have to look quite hard to find the intermediation activity. But some degree of intermediation is always involved which is why the terms financial institution and financial intermediary are some-time used interchangeably.

We said a moment ago that maturity transformation is part of the answer to the question of how intermediaries reconcile the desires of lenders and borrowers. Since lenders want liquidity and borrowers want a loan for a certain, minimum period, then clearly what lenders are willing to lend has to be 'transformed' into something that borrowers want. This raises an interesting (and important) question: 'How are inter-mediaries able to carry out this transformation?' In particular, how are they able to do it in safety, avoiding the risk that lenders may want repayment at short notice when their funds have been lent-on by the intermediary for a long period? This question is obviously most pressing for DTIs where depositors are entitled to repayment *on demand*, i.e. without notice, while borrowers may have borrowed for long periods.

The ability of financial institutions to engage in maturity transformation and to supply the other characteristics of liquidity depends fundamentally upon *size*. The advantages of size come in a number of forms.

> **Maturity transformation:** The conversion of funds lent for a short period into loans of longer duration.

Firstly, with a large number of depositors firms will expect a steady inflow of deposits and a steady outflow of deposits each day. To a large extent the flows will cancel each other out and intermediaries will be subject only to small *net* inflows and outflows. What is more, it is a statistical fact that the behaviour of these flows will be more stable the larger the number of depositors, and the greater will be the confidence that firms can place upon the net flow. Of course, the magnitude of these net flows will change as circumstances change. For example, if competing institutions raise their interest rates, a firm will experience a deterioration in its net flow. But once again, the larger the number of depositors, the more stable and predictable will be the relation-ship between net flows and other variables. Large size therefore reduces the risk to the intermediary of unforeseen outflows and enables it to operate with relatively few very liquid reserve assets. The rest can be made up of illiquid, interest-earning loans.

Secondly, the larger the volume of deposits which a firm controls, the larger the assets it will also be holding. The larger the volume of assets it has, the greater the scope available for arranging those assets in such a way that a proportion matures at regular intervals. It may well be, as with building societies, that each individual asset (mortgage loan) is long term and illiquid when first acquired, but with a very large number of such loans on its books a society can ensure that there is a steady flow of maturing loans. In the last paragraph we saw that large size reduced the risk of an unforeseen outflow of deposits; now we can say that if there were such an unforeseen outflow, large size helps to ensure a steady flow of funds from which to meet it. The more accurate the assessment of net flows, the smaller the proportion of assets that have to be held in very liquid form and the greater the degree of potential maturity transformation.

Let us repeat then, the behaviour of financial firms is similar in that they engage in maturity transformation and they are able to do this for reasons which stem from their size.

The second function which intermediaries perform in the creation of liquidity is *risk transformation* or more precisely *risk reduction*. Risk comes in a number of forms. One can think of risk in terms of 'default' – the possibility that the lender is not able to meet the terms on which it was issued. This may mean an inability to meet interest payments or even an inability to repay the lender at the end of the period. On the other hand, one may wish to emphasise the different ways in which some sort of default may arise. One might then distinguish between 'capital' risk – the possibility that when the lender comes to dispose of the asset its value differs from what had been expected – and 'income' risk – the possibility that the asset pays a return which differs from what had originally been expected or, more subtly, the possibility that its return relative to that on other assets differs from expectations. Notice that we describe 'risk' here as the possibility that actual outcomes *differ* from expectations. Risk does not mean that outcomes have to be *worse* than expectations.

> **Risk transformation:** The reduction in risk that can be achieved by diversification of lending and by screening of borrowers.

Financial intermediaries are able to reduce risk through a number of devices. The two principal ones are diversification and specialist management. We shall see that economies of scale are present here, too, as they were with maturity transformation.

It seems intuitively obvious that holding just one asset is more likely to produce unexpected outcomes than holding a collection or 'portfolio' of assets. We are all familiar with the danger of 'putting all our eggs in one basket'. This is the basis on which savers are encouraged to buy units in a unit trust or to save through a life assurance policy. The managers of the funds can collect the income from a large number of small savers and then distribute it among a much wider variety of securities than an individual saver could possibly do. Precisely the same process is at work with deposit-taking intermediaries. A bank or building society accepts a large number of small deposits, creates a large pool and then distributes that pool among a large number of borrowers who use the loans for many different purposes. (The pool also enables the intermediary to adjust the size of loans to the needs of borrowers which will usually be much larger than the size of the average deposit.) Clearly, the larger the size of the institution, the larger its pool of funds. Since the cost of setting up a loan, or buying securities, is more or less constant regardless of size, large loans and large security purchases have lower unit transaction costs than small ones. A large institution therefore has the advantage that it can diversify widely even though it deals in large investments.

> **Diversification:** The holding of many (rather than a few) assets.

Precisely why and how diversification leads to a reduction in risk is a complex, technical question. Our intuition tells us that it must be something to do with the fact that assets do not all behave in the same way at the same time and that therefore the behaviour of one asset will on some occasions cancel out the behaviour of another. The key certainly does lie in the fact that there is less than perfect 'correlation' between movements in asset prices and returns. What is harder to understand is that by combining assets in a portfolio one can actually reduce the risk of the portfolio below the average risk of the assets which comprise it. We deal with this issue more formally in Appendix I, but Box 1.5 provides a simple illustration of the risk-reducing effect of diversification.

In addition to being able to pool investors' funds and distribute them across a wide diversity of assets, intermediaries offer the risk-reducing benefit of specialist expertise. It is extremely difficult, and therefore costly, for individual savers to research the status of those to whom they might be tempted to lend. Most quality newspapers contain a business section which, especially at weekends, devotes space to company news and share prices, sometimes even offering 'tips'. Even so, in cases like this where information about the borrower is available, it is likely to be of poorer quality than that which an intermediary can acquire through continuous management of funds. And here again economies of scale are at work. As more information (or experience) is acquired it becomes easier to spot the essential characteristics of borrowers and their projects which make them high, medium or low risk and sources of high, medium and low returns.

> **Transaction costs:** The time and/or money used in carrying out the exchange of assets, goods or services.

The third contribution which intermediaries can make to liquidity is their reduction in *transaction costs*. At one extreme, one can imagine the costs, pecuniary and otherwise, of direct lending where an individual lender has to search for a borrower and then arrange for an individually negotiated, legally binding contract to be drawn up. More realistically, one can imagine the costs to a lender of trying to diversify modest savings through numerous holdings of equities on each of which a minimum commission has to be paid. Even assuming a 'buy and hold' policy where no further

Box 1.5

The gains from diversification

Imagine an investor faced with the opportunity to invest in either or both of two shares, A and B, the returns on which behave independently. Suppose that both are expected to yield a return of 20 per cent in 'good' times and 10 per cent in 'bad' times. Assume furthermore that there is a 50 per cent probability of each share striking good and bad conditions. Then it follows that investing wholly in A or wholly in B produces the expected return:

$$K = 0.5(20\%) + 0.5(10\%) = 15\%$$

Notice that although the expected return averaged over a period of time will be 15 per cent per year, in any one year there is a 50 per cent chance of getting a high return and a 50 per cent chance of getting a low return. Savers can be sure that whatever they get it will not be the expected return!

Now consider the possible outcomes if one half of the investor's funds are allocated to each of A and B. Since good and bad conditions can arise independently for each of A and B, it follows that four outcomes are possible, each of course with an equal probability of 0.25. The outcomes and the returns associated with each are:

Outcome	A	B	Return
1	Good	Good	20%
2	Good	Bad	15%
3	Bad	Good	15%
4	Bad	Bad	10%

Over the years, the expected return will be:

$$K = 0.25(20\%) + 0.25(15\%) + 0.25(15\%) + 0.25(10\%) = 15\%$$

The expected return is still 15 per cent, but notice that instead of a zero chance of getting that return in any one year, there is now a 50 per cent chance of getting it. It is now the most likely outcome!

transaction costs are involved until the sale of the equities, the costs will be very high, unit costs rising dramatically with the decreasing size of the purchase. Such costs will be much higher than the 5 per cent initial and 1 per cent per annum management charge that a unit trust management can charge because of the low unit transaction costs it incurs by purchasing large blocks of securities.

The same process is at work with deposit-taking institutions. One standard contract covers each class of deposit. Similarly one standard contract will suffice for a very large number of loans. The institutions' search costs are driven almost to zero for large institutions because their high street presence means that lenders and borrowers bear most of the cost of search by coming to them. For most routine lending and borrowing the cost is limited to the effort of walking in off the street. The cost or 'price' of intermediation by deposit-taking institutions is represented by the 'spread' or differential between the interest rate paid to depositors and the rate charged to lenders.

Suppose, for example, that a borrower were to set out with the intention of borrowing *directly* from a lender and that somewhere in the economy a lender sets out with the intention of lending directly to a borrower. Suppose further that they each have in mind the same acceptable rate of interest, *i*. On top of this, however, the borrower has to pay substantial additional costs (of search, contract, etc.) and from this rate of interest the lender has to deduct similar costs. In both cases these can be expressed as a percentage of the sum lent. Let us call these costs c_b and c_l, respectively. Then it follows that the net return to the lender and the gross cost to the borrower can be written as follows:

$$i_l = i - c_l$$

$$i_b = i + c_b$$

Suppose now that an intermediary is able to bring the two parties together and provide an agreement and carry out all the other administrative work for a cost, c_i, which is less than the total costs of the borrower and lender dealing directly. That is:

$$C_i < (C_1 + C_b)$$

Then it follows that the borrower and lender would be better off dealing through an intermediary, provided that the intermediary's charge for its services, the price of intermediation p_i, were less than the saving in transaction costs. That is, provided that:

$$p_i < (c_1 + c_b) - c_i$$

Typically, deposit intermediaries engage in some element of price discrimination so that for large customers, where the economies of scale are most evident in low unit costs, p_i may be as low as 1 per cent.

In this section we have seen how financial intermediaries can (a) create additional assets and liabilities in an economy by taking funds from lenders and transferring them to borrowers, and (b) make those additional assets and liabilities more attractive to borrowers and lenders than the original assets and liabilities would have been. This describes accurately the fundamental activity of most types of financial intermediary.

However, in Chapter 3 we shall see that there is one group of intermediaries who can go one step further than creating just liquid assets. Banks can create money. This is possible because the liabilities which they create for themselves (assets to the general public, remember) are deposits and in most financial systems these make up the bulk of the money supply. At the moment, it is necessary only to understand *why* the monetary nature of bank liabilities enables banks to create deposits. The 'moneyness' of deposits is important in two ways.

Firstly, it ensures that a decision to lend (an asset decision) leads automatically to the creation of additional liabilities and thus an expansion of the balance sheet. This happens because when a bank makes a loan to a customer and the customer uses that loan to make payment, someone else *must* receive a corresponding addition to his/her bank deposit. Even if the payment was unexpected and the recipient turns her additional deposit into something else (new books, perhaps), the new deposit is not destroyed. It passes to the bookshop, as a *bank* deposit. It cannot escape (unless the recipient chooses to exchange some of it for notes and coin, which simply increases the quantity of money in another way). The deposit created by the loan stays on the collective balance sheet of the banking system. If only one bank lends, of course there is no guarantee that the deposit stays on *its* balance sheet, but if all banks expand their lending, then all banks receive corresponding additional deposits. Collectively, therefore, an expansion of bank loans (assets) is automatically accompanied by the creation of deposits (liabilities).

This is not true for other financial intermediaries. Imagine that a life assurance company were prepared to make me a loan. It creates a loan for me by lending me some of its bank deposits. When I draw on that loan I pass what were the life company's deposits to someone else, and that someone else is most unlikely to be another life company. For the loan to create a matching liability for the life company, I should need to borrow from the life company in order to buy a life policy from them. This is not impossible, but it is unlikely and very far removed from the fact that a borrower from a bank *has virtually no alternative* but to 'redeposit' the loan somewhere in the banking system.

Secondly, and much simpler to understand, even if I did use my life company loan to buy a policy and expand the life company's business, what is expanded is the total number of life insurance policies. And life insurance policies, while they are certainly financial assets and have some degree of liquidity, are certainly not money.

We deal with banks, and their ability to create money, at some length in section 3.3.

1.1.4 Portfolio equilibrium

Another characteristic which financial institutions of all kinds have in common is the need to arrange their portfolios of assets and liabilities so as to maximise some objective – usually, we assume, profit. As private sector firms they will be motivated by profit. At any given volume of business, therefore, it follows from this that firms will be looking to minimise their costs and maximise their revenue. Costs for financial institutions include staff, premises and the cost of attracting deposits. Revenue comes from interest, dividends and other income from their assets, together with other charges which they make to users of the services they provide. We want here to consider the implications of this for the management of institutions' balance sheets.

> **Portfolio:** A collection of assets (or liabilities).

On the deposit side, they will be looking to borrow as cheaply as they can. This is not necessarily the same thing as borrowing at the lowest rate of interest, however. Some very low- or even zero-interest deposits may have substantial costs attached to them if they are held in accounts which themselves are expensive to service. People hold non-interest-bearing sight deposits with banks, for example, but the deposits are paid for by the banks via the cost of the money transmission and other services that go with such accounts.

Attempts to minimise the costs of deposits take many forms. For example, financial institutions are often willing to pay marginally higher interest rates on 'whole-sale' deposits, say sums of over £100,000, on the grounds that the cost per pound attracted is ultimately less than would be the case if the £100,000 were attracted in several small amounts. This results from the administrative costs of 'servicing' customer accounts, even where these are time deposits involving no cheque book or other facilities.

Another example is a variation on the practice of 'price discrimination'. Sometimes, firms calculate that it is worth paying a higher rate of interest in order to attract marginal deposits, provided that the higher rate is confined largely to those marginal deposits alone and does not have to be paid on all those deposits they already have. Thus they offer a higher rate on a new type of account offering in effect a new product. The new product has rules and other features which differentiate it slightly from existing products, and firms hope the different features, combined with depositors' inertia, will prevent a large-scale switch out of existing deposits into the new, higher-yielding ones.

On the asset side of the balance sheet firms will be looking to maximise revenue. Other things being equal, firms will prefer to hold assets with high yields to those with low. Later, in Table 3.3, we shall see for example that a large proportion of bank assets take the form of advances or loans to the public. By comparison, their holdings of other assets are very small indeed. This reflects the fact that the yield on advances is comparatively high. Borrowers are likely to have to pay interest of between 1 and 4 per cent more than banks themselves pay for wholesale deposits. By comparison the current yield on 'investments' is likely to be very close to wholesale deposit rates while notes and coin and deposits at the Bank of England yield nothing at all.

In the circumstances, it seems sensible to ask why institutions bother to hold low- or zero-yielding assets at all. The answer introduces a general principle which plays a part in the behaviour of all financial institutions and of lenders and borrowers. This is that while they will be looking to hold assets which yield a high income, they will also want to hold some assets at least which can be turned very quickly into money should they have to meet an unexpected demand for withdrawals by depositors. Unfortunately, the more liquid an asset, the lower its yield is likely to be. There is thus a trade-off involved, and people will be looking all the time for an 'optimum' mixture of assets and liabilities where 'optimum' means balanced for liquidity and yield or, as it is more frequently put, balanced for risk and return. When people are holding their preferred distributions of assets and liabilities, their portfolios are said to be *in equilibrium*. The idea that portfolios are generally in equilibrium and that disturbances are very quickly accommodated is important in understanding the voluntary behaviour of agents. It is also crucial to an understanding of how the authorities try to influence the behaviour of agents (for monetary policy purposes, for example). For both these reasons we shall be looking in more detail at the structure of institutions' portfolios in Chapters 3 and 4.

1.2 Financial markets

In economics a market is an organisational device which brings together buyers and sellers. Textbooks usually hurry on to point out that a market does not have to have a physical location, though plainly it could do so. For example, until October 1986 trading in stocks and shares in the UK was concentrated on the physical location of the London Stock Exchange trading floor. With the introduction of new technology, however, dealers have since dispersed to their companies' offices. In fact, financial markets offer some of the best examples of buyers and sellers interacting over a widely dispersed geographical area. Markets for foreign exchange, for example, of necessity 'bring together' buyers and sellers in different countries. The latest communication technology now permits financial institutions in the US to deal in shares in Tokyo as readily as they can in New York. This is not just a technological marvel. As we shall see when we come to discuss the regulation of financial activity, the 'internationalisation' of financial markets has serious implications.

> **Financial market:** An organisational framework within which financial instruments can be bought and sold.

1.2.1 Types of product

What is it that is traded in financial markets? Normally, the expression 'financial market' is used in reference to a market wherein some sort of financial product is being traded. By product we simply mean what we have hitherto been referring to as an asset or liability. As a briefer alternative to 'asset and liability' it is common to talk about the trading of financial *claims*.

Claims exist in many specific forms. The specific form which a claim takes is a financial *instrument*. Table 1.1 gives a brief exemplary list of such instruments. The table is useful in that it indicates something of the range of instruments in existence and also because it enables us to distinguish certain broad categories of instrument.

Table 1.1 A selection of instruments

- Bank deposits
- Building society deposits
- National Savings certificates
- Treasury bills
- Government bonds
- Commercial bills
- Equities
- Life insurance policies
- Eurobonds
- Certificates of deposit

It is because instruments differ and therefore meet the needs of different sorts of borrower and lender that we talk of financial markets, i.e. in the plural.

There are various ways in which we can group markets together in order to assess their closeness to one another. Firstly, we could divide our list of instruments into those which can be *traded directly between holders* of such claims and those which cannot. Company shares and government stock, for example, once created can be bought and sold in organised markets without their original issuers ever again being involved. Instruments which can be bought and sold between third parties are known as *securities*. National Savings certificates and building society deposits, by contrast, cannot be bought and sold in this way. The only way to 'dispose' of such an asset is to 'sell' it back to its originator.

> **Discretionary financial saving:** Day-to-day decisions to acquire financial assets of varying kinds and in varying quantities.
>
> **Contractual financial saving:** The regular acquisition of a financial asset of a kind, of an amount and on a date specified in a contract.

Exercise 1.1 **Classifying financial products**

Take the financial section of a weekend newspaper and:

(a) Count the total number of financial products being advertised for savers.

(b) Classify them into those offered by deposit-taking institutions and those offered by non-deposit-taking institutions.

(c) Reclassify them into those which savers can acquire as they wish (or *at their discretion*) and those which they have to buy regularly (or *contractually*).

Alternatively, one could distinguish instruments which are *issued with a fixed rate of interest* for as long as they exist – government bonds, for example – from those assets whose yield varies according to market conditions. The latter category includes a wide range of claims from bank deposits to company shares.

A very popular basis for distinguishing types of instrument is *maturity*. This means the length of time which has to elapse before the claim is repaid. This may be very long. With company shares, for example, it is theoretically infinity. Some government stocks are issued with twenty-five years to maturity. Contrast this with treasury bills which are issued for ninety-one days or even bank deposits which can be demanded immediately or 'at sight'. Traditionally, differences of maturity have been used, as in Table 1.2, to create a distinction between 'capital' markets (markets for long-term claims) and 'money' markets (markets for very short-term claims).

> **Maturity:** The length of time that has to elapse before an asset matures or is repaid. Occasionally 'initial maturity', the time to maturity from the day the asset is first created; more frequently 'residual maturity', the remaining time to maturity reckoned from today.

Table 1.2 'Capital' and 'money' markets

Capital markets	
	● The market for bonds
	● The market for equities
	● The market for mortgages
	● The eurobond market
Money markets	● The discount market
	● The interbank market
	● The certificate of deposit market
	● The local authority market
	● The eurocurrency market

Exercise 1.2

The liquidity of financial assets

Take any six of the financial products which you identified in Exercise 1.1 and rank them for liquidity, beginning with the most and finishing with the least liquid. Use the characteristics we discussed in section 1.1.3 to guide you.

But be warned. As financial innovation continues, as new markets and new types of instrument are developed, the degree of interdependence is increasing. Furthermore, the deregulation of financial markets, a feature of policy in both in the UK and US in the 1980s, has also helped to reduce barriers between financial markets and institutions. In Chapter 3 we shall see that the lowering of demarcations between banks and building societies has had substantial repercussions for UK monetary policy. All of these distinctions between types of financial market are becoming more difficult to maintain.

The behaviour of financial markets, like the behaviour of other markets, can be analysed using the apparatus of conventional economics. We can talk about the supply of, the demand for, the utility and sacrifice involved in consuming and producing financial instruments. However, the way in which we approach the analysis depends upon whether we are dealing with instruments which can be traded between third parties or whether we are dealing with trading between the buyer and the originator of the instrument. In sections 1.2.2 and 1.2.3 we analyse the market for this latter type of instrument. The seller is ultimately responsible for the supply. The buyer is dealing therefore with the creator of the instrument. In section 1.2.4 we shall point out briefly that the details of this analysis are not directly applicable to markets for securities where trade is between third parties as in the markets for company shares, government bonds and so on. The analysis of these very important markets is more complex and is postponed until Chapters 5 and 6.

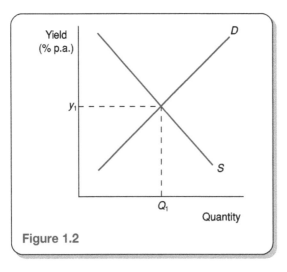

Figure 1.2

1.2.2 The supply of financial instruments

What we have in Table 1.1 is a list of claims which are, obviously, assets to people holding them and liabilities to those who issue them. Sometimes the issuer is an ultimate borrower (as in the case of government stock or company shares), sometimes it is an intermediary (as in the case of building society and bank deposits). For all of these claims there is a market. Sometimes the supply is undertaken by a number of institutions which compete among themselves. This happens when banks and building societies are in competition to offer deposit facilities to members of the public. It happens, too, when a firm makes a new issue of shares. They have to be priced and offered in such a way as to make them attractive to would-be buyers in the light of shares being newly issued by other firms. Sometimes, however, there is a monopoly supplier, as in the case of government stock and National Savings certificates.

The yield that issuers of these instruments have to pay in order to make them attractive is a cost to the issuer. Thus, other things being equal, one would expect the supply of such claims or instruments to fall as yields rise. In Figure 1.2, therefore, because we have yield on the vertical axis, the supply curve slopes downwards to the right.

1.2.3 The demand for financial instruments

As people increase their holdings of instruments, we should expect the marginal utility attaching to each holding to diminish. Thus, as shown in section 1.1.4, there will come a point ('portfolio equilibrium') when the sacrifice involved in holding any claim is just matched by the marginal utility gained from holding it. In such a position, people will increase their holdings of an instrument only if its marginal utility increases. Since a major component of the marginal utility of a financial asset is its yield, we may now say that (starting from equilibrium) there will be an

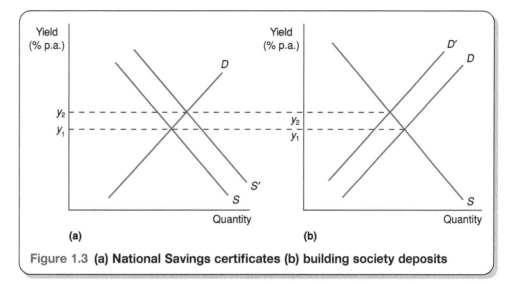

Figure 1.3 (a) National Savings certificates (b) building society deposits

increased willingness to hold any kind of financial instrument if, other things being equal, its yield increases. The demand curve for such assets, therefore, is upward sloping in Figure 1.2, and the market for the claim in question will be in equilibrium at a yield of y_1.

When we talk of financial markets (in the plural) we must be careful not to exaggerate the degree of differentiation. While the instruments in our list above are sometimes very different from one another, for example eurobonds and National Savings certificates, many of the claims are very close substitutes. From this it follows that a disturbance in one market will have a significant effect upon several others. Suppose that the public regards National Savings instruments as close alternatives to building society deposits. Parts (a) and (b) of Figure 1.3 show the market for each initially in equilibrium at a yield of y_1. If the government's borrowing needs then require it to issue more National Savings certificates, the supply curve in (a) will move to S'. The yield will rise towards y_2. Because they are close substitutes, however, this will cause a leftward shift of the demand curve in (b), as people move out of building society deposits towards National Savings. This causes the yield on building society deposits to rise. The transfer of buyers from one market to the other will cease when the yields are again equalised and this, according to the figure, will occur at y_2. The extent of the rise in yields depends upon the slope of the demand curve in (a). This in turn depends upon the willingness of people to move out of building society deposits, i.e. upon the substitutability of building society deposits and National Savings certificates.

1.2.4 Stocks and flows in financial markets

In sections 1.2.2 and 1.2.3 we saw how the basic ideas of supply and demand could be applied to the market for those kinds of financial instruments, like building society deposits, which are not traded between third parties.

Our analysis proceeded exactly as it would do for any other good or service with one exception: the demand and supply curves had the opposite of their normal slope. We must be careful not to exaggerate the importance of this. It arose only because we had 'yield' on the vertical axis where normally we would have 'price'. In fact, even this is not a very significant difference from the usual case. We have already mentioned fixed-interest bonds. In Chapter 6 we shall see that the price of any instrument whose rate of interest is fixed at the time of issue must vary inversely with movements in market interest rates. Thus we could analyse our markets for building society deposits and National Savings certificates as if these instruments bore a fixed rate of interest but fluctuated in price. It would not seem very realistic but it would be analytically quite correct. Then we could have price on the vertical axis and the curves would have their normal slopes. The supply curve for such instruments would slope upwards, showing that as the price rose (and yield fell), ultimate borrowers or intermediaries would be willing to issue more; the demand curve would slope downwards, showing that as the price fell (and yield rose), lenders would be willing to buy more of such instruments.

Let us repeat: the unusual slope of the curves in Figures 1.2 and 1.3 is not important. What is much more important is the fact that the supply curve has any slope at all. What the slope tells us is that more of the instrument in question will be supplied the higher its price (or the lower its yield). This is what one would expect for most goods and services. It is not, however, typical for all financial instruments. The cases we were looking at above involved 'non-securitised instruments'. This means that the supplier of the instrument, the person or firm offering it 'for sale', is also the creator of that instrument. Again, this is what is normally envisaged in market analysis. As the price of a good rises, a profit-maximising firm increases its production so as to equate marginal cost with the (now) higher marginal revenue or price. The increase in price calls forth a flow of additional output. This is what happens when the demand for building society deposits increases. Funds flow into the societies, which happily create new deposits, lowering the rate of interest on those deposits if the inflow is sufficiently large. A sufficiently large outflow of deposits, on the other hand, will require building societies to raise the yield on deposits, as in Figure 1.3(b).

However, in the markets for securities, where financial instruments are traded between third parties, the buyer is rarely buying from the producer of the good. Take, for example, the case of ordinary company shares. A decision to buy shares is not normally a decision to buy new shares from the company that issued them. It is a decision to buy shares from someone who currently holds some of the existing stock of shares and it does nothing to increase their supply. Equally, a generalised increase in demand for ICI shares does nothing directly to increase the supply of ICI shares. It indicates an increased desire on the part of the share-owning public to hold the *existing stock of shares*. Nothing in the immediate future is going to happen to increase the quantity of ICI shares in existence. All that can happen is that this increase in demand causes a rise in price. In terms of supply and demand analysis, whether we have yield or price on the vertical axis, the supply curve will be vertical.

We shall look at the markets for securities in Chapters 5 and 6 and see that their behaviour departs in various ways from that suggested by conventional market analysis.

1.3 Lenders and borrowers

In this section, we want to discuss people's reasons for lending and borrowing and the differing needs of lenders and borrowers that financial intermediaries have to try to meet. In modern economies, where savers make their surplus available to borrowers via financial intermediaries, it is sometimes useful to refer to the savers and borrowers as *ultimate lenders* and *ultimate borrowers*. This enables us to distinguish their behaviour from that of the intermediaries themselves who are also 'lending' (to ultimate borrowers) and 'borrowing' (from ultimate lenders) and frequently lending and borrowing between themselves. It is ultimate lenders and borrowers that we are concerned with here.

> **Ultimate lenders:** Agents whose excess of income over expenditure creates a financial surplus which they are willing to lend.
>
> **Ultimate borrowers:** Agents whose excess of expenditure over income creates a financial deficit which they wish to meet by borrowing.

1.3.1 Saving and lending

In any developed economy there will be people and organisations whose incomes are greater than they need to finance their current consumption. The difference between current income and consumption we call *saving*. The saving could be used to buy 'real' assets, that is to say machinery, industrial premises and equipment, for example, in which case as well as saving they would be *investing*. However, many people will be saving at a level which exceeds their spending on physical investment. Indeed, in the personal sector there will be people who save but undertake no physical investment at all. The difference between saving and physical investment is their *financial surplus*. It is this surplus that is available for *lending*.

What conditions have to be met to induce those with a surplus to lend? We can say that in their choice of asset, lenders will be seeking to minimise risk (often expressed as maximising liquidity) and to maximise return. We know from section 1.1.3 that risk comes in a number of forms. We distinguished, for example, between 'capital' and 'income' risk and said that both might arise from someone else's default or simply from market conditions. One situation which both borrowers and lenders have to anticipate is the risk of needing early repayment (for lenders) and the risk of being called to make early repayment (for borrowers). For lenders this poses a particular form of capital risk and explains why lenders are generally prepared to trade liquidity for return. A lender who needs to dispose of an asset unexpectedly wishes to do so quickly, cheaply and in the knowledge that the proceeds of the sale are fairly certain. These are the joint characteristics of liquidity. In the absence of these characteristics, a lender requiring unexpected repayment faces capital risk since any asset – even a house – can be sold quickly if the seller is prepared to face a sufficiently large capital loss. If we express our objective in liquidity terms, therefore, liquidity and its component characteristics are thus one feature that lenders will wish to maximise, *ceteris paribus*. Alternatively, we can express the same objective as a minimisation of risk.

The second characteristic which lenders will look at, again with a view to maximisation, is *return*. The return on a financial asset may take a number of forms. It may take the form of an interest payment at discrete intervals. This interest payment may be fixed at the outset of the loan or it may vary, but, fixed or variable, it will be paid to the lender for so long as the loan is outstanding. Notice, because it will be important later, that if an asset pays a fixed rate of interest, as do government bonds, for example, then movements in market interest rates will make that asset more or less attractive. If market rates rise above the level paid on a fixed-interest asset, that asset will be less attractive than current alternatives and its price will fall. If market rates fall, it will become more attractive and its price will rise.

Another form which yield may take is the dividend. Unlike a rate of interest which has to be paid for as long as the loan is outstanding, a dividend payment normally reflects the ability of the borrower to pay. Thus in a good year, the borrower may pay the lender a large dividend, but in a poor year the dividend may be small or even non-existent. Entitlement to a dividend, therefore, normally indicates that the lender is sharing in the risk of the borrower's business.

A third source of yield, which may be less obvious than either of these, is the yield that comes from an appreciation in the capital value of the asset. Clearly, many people hold company shares not just for the dividends paid out annually but because they expect the value of the shares to rise over time. Government stock which bears a fixed rate of interest also has a fixed date and a fixed value at which it will be redeemed. If market interest rates have forced the market value of a stock below its redemption value, buying the stock and holding it to redemption will produce a guaranteed capital gain which can be expressed as an annual rate of return over the rest of its life. Some assets, treasury bills for example, have no interest paid on them but are sold 'at a discount' to their redemption value. In this case the yield consists entirely of capital gain.

Thirdly, lenders will wish to minimise transaction costs. There is little point in finding a lending opportunity which seems to offer a superior rate of return if the charges for entering into the commitment absorb the margin over the next best rate of return. This is a problem that confronts many small lenders in particular. The commissions charged for buying stocks and shares, for example, often have a minimum threshold which makes the commission a large fraction of a small purchase of shares. Many personal pension plans sold in the 1980s allowed pension funds to levy charges for setting up the contract, which meant that many savers would have earned a better overall ('net') rate of return by making their own contributions into a mutual fund.

Finally, before leaving this discussion of saving and lending, notice that we sometimes need to distinguish between 'net' and 'gross' lending. We have said that a financial surplus is what people have available to lend. However, people may appear to lend in excess of that surplus. This arises because in any period of time people may be both borrowers and lenders. For example, under tax rules at the time of writing a home-owner with no mortgage may find it profitable not just to lend his or her current financial surplus but to take out a mortgage on the house and to lend the borrowed funds. More importantly, when we come to consider the behaviour of groups of agents, for example the personal sector, we shall find that the aggregate surplus is the difference between a much larger total of individual surpluses and a large number of individual deficits. The amount of 'gross' lending that takes place, therefore, is very much greater than the 'net' lending which must be equal to the financial surplus.

1.3.2 Borrowing

At the same time as some people have income which they do not wish to spend entirely upon current consumption, there will be those firms, people and public authorities whose expenditure plans exceed their income. These plans can be realised only if their owners either draw on past savings or engage in *borrowing*. The plans may be to spend on 'real' assets. These in turn may be of two types: 'investment' or 'capital' goods as bought by firms to assist in producing more goods; or consumer goods, usually of the 'durable' kind whose initial cost is high in relation to income but which will provide a flow of benefits over several years. In certain circumstances, however, one can envisage people borrowing in order to acquire 'financial' assets. This would occur in situations such as the initial sale of BP shares in 1987 where people thought that the gains from acquiring the asset would be greater than the cost of the liability (the debt into which they were entering) by borrowing to buy the shares.

The interests of borrowers are mainly twofold. Firstly, they will wish to minimise *cost*. The cost to the borrower is the yield to the lender and may take any of the forms which we have just been discussing.* It is worth noting, however, that while as a general rule borrowers will obviously be looking to borrow in the cheapest way, they may have preferences about the way in which they meet this cost and therefore about the sort of liabilities they incur. For example, a young firm engaged in rapid expansion may well decide to issue shares. In the early stages, dividend payments may be very small because profits have yet to come through, but shareholders will be rewarded by seeing the capital value of their shares rising with the growth of the company. However, raising the finance by borrowing, either from a

---

* If the loan comes from an intermediary, the cost to the borrower will be the interest rate charged by the intermediary, which will be the yield to the lender *plus* the mark-up added by the intermediary.

Table 1.3 **The objectives of lenders and borrowers**

	Lenders	Borrowers
Return (to lender)	+	−
Risk	−	−
Transaction costs	−	−
Liquidity	+	−

bank or by issuing fixed-interest bonds, will mean paying interest on the loan from the outset. This cash drain could be critical in the early stages of expansion.

By contrast with lenders, borrowers will wish to *maximise the period* for which they have use of the loan. This has two benefits. It reduces the risk that the lender will have to be repaid at a time which is inconvenient to the borrower and also reduces the exposure of the borrower to the risk that funds might become short or very expensive in the future. Like lenders, borrowers will also wish to minimise the (transaction) costs of setting up the deal.

These contrasting interests of lenders and borrowers are summarised in Table 1.3. The signs in brackets indicate whether the lender/borrower is seeking to maximise (+) or minimise (−) the characteristic.

1.3.3 Lending, borrowing and wealth

So far, we have discussed *flows* of lending and borrowing. While flows are very important, we need to remember that flows cause changes in *stocks* and that there are times when stocks matter. For example, a person with a (net) current financial surplus is adding to his or her stock of financial wealth. A person or firm with a (net) current deficit has either to increase their stock of financial liabilities (by borrowing) or to sell some existing financial assets. In either event a financial deficit leads to a reduction in net financial wealth.

Notice that we talk here, as we did with the flows of lending and borrowing, of 'net' positions. People will hold simultaneous debtor and creditor positions. People with mortgages will also have building society deposits. A firm may have a very substantial long-term debt as a result of recent expansion and at the same time be holding a considerable sum in a high-interest bank account.

Why is this the case? Remember that one of the ways in which financial inter-mediaries make a profit is by charging a rate of interest to borrowers which exceeds that which they pay to lenders. At first glance, therefore, it seems strange that people should have a large outstanding debt with an institution at the same time that they hold assets with that institution. Surely, one would think, they would be better off using the assets to pay off at least part of the debt. Suppose that a borrower has savings in the building society equal to half his outstanding mortgage. The interest received on this obviously goes some way to subsidising or reducing the cost of the interest paid to the society on the mortgage. But since the rate of interest received from the savings is less than the rate of interest paid on the mortgage, there would seem to be a benefit in using the savings to pay off half the mortgage debt. However, this overlooks the fact that while the house-buyer has savings with the society, he has access to 'ready money', or at least to 'liquidity'. If he uses the savings to pay off half the mortgage, he is sacrificing the convenience or benefit that liquidity confers. Thus, if we were to persist with the calculation of cost and benefits, we should have to say that paying off half the mortgage would certainly bring a benefit in the saving of interest (equal to the difference in the two rates being paid) but at the same time it would cause a loss of benefit in the access to ready funds. Provided our house-buyer values liquidity more highly than the interest rate saving, then maintaining both the mortgage and the savings simultaneously is entirely rational. Notice that the interest saving is a differential or 'spread' between the rate charged on mortgage lending and the rate paid on building society deposits. We are familiar in other spheres of economics with the idea that people base their allocation decisions upon *relative* prices. We should not therefore be surprised that the same holds true when people make decisions about financial allocations. We shall see later that the behaviour of spreads is very important.

The point which emerges from this discussion is that in making decisions to borrow and to lend, that is to say making decisions to acquire financial liabilities and assets, people are faced with a complex choice. The choice is not just about whether to be either a borrower or a lender but about the amount of both borrowing and lending they should undertake. It also involves a decision about the best mix of types of liability and asset for their particular circumstances. Economists are referring to this decision when they say that people are exercising their *portfolio* choice. As we have just seen, exercising portfolio choice involves arranging the portfolio, the mixture of liabilities and assets, in such a way that, for a given cost, the benefit derived from each asset or liability is equal at the margin. When this is the case people are said to be in *portfolio equilibrium*. The study of the principles underlying portfolio choice is known as *portfolio theory*. There is more on portfolio equilibrium and portfolio theory in Appendix I.

1.4 Summary

A financial system consists of a set of organised markets and institutions together with regulators of those markets and institutions. Their main function is to channel funds between end users of the system: from lenders ('surplus units') to borrowers ('deficit units'). In addition, a financial system provides payments facilities, a variety of services such as insurance, pensions and foreign exchange, together with facilities which allow people to adjust their existing wealth portfolios.

There are many advantages in borrowing and lending via intermediaries and organised markets, compared with borrowing and lending directly between end-users. These include transforming the maturity of short-term savings into longer-term loans, together with the reduction of risk and transaction costs.

Questions for discussion

1 List the functions of a financial system.

2 Distinguish between deficit and surplus units.

3 Distinguish between 'saving' and a 'financial surplus'.

4 Discuss the advantages to deficit and surplus units of using organised financial markets and financial intermediaries.

5 How are financial intermediaries able to engage in maturity transformation?

6 Explain briefly the difference between deposit-taking and non-deposit-taking intermediaries. Give two examples of each.

7 Why do people simultaneously hold financial assets and liabilities?

8 Imagine that a household has a £50,000 mortgage on which its bank currently charges 7 per cent p.a. Suppose that it also has £8,000 in a deposit account which pays 3 per cent p.a. What does this tell you about the value which this household places upon liquidity?

9 Suggest a suitable asset for someone who wished to avoid the following types of risk at all cost: (a) capital risk; (b) income risk.

Further reading

A D Bain, *The Financial System* (Oxford: Blackwell, 2e, 1992) ch. 1

M Buckle and J Thompson, *The UK Financial System* (Manchester: Manchester UP, 4e, 2004) chs. 1 and 2

R Glenn Hubbard, *Money, The Financial System and the Economy* (Reading MA: Addison-Wesley, 3e, 2004)

S I Greenbaum and A V Thakor, *Contemporary Financial Intermediation* (Dryden, 1995) chs. 2 and 3

P G A Howells and K Bain, *The Economics of Money, Banking and Finance* (Harlow: Financial Times Prentice Hall, 3e, 2005) chs. 1 and 2

D S Kidwell, R L Peterson and D Blackwell, *Financial Institutions, Markets and Money* (London: Dryden Press, 6e, 1997)

F S Mishkin, *The Economics of Money, Banking and Financial Markets* (Pearson Addison-Wesley, 7e, 2004) ch. 2

CHAPTER 2

The financial system and the real economy

Objectives

What you will learn in this chapter:

- How financial surpluses and deficits arise out of real economic activity
- How a financial surplus affects the stock of wealth
- How developments in the financial system may affect the level of aggregate demand
- How developments in the financial system may affect the composition of aggregate demand
- How developments in the financial system may affect the allocation of resources

In this chapter we are concerned with the relationship between the financial system and what is sometimes called the 'real' economy. The 'real' economy consists of firms, households and other agencies engaged in the production of goods and services which can either be consumed now or put to use with a view to producing more in future. We think of this as 'real' economic activity because it is using real resources to produce something which people can buy and use, whereas the financial system is mainly concerned either with moving funds around so that those who wish to buy can do so, or with helping people to exchange ownership of the productive resources. The words that we use are chosen obviously to suggest that the activities of the real economy are essential to life. The real economy produces food, heating, lighting, consumer goods, entertainment. The job of the financial system is to facilitate that by making sure that funds are available when and where they are wanted.

This is a reasonable view, so far as it goes. However, there is a danger that we see the financial system as providing a service which merely responds to the demands of the real economy. But this is only one side of the picture. There are many ways in which the behaviour of the financial system affects the behaviour of the real economy. Just think of the way that people respond to stock market booms (by feeling richer and spending more) and to stock market slumps (by hoarding their incomes and cancelling spending plans). Causality works in both ways. The real economy generates financial activity by employing people (who wish to save some of their income) in firms (which wish to borrow for investment purposes).

In the rest of this chapter we look at just four examples (there are many more) of how the real economy and the financial system interact. In the next section, we look at how the real economy generates financial surpluses and deficits which the financial system has to reconcile. In the remaining sections we turn the tables and look at how features of the financial system may affect the real economy. We look at three issues. The first two are concerned with the size and development of the financial system. The third is concerned with the efficiency with which the financial system does its job. In section 2.2 we look at how the financial system may create liquidity or even money, which may in turn affect the level of aggregate spending in the economy. In section 2.3 we consider ways in which the existence of a financial system may affect the composition of total spending in the economy – it may encourage less consumption and more spending on capital goods. In section 2.4 we look at how the performance of the financial system may affect the allocation of resources, in particular funds for investment and management expertise.

2.1 Lending, borrowing and national income

We have noted several times that one of the functions of a financial system is to channel funds from those who wish to lend to those who wish to borrow: in other words from surplus to deficit *units*. We also know that surpluses (and deficits) arise from an inequality between current income and planned expenditure. Notice that they are therefore the outcome of *real* economic activity. They result because people earn incomes from employment which produces goods and services and then make decisions about how much they wish to spend on goods and services. We might go further and suppose that an economy in boom conditions generates more employment, income and output, all of which might in turn be associated with larger surpluses, at least amongst households. Conversely, where the level of economic activity is low, so too is employment and incomes, and many families will find it difficult to make their income stretch to match expenditure. Let us be clear then that one connection between the 'real' economy and the financial system is that it is the real economy that gives rise to the surpluses and deficits which the financial system has to reconcile.

In order to learn more about how a financial system does this, it would be very useful to be able to take a surplus or deficit unit, begin with its income and spending plans and then follow what happens to the resulting surplus/deficit. Unfortunately, it is very difficult to know exactly which are the deficit and surplus units and even more difficult to find out how an individual unit deals with its deficit/surplus. An individual unit is a particular household, or person or firm, and financial information about individual persons, households and firms is understandably confidential. However, if we aggregate individual units into *sectors*, we find that readily available official statistics will tell us both about the size of sectoral surpluses and deficits and about the ways in which they are reconciled. The statistics are imperfect, but it is still worth doing.

The most familiar sectors into which the economy can be divided are those of the national income identity:

$$Y \equiv C + I + G + (X - M) \tag{2.1}$$

Students with some knowledge of macroeconomics will know that 'national income', Y, can be measured either by adding all the incomes earned by factors of production in the course of producing one year's output of newly produced goods and services or by adding all the expenditure on that output (additions to stocks caused by any unsold output are treated as a form of expenditure). In other words, total income and total expenditure are the same thing.

Whether we think of Y as total income or total expenditure, its components appear on the right hand side of the identity (eqn 2.1). In expenditure terms we can say that national income consists of consumption expenditure (by households), C, investment expenditure (by firms), I, public sector expenditure (by government), G, and expenditure on UK exports by customers overseas, X, less any spending on imports, M, which may have been included in the other categories of spending, C, I and G. In *income* terms, then, Y is the sum of incomes paid to households, to firms, to government and to exporters. C, I, G and $(X - M)$ therefore represent the four sectors into which the whole economy can be divided.

Consider now the rather obvious point that while national income must be equal to the total incomes earned by the four sectors (and this must equal *total* expenditure by the four sectors), it does not follow that income and expenditure must be equal for each individual sector. It is possible for any one sector to spend in excess of its income, provided that at least one other sector is prepared to spend less than its income, in order that the equality of *total* income and expenditure is preserved. As a general rule, we think of the household sector as spending less than income, firms and governments as spending more, with the external sector producing whatever difference is necessary to balance the other three.

In the remainder of this section, we are going to look at the household sector in 2004. We shall see how its income exceeded spending, how this difference, with some adjustment, can be used to arrive at a financial surplus, and at what happened to this surplus during the period. We shall also learn some important lessons about the differences between *stocks* and *flows*. Before we begin though, a few words of caution are required. The first is that we shall be using data drawn from official statistics – after all, we want to see what happened in practice. Students who turn to the official statistics themselves, to check on our story (!) or to update it, will find that the official statistics divide the economy into more than four sectors. In particular, what we have lumped together as 'firms' appears as several categories in the statistics. Firms are divided into industrial and commercial companies, and various types of financial firm. Similarly, 'government' appears as two categories – central government and local government. More immediately relevant, data relating to what we call 'households' covers 'households and non-profit institutions serving households'. Roughly, this is 'households *plus* charitable organisations'. None of this is a major problem. It is just an example of what happens when one switches from theory to the real world!

Table 2.1 Income and capital account of the household sector, 2004, £bn

Gross disposable income	768.3		
plus Equity in pension funds	25.7		
Total resources		794.0	
less Consumption		760.7	
Saving			33.3
plus Capital transfers			8.1
less Capital taxes			3.7
Change in net worth			37.7
less Real capital spending			62.3
Net acquisition of financial assets			−24.6

Source: ONS, *UK National Accounts, 2005*, Tables 6.1.6 and 6.1.7

Gross domestic product (GDP) in 2004 amounted to £1164bn. Table 2.1 shows details of households' income and capital account. In the first line, we see households' 'gross disposable income'. This consists mainly of income from employment, *minus* National Insurance contributions and taxes on income but *plus* social security and other benefits received by families. The next line shows a very small item, 'equity in pension funds'. 'Total resources' tells us therefore that households had £794.0bn at their disposal in 2004. (We shall call this 'income' and denote it Y.)

Understandably, most of this was spent on consumption, C. The difference is saving, S. Economists are often interested in saving because it shows how much of current output is not consumed and is therefore available for investment. Thus we sometimes calculate a savings ratio and monitor its behaviour over time. The savings ratio is often expressed as S/Y, but be aware that that Y means 'total resources'. The ratio in 2004 was 4.2 per cent.

Saving, then, is income minus consumption, $Y - C$. The next question is: what happened to this saving in 2004? The first part of the answer is that it was slightly enlarged by the effect of the difference between capital transfers and taxes on capital. They make little difference to our figures, adding £4.4bn to saving. The amount of saving, plus this adjustment, shows the amount that households have available to add to their existing stock of wealth. Thus, £37.7bn is shown as the 'change in net worth'. The second part of the answer is that a significant part of saving was used to buy real capital assets or, as we might say, to carry out real investment. For firms, real investment means the purchase of plant, equipment, vehicles, etc. These are not items which are bought by households. For them, the most commonly purchased real capital assets are newly built houses (not existing houses).

Saving: The difference between income and consumption.

Capital spending in Table 2.1 is shown as £62.3bn, substantially more than the saving available to finance it. The consequence is that households had either to borrow the difference, or alternatively to dispose of financial assets which they had built up in the past. Whichever they chose to do, so far as the accounts are concerned both are described as making a net acquision of financial assets which is *negative* by (–)£24.6bn.

Let us summarise and then highlight some important points. Leaving aside the minor complications of equity in pension funds and capital transfers and taxes, we can generalise what we have just seen so that we can apply it to any sector of any economy. Our general rule is:

$$(Y - C) - I = NAFA \tag{2.2}$$

which says that disposable income *minus* consumption (i.e. saving) *minus* real investment *equals* the sector's net acquisition of financial assets. Notice firstly, therefore, that the surpluses to which we have often referred in this book are not the same as saving. Any financial surplus is what is left *after saving has been used* to *finance real investment*. Notice secondly that we write net *acquisition* of financial assets (NAFA). There are two reasons for this. Firstly, if eqn 2.2 is to be really general in its application, it has to cover cases where saving *minus* investment can be negative or positive, i.e. cases where financial deficits or surpluses occur. By writing net *acquisition* we mean the difference between financial assets bought and sold. For surplus sectors (or units) *NAFA* will be *positive*. Secondly, it may be that our surplus sector has previously only had deficits. Therefore it will have no existing financial assets, only debts or financial liabilities. Its first surplus may be used either to buy financial assets (debts unchanged) or to pay off debts. Both cases are covered by our phrase. *Net* means 'the difference between'. In the former case our surplus sector uses its surplus to buy an asset ('sale' of debt = 0). In the latter case it 'sells' debt (purchase of asset = 0). In each case, there is a (net) gain of asset over liability.

> **Financial surplus or deficit:** The difference between saving and investment in real assets.

In the case of households in 2004, therefore, we know that saving amounted to £33.3bn, giving rise, after real investment and adjustment for capital taxes and transfers, to a financial deficit of –£24.6bn. The next question to which it would be interesting to have an answer is: 'how was this deficit financed?'

For this purpose, we need to turn to what is known as the sector's 'financial account'. This shows the acquisition (disposal) of financial assets and liabilities of various types. When we have allowed for all the acquisitions and disposals, we would expect the financial account to show us that the net acquisition of financial assets exactly matched the deficit of –£24.6bn. We would be quite correct to expect this, but we are again confronted by the complexities of the real world. Information for the income/capital account, from which we derived our financial surplus, comes from sources which are quite different from those on which the financial accounts are based. (And other accounts in the official series are based on yet different sources of information.) Bear in mind also that we are dealing with large absolute figures which represent the behaviour of millions of households. It would be more surprising than not if figures derived from different sources were to turn out to correspond exactly. Generally they do not, so some adjustment is necessary in a column called 'residual error' or 'statistical adjustment'.

The income/capital accounts gave us a figure for households' financial surplus of –£24.6bn. Income data is collected from firms and from the Inland Revenue. Expenditure data is collected largely by survey. Most of the data contained in the financial accounts comes from financial institutions which make statistical returns to the Bank of England (in the case of deposit-taking institutions) or to their various trade organisations (in the case of non-deposit-taking institutions). We shall see in a moment that the financial accounts seem able to trace only £12.8bn of the additional liabilities acquired as a result of the deficit. In other words, there is what is called a 'statistical discrepancy' of £11.8bn. This may seem large, and it may even seem shocking. However, when we look at the 'missing' £11.8bn in the context of the total acquisitions of assets and liabilities it is less than 8 per cent of each and, given the difficulties of data collection we just noted, it is not altogether surprising. There are bigger issues to worry about in reading Table 2.2.

The first is that although households actually had a deficit of £24.6bn, they managed to *acquire* £122.9bn of assets. How is this possible? They could do this because they borrowed much more than they needed to cover the deficit. This is shown in the next line as an acquisition of liabilities of £135.7bn. The way to understand this is firstly to remember that the deficit is the deficit for the household sector in *aggregate*. Individual households will vary widely in their surplus/deficit positions. There will be some that run a surplus, but still choose to borrow to finance some of their spending, meaning that they can acquire more financial assets than their surplus would allow. (Their *net* acquisition must still equal the surplus, but their *gross* acquisition may be larger.) There will be others that run a deficit, but borrow more than they need for this purpose. In other words, we have to distinguish the *net* outcome (which in theory should correspond to the surplus/deficit) from all the individual actions which simply reflect people's continual rearrangement of their existing wealth.

Of the assets that were acquired, £61bn consisted of notes and coin and bank and building society deposits. These taken together are what we usually mean by 'money',

Table 2.2 Financial account of the household sector, 2004, £bn

Acquisition of financial assets		Acquisition of financial liabilities	
Notes and coin	2.6	Loans	75.9
Deposits with banks	45.5	Other liabilities	−0.9
and building societies	12.9	*Net acquisition of liabilities*	75.0
Other deposits	5.6		
Bills and bonds	2.9		
UK company shares	−1.2		
Other shares	3.0		
Mutual funds	8.2		
Life assurance and pension funds	40.0		
Other	3.4		
Net acquisition of assets	122.9		
minus *Acquisition of liabilities*	135.7		
	−12.8		

Source: ONS, *UK National Accounts, 2005*, Table 6.1.8

as we shall see in Chapter 3. Another notable feature is the large accumulation of financial wealth in life assurance and pension funds. This has been a major outlet for financial saving for many years. Another interesting but small item is the figure next to UK company shares. Notice that is negative, meaning that households as a whole have been reducing their direct ownership of shares. This is a trend which began in 2001 following a sharp decline in the stock market. The negative figure of £1.2bn is very much smaller than the figures for 2001 and 2002 and may reflect the fact that some recovery in share prices had begun in 2004.

Net worth: The difference between a person or firm's holdings of assets and liabilities.

We can trace £12.8bn of the net financial liabilities incurred by households in 2004, as well as seeing how they rearranged their financial assets. In acquiring these liabilities, households are acquiring the assets of some other sector. (Mortgage loans are assets of the banking sector.) Note that so far as households are concerned, acquiring these additional liabilities amount to new borrowing which they are undertaking; it is 'new' in the sense that it is additional to any borrowing which they may have done in 2003, for example. Thus (we need to emphasise) it is a *flow*. That is to say it must be measured and expressed with reference to a period of time. Here we have examined the flow in just one year, 2004. This *flow* of new borrowing, or acquisition of liabilities, adds to the existing stock of such liabilities which households already hold. (The same is true of the financial assets that households acquired in the same period.) We might refer to this existing stock as households' existing 'net financial wealth' and it will be a proportion of their total wealth (the rest consisting typically of a house and various consumer durable goods). Notice that the stock is the sum of previous flows and is measured at a particular point in time. Clearly, therefore, the (flow) net acquisition of financial assets causes the stock of assets held to change. Indeed, it is often the case that the change in a stock is equal to the net flow (inflow *minus* outflow) into it. This is rather like a tank of water where the level (the stock) of water rises if there is a net inflow and falls if there is a net outflow. In other words, if we were to compare the stock figures for 2005 with those for 2004, the difference would correspond to the figures in Table 2.2.

However, there is sometimes a complication in financial accounts which arises from the fact that the stock of assets contains some assets which are tradable. They have a market price and this price may fluctuate. Thus the change in the value of a stock of financial assets between two periods of time will be the result of *both* the net acquisition (positive or negative) *and* any change in the market price of the existing assets. Using our current data, for example, the stock of UK company shares held by households in 2005, might not be exactly £1.2bn lower than it was in 2004, because the price of the shares still held may have changed. (In fact, they rose quite sharply between 2004 and 2005.)

Before leaving this discussion of the stock/flow relationship, notice also that the existing stock is always likely to be larger than the current flow (because it has built up over the years). Notice too that there is no requirement that the assets acquired in the current flow are an exact replica of the assets currently held. For example, new assets may be developed and added to the stock for the first time. Other, traditional, assets may then lose their appeal, and while they remain in the stock there may be no new purchases. As rates of return, and levels of risk, on assets vary from time to time, we would expect to see variations in the demand for them. There will be changes in the composition of the flow of newly acquired assets and this will affect the composition of the stock over time.

Exercise 2.1

Imagine that you are the manager of a mutual fund consisting entirely of a portfolio which exactly matches the composition of the FTSE-100 index. At the beginning of the year the value of your fund is £500m. In the first week of the year, you receive £12m in additional funds from investors. In the last week, existing investors withdraw £5m from the fund. During the year, the price of shares in the FTSE-100 index increases by 15 per cent.

(a) Calculate the change in the value of your fund's stock of assets over the year.

(b) What is the net inflow of funds during the year?

(c) How much of the change is explained by the rise in price of assets in the fund?

Answers at end of chapter

Table 2.3 shows the *stock* of financial assets and liabilities held by the household sector *at the end* of 2004. Information on stocks of assets and liabilities comes from balance sheet data. Table 2.3 uses the same categories as Table 2.2, so that comparisons can be made easily. Even the briefest glance reveals that the stocks of assets already held are very much larger than the current flows. The table shows that total financial assets amounted to £3,179bn while financial liabilities amounted to £1,194.4bn. Household financial net worth at end-2004 therefore was £1,984.6bn. We know that it decreased during the year by £12.8bn.

Table 2.3 Financial balance sheet of the household sector, end-2004 £bn

Financial assets		Financial liabilities	
Notes and coin	33.7	Loans – short-term	184.3
Deposits with banks	558.3	– mortgage	874.9
and building societies	156.3	– other long-term	23.8
Other deposits	109.9	*Other liabilities*	111.4
Bills and bonds	51.2	*Total financial liabilities*	1,194.4
UK company shares	343.1		
Other shares	15.8		
Mutual funds	142.7		
Life assurance and	1,668.4		
pension funds			
Other	99.6		
Total financial assets	3,179		

Source: ONS, *UK National Accounts, 2005*, Table 6.1.9

2.2 Financial activity and the level of aggregate demand

We have just seen how activity in the real economy requires the development of a financial system enabling units (or sectors) with a financial surplus to 'dispose' of that surplus by lending it. By lending, the surplus sector acquires financial assets. As we saw in Chapter 1, these assets have varying degrees of liquidity. At one extreme, we have just seen (Table 2.2) that surplus units could acquire notes and coin and bank deposits. In any economy, this amounts to acquiring 'money'. Towards the other extreme (again see Table 2.2), they could add to their holdings in mutual funds. These are certainly not money, but they can be sold back to the mutual fund company very quickly. (Compared with 'real' assets such as land, buildings and consumer durables, therefore, all financial assets could be considered *comparatively* liquid.)

There are at least three ways in which financial developments could affect the level of aggregate demand. The first two involve the creation of liquid assets (including money); the third involves changes in people's financial wealth.

> **Aggregate demand:** The total level of spending in the economy on newly produced goods and services in a given period of time.

As we saw in Chapter 1, one effect of a financial system is to create liquid assets, and it has long been thought that the level of liquidity in an economy has some effect on the level of spending. If this is true, we might consider the hypothesis that an increase in financial activity causes a rise in spending. There are two distinct channels through which this might happen; which matters most has been a matter of controversy between economists for many years. On the one hand, there is the view that it is the expansion of *monetary assets* (bank and building society deposits) that is responsible for the extra spending. This view has often been labelled 'monetarism' and was particularly influential in the UK in the 1980s. The alternative view says that the increase in liquid assets of *any kind* will do the trick, since by definition any liquid asset can be quickly converted to money. This proposition is often associated with the name of J M Keynes and certainly was widely held among economists who followed Keynes in the 1950s and 1960s. We can explore both channels by using the 'equation of exchange', although the equation itself is usually regarded as a building block in monetarist theory.

2.2.1 Money and spending

The equation of exchange says:

$$MsV \equiv PY \tag{2.3}$$

where Ms stands for the total stock of money, P is the general or average level of prices of newly produced goods and services, and Y is the volume of goods and services produced. Note, therefore, that PY is total output valued at market prices. V is given the name 'velocity' and is sometimes said to describe the frequency or speed with which money changes hands. In a modern system where money is largely bank deposits, 'changing hands' is a difficult idea to visualise. It may be better just to think of it as that figure or coefficient which allows the current money stock to be sufficient to buy this year's total output at market prices. Thus:

$$V \equiv PY/Ms \qquad (2.4)$$

Note that we have written the equation using $\equiv$ rather than =. This is because it is an 'identity'. It is true by definition. We make it so by defining PY as the value of output sold and then saying that MsV is the quantity of money *times* the 'number of times it changes hands'. In doing that we have just made MsV stand for total spending, and since spending requires something to be bought (i.e. sold), both sides *must* be equal. No one would argue with this. Since it is true by definition, there is nothing to argue about.

> **Velocity (of circulation):** A ratio (PY/Ms) which expresses the relationship between the quantity of money in circulation in the economy and the value of total output.

However, the equation can be turned into a theory (which allows us to talk about directions of causation and to make predictions) by making some assumptions. If we make the following assumptions, we have turned the equation into part of the theory of 'monetarism'. As we said above, this is controversial.

● V and Y change only very slowly. (In the simplest case, V and Y are fixed.)
● Ms is determined by variables outside the identity – perhaps by the government, or central bank, or even the financial system itself.

Using these assumptions we can make a case for the first channel of influence upon aggregate demand. This is because the assumptions make money into an independent variable whose effects are predictable and *must* fall upon the price level. Box 2.1 shows what happens when the money stock (Ms) expands by 10 per cent when output is increasing at only 2 per cent.

Box 2.1

The quantity theory of money

If by definition $MsV \equiv PY$, then if we turn the variables into growth rates it follows that:

$$Ms + V = p + Y$$

If we specify the behaviour of V (let it grow very slowly at 1 per cent) and Y (assume it grows at 2 per cent), we have a theory which allows us to predict the effect of changes in Ms. Suppose, for example, that Ms grows at 10 per cent, then we have:

$$0.1 + 0.01 = P + 0.02$$

Rearranging gives us

$$P = 0.1 + 0.01 - 0.02 = 0.09$$

an inflation rate of 9 per cent p.a.

Of course, we can change the outcome by changing our assumptions. Suppose, for example, that we relax the restriction on Y. We might, for example, suppose that the economy was suffering heavy unemployment and that there was widespread spare capacity. Y is no longer restricted to slow growth. An increase in spending (MsV) could now cause an increase in Y with little or no effect on P. If, in our example, extra demand was met by an increase in output of 8 per cent, prices would rise by only 3 per cent. Whether the effect of increased spending falls largely on P or on Y is of secondary interest to us, however. What matters is that we have established that if V is fixed (or restricted to slow change), then events in the financial system could cause an increase in spending by causing an increase in the money supply. This will happen if there is an expansion of banks and their deposits.

Exercise 2.2

(a) At the end of 2005, the (M4) money stock in the UK amounted to £1,363bn. For the same year, GDP was approximately £1,211bn. Calculate a figure for the velocity of M4.

(b) At the end of 2005, the Bank of England forecast a rate of growth of 6 per cent for M4 during 2006. Output was expected to grow at about 2 per cent while the Bank was confident of achieving its inflation target of 2 per cent. What did the Bank appear to be expecting to happen to M4 velocity during 2006?

Answers at end of chapter

2.2.2 Liquid assets and spending

An expansion of banking and money is the first channel through which the financial system may affect the level of aggregate demand. The second channel involves non-deposit-taking institutions, though here the mechanism is rather more complex. The liabilities of NDTIs are not money but they are, as we have already seen, relatively liquid assets to their holders. Imagine that NDTIs now develop some new product which is both highly liquid and popular with lenders. As a result, people hold additional liquid assets which, though they are not money, are partial substitutes for money. For example, the new assets cannot be used for spending but if they can be exchanged for money quickly and easily, they are extremely suitable as assets which can be held in case of the need for unforeseen expenditure. If people were previously holding money itself for these 'precautionary' purposes, the new assets, which will pay interest or some other form of reward, may be a superior alternative. Instead of holding money for precautionary purposes, the money can be used for spending. In effect, the creation of money substitutes enables a greater proportion of the money stock to be used for spending, or as a medium of exchange. A given quantity of M permits a higher level of PY. In terms of the equation of exchange, money substitutes permit an increase in V and thus an increase in spending. Doing Exercise 2.3 may help to clarify the process.

Exercise 2.3

Imagine an economy in which *there are no liquid assets* except money. Imagine now a family whose monthly income of £2,000 is paid into their bank account on the first day of the month. Suppose further that their expenditure is also £2,000 per month and that it takes place at a constant rate during the month. Most of their wealth consists of a house, a car and other consumer durables. But they also have £1,000 in bank deposits, saved from the past, which they feel is necessary to hold for precautionary purposes.

1 Draw a sketch showing how the size of their bank deposit varies over a two-month period.

2 Calculate their average holdings of money over one month (ignore any notes and coin).

3 Calculate a monthly velocity figure for their holdings of money (remember: velocity = spending ÷ money holdings).

Now imagine that an NDTI emerges which offers units in a mutual fund. These units pay a small income and promise a capital gain if held over a long period. Furthermore, they can be sold back to the company within seventy-two hours. Suppose that our family now decide that their precautionary requirements can be met by cutting their minimum bank deposits to just £100 and holding £900 worth of fund units instead. Repeat steps 1–3.

Suppose that the £900 of deposits passed to the mutual fund company go to an ultimate borrower who spends it with the same velocity as our family. How much additional expenditure is generated from the £900?

Answers at the end of the chapter

In summary, then, we may say that an expansion of the financial system is likely to lead to an increase in the availability of liquid assets. Such an increase in liquid assets is likely to increase the level of spending in the economy whether there is an increase in monetary assets or in non-money assets. Using the equation of exchange, the former channel is represented by an increase in M_s; the latter involves an increase in V.

2.2.3 Financial wealth and spending

In the first part of this chapter, we saw that saving out of income enabled people to add to their wealth. Saving would add to *real* wealth if it was used to finance investment in real capital goods; saving would add to financial wealth if it gave rise to a financial surplus. Clearly the decision to divide income between consumption and saving is an important one and one which firms and households will take very seriously. It seems reasonable to suppose that a household, for example, will have a level of consumption which reflects current income, and perhaps the income which it expects to earn in future, as well as the 'standard of living' which is regarded as normal for households with similar incomes, living in the same area and so on. Cultural norms and traditions, as well as economics, play a part.

In addition to these factors, a household may have a target level of wealth. This is a level of wealth which it wishes to accumulate, perhaps to pass to the next generation, or to spend in retirement, or simply because it gives a sense of security in an uncertain world. If a household is a long way from this target, therefore, it seems reasonable to suppose that it will see saving (and consuming less) as a greater priority than if it were near to its target. All this is just a way of saying that the wealthier a household feels, the more inclined it will be to spend on consumption. For any given level of income, therefore, consumption will be a higher proportion of income when people feel 'wealthy'.

As we have been pointing out since the beginning of this book, a major part of people's wealth consists of financial assets of many kinds. As financial wealth increases, so too, other things being equal, does total wealth. Financial surpluses add to financial wealth, but financial surpluses (and deficits) are not the only reason for changes in financial wealth. We have noted already that many financial assets are traded in organised markets. Because they are traded, their price can go up and down. As the price of tradable assets rises, the owners of those assets enjoy an increase in financial (and maybe total) wealth. If all our theorising is correct, we might then expect that consumption will be positively affected (and saving negatively affected) by price rises in asset markets. In October 1987, the price of ordinary shares in the UK and US fell by approximately 30 per cent in just two days. Central banks around the world reduced interest rates because they feared that this sharp drop in financial wealth would cause a fall in aggregate demand and the possibility of recession. The same fears were revived exactly ten years later in the autumn of 1997, when prices in South East Asian stock markets fell sharply. Prices elsewhere, however, were little affected and by January 1999, shares on the New York exchange had doubled in value since the middle of 1996. At the same time, aggregate household saving had fallen to zero as US households went on a consumer boom, fuelled in part by this unprecedented increase in financial wealth.

In January 2001 the long stock-market boom came to an end in the UK and the US. Over the next two years, the FTSE-100 index of stock prices fell by 50 per cent. This caused a great deal of concern for people nearing retirement who were relying on their financial wealth to provide them with a future pension. It caused a great deal of concern for pension funds which found they were committed to paying pensions which *their* investments could no longer support. Above all, it caused a great deal of concern for the Bank of England (and the US Federal Reserve) which both feared that the erosion of people's wealth would lead them to cut their consumption. For this reason, both central banks cut interest rates repeatedly throughout 2001.

2.3 The composition of aggregate demand

In Chapter 1 we saw that some people have incomes which exceed that which they require for current composition. This excess is saving. That saving may simply be 'hoarded' (i.e. not spent on anything), or it may be used to finance the saver's

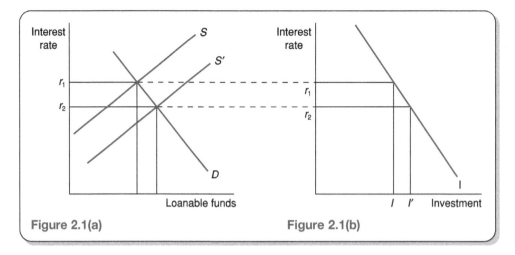

Figure 2.1(a)   Figure 2.1(b)

capital spending, or it may be lent to others to finance their capital spending. We also said that borrowers and lenders had different motives and therefore different needs. Broadly, lenders like to maximise liquidity and yield while borrowers like to maximise the length of their borrowing while paying the minimum cost. If we adopt the customary device in economics of assuming other things are equal, we can show how, in Figure 2.1(a), the willingness of lenders to lend and of borrowers to borrow will vary with the rate of interest on borrowing and lending. Other things being equal, the demand for 'loanable funds' by borrowers will be inversely related to interest rate (the price they have to pay), while the supply will be positively related.

Notice that the stability of these curves is not without controversy, however. In Figure 2.1(a) an increase in income will cause the supply curve to shift to the right. In addition, some would argue that the demand curve is unstable, shifting outwards as borrowers sense a more 'profitable' future for the projects they hope to finance, and in towards the origin as their outlook becomes more pessimistic.

In addition to the level of income and the state of 'expectations', the positions of the curves will be influenced by the quantity and nature of financial intermediation. In Figure 2.1(a) the supply of lending is equal to the demand for lending at an interest rate r_1. At r_1, given their level of income at the current level of risk and inconvenience involved in allowing others the use of their funds, savers are prepared to lend just the amount that borrowers wish to borrow. Suppose now though that some form of financial innovation occurs which savers find particularly attractive. If the rate of interest remains at r_1, more lending will be forthcoming. The same would be true for any level of yield which we care to choose, and the curve showing the supply of lending needs to be redrawn at S'. At r_1, the supply of lending now exceeds the demand for it and we should expect the rate of interest to fall, and demand for funds to increase, until both become equal again at r_2. Other things being equal, we may say that an increase in the volume of intermediation will increase the supply of funds and lower the cost and increase the volume of borrowing.

Look at the situation now from the angle of the 'real' economy. Profit-maximising firms will undertake all those projects whose net present value is positive, when the earnings are discounted at the current rate of interest. On the customary assumption that more projects will pass this test when interest rates are low than when they are high, the volume of investment spending will be negatively sloped as in Figure 2.1(b). If, as in Figure 2.1(a), intermediation makes lending more attractive, increasing the supply and lowering the price (the rate of interest), then Figure 2.1(b) shows there will be an increase in investment, I.

In summary, the development of financial intermediation in this example has had no effect upon the *level* of aggregate demand, but has shifted its *composition*. There is less current consumption, but more saving and more investment for future production. Seen like this, financial intermediation can have implications for the balance of production in an economy (between consumption and investment goods) and upon the rate of growth of the economy if more resources are devoted to investment than would otherwise have been the case.

2.4 The financial system and resource allocation

In an ideal world, we should like to think that the financial system functions in such a way that it channels funds from lenders to their most productive use. Where the funds are borrowed for real investment projects, for example, these should be the projects which society values most. For this to happen, a number of conditions have to be met. If we assume that they are met, we are assuming that the financial system has the characteristics of a *perfectly competitive* system. The assumptions are:

- there are many lenders and borrowers;
- all lenders and borrowers have perfect information;
- new lenders and borrowers can enter the market without restraint;
- there are no taxes;
- there are no costs to be borne (or benefits to be enjoyed) by people outside the loan contract.

In this setting, lenders know where they can find the best returns. (We would normally say 'best returns for a given level of risk' but with the assumption of perfect information there is strictly speaking no risk!) The best returns will be offered by the borrowers whose projects earn the highest rates of profit. These high profits will be available because of the high price which customers are prepared to pay for the product which is produced. If there are no taxes, this price represents the marginal benefit which consumers derive from the good. With no externalities, there are no hidden costs of production being carried by other members of society. Since lenders know where the best returns are, they will ensure that there is a steady flow of funds towards these activities which society seems to value highly. The supply of funds competing for these high returns will encourage firms to expand their activities. With expansion, the rate of profit may fall and the rate of return offered to lenders may also fall. It may fall to a point where the existing lenders are just happy with the return. There is no incentive for additional lenders to join in. Expansion stops, but only after society's need for this desirable product or service has been met. Looking at the other end of the spectrum, firms whose profits do not enable them to pay at least the minimum rate of return required by lenders will find it impossible to obtain funds for expansion and may, in the long run, be forced to contract. So long as our assumptions hold, then we can be confident that the pressures on declining firms represent the preferences of 'society at large' and that the decline is part of the mechanism whereby funds are directed towards the activities that society values most highly and away from those that are less highly rated.

In practice, however, life is neither so simple nor so benevolent. There are a number of respects in which the financial system fails to match the assumptions of perfect competition. We shall consider just some of these. We shall then show how the failures affect the allocation of funds and also, briefly, how the failures may also affect the allocation of management expertise.

Traditionally, financial activity has been subject to extensive regulation by government. This is partly because of something called 'asymmetric information'. In this case, borrowers have better information about the likely risk and return from their projects than lenders have and so some degree of regulation is necessary to prevent lenders from being exploited. Regulation is also thought to be necessary to prevent financial institutions from taking on too much risk. This is because the costs associated with the failure of a financial firm, especially if it is a bank, are very high. Although the tendency has been to reduce the extent of financial regulation in recent years, rules about the type and volume of business that financial firms can do remain. The next chapter provides some examples in the case of banks and building societies.

Such regulation, drawing dividing lines between different types of institution, reduces competition. A surplus, for example, of loanable funds in one part of the system cannot be made available to satisfy excess demand elsewhere. For many years (before 1986 when steps were taken to broaden the borrowing and lending powers of building societies) it was argued that the UK financial system was biased towards channelling funds into the domestic property market and against supplying cheap funds to industry. The result, it was said, was to produce a booming housing market and a low rate of growth of productivity and output. The situation arose because building societies offered savings products which were very attractive to households (partly because of their tax treatment). Thus building societies received large flows of funds which they could lend quite cheaply to people who wished to buy (largely secondhand) unproductive assets. Meanwhile firms (even firms wishing to buy buildings) had to borrow elsewhere at higher rates of interest. As the next chapter shows, the 1986 Building Societies Act, and later legislation, allowed building societies more freedom in their source and use of funds, but restrictions remain and building societies still do very little 'commercial' lending.

In this one example, we see that information is not perfectly available to all, lenders and borrowers are not entirely free to lend to and borrow from whomsoever they wish, and taxes can certainly influence decisions. As a result, the flow of funds can be distorted.

A different illustration is provided by securities markets, the market for ordinary company shares, for example. The shareholders of a firm are its legal owners and they appoint the Board of Directors who in turn give general direction to a firm and appoint its managers. Taking control of a firm thus requires either ownership of, or influence over, at least 50 per cent of the ordinary shares. In a takeover battle, this is the target for the 'predator' firm. Clearly, the higher the price of a firm's shares, the more costly it is to buy 50 per cent. Thus, other things being equal, a high share price provides an element of security against takeover, while a low share price may invite predators.

In theory, the price of a company's shares should reflect the 'fundamental value' of the firm. As we explain in Chapter 6, this means that the price should be determined by the profits that the firm can earn from its assets. As above, the level of profit is seen as some indicator of the value which society places on the firm's activities. Low profits, and a low share price, indicate that the firm is not providing goods or services which people want particularly strongly, or that it is not doing so efficiently. In these circumstances, it could be argued, it might be a good idea if the firm were taken over (by another firm with high profits and a high share price) and reorganised into a more valuable productive unit. In these circumstances, a takeover is one way of bringing superior management expertise to a poorly performing firm. It might be uncomfortable for the management (and workers) of the firm being taken over, but there would be a sound economic rationale. Notice though that the rationale depends critically upon share prices. For the process to work correctly, a company's share price has to accurately reflect the performance of its underlying assets. If the predator firm has a high share price for reasons not associated with its assets' performance, there can be no guarantee of superior management. Equally, if the target firm has a low share price for reasons which have little to do with its economic performance, this may be no indication of poor management expertise. So far as getting the best management resources to places where they are most needed, the results of takeovers in these circumstances will be a lottery.

A further consequence of mispricing can be seen in the cost of capital to a firm. Imagine a firm whose capital structure is financed entirely by the issue of ordinary shares. If the firm wishes to expand by raising new capital, the rate of return to existing shareholders tells us the rate that will have to be available on the new shares. The shareholders' return, in other words, is the firm's cost of capital. As we shall see in Chapter 6 (eqn 6.14), this rate of return varies inversely with the price of the shares. Thus, a firm whose share price is 'high' can raise new funds more cheaply than when the price is 'low'. (Think of this as the difference between the number of pounds that the firm can buy in return for a given dividend payment.) With a low cost of capital a firm may be encouraged to expand, while if capital is costly it may be deterred. As we said above, provided that the price of shares reflects the 'fundamentals' of the business, a 'high' or 'low' price conveys a signal to the firm that will ultimately benefit society. But if the price has nothing to do with a firm's earnings and therefore nothing to do with the utility that consumers derive from its products, firms may be encouraged to expand or contract with no corresponding benefit to the community at large.

An extreme example of this was provided by the 'dot.com' boom of 2000, when investors queued up to buy internet businesses which were being floated on the stock exchange with no earnings history at all, and no prospect of making a profit for some years. When the flotation of Lastminute.com was announced in March 2000 the response was so enthusiastic that the issuing bank revised the offer price, raising it by 67 per cent. While companies like Lastminute.com found investors fighting to supply it with funds, the prices of utility companies (water, gas, electricity, etc.) were depressed to the point that some lost their position in the FTSE-100 index. How much of investors' capital was to be wasted in this craze became apparent a year later. As one broker later said, with the benefit of hindsight: 'We all invested in a few [dot.coms]. You look at it now and think you must have been a bit crackers . . .' (10 March 2001, *Financial Times*).

So far, we have considered several ways in which the financial system can contribute to the functioning of a developed economy. In recent years, however, there has been a growth of interest in the way in which financial systems may contribute to the development of low-income countries. Clearly, a less-developed country should benefit from a financial system which encourages lending and borrowing in the same way that a developed economy should benefit. There should be more saving and investment, less consumption and a higher rate of economic growth (as we described in section 2.3). But in many low-income countries we find that governments impose many restrictions on the functioning of the financial system and even interfere directly in its working. This is a situation that has come to be known as 'financial repression'. A common example of such interference is a ceiling (or 'cap') on interest rates to hold them below the market clearing level. Sometimes this is done in the misguided belief that by keeping the cost of borrowing artificially low, firms will be encouraged to borrow and invest and so raise the level of productivity. Sometimes, however, it is simply a way of making it cheaper for the government itself to borrow in order to finance a large budget deficit. Whatever the reason for such a cap, the effects on investment and growth are usually negative for two reasons: one fairly obvious, the other more complex.

To understand the first problem, we have to visualise a diagram rather like Figure 2.1a but with only a single supply curve. Instead of the rate of interest settling where the demand and supply curves intersect, a rate of interest below the market-clearing rate is imposed. There is an excess demand for funds. (This low rate of interest encourages firms to borrow for investment, but it discourages lending.) Since firms can only borrow what is lent, the low price has only succeeded in limiting investment.

The second problem begins with the excess demand. The standard test of a worthwhile investment project is that its rate of return should equal or exceed the cost of capital. With a low rate of interest, the threshold test is set very low and there are potentially many profitable projects amongst which the limited funds must be allocated. Furthermore, many of these potentially profitable projects will have low rates of return (equal to or just above the low rate of interest) indicating that they have low productivity and will contribute little to increasing the economy's rate of economic growth. In short, the average productivity of the potential projects will be lower than it would be if the test rate were set higher (say, at the market-clearing level). The question then is: how are lenders to allocate the limited funds? They may do it by lending to the lowest risk projects (which are also likely to be low productivity); they may lend 'by name', i.e. to borrowers with an established reputation for being creditworthy; they may lend to firms whose owners occupy a powerful political position and may be able to bring more business in future; or they may lend to firms whose owners are prepared to pay bribes. From an economic viewpoint, it does not matter much which method is used. The point is that the average productivity of the potential projects is low and lenders have no mechanism at their disposal which is bound to select only the few genuinely high-productivity schemes.

So, not only will the *quantity* of investment funds be limited, they are likely to be channelled into relatively poor-*quality* projects. Even if the financial repression is well-meant (i.e. to encourage development) it is more likely to do the opposite.

2.5 Summary

The financial system and the 'real' economy can interact in a number of ways. Firstly, it is in the real economy that people earn and spend incomes. Earning and spending generates surpluses and deficits, and it is a prime function of a financial system that it can reconcile those surpluses and deficits by creating for lenders and borrowers those assets and liabilities which most closely match their preferences for risk and return. Secondly, in doing this job, the financial system creates both liquidity and money proper. An expanding real economy requires additional liquidity, but it is at least theoretically possible that the financial system can generate additional spending power, in advance of the growth of output, which has the effect of raising the level of aggregate demand, with an effect on the price level or on output which depends on circumstances.

Thirdly, by making lending and borrowing easier, a financial system must also make it cheaper. Either more funds are available at the going price (than would otherwise be) or the same funds are available at a lower price. The price here is the rate of interest. Whichever effect dominates, the result will be an increase in the level of saving and investment. This changes the *composition* of aggregate demand, and may increase the future rate of growth of output.

Finally, regardless of the *volume* of lending and borrowing which it encourages, the financial system may be efficient in directing the funds to their most productive use or it may not. The system is not perfect. Not everyone knows the opportunities available; not everyone can get access to them. The tax system is not always neutral between different types of lending/borrowing, and government regulation, designed to protect lenders and borrowers, may also create distortions. Furthermore, we cannot be certain that financial markets always price financial assets 'correctly', in relation to their fundamental values. Where this happens, the ownership of the underlying assets may change for no good reason.

Questions for discussion

1 Distinguish between 'saving', 'lending' and a 'financial surplus'.

2 A financial surplus *must* result in the net acquisition of financial assets. Assume that you are in normal employment and that you regularly run a financial surplus. Assume further that you make no conscious decision to buy financial assets. What financial assets will you inevitably acquire?

3 If your income and capital account showed that you had made a 'negative net acquisition of financial assets', what would this mean in practice?

4 Using the latest available figures, find the value of households' net acquisition of UK ordinary company shares. How does this acquisition figure compare with the stock of ordinary company shares already held? What were the most popular assets acquired by households?

5 Outline three ways in which the behaviour of the financial system could affect the level of aggregate demand in the economy.

6 Suppose that prices in the US stock market suffer a major collapse. What effect would you expect this to have upon the rest of the US economy and the economies of other developed countries?

7 Why does a company's share price matter in a takeover battle? If you were the financial director of a predator firm, what would you want to happen to your firm's share price? Might you be able to influence it in any way?

8 Why might financial systems fail to allocate resources to their most desirable use?

Further reading

A D Bain, *The Financial System* (Oxford: Blackwell, 2e, 1992) ch. 2

M Buckle and J Thompson, *The UK Financial System* (Manchester: Manchester UP, 4e, 2004) chs. 1 and 16

P G A Howells and K Bain, *The Economics of Money, Banking and Finance* (Harlow: Financial Times Prentice Hall, 3e, 2005) ch. 1

P J Montiel, *Macroeconomics in Emerging Markets* (Cambridge: CUP, 2003) ch. 12

A M Santomero and D F Babbell, *Financial Markets, Instruments and Institutions* (McGraw-Hill, 2e, 2001) chs. 1 and 2

Answers to exercises

2.1 (a) £83.8 million (or 16.8%); (b) £7m; (c) £76.8 million.

2.2 (a) Initial velocity was 0.888; (b) it was expected to fall to about 0.870 (i.e. by about 2 per cent).

2.3 Initial average holdings of money are £2,000 and velocity is 1.0. After the change, money holdings are £1,100 and velocity is 1.82. The loan will finance £1,636 of spending.

CHAPTER 3

Deposit-taking institutions

Objectives

What you will learn in this chapter:

- The functions of the central bank
- The functions of different types of commercial bank
- How banking activity can affect the quantity of money in the economy
- How central banks can influence the money-creation process
- The functions of building societies
- How competition between deposit-taking institutions has led to the practice of 'liability management' and how this has made the conduct of monetary policy more difficult

There is no universally accepted method of classification where financial intermediaries are concerned. However, it is quite common to distinguish between deposit-taking institutions (DTIs) and non-deposit-taking institutions (NDTIs). There are three reasons for this. Firstly, the deposit liabilities of DTIs (or at least a large subset of them) usually form the bulk of a country's money supply. The quantity and growth of these deposits are often of considerable policy interest to the government and central bank and so DTIs are often subject to pressures and influences which do not apply to NDTIs. Secondly, because deposit liabilities are money, the failure of a DTI means that people lose, at least temporarily, access to the means of payment. This can be very serious and so DTIs are usually subject to supervision and regulation which is not applied to NDTIs. Lastly, customers hold deposits for reasons which are rather different from the reasons which cause them to hold other types of financial product. For example, changes in the quantity of bank and building society deposits which people hold are often the *result* of fluctuations in their income and day-to-day spending (fluctuations in their 'net financial surplus') and the fact that they have long-term commitments to holding or buying other types of financial asset. In that sense deposit holdings are a residual and act as a buffer, increasing when there is a surplus and declining when there is a deficit. Deposit holdings are sometimes said to be *discretionary* because people are free to make decisions about the quantity they can hold, from day to day. By contrast, the decisions to acquire other types of financial asset (pension funds, life assurance, etc.) often involve

Table 3.1 **The classification of financial intermediaries**

Banks (under the FSMA, 2000)		
The Banking Department of the Bank of England	⎱ MFIs	
Building societies	⎰	⎱ DTIs
Credit unions		
Friendly societies		⎰
Insurance companies – 'Life' or long-term		
– 'General'		
Pension funds		⎱ NDTIs
Unit trusts		
Investment trusts		⎰

entering into a contract which stipulates regular payments to the NDTI and the terms on which withdrawals can take place. The flow of funds into and out of NDTIs is therefore often described as *contractual*. The discretionary or contractual nature of flows has important effects upon the way that DTIs and NDTIs behave towards their assets. In other words, the balance sheets of DTIs and NDTIs are very different.

It should be clear from what we have just been saying that 'DTIs' is a phrase which must overlap substantially with 'banks'. Table 3.1 shows the relationship between these terms more precisely. Note that some DTIs are *not* banks. In the UK, the obvious example is building societies. They differ from banks in their legal status and in the regulations to which they are subject. Nonetheless, their deposits have been part of the officially defined money supply since July 1989 and their clients certainly use them in the same way that they would use banks. This means that their balance sheets also closely resemble those of banks. Hence, it is very useful to have a category which enables us to put banks and building societies together. We do this with the term 'monetary financial institutions' or MFIs. Table 3.1 shows how banks fit within the broader category of MFIs, which in turn fit within the broader category of DTIs. Together with NDTIs, DTIs make up what we are calling 'financial institutions'.

Before we begin looking at any specific type of financial institution, however, a few further words of clarification are necessary. One consequence of the liberalisation of financial market activity in Europe during the 1980s has been the merger of specialist financial institutions into conglomerates offering a wide range of financial services. This in turn has led non-merging firms to diversify their own activities by setting up subsidiaries. Thus banks have taken on insurance, fund management and market-making roles while insurance companies have become deposit-takers. 'Bankassurance' is a term sometimes used to describe this conglomerate activity. In short, it is no longer possible to find a firm which functions uniquely as a bank. Similarly, it is impossible to find a firm which functions uniquely as an insurer or fund manager. Rather than thinking about different types of 'institution', we should probably be thinking about different types of financial activity, all or most of them being hosted within a major financial firm.

By way of illustration, Box 3.1 shows the structure and activities of the Royal Bank of Scotland (RBS) Group in 2006.

Box 3.1   The RBS Group in 2006

Retail banking	Citizens	RBS Insurance	Direct Retail	Manufacturing	Wealth management	Ulster Bank	Corporate banking and financial markets
Banking, insurance and financial services for individuals and small businesses	Retail and corporate banking activities through its branch network in 13 states in the northeastern US and through non-branch offices in other states.	Sells and underwrites retail, commercial and wholesale insurance on the telephone, the internet, and through brokers and intermediaries.	Retail and wholesale insurance via phone and the internet	Technology support and payment mechanisms	Private banking and offshore banking services	Retail and wholesale banking services to clients in Northern Ireland	Banking services to firms, derivatives, forex money market, bond and gilt market making
UK financial services	*US banking*	*Insurance*	*Internet banking*	*Support services*	*Banking services for overseas*	*NI financial services*	*Corporate and investment banking*

In the days when banks were the only institutions whose liabilities were counted as 'money', one used to be able to group the rest of the private sector (in effect, banks' clients) as the 'non-bank private sector' or NBPS. Since 1989, however, when the official measure of broad money became M4 and included building society deposits, the corresponding expression became the 'non-bank, non-building society private sector'! Fortunately, this has come to be shortened to 'M4 private sector' or M4PS. It might loosely be translated as 'the general public'.

In the remainder of this chapter, we shall focus on the Bank of England and then on banks and building societies. In Chapter 4, we shall focus on the behaviour of non-deposit-taking institutions. In both chapters we begin with descriptive material and then move to issues of economic importance.

3.1 The Bank of England

The Bank of England is the UK's central bank. At various times central banks are responsible for some or all of the following:

- the conduct of monetary policy;
- banker to the commercial banking system;
- banker to the government;
- supervisor of the banking system;
- manager of the national debt;
- manager of the foreign exchange reserves;
- issuer of the national currency.

In recent years, there has been a tendency towards giving central banks increased independence in their conduct of monetary policy and a mandate which requires them to focus on price stability ahead of all other objectives. Where this has happened (as in New Zealand, Canada, Chile, Mexico, France and in the UK since 1997) it can create conflicts between the monetary policy and other roles. For example, a central bank whose charter requires it to use every available monetary instrument to achieve the single target of a low rate of inflation will find that it has to make frequent *changes* to interest rates and sometimes push them to *high levels*. The first of these causes bond prices to fluctuate (see section 6.2.1), which may reduce the demand for government bonds and make it difficult for the central bank to manage the national debt as it would wish if it were also charged with that responsibility. The latter may cause some bank borrowers to default, and a bank which already has some poorly performing loans might be pushed into insolvency. If the central bank were also responsible for supervising and maintaining stability of the banking system, it may be reluctant to raise interest rates as required by monetary policy.

These potential conflicts of interest explain why the more independent central banks, charged with the conduct of a strict anti-inflationary monetary policy, tend *not* to have the full range of responsibilities listed above. (There is little point in trying to make the central bank more powerful in its anti-inflation role by making it independent of government if it is still going to have other responsibilities which interfere with the conduct of monetary policy.) They also explain why the supervisory and debt management functions were removed from the Bank of England when it became more independent in 1997.

In the rest of this section we shall look briefly at each function and then, where appropriate, explain the Bank of England's current role.

3.1.1 The conduct of monetary policy

No central bank can avoid some involvement with the conduct of monetary policy. This is because the conduct of monetary policy *must* involve the setting of short-term interest rates, and this is done by the central bank using its role in the money markets, exploiting its position as banker to the rest of the banking system (see section 5.3). However, while the setting of rates must involve the central bank, the decision as to what rate to set may be made elsewhere. This is what used to happen in the case of the Bank of England until the mid-1990s. The Bank of England was formally nationalised in 1947 and from then until 1997 the level of interest rates was determined formally by the Chancellor of the Exchequer, advised by both the Treasury and the Bank of England. However, during the 1970s and 1980s evidence seemed to accumulate that linked low inflation with central bank independence of government. This led to tentative steps towards giving the Bank of England more responsibility for setting interest rates, independently of the government's preferences. Firstly, in November 1993, it was agreed that the Bank would have discretion in the *timing* of interest rate changes, though the change itself still needed the Chancellor's agreement.

Next, in April 1994, it was decided that minutes of the monthly meetings between the Chancellor and the Governor of the Bank of England should be published promptly. It was argued that this would serve two purposes. Firstly, it would reveal the reasons for interest rate changes and thus provide information to agents which would enable them to make their own judgement about the future trend of interest rates. Secondly, the minutes would reveal any difference of opinion between Chancellor and Governor and observers would be able to see for themselves whether short-term political considerations were entering into the decision. Thus, it was hoped, the Chancellor would be less likely to argue for a particular interest rate decision on 'political' grounds and this would increase the Bank of England's 'credibility' in the fight against inflation.

However, the major step towards independence came in May 1997 when it was announced by the new Labour government that the Bank would have complete independence in its setting of whatever interest rates were required to achieve and maintain an inflation target of 2.5 per cent (+/− 1 per cent). The decision was placed in the hands of a Monetary Policy Committee (MPC) consisting of nine members: the Governor of the Bank and four other senior Bank personnel, and four specialists appointed by the Chancellor of the Exchequer. The Governor retains the casting vote. There is a strong emphasis on accountability, with the minutes of the MPC's monthly meetings (and voting record) being published, along with a quarterly *Inflation Report* which contains the evidence about inflationary trends upon which the MPC is basing its decision. Notice though that while this independence marks a major transition from the arrangements between 1947 and 1993, it falls short of the degree of independence enjoyed by some other central banks. In particular, the Bank of England is limited to 'instrument independence' – it is free to set the level of interest rates required to achieve a target, but the target is set by the government. This contrasts with the instrument *and* 'goal independence' of the European Central Bank (ECB) and the Federal Reserve (in the US) which also set what they think is the appropriate target.

> **Instrument independence:** The freedom of the central bank to take whatever steps it thinks necessary to achieve the goal laid down by government.
>
> **Full independence:** The freedom of the central bank to choose *both* the goal (usually a target rate of inflation) and the steps necessary to achieve it.

The trend towards increasing central bank independence has its origin in the observation that there is a positive correlation between the political independence of central banks and low rates of inflation. Indicators of political independence include such things as the role of government in appointing members of the central bank board, government representation on the board, the length of term of the senior bank officers compared with government, and the details of the bank's charter. The earliest work was done by Bade and Parkin (1985), who found this correlation across twelve OECD countries. Grilli *et al.* (1991) extended the study by adding indicators of *economic* independence (e.g. the government's ability to borrow from the central bank). They found that political independence correlated with low inflation in the 1970s while economic independence seemed more important in the 1980s. Later studies (Alesina and Summers, 1993) extended the measures of independence and the countries examined. The basic hypothesis continued to be confirmed.

The theory behind the hypothesis contained two elements. The first is that democratically elected governments have an incentive to run monetary policy with a bias towards inflation. This is because the short-term effect of a monetary expansion, especially if it is unexpected, is usually to reduce unemployment and increase output. These are both results which impress voters and thus increase the popularity of governments, even though the employment and output effects do not last. When the positive 'real' effects have worn off, the community is left with a higher price level and agents who expect that prices will continue to rise. Policy has then to be switched to deflation in order to reverse these expectations. Since it does not have to appeal to voters, a central bank should be able to resist pressure for undesirable monetary expansion.

The second argument was known as the 'time-inconsistency' problem and is based on the fact that society's wellbeing is improved by *both* low inflation and low unemployment. Hence, once the policy-maker has achieved low inflation, he automatically has an incentive to expand the economy to improve the unemployment position. But this only serves to increase inflation again so that, over time, a policy-maker with *discretion to choose* the instrument settings will deliver a higher rate of inflation on average than would be the case if he were *constrained* to minimise inflation.

On the face of it, both the theory and the evidence look sound. But there are criticisms of both. The major one is probably that the empirical studies do not look at other (non-central bank) factors which may play a part in a country's predisposition towards inflation. For example, in Germany, whose central bank was often portrayed as the ideal model of independence, there is a widespread fear and dislike of inflation. This stems from historical episodes, in 1921–23 and 1948, when inflation wiped out the savings of millions of people and reduced transactions to barter. Understandably, trade unions, employers and consumers are strongly opposed to any development which might foreshadow rising prices, and this undoubtedly gave the Bundesbank a relatively easy task, with or without independence. (It remains to be seen whether the ECB, modelled on the Bundesbank, will enjoy such widespread popular support.)

There are problems on the theory side too. Firstly, the beneficial effects on output and employment are purely temporary because agents are assumed to be well-informed and realise that the higher money wages they are being paid to attract them into work are quickly offset by rising prices. Realising that their *real* wage has not risen they withdraw again from employment. Even so, the theory says that governments have a *continuing* incentive to trick people into work by monetary expansion. This suggests that agents can learn about the difference between real and money wages but apparently cannot learn not to vote for governments that keep tricking them. It seems that agents are quick to learn some things but not others. There is some contradiction here.

Secondly, the incentives in the time inconsistency problem apply to *all* policy-makers. Putting the decision in the hands of a central bank rather than government in itself changes nothing. What is required is something additional, namely a central bank that ignores the benefits of surprise expansions. This is sometimes called a 'conservative' central bank. But it is not obvious why a central bank should find it easier to be 'conservative' than a politician who knows that surprise expansions do not fool the electorate.

3.1.2 Banker to the commercial banking system

Later in this chapter we shall emphasise that a country's money supply is dominated by bank deposits (notes and coin make up only a small proportion of the total). Thus, while some bank deposits may be held as a form of saving, many deposits ('sight' deposits in particular) will be held as their owners need them as a means of payment. In the course of the average working day, customers of one bank will make payments to other customers of the same bank, but also to customers of other banks in the system. Payments between customers of bank A and bank B require some means whereby funds can be moved between the two banks. This is done in most systems by commercial banks holding their own accounts at the central bank. A payment from customer A to customer B is then matched by the central bank debiting the account of bank A and crediting the corresponding sum to bank B.

Furthermore, the willingness of the general public to hold bank deposits and regard them as 'money' (something which we all take for granted today) depends ultimately on the confidence that deposits can *always* be converted to notes and coin on demand. However, banks could not operate at a profit if for every deposit (liability) they had to hold corresponding cash (assets), since notes and coin do not pay interest. In practice, they hold only a small, carefully calculated fraction of cash to deposits. (A *very* small fraction, as we shall see in the next section.) This opens up the possibility, in theory at least, that a bank could find itself in a position where it could not meet an unexpectedly large demand for cash withdrawals. This could cause a panic in which depositors generally tried to withdraw cash all at once and banks, which were perfectly sound commercially, would nonetheless be forced out of business. (The consequences of bank failure are discussed further under the question of supervision below.) For this reason, the central bank occupies the role of *lender of last resort*. Just as the general public can borrow from commercial banks, so commercial banks can borrow from the central bank.

Lender of last resort: The ultimate provider of reserves to the banking system.

The Bank of England's balance sheet is shown in Table 3.2.

Table 3.2 Bank of England balance sheet, end 2005, £m

Banking Department	
Liabilities and capital	
Capital	14
Public deposits	615
Bankers' deposits	3,117
Reserve and other accounts	21,095
	24,841
Assets	
Government securities	2,126
Advances and other accounts	14,977
Premises, equipment, other securities	7,737
Notes and coin	1
	24,841
Issue Department	
Liabilities	
Notes in circulation	39,329
Notes in banking department	1
	39,330
Assets	
Government securities	13,370
Other securities	25,960
	39,330

Source: Adapted from ONS, *Financial Statistics February 2006*, table 4.2A

The relationship between the balance sheets of commercial banks and the central bank, and the effects on both of various flows, are examined further in section 3.4.

3.1.3 Banker to the government

In some, but not all, financial systems the government holds its accounts with the central bank rather than with the commercial banks. Where this is the case, payments between the government and the private sector will involve transfers inside the central bank between the government's accounts and the accounts held by commercial banks. For example, if customers of bank A make net payments to the government (as they will when paying taxes, for example), funds are debited from bank A's account at the central bank and credited to the government account. In fact, if there are net payments (payments in excess of receipts) from the whole of the private sector to government (as there are on occasions), the whole of the commercial banking system may find itself being debited to the point where there is a serious shortage of funds available to commercial banks. On the other hand, net payments from government to the private sector as a whole will lead to an expansion of commercial bank deposits at the central bank.

3.1.4 Supervisor of the banking system

Central banks are often responsible for the supervision of the banking system. This involves some form of licensing, control over the appointment of directors of commercial banks and the laying down and monitoring of key financial ratios in commercial banks' balance sheets. The reason for all supervision of financial institutions originates with 'asymmetric information' – the fact that customers of the institutions are less well informed and thus more at a disadvantage about the affairs of the intermediary than the intermediary is itself.

The case for banking supervision is further strengthened by worries about the consequences of bank failure. It is widely felt that bank failures are especially serious and damaging to the economy. If an insurance company becomes insolvent, for example, policyholders will find that they no longer have the cover for which they had paid their latest premium. There is plainly a loss to policyholders, consisting of the wasted premium plus the risk of temporary lack of cover, plus the inconvenience of finding a new policy. However, this loss is not likely to affect their behaviour in any dramatic way and it is unlikely that the failure of one insurance company will have direct repercussions on others. The failure of a bank, however, means that many depositors will lose not just some fraction of their wealth but also their *means of payment*. This again originates from bank deposits functioning as money. If they lose their means of payment, people are bound to take instant steps to remedy the situation. This will involve the rapid sale of other assets. The price of these assets is then bound to fall, and since other financial institutions hold these assets as part of their portfolio, the value of their assets declines and they in turn could become insolvent. This chain of events is a way of saying that the 'negative externalities' of bank failure can be severe.

For this reason, banks generally enjoy two advantages over other financial institutions. The first is that they have access to a 'lender of last resort facility' provided by the central bank (discussed in 3.1.2 above). The second is a system of deposit insurance, operated by the banking supervisory body, whereby clients of a bank which fails are guaranteed that at least a proportion of their deposits will be safe. Box 3.2 gives a summary of the terms that apply to deposit insurance in the UK at the time of writing.

Box 3.2

UK deposit insurance in 2005

The scheme, operated by the FSA, covers banks, building societies and credit unions (deposit-taking firms) listed on the FSA's Register of Authorised Firms. If a bank, building society or credit union goes out of business, the scheme pays the first £2,000 in full of the amount that clients have on deposit. It also pays 90 per cent of the next £33,000. This means a maximum compensation of £31,700.

If depositors have more than £35,000 deposited in a bank, building society or credit union, the extra amount (above £35,000) is not eligible for compensation. How much of this extra amount a depositor will recover from an insolvent bank, building society or credit union will depend on how much of the bank, building society or credit union's assets can be recovered.

Source: www.fsa.gov.uk

Given these advantages, it is not surprising that banks must be prepared to accept a high degree of supervision in return. If this were not the case, it would be at least a possibility that banks might behave in a reckless manner, in pursuit of additional profit, knowing that if their schemes went wrong, the lender of last resort might help them, while the supervisory body would protect bank depositors from losing all their deposits. (The idea that protection schemes can encourage people or firms to behave more recklessly than they would otherwise is known as 'moral hazard' and is discussed in connection with insurance companies in the next chapter.)

The need for supervision may be widely accepted, but it does not have to be done by the central bank. As we noted above, supervision of the banking system is one of the activities which can potentially give rise to conflicts of interest if carried out by a central bank which has independent responsibility for the conduct of monetary policy. In Germany, for example, the responsibility for banking supervision rests with the *Aufsichtsamt*, the Federal Banking Supervisory Office. In the UK, supervision of the banking system has traditionally been carried out by the Bank of England. Its most recent authority stemmed from the Banking Act 1987 which required the Bank of England to exercise the following powers:

- licensing of all deposit-taking institutions (except building societies);
- ensuring that institutions have adequate *capital, liquidity and controls*;
- ensuring they make adequate provision for bad debts;
- checking that directors of banking institutions are 'fit and proper persons'.

With the changes to the Bank of England's responsibility for monetary policy in 1997, these powers (together with many staff) were transferred by the Bank of England Act in June 1998 to a newly established Financial Services Authority (FSA), which eventually became responsible for the supervision of all financial intermediaries in 2001.

Banking, like most forms of financial intermediation, is increasingly an international activity. Banks with headquarters in one country, for example, may operate subsidiaries in many others. This poses a problem for supervisors, partly because differences between national rules may lead to distortions in the pattern of banking activity whereby banks concentrate certain types of business in those countries where regulation is lightest, and partly because there is a danger that foreign subsidiaries 'fall between the cracks' when it comes to supervision: the home authority cannot exercise supervision in the host country, while the host country supervisor may not feel a responsibility for foreign banks. Thus much activity in recent years has gone into the international co-ordination of banking supervision. For example, the capital tests imposed by the FSA are derived from the EC Capital Adequacy Directive, 1996, while the EC Second Banking Co-ordination Directive, 1993, places the responsibility for supervision of overseas branches on the home supervisor but lays down rules to ensure the co-operation between home and host authorities. Thus branches of banks with headquarters in other EU states are permitted to operate in the UK on the strength of the licence issued in the home country. The general issue of financial regulation and supervision is discussed further in Chapter 13.

3.1.5 Management of the national debt

Another activity which is sometimes the responsibility of the central bank is the management of the national debt. In most years since 1945, the UK government has run a budget deficit and the national debt is the accumulation of successive annual borrowings. At the end of 2003, the UK debt stood at £470bn or approximately 43 per cent of GDP.

Decisions have to be made therefore about both the funding of new, annual deficits and the refinancing of that fraction of the existing debt which matures each year. Both can be financed in a number of ways, each with different monetary consequences. For example, funds can be raised by sales of marketable debt (treasury bills and government bonds) or non-marketable debt (National Savings products in the UK). Within each of these categories, there are further decisions to be made. Treasury bills generally have an initial maturity of ninety-one days and are therefore highly liquid. Bonds may have an initial maturity of five years or up to twenty-five years. A decision to issue mainly long-dated bonds, for example, means that the overall maturity structure of the national debt is lengthened, as long-dated bonds form an increasing proportion of the total. This might cause long-term interest rates to rise relative to short and, since long-dated assets are less liquid than short-dated ones, the supply of liquid assets will diminish relative to less liquid ones. The opposite consequences will follow if the authorities fund the national debt by the issue of short-dated bills. Lengthening the average maturity of the debt is confusingly called 'funding', while shortening it is unattractively called 'unfunding'. If the quantity of liquid assets, not just money, in the economy has any effect upon people's willingness to spend, then 'unfunding' could be one part of an expansionary part monetary policy. 'Funding' would be associated with a tightening of monetary policy.

Once issued, bonds can be bought and sold and may pass through many hands in the course of their lifetime. This means that the central bank, if it is responsible for debt management, will have to maintain an up-to-date register of bond ownership and make efficient provision for the payment of bond interest to current holders.

Debt management was one of the oldest functions of the Bank of England. But in April 1998 it was transferred to a new Debt Management Office, an executive agency of the UK Treasury. The reason for the transfer lies in the assumption that holders of government bonds are 'capital risk averse'. This means that they buy bonds partly for the secure interest they pay and also in the hope that their prices will not fluctuate beyond narrow limits. But as Chapter 6 shows, bond prices *must* fluctuate (inversely) with interest rates. A central bank whose primary function is the control of inflation must be free to change interest as often as it likes. The argument is that it might hesitate to do that if it is also trying to maximise the sale of government bonds *and* it believes that buyers might be frightened off by price volatility. Without responsibility for debt management, the Bank of England has more freedom to set interest rates as it thinks appropriate for its anti-inflation policy.

3.1.6 Manager of the foreign exchange reserves

Central banks frequently act as agents of their government in the management of foreign exchange reserves. 'Management' is necessary since governments normally have some policy towards the exchange rate. Even if they do not operate a fixed exchange rate policy, governments will normally want to prevent sharp day-to-day fluctuations in the exchange rate. Resisting a rise in the value of the domestic currency means that the authorities have to enter the foreign exchange market and sell the domestic currency for foreign currency. Resisting a fall in the value of the domestic currency means selling foreign exchange.

In the UK, management of the foreign exchange reserves rests with the Bank of England.

3.1.7 Currency issue

Central banks are commonly responsible for the issue of some or all of a country's notes and coin. In the UK, for example, the Bank of England designs, prints and issues the country's banknotes. There is no policy to limit the note issue. Notes are issued on demand to commercial banks, which pay for them by surrendering some of their deposits at the Bank. The process is analogous to commercial bank customers withdrawing deposits in the form of cash. Such constraints as there are on the note issue are constraints upon the *demand* for money as a whole, and as we have already seen, deposits form a much larger proportion of the money stock as a whole than do currency notes. Since the cost of producing a banknote is considerably less than its face value, there is a substantial profit to be made from the printing and issue. This known as 'seignorage' and is paid, in the UK, to the Treasury.

Some central banks are responsible also for the issue of coins, but in the UK this is the responsibility of the Royal Mint.

3.2 Banks

As Table 3.1 shows, the term 'banks' covers a wide variety of institutions whose principal function is to accept deposits and make loans. All deposit-taking institutions require a licence which is granted by the FSA under the Financial Markets and Services Act (FSMA), 2000. But not all deposit-taking institutions are 'banks'. For example, insurance companies often hold deposits on behalf of their clients in the course of arranging cover and settling claims. These are excluded from the definition of 'bank', together with building societies, credit unions and friendly societies. The banking department of the Bank of England is also excluded (a change since 2000). The category does, though, include the supermarkets and other retail stores which have started to offer basic banking services in recent years. Examples are Sainsbury's Bank plc and Marks and Spencer Financial Services plc. It also includes branches of foreign banks whose licences are granted by regulators in their home countries but which meet the terms of what is known as 'schedule 3' of the FSMA, 2000.

If we add building societies and the banking department of the Bank of England to 'banks', we have a category known as 'monetary financial institutions' (MFIs). These are institutions whose deposits feature in official measures of the country's money supply. If we then add to this category the credit unions and friendly societies mentioned earlier, we have 'deposit-taking institutions'.

The FSA website (www.fsa.gov.uk/pubs/list_banks/2005/lob_apr05.pdf) maintains a list of institutions making up the category of 'banks'. The constituents are grouped together by nationality of the head office. The list numbers approximately 500. Table 3.3 shows the consolidated balance sheet of banks operating in the UK.

In years gone by, it used to be possible (and useful) to classify banking firms by the kind of banking business that they did. Thus we used to speak of 'clearing banks'. These contrasted with 'merchant banks', 'discount houses' and so on. However, since the 1980s there has been a remarkable trend towards merger and the globalisation of banking activity, with the result that the major retail banking firms now include not just a retail banking division but also divisions specialising in other forms of banking (and even divisions specialising in non-banking activity, as we saw in Box 3.1).

In Figure 3.1, we have divided banking activities into four main groups. *Retail banking* involves the provision of loan and deposits facilities to the personal or household sector. It also includes banks which provide similar services to small and medium-sized firms. Both types of activity include payment services, and so banks operating in both parts of the retail sector are heavily involved in the payments mechanism. Under the heading of *wholesale banking* we have 'corporate banks' which provide loan and deposits facilities to large corporate clients and also a large range of fee-based financial advice of relevance to the major plcs. In addition, we have a range of institutions, known as 'investment banks', whose principal activities have little direct contact with conventional banking activity at all (loans and deposits)

Table 3.3 Banks in the UK – assets and liabilities (£m, end-December 2005)

Assets		% of total	Liabilities and capital		% of total
Notes and coin	9,501	0.17	Deposits	3,465,704[1]	62.70
			CDs	507,959	9.19
Operational deposits at the Bank of England	1,388	0.035	Repurchase agreements	1,008,858	18.25
Cash ratio deposits	1,949	0.025	Other	205,505	3.72
Market loans and CDs	960,085	17.37	Capital etc.	338,835	6.13
Bills	41,831	0.75			
Acceptances	1,774	0.32			
Repurchase agreements	1,245,043	22.53			
Investments	722,053	13.06			
Advances	2,324,241	42.05			
Other	218,996	3.96			
	5,526,861	100.0[2]		5,526,861	100.0[2]

[1] Includes sterling sight deposits of £883,315 equal to 16% of total liabilities.
[2] Percentages may not sum to 100 owing to rounding.

Source: Adapted from ONS, *Financial Statistics February 2006*, table 4.3A

	Retail banking		Wholesale banking	
	Personal	Small business	Corporate	Investment
Retail banks				
– the 'Big Five'	●	●	●	●
– others	●	◌	◌	
Wholesale banks				
– UK 'merchant banks'			●	●
– Foreign banks			●	●

Key: ● = heavily involved; ◌ = limited involvement

Figure 3.1 A taxonomy of banking

but are concerned mainly with the operation of security markets. Neither category of wholesale bank is involved in the operation of the payments mechanism.

What Figure 3.1 also shows is that retail banking is dominated by the so-called 'Big Five': HSBC, LloydsTSB, Royal Bank of Scotland, Barclays and HBOS. It also shows that these major banking groups are heavily involved in all four types of banking activity (remember that Box 3.1 showed the structure of RBS). The 'other' retail banks include the Abbey and other former building societies, and some Scottish banks. These too are engaged in business and corporate banking, though only on a limited scale and none plays any role in investment banking.

While institutions which provide retail banking services may also be involved in wholesale banking, it is not true that banks which specialise in wholesale banking provide retail services. What Figure 3.1 shows is that 'wholesale banks' can be divided into two groups, largely on the basis of ownership, and that both groups commonly operate in both areas of wholesale banking. 'UK merchant banks' are banks which had their origins in the finance of foreign trade many years ago. Some among them were known as 'acceptance houses' because they made a large part of their income from 'accepting' or guaranteeing bills of exchange. Others began as 'discount houses' whose main purpose was to discount the accepted bills for cash. Following centuries of amalgamation and diversification, both these functions and many more relating to the needs of large firms rather than households are now provided by these banks. 'Foreign banks' are branches of large international banks which also specialise in corporate and investment banking services. We turn now to the features of retail and wholesale banking in more detail.

The term *retail bank* covers about a dozen banks in total. At the centre of their activities is the provision of a money transmission service using the cheque-clearing and electronic systems. For this reason, many individuals and firms find a cheque account with a retail bank to be indispensable even if, for savings purposes, they prefer to hold accounts with other banks or building societies. The consequence of this is that retail banks have a very large number of accounts but the average size of the accounts is comparatively small. Sight deposits form a large proportion of total deposits and the majority of these deposits are in sterling.

Having a large number of accounts makes for very stable behaviour among depositors, but the small size of the deposits and their 'active' nature makes them an expensive source of funds for the banks. Three consequences have followed from this in recent years.

Firstly, retail banks have made great strides in automating the basic banking functions of taking in and paying out cash and providing account information. The first automated teller machines (ATMs), or 'cash dispensers' as they are often called, were introduced in 1967 when they did little more than give the customer access to cash in a fixed amount. By 1977 there were about 1,300 machines, which by then offered customers a choice of withdrawal amounts together with a statement of current balance. By 2004 there were 57,000 machines. About 60 per cent (34,000) of the machines are owned and operated by banks and about 19,000 of those are sited on bank premises but the growth in these locations is now very slow. The remainder are sited in 'remote' locations such as supermarkets, railway stations, filling stations, etc. and growth is much more rapid in these sites, new machines being opened at the rate of around 1,000 a year. Most of these are being opened by 'independent' operators (i.e. non-banks, non-building societies) who usually charge for their use. Although still primarily used for access to cash (there were 2.6bn withdrawals averaging £64 in 2004), these machines now offer a wide range of services, from the ordering of statements and cheque books to changing PIN numbers. Although not yet in use in the UK, machines exist which can scan a cheque and credit specified amounts across a number of accounts. In some branches, machines with touch-sensitive screens provide on-screen links to a variety of product descriptions, take customers through a series of questions and answers before recommending a product or providing a quotation, and can create a video-conferencing link with staff at a central location to deal with more complex enquiries.

The automation of cash handling also explains another trend which the UK has seen in retail banking since 1990. This is the practice of supermarkets like Tesco and Sainsbury and multiple retailers like Marks and Spencer of offering deposit, cash withdrawal and loan facilities. Such activities represent the core of traditional banking business. The advantage to the stores is that such services provide an additional convenience to customers which may encourage them to shop there. The reason for this is that technological innovation has lowered barriers to entry. Given some sort of cash-handling interface, all that is necessary is a computer network which can keep track of cash transactions centrally. For banks, the interface is increasingly a machine or ATM. For supermarkets, it is staff at the checkout already handling large quantities of cash. As stores have linked their checkouts to a computer network for stock ordering purposes, it has become a fairly cheap matter of some additional programming and software to track the inflow of deposits and withdrawal of cash alongside the inflow of money and giving of change in the normal process of buying and selling. This is very different from the days when cash handling required large numbers of staff operating from specialised premises. To begin with, retail stores acted as agents of existing banks (and still do for the more sophisticated financial products that they offer). But Tesco, Sainsbury and M&S all now have a deposit-taking licence and, on that definition, are 'banks' too.

The payment system has also been largely automated. From 1992 to 2005, payments by cheque declined from 22 per cent of total payments by volume to 12 per cent, while debit/credit card and electronic payments rose from 13 per cent to 38 per cent and from 3.5 per cent to 33.2 per cent respectively.

A second trend which reflects retail banks' attempts to reduce costs is the closure of bank branches. The total number of UK branches fell by 20 per cent between 1995 and 2003, to about 14,000. This trend itself owes something to the automation process we have just described since it is now possible for clients to carry out many of their banking operations by telephone and via the internet. In April 2000, for example, Barclays was quoted as having 1.2m telephone banking customers and 800,000 online accounts. The latter had grown at a staggering rate from just 20,000 a year earlier. There is therefore some truth in banks' assertion that the decline of branch banking is demand-led, by customer preference. On the other hand, it is interesting that building societies, which enjoyed the same benefits of automation, closed only 5 per cent of branches in the same period. It is also interesting that up until 2000 the closures were mainly in sparsely populated areas but since 2000 the majority of closures have occurred in urban locations, often inner-city areas which suffer from low incomes and other disadvantages.

A third recent trend, aimed more at generating additional income than reducing costs, can be seen in the exploitation of branches that have remained open and in particular in those into which banks have put most investment. These lie mainly in major centres of population. No doubt this reflects the familiar banking economies of scale again. But it also means that these branches are open to a large potential market for a whole range of financial products and services. A careful examination of any of these branches confirms that traditional banking functions (deposits and cash withdrawals) occupy a minority of space in large banking halls which were originally designed for a very labour-intensive operation. The reduction in cashiers and counter space has been facilitated by the development of ATMs which will also be found inside the banking hall, offering the full range of services we referred to above. The remaining space, typically half the floor area, will be devoted to the marketing of a range of products and services, some of which (foreign exchange, personal loans, trustee and executorship) are traditional activities, while some (insurance, mortgages, pensions, mutual funds) most decidedly are not but represent the movement towards universal banking that we discussed at the beginning of this chapter.

By contrast, wholesale banks are less heavily engaged in the traditional banking business of deposit taking and loan making. This is especially true of those that specialise in investment banking and asset management. Where deposits are concerned, these are much fewer in number but individually much larger than for retail banks. A high proportion is also denominated in foreign currencies (nearly 80 per cent of the total, compared with 25 per cent for retail banks). The vast majority (by value) are time deposits and so wholesale banks are much less exposed to the risk of unforeseen withdrawals and hold very few truly liquid assets. They hold no operational deposits at the Bank of England, preferring where necessary to hold deposits with the Big Four retail banks. The high proportion of time deposits means that the degree of 'maturity transformation' is markedly less than for retail banks. Finally, recall that we noted earlier that the Bank of England lists approximately 500 banks operating in the UK. Since retail banking services are provided by the Big Five plus, at most, eight other institutions, it follows that wholesale banks are extremely numerous. The fact that they are mainly invisible (except to visitors to the City of London and Canary Wharf) simply tells us that the bulk of their activities does not require a branch network.

As Figure 3.1 shows, 'wholesale banking' refers to a range of activities. 'Corporate banking' refers to the provision of banking services to large firms. In many cases, these services are scaled-up versions of the banking services provided by retail banks to households. The deposits are large, generally time, deposits; the loans are also large and may take the form of overdrafts or may be long-term lending secured on specified assets. The banks also provide advice, but it is advice relevant to the operations of large firms – on hedging foreign currency risk, for example, or using financial derivatives, or making a major investment decision.

'Investment banking', by contrast, has little obvious contact with traditional banking. Investment banks are heavily involved in security market operations. They employ 'analysts' whose job it is to study corporate trends and identify firms as over- or under-valued, or as high-growth and low-growth, high-risk and low-risk, etc. The results of the research are provided to clients who are often managers of mutual funds. The banks will sometimes be 'market makers' in equity or bond markets. Because of this expertise, they will usually handle the issue of new securities on behalf of companies wishing to become limited companies for the first time or which wish to raise additional capital for expansion. Their most high-profile work, which does occasionally bring them to public attention, involves their negotiating on behalf of clients during mergers and acquisitions or 'M&As'.

This particular mix of activities has given rise to the allegation that there are potential conflicts of interest in investment banking because analysts will be reluctant to write adverse reports about companies which are clients for the investment banks' other services. In 2002 several Wall Street investment banks achieved notoriety when it was revealed that their analysts were writing favourable reports (for fund managers and other investors) about firms that they privately regarded as very bad value. These reports obviously pleased the firms in question, which then favoured the banks with other business, in particular using the banks to handle new issues of securities and to advise on mergers, etc. In April 2003, Citigroup, CSFB and Merrill Lynch agreed to pay $880m in fines after an investigation by the US Securities and Exchange Commission and the New York attorney general.

Banks' income is earned from two principal sources. The lending rates are higher than deposit rates and this 'spread' forms the traditional source of profit for banks. But increasingly banks earn income from charging fees for advice and other services. Fee income is generally more important to wholesale banks, and especially to investment banks, than it is to retail banks where deposit taking and lending remains a large part of the banks' business.

3.3 Banks and the creation of money

For the authorities, and for most economists too, the significance of deposit-taking institutions lies in the fact that the deposits which they hold function as money. As Table 3.4 shows, the current official measure of broad money, M4, contains bank and building society deposits. Furthermore, these deposits make up 96 per cent of M4. It follows therefore that an expansion of bank and building society activity, where this involves an expansion of deposits, automatically involves an increase in the stock of money with the possibility that this in turn leads to an increase in aggregate demand and in output and/or prices. In this section we want to look firstly at why banks have

Table 3.4 Monetary aggregates – definition and magnitude, 2006, end-January

Symbol	Definition	Magnitude (£bn)
M0	Notes and coin outside the Bank of England + banks' operational deposits at the Bank of England	46
M4	Notes and coin in circulation with the non-bank, non-building society private sector[1] + M4PS holdings of sterling bank sight deposits + M4PS holdings of sterling bank time deposits and CDs + M4PS holdings of building society deposits – building society holdings of bank deposits, CDs and notes and coin	1,365

[1] The expression 'M4 private sector' is often used as a substitute for 'non-bank, non-building society private sector'.

Source: Bank of England, interactive database: series LPMAVAD and LPMAUYN an interest in expanding the volume of deposits and thereby the stock of money. Secondly, we shall look at how they are able to do it. In section 3.4 we shall look at some of the possible constraints on deposits and monetary expansion.

3.3.1 Why banks create money

The answer to the first, or 'why', question begins with a recognition that banks are private sector, profit-making organisations with obligations to shareholders to increase profits over time. Thus they will always be looking for ways of expanding their balance sheets provided this leads to extra profit. Look again at Table 3.3, which shows the aggregate balance sheet of a large number of banks. Notice that assets are composed of various forms of lending: to the personal sector, the commercial sector, the government or the Bank of England. The liabilities side is dominated by deposits. Notice also that we can express any class of asset as a proportion of total assets or liabilities and remember too that in Chapter 1 we said that these ratios are arrived at as a matter of deliberate choice and are assumed to represent portfolio equilibrium.

Box 3.3

Loans create deposits in a multi-bank system

Bank A

Assets		Liabilities	
Notes and coin	C_b	Capital and shareholders' funds	S_f
Deposits at the central bank	D_b (−)	Customer deposits	D_p
Loans to the public sector	L_g		
Loans to the general public	L_p (+)		

Bank B

Assets		Liabilities	
Notes and coin	C_b	Capital and shareholders' funds	S_f
Deposits at the central bank	D_b (+)	Customer deposits	D_p (+)
Loans to the public sector	L_g		
Loans to the general public	L_p		

Box 3.3 helps us understand some of the basic principles in the money-creation process. It shows the balance sheets of two commercial banks, A and B. Although simplified, these are an accurate representation of the information in Table 3.3. Firstly, on the asset side, we see that banks hold two essential sources of instant liquidity, notes and coin (C_b) and deposits at the central bank (D_b). (The latter are the 'operational deposits'. 'Cash ratio deposits' are not relevant here and are omitted.) The remaining assets are loans of some sort, which must be either to the government or public sector (L_g) or to the M4 private sector (L_p). (In practice, these may be 'advances' or they may be 'investments' – securities which banks hold, but these are just different forms of lending.) On the liabilities side, the essentials are similarly preserved. Liabilities are dominated by M4 private sector deposits of some form (D_p). We have said that the balance (or ratio) between various assets and liabilities is something which is likely to have been arrived at as an act of deliberate decision by banks. One key ratio is what we shall call the *reserve ratio, R.* This is the ratio of immediately available liquid assets to deposit liabilities. Thus $R = (C_b + D_b) \div D_p$. This is a key ratio because the profitability of the banking system depends upon banks being able to make loans of varying terms to maturity while holding deposits of shorter maturity (the maturity transformation principle that we discussed in 1.1.3).

> **Reserves:** Banks' holdings of notes and coin *plus* operational deposits at the central bank.
>
> **Reserve ratio:** Bank reserves *divided by* customer deposits.

In order to do this, banks need to know that they can meet any demand from their depositors for convertibility of their deposits into cash. This convertibility must be instant for 'sight' or 'demand' deposits. (For retail banks, sight deposits can be as high as 50 per cent of total sterling deposits.) Thus, profitability demands the reserve ratio be kept to a minimum while confidence in the banking system requires that it should never fall too low! Remember (see Table 3.4) that broad money is defined as bank (including building society) deposits of the M4PS (D_p) *plus* notes and coin held by the M4PS (C_p). The money stock, $M_s = D_p + C_p$. The ability of banks' behaviour to influence the money stock thus focuses upon their ability to cause changes in the quantity of customer deposits (D_p).

Imagine now that a customer of an individual bank, A, applies successfully for a personal loan. Until he begins to write cheques, i.e. to spend, nothing has happened to the balance sheet. As the loan facility is *used*, however, two things begin to happen simultaneously. The figure for loans begins to tick up as the customer's borrowing increases. At the same time, the figure for deposits at the Bank of England falls by an equal amount as the recipients of the cheques pay them into their accounts at different banks and the cheques are presented for payment at the issuing bank. When the loan facility is fully used, the composition of assets will have changed. Advances will be larger by the amount of the loan (+) and the bank's operational balances will be smaller by the same amount (−).

Notice that the size of the balance sheet has not changed but its composition and therefore the ratios have. As a result of the loan, D_b is reduced. If $(C_b + D_b) \div D_p$ is the *reserve ratio*, then with D_p unchanged, the ratio is reduced. Notice also that since the bank charges interest on advances but gets none for its notes and coin and a low rate on balances at the Bank of England, its operations are now more profitable. Expanding its lending in this way is, on the face of it, clearly in the bank's commercial interest.

Granted that the expansion of lending may be profitable, how does it affect the money supply? Remember that the money supply consists overwhelmingly of bank deposits. Clearly, as far as our lending bank is concerned, nothing has happened to the money supply. The changes have been entirely on the asset side of the balance sheet. But remember that this change in the composition of assets came about because the borrower *used* his loan facility. Operational balances were reduced (and advances increased) by the fact that the borrower wrote cheques which other people paid into their accounts at other banks. If we were to look at the balance sheets of these other banks, we should find that their customers' deposits had increased (+) and that this increase was matched on the asset side by an increase in their operational balances at the Bank of England (+).

Other things being equal, an increase in lending raises profits and the supply of money. Provided there is a demand for bank lending at a profitable rate of interest, from customers that banks think creditworthy, we can see why it will always be difficult for the authorities to control monetary expansion.

3.3.2 How banks create money

We have just seen that if an individual bank increases its lending, other things being equal, the money supply will expand. When we talk of an increase in bank lending leading to monetary expansion, however, we are not normally talking about the behaviour of an individual bank but about banks as a whole. However, the process remains essentially the same. Imagine bank A grants an overdraft as before, but that banks B, C . . . n are doing the same. If the borrower of bank A uses the overdraft to pay people who bank with banks B, C, etc., then the increase in the money supply appears in their deposits just as it did in the single bank case. The difference, of course, is that borrowers from banks B, C . . . n are paying clients of bank A and so part of the increase in money supply will appear in bank A's deposits.

Notice, however, that all the time this expansion is taking place, the composition of the aggregate balance sheet must be changing. Each individual bank does as our single bank did. It lends to a customer whose spending leads to an increase in 'advances' at the expense of 'operational balances'. If banks in general are doing this, however, each individual bank will be receiving additional customer deposits and corresponding operational balances. Remember though that each bank was able to lend only by running down operational balances in order to make advances. Therefore, each time it receives new deposits and operational balances, the additional balances serve only to replace the balances used to increase its own advances. If we were to inspect the balance sheet at intervals as this process continued over time we should find that operational balances were constant (though their ownership would be oscillating between banks) while the increases appeared in deposits (on the liabilities side) matched by advances (on the asset side). The balance sheet is expanding, but the ratio of operational balances to total assets/liabilities is falling. The process is illustrated in Exercise 3.1.

Clearly, then, the answer to our question of how banks create money is that they do so by increasing their lending, provided that they are prepared to accept a change in their portfolio composition. Specifically, this means provided they are prepared to work with a smaller reserve ratio.

> **Sight deposits:** Deposits which can be used without notice to make payments or to exchange for notes and coin.

Exercise 3.1 Loans create deposits

Imagine a system in which there are just three banks, A, B and C, whose balance sheets are shown below.

Bank A		Bank B		Bank C	
L	A	L	A	L	A
$D_p = 1{,}000$	$C_b = 10$	$D_p = 1{,}000$	$C_b = 10$	$D_p = 1{,}000$	$C_b = 10$
	$D_b = 40$		$D_b = 40$		$D_b = 40$
	$L_p = 950$		$L_p = 950$		$L_p = 950$

where D_p are customer deposits, C_b is cash (notes and coin) held by banks, D_b are banks' deposits at the central bank, and L_p are advances (loans) to customers. Bank reserves, R, consist of $C_b + D_b$, and a bank's reserve ratio is thus R/D_p. Assume that banks' customers are holding notes and coin (C_p) of 500.

(a) What is the size of the money stock, $C_p + D_p$?

(b) Calculate the reserve ratio, R/D_p, for each bank and for the system as a whole.

Suppose now that bank A increases its advances (L_p) by 10 and its customers use this lending to pay 5 to clients of bank C and 5 to clients of bank B.

(c) Show the new balance sheet position for each bank.

(d) By how much has the money supply increased?

(e) Calculate the new reserve ratio for each individual bank and the aggregate reserve ratio.

Suppose now that bank B also increases its lending by 10 and that its customers pay 5 each to clients of A and C, and that bank C increases its lending by 10 and payments are made equally to clients of A and B.

(f) What is the size of the money stock now?

(g) What is the reserve ratio for each bank?

(h) What is the aggregate reserve ratio?

Answers at end of chapter

However, the dangers of doing this are obvious. Remember that the need for reserves arises fundamentally from the need to be able to meet unforeseen demand for deposit convertibility. Any suggestion that a bank could *not* meet these demands would immediately result in depositors at that bank rushing to withdraw cash. No bank could meet a *general* withdrawal of cash of this kind, and the inability to pay would not only cause the first bank to fail but would almost certainly cause the rapid spread of similar demand to other banks which would also fail. (This is another example of the 'negative externalities' of bank failure that we discussed in section 3.1.4.)

> **Time deposits:** Deposits which can be withdrawn from a bank only after a specified period of time.

Because of the dangers of insufficient liquidity, some monetary authorities *impose* a minimum reserve ratio. Where this happens, the ratio is said to be *mandatory*. In the UK the ratio is a matter of choice for banks themselves (though the Bank of England must be informed in advance of any proposed change). In the UK case, therefore, the ratio is said to be *prudential*. A glance at Table 3.3 shows that for UK banks as a whole the ratio of reserves to total liabilities is just over 0.2 per cent (0.17 + 0.035). This looks astonishingly (dangerously?) low. But remember that Table 3.3 is the consolidated balance sheet for the *whole* banking system and we know that banks vary greatly in their activities.

> **A mandatory reserve ratio:** A ratio of reserves to customer deposits, which banks are *required by law* to maintain.
>
> **A prudential reserve ratio:** A ratio of reserves to deposits which banks can choose for themselves *in the light of their own experience*.

For some banks in the system deposits are only a small proportion of the balance sheet, and sight deposits (where the risk of unforeseen withdrawal is greatest) are virtually zero. If we calculate the reserve ratio strictly using deposit liabilities (only) in the denominator, the ratio rises to 0.3 per cent, and if we calculate it solely on sterling sight deposits, the ratio jumps to 1.2 per cent. Be that as it may, availability of reserves *could* obviously set a potential limit to the expansion of loans and deposits.

In most monetary systems however, including that of the UK, the *quantity* of reserves is not a binding constraint. Reserves can always be obtained from the central bank, albeit at a *price*. In section 3.4.1 we look at how the *price* of reserves may be a constraint on monetary expansion and in 3.4.3 we look at why the authorities do not try to control the *quantity*. For the moment, we merely wish to see how the authorities' creation of reserves permits banks to expand their lending, and deposits and the money supply.

Box 3.4 sets out a simplified version of the Bank of England's balance sheet, following the simplified style that we adopted for commercial banks above.

Box 3.4

The Bank of England's balance sheet

Assets		Liabilities	
Loans to commercial banks	CBL_b	Commercial banks' deposits	D_b
Loans to government	CBL_g	Government deposits	D_g
Holdings of government debt	B_g	Notes and coin in circulation	C_p

Flows of funds through this balance sheet have very similar effects to those that we saw with commercial banks. For example, if the central bank extends loans to its customers, those who receive payments from those customers will find their deposits increase. Imagine, for example, that the central bank extends loans to the government. As the loans are drawn, CBL_g increases, but the government makes purchases from the private sector so that D_p at the commercial banks must increase by the same amount. When the M4 private sector receives these funds, commercial banks' own deposits at the central bank are also credited. The end result (looking at both sets of balance sheets) reads: $CBL_g(+)$, $D_p(+)$, $D_b(+)$. Notice that D_b appears twice: in the commercial banks' balance sheet (as an asset) and in the central bank's balance sheet (as a liability). Notice also that the balance sheets still balance: there is a (+) on each side of both balance sheets. Most importantly, notice that commercial bank reserves, D_b, have increased. Much the same sequence occurs if the central bank lends to commercial banks. As commercial banks draw on the loan facility, CBL_b increases. But this can happen only when banks make payments to someone. Again the recipients must be the M4 private sector ('the general public'). Thus D_p increases and the Bank of England credits commercial banks with the corresponding deposits, D_b.

If the central bank buys government debt (bills or bonds), the flows are different, but the results are the same: B_g increases by the amount of the purchase. If the debt was bought from banks, then CBL_g in Box 3.3 falls by the same amount. (The bills and bonds appear under 'bills' and 'investments' in Table 3.3.) When the central bank purchases the debt, it credits the commercial banks with funds equal to the amount of the transaction. Thus, while CBL_g falls, D_b increases by the same amount. (Check again that the two balance sheets still balance. $B_g(+)$ and $D_b(+)$ expand the balance sheet at the central bank. $L_g(-)$ is offset by $D_b(+)$ at the commercial banks.) Commercial banks have more reserves.

If the government debt is bought from the general public, CBL_g increases as before. But this is matched by payments to the M4PS, so D_b also increases. The addition to D_b is matched when the central bank credits commercial banks with the amount of the purchase (D_b). This time then we have: $CBL_g(+)$, $D_p(+)$, $D_b(+)$. Once again, commercial banks have additional reserves.

Notice one further possibility. The central bank can always make additional reserves available to commercial banks by short-term loans, secured on 'investments' held by the commercial banks. This is done through what is known as a 'repurchase agreement' or 'repo'. This is now common practice, and we explain it in more detail when we discuss the functioning of money markets in Chapter 5. A repurchase agreement involves a temporary sale of securities (most probably government bonds) from commercial banks to the central bank. At the time of sale, both parties make an agreement that the seller will buy back the securities in the near future at a price which is more than that of the original sale. The difference is the 'price' of the loan. In Chapter 5 we shall see that this price can be expressed as a rate of interest. In terms of balance sheets, these events give us: $CBL_b(+)$ and $D_b(+)$.

Thus, there are many ways in which the central bank can make reserves available to commercial banks. Remember, we emphasised earlier that in practice central banks do generally make reserves available, as and when they are required. The *quantity* of reserves is not usually a constraint on bank lending. But in making additional reserves available, the central bank can set the *price*. After all, in the event of a general shortage, the central bank is the monopoly supplier of reserves. (Bank A may bid customer deposits from bank B and the movement of D_p will be matched by movements of D_b. But what bank A gains, bank B loses. This is no solution to a *general* shortage.) For this reason, the central bank is sometimes said to be acting in this role as 'lender of last resort' (see section 3.1).

The 'price' in such cases is the rate of interest at which reserves are made available. We have just seen in the case of repos that the difference between the prices of sale and repurchase is the cost of the loan. In all the other cases too, the central bank can set the rate of interest at which funds are made available to the banking system. When it buys government debt, for example, the price which it pays for the bonds sets a rate of return in the bond market. (The relationship between bond prices and rates of return is discussed in Chapter 6.) When it lends to government, again, it sets a rate of interest. Whatever the mechanism it chooses, the central bank is setting the price at which reserves are available. Since reserves are an essential input into banking operations, the cost of those reserves represents a benchmark rate, to which banks relate all other rates. The price of reserves is given different names in different systems. Sometimes it is known as 'base rate', or 'minimum lending rate', or sometimes as 'repo rate' and sometimes as the 'rediscount rate'. Whatever the name, banks set their lending rates by adding appropriate mark-ups to this key rate while paying rates on deposits which are below this rate. Notice that if these mark-ups are generally maintained, a rise in the repo rate will cause all rates to rise, while a cut in the rate will cause all rates to fall. The central bank has considerable power over interest rates.

3.4 Constraints on bank lending

We have just seen that banks have the power to create money through lending and that they will frequently have a commercial interest in so doing. Why then does the money supply not grow very much faster than in fact it does? There are three sources of constraint: the first two we might call 'demand' constraints and the third we can think of as a 'supply' constraint. Both types of constraint can form the basis for monetary control techniques.

3.4.1 The demand for bank lending

The first limitation on banks' ability to lend is the *demand for bank lending*. As we just remarked, banks charge interest on bank loans. Conventionally, we would expect people to borrow up to the point where the utility gained from the last pound borrowed is just equal to the cost of borrowing it. The utility of a bank loan lies not in the money itself, of course, but in the goods that can be purchased with it. Since the marginal utility of most goods is assumed to decrease with increasing quantities of the good, it follows that the utility associated with each addition to one's borrowing also diminishes. In short, we should expect the demand for bank lending to vary inversely with the rate of interest charged. In these circumstances, we can see the importance of the central bank's lender of last resort role.

Imagine, for example, that the authorities were pursuing a policy of targeting the growth of money and/or credit, and that the current rate of expansion threatened to exceed the target. The rapid expansion would mean that the banking system would frequently need additional reserves. As we have said, these will always be forthcoming, but in the present circumstances the appropriate response from the central bank would be to raise the rate of interest at which they are supplied. Banks would then know that their profitability would diminish if they continued to lend at current rates of interest while having to pay a higher price for reserves. In practice, banks will raise all their interest rates once the central bank raises its dealing rate. If there is some price elasticity in the demand for loans, the demand for new loans will diminish. New loans (and deposits) will still be created, but their *rate of growth* will be less than before. This explains why we frequently see interest rates going up in times of rapid credit expansion while cuts in interest rates occur when money and credit growth is slow, especially if this looks likely to be an early warning of recession.

This is not to say that demand is necessarily elastic with respect to the rate of interest. Recent experience suggests it is not. Nor does it mean that demand is stable. Many things, for example changes in income and wealth, and expectations about future interest rates, may cause the demand curve for bank lending to move. What we do wish to note is that, other things being equal, the demand for bank lending will vary inversely with interest rates and that banks cannot lend unless people wish to borrow.

3.4.2 The demand for money

A second factor limiting banks' ability to expand the total stock of bank deposits is the *demand for money*. Be careful to distinguish this from the demand for lending we have just discussed. The demand for bank lending gives rise to a flow (of new bank loans). If the flow of new loans exceeds the rate at which existing loans are being repaid, there will be an increase in the stock of bank deposits. The question at issue here is the willingness of people to hold an expanding stock of bank deposits. Plainly, the simplest case is that where people are willing to hold exactly that expanding stock of deposits which results from other people's decisions to borrow. Both sets of demand conditions are consistent. But suppose this were not the case.

Imagine firstly that we have a demand for bank lending at some level set by the rate of interest charged on that lending, other conditions for the moment being given. We might refer to this as the *ex ante* demand for bank lending. Suppose secondly that we have a demand for money, *ex ante*, which is less than that required to hold the growing stock of bank deposits. How is the position to be reconciled?

Remember to begin with that the demand for bank lending is a demand which results from a desire to buy goods or services. Therefore, quite obviously, there is no problem about the new deposits being wanted at this stage. Neither can there be a problem at the next stage. The borrower passes the newly created deposit to the seller of the goods who is willing to take it in payment. Indeed, it is worth emphasising that from the seller's point of view, he is simply receiving 'money'; he has no way of knowing when, where or how it was created.

Momentarily at least, the deposit is willingly accepted by the seller. Now comes the crux of the issue. The seller has given up goods in exchange for an increase in his bank deposit. There has been a rearrangement of his wealth. A decision now has to be made about whether this rearrangement is acceptable for the time being or whether some further rearrangement might be more satisfactory. The seller may be entirely happy with the position or, as we began this discussion by assuming, he may decide that he does not want to hold so much wealth in the form of money. If this is indeed the case, he has obviously a wide range of choices available to him. Even limiting the choice to alternative financial assets still opens up many opportunities. He might prefer a building society deposit or a National Savings instrument or government bonds or equities. Buying any of these reduces his holdings of money.

Now we have to break out from this story of the individual and imagine that what we have described is general. A general attempt to reduce money holdings in this way adds to the demand for these alternative financial assets, pushing up prices and pushing down yields. As this process goes on, two consequences will follow. Firstly, as yields fall on these alternative assets, the attraction of money rises relative to them. Secondly, these falling yields mean that it is becoming cheaper for firms and individuals to borrow by issuing new claims like bonds and equities or going to building societies, by comparison with borrowing from banks. The demand for bank lending will fall, not because of a rise in the 'own' rate of interest on bank loans but because the fall in interest rates elsewhere has caused a relative rise in bank interest rates. Because the cost of alternative forms of borrowing has fallen, the demand curve for bank lending shifts to the left. We should now be able to see that an inconsistency between the demand for bank lending and the demand for the money stock created by that bank lending is reconciled by two simultaneous mechanisms.

Firstly, as yields fall on non-money instruments the demand for money will increase. Secondly, as these yields and therefore the cost of non-bank borrowing fall, the demand for bank lending is reduced.

3.4.3 The monetary base

In section 3.3.2 we saw that with fixed reserves banks could increase their lending only if they were prepared to operate at lower ratios of reserves: deposits. Until now we have assumed that banks decide for themselves the appropriate ratio in the light of their desire for profit and need for liquidity. The ratio is said to be a matter of 'commercial prudence' and is said to be 'non-mandatory' to distinguish it from the possible alternative, namely, that the ratio be written into banking law. A non-mandatory ratio has operated in the UK for many years. This means that, strictly speaking, banks could at any time increase their lending quite sharply provided they were happy to incur the risk in so doing. However, under the current monetary control arrangements banks have agreed to advise the Bank of England in advance of any significant change in their decision to hold operational balances. Thus, we may repeat that if the authorities decline to increase the supply of base money, banks are constrained in the amount of lending they can undertake. To emphasise this point, we can look briefly at some of the steps that banks might think of taking in order to circumvent the constraint. We shall see that they will not work.

Our first thought might be that an individual bank which was short of base money could raise the rate of interest it offered to depositors. It would gain deposits, matched exactly of course by additional operational balances. Since operational balances were previously only a very small proportion of deposits, this addition to both in the ratio of 1:1 must raise the overall ratio. The bank is then free to expand its lending until the ratio again falls to the critical level.

What is the difficulty? It is that these additional deposits can come only from some other bank. Any bank which loses deposits loses balances in equal measure and so its ratio deteriorates. Thus, if the original problem was that the monetary sector as a whole was critically short of base money, the attempt by individual banks to improve their own position by raising interest rates will be self-defeating. The monetary sector as a whole cannot gain balances by bidding for deposits. Let us consider an illustration.

Exercise 3.2

Assume that the money supply is made up as follows and that the components pay the rate of interest indicated:

	£bn	Interest rate % p.a.
Notes and coin in circulation with the public	50	0
Bank sight deposits	300	0
Bank time deposits (1 month)	200	5
Bank time deposits (3 month)	150	6
Bank CDs (3 month)	50	4
Building society deposits	250	7
	1,000	

(a) Calculate the weighted average rate of interest on money as a whole.

(b) Assume now that banks begin to pay interest on sight deposits at 3 per cent p.a. What is the new weighted average interest rate?

Answers at end of chapter

Let us suppose that for each bank and for the system as a whole the reserve ratio is 5 per cent or 1/20 and that each bank has deposit liabilities (D_p) of 1,000. Reserves for each bank consist of cash (C_b) of 10 and deposits at the central bank (D_b) of 40. Imagine now that banks feel this is too low and that bank A tries to improve its situation by bidding deposits of 10 from each of B and C. If bank A succeeds, its customer deposits rise to 1,020 matched by an increase in its deposits at the central bank from 40 to 60. Bank A's reserve ratio has increased dramatically to 6.86 per cent (= 60 + 10 ÷ 1,020). But total reserves in the system are unchanged: Bank A's position has improved only because the position for B and C has deteriorated. If B and C now retaliate by trying to retrieve their lost deposits from A, the aggregate position will still be unchanged, individual ratios will be returned to 5 per cent, but there is a distinct possibility that interest rates will have been bid up in the competition for deposits.

The second possibility is that a bank could rearrange its assets by selling securities. Assume that it sells to people who bank elsewhere. When their cheques are cleared our bank will have fewer securities but more operational balances to its credit and its position will have improved. Customers of other banks will have more securities, fewer bank deposits and their banks will have fewer operational balances. As a solution to a general shortage of balances, however, the fallacy is already apparent because it is very similar to the previous case. If all banks sell securities, they will all lose deposits and balances as their own customers buy securities. Of course, they will retrieve some of those balances from their own security sales, but the message is clear. The total stock of D_b will not increase.

Will anything have changed? Since banks have sold securities to people who surrender deposits for them, the fixed stock of balances will be larger in proportion. The ratio will have improved, but this is no solution to the original problem which was that banks wanted to expand their business by lending more. In fact, their balance sheets are now smaller by the loss of securities on the asset side and of deposit liabilities. Notice also that this generalised sale of securities by banks is likely to have driven down their price and therefore to have pushed up interest rates.

A third possibility also involves a rearrangement of assets. Banks could call in funds lent 'at call' to the money market ('market loans' in Table 3.3). Holders of the funds, generally other banks, have no option but to repay. Some of their operational balances are therefore transferred to the rest of the monetary sector and banks initially appear to have achieved what they want: more deposits at the central bank, fewer market loans and a more favourable ratio which would allow them to lend more.

However, the shortage of liquidity is transferred to banks active in the money market. Normally to raise funds the banks could think of selling off bills, but with a *general* shortage of liquidity the only possible buyer is the Bank of England. As we have seen, the Bank agrees always to provide assistance in such circumstances, though as a monopoly buyer of bills/monopoly supplier of liquidity it can impose its own terms. But if we start, as we did, with the assumption that the authorities were not willing to expand the quantity of base money, then the Bank is going to refuse assistance.

The money market banks would then be obliged to pay whatever level of interest was required to prevent other banks demanding money at call, i.e. that rate of interest on call money which persuaded banks not to use this route to increase their balances at the Bank but to forgo instead their intention of increased lending. Conceivably, interest rates could rise very high indeed.

What this discussion reveals is twofold. Firstly, that the monetary sector can expand its assets and liabilities up to a limit imposed by its available reserves. The desired ratio of reserves:deposits may be a matter of commercial prudence and may therefore vary in the light of circumstances (as in the UK) or it could be 'mandatory', imposed as a matter of regulation by the monetary authorities. Whatever its origin, however, there will at any time be some such ratio which banks will wish to observe.

Secondly, because the reserves in question – notes and coin and balances at the Bank of England – are liabilities of the Bank of England, the Bank is itself the sole supplier of such reserves. The fact that all banks require some reserves in the form of bankers' deposits at the Bank of England makes such deposits an essential input into the money-creation process. If the authorities refuse to increase the size of the monetary base, therefore, there must come a point at which further lending, and monetary growth, are inhibited.

In a system where the authorities exercise rigid control over the size of the monetary base, leaving interest rates to settle at whatever level matches the demand for loans to banks' ability to supply them, the money supply is said to be *exogenously* determined. 'Exogenous' means that the money supply is determined 'outside of' or independently of the rest of the economic system. It is imposed, in effect, by the authorities. This is the sort of system that underlies the vertical money supply curve which is often drawn in diagrams showing the interaction between money supply and money demand. In the alternative case, where the central bank supplies whatever reserves banks require to enable them to lend, hoping that setting the level of interest rates will curb the demand for bank lending, the money supply is said to be *endogenously* determined. The central bank sets the price of bank loans and the money supply is then determined within the economic system by those variables which give rise to agents' demand for bank loans.

It should be clear by now that in most monetary systems the money supply is endogenously determined. The central bank supplies reserves on demand but sets the price. At that price the quantity of money and credit will depend upon the demand for it. Nonetheless, the joint facts (a) that sound banking requires banks to hold a minimum level of reserves and (b) that the central bank is a monopoly supplier of reserves have led many textbooks (and some commentators) to describe the money supply process as though it were exogenous. (The vertical supply curve just mentioned is a case in point.) In these circumstances, the money supply is shown to be determined by the quantity of reserves, fixed by the central bank, and a deposit or credit 'multiplier'. Notice that in this model it is the *quantity* of reserves which the central bank is assumed to control. A monetary policy based upon this model, i.e. one in which the central bank fixes the quantity rather than price of reserves, is known as 'monetary base control' and was actively promoted by some economists in a debate about monetary policy in the UK in 1981. We know that it was rejected, and the reasons are given in Box 3.5.

Box 3.5 | **Monetary base control rejected**

Virtually every monetary economist believes that the CB [central bank] can control the monetary base . . . Almost all those who have worked in a CB believe that this view is totally mistaken. (Goodhart, 1994 p. 1424)

The base–multiplier model of money supply determination is presented in almost every macroeconomics textbook as the only explanation of money supply determination. Furthermore, it is *implied* in all those texts which, lacking a formal model, still present the money supply as a curve drawn vertically in interest–money space. And yet, as Goodhart says, no central bank uses open market operations with a view to changing the size of the base in order to achieve a multiple change in deposits. Even in 1981, at the 'high tide of monetarism' when monetary targets were adopted universally, the Bank of England considered explicitly moving to a system of monetary base control (MBC) and just as explicitly rejected it. Why the model continues to dominate in textbooks when the real world consistently rejects it is an issue we do not have time to discuss, but we can offer a number of reasons for the rejection.

- Firstly, MBC is a quantity control. In a pure system of MBC, supply would be fixed (some positive interest elasticity notwithstanding) and fluctuations in demand would have to be absorbed entirely by price. If the authorities were trying to target the base over very short periods, the fluctuations in short-term interest rates could be extreme. The authorities are always reluctant to create situations in which interest rates may be volatile. Targeting the base, averaged over a longer period, would ease this problem by allowing some day-to-day flexibility in quantities, but so long as quantities are targeted rather than price, price must fluctuate.

- Secondly, while the base consists of liabilities of the central bank and one might expect the central bank to be fully in control of its own liabilities, this is not always the case. Essentially, the central bank has to *know* in advance what will happen to its liabilities in the course of ordinary transactions in order to supplement or reduce them. The main problem arises with D_b which will change every time there are net payments between the public and private sectors. Most central banks make daily predictions about these flows and inform banks and money markets of their plans to relieve shortages or to mop up excess liquidity. It is quite common for the financial press to report the predictions and outcomes. The errors are very large.

- Thirdly, even if the central bank *knew* what effect spontaneous transactions were going to have on the base, this does not mean that it could take the appropriate measures. Knowledge that the base was going to expand more rapidly than desired does not mean that the Bank can suddenly organise a bond issue in order to offset it. Again, this problem becomes more acute the shorter the targeting period. But even if the aim were to achieve an average rate of growth on a quarterly basis, frequent sales of government debt could be very disruptive to financial markets. To ensure the sale of the correct *quantity*, governments would have to adopt a pure auction form of sale and thus would have to accept the market clearing price. Once again we are back to volatile interest rates, this time at the longer end of the spectrum.

- Fourthly, in some systems there would need to be major structural changes. For example, it is doubtful whether MBC is compatible with an overdraft system of borrowing where banks agree maximum credit limits with their clients who then use whatever fraction of the limit they need. In the aggregate, this is often of the order of 50–60 per cent. A tightening of monetary policy would inevitably mean that firms would want to use more of their overdrafts, and banks (unable to get reserves) would then face the choice of either allowing the loans and breaching the reserve ratio requirement or defaulting on their promises to borrowers. MBC would also require governments to bank with the commercial banking system rather than the central bank so that payments between the public and private sectors would not cause continuous and large fluctuations in D_b.

- Fifthly, there is an asymmetry in the operation of MBC caused by the fact that most bank assets are non-marketable. This means that an open market purchase of debt will increase D_p, D_b and a (the banks' reserve ratio – see below) as predicted and banks, being more liquid, can try to increase their lending. But a *sale*, causing a reduction in D_p, D_g and a, requires banks to reduce loans. However, loans are not, as a rule, marketable. They can be reduced only by insisting on repayment (or refusing to renew). This is likely to prove very disruptive to trade, resulting in bankruptcies.

- Sixthly, since cash pays no interest, then reserve requirements act as a tax on bank intermediation since they increase its cost. This occurs because the remaining, *earning*, assets have to earn a higher return to compensate for the zero return on cash (and what is often a below-market rate on operational balances at the central bank). This increases the spread between deposit and lending rates, which many would regard as the appropriate way of calculating the cost of intermediation. As with any tax, the supply curve is shifted to the left. Less intermediation is 'bought' and 'sold' and at a higher price than would otherwise be the case.

- Finally, MBC raises doubts over the central bank's lender of last resort role. As we have seen, bank deposits are convertible into cash on demand (albeit with interest penalties in some cases). However, the flows that we have discussed in this section could mean that perfectly well-run and solvent banks might find themselves short of reserves. Would the central bank still offer the convertibility guarantee if such a shortage arose, as it well might, in a period of tight MBC?

Nonetheless, because it remains an extremely influential view of the money supply process, we need to know its essential features. In fact, we know how the central bank could fix the quantity of reserves if it so chose, so our main interest in this model is the idea of some multiplier relationship between reserves and deposits. Before we begin, notice that policy based upon this model is known as 'monetary *base* control' (not *reserve* control). This is because bank reserves and what is known as the 'monetary base' overlap to a considerable extent. This can be seen by looking back at Table 3.4, where the monetary base (M0) is shown to comprise notes and coin outside the central bank (i.e. with banks and with the general public) plus banks' deposits at the central bank. Using our earlier abbreviations, the monetary base = $D_b + C_b + C_p$, while bank reserves comprise only the first two, $D_b + C_b$. If we assume that the general public's demand for notes and coin is stable (maybe a fraction of their deposits, D_p), then in practice controlling the quantity of reserves amounts to controlling M0, the monetary base.

We turn now to the 'base–multiplier' model of money supply determination. All it requires is some manipulation of terms with which we are already familiar.

Suppose that

$$M = D_p + C_p$$

where M is the money supply, D_p are bank deposits held by the public and C_p is the public's holdings of notes and coin. Suppose also that

$$B = D_b + C_b + C_p$$

where B is the wide monetary base, D_b are bankers' deposits (operational balances), C_b is banks' holdings of notes and coin and C_p is, as before, the public's holdings of notes and coin. Let that part of the monetary base held by banks be called 'reserves', R, so that

$$R = D_b + C_b$$

and therefore

$$B = R + C_p$$

Suppose that banks operate with a desired ratio, a, of reserves to deposit liabilities, 'the reserve ratio'

$$R/D_p = a$$

and that the public holds a desired ratio, b, of notes and coin to its deposits, 'the cash ratio'

$$C_p/D_p = b$$

Then we can show that the relationship between the quantity of base money in existence and the outstanding money supply depends numerically upon the magnitude of the ratios a and b. Also we can show that a change in the supply of base will cause a predictable change in the money supply, also dependent in size upon these magnitudes. Firstly, the ratio of money supply to monetary base is

$$\frac{M}{B} = \frac{D_p + C_p}{R + C_p}$$

Dividing through by D_p gives

$$\frac{M}{B} = \frac{D_p/C_p + C_p/D_p}{R/D_p + C_p/D_p}$$

Notice that $D_p/D_p = 1$, while C_p/D_p is the public's cash ratio b, while R/D_p is the banks' reserve ratio, a. Thus

$$\frac{M}{B} = \frac{1 + a}{a + b}$$

and therefore

$$M = (1 + b)/(a + b) \times B$$

and

$$\Delta M = (1 + b)/(a + b) \times \Delta B$$

The expression $(1 + b)/(a + b)$ is sometimes represented by m and referred to as the bank deposit multiplier.

Clearly, if the ratios a and b are stable, there is a precise relationship between M and B and changes in B will have a totally predictable effect upon M. Equally clearly, in these circumstances the quantity of B will be a constraint upon M. If the supply of base is fixed, banks cannot increase their lending without sacrificing the ratio a. Let us repeat, this is not a satisfactory account of the way in which the money supply is determined in practice and the reasons for not basing monetary control techniques upon it are given in Box 3.5.

3.5 Building societies

The history, function and regulation of building societies distinguishes them quite clearly from banks. They are, however, deposit-taking institutions and since 1989, when M4 replaced M3 as the official measure of broad money, their deposits have been unambiguously 'money'.

Building societies began, in the eighteenth century, as friendly or mutual societies into which members made periodic payments to finance the building of houses in their immediate locality. The origins are important because they help explain a number of otherwise curious features of the societies. Their friendly society status means that they have no shareholders in the normal sense of the term. A society has no 'owners' but has 'members' who lend to the society by buying shares which are in effect deposits. This partly explains why, although functioning for many recent years in ways similar to banks, they have been exempt from regulations applying to banks and were supervised by the Registrar of Friendly Societies rather than by the Bank of England. Even now, under the FSA, the regulations applying to building societies are different from those governing banks. Their mutual nature also explains why, until 1983, the Building Societies' Association (BSA) was able to operate a system of 'recommended (interest) rates', a form of cartel which would have been illegal for public companies. Their origins as providers of housing finance combined with the advantages of mutual status also help explain why, in spite of rapid growth, their business remains overwhelmingly concentrated in lending for house purchase.

As we noted above, the societies' deposits were first admitted to the official measure of broad money in 1989. For most of the 1980s, the treatment of building society deposits was something of a problem. Undoubtedly depositors themselves saw the deposits as money. They could go into a building society branch and draw cash on demand. For larger purchases they could obtain, also on demand, a cheque signed by the manager payable to whomsoever they nominated. In the first case, though, it was the cash which was money, while in the second case careful examination of the cheque would show that it was drawn on the building society's *bank*. It was the building society's *bank* deposit which was functioning as money, not a deposit with the society itself.

As we shall see in the next section, competition between banks and building societies drove their products closer and closer together during the 1980s. Eventually, the Building Societies Act 1986 removed some of the formal distinctions. Most importantly it allowed building societies to issue cheque guarantee cards (so their own deposits became instantly acceptable as means of payment), and it provided for societies to 'incorporate' themselves as banks. At the time, building society deposits were included in a measure of 'liquidity', 'PSL2', but not in M3. After the 1986 Act this differential treatment of building society deposits became very difficult to sustain. A change was finally forced by the decision of the Abbey National Building Society, at the time the second largest society, to convert to banking status in 1989. This would have meant an overnight increase in M3 of about 11 per cent. This large break in the series persuaded the Bank of England to discontinue publication of the M3 measure and to treat M4, first published in 1987 as a replacement for PSL2, as the official measure of broad money. Thus, *from a monetary point of view* the societies have become indistinguishable from banks.

A brief history of UK monetary aggregates is provided in the appendix to this chapter and the history of building society deposits in the 1980s is a good illustration of how 'custom and practice' determine what assets should count as money and how this custom and practice is continually changing.

As Table 3.5 shows, at the end of 2004 building society assets totalled £243bn. This was a sharp drop from their peak of £309bn in July 1995 and is explained by the conversion of some major societies into banks (see Box 3.6). Prior to these mass conversions, and since 1998, the figures show an annual growth rate of 8–9 per cent p.a.

As Table 3.5 shows, 'loans and investments' which consist overwhelmingly of mortgage loans for the purchase of property, amount to more than 80 per cent of building society assets. The societies provide about 80 per cent of total lending for private house purchase, though this figure has fluctuated since 1981 as banks entered, retreated from and then re-entered the mortgage market.

This concentration on long-term mortgage lending means that societies provide a good illustration of the degree of maturity transformation that is possible. However,

Table 3.5 **Building societies – assets and liabilities (£m, end-2004)**

Assets		Liabilities	
Notes and coin	580	Retail shares and deposits	160,456
Sterling deposits with banks	18,162	Certificates of deposit	13,106
British government bonds	1,030	Commercial paper	27,783
Other liquid assets	25,067	Bank borrowing	922
Loans and investments	195,807	Bonds and other wholesale	21,528
Other	2,421	Other (incl. reserves)	19,272
Total	243,067	Total	243,067

Source: Adapted from ONS, *Financial Statistics February 2006*, table 4.4A this should not be exaggerated. While a new mortgage loan may typically be for twenty-five to thirty years, societies hold a portfolio of existing mortgages at various stages of maturity. They will obviously arrange their affairs so as to ensure a steady stream of maturing loans. In addition, very few mortgages last their full term. People sell and move house frequently. The average life of a building society mortgage is about eight years. Until the early 1980s, societies commonly restricted their lending on individual purchases to 84 per cent of the estimated value of the property. In the increasingly competitive environment after 1983, this crept slowly upwards and 100 per cent mortgages became quite common by 1989. Following a collapse in the UK housing market in the early 1990s, the normal ratio has since settled back to 90 per cent.

With the exception of 'other assets', comprising land, buildings and equipment, building society non-mortgage assets are generally very liquid. 'British government securities' consist of central government bonds, almost all with less than five years to maturity. More than one-half of 'short-term assets' are bank deposits. Under the Registrar's rules, societies are required to maintain a minimum ratio of 7.5 per cent of liquid assets (roughly British government securities plus 'short-term assets') to total assets. However, we can see from Table 3.5, the ratio in 2004 was nearly three times the required minimum at 18.5 per cent. Indeed, societies have traditionally operated with a liquid assets ratio in the range of 15–20 per cent. There are several reasons for this. The retail, short maturity, nature of most building society liabilities and the need to maintain public confidence are obviously relevant. Less obvious, but important, is the fact that because interest rate changes are administratively expensive, building society interest rates are 'sticky' in comparison with those of some of their competitors like banks and National Savings. Consequently the inflow of funds is sometimes erratic. If the inflow falls short of mortgage lending plans, a generous cushion of liquid assets can be run down in order to preserve a steady outflow of mortgage lending. In 2004 the net inflow of funds was £23.6bn, including £13.2bn of new shares and deposits and £7.8bn from wholesale sources.

Finally, the 1986 Act gave societies the power to seek 'incorporation', subject to their giving adequate notice of their intention and subject to a vote by their members. Incorporation would mean their becoming public limited companies. They would then have shareholders, rather than members, and would be able to raise additional capital for expansion in the normal commercial way by issuing additional shares. They would, in effect, become banks.

The first building society to make the change was the Abbey National in 1989. Although other societies also announced their interest in conversion at the time, the momentum did not fully develop until 1997, when the conversion of several major societies in that single year led to a sharp, but temporary, contraction in the building society sector. A list of major conversions is provided in Box 3.6.

We have seen that the Abbey National Building Society was the first to abandon mutual status and convert to a plc in 1989 (and in 2003 changed its name again to 'Abbey'). Several other major societies considered doing the same at the time, but as Box 3.6 shows, it was not until the mid-1990s that 'demutualisation' either by merger with an existing bank or by incorporation really gathered pace.

Box 3.6	Following the Building Societies Act 1986, a number of major building societies decided either to incorporate as banks or to merge with existing banks. The major conversions (with dates) were:

Abbey National B.S.	incorporated as bank	July 1989
Cheltenham and Gloucester B.S.	joined Lloyds Bank Group	July 1995
National and Provincial B.S.	joined Abbey National Bank	August 1996
Alliance and Leicester B.S.	incorporated as bank	April 1997
Halifax B.S.	incorporated as bank	June 1997
Woolwich B.S.	incorporated as bank	July 1997
Bristol and West B.S.	joined Bank of Ireland Group	July 1997
Northern Rock	incorporated as a bank	October 1997
Birmingham Midshires B.S.	joined Halifax Bank	March 1999
Bradford and Bingley	incorporated as a bank	December 2000

The reasons commonly given for abandoning mutual status all related to the competitive environment which had developed for mortgage lending in particular, and other financial services generally. The central argument was that a plc could raise capital by issuing shares. This in turn would enable the firm both to expand and to diversify by offering a wider range of services and would thus make it better able to compete. (The Alliance and Leicester Building Society, which incorporated in 1997, gave as one reason its desire to enter the personal pensions market.) The competitors were existing (UK) banks and also European financial institutions which it was thought would try to expand in the UK as the single financial market developed.

3.6 Liability management

'Liability management' refers to the attention which financial intermediaries give to the size and composition of their liabilities. Thus it is a term which can be used to describe the behaviour of any financial intermediary, though in practice it is used most frequently to describe the increasing attention given by banks and building societies to their deposit liabilities since the 1970s.

> **Liability management:** The practice of varying the interest rate and other terms applying to liabilities (usually deposits) in order to vary the composition and quantity of liabilities.

Before the introduction in 1971 of the package of monetary control measures known as *Competition and Credit Control*, banks generally accepted the size and composition of their deposits as given. Profitability thus depended upon the skill with which banks could employ those deposits, i.e. upon *asset* management. This passive approach to liabilities arose partly from banks' monopoly of the payments mechanism – people had to have bank deposits in order to make payment by cheque – and partly from the uncompetitive nature of the banking system before 1971. Until 1971, banks had operated an interest rate cartel which made it impossible for banks to 'manage' (i.e. bid for) deposits in any significant way. Competition and Credit Control swept this away and at the same time removed direct controls on the supply of bank lending. For the first time, banks were free to respond to the market demand for loans provided they could obtain an adequate supply of deposits. The early 1970s were therefore marked by a dramatic expansion in bank lending (and money supply) and by a general rise in the rate of interest paid on 'wholesale', that is to say large, usually time, deposits of firms. Furthermore, competition meant that the rates paid on these deposits became increasingly market-related, rising and falling as the level of official short-term interest rates rose and fell. We shall return to the consequences of this in a moment.

The second phase of liability management came in the 1980s. Where previously the competition had been between banks, it now spread to embrace the boundary between banks and building societies, and the competition was for 'retail' rather than wholesale deposits. The initial stimulus came from the problems which banks encountered with their sovereign lending at the end of the 1970s. Looking for a more secure and profitable alternative, their attention was attracted to domestic mortgages for which there was often an unsatisfied demand resulting from building societies' uncompetitive practices in holding mortgage and deposit rates below market-clearing levels, with the inevitable queuing for and rationing of mortgages.

As we saw in the last section, the societies responded to this invasion of their traditional territory by abandoning their interest cartel, by offering features which made their deposits increasingly similar to those of banks, and by lobbying for changes in restrictive legislation. The result of all this was the further spread of market-related interest payments on bank deposits. In 1975 the interest-bearing fraction of M3 was 0.65; it rose to 0.72 by 1981 and to 0.81 by 1989. When M3 was then replaced by M4, the interest-bearing proportion jumped from 0.81 to 0.89. By the end of 1992 it had risen to 0.92.

> **Money's own rate:** The rate of interest paid on money itself. Usually calculated as the average of the rates paid on its component parts, weighted by their proportion of the total.

The monetary implications of liability management are numerous but can be grouped under two headings. Firstly, as interest-bearing deposits increase as a proportion of broad money, it follows that the *weighted average* rate on money as a whole is increasing. Money is more attractive when interest of, say, 10 per cent is paid on 95 per cent of it than it is when 10 per cent is paid on only half of it. At any given level of market interest rates, therefore, the rate on money (money's 'own rate') was rising. Furthermore, it was rising *relative* to all other interest rates. Thus money's own rate was rising relative to that paid on non-money assets (making money more attractive relative to other assets); it was also rising relative to the rate charged on bank advances. In some cases this made bank borrowing seem preferable to using accumulated savings. As a result of what we might call the rise in money's own rate, therefore, both the demand for bank borrowing *and* the demand for money increased. Both of these trends were associated with the fall in velocity of M3 in the early 1980s which led to the end of broad money targeting in 1985.

The second consequence of liability management was that money's own rate came to be more market-related. Thus, when the authorities raised (for example) short-term interest rates, money's own rate went up more or less in step. The implications of this for monetary control were profound, since controlling the growth of bank lending and the money supply by changing the level of official interest rates relies heavily upon being able to change *relative* interest rates. Consider again what we said in sections 3.4.1 and 3.4.2 about constraints on bank lending. To reduce the flow of new loans (and new deposits), the central bank raises its official dealing rate and banks raise the rates they charge (and pay) to customers. In section 3.4.1, we noted that this should reduce the demand for new loans since the rate of interest is the 'price' of the loan. However, the demand for new loans will be reduced much more sharply if the rate charged on loans rises not just in an absolute sense but *relative* to the rate paid on deposits. If this happens, people will be more inclined to finance their spending by the use of existing deposits than by taking out new loans. Furthermore, if the rate on non-money assets (bonds, bills, etc.) increases along with the loan rate, non-money assets become more attractive than deposits at the margin. This causes people to be more willing to buy bonds (than hold money – we move now to section 3.4.2). But bonds which many of us hold as assets are issued by firms and government as a means of *borrowing*. Borrowing by selling new bonds to an eager public is a partial alternative to borrowing from banks. Thus, not only do bank loans become dearer, non-bank finance becomes easier to get. Two forces act to reduce the demand for new loans (and the flow of new deposits). Notice how a change in the *demand for money* affects the *supply of non-bank finance*. But it happens only if interest rates on loans and on non-money assets change, while money's own rate stays unchanged (or changes only slightly or with a long delay). If liability management leads to money's own rate being very flexible, an increase in interest rates has comparatively little effect on the demand for loans (and the creation of new deposits). Liability management, and the inability to manipulate relative interest rates, was one of the developments behind the decision to abandon monetary targets in 1985.

Like most financial practices, liability management is a worldwide phenomenon and like many financial practices it has often been encouraged by regulations which deposit-taking institutions have found irksome. In the US, for example, the Federal Reserve imposes mandatory reserve ratios on bank deposits, the ratios varying between different types of deposit. For obvious reasons, sight deposits carry the highest reserve requirement while time deposits carry a lower requirement, diminishing as the term of the deposit lengthens. Recall that we noted earlier the desire of banks to hold the minimum of reserves, since reserves are not interest-earning. Clearly in the US system it would suit banks to encourage customers to hold time rather than sight deposits. The problem with this from the customer's point of view is that she needs sight deposits in order to make payments, and from the bank's point of view this poses a problem in that the extra interest which will have to be paid to induce her to manage with fewer sight deposits will reduce the profits available from being able to switch reserves to income-earning use. The 'sweep account' is the answer. Under this arrangement a customer holds both a sight and time deposit and both are monitored continuously by a computer program which automatically sweeps any surplus sight deposits into the time deposit account and can be set if necessary to sweep the whole of the sight deposit account into the time deposit account overnight. *On average*, therefore, the customer holds, and the bank is liable for, a lower level of sight deposits, and funds that would otherwise be non-interest-earning reserves can be switched to more profitable use.

While profit can be earned from financial innovation, which means while there is competition between financial institutions and while governments and central banks impose regulations on financial activity, liability management seems bound to continue.

Questions for discussion

1 Distinguish between deposit-taking and non-deposit-taking institutions and explain the difference between 'discretionary' and 'contractual' saving.

2 Explain what is meant by the 'M4 private sector'. What is the relevance of this concept to the definition of 'broad money'?

3 Distinguish between M0 and M4.

4 Why might conflicts arise between some functions of the central bank?

5 Distinguish between 'mandatory' and 'prudential' reserve ratios. Using a simplified balance sheet, show how (a) the stock of money and (b) the reserve ratio of the commercial banking system are affected by an expansion of bank loans.

6 Explain what is meant by 'lender of last resort' and show how this role enables the central bank to influence the level of short-term interest rates.

7 How does a rise in interest rates affect the flow of new loans and the creation of new deposits?

8 Give a brief account of the base–multiplier model of money supply determination.

9 Compare and contrast (a) the functions and (b) the balance sheets of banks and building societies.

Further reading

A Alesina and L H Summers, 'Central bank independence and macroeconomic performance', *Journal of Money, Credit and Banking*, 25 (2), 1993, 151–62

R Bade and M Parkin, 'Central bank laws and monetary policy', Department of Economics, University of Western Outario, 1985, mimeo

Bank of England, *The Bank of England*, Bank of England Fact Sheet, August 1998 (also available at the Bank's web site)

Bank of England, 'The Bank of England Act', *Bank of England Quarterly Bulletin*, 38 (2), May 1998 (also available at the Bank's web site)

Bank of England, 'The transmission mechanism of monetary policy', *Bank of England Quarterly Bulletin*, 39 (2), May 1999 (also available at the Bank's web site)

Bank of England, 'Reform of the Bank of England's operations in the sterling money markets', *Bank of England Quarterly Bulletin*, 44 (2), Summer 2004 (also available at the Bank's web site)

C R Bean and N Jenkinson, 'The formulation of monetary policy at the Bank of England', *Bank of England Quarterly Bulletin*, 41 (4), November 2001 (also available at the Bank's web site)

M Buckle and J Thompson, *The UK Financial System* (Manchester: Manchester UP, 4e, 2004) chs. 3–5

A Budd, 'The role and operations of the Bank of England Monetary Policy Committee', *The Economic Journal*, 108 (451), November 1998, 1783–94

A Cukierman, 'Central bank independence and monetary control', *Economic Journal*, 104 (427), November 1994, 1437–48

C A E Goodhart, 'What should central banks do? What should be their macroeconomic objectives and operations?', *Economic Journal*, 104 (427), November 1994, 1424–36

C A E Goodhart, *The Central Bank and the Financial System* (Basingstoke: Macmillan, 1995)

V Grilli, D Maciandaro and G Tabellini, 'Political and public finance policies in the industrial countries', *Economic Policy*, 13, October 1991, 341–76

P G A Howells and K Bain, *The Economics of Money, Banking and Finance: A European Text* (Harlow: Financial Times Prentice Hall, 3e, 2005) chs. 3 and 12

http://www.bankofengland.co.uk

http://www.dmo.gov.uk

http://www.fsa.gov.uk/bank

http://www.apacs.org.uk

Answers to exercises

3.1 (a) 1,000 + 1,000 + 1,000 + 500 = 3,500.
  (b) 50/1,000 = 5%; 150/3,000 = 5%.
  (d) 10.
  (e) A: 40/1,000 = 4%; B: 55/1,005 = 5.47%; C: 55/1,005 = 5.47%; Agg: 150/3,010 = 4.98%.
  (f) 1,010 + 1,010 + 1,010 + 500 = 3,530.
  (g) 50/1,010 = 4.95%.
  (h) 150/3,030 = 4.95%.

3.2 (a) Initially, (50/1,000 × 0) + (300/1,000 × 0) + (200/1,000 × 5) + (150/1,000 × 6) + (50/1,000 × 4) + (250/1,000 × 7) = 3.85%.
  (b) Afterwards, (50/1,000 × 0) + (300/1,000 × 3) + (200/1,000 × 5) + (150/1,000 × 4) + (50/1,000 × 4) = (250/1,000 × 7) = 4.75%.

A history of UK monetary aggregates

Name	Components	First published	Discontinued	Targeted
DCE (domestic credit expansion)	Changes in £ bank lending to the NBPS[1] + £ bank lending to the public sector	Dec. 1972	March 1986	1967–9 1976–9
M0 (wide monetary base)	Notes and coin in circulation + banks' operational balances	June 1981		1984–present
NIBM1 (non-interest bearing M1)	Notes and coin in circulation + NBPS non-interest bearing £ bank sight deposits	June 1975	Feb. 1991	
M1	NIBM1 + NBPS interest bearing £ sight bank deposits	Dec. 1970	July 1989	1982–4
M2	NIBM1 + NBPS interest bearing retail £ deposits with banks and building societies + National Savings ordinary accounts	Sept. 1982[2]		
M3 (£M3 until May 1987)	M1 + NBPS £ bank time deposits + NBPS holdings of £ CDs with banks	March 1977[3]	July 1989	1976–86
M3c (M3 until May 1987)	M3 + NBPS foreign currency bank deposits	Dec. 1970[3]	July 1989	

Name	Components	First published	Discontinued	Targeted
PSL1	M3 – NBPS £ bank time deposits original maturity > 2yrs + NBPS holdings of bank bills, treasury bills, local authority deposits and certificates of tax deposits	Sept. 1979	May 1987	
PSL2	PSL1 + NBPS building society £ deposits (excl. term shares) + short-term National Savings instruments	Sept. 1979	May 1987	1982–4
M4	M3 + NBPS building society £ shares, deposits and CDs – building society holdings of bank deposits, CDs and notes and coin	May 1987		
M4c	M4 + NBNBSPS[4] bank and building society foreign currency deposits	May 1987	May 1991	
M3H	M4c + public corporations' holdings of bank and building society foreign currency deposits	August 1992		
M5	M4 + NBPS holdings of bank bills, treasury bills, local authority deposits and certificates of tax deposits + short-term National Savings instruments – building society holdings of bank deposits. CDs and notes and coin	May 1987	May 1991	

Notes:
[1] NBPS = non-bank private sector.
[2] Not to be confused with an earlier M2 aggregate (Dec. 1970–Dec. 1971) which was midway between M1 and M3 in the range of deposits included.
[3] M1 and M3 included public sector £ bank deposits until March 1984.
[4] NBNBSPS = Non-bank non-building society private sector ('M4 private sector').

Source: *Bank of England Quarterly Bulletin*, various issues.

CHAPTER 4

Non-deposit-taking institutions

Objectives

What you will learn in this chapter:

- What services are provided by each of the main categories of non-deposit-taking intermediary
- What assets are held by each
- The comparative size of each as measured by total assets and inflows of funds
- Where they directed their funds in 2004/5
- How some NDTIs have become involved recently in a number of controversial issues

At the beginning of Chapter 3, we divided financial institutions into two groups: those whose liabilities were largely deposits (DTIs) and those whose liabilities took some other form (NDTIs). In this chapter we devote sections 4.1–4.4 to an examination of each of the major types of non-deposit-taking institution. We shall describe the services offered by each NDTI, look at its balance sheet, and explain the regulatory framework to which it is subject. Remember, as we said in the opening to Chapter 3, that 'financial institution' does not correspond to 'financial firm'; a particular type of financial institution is better understood as a particular type of financial activity undertaken by a specialist subsidiary of a large financial corporation which may be engaged in a wide variety of activities.

We are familiar (since Chapter 2) with the distinction between stock and flow data. Balance sheets show us the (asset) stock position for each type of NDTI and this gives us an indication of what each type of institution has done with the funds it has received in the past. Stock data is the basis of the pie charts distributed through-out this chapter. However, we are also interested in the magnitude of *new* funds which NDTIs receive each year and in the destination of these funds. These funds are used to buy additional assets, or to make what is called in the official statistics '*net acquisitions*' of assets (see Box 4.1). In section 4.5, therefore, we compare the *flows* of funds passing through different types of NDTI in recent times. By looking at the assets which they acquire we can tell which NDTIs are mainly responsible for financing different types of activity.

Box 4.1

Measuring financial activity

UK official statistics on financial activity use the following terms, which must be carefully distinguished:

Holdings at year end: refers to the *stock* of assets (or liabilities) at a particular moment. It is the data that is used to compile a balance sheet of assets and liabilities.

Net acquisitions: refers to the quantity of assets (or liabilities) acquired during a period. This is *flow* data and for financial institutions it must match the inflow of funds from savers during the period in question.

Turnover: The total value of transactions (the sum of purchases *and* sales) during a period of time. This is also *flow* data, but the figures will normally be much larger than those showing net acquisitions.

In addition to data showing assets accumulated and assets recently acquired, there is a third set of data whose examination we postpone until Chapter 6, where we look at the functioning of capital markets. This is data for *turnover*. Turnover refers to the total purchases and sales of assets (or liabilities) and will usually be much greater than any figures for net acquisitions. This is easily understood if one imagines a unit trust manager with an inflow of funds of £100m which he has to allocate between additional assets. £100m will be the figure for net acquisitions, but in order to achieve precisely the portfolio which he thinks best, he may very well sell £200m of his existing holdings and buy £300m of assets in total. The fund's turnover in this case is £500m.

In order that we do not have to repeat ourselves for every type of NDTI, let us just remember that howsoever they differ from deposit-taking institutions, NDTIs all engage in the principal features of financial intermediaries:

- They create assets for lenders and liabilities for borrowers which are more attractive than would be the case if the parties had to deal directly.
- They do this in part by 'maturity transformation'.
- This in turn depends upon large size which enables them to pool and diversify risk.

What distinguishes the institutions is the manner and scale in which this is done.

In Chapter 1 we discussed the advantages to both lenders and borrowers of using financial intermediaries and paying for their services. The NDTIs we are about to look at are differentiated partly by the very specific services which they offer. The one thing which they all offer to lenders, however, is the risk-reducing effect of diversification.

4.1 Insurance companies

We need firstly to recognise that insurance companies as a group are engaged in two quite distinct forms of business: *long term* and *general*. So distinct are these forms of business that many insurance companies specialise in one or the other. Some of the largest firms, however, deal in both. Long-term insurance is also sometimes referred to as *life* insurance, although it includes activity which is not strictly life-related, and the firms that specialise in long-term insurance are often called 'life offices'.

We shall see in a moment why their activities are quite distinct. What they have in common, however, and the reason that they are treated together, is the fact that they all provide insurance against financial loss. They do this by collecting *premiums* or contributions from large numbers of people in return for an agreement to compensate the policyholder in the event of a specified event occurring within a specified time. Such an event might be theft, fire, illness or even death; within the next year, the next many years or even within a lifetime. The level of premium paid to insure against an event depends obviously upon the likelihood or risk of the event occurring and the level of compensation or benefit to be paid when it does. Alternatively, we may say that for a given level of benefit, the premium will be determined by the risk, or more briefly still, that the premium : benefit ratio is a function of risk. However, the payment of premiums creates a pool of funds at the companies' disposal, awaiting claims to be made against it. Provided sufficient funds are available or can be easily recovered in order to meet unexpected claims, this pool of funds can be invested in earning assets by the companies to provide a further source of income. Thus their investment success is a second factor which influences the ratio of premium : benefit levels.

> **Asymmetric information:** A situation where one party to a financial transaction has better information than the other about factors relevant to the transaction.

Since the premium : benefit ratio is one of the main criteria on which clients are likely to choose an insurance company, the management of risk is clearly very important for insurance companies. It is also quite difficult for reasons arising out of *asymmetric information*. There is often an inequality in the information available to the two parties in any financial transaction. In section 3.1.4, for example, we noted that intermediaries (banks in that case) often have better knowledge about the risk to which they are going to put funds than do the savers who lend them. This is a major reason for regulating the behaviour of financial institutions. In the case of insurance, however, the more obvious asymmetry arises between the insurance company itself and the insured. Typically, and especially in general insurance, it is the insured who has the better information since he knows his activities and the risks involved in much greater detail than the insurance company does.

This particular asymmetry gives rise to two specific problems. The first is *moral hazard*. This arises when an insured person becomes less careful about her actions precisely because she is insured. Since safety measures typically have a cost, it might be tempting to some people to cut down on these measures, knowing that the insurance company will have to pay in the event of an accident. The other problem is described as *adverse selection*. This arises when the riskiest clients express the strongest demand for insurance products. The insurance company does not normally have the information to distinguish very accurately between customers of different degrees of risk. It has thus to set a price for its contracts (the premiums) which it hopes will provide a positive return for the *average* level of risk to which it is exposed. But potential customers, seeing the uniform price, will divide into those who will take the contract because they think the premium is good value (knowing themselves to be high-risk) and those who will reject the contract because the premium is too high (knowing themselves to be low-risk). The average risk that the company actually faces is thus increased because the contracts that are actually written are dominated by high-risk (relative to the premiums) clients.

Moral hazard: The situation where being insured encourages someone to behave more recklessly than they would have done without the insurance.

Adverse selection: The situation where those who pose the highest risks are the ones most likely to take out insurance.

Both problems can be tackled to some degree by *risk screening*. Typically, this involves the study of past statistics on client characteristics and outcomes. It may be possible to identify groups of clients as having differing degrees of risk and then charging them risk-based premiums. Where screening is difficult or impossible, moral hazard-type behaviour can be discouraged by imposing a *deductible amount* (commonly referred to as an 'excess') which the insured has to pay for himself. This gives the insured a financial incentive to behave with caution. Similarly, *restrictive covenants* can be imposed which make the contract void if the insured behaves in a completely inappropriate way. Motor insurance provides a good example of these responses to the asymmetric information problem. Age, past record and type of car are used to screen drivers for risk, to the level of which premiums are then related; motor policies often pay for damage only in excess of a certain value and they also contain clauses forbidding the use of the vehicle for anything other than normal or 'domestic' use.

General insurance covers such things as accident, vehicles, goods in transit, damage to property, various forms of liability, fire and natural forces, and legal expenses. Classes of long-term insurance include life and annuity, permanent health, marriage and birth. One class of long-term business is pension fund management. This does not in itself involve companies undertaking insurance risks but acknowledges that the skills required for the operation of the life insurance business are similar to those needed to run pension funds. Thus, over the years, many life assurance companies have taken on the management of pension funds on behalf of firms and other institutions. When we come to consider the activities of insurance companies as a form of financial intermediation, this distinction between the two types of business will be crucial.

Firstly, though, let us get some idea of the size of the insurance business. As with all financial magnitudes, we can consider both *flows* and *stocks*. In the course of 2004, net investment by insurance companies was approximately £33bn. Long-term insurance companies received the greater part of this inflow: roughly £25bn compared with £8bn received by general funds. Later, in Table 4.1, we shall look further at what assets insurance companies acquired and compare these acquisitions with those of other NDTIs.

When we look at stocks, we can see from Figure 4.1 (by adding up all the assets in both pie charts) that total assets/liabilities at the end of 2004 amounted to £1079bn. Of these, £112bn were held by general insurance companies and £967bn belonged to long-term funds.

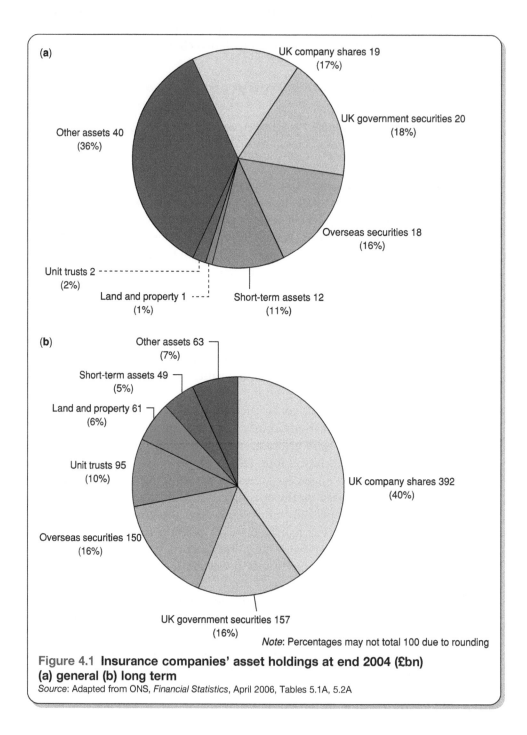

(a)

UK company shares 19
(17%)

UK government securities 20
(18%)

Other assets 40
(36%)

Overseas securities 18
(16%)

Unit trusts 2
(2%)

Land and property 1
(1%)

Short-term assets 12
(11%)

(b)

Other assets 63
(7%)

Short-term assets 49
(5%)

Land and property 61
(6%)

Unit trusts 95
(10%)

UK company shares 392
(40%)

Overseas securities 150
(16%)

UK government securities 157
(16%)

Note: Percentages may not total 100 due to rounding

**Figure 4.1 Insurance companies' asset holdings at end 2004 (£bn)
(a) general (b) long term**
Source: Adapted from ONS, *Financial Statistics*, April 2006, Tables 5.1A, 5.2A

Figure 4.1(a) shows the assets held at the end of 2004 by firms conducting general insurance business. The two most conspicuous features are the large holdings of UK shares, amounting to nearly 17 per cent of total assets, and of overseas shares, accounting for another 16 per cent. Given that the purpose of a general insurance company is to provide a pool of funds from which to meet claims which are by their nature uncertain: and given also that their policies are mainly short term – clients can terminate or renew annually – this proportion of long-term assets may be surprising. However, this overlooks two points. Firstly, while it may be true that individual clients can and do terminate contracts frequently, they do this to move from one company to another: every year each company loses existing customers but gains new ones. Rather like banks, in the aggregate, premium income is fairly stable. Secondly, during the 1980 and 90s it became common for firms to make 'underwriting losses'. That is to say that their premium income was insufficient to meet claims and the difference has therefore had to be met from investment income. This has made the profitability of investment very important. Thus the companies' approach to investment has been to ensure that there is sufficient availability of short-term assets to meet unforeseen contingencies and then to maximise holdings of long-dated, higher-yielding assets.

If we were to look at both stocks and flows together for the most recent years, say 2000 to 2004, insurance companies have tended to dispose of UK *ordinary* company shares and government securities (a trend now reversed). What the figures obscure, however, is a switch from ordinary company shares into preference shares and corporate bonds. This is a useful reminder that stock figures are a snapshot of the position at a particular moment: the flow figures will often reveal that the stock is in the course of changing. Notice, though, that while flow figures are useful in telling us the directions in which companies channel the funds they most recently received, they do not tell us how active those companies are in any particular market. In Chapter 6, for example, we shall see from turnover data that insurance companies can be very important traders of company securities even if their *net* acquisitions (positive or negative) are small.

Figure 4.1(b) shows the aggregate portfolio for long-term insurance companies. The conspicuous features are like those for general insurance companies. There is a very heavy concentration on securities of all types, amounting to 72 per cent of the whole portfolio. However, they have larger holdings of land and property. There is also a difference when we come to consider 'short-term assets'. At 5 per cent of total assets for long-term funds, they form a smaller proportion than they do for general insurance companies and this suggests that the latter are more liquid. In fact, the difference is even larger than it appears since 'other assets' is a much larger category for general insurance companies and this too is made up largely of short-term and fairly liquid assets (agents and reinsurance balances, for example). The message is that long-term insurance funds hold a much higher proportion of longer-term assets than do general funds. To understand why they do so, it is necessary to consider the nature of a long-term fund's liabilities.

As we said earlier, long-term insurance contracts enable people to insure against such events as death or permanent illness or disablement. For obvious reasons, life (i.e. death)-related contracts dominate. These may be of various forms. A person can insure against death within a specified period, the policy paying nothing if the insured survives. This is known as *term insurance*. Alternatively a *whole-of-life* policy insures against death at any time. An *endowment* policy pays a capital sum to the insured at a specified time in the future, or on death if earlier. This sum may be a guaranteed absolute amount, in which case the insured has a policy 'without profits', or there may be a guaranteed minimum plus an entitlement to share in the company's annual profits. On this 'with profits' type of policy the shares accrue as annual bonuses and are paid with the guaranteed minimum on termination of the policy. Under an *annuity* policy the company pays a regular income to the insured for a specified period up until death, in return either for a lump sum payment or regular contributions earlier in life. This cannot be an exhaustive list (see Box 4.2) since, like other financial intermediaries, insurance companies are continually developing new products. Nonetheless it makes two features of long-term insurance policies very clear.

Box 4.2 | **Types of life assurance product**

Annuity: A policy which provides the holder with a regular stream of payments from some specified date until death. An annuity is purchased by a large lump sum payment (often at the point of retirement) though the lump sum may be accumulated by regular payments into a fund previously established for the purpose.

Endowment: A policy requiring regular contributions which pays a specified sum on a specified date or on the death of the insured if this should occur earlier. This is a long-term savings product, with an element of insurance, often sold in conjunction with some fixed-term loan (e.g. a mortgage) in order that the specified sum will pay off the loan.

Term assurance: A policy requiring regular contributions which makes a payment to a named survivor if the insured dies within a specified period. If the insured lives beyond the specified date, nothing is paid. The only life assurance product which provides no element of saving.

Whole of life: A policy, normally requiring regular contributions, which makes a payment to a named survivor only on the death of the insured.

The first is that they are *contractual*. People taking out policies of the kind just described are committing themselves to paying premiums as part of a long-term contract. They can, of course, cease payment at any time, but they break the contract and forgo virtually all the benefits since very little compensation is usually available for the premiums which have already been paid. Secondly, unlike general insurance, the motivation behind many life-related policies is essentially a desire to save for the future, either for one's own benefit or for the benefit of dependants. This means, of course, that life insurance companies, while obviously offering products that are distinct by virtue of their pure insurance element, are to some extent in competition with other intermediaries whose function is mainly to attract long-term savings.

The nature of these policies determines the risks to which long-term funds are exposed. Actuarial predictions of a country's mortality record are now very reliable, but it is at least a theoretical risk that the record could deteriorate unexpectedly. A bit more likely is the possibility that a change in the savings products offered by other inter-mediaries could cause an increase in the early terminations or 'surrender' of policies as savers switch to the other products. Conceivably a company could underestimate its future operating costs. The most serious risk faced by long-term insurance funds, however, is that future economic and financial conditions cause the future yield on their portfolio to fall below expectations. The probability of such an event may be low, but the consequences would be serious since investment income for long-term funds is approximately half as large as their total premium income. We shall see in a moment that the fall in stock market values in 2001 and 2002, and the persistence of low inflation and interest rates since the mid-90s has had a serious effect on the solvency of life assurance companies, and has caused a great deal of concern to clients holding 'with profits' products and to the UK's Financial Services Authority.

In the circumstances, the composition of assets is not hard to explain. Their liabilities are long term and the probabilities of both unforeseen shortfalls of income and unanticipated paying out of benefits are low. The need for short-term, highly liquid assets is low. On the other hand, they are in competition with other forms of long-term saving. For this purpose they need to maximise yield and in particular their contracts need to produce 'real' returns, i.e. returns which exceed the rate of inflation. The emphasis upon company securities therefore is to be expected. However, while a narrow range of assets may maximise yield, it also increases the exposure to risk. This can be reduced by diversifying, in particular to achieve a mix of assets whose values would not all be expected to move in the same direction at once. Fixed-interest securities would be immune at least to some of the difficulties that might affect companies' trading performance.

During 2004, long-term insurance companies bought about 15.4bn of UK govern-ment securities and exchanged about £7bn of UK ordinary company shares for preference and fixed-interest securities. Within the category of overseas securities there was a marked shift towards company shares (of all kinds) and away from govern-ment bonds.

From 1 December 2001, the Financial Services Authority (FSA), which was set up by the Financial Services and Markets Act of 2000, took over the prudential regulation of all insurance companies and the conduct of business regulation of life insurance companies in the UK. Before this, insurance firms had been regulated for prudential purposes under the Insurance Companies Act of 1982, while the conduct of business of life insurance firms had been covered by the Financial Services Act of 1986. The 1982 Act had made it an offence for anyone to conduct insurance business in the UK without authorisation and resulted from concern following the collapse of several (mainly general insurance) companies in the 1970s. Under the Financial Services and Markets Act, the power of authorisation passed to the FSA. Authorisation is granted to each company with respect to particular classes of insurance business. In addition to providing authorisation, the FSA monitors the performance of companies, in particular with respect to solvency margins, and has the power to intervene in various ways: it may require a change in investment strategy, prevent the issuing or renewing of policies and, of course, ultimately, withdraw authorisation. The ability to monitor and to intervene stems from the requirement that companies provide specified annual information relating to the conduct of their business. In the event that a company should fail, in spite of this scrutiny, policyholders have some degree of protection under the Financial Services and Markets Act, which also contains regulations on the marketing of insurance products. For example, it laid down standards relating to advertising, and specified a minimum 'cooling-off' period.

The fact that so many insurance products contain a substantial savings element explains the inclusion of conduct of business regulation firstly in the Financial Services Act 1986 and now in the Financial Services and Markets Act 2000. The various changes to the regulatory regimes over the past twenty years have made little difference to the behaviour of the companies so far as the production of policies and their conduct of business are concerned, but they have imposed constraints on the marketing of what are now clearly seen as forms of saving.

Recent problems such as with the life insurance company Equitable Life and with the possible insolvency of a number of large insurance companies have meant that much of the FSA's energies in its early life have been devoted to the insurance sector. In addition, the creation of the FSA as a single regulator of financial services highlighted significant differences between the regulation of insurance and other sectors in respect of similar types of risk. Consequently, a project was initiated in September 2001 to overhaul insurance regulation. In November 2001 a report was submitted to the Economic Secretary to the Treasury outlining the agenda for strengthening insurance regulation and listing actions the FSA already had in hand. The main problem that came to light (and preoccupied the FSA's insurance division from 2001 to 2005) was the treatment of what were called 'with profits' investors. We return to this and other problems of NDTI behaviour in Chapter 13, where we discuss the regulation of financial markets and institutions.

4.2 Pension funds

After their retirement from employment, most people in the UK can expect to receive some form of pension. This comes in one of three forms: a flat-rate pension paid by the state to everyone above a certain age; an occupational pension provided from a fund to which the employer and employee have contributed; a personal pension paid from a fund to which the individual has made contributions. As we shall see, only the second and third forms strictly involve financial intermediation. This is because the first of these operates on 'pay as you go' principles, while payments under the latter are made from an accumulated fund of savings.

> **Funded pension schemes:** Schemes where payments to pensioners are made out of the income earned by a fund of savings which has been built up in earlier years by (usually regular) savings contributions.
>
> **Unfunded pension schemes:** Schemes where payments to pensioners are financed by *simultaneous* contributions from those in work. Such schemes are often called 'pay as you go' or PAYG schemes.

Consider firstly the flat-rate state pension. This is paid for out of general taxation and although those drawing a pension may feel that they have contributed to its cost by virtue of their earlier contributions, the state scheme in fact operates on a 'pay as you go' (PAYG) basis. The current level of contributions is set at whatever level is necessary to pay for the current number and level of pension payments. Each generation of workers is in effect paying for its predecessors' pensions, in the hope that the next generation will pay for theirs. Crucially, no pool of investible funds is created.

Other pensions which are organised on PAYG principles include most public sector occupational schemes like those for teachers, the Civil Service and National Health Service employees and the state earnings-related pension scheme (SERPS) which began in 1978.

However, the PAYG principle is not thought to be suitable for private sector occupational schemes. In the public sector, the government can be relied upon always to raise the funds necessary to honour its pension obligations through taxation. Private firms, by contrast, might find their existing workforce too small to pay for their existing pensioners or they might even go bankrupt. Therefore, the practice with the private sector is for employers and employees to make contributions to a fund at a rate which, combined with judicious investment of the fund, should be sufficient to meet obligations to current employees at some point in the future. Since the fund is kept strictly separate from the firm's own assets, employees' pensions should remain secure even if the firm ceases trading. The scandal surrounding the late Robert Maxwell's group of companies is based upon the fact that he approved the (mis)use of pensioners' funds by the companies themselves. We return to this later when we discuss the regulation of financial activity in Chapter 13.

Pension schemes of this kind are referred to as 'funded' schemes and crucially for our purposes they involve the accumulation of a fund of assets. These assets are someone else's liabilities. Hence funded pension schemes are involved in channelling funds from savers to borrowers: directly if the fund buys newly issued liabilities; indirectly if it buys liabilities issued in the past, from their current holders. We shall say more about whose liabilities are held by pension funds in a moment. But notice, before we go on, that an occupational pension fund can be confident of the source and scale of its contributions since these are a contractual obligation for employer and all employees. In this sense a pension fund is very different from a bank or building society where the inflows of funds are entirely at savers' discretion and tend to be 'residual', i.e. made after all other types of saving expenditures. There are two types of funded scheme and the difference has become extremely important in the past few years.

The first type of arrangement is known as a 'defined benefit' (DB) scheme because the rules of the scheme specify at the outset what a pensioner can expect to receive, provided he or she maintains the required level of contribution. For example, most DB schemes award a pension equal to some proportion of 'final salary'. 'Final salary' might be defined as the average salary of an employee's last three years of employment. The contract might then specify that each year of service entitles the employee to, say, one-eightieth of that figure. There may or may not be a provision for periodic inflation-related reviews or even for index-linking. Given then that the fund's future obligations per retired employee are known, its total obligations are a matter of actuarial calculation, involving the current size of the workforce, its age distribution, the average life expectancy after retirement, and other factors which are largely predictable – including the rate of return on, and thus the growth of, the underlying fund.

The idea behind a DB fund, therefore, is that contributions (from employer and employee) are set at such a level that they will build up a savings fund over the years which will be sufficient to provide the defined benefits for the pensioner. Notice, however, that the growth rate of the fund does not depend solely upon the level of contributions. It also depends on what happens to the value of the assets in which the fund invests. Until the 1930s, it was common for pension funds to invest largely in fixed-interest government bonds. These provided a nominal rate of return of 3–4 per cent p.a. and, with the low inflation of those years, a real rate of return of 2–3 per cent. After the Second World War, with inflation running at much higher levels, pension fund managers switched increasingly to holding company shares because the market value of the shares should increase with the growth of company dividends and these in turn should reflect both the rising level of prices and the growth in firms' productivity. They might be riskier than bonds, but risk could be contained by diversification (see Appendix I). By the 1990s, experience suggested nominal rates of return for a well-diversified fund could be 7–10 per cent p.a. Indeed, during the 1990s, some funds grew so quickly as a result of rising stock market values that employers took 'pension holidays' – short periods in which they stopped making contributions to the fund because the contributions were not necessary. Alas, when markets collapsed in 2000 and continued to fall in 2001 and 2002, the value of the invested funds shrank dramatically and it quickly became clear that the principle of a funded pension scheme was in danger of being undermined. A new expression entered the language of the pensions industry: the 'pension fund deficit'. This was calculated as the difference between the current value of the fund and the size of the fund that would be required if the firm were to cease trading and still be able to meet all its current pension obligations. This deficit was a liability of the firm and had to be declared as such on its annual balance sheet statement. This in turn reduced the value of the firm and the value of its shares. Understandably this caused a great deal of alarm among firms operating such schemes. We return to this later. For now, the important thing to note is that the sharp decline in stock market values was a powerful reminder that *under DB arrangements the risk attached to making future pension payments rests with the employer.*

The second type of funded scheme, known as a 'defined contribution' (DC) arrangement, places the risk largely upon the employee. This is because the scheme lays down the contribution rates for employer and employees but makes no stipulation about the level of benefit which will be forthcoming at the point of retirement. As in a DB scheme, the contributions go together to build up a fund which grows at a rate determined in part by what happens to the fund's investments. When the employee retires, however, he receives a lump sum which is his share in the value of the fund, whatever it may be at that particular time. In recent years, someone retiring in mid-1999 would have received 50 per cent more than a person with the same contribution record, working for the same firm and retiring at the same age in mid-2001. Given the problems (for firms) caused in recent years by schemes based on defined benefits, it is not surprising that many firms have begun to switch from DB to DC arrangements.

The flat-rate state pension in the UK is intended to provide only a minimum level of retirement income. Most people wish therefore to make additional provision and for many, as we have seen, this is provided by an occupational pension based upon an accumulated fund of investments. However, not all employers operate such a scheme. For this reason, the government introduced a state earnings-related pension scheme (SERPS) in 1978. This too was to be funded from general taxation on a PAYG basis. By 1988, however, there were fears that taxation (at levels which people were prepared to pay) was unlikely to be sufficient to pay for these pensions. The main reasons for this were that average life expectancy was increasing (meaning that people would have a longer retirement during which to draw their pension) and that the birth rate was declining (meaning that the number of working people paying the taxes to pay the pensions would eventually fall). Indeed, at the time of writing, there are some doubts that the core, flat-rate state scheme can continue to be financed by taxation in its present form. This is an even larger problem for a number of continental countries where PAYG arrangements are much more widespread than in the UK.

In April 1988, therefore, the decision was taken to encourage the private provision of pensions, not linked to employment. The desirability of such a move was reinforced by arguments that existing occupational schemes were too rigid. Typically, an employee who moved jobs, in the private sector, would be forced to terminate his existing occupational scheme and begin another with the new employer. Like most contractual investment schemes, pension funds pay the biggest rewards to those who contribute for a long period. Thus, it was argued, people were deterred from moving jobs because of the difficulty in building up a long-term pension fund. Existing pension arrangements, in other words, reduced labour market mobility. The desirable alternative, it was felt, was for people to build up their own pension fund (a *personal* rather than occupational pension) which they could take with them every time they moved. As a further step towards the 'privatising' of pensions it was also made possible for workers in an occupational scheme to make additional voluntary contributions, with the customary tax advantages, into a private scheme operating alongside that offered by the employer.

'Encouraging' such provision amounted to opening up the pension market to a wide range of institutions, including banks and building societies, as well as life assurance and traditional pension funds. (This provides another example of what we said at the beginning of Chapter 3 – a pension fund is a financial activity, not a distinctive type of financial firm.) Inevitably, perhaps, a great deal of effort went into the sale of pensions, many of which were sold on commission, and what began as a sensible project to provide certain groups of people with more flexible pension arrangements and higher levels of retirement income soon developed a reputation for the unscrupulous selling of personal pensions to those for whom they were not suitable. The main examples were cases where people with many years of contributions to an occupational scheme were persuaded to switch to private provision. It was always unlikely that personal pension products could provide larger benefits than occupational schemes, since an employee in an occupational scheme benefited from the fact that the employer also contributed. Furthermore, using the terms that we have explained above, these private pensions were all funded schemes based on defined contributions. Inevitably, therefore, some of those who switched to a private pension scheme gave up not only their employer's contribution to their retirement income but also his willingness to bear the risk that the fund might not be large enough to pay the target income. Fortunately, it is possible to establish retrospectively those cases where personal pensions were 'missold'. In 1995, the Personal Investment Authority (see Chapter 13) insisted that pension funds should do precisely that and it estimated that there were more than 300,000 'priority' cases where compensation was urgently required.

As with other intermediaries, the nature of pension fund liabilities influences the composition of the asset portfolio. If the purpose of the fund is to collect 'lifetime' contributions in order to pay a pension that is related to final salary or earnings, it is obviously a fundamental requirement that an employee's contributions be invested in a manner which keeps their value at least in line with rising real earnings. As we saw with long-term insurance funds, this inevitably means an emphasis upon company securities.

Figure 4.2 shows the composition of pension funds' portfolios in 2004. Notice firstly that at £761bn the market value of pension fund assets at the end of 2004 was second only to that of long-term insurance funds. Of this total, UK company securities accounted for over 29 per cent, and overseas securities, by far the greater part of which are also company shares, accounted for nearly 23 per cent. UK government

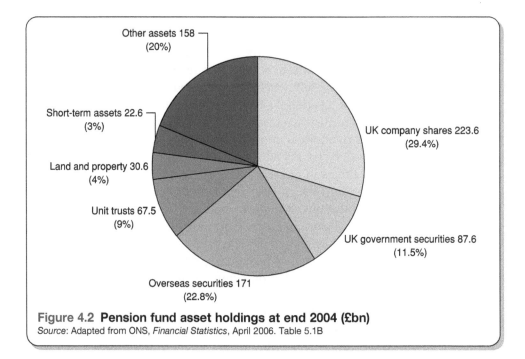

Figure 4.2 Pension fund asset holdings at end 2004 (£bn)
Source: Adapted from ONS, *Financial Statistics*, April 2006. Table 5.1B

Table 4.1 **NDTIs – some comparative features, end 2001**

	Insurance companies		Pension funds	Unit trusts	Investment trusts
	General	Long-term			
Assets	109.7	967.3	760.9	279.2	48.1
Growth 2000–04 % p.a. (compound)	1.2	0.3	0.4	1.7	−6.0
UK co. securities					
– holdings	18.5	392	223.6	161.2	25
– acquisitions	2.1	3.3	−10.9	7.4	−2.5
UK govt securities					
– holdings	19.7	157	87.6	9.8	0.5
– acquisitions	−0.2	15.4	0.5	0.9	−0.1
Overseas securities					
– holdings	18.2	150	171	98.1	21
– acquisitions	0.9	6.7	9.4	5.0	−0.9
Net inflow of funds	7.7	25.3	11.7	16.2	−3.4

Notes and sources: All figures in £bn except growth rates. Holdings at end 2004, acquisitions and net inflows during 2004. Figures taken or calculated from ONS, *Financial Statistics*, April 2006, section 5.

securities also formed a significant proportion at 11.5 per cent. The rate of acquisition of these various classes of assets has varied from year to year. Since 1980, the proportion of overseas securities in pension fund portfolios has tended to rise, inviting the same criticism – that pension funds have hindered the financing of UK industry – that we saw levelled at life assurance companies. What Table 4.1 shows is that 2004 saw a marked shift out of UK company securities. Total net investment in 2004 was £11.7bn. Much of this, and the funds switched out of UK shares, went into unit trusts and 'other' assets.

Most of the funds flowing into pension fund schemes are contractual; employees have had little choice about contributing to such schemes. Contributions have also been comparatively favoured by tax treatment. Successive governments have been very careful to ensure that the benefits bought from a pension fund are taxed only once and strictly as deferred earned income. Contributions up to 17.5 per cent of annual income are exempt from income tax and pension funds pay no capital gains or income tax on their investments. The benefits paid from the fund are taxed at the rate appropriate to the pensioner's circumstances.

Just as the tax position of pension funds is straightforward, so too, comparatively speaking, is the regulatory framework. Most pension funds are strictly speaking trusts. Their activities are therefore circumscribed by the terms of a trust deed and this deed itself must comply with legislation governing the conduct of trusts. Any member of the scheme who feels that the terms of the trust are being abused can seek redress under trust law. To be exempt from taxation the trust must meet Inland Revenue conditions relating to contributions and benefit entitlement.

This leaves pension funds with a wide range of powers over the selection and management of investments, and this has attracted a degree of adverse attention in recent years. The first worry was noted by the Wilson Committee (1980). This was that pension funds, like life insurance companies, were too willing to invest in overseas companies, by implication 'starving' British industry of capital. The Wilson Committee found the case unproven, but the Labour Party and the trade union movement suggested at the time that tax concessions available to pension funds should be made conditional upon the repatriation of some of their overseas investment. More recently, concern has grown in many quarters about the ethics of certain types of investment. With hindsight, the beginnings can be seen with the British Rail Pension Fund's purchase of paintings in the mid-1970s. Although their capital appreciation might eventually benefit pensioners, it was felt inappropriate by some that a fund should invest in 'unproductive' assets. In 1984, the National Union of Mineworkers fought an unsuccessful legal battle to prevent their pension fund managers from investing in alternative, i.e. competing, energy sources. More recently, investments in tobacco, drug and oil companies and in firms using animals for experimentation have been the subject of protest and workers have tried to influence their pension fund managers away from these.

4.3 Unit trusts

The purpose of a unit trust is to accept funds from individuals or companies and to invest those funds in a wide variety of assets. Contributors to the trust then have a share in the income and capital appreciation of the underlying assets. To understand the mechanism whereby contributors share in the benefits of belonging to the trust we need to understand the concept of a *unit*. Imagine that a newly formed trust advertises units for sale to savers. It must advertise those units at a price. The price is not important except in so far as it determines the number of units to be created after subscriptions have been received. Prices of 50p and £1 are common for units in a newly established trust; we will choose 50p for our illustration. The advertisement will give some indication of the objectives of the trust. These might be capital growth or income or 'general' – a combination of both. It will also give some indication of the range of assets in which it expects to invest: 'health', 'technology', 'recovery situations', 'European' are examples. Suppose now that the trust receives £5m of subscriptions. Ignoring the question of expenses for the time being, it will create 10 million 50p units which will be distributed to savers in proportion to the funds they subscribed and it will buy £5m of appropriate assets.

As the price of the underlying assets changes, the value of the units will change and will be calculated (again ignoring expenses) by dividing the current value of the assets by the number of units in existence. Such calculations are normally done daily and are published in financial and other quality newspapers. The income generated by the assets is accumulated and paid out at intervals, the amount paid on each unit again roughly corresponding to total income divided by the number of units in existence.

However, the number of units need not remain fixed. Unit trusts are one example of what is known as an open-ended mutual fund. This means that new savers can join the trust at any time, and that existing savers can increase their holdings of units. Indeed, many trusts encourage regular saving through fixed monthly contributions. If, as is usual, the inflow of funds exceeds the rate at which people wish to relinquish their units, the trust creates new units at the going price. If the value of existing units has risen to 75p for example, new subscribers will 'buy' newly created units at 75p and the number they purchase will be equal to the amount they wish to invest divided by 75p. The new funds will be used by the trust to buy additional assets. In this crucial respect, 'open ended investments companies' (OEICs) are similar to unit trusts. Although they have a different legal structure, OEICs share the characteristic that when there is a net flow of savings into the fund, the fund expands; when there are net withdrawals, the fund contracts.

The attractions to savers are several. Firstly, a small saver is able to minimise risk by investing quite cheaply in a much wider range of assets than would be possible by direct investment. Suppose, for example, that one wished to hold company shares. If you look at Figure A1.3 in Appendix I you will see that most of the benefits that diversification offers in the reduction of risk can be achieved with a portfolio of 'only' fifteen to twenty different shares. However, brokerage fees make the purchase of less than, say, £5,000 worth of a share very expensive. The minimum cost of a fifteen-share portfolio is likely therefore to be nearly £75,000. The minimum investment in a unit trust is commonly £500 as a lump sum and £20 as a regular monthly contribution. And for this, a saver can have a very small share in the performance of over 100 companies.

> **Open-ended fund:** A fund which will expand in response to new contributions and contract in response to withdrawals. The value of shares in the fund corresponds to the value of the underlying assets.
>
> **Closed-ended fund:** A fund with a fixed number of shares. The value (not the number) of the shares responds to inflows and withdrawals and thus may differ from the value of the underlying assets.

Secondly, holdings of units can be liquidated quite quickly. After purchasing units, the owner receives a certificate stating the number of units purchased. This certificate normally carries on the reverse side a form of renunciation. The sale of units merely requires the completion of this form and its return to the trust. A seller would normally expect to receive the current market value of the units within fourteen days. Notice that the buying and selling of units can take place only between the trust and the original purchaser. They cannot be transferred by the purchaser and thus there is no secondary market and the market value of the units is determined solely by the performance of the underlying assets themselves. Since new units are created in response to an inflow of funds (and existing units cancelled in response to an outflow), there can be no excess demand or supply and so demand for the units has no effect upon their price.

Each individual trust is always the responsibility of two companies. Firstly, there is the company responsible for the day-to-day management of the trust. This may be a specialist unit trust company or it may be part of some other large financial grouping, a subsidiary of a retail or merchant bank for example. The management company will make the detailed investment decisions, accept funds from investors, issue certificates of unit ownership and pay income to investors as appropriate.

In addition to its managing company, each trust has a trustee. These are mainly specialist subsidiaries of major banks. The job of the trustee is to see that the fund is managed within the terms of its 'trustee deed'. This deed specifies the objectives of the trust and lays down broad conditions governing the management of the funds. There is an obvious sense, therefore, in which the trustee company is acting as guardian of the unit holders' interests.

For simplicity we have so far ignored the expenses of running a unit trust. However, both the management and the trustee companies will expect a reward for their services. For the management company, this comes from two sources. Firstly, there is the 'spread', the difference between the bid (the trust's buying) and offer (the trust's selling) prices. Unit trusts are permitted to operate a spread as wide as 15 per cent of the net asset value of the fund. Thus in our example above, where we calculated the unit price at 75p, the bid price could be as low as 64p while the offer price could be 86p. However, competition between management companies normally keeps the spread to within 5–6 per cent. In addition, the management company may charge an annual fee of 0.5–1 per cent of net asset value. This would normally be deducted from dividend income before calculating the income available for distribution to unit holders. The trustee company will also be paid an annual fee, normally calculated as a very small percentage on the net asset value of the trust.

Details of unit trust prices are published every day in the *Financial Times*. Box 4.3 shows details of the first three unit trust funds in the list operated by AXA Framlington, and illustrates all the points we have been making. The first column tells us that among the funds operated by the company are one concentrating on capital growth amongst US shares, one on biotechnology companies, and another focused on firms showing some 'special' features – usually suggesting high growth prospects. The next column tells us that the managers make an initial charge of 5.25 per cent to buyers of units. This is reflected in the fact that savers could buy the US growth units, for example, for 178.8p but would be able to sell them for 5.25 per cent less (168.8p). The fifth column tells us that the value of the underlying assets (and thus of the units) increased (+) by 2.6p during the last valuation period. Information at the top of the table tells us that the units are revalued at 12 noon (1200) every day and that the managers will deal with clients at the price that is fixed at the first valuation *after* the receipt of instructions to buy or sell ('F' or 'forward' pricing). The final column shows the yield on the units, calculated from the dividend yield being paid by the underlying shares. For the US units, this is zero, which is often the case where shares are being selected solely for their growth prospects. (They may be shares in very young companies which are using every penny of profit to finance new investment.) If we look a bit further down we can see that the UK Select Opps pay a very small dividend yield of 0.59 per cent.

Source: Financial Times, 27/28 May 2006

The rate of growth of unit trusts has been erratic. The first unit trust in the UK was established in 1932 by the M & G management company. Growth was slow until the early 1960s. Between 1960 and 1970, however, total assets grew sevenfold. In the 1970s, assets grew only fourfold and there was a sharp setback in 1973 and 1974. From £5bn in 1980, assets have grown to £279.2bn by 2004. Their pattern of growth suggests quite clearly, and quite reasonably, that the growth of unit trusts depends on the performance of stock markets and on the public's perception of the benefits of equity investment.

Figure 4.3 shows the distribution of unit trust assets at the end of 2004. At the end of 2004, over 90 per cent of unit trust assets were company securities (UK and

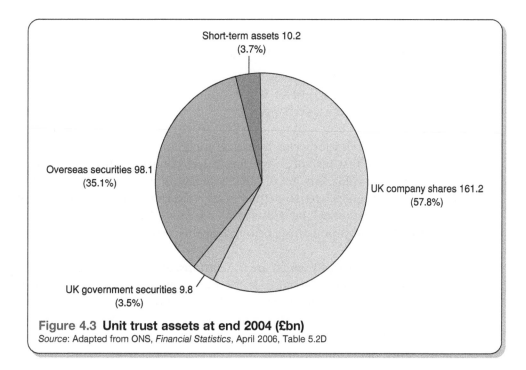

Figure 4.3 Unit trust assets at end 2004 (£bn)
Source: Adapted from ONS, *Financial Statistics*, April 2006, Table 5.2D

overseas). After holdings of short-term assets (3.7 per cent and mainly cash and bank deposits), only UK government securities formed a significant category (3.5 per cent). What the figure does not reveal is the shift in the balance that occurred during the 1980s towards overseas securities, prompted initially by the relaxation of exchange controls in 1979 and encouraged subsequently by the strong performance of some overseas economies and stock markets. Neither does it reveal the decline in holdings of short-term assets, from over 10 per cent of the total in 1978. It will be interesting to see whether the recent (2006) increased volatility of stock markets leads to a reversion of liquidity levels to those seen in the late 1970s.

Total assets in 2004 amounted to £279.3bn. This was an increase over 2003 of £24.2bn. This was in spite of a net inflow of funds (and net acquisition of assets) of only £16.2bn. The difference (£8bn) resulted from the increase in the value of *existing* assets, as stock markets throughout the western world showed a rapid rise. Remember though what we said about the flow of funds through insurance companies. The purchase of assets with new funds is no reliable indication of the total scale of buying and selling activity. Unit trust managements are continually rearranging their portfolios with the aim of maximising performance and so turnover figures will be much larger than net acquisitions.

In the UK a distinction is made between 'authorised' and 'non-authorised' unit trusts. Since December 2001, authorisation has been in the hands of the Financial Services Authority and depends upon a trust's deed meeting at least the following conditions:

- there must be no investment in property or commodities;
- the trust must not hold more than 10 per cent of the total capital of any one company;
- the trust must not normally invest more than 5 per cent of its portfolio in any one company;
- at least 75 per cent of the portfolio must be invested in shares quoted on a recognised stock exchange.

Responsibility for seeing that these conditions are complied with post-authorisation lies in the first instance with the trustee company. However, under the Financial Services and Markets Act of 2000 complaints about any aspect of the conduct of a unit trust can be referred to the FSA, as is the case with all regulated financial services. The Association of Unit Trusts and Investment Funds (AUTIF) is a professional body to which most unit trusts belong and this also exercises a degree of supervision of its members.

Those unit trusts which are 'unauthorised' normally owe their status to the fact either that they invest in unauthorised assets such as property or commodities, or that they are managed from an offshore location and therefore are not subject to UK regulation. Unauthorised trusts are prevented from advertising units for sale to the general public although they may write privately inviting subscriptions from a very limited range of institutions.

4.4 Investment trusts

Investment trusts differ from all the other institutions we have discussed in this chapter in a number of significant ways. The chief of these is that while all previous intermediaries are 'open ended', investment trusts are 'closed'. By open ended we mean that any number of customers, savers or subscribers can lend any volume of funds to the intermediary at any time. For example, people can increase their aggregate building society deposits, or buy more life assurance or more unit trusts without any limit, except that which they themselves choose, having regard to their wealth, the return on saving and so on. Furthermore, any increase in this lending will mean more funds are made available to ultimate users.

In the case of investment trusts, however, what savers buy is shares in a trust which is in effect a company whose business happens to be holding stocks and shares. At any moment, the total number of a trust's shares in issue is fixed. Thus new savers can buy shares only from existing holders. When we hear of a sustained flow of funds 'into' investment trusts, we must recognise that extra funds do not go into the trust at all (except in one case we shall come to in a moment). There is no increase in lending by the trust to ultimate users; all that happens is that the market price of the trust's shares rises. Equally, if savers decided to 'move out of' investment trusts, this would simply mean a fall in the market price of the trust's shares. It would not mean that the trust itself had to make payments to savers. As we shall see, this immunity from savers' redemptions is reflected in the composition of trusts' assets.

The fact that investment trusts do not continually take in new funds and channel them to ultimate borrowers obviously raises the question of whether they should be considered as financial intermediaries at all. The reasons for doing so are twofold. Firstly, there must at least once have been a flow of funds from savers to the trust and on to borrowers, when the trust was first established. Also, of course, a trust is at liberty to raise new capital by an issue of additional ordinary or debenture shares. When trusts are popular among investors and the market value of their shares is 'high', raising new capital is comparatively cheap (we look at the reasons for this in Chapter 6). Thus a flow of funds into trusts' shares, pushing up their price, may result in new issues of shares in the trust and a flow of additional funds into the trust itself. This is the case we anticipated in the last paragraph.

Secondly, even with only sporadic injections of new funds, investment trusts may still be active traders in the markets for financial assets. With all the previous intermediaries we looked at, we warned that we cannot judge the volume of buying and selling of assets which an intermediary carries out just from looking at the inflow of new funds. In the case of investment trusts, this warning needs repeating with force. Even without an inflow of funds from savers, trusts have income from dividends and interest on their assets and from capital gains. After the deduction of operating costs and payments to shareholders, this is put to reserve. From this reserve and from the immediate disposal of existing assets, trusts can make acquisitions of new assets. Investment trusts are in fact very active in the market for new issues of shares and in this respect are channelling funds to ultimate borrowers. Although their business is not one of short-term speculation, they are, however, active traders in stocks and shares. As we shall see in Chapter 6, trading in *existing* stocks helps to maintain their liquidity, makes them attractive to savers and thereby lowers the cost to borrowers of raising new capital in this way.

Their 'closed' nature is one feature which distinguishes investment trusts from other types of intermediary. Their legal status and their regulatory framework are others. They are not trusts at all in the sense that unit trusts are. There is no trust deed, no trustee and the saver's claim upon the assets of the trust is only the very general claim that any shareholder has upon a company. Indeed, being a limited company makes an investment trust subject to the relevant Companies Acts and it is these which principally constrain the trusts' conduct of business. In addition, the Stock Exchange imposes conditions on companies wanting a listing. These extend to very broad guidelines on the nature of investments and would also affect trusts considering merger. Lastly, the Inland Revenue 'approves' investment trusts for purposes of tax treatment (principally their exemption from capital gains tax on disposal) and this approval is conditional upon very limited portfolio requirements being met.

Investment trusts, therefore, are not regulated by the Financial Services Authority as are unit trusts. This became an issue in a recent financial markets scandal – that of split capital investment trusts (see Box 13.2).

The first trust was established in 1868. By comparison with other intermediaries, growth has been slow, at least until the 1980s when the value of investment trusts' assets almost doubled (1981–86). A feature throughout their history has been a very high level of investment in overseas securities. The reason for this seems to have been that until 1914, the return on UK securities was very low, rarely more than 3 per cent, and better returns could almost always be obtained abroad. However, these were generally riskier and since many savers lacked the necessary information and confidence to invest overseas, it seemed a natural role for investment trusts that they should provide an indirect route into overseas markets for small investors who would benefit from the trust's professional management. The overseas weighting fell from the end of the First World War until the early 1950s, since when it has grown steadily, increasing sharply again in the 1980s after the removal of exchange control in 1979.

At the end of 1997, aggregate investment trust assets amounted to £60.4bn and the number of trusts to about 150. The number of trusts has been falling, though only slowly, mainly as a result of mergers. As a company, each trust has a board of directors responsible for the broad outline of investment policy. The day-to-day administration, however, is often left to professional management companies. Some of these companies manage several trusts. As Figure 4.4 shows, the assets of investment trusts are overwhelmingly company securities; there are very few government securities. Overseas company securities take almost as large a share as UK company securities. The small holdings of government debt and of net short-term assets (mainly bank deposits) are a reflection of the point we observed earlier, namely that investment trusts are not subject to savers' redemptions.

We noted earlier that the immediate effect of increased investment in investment trusts would be to push up the price of their shares without resulting in any extra

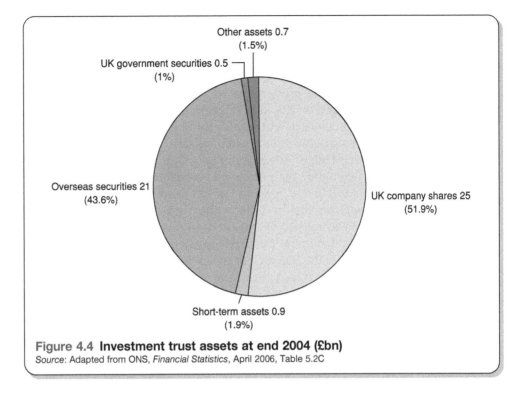

Figure 4.4 Investment trust assets at end 2004 (£bn)
Source: Adapted from ONS, *Financial Statistics*, April 2006, Table 5.2C

flow of funds from savers to borrowers. This obviously amounts to saying that the market value of investment trust shares is determined by the demand for them and not (as with units in a unit trust) by the performance of the underlying assets. Even so, we would expect the resulting market valuation to pay some attention to the underlying assets since the reason for buying investment trust shares is to participate in the income and capital gains resulting from the managers' investment performance. Nonetheless, it is a general and interesting phenomenon of investment trust shares that they stand 'at a discount' to the net asset value of the trust. On the face of it, this offers a potential bidder the opportunity to acquire a complete portfolio of assets at a discount to their value by taking over the trust by buying up all its shares. To understand how such a discount can persist we have to consider the value of a trust's shares from a buyer's point of view.

Consider firstly the ordinary investor who wants shares in a trust so as to have a claim on a much wider portfolio of shares than she could afford by investing directly. She has this advantage, but set against it she has to accept that management charges and corporation tax will be charged against trust income. This obviously reduces the income below what it would have been had she been able to hold the assets directly. Now consider the shares as seen by a potential bidder for the whole trust; most likely this would itself be a financial institution. If it held the shares intact it would suffer the same disadvantage that our ordinary investor encountered. If it liquidated the trust, however, in order to hold the underlying assets directly, it would face liquidation costs including compensation to the existing management.

4.5 NDTIs and the flow of funds

In the previous sections of this chapter, we have looked at a variety of types of non-deposit-taking financial intermediation. We have seen what assets have been accumulated in the process and we can make a judgement about relative size, at least when judged by the total stock of assets that has been accumulated. However, while stock data tells us a great deal about what has happened in the past, it is often useful to look at flow data as well, especially if there is any reason to believe that current activity might differ from past trends.

Table 4.1 combines both stock and flow data for different types of NDTI. Comparing the information in the first and last lines shows immediately that different pictures can be drawn from the two different data sources. The first line shows the total stocks of assets held at the end of 2004 and on this basis long-term or life assurance companies clearly dominate, followed closely by pension funds. But if we rephrase our question 'who is the biggest?' to mean 'who took the largest slice of savings during 2004?', the answer is that life assurance companies still came first, but the next most important destination for savings was unit trusts. General insurance came a rather distant fourth. The second line in the table shows the annual percentage rate of growth for these different intermediaries over the period 2000–04. This is essentially looking at the net inflow of funds during this four-year period rather than looking just at 2004. Notice that investment trusts contracted over the period (and in 2004 itself). The most rapid growth was in unit trusts, which grew at 1.7 per cent p.a. Clearly, taking either stock or flow data in isolation can present a very misleading picture.

Table 4.1 also enables us to compare the holdings of different types of asset across NDTIs (showing where funds have gone in the past) and the acquisition of these assets (showing where the inflow of funds went during 2004). Notice that the table does not list all the categories of assets acquired, and so adding the figures for the different acquisitions in the table does not produce a figure which matches the net inflow of funds.

If we are interested in the financing of UK industry, we might care to note firstly that life assurance companies and pension funds are the major holders of UK company securities. This is hardly surprising since we have already seen that these are the dominant intermediaries by asset size. Much more interesting is the fact that these organisations appear to have had quite different views about the attractiveness of UK company securities during 2003. Insurance companies were buyers, while pension funds made net disposals. The other major holders (and buyers) were unit trusts.

Looking at UK government finance we see again the importance of long-term insurance and pension funds in accumulating holdings of government bonds. Once again the acquisitions data is interesting since it shows that in 2004 long-term insurance companies were buying £15.4bn of government bonds, more than half their net inflow of funds. Other institutions bought very few.

Exercise 4.1

Using the data in Table 4.1, calculate for each NDTI the proportion of its total assets made up of (a) UK company securities, (b) UK government securities and (c) overseas securities. Make a note of any significant difference in the proportions.

4.6 Summary

In this chapter we have looked at the activities of financial institutions which accept and hold savers' funds in some form other than deposits. In some cases these non-deposit-taking financial intermediaries offer some particular additional service – insurance is an example – but they all offer a home for people's savings. The fact that their liabilities are not deposits obviously distinguishes them from the banks or monetary financial institutions that we looked at in the last chapter. A second distinction is that their inflows of funds tend to be much steadier than those of banks since they are often contractual – savers have made an agreement to make regular payments on a long-term basis. For some, insurance companies and pension funds for example, the outflows are also more predictable, depending largely upon the age structure of the population. The fact that these flows are very stable and that savers are making long-term contracts gives rise to a third distinction between MFIs and NDTIs. The latter hold long-term assets such as stocks and bonds, whereas the former's assets consist of short-term loans to households and firms. Thus, when we talk about 'the institutions' whose decisions are so important in stock and bond markets, it is these NDTIs that we are referring to rather than banks.

We looked at the total size and distribution of their assets. These assets have been acquired over many years and enable us to see that these institutions have been especially important in the funding of firms and government over the years. If we concentrate on flows of funds within the last few years, the same appears to be broadly true, but it is always possible for flows in one particular year to be different from those which have built up the stock of assets, especially if institutions think that one type of asset is likely to produce better returns than another in the near future.

Questions for discussion

1 Briefly summarise the key differences between DTIs and NDTIs.

2 What different things are savers looking for when they hold funds with (a) DTIs and (b) NDTIs?

3 Distinguish between funded and unfunded pension schemes. Would you worry if you were a member of the latter?

4 When looking at the assets of financial firms, distinguish between 'holdings at year end', 'net acquisitions' and 'turnover'. Which category of figures is always likely to be the smallest?

5 Suppose that mortality rates suddenly became less predictable. How would you expect that to affect long-term insurance companies' choice of assets?

6 Explain how insurance companies try to deal with the problems of moral hazard and adverse selection.

7 Why do shares in closed-ended mutual funds often sell for less than the value of their underlying assets?

Further reading

M Buckle and J Thompson, *The UK Financial System* (Manchester: Manchester UP, 4e, 2004) chs. 6 and 16

E Philip Davis, *Institutional Investors* (Cambridge MA: MIT Press)

R Glenn Hubbard, *Money, the Financial System and the Economy* (Reading MA: Addison-Wesley, 2e, 1997) chs. 12–14

P G A Howells and K Bain, *The Economics of Money, Banking and Finance* (Harlow: Financial Times Prentice Hall, 3e, 2005) chs. 15 and 16

E H Neave, *Financial Systems: Principles and Organisation* (London: Routledge, 1997)

K Pilbeam, *Finance and Financial Markets* (London: Macmillan, 1998)

'Sandler Report' (2002) at www.hm-treasury.gov.uk/documents/financial_services/savings/fin_sav_sand.cfm

The money markets

What you will learn in this chapter:

- Who uses the money markets and for what purpose
- What the various money markets are
- How different money market instruments are priced
- Why 'money market operations' are important to central banks
- How to read, interpret and analyse data relating to the money market

In Chapters 3 and 4 we have been looking at the major groups of institutions that participate in the financial system. In this chapter, and in Chapters 6, 8 and 9, we shall look at the markets in which these institutions operate. Financial institutions are not the only participants, of course. All financial markets (not just the money markets) involve brokers, market-makers, speculators, as well as the ultimate borrowers and lenders – firms, governments and occasionally households. Box 5.1 provides a list of the major market participants and their functions. The box makes it clear why financial markets tend to be dominated by institutions (DTIs and NDTIs) rather than individuals.

It is common to talk of two groups of domestic financial markets: the money markets and the capital markets. In one sense this is misleading. In both markets what is offered for sale is debts or claims, in exchange for money. In both markets it is money that is being borrowed. The difference which justifies the labels is the period to maturity of the debts or, more simply, the length of time for which the funds are borrowed. In the money markets, funds are borrowed for a short period, i.e. less than one year; in the capital markets, funds are borrowed for long-term use, in some cases indeed with no promise of ever being repaid. Although the distinction is useful and well recognised, it does not of course constrain people's behaviour. Some institutions – banks and building societies, for example – are accustomed to working in money markets, while others, like pension funds, are accustomed to capital markets, but these boundaries are occasionally crossed when commercial circumstances require. Certainly, ultimate borrowers and lenders are free to switch as the advantage of doing so presents itself. Firms may, as a rule, prefer to raise capital by issuing long-term bonds,

| Box 5.1 | ## Market participants |

Ultimate lenders and borrowers

Ultimate lenders are households and firms with a financial surplus which they want to lend, while ultimate borrowers are firms and governments with a financial deficit which need to borrow. It is not usual for ultimate lenders and borrowers to participate in markets directly. As a rule they deal through an intermediary which performs one or other of the following functions.

Broker

Strictly speaking a broker is someone who brings together two parties with a coincidence of wants. In practice, however, brokers tend to act as agents of lenders or buyers of a financial service. Thus, they may undertake to find the best price for someone who wishes to buy or sell securities or to find the best insurance policy, for example.

Issuing house

An intermediary who undertakes to issue new securities on behalf of a borrower. An issuing house thus acts as agent for the borrower in financial markets. In the UK, the task is usually carried out by merchant or investment banks (see Chapter 3).

Market-maker

An intermediary who holds stocks of securities and quotes a price at which each of the securities may be bought and sold. Market-making is usually performed by the securities divisions of the major banks (see Chapter 3).

In addition to borrowers, lenders and their agents there are:

Arbitrageurs

An arbitrageur is someone who buys and sells financial assets in order to make a profit from pricing anomalies. Anomalies occur when the same asset is priced differently in two markets at the same time. Because financial markets are well informed and highly competitive, such anomalies are usually very small and short-lived. Thus, to make a serious profit, an arbitrageur has usually to move large sums of money and very quickly. Notice, since the anomalies are known, there is no risk to arbitrage. This distinguishes arbitrage from speculation.

Speculators

A speculator is one who takes a position, believing he knows better than the market. Since he may well be wrong, a speculator is taking a risk. He may buy share A expecting it to rise in price, only to find that it falls.

Hedgers

A hedger is someone who buys or sells a financial asset to avoid risk. An importer who knows she will have to pay for goods in $US in three months' time may contract today to buy the dollars at a known price in sterling for delivery in three months' time. This avoids the risk that sterling's value against the dollar may fall before the payment is due.

but as we shall see in Chapter 6, there may be circumstances where it is preferable to raise short-term money instead.

It is sometimes the practice to divide these markets even further. In the case of money markets, for example, we sometimes distinguish as follows:

(a) the discount (or 'traditional') market;

(b) the interbank market;

(c) the certificate of deposit market;

(d) the gilt repo market;

(e) the local authority market;

(f) the eurocurrency markets.

Items (b) to (f) have traditionally been grouped under the heading of 'parallel markets'. This is a reflection of the fact that the discount market is the oldest of the markets and for many years was the largest. It used also to be the market in which central banks used their power to set interest rates. It has no special significance today.

Clearly, the divisions among this group of short-term markets will be even less watertight than they are between these and the capital markets. While there may be some segmentation between money and capital markets, there is very little segmentation *within* each group. This means that a change to interest rates in one market will be transmitted very quickly through all money markets. In other words, money market rates are highly correlated. We shall see that this correlation is frequently exploited by central banks which can cause an instant change in all short-term interest rates by dealing in just one market. Because these markets are highly competitive and interest rates are highly correlated, there are very small differences in the return on different money market instruments. This means we need some way of expressing very small differences in interest rates. This is done by referring to 'basis points'. A basis point is 1/100 of 1 per cent.

> **Basis point:** A very fine measure of interest rates. Equal to one hundredth of one percentage point.

Finally, before we begin to look at any financial market, we need to understand that some markets have to fulfil two functions. They have to achieve a primary function of absorbing newly issued securities, which enable borrowers to raise new funds; they also have to carry out a secondary function of allowing holders of *existing* securities to sell them to those who wish to buy. Secondary trading does not raise new funds, of course; it merely redistributes the ownership of loans which were made in the past. But the fact that lenders can sell their loans cheaply and easily in a secondary market may make them much more willing to lend. An active secondary market may do much to increase the supply of lending while reducing its price. While both the primary and secondary trading take place in the same market, the practice has developed of talking about a primary market for a given type of security and a secondary market, as though they were somehow different in location, design and rules.

> **Primary market:** A market for *newly issued* securities.
>
> **Secondary market:** The market for *existing* securities.

While the way in which a market fulfils its primary role is obviously very important to borrowers, every market is dominated by secondary trading.

In section 5.1 we shall look at the characteristics of the discount market. We look at this in some detail for two reasons. Firstly, until very recently the discount market was the money market in which the Bank of England carried out its interest-setting activities, and it remains important from that point of view. Secondly, much of what we learn about the discount market can be carried forward, without repetition, to our discussion of the parallel money markets in section 5.2. In section 5.3 we look at the way in which central banks, and the Bank of England in particular, can exploit their power in the money markets to set short-term interest rates.

5.1 The discount market

In the discount market funds are raised by issuing bills, 'at a discount' to their eventual redemption or maturity value. We shall look at the characteristics of bills more carefully in a moment. Transactions in the discount market are normally very large, enabling profits to be made from deals involving differentials in discount rates of small fractions of 1 per cent. The market has no physical location, relying almost exclusively on telephone contact between operators and, therefore, on verbal contracts.

As with any market, we can think in terms of a source of supply and a source of demand. In theory, bills can be issued by anyone, but in practice they are issued mainly by large corporations (commercial bills) and by the government (treasury bills). The main buyers and holders of bills used to be a highly specialised group of banks known as discount houses. Their central role came about because traditionally the Bank of England dealt only with the discount houses (rather than with the banks or financial institutions as a whole). In 1997, when the Bank began dealing directly with a wide range of banks, retail and wholesale, the discount houses lost their special position and were generally absorbed into the banks that we described in Chapter 3 as investment banks. This means that treasury and other eligible bills are now widely held throughout the banking system. As we said in section 3.3, this is one of the reasons why banks can manage with such a low ratio of primary reserves. The existence of an active discount market, together with the distinctive characteristics of bills (we look at these in a moment), means that these assets are highly liquid. In the event of a shortage of primary reserves (cash and deposits with the central bank) banks can sell bills very quickly and for a price which is virtually certain.

Bills are certificates containing a promise to pay a specified sum of money to the holder at a specified time in the future. After issue they can be traded (they are thus 'securities') and so the holder at the time of redemption need not be the person to whom the bill was originally issued. Compared with other financial instruments, bills have a number of distinctive features.

Firstly, bills are issued in large denominations. The minimum is £5,000, but few treasury bills are issued for less than £250,000 and most bills are much larger than this, up to a maximum normally of £1m.

Secondly, they are a highly liquid form of asset. This is due firstly to their short maturity (treasury bills are normally issued for ninety-one days) together with the fact that they can be quickly bought and sold before maturity in a highly organised market. It is reinforced further by the fact that they have a low default risk. In the case of treasury bills the reason for this is obvious, but commercial bills can acquire a similar status. We saw earlier that commercial bills are frequently 'accepted' by a bank at the time of issue. Accepting bills was once the principal function of those merchant banks which are still sometimes referred to as acceptance houses (see section 3.2); it is now carried out by a large number of banks. Bills which have been accepted by one of the major banks, recognised for this purpose by the Bank of England, acquire the ultimate standing, along with treasury bills, of being 'eligible' bills. The immediate significance of this is that they are eligible for discount at the Bank of England. Eligible bills, particularly treasury bills, are the nearest examples in practice of risk-free securities. They are short term and so need be held only for a short period to redemption, at which point they deliver a known rate of return; the potential default risk is also minimal, requiring as it does a repudiation of the bill by the government or by a major bank.

Thirdly, the reward to the lender for holding a bill to redemption comes in a form which resembles a capital gain rather than a conventional rate of interest. This is because bills are issued 'at a discount' to their redemption value. For example, the government might make an issue of £100,000 ninety-one-day bills, each at a discount of £1,000. This would mean that a buyer would pay £99,000 and receive £99,000 plus £1,000 in three months' time. However, it is obviously essential to have some way of comparing the cost and reward of borrowing and lending in this way with other methods which pay interest. This is done by calculating a rate of discount. The appropriate formula is

$$d = (R - P)/R \cdot n \tag{5.1}$$

where d is the rate of discount, R the redemption value, P the initial price of the bill and n the time to redemption in years. In the present example, therefore,

$$d = (100,000 - 99,000)/100,000 \times 0.25$$
$$= 1,000/25,000 = 0.04 = 4\% \text{ p.a.}$$

Although comparable with an annual rate of interest, however, this rate of discount is not identical. Notice that this calculation features the reward (£1,000) as a proportion of the redemption value (£100,000). In calculating a rate of interest, by contrast, we would normally express the reward as a proportion of the outlay, here £99,000. The formula would be

$$i = (R - P)/P \cdot n \tag{5.2}$$

Table 5.1 **Returns on money market instruments**

The discount market	
– Treasury bills	d
– Commercial bills	d
Commercial paper	d
Certificates of deposit	y
Interbank deposits	y
Money market deposits	y
Repurchase agreements	y

In the present case i would take the value 4.04 per cent p.a. It is important to remember, therefore, when comparing returns on money market instruments that a rate of discount will always indicate a slightly higher equivalent rate of interest. Money market instruments whose rate of return is expressed as a conventional rate of interest are said to be 'quoted on a yield basis'. Table 5.1 lists a variety of money markets, showing those whose returns are quoted thus (y) and those where the return is expressed as a rate of discount (d).

Fourthly, since the return for holding a bill to redemption is known at the time of issue, bills are *fixed-interest securities*. In common with all fixed-interest securities, therefore, their price will change with any change in market or current interest rates. We shall see more formally why this is the case when we discuss bonds in Chapter 6, but it is a relationship which is easy to grasp intuitively if we just consider the position of a holder of existing bills. These will have been issued with a fixed redemption value and we must assume that the holder calculated that this would give him a return equal or similar to alternative returns currently available. If market rates now rise, there will be instruments newly available with the higher return. Indeed, newly issued bills will have to carry a larger discount to match the higher market rates. In the circumstances, ignoring transaction costs, it will pay existing holders to sell their old bills in order to buy the new, higher-yielding instruments. The price of existing bills will therefore fall. As their price falls, however, a larger differential between their current and redemption price emerges. Eventually their price will fall until they yield a rate of return similar to that available on new ones.

Lastly, with no change in interest rates, the market price of a bill will approach its redemption price as the period to redemption shortens. Again, this may seem intuitively obvious. The redemption value is fixed. If the price were to remain constant, the gain received on redemption would be constant. However, with the period to maturity diminishing this would represent an ever-increasing rate of return. It can be seen clearly by considering the expression for the rate of discount above. If market interest rates are unchanged, then d is given. R is given also. As redemption approaches, the value of n diminishes. With n diminishing and R constant, the value of the denominator will fall. If the value of the whole expression, d, is to remain constant, the value of the numerator must also fall. With R given, this can happen only if P rises.

Given the expression for finding the rate of discount (5.1), we can easily find the price by rearranging as follows:

$$P = R - d(R \cdot n) \qquad\qquad (5.3)$$

Exercise 5.1

Rates of discount and rates of interest

The current rate of discount on treasury bills is quoted at 11 per cent.

(a) Calculate the price of a newly issued, ninety-one-day treasury bill for £100,000.

(b) Assuming that interest rates remain unchanged, what will its price be when there are 36 days left to redemption?

(c) The interest rate currently quoted on three-month local authority deposits is 11.5 per cent. Is this better or worse than the return on treasury bills?

(d) What would be the price of a newly issued, ninety-one-day treasury bill if interest rates generally rose by 1 per cent?

Answers at end of chapter

We now know that bills are short-term instruments, issued to raise funds for periods of up to one year, and that they are issued at a discount where the discount provides the return to the holder of the bill. If interest rates change, this must be reflected in the money markets as in all others. A rise in interest rates causes bill prices to fall, while falling interest rates will boost bill prices.

However, when we talk of a 'market', we normally think of prices changing because of changes in supply and demand. It might be useful, therefore, to see how we can analyse the operation of the discount market, using a supply and demand framework but maintaining a focus upon short-term interest rates. (This will be a useful investment for the future, since much of the analysis can be applied to other financial markets in which we are interested.) We begin with the supply side of the market and then turn to demand.

Compared with markets for goods and services, financial markets display a few curious features. The first of these is that what we refer to as the 'supply' of bills is in fact a stock rather than a flow. There is, more or less continuously, a flow of newly issued bills and a flow of bills maturing (i.e. ceasing to exist) and the relative sizes of these flows will cause the stock to expand or contract. But we cannot in this case take the flow of newly issued bills, or even the net flow (new issues minus redemptions) as the supply and learn anything useful from it about the operation of the market. We have to take the supply of bills to be the existing stock because, as we said above, bills are securities which can be traded. People can buy and sell existing bills. What is more, the stock of existing bills is much larger than current flows and therefore most transactions will involve existing bills.

In Figure 5.1 we have the price of bills on the vertical axis and the stock of bills on the horizontal axis. Because we are treating it as a stock, the supply of bills is

Figure 5.1

drawn vertically, at S_0. However, as we said earlier, this stock may expand or contract depending upon the net flow of newly issued bills. As the stock expands, the supply curve will shift to the right, to S_1, and as it contracts it will shift to the left to S_2.

What causes the supply curve to shift? We know that bills are a form of short-term finance and that they are issued by firms (usually large corporations) and central government. In other countries, local authorities and/or public utilities are major users of bill finance but this is not the case in the UK. For small firms, and especially for households, the issuing costs and the minimum bill denominations are too large. The obvious answer to our question, therefore, is that the supply curve shifts to the right as a result of *net* new issues (i.e. newly issued bills exceeding bills maturing) and to the left as a result of net redemptions. We can, perhaps, separate long-term influences on supply from short-term influences. In the long run, we expect the economy to grow in real terms. Output increases and firms expand. As they expand, they require more finance and some of that will be short-term finance. Over time, therefore, *other things being equal*, one would expect firms to make net issues of bills. The picture is not quite so clear cut with central government, however, since the expansion of central government is neither so smooth nor so guaranteed. Different governments, for example, have different views about the size of the state. However, we can say that *if* central government activity remains a constant fraction of the total economy, the government's need for short-term finance will also expand over time. Notice also that the price level will affect the quantity of bills which both governments and firms need to issue. It is *nominal* spending, the amount in money terms, not real terms, that needs to be financed. So inflation will also have an effect on the rate at which the supply curve shifts.

More interesting are the short-term influences on supply. Bills are just one form of finance (they are only one source even of short-term finance). This means that the decision to borrow by issuing bills will depend, especially for competitive firms, to some extent on the cost of alternative sources of borrowing. This in turn means looking at relative interest rates as well as at any changes which may occur to costs of issuing bills. A rise in the cost of alternative sources of funds will cause an increase in the incentive to borrow via bills, especially if it is alternative short-term funds which become costlier.

Although bills are a source of short-term finance, the behaviour of interest rates on long-term instruments could also be relevant. Suppose that longer-term rates are expected to fall. In these circumstances, firms which require medium and long-term finance, which they might get by issuing bonds, might decide to defer committing themselves now to current longer-term rates. Although there may be disadvantages to using short-term finance for longer-term projects, these might be outweighed by borrowing short just now, so as to be in a position in the near future to issue longer-term debt when long-term rates have fallen.

Finally, we need to understand that the issue of treasury bills by government is a form of residual finance. That is, bills are issued from week to week to cover any shortfall that may occur between expenditure and revenue from taxation, charges and longer-term borrowing. In the very short term (meaning week to week) therefore, there may be sharp fluctuations in treasury bill sales resulting from the uneven timing of government receipts and payments.

All of these influences on supply are summarised in Box 5.2, together with influences on demand. Note two things. Firstly, the influences are all described as though they are shifting the supply curve to the right. It is easy to see how they could cause leftward shifts. Secondly, these are described as influences on the bills' market, but we noted that all the markets for money are closely related. These influences might be felt first in the bills market, but they will affect the parallel markets too.

Box 5.2   **Supply and demand influences in the bills' market**

		Supply		Demand
Long term	S_1	Economic growth	D_1	Economic growth
	S_2	Inflation	D_2	Inflation
Short term	S_3	Expected fall in interest rates	D_3	Increase in liquidity preference
	S_4	Rise in interest rates on alternative sources of funds	D_4	Excess liquidity in banking system
	S_5	Residual financing of PSNCR	D_5	Fall in yields on alternative assets

---

In Figure 5.1 we also have a demand curve for bills, D_0. This expresses the willingness of buyers of bills to hold the existing stock. It is negatively sloped with respect to price because of the inverse relationship between bill prices and rates of discount. At low prices, i.e. at large rates of discount, *ceteris paribus*, holders will be willing to hold more bills than they would at low rates of discount, i.e. at high prices.

What might cause the demand curve to shift? Again, we can expect long-term influences such as increasing income, prices and wealth to cause a rightward shift of the demand curve. In addition, there may be short-term causes of increased preference for bills. We emphasised earlier that bills are a very liquid form of asset. They carry negligible risk, a known rate of return if held to their redemption which occurs always in the near future, and there is a ready market for them. It is a reasonable supposition, therefore, that anything that increases the community's demand for liquid assets relative to other forms of wealth will cause a rise in the demand for bills. Uncertainty about the future value of other financial assets, or about the timing of important receipts and payments, are examples.

One of the most important short-term influences on the demand for money market instruments of all kinds is referred to in Box 5.2 as excess liquidity in the banking system. Since banking system liquidity changes from day to day, with major implications for the money markets, we need to look at how the two are connected. We shall stay with the discount market as our example of the market which most directly feels the impact of these banking system fluctuations, but all money markets will be affected to some degree.

Bills are held mainly by financial institutions which see them as highly liquid, interest-bearing assets, and especially by discount houses for which holding bills is a specialist and major activity. Most important of all, therefore, will be changes in the factors determining discount houses' willingness and ability to buy bills and this, in turn, depends upon the ability of other monetary financial institutions to lend 'surplus' funds to the discount houses in order to finance the purchase. The demand for bills, in other words, depends upon the liquidity of the rest of the banking system.

When we talk of the 'liquidity of the banking system' we refer to the supply of bank reserves relative to their liabilities or relative to their other assets. Essentially, this means relative to deposits or to loans. As we saw in Chapter 3, it is normally expressed as a ratio of reserves to deposits, R/D_p. If reserves are plentiful, some can be lent to the money markets (and discount houses will then have funds to buy bills); if reserves are scarce, existing loans to the discount market (money lent 'at call') will be recalled and discount houses will have to sell bills. The flows of funds which cause changes in banks' liquidity positions are many and varied. Notice, though, that since we are talking about reserves, $R \ (= C_b + D_b)$, we are talking about changes in the monetary base, $B \ (= C_b + D_b + C_p)$. Box 3.4 showed us that the components of the monetary base are all liabilities of the central bank. They will change, therefore, whenever there is a change in central bank assets. A look back at Box 3.4 shows that one component of central bank assets is loans to the government. This lending will increase if the central bank either buys bonds directly from the government at the time of issue or buys them from other holders subsequently. In either event, the payment for the bonds is deposited in a bank which then has larger customer deposits (D_p), but, more importantly, it has an equal increase in reserves (D_b).

Since most governments run annual deficits, central banks can always add to the monetary base by their acquisition of government debt. This they do on a continuous but limited basis. This steady source of new monetary base clearly adds to the liquidity of the banking system over time. But this does no more than allow it to expand to accommodate the needs of increasing trade and economic expansion. If this is all that the expansion does, of course, it will have little effect on money markets since it will be meeting the banking system's requirements for additional reserves with which to carry out its day-to-day banking operations. What we are concerned with here is fluctuations around this trend: short-term changes in the liquidity of the system which lead to temporary shortages (or surpluses) in bank reserves. It is these fluctuations which have an effect on the flow of 'call money' into and out of the discount market.

The principal source of these fluctuations is the net flow of funds between the government (often called 'the exchequer' for this purpose) and the private sector. The government buys goods and services and hires labour from the private sector, while the latter pays taxes and other charges to the government. It may well be that there is a net flow towards the private sector, over the year; but on a short-term basis these flows could go in either direction. Since the exchequer accounts are held at the Bank of England, a net flow changes the volume of deposits and the liquidity of the system.

To understand this fully, we may need again to refer back to the balance sheets of commercial banks and the central bank in Boxes 3.3 and 3.4 respectively. Any net payments from the general public to the government cause a reduction in their deposits at commercial banks ($-D_p$). At the central bank, government deposits increase by the same amount ($+D_g$). What is crucial, though, is what happens to commercial bank deposits at the central bank. These are debited by the same amount ($-D_b$). This is the source of the liquidity shortage. In Chapter 3, we noted that D_b is very small relative to D_p. Therefore, anything which causes an equal absolute reduction in both is going to have a dramatic effect in lowering the D_b/D_p ratio. In this example, commercial banks, especially the deposit-taking retail banks, will be looking for ways to restore D_b, and the first course of action will be to recall funds from the discount market. A shortage of this kind will occur whenever there are net payments to the exchequer from the general public. These transfers may be 'spontaneous', the result of tax payments perhaps, or they could be induced by the sale of government bonds to the general public. These and other short-term influences on the state of liquidity in the discount and other money markets are given in Box 5.2. They are described in the form in which they give rise to a money market surplus. In terms of demand curve shifts, therefore, the events as described in Box 5.2 will cause a rightward shift. But it is a comparatively easy task to reverse the direction of the influences. When their effects are reversed, these events will reduce liquidity in the money markets and the demand curve will shift to the left.

These long-term and short-term influences on demand are also summarised in Box 5.3. (Indeed, the contents of Box 5.3 should be interpreted as an expansion of point 'D_4' in Box 5.2.) In Box 5.3, the events are described in a form which causes the demand curve to shift to the left. It is assumed, for example, that the events of Box 5.3 have created a *shortage* of liquidity in the banking system.

Information about selected instruments in the London money markets is published by the *Financial Times* on its 'Market Data' page. Box 5.4 contains the relevant information for 31 May 2006 and illustrates a number of points we have made so far.

| Box 5.3 | **Flows affecting the liquidity of the banking system** |

Exchequer transactions

- *Net payments to the exchequer*: When the private sector makes net payments to the central government, banks' balances at the Bank of England are debited while exchequer accounts are credited by the same amount.

- *Net official sales of gilts*: The net purchase of government bonds by the private sector is just one way in which net payments may be made to central government with the consequences described above.

- *Net receipts of sterling on the Exchange Equalisation Account (EEA)*: If the EEA intervenes to support sterling, it sells foreign currency in exchange for sterling which is drained from the market.

Change in the note issue

When the public makes net drawings of banknotes, retail banks replenish their holdings from the Bank, which debits banks' balances.

Bills maturing in official hands/sales of treasury bills

When bills held by the Bank mature, payment flows to the central bank from those who issued the bills. The purchase of treasury bills at the weekly tender requires a flow from the market to the Bank.

Unwinding of previous assistance

If the Bank has provided earlier help, perhaps by lending, to the discount market, the end of that help (the repayment of the loan) requires a flow of funds from the market to the Bank.

Bankers' balances below target

If the previous day's clearing has left banks' balances at the Bank below their preferred level (see section 3.4.1), banks will withdraw funds from the discount market. Such a situation will tend to recur when banks are expanding their lending.

Other flows

The Bank of England has a small number of other accounts (overseas central banks, for example). Flows into and out of these accounts will sometimes reduce the liquidity of the UK discount market.

Notice firstly that it gives the rates of return on various money market instruments with maturities ranging from overnight up to one year. A quick glance at the table confirms our earlier point about the differences between money market rates being very small. Not all instruments are available for all maturities, but most are available for one month and three months. We noted earlier that interest rates can be divided into parts of 1/100, but the table shows that the London money market still quotes rates in 1/32 fractions of 1 per cent.

Box 5.4 | **London money market rates**

UK INTEREST RATES

May 31	Over-night	7 days notice	One month	Three months	Six months	One year
Interbank Sterling	$4\frac{11}{16} - 4\frac{9}{16}$	$4\frac{21}{32} - 4\frac{9}{16}$	$4\frac{21}{32} - 4\frac{9}{16}$	$4\frac{23}{32} - 4\frac{5}{8}$	$4\frac{25}{32} - 4\frac{11}{16}$	$4\frac{15}{16} - 4\frac{27}{32}$
BBA Sterling	$4\frac{21}{32}$	$4\frac{21}{32}$	$4\frac{21}{32}$	$4\frac{23}{32}$	$4\frac{25}{32}$	$4\frac{15}{16}$
Sterling CDs			$4\frac{5}{8} - 4\frac{19}{32}$	$4\frac{11}{16} - 4\frac{21}{32}$	$4\frac{3}{4} - 4\frac{23}{32}$	$4\frac{15}{16} - 4\frac{29}{32}$
Treasury Bills			$4\frac{5}{8} - 4\frac{19}{32}$	$4\frac{11}{16} - 4\frac{21}{32}$		
Bank Bills			$4\frac{5}{8} - 4\frac{19}{32}$	$4\frac{11}{16} - 4\frac{21}{32}$		
†Local authority deps.		$4\frac{5}{8} - 4\frac{1}{2}$	$4\frac{5}{8} - 4\frac{9}{16}$	$4\frac{11}{16} - 4\frac{5}{8}$	$4\frac{3}{4} - 4\frac{11}{16}$	$4\frac{15}{16} - 4\frac{7}{8}$
Discount Market deps.	$4\frac{21}{32} - 4\frac{9}{16}$	$4\frac{5}{8} - 4\frac{9}{16}$				

Av. tndr rate of discount May 26, 4.5129pc. ECGD fixed rate Stlg. Export Finance. make up day Apr 29, 2006. Reference rate for period Apr 29, 2006 to May 31, 2005, Scheme V 4.701%. Finance House Base Rate 5pc for Apr 2006
UK clearing bank base lending rate $4\frac{1}{2}$ per cent from Aug 4, 2005

	Up to 1 month	1–3 months	3–6 months	6–9 months	9–12 months
Certs of Tax dep. (£100,000)	1	$3\frac{1}{2}$	$3\frac{1}{4}$	3	3

Certs of Tax dep. under £100,000 is 1pc. Deposits withdrawn for cash $\frac{1}{2}$pc.

Source: Reuters, RBS, †Tradition (UK) Ltd. **FT**

5.2 The 'parallel' markets

The parallel markets are also markets for short-term money. They therefore share many of the characteristics of the traditional, discount, market. Deals are done for very large sums at very small rates of profit. Most of the participants, banks and discount houses, are common to both the traditional and parallel markets. In this section we shall provide a brief description of each of the markets and follow that with a discussion of the significance of the parallel markets as a group.

5.2.1 The interbank market

As its name suggests, the interbank market is a market through which banks lend to each other. Like the discount market this provides individual banks with an outlet for surplus funds and a source of borrowing when their reserves are low. It is a wholesale market. Deals are usually measured in £ms. The market developed in the 1960s, involving firstly overseas banks, and later merchant banks and discount houses. Now it is used by all types of banks and it is not uncommon for NDTIs as well to lend surplus funds through this market.

The loans are normally for very short periods, from overnight to fourteen days, though some lending for three, six months and one year occurs. Naturally, given the degree of overlap, there is some connection between interbank interest rates and rates in the traditional market. If banks are short of liquidity they will lend less to both markets and rates will rise; if the Bank of England readily provides funds to the discount market, houses will offer less attractive terms to other banks which will deposit instead with the parallel markets, causing rates there to fall. However, interbank rates are generally slightly higher and certainly more volatile than rates in the traditional market. Loans are unsecured and there is no lender of last resort. Also, the range of participants is much wider than in the traditional market. Lesser banks will expect to pay slightly more for funds than the major retail banks. In periods of great shortage of liquidity, the needs of banks which do not have sufficient funds with the traditional market have driven overnight rates to more than 100 per cent. Interestingly, operating in the opposite direction, the oversubscription of several new share issues in the 1980s and 1990s saw seven-day rates dip. While they were completing the administration of the sale, issuing houses deposited subscribers' money in the interbank market. The rate of interest paid on interbank loans is known as London InterBank Offer Rate or LIBOR. It is an important point of reference to banks because it is probably the best indication to them of the cost of raising immediate marginal funds. Numerous bank interest rates are therefore tied to LIBOR, particularly to the rate for three-month deposits.

Unlike other instruments 'traded' in the money markets, interbank deposits are not negotiable. They cannot be bought and sold between third parties. A lending bank which wishes to retrieve its funds simply withdraws the deposit from the bank to which it was lent. In this case, therefore, the distinction between primary and secondary markets is irrelevant.

5.2.2 The market for certificates of deposit

A certificate of deposit (CD) states that a deposit has been made with a bank for a fixed period of time, at the end of which it will be repaid with interest. It is, in effect, a receipt for a time deposit. This explains, incidentally, why CDs appear in definitions of the money supply such as M4. It is not the certificate as such that we wish to include but the underlying deposit, which is a time deposit just like all other time deposits that appear in such definitions. An institution is said to 'issue' a CD when it accepts a deposit and to 'hold' a CD when it itself makes a deposit or buys a certificate in the secondary market. From an institution's point of view, therefore, issued CDs are liabilities; held CDs are assets.

A CD might be described thus, '£50,000 three-month CD at 10 per cent'. This would mean the holder would receive £50,000 plus 0.25×10 per cent, i.e. £51,250, at the end of the period. The advantage to the depositor is that the certificate is tradable so that, although the deposit is made for a fixed period, he can have use of the funds earlier by selling the certificate to a third party at a price which will reflect the period to run to maturity and the current level of interest rates. The advantage to the bank is that it has the use of a deposit for a fixed period but, because of the flexibility given to the lender, at a slightly lower price than it would have had to pay for a normal time deposit.

Unlike bills, CDs are priced on a *yield* basis. The rate of interest paid on CDs is often linked to interbank rate. If LIBOR is 9.75 per cent, for example, the CD described above might be paying 10 per cent because it is quoted as paying LIBOR plus 25 basis points. In the circumstances, the 10 per cent payable at maturity is similar to the coupon rate (c) on a conventional bond, except that the coupon is paid just once, at maturity. The maturity, or redemption value (R) of the CD if held to maturity will be:

$$R = D \times (1 + c \cdot n) \tag{5.4}$$

where D is the value of the initial deposit and n is the original maturity expressed as a fraction of a year. Thus, at redemption, our £50,000 CD above will be worth:

£50,000 × (1 + 0.1(0.25)) = £51,250

The market price of the CD now is found by discounting the redemption value by the rate of interest currently available on similar assets, adjusted for the residual maturity. As an exercise we can just check that if we are pricing this CD on the day of issue and short-term interest rates are the same as the coupon rate on the CD (10 per cent), then the value of the CD now is £50,000, the price we have paid for it. The formula is:

$$P = \frac{R}{1 + i \cdot n} \tag{5.5}$$

and the result is £51,250 ÷ (1 + 0.1(0.25)) = £50,000.

Notice that if all else remains the same, the market price will rise as the residual maturity shortens. We saw this with bills and it happens here for the same reason. Because the CD is issued with a fixed rate of interest, its maturity value is fixed from the outset. The shorter the period one has to wait for the £1,250 profit, the higher the rate of return one earns. But if interest rates generally are unchanged, this cannot be. The rate of return cannot be out of line with returns on other similar assets. And what keeps it in line is the price which people are willing to pay for the CD as it nears maturity. Exercise 5.2 asks you to calculate the price of this same CD when there are just 36 days left to maturity.

Exercise 5.2

(a) Find the price of a three-month £50,000 CD, paying 10 per cent, if it has 36 days to maturity and short-term interest rates are 10 per cent.

(b) Find the price of this same CD if short-term interest rates fall to 8 per cent.

Answers at end of chapter

Another similarity with bills (again because the CD is a fixed-interest instrument) is that changes in market interest rates will cause a change in price. We can see this by using eqn 5.5 again. Suppose that market rates rise to 12 per cent (on the same day that the CD is issued!). Then:

$P = £51,250 ÷ (1 + 0.12(0.25)) = £51,250 ÷ 1.03 = £49,757$

If we needed to sell our £50,000 CD instantly, we should be able to get only £49,757 for it.

Finally, given the pricing equation (5.5), it follows that if we know the current market price of a CD of given size and coupon, and given maturity, we can find its current yield. This is done by taking the difference between the market price and the redemption value, as a percentage of the purchase price, and adjusting that percentage to an annualised rate:

$$i = \left(\frac{R}{P} - 1 \right) \cdot \frac{1}{n} \tag{5.6}$$

Notice (by rearranging the terms) that eqn 5.5 is exactly equivalent to eqn 5.2, the equation for calculating the rate of return on a yield basis rather than a discount basis. As we said at the beginning of this section, the difference in quotation method is the major difference between a bill and a CD.

Exercise 5.3

A three-month CD for £100,000 at 6 per cent matures in 73 days. It is currently trading at £99,000. What rate of return is this CD currently offering?

Answer at end of chapter

Certificates of deposit are another means of short-term, wholesale lending and borrowing. Three- and six-month maturities are common. Some CDs are issued for one year and even for two years but the market for these is comparatively thin. This has led to the practice of banks issuing 'roll-over' CDs, i.e. six-month CDs with a guarantee of further renewal on specified terms. The minimum value is £50,000.

A market in CDs began in 1966 with dollar certificates. The first sterling CDs were traded in 1968 when foreign banks, some merchant banks and discount houses began issuing and holding CDs. They were quickly joined by other banks, including the clearing banks, in 1971. During the 1970s the market developed dramatically. As we saw in earlier chapters, CDs are now issued by a wide variety of banks and since 1983 by building societies. It is quite common for a bank both to have issued and to hold CDs, though normally of differing maturities. It will issue CDs with a maturity expected to coincide with a liquidity surplus and hold CDs expected to mature at a time of shortage.

5.2.3 The commercial paper market

As Table 5.1 shows, commercial paper (CP) is the other money market instrument whose return is expressed on a discount basis. Commercial paper is issued by large corporations as a form of short-term borrowing. Its initial maturity is usually between seven and forty-five days. It is sold at a discount to its maturity value, and the return is thus calculated in exactly the same way as for bills, in eqn 5.1. Commercial paper is normally unsecured against any specific assets and firms wishing to use the commercial paper market will usually seek a credit rating from one or other of the credit rating agencies, since a high rating will mean that such paper can be issued at a smaller discount, often amounting to the equivalent of 1 per cent. As a source of finance, commercial paper serves a similar purpose to commercial bills (and is priced in the same way). Thus, in countries like the UK where there is a highly developed discount, or bills, market, the market for commercial paper is relatively small. By contrast, in France and the US, where the commercial bill market is less developed, the commercial paper market is very large. The main difference between commercial paper and commercial bills lies in the manner of their creation. A firm borrows via a commercial bill when it agrees to 'accept' a bill which is 'drawn' by a creditor. The bill originates with the lender. A firm borrows via commercial paper when it issues the paper itself.

5.2.4 The local authority market

As its name implies, this is a market in which funds are lent to local authorities. Strictly speaking, we are interested here only in one part of the market, that part which supplies local authorities with short-term 'money' through bills and deposits. We need to remember that local authorities are also active in the 'capital' markets where they borrow by the issue of stocks, bonds and mortgages.

Bills are issued with maturities of three and six months. They are in most respects similar to treasury bills, including the eligibility for rediscount at the Bank of England. Consequently they are held and traded by those active in the traditional bill market and yields are always very close to treasury bill yields.

However, deposits are a much larger source of funds than are bills. They are normally short and fixed term, though some are overnight ('at call') deposits and some are for 364 days. As we must now expect, the size of the deposits is large, usually over £50,000, with £1m quite common. The deposits once made cannot, unlike CDs, be traded.

The source of deposits ranges from banks lending their own surpluses, to large firms and other financial institutions and to institutions arranging deposits for overseas depositors. Given the size of the deposits and the other terms and conditions, local authority deposits are bound to function for lenders as an alternative to deposits in the interbank market.

5.2.5 Repurchase agreements

A repurchase agreement is an agreement to buy any securities from a seller on the understanding that they will be repurchased at some specified price and time in the future. However, since the length of any repurchase agreement (or 'repo') is likely to be short, a matter of months at most, it is customary to think of repos as a form of short-term finance and therefore, logically, as being an alternative to other money market transactions. In section 5.3 we shall note that the Bank of England now conducts 'gilt repos' as a means of influencing money market interest rates. 'Gilts' are government bonds, with long initial maturities (and thus we discuss them in the next chapter), but the Bank of England seeks to influence money market rates by conducting short-term repos in gilts of any residual maturity (provided that it exceeds the term of the repo). Since the effect of the repo deal falls upon money market prices and yields, it is normal to regard such repos as money market deals.

In a repo, the seller is the equivalent of the borrower and the buyer is the lender. The repurchase price is higher than the initial sale price, and the difference in price constitutes the return to the lender. Deals are quoted on a yield basis, using eqn 5.2. Thus if the Bank of England agrees to a gilt repurchase deal with a commercial bank, it may buy the bonds for £1m, agreeing to resell in fourteen days for £1.002m. If so, the yield can be found as follows:

$$i = (1.002 - 1.0) \div (1.0 \times 0.038) = 5.26\%$$

In this example, the sale price of £1m is likely to be slightly less than the market value of the bonds at the time of purchase. This margin offers some protection to the lender in case the borrower goes bankrupt or defaults for some other reason. The size of the risk, and thus this margin, depends in large part upon the status of the borrower, but it also depends upon the precise nature of the contract. Some repo deals are genuine sales. In these circumstances, the lender owns the securities and can sell them in the case of default. In some repo contracts, however, what is created is more strictly a collateralised loan with securities acting as collateral while remaining in the legal ownership of the borrower. In the case of default, the lender has only a general claim on the lender and so the margin is likely to be greater.

5.2.6 The euromarkets

So far, we have discussed a variety of money market instruments which enable short-term lending and borrowing to take place in the domestic currency – that is, the currency of the country in which the markets are located. However, in recent years some of the fastest growing markets have been the so-called 'eurocurrency' markets. These are markets in which the borrowing and lending that takes place is denominated in a currency of some other country. Generally speaking, the instruments available for this type of transaction are the same as those which we have just discussed. However, where such instruments are denominated in some other currency, they are identified by the prefix 'euro-', though this is clearly a misnomer since the currency can be *any* currency (US or Hong Kong dollars, or yen, for example) and the trading can be taking place anywhere (in New York or Tokyo or Hong Kong), not just in Europe. A eurocurrency instrument is in fact *any* instrument denominated in a currency which differs from that of the country in which it is traded. Thus it follows that 'euro-' instruments can be found all over the world and have no obvious connection whatever with Europe. The 'euro-' prefix is just a reminder that the practice of trading instruments denominated in foreign currencies began with the US$ being traded in Europe. Since dollar deposits first began to be held in European banks in the late 1960s, the eurocurrency markets have grown rapidly, the stock of eurocurrency assets being estimated by 1995 at over $6,000bn. In the 1980s alone they expanded over threefold. The euro*currency* markets predate the markets for euro*bonds* (which we discuss in Chapter 10). Why did eurocurrency markets develop and what, if any, is their significance?

> **Eurocurrency:** Currency held outside its country of origin. A eurocurrency instrument is an instrument denominated in a currency different from that of the country in which it is trading.

Under the Bretton Woods system of fixed exchange rates established after the Second World War, the US$ functioned as an intervention currency, an international means of payment and store of value. The worldwide demand for dollars was met by a combination of US balance of payments deficits and dollar borrowings from US banks, the resulting deposits being held until the early 1960s, mainly with US banks. In the mid-1960s, however, the US authorities began to impose controls on currency outflows which limited access to these (US-stored) deposits for overseas owners. This combined with two further, long-running disadvantages. The first was 'regulation Q' which limited interest payments on deposits. The second, mainly relevant to Eastern bloc countries, was the risk that dollar deposits might be impounded for political reasons. The result was that non-US owners of dollar deposits began to place them with European banks and, later, with European subsidiaries of US banks.

Since reserve, deposit insurance, capital and other regulatory requirements are usually imposed with respect to banks' holdings of deposits in the domestic currency and act as a tax on deposit business, a further contributory factor to the long-term growth of eurocurrency business was the ability of eurobanks to offer their services at more competitive rates than domestic institutions. 'Eurobanks' is actually something of a misnomer. Most are departments or subsidiaries of major banks with a clear national identity. Most countries are involved, although the largest shares lie with banks whose headquarters are in Japan or the US.

There is nothing fundamentally different between a bank which specialises in eurocurrency business and a bank which concentrates on domestic deposits and lending, from an economic point of view. Both help channel funds between surplus and deficit units and, in so far as they create assets and liabilities which are more attractive to end-users than would be the case if the latter dealt directly with each other, they help to mobilise funds which might otherwise have lain idle. One potential consequence of the development of eurocurrency markets, however, is that they contribute to the difficulties which central banks face in operating their domestic monetary policy. We shall see in section 5.3 that direct controls on bank lending have been out of fashion for the past twenty years. One reason for this is that such controls can apply only to domestic banks conducting their business in sterling. With no foreign exchange controls and active eurocurrency markets, it is an easy task for a UK bank, denied the ability to lend to a customer in sterling, to arrange a eurocurrency loan with a subsidiary and then swap the proceeds into sterling. In section 3.4.3 we discussed the possibility of the central bank controlling the quantity of bank reserves in order to restrict lending. This too would suffer the same fate. UK banks would simply divert business to banks offering eurocurrency facilities and take a commission on the deal.

5.2.7 The significance of the parallel markets

In section 3.3.2 we noted that central banks generally implement monetary policy by setting the rate of interest at which they make reserve assets available to the banking system. As we shall see in a moment, one significance of the parallel markets is that they make a central bank's monetary control operations, at least in principle, more difficult and they do this in at least two ways. A second feature of these markets is their widening of the range and reduction in the cost of lending and borrowing facilities. We shall look at each of these in turn.

Firstly, the development of parallel markets has diminished the impact of the Bank of England's official operations. In the gilt repo market (and previously in the discount market) the Bank of England takes advantage of day-to-day flows of funds between the public and private sectors to indicate the way in which it wishes to see short-term interest rates move. It is able to do this because the repo market is a front-line source of liquidity to banks in the event of a shortage. When banks are short of funds or require earlier borrowing to be refinanced, the Bank of England relieves the shortage at that rate of interest in the repo market which it thinks appropriate, nudging rates upwards perhaps to reduce the demand for bank lending or lowering them to counteract a rising exchange rate.

With the growth of the parallel markets, however, there are many sources of funds immediately available to individual banks and the Bank of England need no longer be the immediate source of funds to any financial institution. As we have seen above, all deposit-takers have substantial short-term funds lent to each other. In Table 3.3 these are shown under assets as 'market loans and CDs'. In these markets the Bank has no direct control over interest rates. Individual banks (and other financial intermediaries) can alleviate liquidity shortages through these markets without the Bank having an opportunity to influence rates. Some indication of the relative importance of the parallel as opposed to traditional markets is the widespread use of LIBOR, rather than repo rate, by financial institutions as a basis for calculating their lending and deposit rates. Furthermore, in a period of a domestic monetary squeeze, it will be possible, and may be cheaper, to borrow in eurocurrency markets. With a well-developed sterling spot market and no exchange control, it is then a simple and cheap operation to swap foreign currency for sterling from the Exchange Equalisation Account. Unless the authorities react by selling government debt to the non-bank private sector on a sufficient scale (with whatever interest rate consequences may follow), the money supply will increase.

Of course, a general liquidity shortage cannot be alleviated by banks withdrawing loans from each other. Eventually the Bank will be required as lender of last resort. But the existence of numerous alternative markets for short-term funds means the opportunity for intervention may be subject to a time lag.

Granted that the parallel markets may reduce the ability of short-term interest rate changes to influence monetary growth, by changing the relationship between money and spending (i.e. velocity), they may also alter the significance of any monetary growth which does occur.

For example, imagine a situation of a 'tight' domestic monetary policy, in which UK banks are operating at or near the limit of their desired reserve ratio. An overseas bank then raises its interest rate to attract (euro)sterling deposits. These are withdrawn from a UK bank by the M4 private sector (M4PS): M4PS bank deposits, the UK money supply and bankers' balances all fall by an equal amount. The foreign bank gains the sterling deposits. Suppose now that it lends 90 per cent of that deposit in sterling to a UK resident who spends it in such a way that it is redeposited with the UK bank; also that the remaining 10 per cent is held by the overseas bank as an interest-bearing deposit with the UK bank. The UK bank's deposits and balances are restored; it continues as before. However, the original stock of bankers' balances has financed an additional round of spending. In actual fact this has been achieved even though the measured money stock has fallen! Remember, when the sterling was redeposited with the UK bank only 90 per cent of it was credited to the M4PS; 10 per cent was deposited in the name of the overseas bank and is not included in normal definitions of the money supply. This shows how intermediation via euromarket banks can increase the volume of spending for a given monetary base. Since it does this without increasing the money supply, it is raising the velocity of the existing stocks. To this extent it is a further indication of the way in which continuous innovation affects the 'information content' of key indicators. Here, the recorded money supply falls while spending increases.

Another difficulty for monetary control is posed by the very narrow 'spread' (between borrowing and deposit rates) that exists in these competitive markets. Given that borrowed funds can always be placed on deposit, the spread could be regarded as the real cost of borrowing. Granted that there is always an advantage in having liquid funds available, if the spread is low enough customers may choose to hold large volumes of funds on deposit rather than repay outstanding borrowing. The demand for money and the recorded money supply figures rise accordingly. This increase is clearly associated with an increase in liquidity but it is no longer clear what this implies. It may be a preliminary to higher levels of spending or may be simply a shift in portfolio preferences towards more liquid forms of wealth.

The second and obvious consequence of the growth of the parallel markets is the widening of lending and borrowing opportunities that have been created. We should expect this to reduce the cost and increase the volume of lending and borrowing with possible consequences for both the balance between consumption and saving and the level of aggregate demand. The consequences are difficult to prove quantitatively. The ratio of saving to aggregate income changes for several reasons; the level of aggregated demand generally increases over time, again for reasons other than the volume and cost of financial transactions. All we can say is that *ceteris paribus* we should expect consequences of these kinds and then look at specific developments which would seem to illustrate the possibilities.

One obvious example is the market for (sterling and eurocurrency) CDs. We said earlier that CDs brought clear advantages to both sides of the market. Lenders could get a rate of interest very close to that available on corresponding time deposits knowing, nonetheless, that they could recover use of the funds by selling the CDs. Banks, and eventually borrowers, had the advantage that the rate of interest they paid for the deposit would be slightly less than that on a conventional time deposit.

A second example is provided by the interbank market. Before the development of the interbank market, there were significant gaps in the maturity structure of many banks' asset portfolios. Put simply, it was difficult to find outlets for short- to medium-term lending whose self-liquidation at a definite time could be relied upon. It was possible to lend overnight to the traditional market and in theory at short term through overdrafts. However, the termination of overdrafts is a painful process. The development of the interbank market enabled banks to lend for specified periods of time, repayment to coincide with what they expected to be periods of shortage. They could match their lending more closely with their borrowing, much of which was for specified periods of time. This 'maturity matching' reduces risk and therefore the need for low- or zero-yielding reserves. Once again, the tendency is to reduce costs and expand the flow of business.

This growth of alternative markets for short-term money and the instruments that go with them has made the supply and demand for short-term money extremely competitive. As we have said many times in this section, 'wholesale' deals are often done on extremely small commissions or to profit from extremely small interest rate differentials. With such a variety of similar instruments and competitive rates it is difficult and costly in time for all participants to know exactly the best terms and rates. This has stimulated the development of two professions. The first is that of money brokers, firms which offer for very small commissions on very large deals to put lenders and borrowers in touch with their most advantageous counterparts. Indeed, it is normal practice for money brokers to search out, by phoning round, those institutions with funds to lend and borrow. It has also encouraged interest arbitrageurs. Arbitrage involves making a profit by borrowing from one source solely to lend to another to take advantage of interest differentials. Notice that, in contrast to speculation, no gamble is being taken on future events. The rate of interest on the borrowed funds is known, as is the rate at which the funds can be lent. The only possible risk is that one or both might change while the deal was being made. By directing funds from low-interest source to higher-interest outlets, interest arbitrage, like money broking, should help to remove anomalous interest rate differentials.

5.3 Monetary policy and the money markets

We noted in Chapter 3 that while there have been changes in the functions of central banks in recent years, one activity in which all central banks remain involved is the operation of monetary policy. Monetary policy involves controlling the price and quantity of money and credit with a view to achieving some desired objective for the macroeconomy. Remember that it is bank loans which create money and so the rate at which *net* new loans (new loans made *minus* existing loans repaid) are created determines the rate of expansion of money and credit. Although there seems in practice to be a large variety of techniques which can be used for this purpose, there are basically only two ways in which this rate of expansion can be influenced, and the techniques must fall into one or other category. Broadly speaking, the flow of money and credit can be constrained by operating upon either supply or demand conditions. That is by:

- limiting banks' ability to create loans;
- limiting the demand for loans.

The traditional textbook example of restraining banks' ability to lend involves the central bank manipulating the quantity of bank reserves. Since loans and deposits are assumed to be linked to reserves via a stable 'bank deposit multiplier', a change in reserves produces a multiple change in loans and deposits. The modern version of this technique is called monetary base control and we looked at it in some detail in section 3.4.3. In the 1970s, the UK attempted to control the flow of new loans more 'directly' using a device called the 'supplementary special deposit scheme' ('the corset'). Under the rules of the SSD scheme, banks were asked to restrict the rate of expansion of their lending to a target range specified by the Bank of England and the UK Treasury. They could adopt whatever method of rationing they found most effective, but if their lending overshot the limits, they were effectively 'fined' by having to hold additional (non-interest-bearing) deposits at the Bank of England. Such direct controls have been out of fashion since the end of the 1970s.

In section 3.4.1 we also noted that banks cannot make loans if people do not wish to borrow. Thus, if the central bank can limit the demand for (net new) loans, it can limit the rate of monetary expansion. The modern version of loan demand limitation involves the use of short-term interest rates. Raising rates causes the demand for new loans to diminish and reduces the rate of monetary expansion. There have also been attempts at 'direct' control of the demand for loans. During the 1950s, for example, attempts were made to limit the demand for credit by specifying minimum deposit terms and maximum repayment periods for consumer credit. Again, such direct intervention has been unfashionable for many years.

> **Monetary policy instruments:** Variables which are directly under the control of the monetary authorities.

In principle, then, monetary policy comes down to controlling either the availability of reserves (or monetary base) or the level of interest rates. Both of these require day-to-day action by the central bank and so involvement with monetary policy is inescapable.

Interest rates and the quantity of reserves are known as *instruments* of monetary policy. As we said above, they are used with the intention of producing some desirable macroeconomic outcome. This outcome is usually listed as one or more *objectives*. For example, the desired outcome may involve some combination of values for the rate of inflation, the level of unemployment and the rate of economic growth. As we noted in Chapter 3, the fashion in recent years has been to revise the rules whereby central banks operate in order to give them independence to pursue mainly one objective: a low rate of inflation.

Policy objectives: The ultimate goals or objectives of economic policy.

However, the connection between monetary conditions and the rate of inflation (and the connection with unemployment and economic growth too, for that matter) is indirect, it may not be constant over time, and it operates with a considerable time lag. Thus, changing the instruments today in response to the *current* rate of inflation may be too late. Indeed, by the time any new settings start to take effect, the rate of inflation may have changed and we may find the new instrument settings pushing in the wrong direction. For this reason, central banks have often operated with some *intermediate targets*. These are variables which respond to instrument settings rather more directly and quickly, but have a predictable relationship with the ultimate objective. Thus, if one can keep an intermediate target on track, this may be a good indicator that the ultimate objective will be at least approximately achieved. During the 1970s and 1980s, the intermediate target in most countries was the rate of growth of some measure of the money supply, and policy instruments were adjusted to keep this within some target range. During the 1980s, however, the link between the quantity of money, the growth of spending and the rate of inflation broke down. Many countries, including the UK from 1986 to 1992, refocused attention on the exchange rate. Since 1992, the Bank of England has dispensed with intermediate targets and has focused directly on the ultimate objective of inflation. 'Inflation targeting' involves looking at a very wide range of intermediate 'indicators' (rather than 'targets') in order to make a forecast of the future path of inflation on current instrument settings. The instruments are then adjusted, if necessary, in the light of the forecast. An explanation of inflation targeting in the UK is provided by Vickers (1998) and details of the way in which the Bank of England Monetary Policy Committee arrives at its monthly decisions are given by Budd (1998).

Intermediate targets: Variables which are affected directly by policy instruments and form a reliable connection with the objectives of policy.

So far in this section we have suggested that central banks have a choice of two policy instruments: the quantity of reserves and the rate of interest. In practice, however, a general consensus has emerged among central banks that their powers are limited to the setting of short-term nominal interest rates. The reasons for this are mainly practical and can be summed up in the reasons for rejecting monetary base control. We did this in Box 3.5. However, there is also a theoretical reason. Operating on the quantity of reserves or the level of interest rates can be regarded as policies drawn from each extreme end of a spectrum. It would be possible to employ a mix of these instruments at different times.

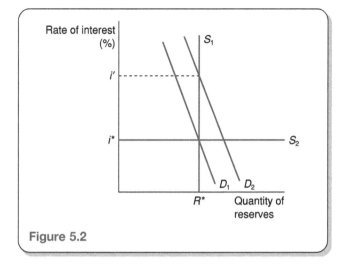

Figure 5.2

To understand the difference involved in choosing between these instruments, consider Figure 5.2. At one end of the spectrum, the central bank can set the quantity of reserves and refuse to adjust it in response to any changes in demand. In this case, the supply of reserves is shown by the vertical supply curve S_1 in the diagram and the quantity of reserves is R^*. Banks' demand for these reserves is shown by the demand curve, D_1. Notice that the demand curve is drawn steeply. Provided that banks offer free convertibility between deposits and notes and coin (and we saw in Chapter 3 that their ability to do this is crucial to confidence in the system), their demand for reserves is very inelastic. To begin with, we have an equilibrium position at a (short-term nominal) rate of interest at i^*. Suppose now that banks demand more reserves. Remember: this could be because their clients are making net payments to government or it could simply be that they have increased their lending (for commercial reasons) and now need additional reserves to hold against the extra deposits. The demand curve shifts outwards to D_2. *Given the inelasticity of demand*, interest rates could rise very quickly indeed and to very high levels. i' is the example in the diagram. Demand is inelastic because banks must be able to ensure convertibility. And since their liquidity position is calculated when interbank settlements take place at the end of each day, they need the reserves instantly. Faced with a shortage of reserves, banks will bid aggressively for short-term funds. For every £1 gained in customer deposits, there is an equal gain in deposits at the central bank. This one-for-one gain raises the D_b/D_p ratio. But in a situation where reserves are in *generally* short supply, bidding for deposits will not solve the problem. What one bank gains, another bank loses. But while attempts by individual banks to gain reserves will be self-defeating, they will push up short-term rates sharply.

At the other end of the spectrum, the central bank may respond to the increase in demand by providing additional reserves which completely accommodate the demand. This it *must* do if it wishes the rate of interest, i^*, to continue. Such a situation is shown in the diagram by the supply curve S_2, drawn horizontally at the going rate of interest.

Between these two extremes, obviously, it is possible for the central bank to respond to a shortage by meeting some of the excess demand which will allow the remaining shortage to bid up interest rates, but only to modest levels. We could draw an upward-sloping curve in the diagram.

What this discussion reveals is that the central bank occupies a critical position in the monetary system by virtue of its position as a monopoly supplier of liquidity in the event of a system-wide shortage. In such a situation, it is genuinely a lender of last resort.

Figure 5.2 tells us that the central bank can exercise this power just like any other monopolist: it can fix the quantity or it can fix the price of what it supplies. Fixing one determines the other, but this does not mean that the choice does not matter. Firstly, it can fix the quantity of reserves and let the price (the rate of interest) adjust to shocks in demand. Alternatively, it can fix the price, in which case it is the quantity of reserves that will respond to shocks. Given the inelasticity of the demand curve, fixing the quantity is likely to result in sharp fluctuations in price. In general, central banks have come to the conclusion that it is likely to be less disruptive to economic life in general to allow a certain degree of fluctuation in the quantity of reserves than to have interest rates moving sharply from day to day. This means that the selected monetary policy instrument for most central banks is the rate of interest. Central banks set the level of short-term interest rates which they hope will produce the appropriate value for their intermediate target – the growth of money, or credit, or asset prices, or the level of exchange rates – and provide whatever quantity of reserves banks require in the light of the demand for loans. This demand for loans will depend, among other things, upon the rate of interest which banks charge to borrowers. This is not the same rate that the central bank targets, but it is linked to it in such a way that changes in the official rate are reflected in the loan rate. The official rate is the price at which the central bank is willing to supply reserves. The cost of reserves is part of the costs of production for banks. The rate they charge on loans will be built up from the official or 'base' rate by the addition of a margin for profit and then a series of premia reflecting the riskiness of the borrower, the length of the loan and so on. The loan rate, in other words, is equal to the base rate plus a 'mark-up'. Provided the mark-up is constant, any change in the base rate must be matched by a change in the loan rate.

The position of any monopolist is inevitably a powerful one, especially if it is supplying something as crucial as the liquidity necessary to ensure the stability of a country's banking system. However, we must not get carried away with the idea that because it has considerable power to bring about the rate of interest it thinks appropriate, its choice of what is an appropriate interest rate is unconstrained. Even an independent central bank is independent only of government influence. It cannot ignore the rest of the world. The constraints which central banks face in choosing the appropriate level of interest rates are discussed in section 7.6.

Given their choice of the level of rates appropriate for the circumstances, central banks set that level through their 'official' operations in a country's money markets. Exactly how this is done and exactly which of the many short-term interest rates is involved varies between countries. However, once again, there has been considerable convergence in recent years. Essentially, there are three possible ways of making reserves available and setting their price. These are:

- lending via the 'discount window';
- open market operations;
- repurchase agreements.

'Discount window' lending refers to the situation where the central bank lends directly to banks. The loan is usually secured against some collateral. (In the days before parallel markets this collateral was always bills. Since the loan was usually less than the value of the collateral, it was 'at a discount'.) In most systems, discount window borrowing is limited to specified institutions. In the US, for example, it was restricted to member banks of the Federal Reserve System until 1978. In the UK, such loans were available only to the subset of banks known as discount houses until 1998 (though discount window lending largely ceased in the UK in 1981). The loans are for short periods, usually a matter of days. The rate which the central bank currently charges on such loans is widely advertised. Banks know the cost of the loan in advance.

In recent years, there has been a convergence of central banking operating techniques away from discount window lending towards more 'market-based' methods of intervention. Assistance via the discount window requires the authorities to make a lot of decisions themselves. These decisions might or might not be appropriate, in the light of market conditions. For example, discount window lending requires the authorities to decide from time to time on the rate which they charge and to 'post' this, i.e. make it known to everyone, continuously. In making this decision, the central bank will make an assessment of the likely rate of expansion of money and credit and the likely degree of shortage of reserves for the foreseeable future. However, it may be wrong in its estimate. It might, for example, overestimate the likely shortage. It then sets the discount rate 'too low'. Having set the rate, it is obliged to supply reserves at that rate to all eligible borrowers. If for commercial banks the rate is 'low' relative to what they can charge for loans, they are likely to borrow a great deal of reserves and expand their lending rapidly. There is a monetary expansion which the central bank did not intend. Given this rapid expansion, the central bank may then decide to raise the discount rate, say by 50 basis points (bps). But in doing this, they may underestimate the degree of liquidity in the market. If there is no shortage of reserves, banks will not need to borrow from the discount window and loan rates will not rise. Establishing the appropriate discount rate is a technical problem. In some countries there has been a political problem too.

Because central banks have to post or announce the rate for discount window borrowing, it is obvious that the central bank is setting interest rates. In some countries, where the central bank is closely linked to government, this looks like government setting of interest rates. During the 1980s there was a general movement in economic policy making towards a general belief that 'markets know best'. In a period when markets were generally being liberalised, such explicit intervention in money market interest rates looked odd. For all these reasons, central banks moved in the 1980s toward operating techniques which gave a larger role to market forces (or at least appeared to do so). Such techniques include open market operations and repurchase agreements. We shall explain both of these by looking at the development of the Bank of England's money market operations in recent years. The years from 1981 to 1996 mark the high point of open market operations, while the move to repurchase agreements began in 1997.

On taking office in 1979, the Conservative government launched a major review of the recent operation of UK monetary policy and of possible alternatives. In the light of the subsequent Green Paper (1980), the Bank of England rejected the possibility of moving towards monetary base control (for all the reasons we have seen above and in Box 3.5) and reaffirmed its commitment to interest rate setting. The operating techniques were, however, changed. The Bank abandoned its previous practice of providing liquidity to the banking system by lending to the discount houses at a preannounced rate of interest (known at the time as Minimum Lending Rate). Instead, it set out to make more use of market forces. This involved making a twice daily forecast of the money markets' liquidity position. This involved taking account of the influences listed above in Box 5.3. In the light of the resulting forecast, it then stated that it would be willing to provide assistance (in the case of a shortage) by making outright purchases of treasury and eligible commercial bills. The maturity of the bills was restricted to the very short end of the maturity spectrum (less than fourteen days), and transactions in bills were confined to the Bank and the discount houses.

Open market operations: The purchase (or sale) of any asset in the open market.

Crucially, there was no announcement of a purchase price for these bills and thus the discount houses (and money markets) could not know in advance what rate of discount the Bank was going to impose. The discount houses had to set their own offer price and the argument was that this would tell the Bank something about the degree of liquidity shortage (low offer prices indicating a major shortage, for example). In the circumstances of general liquidity shortage, the Bank would be the monopoly *buyer* of bills and could set its own price. If it wished to raise money market rates, it would reject the bills offered by the discount market and invite a resubmission at lower prices. (Again, the new prices had to be set by the discount houses.) In practice, the first submission of bills for sale would usually be made at prices closely equivalent to the existing discount rate. If the Bank wanted interest rates to remain unchanged, it simply bought all the bills at prices reflecting the going discount rate (making the supply of liquidity perfectly elastic at the going rate of interest). Whatever the Bank's response, notice that there was never any doubt that liquidity would be forthcoming. Supplied with liquid funds, the discount houses could then meet any demand from the rest of the banking system for repayment of money at call. The rest of the system would get the additional reserves.

Referring to post-1981 operating techniques as 'open market operations', however, is exaggerating slightly. An open market is one to which everyone has access. As we have seen, after 1981 the Bank of England was creating a market for bills between itself and the discount houses. As far as prices and rates of discount were concerned, however, the effects would probably have been the same, even if the Bank had dealt with everyone operating in the discount market. Nonetheless, the next step in the movement towards market-based methods of intervention would involve the widening of institutions with which the Bank was willing to deal. This came in 1997 and, when it did, it meant of course that the Bank was beginning to deal directly with those institutions which were experiencing the initial liquidity shortages and surpluses.

In 1996 the Bank announced that from March 1997 it would deal not just with discount houses but with banks, building societies and securities houses. Further-more, instead of confining its transactions to treasury and 'eligible' commercial bills (which were not widely held outside the discount houses), it announced that it would also enter into repo agreements in government bonds (which were). Strictly speak-ing, government bonds are not money market instruments. This is because they are issued for much longer periods of maturity (and we deal with them as capital market instruments in the next chapter). As we saw in section 5.2, a repo deal is just another form of collateralised loan. In offering to deal in gilt repos, the Bank of England was offering to relieve a shortage of liquidity (for example) by purchas-ing government bonds for a given price and to hold them for a set period (usually fourteen days), subject to the agreement of the seller to repurchase them on a set date for a price higher than that for which they were sold. Equation 5.2 shows how the sale price, the duration and the repurchase price can be used to calculate an equivalent rate of interest.

In 2005 the Bank announced a further series of reforms to its money market operations, and these took effect from 18 May 2006. Under these arrangements, the Bank still supplies liquidity by repo deals, but now of seven-day maturity. However, these deals are carried out only once a week, instead of daily. Deals are carried out on Thursdays because the terms of the repo are still intended to be the method by which the Bank sets interest rates and so the deals have to take place immediately after any possible decision by the Monetary Policy Committee (which is also made on a Thursday). With additional liquidity being available only on a weekly basis, there obviously had to be further changes to accommodate banks' requirements on the days in-between.

These came in two forms. Firstly, there was an easing of the liquidity conditions that banks have to meet. The prudential ratio remains (see section 3.3.2) but instead of banks having to observe this ratio at the close of business *every day*, it is now sufficient that they observe this ratio *on average* over the period between Monet-ary Policy Committee (MPC) meetings. Furthermore, they have a margin of error of +/−1 per cent. Also, for the first time in UK monetary history, the deposits held at the Bank of England pay interest (at a rate which is the rate set by the MPC at its last meeting). The penalties for missing the target are that reserves in excess of the ratio (+1 per cent) pay no interest while a shortfall of reserves greater than 1 per cent of the target leads to the bank being charged interest on the deficit charged at a rate equal to twice the MPC's current rate.

Secondly, the Bank created 'standing facilities' consisting of a borrowing and deposit facilities. The first of these enables banks to borrow on a day-to-day basis to top up their reserves when necessary. This costs them the MPC rate +25bp. The deposit facility enables them to hold 'spare' funds at the central bank on which they can draw to top up reserves. According to the Bank of England, the main purpose of the reforms is to reduce day-to-day volatility in interbank rates. Notice two things. Firstly, interbank rates cannot move away from the official rate by more than 25bp points because banks can always borrow from or lend to the Bank of England at those rates. Secondly, all these rates (and the interest on reserves and the penalty rate) are linked directly to the MPC's rate. Any decision by the MPC to change the official rates will have an immediate effect on the rate charged to banks for additional reserves as it has always done.

We should also note that all the reforms of the past ten years (extending its operating procedures to include most DTIs, switching to the use of gilt repos and now introducing an averaging requirement with standing facilities) have resulted in the Bank shifting its money market operations away from their traditional focus on the discount market, and in so doing has put them on a similar footing to those in other European centres. It may be significant that its procedures are now very similar to those currently used by the European Central Bank.

5.4 Summary

The money markets are markets in which funds are lent and borrowed for short periods, usually a matter of months, but sometimes for no more than a day. In some cases the loans take the form of securities which can be traded between third parties. In such cases, the return to the holder will come in the form of the difference between what was paid for it and the price received either at maturity or when it is re-sold. With such instruments, a change in market price means a change in the rate of return. Some money market instruments have their return quoted on a 'discount' basis and some on a 'yield' basis, which means we must be careful in making comparisons.

In most countries, the primary instrument of monetary policy is the level of some designated, short-term interest rate. Whichever rate is chosen, it will be determined in one or other of the money markets. This means that central banks are active participants in money markets. In the event of a general shortage of liquidity, which they can themselves create if they wish, they become the monopoly suppliers of short-term funds and this gives them considerable power to influence money market rates as a whole. In the UK, the Bank of England used to operate mainly in the discount market, setting treasury bill rate via its transactions with discount houses. Because money market instruments are close substitutes for one another, this would affect all short-term rates to a large degree. Since 1997, however, it has exercised its influence directly across a wider range of money markets by dealing with a wider range of institutions.

Questions for discussion

1 How do money markets differ from capital markets? Who are the main users of money markets?

2 What is the difference between money market instruments quoted 'on a discount basis' and 'on a yield basis'? Suppose that one-month treasury bills and one-month CDs are both quoted as having a rate of return of 5 per cent. Which gives the higher return to an investor?

3 Suppose the expectation develops that long-term interest rates are likely to fall in future. What is this likely to do to the *supply* of commercial paper and why?

4 Suppose that the government makes a major sale of bonds to the M4 private sector. Explain the likely effect of this on (a) the liquidity of the banking system and (b) the demand for money market instruments.

5 Discuss the various ways in which the central bank could respond to the money market developments identified in (4).

6 Imagine that the central bank is concerned about the rate of growth of credit in the economy. Explain how it might use its position in the repo market to tackle this problem. Work an example to illustrate how it might use gilt repos to raise interest rates from 5 per cent to 5.5 per cent.

Further reading

A D Bain, *The Financial System* (Oxford: Blackwell, 2e, 1992) ch. 12

Bank of England, 'The first year of the gilt repo market', *Bank of England Quarterly Bulletin*, 37 (2), May 1997

Bank of England, 'Changes at the Bank of England', *Bank of England Quarterly Bulletin*, 37 (3), August 1997

Bank of England, factsheet, 'Monetary Policy' (www.bankofengland.co.uk/factmpol.pdf)

Bank of England, 'The transmission mechanism of monetary policy', *Bank of England Quarterly Bulletin*, 39 (2), May 1999

Bank of England, 'Implementing monetary policy: reforms to the Bank of England's operations in the money market', *Bank of England Quarterly Bulletin*, 45 (2), Summer 2005

C Bean, 'The new UK monetary arrangements: a view from the literature', *Economic Journal*, 108 (451), November 1998

M Buckle and J Thompson, *The UK Financial System* (Manchester: Manchester UP, 4e, 2004) ch. 10

A Budd, 'The role and operations of the Bank of England Monetary Policy Committee', *Economic Journal*, 108 (451), November 1998

P G A Howells and K Bain, *The Economics of Money, Banking and Finance: A European Text* (Harlow: Financial Times Prentice Hall, 3e, 2005) ch. 15

K Pilbeam, *Finance and Financial Markets* (London: Macmillan, 2e, 2005) ch. 5

J Vickers, 'Inflation targeting in practice: the UK experience', *Bank of England Quarterly Bulletin*, 38 (4), November 1998

http://www.bankofengland.co.uk

http://www.dmo.gov.uk

Answers to exercises

5.1 (a) £97,250; (b) £98,900; (c) better (equivalent treasury bill rate = 11.3%); (d) £97,000.

5.2 (a) £50,749; (b) £50,848.

5.3 12.63%.

The capital markets

What you will learn in this chapter:

- What the capital markets are, who uses them and why they are important
- The characteristics of the instruments traded in the capital markets
- The arrangements for trading these instruments
- Some basic principles relating to the pricing of these instruments
- What causes their prices to change
- How to read and analyse news and data relating to capital markets

Capital markets provide funds for long-term use. There is no strict definition of 'long term' but the original maturity of the debts will usually be more than five years. The main instruments which are traded in these markets are bonds and equities or company shares. Many bonds are issued with a projected life of more than twenty years, while a company's shares have no specified maturity but continue for as long as the firm exists.

In this chapter we shall start by looking at who uses the capital markets and why the behaviour of these markets is important. In section 6.2 we shall look at the particular characteristics of bonds and equities and at the way in which they are bought and sold in the UK. In section 6.3 we focus on bonds, looking at factors influencing supply and demand and at the basics of bond pricing. In section 6.4 we do the same for equities. We shall see that demand fluctuates with changing views of what these securities are worth. This takes us into the theory of asset valuation. It involves some fairly simple arithmetic and some ideas which we explain more fully, for those who are interested, in Appendix I: Portfolio theory. In section 6.5 we shall look at some typical real world events that cause security prices to change and see whether our theory helps us to understand *why* these events affect prices. In section 6.6 we look at the way in which information about shares and bonds is reported.

6.1 The importance of capital markets

Like short-term borrowing, long-term borrowing can be done in a number of ways. In this chapter we focus on two common sources of long-term funds – equities, or ordinary company shares, and fixed-interest bonds. We look at the characteristics of these instruments in more detail in the next section. Most long-term borrowing in any economy is carried out by government and firms. The only long-term borrowing in which households engage is when they take out a mortgage loan to buy a house, and although these loans typically have an initial maturity of 20–25 years, the majority are repaid within eight years when borrowers sell, move house, and take out a new mortgage. Table 6.1 shows the *net* amount (new issues minus redemptions) raised by government and firms in sterling capital markets in 2004 and 2005. The table shows two things of interest. The first is the dominance of fixed-interest securities ('bonds') compared with shares in the financing of firms. Indeed, in both years, firms have reduced the number of shares outstanding by buying back some of their earlier issues. The second is that the UK government is a very large borrower, also borrowing by the issue of bonds. It is not always easy to remember the importance of bond finance when the media pay so much attention to what is happening in share markets and so little to what is happening in the much larger bond markets.

What the table does not show is that while the funds raised by firms may look large, they are in fact a very small proportion of firms' capital requirements each year. More than half of the net investment carried out by UK firms is regularly financed by internal funds, that is, by 'ploughing back' a substantial fraction of profits. In addition to this, firms borrow from banks: the proportion of investment financed by new issues of securities is rarely more than 20 per cent.

Given that firms raise so little capital from them directly, it is tempting to argue that the behaviour of capital markets is of little importance. However, we must firstly remember that firms using internal funds, if they are performing the calculations correctly, should be taking the level of yields on alternative financial assets as an indication of the opportunity cost of using these funds. Secondly, we must remember that when firms do make new issues of securities in order to raise new funds for investment, they have to issue those securities on terms which make them attractive

Table 6.1 Net amounts raised in sterling capital markets, 2004–05, £m

	Firms[1]			Government[2]
	Shares	*Bonds*	*Commercial Paper*	*Bonds*
2004	−789	63,746	4,845	49,651
2005	−4,504	87,699	8,963	50,025

[1] Funds raised by all firms (UK and overseas) on the London Stock Exchange and Alternative Investment Market.
[2] Data for financial years 2003/04 and 2004/05

Source: ONS, *Financial Statistics*, March 2006, Tables 1.2c, 6.2b and 6.2c to lenders, and that means issuing them on terms which compete with those available on existing securities. If share prices are high, for example, new shares can be issued at a 'high' price and the cost of new capital will therefore be low. Thirdly, the existence of an active secondary market has the effect of making securities very liquid. Even large quantities can be bought and sold quickly and with low brokerage charges. This makes them much more attractive to investors, lowers the return which they require, and (again) keeps down the cost of capital to firms. Furthermore, the behaviour of financial markets may have some indirect effect upon firms' behaviour by their impact upon the general state of 'confidence' in the economy. Whatever its objective relevance to firms' spending plans, it is hard to imagine that the 40 per cent fall in stock prices in 2001 and 2002 did not cause most people, firms included, to be less certain about the future. Lastly, it should be remembered that securities are assets in the portfolios of individuals and of financial institutions. General price movements, therefore, cause changes in wealth. People may change their spending plans as security prices rise or fall; certainly banks and other financial institutions will revise their lending plans as the value of their assets rises and falls. The long boom in the US economy during the 1990s was thought by many to have been due to the steady rise in the stock market. During 2005 and 2006, central banks monitored closely the recovery in share prices for signs that it might be encouraging too fast a rise in consumer spending.

6.2 Characteristics of bonds and equities

6.2.1 Bonds

Bonds are normally issued with a fixed period to maturity. Many are issued to mature in ten or even twenty years' time, but there are some government bonds in existence which will never be redeemed. The year of maturity normally forms part of the bond's title. Obviously, as time passes, the *residual maturity* of any bond shortens. It is common to classify bonds by their residual maturity. Bonds with lives up to five years are called 'shorts'; from five to fifteen are 'mediums'; over fifteen are 'longs'.

Secondly, bonds pay a fixed rate of interest. This interest payment is known as the coupon and is normally made in two instalments, at six-monthly intervals, each equal to half the rate specified in the bond's coupon. The coupon divided by the par value of the bond (£100) gives the coupon rate on the bond. We can illustrate both these points by reference to the government bond known as Treasury 8% 2015. Its title tells us that it will be redeemed in the year 2015 and that until then it will pay £4 every six months to whoever is the registered owner. Thus someone buying such a bond for £100 at the time of issue, intending to hold it to redemption, is guaranteed a return of £8 p.a., or 8 per cent of its *par value*.

Thirdly, the par or redemption value of bonds in the UK is commonly £100. In principle this will also be the price at which bonds are first issued. However, since the preparations for sale take time, market conditions may change in such a way as to make the bonds unattractive at their existing coupon at the time they are offered for sale. They will then have to be sold at a discount to £100, in order to make the coupon rate approximate the going market rate of interest. If, by contrast, market interest rates fall, the coupon may make the bond attractive at a price above £100. In these cases the issuers are making a last-minute adjustment to the price which they hope will make the bonds acceptable to the market. In 1987 the Bank of England began a series of experiments in the auctioning of new bonds. This was going one stage further and effectively allowing the market to price new issues, rather than setting a price and then seeing how many can be sold at that price.

Fourthly, because the coupon is fixed at the outset, bond prices must fluctuate inversely with market interest rates. When we look at the demand for bonds in section 6.3 we shall see precisely why this is the case, but for the moment we can adopt the same reasoning that we adopted with bills. If market rates rise, people will prefer to hold the new, higher-yielding issues in preference to existing bonds. Existing bonds will be sold and their price will fall. Eventually, existing bonds with various coupons will be willingly held, but only when their price has fallen to the point where the coupon expressed as a percentage *of the current price* approximates the new market rate. We can see this immediately by taking an example such as Consols 2.5%. These are *irredeemable* bonds which pay a fixed coupon of £2.50 a year and will never be redeemed. Let us suppose that market interest rates are 10 per cent. Why should anyone hold an asset paying £2.50? The answer of course is that it all depends on the price. If its price is sufficiently low that £2.50 approximates the market rate, there will be buyers. (In this case the price will need to be c. £25.)

Fifthly, we need to note that the yield on bonds can be expressed and is commonly published in two forms: the *redemption yield* and the *running* or *interest yield*. The redemption yield is the annualised yield on a bond held to redemption while the running or interest yield is the coupon expressed as a percentage of the purchase price. To understand why they differ, remember what we said about the price of a bond standing at a discount or a premium to its redemption value depending on whether its coupon was less or greater than the current rate of interest. If we buy a stock with a coupon higher than the current rate of interest (a 'high-coupon' stock), its price will stand at a premium to its redemption value. For as long as we hold it we shall enjoy a series of large coupon payments. Dividing those payments by the price we paid for the bond gives us the running yield. However, if we hold it to redemption we shall receive only £100 for it. This will be less than the price we paid and we shall find that we have made a capital loss. The redemption yield annualises this gain/loss and adds it to/subtracts it from the interest yield. On 28 April 2006, the price of Treasury 9% 2012 was £122.87. The redemption yield was 4.74 per cent (in line with other very low-risk interest rates at the time) while the running (or interest) yield was 7.32 per cent.

Running yield (or interest yield): The return on a bond taking account only of the coupon payments.

Redemption yield (or yield to maturity): The return on a bond taking account of the coupon cash flows and the capital gain or loss at redemption.

Treasury 8% 2015 is a bond issued by the government. Such bonds are often called gilts or gilt-edged stock. Bonds issued by firms are usually called corporate bonds or loan stock. Their characteristics are essentially the same as those of government bonds. In most cases, however, the yields on corporate bonds tend to be higher than those on gilts, reflecting the fact that even the largest and best-established companies could fail, while governments, in developed economies at least, are not likely to default. One ingenious way of trying to predict the immediate future for the economy involves comparing the yields on corporate bonds with those on gilts. If the economy is entering a recession, for example, it is assumed that firms face larger risks than when the economy is in an upswing and the risk attaching to their bonds should rise and fall in parallel. By contrast, governments' ability to pay interest and to redeem maturing bonds is unaffected by the state of the economy. Thus if we plot the differential, or spread, between yields on corporate bonds and yields on gilts, a widening of the spread would suggest the economy is moving into recession; a narrowing would suggest that the economy is about to experience a boom. Notice though that what happens to these yields is determined by operators in financial markets. Strictly speaking, therefore, the behaviour of this spread is not telling us for sure what will happen; it is telling us only what *financial markets think* the economy is about to do. This is just one example of a recent tendency among economists (and policymakers) to regard financial markets as a source of reliable information. In section 7.8 we shall see that the spread between yields on long-term gilts and short-term gilts (the 'term structure of interest rates') is sometimes used to predict the future path of inflation.

The characteristics which we have just described are those of fixed-interest sterling bonds – bonds denominated in sterling and issued in the UK. Such bonds, and their counterparts in other countries, are sometimes called straights or plain vanilla bonds, in order to distinguish them from the more exotic variants which we come to in a moment. For most of this chapter we shall take these as typical of the whole category of bonds. Nonetheless, the past few years have seen numerous innovations in bonds, as in other financial instruments. The latest developments have been the issue of bonds denominated in euros and the 'stripping' of coupon payments from conventional bonds. But long before these innovations, many variations on the simple fixed-term, fixed-interest bond had emerged. Some of these are described in the following list.

Callable and putable bonds

Callable bonds can be redeemed at the issuer's discretion prior to the specified redemption date. Putable bonds can be sold back to the issuer on specified dates, prior to the redemption date.

Convertibles

These are usually corporate bonds, issued with the option for holders to convert into some other asset on specified terms at a future date. Conversion is usually into equities in the firm, though it may sometimes be into floating rate notes.

Eurobonds

Eurobonds are bonds issued in a country other than that of the currency of denomination. Thus bonds issued in US$ in London are eurobonds, as are yen bonds issued in New York. The bonds themselves may be straights, that is fixed-interest, fixed-redemption bonds like the sterling ones described above, or they may come in any of the variations listed here. Eurobonds are issued by governments but more usually by corporations. (Not to be confused with euro bonds.)

Euro bonds

These are bonds denominated in euros and issued in the euro currency area. The Italian government issued the first euro bond in March 1997. There is no reason why bonds denominated in euros should not be issued outside the euro currency area. These would be euro eurobonds. (Not to be confused with eurobonds.)

Floating rate notes (FRNs)

These are corporate bonds where the coupon can be adjusted at pre-determined intervals. The adjustment will be made by reference to some benchmark rate, specified when the bond is first issued. An FRN might specify, for example, that its coupon should be fifty basis points above six-month treasury bill rate, or six-month LIBOR, adjusted every six months. FRNs are, in part, a response to high and variable inflation rates.

Foreign bonds

These are corporate bonds, issued in the country of denomination, by a firm based outside that country. Thus, a US firm might issue a sterling bond in London. Foreign bonds are often given colourful names, based upon the currency in which they are issued. The US firm here would be said to have issued 'Bulldog' bonds. A UK firm issuing US$ bonds in the US is issuing 'Yankee' bonds.

Index-linked bonds

In the UK, these were first issued by the government in 1981 in response to high and variable rates of inflation. While other bonds have a redemption value fixed in nominal terms and therefore suffer a decline in real value as a result of inflation, both the value and the coupon of an index-linked bond are uprated each year in line with lagged changes in a specified price index. For example, assume that the rate of inflation in the relevant time period turns out to have been 4 per cent p.a. An index-linked 2 per cent bond will actually pay a coupon of £2.08, and its redemption value will be adjusted from £100 to £104.

Junk bonds

Junk refers not to the type of bond but to its quality. Junk bonds are corporate bonds whose issuers are regarded by bond credit rating agencies as being of high risk. Thus they may be fixed-interest, convertibles, FRNs, eurobonds, etc., but they will carry a rate of interest at least 200 basis points above that for the corresponding bonds issued by high-quality borrowers. We return to credit ratings in the next section.

Strips

Stripping refers to the breaking up of a bond into its component coupon payments and its redemption value. Thus a ten-year bond, paying semi-annual coupons, would make twenty-one strips. Each strip is then sold as a zero-coupon bond. That is, it pays no interest but is sold at a discount to the payment that will eventually be received. In this sense, it is like a long-dated bill. The strips entitling holders to the early coupon payments from our ten-year bond will have a small discount while the strips giving the holders the coupons due in eight, nine, ten years and the strip giving the holder the £100 paid on redemption will sell at large discounts. Because the payment comes at the end of the investment period, strips will have a 'duration' (see below) which is longer than that of a whole bond of corresponding maturity. Its price will therefore be more interest-sensitive and this has attractions for investors who want to take a position based on the belief that interest rates will fall in future. Furthermore, the fact that the return comes in the form of capital appreciation rather than periodic income payments will have tax advantages for some investors. A strips market for government bonds began in the UK in December 1997. The strips are created from conventional bonds by gilt-edge market makers.

6.2.2 Equities

'Equities' is a commonly used alternative name for company shares, though strictly it should be used only for *ordinary* shares. Ordinary shares give their holders claims to variable future streams of income, paid out of company profits and commonly known as dividends. The owners of equity stock are legal owners of the firm. The law requires that the company provides them with specified information in the annual report and accounts and that the firm must hold an annual general meeting at which the directors' conduct of the firm's affairs is subject to approval by such shareholders, each of whom has a number of votes matching the size of his shareholding. Preference shares pay a fixed dividend and in many ways are more like bonds. They confer no voting rights.

Ordinary shareholders have no preferential claim upon a firm's profits or its assets. They are entitled to a share only in those profits which remain after bondholders and preference shareholders have been paid; if the firm goes into liquidation, shareholders have a claim on any remaining assets only after prior claimants have been paid. Obviously, therefore, ordinary shareholders are exposed to much greater risk than are bondholders and preference shareholders. However, they also face the prospect of greater benefits. Remember that a shareholding is a part ownership of the firm. In normal circumstances the monetary value of the firm will grow as a result of both real expansion and inflation. If the value of the whole firm increases, so too must the value of the shares in it. In the long run, the value of shares should increase where the value of bonds will not. Also, in a year when the firm does well, bondholders will receive only their guaranteed interest, leaving perhaps a substantial surplus to be divided among shareholders.

For precisely this reason, the proportion of bond finance to equity finance within a firm (sometimes called the debt:equity ratio or gearing) affects the variability of returns to shareholders. Clearly, the higher the proportion of bond finance, the larger the fixed annual sum to be paid as interest; equally, the fewer are the shares over which remaining profit has to be spread. Once profits exceed the level necessary to pay the interest, therefore, the whole of any marginal addition to profit accrues to this small number of shareholders. On the other hand, if profits fall, the whole of the fall has to be borne by a reduction in payments to this small number of shareholders. The higher the debt : equity ratio, the greater the variability in dividend payments to shareholders, and since the uncertainty of magnitude of future dividend payments is normally said to be part of the risk of owning shares, shares in 'highly geared' companies are normally regarded as riskier than those in 'low geared' companies.

> **Gearing:** The amount of debt, relative to equity, in a firm's capital structure. Usually expressed as the ratio of debt to equity, D/E, or debt to total capital D/(D + E).

To understand how share price behaviour is reported and analysed we might imagine the following firm whose issued capital consists entirely of 50 million ordinary shares. Suppose that its pre-tax profits in the last financial year amounted to £4m and that the directors decided to distribute three-quarters of that as dividends to shareholders, retaining the rest for future use within the firm. If the market price of each share is £4, we have the following information expressed in the language of the market.

Shares in issue	= 50 million
Market price	= £4
Market capitalisation	= £200m
Earnings	= £4m
Earnings per share	= 8p
Distributed profit	= £3m
Dividend per share	= 6p
Payout ratio	0.75
Dividend yield	= 1.5 per cent
Earnings yield	= 2.0 per cent
Price/earnings or *P/E* ratio	= 50

The first two items need no explanation. *Market capitalisation* is the market's valuation of the firm and is found by multiplying the number of shares by their market price. *Earnings* are profits. Earnings may be quoted pre- or post-tax. Obviously, for most purposes the post-tax figure is the more useful, but it is very difficult for analysts to know exactly what a firm's tax position is. Thus, earnings figures quoted post-tax are often accompanied by the assumption that the firm is liable for tax at the going rate of corporation tax. *Earnings per share* are profits divided by the number of shares in issue, here 8p per share.

In our example the directors have chosen to pay out three-quarters of earnings (the *payout ratio*) as dividends to shareholders. The *dividend per share*, therefore, is 6p (£3m/50 million). At the current price of the share that provides a *dividend yield* of

1.5 per cent (6p/£4). Notice that if the market price of the share rises, dividends being unchanged, the dividend yield will fall; it will rise, dividends unchanged, when the share price falls. Notice also the elementary point that we cannot judge a share to be 'cheap' or 'dear' just by looking at its price. Penny shares may be regarded as dear if they pay no dividend; a share at £5 may pay a sufficiently large dividend to have a large dividend yield. It might then be thought of as cheap.

Earnings which are retained within the firm may also benefit shareholders in the long run. One could make a case for saying the higher the retained earnings, the higher the rate of new investment, the more rapid the growth of the firm and the more rapid the capital appreciation of its shares. Accepting this argument means that a share should be valued according to both the dividend which is paid now and the earnings retained 'on the shareholders' behalf'. This is the purpose of calculating an *earnings yield*, in this example 2.0 per cent ((£4m/50 million)/£4).

The *price/earnings ratio* is the reciprocal of the earnings yield. Accordingly, it conveys the same information but avoids the use of percentages. Notice the use to which such a measure may be put. If a firm has a high P/E ratio, the indication is that the market values it highly for some reason other than current earnings. The usual presumption is that future earnings are likely to grow rapidly and the price has been bid up in anticipation. In the circumstances one might therefore regard the share as 'dear'. Shares of another company in the same sector might be judged 'cheap' if their P/E ratio were low by comparison (for no obvious reason).

6.2.3 The trading of bonds and equities

As with money market instruments, we can distinguish primary markets for bonds and equities – markets in which newly issued instruments are bought – and secondary markets – markets in which existing or secondhand instruments are traded. In this section we look at primary and secondary markets for bonds and then for equities.

In most bond markets throughout the world there are differences between the institutional arrangements for the issue and trading of government bonds and corporate bonds. This is because (as we have seen) governments are very large borrowers. Thus it is essential that they should always be assured of being able to sell the debt they require and thus that there should be an active market in which investors have the utmost confidence. It is a characteristic of government bond markets, therefore, that they are subject to a high level of supervision and regulation, either by the central bank or by some agency of government. The different institutional arrangements have little effect upon the characteristics of the bonds and certainly have no effect upon the mathematics of bond pricing, yield calculations, etc. Since it is the government bond that dominates in the UK, and because there have recently been a number of changes in the arrangements for trading in government bonds, we shall start there and add some words about the corporate bond market at the end.

The primary market for government bonds involves the UK government's Debt Management Office or DMO and a group of sixteen 'Gilt Edge Market Makers' or GEMMs. The DMO is an executive agency of the UK Treasury. It began operations in April 1998, taking over the government debt operations which previously had been carried out by the Bank of England (see section 3.1). The methods by which it issues new government debt remain unchanged from those previously used by the Bank, and the DMO continues to use the systems developed by the Bank for settling transactions in new debt and for registering ownership (of new and existing debt).

The DMO is responsible for deciding the type of bonds to be issued, the terms of the issue and the timing of such issues. The traditional method, still used, is the sale by tender in which the DMO offers a specified quantity of stock for sale on a particular day at a minimum price and invites bids. If the offer is undersubscribed, all bids are accepted; if it is oversubscribed, the highest bids are accepted but at a common price – usually the minimum bid price necessary to clear the sale. If the offer is undersubscribed, the DMO retains the unsold stock and releases it onto the market subsequently, when conditions permit. Stock issued in such a way is known as *tap stock*.

The second method of issue involves the auction of stock in which no minimum price is set. The stock is sold to the highest bidders at the price they bid. This is a method which was first used in 1987 and represents a distinct stage in the evolution of debt management policy. From the point of view of the money supply and credit aggregates, sales by auction have the advantage that the DMO can be confident that it will be able to sell a given *volume* of debt since the price will adjust to ensure that this is so. Thus, the desire to sell a given volume of stock consistent with targets for the money supply can generally be met. With a sale by tender the price is set, with the result that the volume of sales becomes uncertain. The two methods simply illustrate the age-old principle that one can control the price or the quantity, but not both.

The third method of issue is for the DMO to 'buy' the stock itself and to release it to the market as conditions permit: the 'tap' method of issue.

When new issues are made, many of the bonds will be bought by GEMMs. These are usually part of a securities dealing firm (itself often part of a major banking group) which will deal in all types of securities. However, GEMMs' activities must be kept separate from the company's other securities trading. They must not themselves deal in equities. They can deal in corporate bonds, but not in bonds which have the option to convert to equities. They are subject to capital adequacy requirements, laid down by the DMO. They are committed to making 'continuous and effective two-way prices' at which they are prepared to deal up to a specified market size.

In return for these obligations, they have borrowing facilities at the Bank of England, access to a system of 'inter-dealer brokers', and a facility for making 'late' bids at government bond auctions. Inter-dealer brokers (IDBs) are intermediaries who buy and sell stock from and to GEMMs in conditions of anonymity. This enables a GEMM which has purchased (for example) a large quantity of one particular bond to sell parts of it to other GEMMs without their knowing that it has excess stock and deliberately lowering their bid prices. All of these intricate arrangements are meant to ensure that there is always a ready and stable market for government bonds. New issues of government bonds may be bought by anyone – many will go directly to banks and other financial institutions – but the DMO–GEMM relationship ensures that whatever the interest shown by the rest of the financial system, the government can always borrow on reasonable terms.

The secondary market in bonds revolves around the gilt-edge market makers. As we have seen, GEMMS are usually a part of larger firms, often banking groups which deal in securities of all kinds. Securities trading in the UK underwent a major upheaval in 1986 with a series of changes which acquired the name of 'Big Bang'. The main consequence of Big Bang of relevance here is that it ended the tradition of 'single capacity' trading. In single capacity trading a strict line is drawn between brokers, who buy and sell securities on behalf of clients, and jobbers, who hold stocks of securities from which they buy and sell to brokers. After 1986, firms, known as market-makers, could act in a dual capacity. This meant that they could 'make a market', that is they could hold stocks of securities from which they would buy and sell, like jobbers, but usually on a much bigger scale. But acting in a dual capacity meant that they could buy and sell direct to investors, instead of dealing via an intermediary broker. They could also trade in securities on their own account, for their own profit.

We saw earlier that GEMMs undertake to quote continuous two-way prices. This means that bond holders know at any moment the price at which they can sell bonds and the price at which they could buy more. Thus the UK bond market is an example of what is known technically as a 'quote-driven' or 'dealer' market. This contrasts with a 'matching' or 'order-driven' market, which we shall refer to again in connection with share trading below. The market has no physical location. Most GEMMs display the prices at which they are prepared to deal on screens linked to SEAQ, the Stock Exchange Automated Quotation System. Private investors, without access to such screens, can obtain prices over the phone. Orders to buy and sell, likewise, are taken over the phone.

During the 1980s, the Bank of England and the London Stock Exchange developed a computerised system of trading and settlement for the gilts market, known as the Central Gilts Office, or CGO. This has links to more than 100 financial firms, including the GEMMs and IDBs, banks and major holders of government debt. Transactions through the CGO are settled on the same day. For private clients and firms without direct links to the CGO, settlement normally takes place within three days. The CGO was originally intended as a facility for wholesale trading, but in 1997 it was upgraded to handle trades in gilt repo (see section 5.2) and to make it accessible to a wider range of dealers. Many 'retail' brokers who specialise in private client business now have access to CGO facilities either directly or as 'sponsored' members.

One measure of market efficiency is the level of transaction cost. Prior to 1986, gilt transactions involved the payment of a commission on each sale/purchase. In addition, jobbers quoted one price for a purchase (by the investor) and a lower price for a sale. The difference, or spread, was another source of income for jobbers. Since 1986 commissions have largely disappeared. Furthermore, spreads have declined by about a half. It now costs about £600 to trade £1m of gilts. This is much less, incidentally, than the cost of trading company shares. These relatively low transaction costs, combined with the short time required for settlement, means that government bonds are highly liquid assets. This is true even for long-dated bonds.

In the last quarter of 2005 there were about 2,100 trades a day involving GEMMs and their clients, and about 317 deals per day between GEMMs themselves. The average size of the deals was about £3.8m for transactions with customers. Deals between

GEMMs, 'intra-market' business, were much larger at £18m. The value of total trades, or 'turnover', per day was about £13bn. By far the largest share of government debt is held by financial institutions. Over 50 per cent is held by life assurance and pension funds (see Chapter 4), while banks and building societies hold about 5 per cent (see Chapter 3), mainly at the very short end of the spectrum. About 10 per cent of the total is held by private investors and trusts.

The introduction of the euro in January 1999 automatically created a large, unified market for government bonds denominated in euros. Since these are close substitutes for sterling bonds, traders in the UK were bound to keep a close watch on developments in the prices and yields of European bonds, just as they had previously kept a close watch on the deutschmark bond market. To facilitate comparisons and calculations, the practice of quoting UK bond prices in fractions of a pound ('1/32') was discontinued. UK bond prices are now quoted in pounds and decimals.

The secondary market for corporate bonds is much smaller than the market for gilts. The value of bonds outstanding is much smaller, the volume of trading is lower and so one obvious feature of the market is that it is less liquid. This is one of the reasons, together with the higher risk associated with private corporations, why corporate bond yields tend to be higher than gilt yields. Many GEMMs deal in corporate bonds, especially in the larger issues; however, corporate bond dealing is not confined to GEMMs but is carried out by market-makers who otherwise deal in equities. New issues of corporate bonds are usually made by equity market-makers, i.e. by investment banks.

In recent years, two circumstances have worked against the expansion of the sterling corporate bond market. The first was the period of volatile inflation and interest rates in the 1970s and early 1980s. When interest rates were high, firms were reluctant to issue high coupon bonds which would lock them into paying high interest rates for years into the future when interest rates might have fallen while high rates of inflation deterred investors from buying fixed-interest securities generally. (The same circumstance encouraged the UK government to introduce index-linked bonds.) The second is the growth of the eurobond market. Like gilts, sterling corporate bonds pay interest net of tax and their ownership is registered. For many investors, there is an advantage in receiving interest without deduction of tax and in holding bonds anonymously. Eurobonds provide both of these facilities, with the result that UK corporations now often find it convenient to issue sterling eurobonds – bonds denominated in sterling but issued overseas.

The primary market for equities enables firms to issue new shares, normally in order to raise funds to finance an expansion. Sometimes this will involve a privately owned firm (a non-plc) seeking a stock exchange *listing*. This requires that it meets certain requirements laid down by the relevant exchange. It will have to have an established trading record, be prepared to publish key financial information, including an annual report, on set dates and hold an annual general meeting to which all shareholders are invited. When a privately owned firm achieves a listing and sells shares, its ownership will pass to the holders of the shares. In the UK, the major market for equities is the London Stock Exchange (LSE). However, because of the strict criteria which firms have to meet for an LSE listing, it has often been argued that the costs of entry are too high for small and medium-size firms. From 1980 to 1996 the LSE was supplemented by the Unlisted Securities Market (USM), which had lower listing requirements. The two were merged in 1996 when European Community directives, intended to harmonise listing requirements across Europe, lowered the criteria for access to the LSE to the point where there was little difference between the LSE and the USM. The need for a subsidiary market with less demanding criteria and lower entry costs did not disappear, however. Since 1995, this has been provided by the Alternative Investment Market or AIM.

A less dramatic case than that of firms seeking an initial listing arises when firms which are already listed, and whose shares are already widely owned, wish to issue more shares in order to finance an expansion. This involves what is called a rights issue, since existing shareholders must be given the right to buy the new shares in proportion to the size of their existing shareholding. Behind this lies the view that a shareholder in any company should be able to protect his proportionate share in the company: this should not be diluted unless the shareholder so decides. He can so decide by declining to take up his rights to the new shares by selling the rights. In all cases, whether it is a firm seeking to go public for the first time or a firm making a rights issue, the issue of new shares will normally be managed by an issuing house, usually an investment bank which specialises in this activity. The issuing house charges a fee for handling the publicity and administration of the sale and for advising the firm about the price of the shares and the timing of the sale. With the exception of rights issues, new issues will usually be underwritten by the issuing house. This means that it guarantees the company that the desired funds will be raised, even if some of the shares remain unsold. In these circumstances, it takes up the shares itself or, in the case of a large issue, it arranges in advance with other investment banks that they will collectively take up any unsold stock.

There are various ways of marketing new issues. The simplest is the *offer for sale*, where an issuing house buys the whole of the issue at an agreed price and then resells the shares to the general public, over a period of time, for the best price that it can get. An *offer for sale by tender* is similar except that the general public is invited to make a bid for the shares subject to a minimum specified price. Tenders are ranked in descending order of price and the lowest price is identified at which the whole issue would sell out. All bidders above that price are then allotted shares at that price (the striking price) regardless of the price they may have bid. A *placing* involves the issuing house placing the shares with investors, usually the large institutions, whom it knows will be interested in the type of share in question.

However, trading in the primary market is dwarfed by the buying and selling of existing shares. And it is this activity that is widely reported in the media every day. The scale of the difference between new issue activity, where new funds are raised, and turnover in existing equities can be seen in Table 6.2. This shows that in 2005, UK corporations raised £18,692m by issuing new shares in London, while the turnover in existing company shares was approximately 25 times as large.

Given the overwhelming magnitude of transactions in existing shares when compared with activity which raises new funds, it is easy to dismiss the activities of stock exchanges as little more than a form of gambling. Undoubtedly, there are many

Table 6.2 Ordinary company shares, new issues and turnover, 2005, £m

New issues of ordinary company shares[1]	18,692
Turnover in ordinary shares by:	
Pension funds	155,876
Life assurance	140,985
Investment trusts	18,035
Unit trusts	154,425
Total	469,321
New issues: turnover	0.04

[1] *Before redemptions. (UK firms only).*

Source: ONS, *Financial Statistics*, March 2006, Tables 5.3a and 6.2a

investors whose only interest lies in the secondary market and only then in what is going to happen to selected share prices in the short run. However, while the motives of some may be greed and little else, the combined activities of all may mean that stock market performance is both important to us all and generally beneficial from an economic point of view. We have already mentioned some of the consequences:

- An active stock market transforms equities from being a very long-term form of investment into highly liquid assets. This undoubtedly increases the availability of long-term funds to firms and reduces the cost.

- If individual share prices generally reflect the performance of their firms, then successful, well-managed firms will have a high share price and a high market value. Poorly performing firms will be valued accordingly. A depressed share price usually makes a firm a target for takeover. In a takeover, the management of the target firm is usually replaced and thus one might argue that an active stock market is one way of promoting the efficient management of firms.

- Changes in the general level of share prices affect people's wealth, directly (for shareholders) and indirectly (for those with pensions and life assurance policies). They also affect consumers' and firms' confidence. A booming stock market reinforces a booming economy and vice versa.

- When share prices are high, new issues can be made at a high price. This brings in a large volume of new funds for each additional dividend payment that a firm is committing itself to in future. The cost of new capital, in other words, is low. The cost of capital is high when share prices are low. It may be true that little capital is raised through new issues (compared with retained profit, for example), but even when using retained profit to finance new investment projects, a rational, profit-maximising firm should still be evaluating new projects in the light of the cost of capital. Internal funds are not free. They have an opportunity cost which is the return they could have earned by being invested elsewhere, including investment in the shares of other firms.

Like the bond market that we looked at above, the secondary market for company shares was dramatically affected by the Big Bang reforms of 1986, and the trading arrangements in place at the moment still show the legacy of those reforms. The buying and selling of equities is done largely through market-makers who act in a dual capacity. They quote continuous two-way prices for the shares in which they deal. Market-makers in the London Stock Exchange are usually divisions of major banking groups. Buying and selling prices are displayed on computer screens using the London Stock Exchange's SEAQ system. Because market-makers hold their own inventories of stock and quote continuous prices, the London Exchange is said to be a 'quote-driven' rather than an 'order-driven' (also called 'matching' or 'auction') market.

In this respect, London is unusual. Most stock exchanges – including those of continental Europe, many of which have recently undergone drastic modernisation – are order-driven markets. Tokyo and New York mix both systems. In an order-driven market, buyers and sellers submit orders to the market-maker specifying respectively an upper and lower limit at which they are prepared to trade. Buy orders are then matched to sell orders, so far as possible, by computer and a price is struck and declared. Any offers which cannot be executed at that price are kept until the price moves within their limit or the instruction to buy or sell is withdrawn. Compared with the quote-driven or dealer system it is immediately apparent that the order-driven system distributes the risk associated with holding shares rather differently. In a dealer system, the dealer holds inventories of stocks on his own behalf, to which he adds the sell stocks that he receives and from which he executes buy orders. Clearly the price of this inventory will fluctuate with changes in the market price of stocks. Meanwhile, the buyer/seller has the advantage of knowing with certainty the price at which his order will be executed. In an auction system, the market-maker holds no significant inventories and accepts no stocks except in so far as he matches them instantly with a buyer. The counterparties to the transaction, however, cannot know in advance the exact price at which their order will be carried out. The risk to the latter is moderated by the setting of price limits and by the fact that auction markets, just like dealer markets, display continuous and detailed trading information on screen which enables potential buyers and sellers to see the price at which the last trade was carried out and any trend that might be developing. Partly because the market-maker faces less risk, while the shareholder faces more, order-driven markets are generally cheaper to operate. Commissions and spreads between the bid and offer prices are lower in Frankfurt and Paris than in London, for example.

In October 1997, the London Stock Exchange launched a limited order-driven dealing facility. Known as 'SETS' (Stock Exchange Electronic Dealing System), it covered the shares of 126 larger companies (most of them included in the FTSE-100 index). The results so far have been mixed, especially for small investors. On average, the bid–offer spread has fallen from around 0.6 per cent to 0.4, but there have been cases where such spreads (normally less than 1 per cent) have jumped to nearly 10 per cent. The problem, it seems, lies with insufficient orders. Clearly, if orders are few, there is a chance that the only matching order is at a very disadvantageous price. Part of the problem may well be that with two systems running side by side, not enough people were attracted to the order-driven system and once it emerged that prices could behave erratically, fewer still were attracted by low dealing costs. Problems seem to have been worst at the beginning and end of the day. (There were even rumours that some investors were putting in 'buy' orders at absurdly low prices at the end of the day, hoping to pick up a bargain from some unsuspecting investor who placed a 'sell' order early the following morning when there might be no buyers for the shares.) It remains to be seen whether London will move to order-driven trading as the norm. The main lesson may be that running the two systems in parallel is the worst of all possible options.

6.3 Bonds: supply, demand and price

At any particular time the total quantity of securities available for purchase consists of those securities which firms and other organisations are issuing to finance current borrowing needs, together with all those securities issued in the past. Thus, as with bills, we must recognise that by far the greater part of securities offered for sale at any particular time are existing or 'second-hand' securities. This contrasts with our normal assumption in economics that 'supply' refers to a flow of something taking place over a period of time. The supply of securities is a stock.

This means of course that a decision by an investor to purchase shares or government bonds is not normally a decision which involves making new funds available to a borrower. The borrowing and lending which brought the securities into existence was done in the past, maybe a long time ago. A decision today to buy, say, Marks and Spencer shares is a decision to accept ownership of an existing debt, transferred from someone else who may also not have been the original lender.

In these circumstances it is perhaps tempting to view the immense trade in existing securities that takes place each day as unimportant to organisations' borrowing needs and therefore to the real economy. However, a well-developed and active market for existing securities, the secondary market, is important in supporting the market for new issues of securities, the primary market. People are willing to buy new issues on the existing terms precisely because they know there is an active secondary market in which they can transfer the debt if they wish. We shall also see in a moment that trading in the existing stock of securities effectively determines the cost and other terms on which new capital can be raised.

In Figure 6.1 we have depicted the stock of some existing bonds as a vertical line. The figure also includes a demand curve showing equilibrium between the stock of bonds in existence and the demand for it at a price P. We need to be careful in our interpretation of this equilibrium. Remember that the supply curve S indicates a fixed stock. Equilibrium must therefore mean that this stock of bonds is willingly held at the price P. However, this does not mean that no trading is taking place. It is quite possible that some people feel that the price is rather high (in the light of conditions which we shall discuss more fully in a moment). They will be selling. But provided that these sellers are matched by an equal number of buyers who judge that the bond is cheap, the total stock of bonds will still be held at the current price which will be stable.

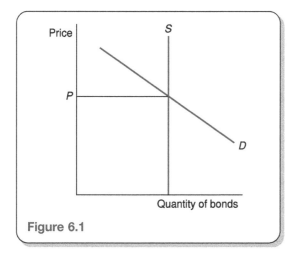

Figure 6.1

Notice that we have drawn the supply curve vertically. This is because we are looking at the market in the short run and in the short run the stock is fixed *independently of the price of the bonds*. This is different from the normal case in economics where we are often looking at the supply of a good being produced by a firm. In this case a rise in price is usually assumed to cause an increase in output and so we draw the supply curve with an upward slope.

However, over a longer period, the stock of bonds can expand as the result of several forces which we might distinguish as 'long-run' and 'medium-run'. In the long run, rising real income and wealth will themselves encourage more borrowing and lending and, other things being equal, bonds will share in that expansion in proportion to their existing importance to firms' borrowing needs. Although the UK has recently seen years of budget surplus, the historical norm has been for deficits or 'positive' public sector net cash requirements (PSNCRs). As regards the supply of government bonds, therefore, this has been a major influence in the long run.

For medium-term changes we have to look to factors which cause a change in the attractiveness of this form of borrowing relative to other forms. Conceivably the cost of alternative forms of borrowing, from banks for example, could rise relative to the cost of issuing bonds. More likely, in practice, are changes in non-price variables. At various times, in response to monetary policy, banks have had either to ration their lending or direct it to favoured areas of the economy. This would push some marginal financing decisions towards bond or equity finance. Changes in the structure of the securities markets, making them larger, more competitive, operating with lower commissions and so on, might have the same effect. This was one of the arguments in favour of the changes introduced to the London Stock Exchange in October 1986.

We noted above that the public sector's annual borrowing requirement was the major source of bond issues in the long run. In the short run, policy decisions will lead to variations in the proportion of the PSNCR that is funded by bond sales. A tight monetary policy, for example, would require the PSNCR to be largely funded by bond issues, or even to be 'overfunded'. Companies will try to issue fixed-interest

Box 6.1 **Increases in the stocks of equities and bonds – long- and medium-run influences**

	Equities	Bonds
Long-run	1. Economic growth 2. Inflation	1. Economic growth 2. Inflation 3. PSNCR

Medium-run	3. Rise in cost of alternative
	   sources of capital
	4. Reimposition of bank lending
	   controls
	5. Reduction in new issue costs
	6. High equity prices
		4. Rise in cost of alternative
		   sources of capital
		5. Reimposition of bank lending
		   controls
		6. Reduction in new issue costs
		7. Tighter monetary policy
		8. Expected higher future
		   interest rates
		9. High bond prices

debt when interest rates are low, or at least when they expect that the probability of higher future rates is greater than the probability of lower future rates. These supply influences are summarised in Box 6.1, as though acting to increase supply. When they do so, the stock of bonds will expand and the supply curve will shift to the right, as in Figure 6.2. A useful exercise would be to work out how each of the influences could work in reverse and shift the supply curve to the left.

We said above that we draw the supply curve vertically because we are looking at the situation in the short run where the stock of bonds cannot increase in response

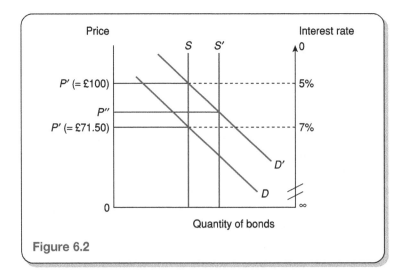

Figure 6.2

to a rise in price. However, before we leave this discussion of supply, we need to note that there is one way in which price may have an effect upon the supply of bonds but this can only happen in the medium or long term. In order to understand this, we have to start thinking about some of the factors that underlie demand.

In Figure 6.2 we have a demand curve, D, intersecting the supply curve for a bond at a price P. Notice that the demand curve slopes downward, in the normal way. This is because bonds pay a fixed income stream (see section 6.2.1) in the form of a coupon. Clearly, the lower the price at which this fixed income stream can be purchased, the more attractive it will be and thus the greater the demand. More precisely, the lower the price at which the income stream can be purchased, the higher the rate of return the bond holder will receive. This amounts to saying that for any individual bond, the price corresponds to a unique rate of return (expressed as the running or interest yield) and that the price and rate of return vary inversely. In Figure 6.2, therefore, we have assumed that we are looking at a bond with a 5 per cent coupon whose current market price is £71.50. At this price the running yield is 7 per cent (= 5/71.50). We have marked this on the right-hand axis. Suppose something happens to shift the demand curve to D'. The price rises to P' and the return falls. If the price rises to £100, the running yield falls to 5 per cent. This increase in the price of the bond indicates two related things to the issuer (or borrower): firstly, it indicates that any new 5 per cent bond can be sold to raise £100 rather than £71.50; secondly it shows that £100 can be raised for an interest rate of 5 per cent rather than 7 per cent. Whichever way we look at it, the cost of borrowing by issuing new bonds has fallen. Clearly, in these circumstances (and assuming nothing else has changed) borrowers will be encouraged to issue more bonds. In these circumstances, the stock of bonds increases (by the size of the new issue) and the supply curve moves to S'. The increase in the supply may have the effect of lowering the price (to P'') and raising the yield (the end result depends on the elasticity of the demand curve and the scale of the new issue). The fact remains, however, that the borrower can borrow more cheaply than otherwise would have been the case. Hence, an increase in price *could* result in an increase in supply but this is shown by a *shift* in the curve to S', and not, as more normally, by a movement *along* an upward-sloping supply curve.

Figure 6.2 teaches us three very important lessons:

- The first is that (*ceteris paribus*) the return on a security varies inversely with its price.
- Trading in an existing security determines the price at which new capital can be raised.
- (If we ignore transaction costs) the yield on a security is simultaneously the rate of return to investors and the cost of capital for borrowers.

In Figure 6.2, we have seen that the price that investors are willing to pay for a bond is mathematically linked to the rate of return that they receive. In fact, the orthodox theory of asset pricing says that it is the required rate of return that *determines* the price that people are willing to pay. Formally speaking, the price that people are willing to pay is the value (more strictly, the *present value*) that they place upon the future payments. We look at how this is arrived at in the next few paragraphs. The theory and techniques that we draw upon are explained more fully in Appendix I: Portfolio theory.

In the calculation of a present value for the future stream of income flowing from a bond, the size of the coupon payments will obviously be crucial. Other things being equal, a bond with a 15 per cent coupon will have a higher market price than one with a 10 per cent coupon. As a first attempt at a valuation we might be tempted simply to sum the future payments. However, this overlooks a fundamental principle of economics and finance, namely that a payment at some time in the future is worth less than the same payment now. This is not because of inflation (although the presence of inflation reinforces the point). Even in a zero-inflation world the principle would hold, as we explain in Appendix I: Portfolio theory. The reason that £5, say, today is worth more than £5 in a year's time is that the £5 today could be put to some immediate use. Waiting for one year causes us a 'loss' equal to the pleasure, satisfaction or whatever which could have been enjoyed by using the £5 in the intervening year.

The practice is therefore to discount future income payments by using a formula which takes the current rate of interest to represent the cost of waiting and recognises that the loss increases with the length of the wait. Notice that the rate of interest here is the nominal rate. Notice also that since its function is to represent the cost to us of not having the funds immediately available, it must be the rate of interest that could be earned in the market now on other assets of similar risk and duration to the bond. And this means that we can also think of it as the rate of return that we would require (since we can get it elsewhere) to induce us to hold the bond. (These equivalencies are discussed further in Appendix I: Portfolio theory.) Other things being equal, we should expect nominal interest rates to rise and fall with increases and decreases in the rate of inflation (i.e. we should expect real rates to be fairly stable). With high rates of inflation, therefore, we should expect high nominal interest rates. As we shall see, this will lower our present valuation of any future stream of income and explains why bond prices are sensitive to, among other things, expectations of inflation.

The (discounted) present value of a payment in one year's time is given by

$$C \times \frac{1}{1+i} \tag{6.1}$$

where C is the coupon payment and i is the rate of interest. (Throughout our examples, we assume that bonds pay a single coupon, annually. In practice, many pay half the coupon at six-monthly intervals.) Take the case of the 15 per cent bond mentioned earlier. Assume that the next coupon payment is exactly a year away, and that interest rates are currently 10 per cent. The present value of the next coupon payment would be £15/(1 + 0.10) or £13.63. The value of the same payment in two years' time is given by

$$C \times \frac{1}{(1+i)^2} \tag{6.2}$$

Thus it follows that the value of the whole stream of payments is the sum of this progression. If P is the present value or price of the bond, then

$$P = \sum_{t=1}^{n} C \times \frac{1}{(1 + i)^t} \tag{6.3}$$

In the case of an irredeemable bond, the payments go on for ever and t tends to infinity. This means that the series

$$C \times \frac{1}{(1 + i)^t} \tag{6.4}$$

is converging on zero and the present value P of the sum of the series can be more conveniently written as

$$P = C/i \tag{6.5}$$

This can be confirmed by taking the coupon of any undated government bond from the *Financial Times* and dividing it by the current long-term rate of interest.

Exercise 6.1

(a) On 6 May 2006, long-term interest rates were about 4.6 per cent. Calculate a price for the undated bonds 'Treasury $2\frac{1}{2}$%' on that day.

(b) What would the price have been if long-term interest rates had been 1.6 per cent?

Answers at end of chapter

However, most bonds in fact mature and so our formula has to include a valuation of the payment received on maturity. In this case P is found as follows:

$$P = \sum_{t=1}^{n} C \times \frac{1}{(1 + i)^t} + \left[M \times \frac{1}{(1 + i)^n} \right] \tag{6.6}$$

where M is the maturity value of the bond.
Or, more compactly,

$$P = \sum \frac{C}{(1 + i)^t} + \frac{M}{(1 + i)^n} \tag{6.7}$$

Remember that in calculating P we have assumed that the next coupon payment is one year away. This is a way of saying that the last coupon payment has just been made. In practice, however, we shall often want to price bonds at dates which lie between two coupon payments. We might want to price a bond, for example, where three months have elapsed since the last coupon payment (and there are three months to run to the next half-coupon payment, or nine months to the next full payment). If we continue with our assumption of single, annual coupon payments, it is clear that if we buy a bond three months after its last coupon payment, we have to wait only nine months to get the next coupon, and waiting nine months for a given payment is better than waiting a whole year. (On the face of it, we would do best if we bought bonds which had, say, only a month to go before the next coupon payment and then sold them after one month in order to buy more bonds near their payment date.) And of course we can do precisely that; and so can everyone else. The result is that the price that investors actually have to pay for a bond reflects not just the elements in eqn 6.6 and eqn 6.7 but also the position of the transaction date relative to the coupon payment. In effect, the behaviour of the bond's price reflects the amount of accrued interest, that is to say, the share of the coupon that is represented by the number of days since the last coupon payment divided by the coupon payment period. If we are three months into an annual cycle, the price that we pay should include a premium equal to $^1/_4 \times C$. This ensures that one-quarter of the coupon goes to the seller of the bond, who has, after all, held the bond for three months of the coupon cycle.

> **'Clean' price:** The price of a bond ignoring any interest which may have accrued since the last coupon payment.

The need to allow for accrued interest introduces the distinction between 'clean' and 'dirty' bond prices. The clean price is the price without accrued interest. In practice, the clean price will be the price we should pay if we bought the bond immediately after a coupon payment, so that we would have to wait for the entire payment period before receiving the next payment. P in eqn 6.6 and eqn 6.7 is a clean price, since we calculated it on the assumption that we had to wait a year for the coupon. The dirty price is always the price we actually pay and it will normally include accrued interest in addition to the clean price.

> **'Dirty' price:** The price of a bond, including any accrued interest.

At first sight, it may seem strange to use bond pricing formulae (like eqn 6.6 and eqn 6.7) which give us a price which will only rarely be the price that people actually pay, but there is a logic to it. First of all, it is quite easy to calculate accrued interest and to add it to the clean price. There are no unknowns or uncertainties. The premium is simply the fraction of the payment period times the coupon payment. The coupon payment and period are both fixed and the fraction can be calculated from a calendar. The interesting influences on a bond's price are the variables whose values can change: in particular interest rates and (we shall see later) expectations about changes in interest rates. Because it is the clean price which is subject to unpredictable changes, bond prices quoted in the financial press are usually clean prices.

In Box 6.2 and Exercise 6.2, we have two 8% bonds. The bond in Box 6.2 matures in three years, while the bond in the exercise matures in five years. The box shows the price of the three-year bond when interest rates are 6 per cent and again when they are 9 per cent, while the exercise requires the price of the five-year bond to be calculated for each of these interest rates.

Exercise 6.2

Using the approach adopted in Box 6.2, calculate the price of an 8% bond with five years to maturity when interest rates are 6 per cent and again when they are 9 per cent. Compare the results carefully with those in Box 6.2.

Answers at end of chapter

The results in Box 6.2 (and in Exercise 6.2) lead us to three important conclusions. All three are concerned with the relationship between interest rates and bond prices. The first we have met before. It is that:

A rise in interest rates causes a fall in bond prices and vice versa.

Box 6.2

Interest rates and bond prices

Imagine an 8% bond which matures for £100 in three years' time. Interest rates are currently 6 per cent. We assume that a coupon payment has just been made, so that an investor holding the bond to redemption receives three coupon payments and the maturity value. Using eqn 6.7 we can write:

$$P = \sum_{t=1}^{3} \frac{8}{(1 + 0.06)^t} + \frac{100}{(1 + 0.06)^3}$$

However, in Appendix I we show that the first part of this expression, the value of any series of regular payments, could be found using:

$$PV = \frac{A}{i} \times \left(1 - \frac{1}{(1 + i)^n}\right) \tag{A1.5}$$

Substituting values, we have:

$$P = \frac{8}{0.06}\left(1 - \frac{1}{(1 + 0.06)^3}\right) + \frac{100}{(1 + 0.06)^3}$$

which gives us:

$$P = 133.33 \times \left(1 - \frac{1}{1.191}\right) + \frac{100}{1.191}$$

$$= (133.33 \times 0.16) + 83.963$$

$$= 21.33 + 83.96 = £105.30$$

If we repeat the last stage of this calculation, but setting the interest rate to 9 per cent, we have:

$$P = \frac{8}{0.09} \times \left(1 - \frac{1}{(1 + 0.09)^3}\right) + \frac{100}{(1 + 0.09)^3}$$

and the result is:

$$P = 88.88 \times \left(1 - \frac{1}{1.295}\right) + \frac{100}{1.295}$$

$$= (88.88 \times 0.228) + 77.22$$

$$= 20.264 + 77.22 = £97.48$$

The second is that:

> *When the rate of interest exceeds the coupon rate, the price of the bond stands at a 'discount' to its maturity value; when the rate of interest is below the coupon rate, the price stands at a premium.*

If we continue with our assumption that the maturity or redemption value is £100, and if we let *c* stand for the coupon rate, we can summarise this particular rule as follows:

$i > c, P < 100$

$i < c, P > 100$

The third is that:

> *The longer the residual maturity of a bond, other things being equal, the greater is the sensitivity of its price to changes in interest rates.*

In each of our cases above, the level of interest rates changed by three percentage points. The price change for the three-year bond was about £8, while the price change for the five-year bond was over £12.

The extent of this sensitivity to interest rate changes is expressed by the concept of 'duration'. The duration of a bond can be calculated, though the mathematics are beyond the scope of a book like this (see Howells and Bain, 2005, ch. 16; or Pilbeam, 2005, ch. 6). Duration is defined as the weighted average maturity of a bond. The logic behind the idea of 'weighted average maturity' is that for bonds which pay regular coupons, the total cash flow from that bond is spread over a period (from now to the date of maturity). Depending upon the characteristics of the bond, this cash flow could be heavily weighted towards the immediate future or towards the more distant future. (The 'strips' we mentioned earlier in this chapter have just one payment at the end of their life, which gives them a longer duration than the bond from which they were created.) Since changes in the discount rate always have a larger effect upon distant payments than upon short ones, a bond where the weight of payments is soon should be less interest-sensitive than a bond where the weight of payments lies further away. Duration, therefore, is trying to capture the *average* time that it takes to receive the cashflow.

Duration is mainly determined by the residual maturity of a bond. However, other things being equal, duration increases with lower coupons and, again other things being equal, it is higher for lower redemption yields. It follows that if you wish to hold bonds whose price has the maximum exposure to interest changes (because you expect interest rates to fall, for example), you should concentrate on long-dated, low-coupon stock and buy the bonds with the lowest redemption yield in that group!

What we have just seen is that if we know the appropriate market rate of interest, that is to say the rate of interest on assets of similar maturity and risk, we can find the price of a bond. Equally, of course, it follows that if we know the price at which a bond is trading, we can calculate the rate of return on that bond. This is very easily seen for an irredeemable bond. We simply rearrange eqn 6.5 so that the rate of interest appears on the left-hand side. Thus, if the current price of an irredeemable bond with a $2^1/_2$% coupon is £60, the rate of interest received by the holder is:

$$i = C/P \tag{6.8}$$

In this case, £2.50 ÷ £60 = 4.17 per cent.

However, as we saw earlier, the return on bonds can be expressed in at least two forms. Firstly, we can calculate the 'running' or 'interest' yield. This is what we have just calculated using eqn 6.8. Alternatively, we can calculate the 'redemption' yield or 'yield to maturity'. This takes account of the fact that most bonds trade at a price which is different from their maturity value. Thus, if we hold them to maturity, we shall make a capital gain (or loss) and this has to be added to the return which we earn from the coupon payments. In Box 6.2, for example, if market interest rates were 6 per cent, we would have paid £105.30 for a bond maturing in three years. If we calculated the interest yield, this would give us 8 ÷ 105.30 = 7.6 per cent. But this takes no account of the fact that if we hold the bond to maturity we shall make a capital loss of £5.30 or approximately £1.77 per year. In most cases we should wish to take this into account by calculating the redemption yield. (Notice that since irredeemable bonds have no redemption date, we can *only* calculate an interest yield. Equation 6.8 is the only expression we ever need for calculating the return on undated bonds.)

Unfortunately, calculating the redemption yield is no simple task. It has to be done by iteration or 'trial and error'. It can be done quickly by computer, but only then because a computer can perform hundreds of iterations per second.

To understand how we find the redemption yield, look again at eqn 6.7. We know P, the market price, and C, the coupon. We also know n, the term to maturity (and thus the number of coupon payments) and M the maturity value. Finding the redemption yield involves finding a value for i which makes the present value of the stream of coupon payments and the maturity value equal to the current market price. The technique involves four steps:

1. Choose a rate of interest which is bound to give a value (PV_1) which is less than the market price (i.e. choose a value of i that is too high).

2. Choose a rate of interest which is bound to give a value (PV_2) which is greater than the market price (i.e. choose a value of i that is too low).

3. See where the current market price falls, between the two calculated values PV_1 and PV_2.

4. Choose a new interest rate which falls between the two previous rates in the same position as the market price falls between PV_1 and PV_2.

Box 6.3 provides an example of how it is done.

In practice, when we talk about bond yields it is the redemption yield that we are interested in. Bonds of similar risk and similar residual maturity will usually have redemption yields which are very close together; furthermore, these redemption yields will be equal (or very close) to the rate of return on all other assets of similar risk and maturity. In other words, bond redemption yields (and therefore prices) must

| Box 6.3 | Finding redemption yields |

A 6% bond, with three years to maturity, is trading at £92.40. What is its redemption yield? (Assume that a coupon has just been paid: there are three coupon payments left.)

Step 1
Notice that the bond is trading at a discount to its redemption value. We know from our earlier discussion that this means the rate we are looking for is greater than the coupon rate. If we want to be sure that our first trial redemption rate is 'too high', we might start with 10 per cent. If we follow the procedures we adopted in Box 6.2, we shall find that a trial rate of 10 per cent gives us a present value for the coupon payments of £14.93, and a *PV* for the maturity value of £75.13. The present value of both (PV_1) is thus £90.01.

Step 2
£90.01 is fairly close to the market price of £92.40, suggesting that 10 per cent is not far from the true yield to redemption. In order to get a present value which is above the market price, we shall not need to pitch our second trial rate very far below the first. We might try 8 per cent. This gives a *PV* for the coupon payments of £15.43 and a *PV* for the maturity value of £79.38. Thus PV_2 = £94.81.

Step 3
$PV_2 - PV_1$ = £94.81 – £90.01 = £4.80. If we now look at the market price of £92.40, we can see that it is £2.39 more than PV_1. £2.39 is very close to one half of £4.80, i.e. it is half-way between the two trial *PV*s. (Our calculations have involved a very small amount of rounding, which a computer would avoid.) This suggests that we should try a figure for redemption yield half-way between our two trial rates.

Step 4
If we do the calculations once more, using an interest rate of 9 per cent, we find that the present value of the coupon payments is £15.18, while the *PV* of the maturity value is £77.22. A redemption yield of 9 per cent makes the present value of the coupon and redemption payments just equal to the market price of £92.40.

reflect market conditions. This need not be true of the interest or running yields on bonds. These can show significant divergence across individual bonds and between individual bonds and other assets. We shall notice this when we look at bond price data in section 6.6.

As we saw in Chapter 4, the major holders of government bonds are long-term insurance funds, followed closely by pension funds and more distantly by building societies and general insurance companies. Discount houses are also significant holders of bonds. As a general rule the attractiveness of such assets lies in their guaranteed rate of return if held to redemption. For intermediaries with long-term liabilities, holding to redemption is invariably the rule. The short-term liabilities of building societies and discount houses, however, mean that they might in certain circumstances be forced into the sale of some gilt holdings. The effect of this is shown in their preference for short-dated bonds whose prices, as we have just seen, are less volatile. In addition to their secure returns, bonds are also extremely marketable. Approximately 60 per cent of London Stock Exchange transactions, measured by value, are in government bonds.

For some investors, the tax treatment of government bonds may also be an attraction. No capital gains tax is payable on government bonds provided that their holders are deemed to be holding them as an investment and not to be actively trading in them for profit. (Banks and building societies are so regarded, incidentally, and their capital gains on gilts are taxed as profit.) Remember that 'low-coupon' bonds will be trading at a discount to their redemption value. Thus a large part of their redemption yield is made up of the eventual capital gain to be made at maturity. This gain we have seen is not taxable while the coupon payments themselves are taxed at the investor's marginal rate of income tax. Such bonds are obviously attractive to investors who expect their capital gains to exceed the current tax-free threshold and in particular to those who also pay income tax at above the minimum rate. This tax treatment creates a rather specialised demand for low-coupon stocks. This raises their price relative to other stocks and explains why their (pre-tax) redemption yields appear to be out of line with (i.e. below) those on higher-coupon stocks.

Granted the attraction of fixed-interest bonds is the secure income that they yield, we know that their price fluctuates with changes in interest rates. This gives rise inevitably to capital gains and losses on bonds not held to redemption and this encourages a certain amount of trading for capital gain, particularly when, as in the 1970s and 1980s, nominal interest rates were volatile.

In Figure 6.3 we have drawn the supply curve for bonds vertically at S. The demand curve slopes downwards, suggesting that, other things being equal, holders of bonds will be willing to hold more at lower prices (and higher yields) than at higher prices (and lower yields). The equilibrium price is at P and yields are at some corresponding, given, level. What is likely to cause the demand curve to shift? Taking long-term influences, first of all, we should expect the demand curve to shift outwards with increasing income and wealth. Other things being equal, we should expect people and firms to wish to maintain the current balance of their portfolios. If portfolios are

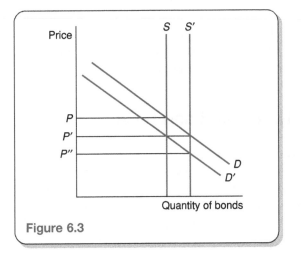

Figure 6.3

growing, then the demand for bonds will expand in proportion. Notice that this means that in the long term the supply curve can also shift to the right without necessarily inducing any rise in yields (fall in prices). Governments have sometimes worried about the interest rate consequences of financing the PSNCR by bond sales which continually add to the stock of bonds. These worries obviously overlook this elementary point that the demand curve is also shifting to the right.

As we have seen, the price that people are prepared to pay for bonds is equivalent to the value that they place upon the income stream that it gives them. For a given coupon and redemption value, eqn 6.7 tells us that this value in turn depends upon the rate of interest at which the coupons and redemption values are discounted. As always, the rate at which we discount is the rate of return that we require from the asset, and this is the rate that we could get on comparable alternative assets. In short, therefore, the price of bonds will vary inversely with interest rates. In our diagrams, the demand curve moves outwards when interest rates fall, and vice versa.

Clearly, if the price of bonds fluctuates in response to interest rates, investors who intend to sell before redemption can make a capital gain or a capital loss. For example, someone holding fifteen-year bonds for a five-year period will find that she has made a loss if long-term interest rates fall over the five-year period. Someone who buys two-year bonds, intending to hold them for six months, will make a capital gain if short-term interest rates fall. The way to make these capital gains (avoid losses) is to buy (sell) just before interest rates change. This, in turn, means buying (selling) whenever an interest rate change is *expected*. If this is true, notice that it is not actual interest rate changes that cause a change in price but only *expectations* of an interest rate change. This explains why bond prices often rise and fall, even when interest rates do not actually change. It also explains why certain events seem to be regularly linked to changes in bond prices. For example, if the latest figures on unemployment or wage settlements suggest that the rate of inflation might be about to increase, bond prices will fall if the market jumps to the conclusion that these signs of inflation are also signs that the central bank may be about to raise interest rates. Alternatively, a sharp appreciation in the external value of the currency might lead markets to expect a cut in interest rates in the near future. If so, the expectation itself will be enough to cause bond prices to rise. We shall look at some more examples in section 6.5 where we shall see (a) how relevant events bring us always back to interest rates and (b) how often our interpretation of relevant events involves having to make an estimate about government thinking and policy.

6.4 Equities: supply, demand and price

In this section we look at how a value can be arrived at for equities or ordinary company shares. In doing this, we shall see that there are many similarities with the valuation of bonds. The first of these is that the market price must be the outcome of the interaction between supply and demand: the current price of a share is that price at which investors are just willing (in the aggregate) to hold the existing stock of shares.

Notice that this immediately introduces another major similarity with bonds; that we treat supply as a *stock*. The current price represents the value that investors place upon the *existing* quantity of shares and these shares may have come into existence recently or long ago. If that valuation changes, then the price will rise but nothing happens to the quantity of shares; likewise a fall in the value that investors place upon them simply changes the market price without changing the quantity. Therefore, as with bonds, we draw the supply curve vertically.

But remember the other points that we made in connection with the supply of bonds. We said that the supply of bonds is not fixed forever. So, if we think about developments in the long run we would probably expect that the economy will grow and with that growth existing firms will expand and new firms will be formed. In both cases, new long-term funds will have to be raised and this will lead to new issues of shares. The stock will expand and the supply curve will shift to the right.

Even in the shorter (let us call it the medium) term, the stock of shares may expand if firms see that this is an attractive way to raise funds. This could happen if other forms of finance become more expensive or if investors become more enthusiastic about share ownership. In the latter case, there is an increase in demand for all shares and so their prices will rise. Look again at Figure 6.2 and the discussion that follows it. In that discussion, we said that if demand increases the price of the bond will rise and, *if nothing else changes*, investors will earn a lower rate of return. Furthermore, we went on to say, this lower rate of return that investors are prepared to accept amounts to a lowering of the cost that a borrower has to pay if she chooses to raise additional funds by issuing new bonds. So it is with shares. When share prices are high (relative to the income they pay), then the cost of equity finance is low, and vice versa. Thus, when stock markets are booming we tend to see more new issues of shares and this will also increase the stock (and shift the supply curve).

Finally, in this comparison with bonds, recall that we said that when the price is stable, the stock to which it belongs is willingly held. There may be people at the margin willing to sell their holdings of the stock, but these are just matched by people wishing to buy. In the aggregate, there is agreement that the current market price represents the correct value for the share. But what does this mean? What leads the market to agree that one particular price is appropriate?

As with bonds, the price of shares is determined by the value that the market places upon a future stream of income. How is that value arrived at?

Like bonds, there is the size of the income payments. But now we start to meet some differences between bonds and equities. With ordinary shares, the income payments will vary depending upon the success of the firm and its dividend policy. Thus the income payments are strictly speaking uncertain and so there is an element of risk which is not present in the case of bonds. A further contrast with bonds is that dividends might reasonably be expected to grow over time, as the firm expands but also as the result of inflation. If the *dividend yield* (dividend ÷ price) is to stay at a normal level, the price of the share itself must be expected to rise. Thus the return from ordinary shares comes from two distinct sources. The first is the current dividend, producing the current dividend yield; the second is the capital growth or capital appreciation. We shall see shortly, in eqn 6.14, how we can disaggregate the total

---

Box 6.4   **The dividend irrelevance theorem**

It seems intuitively obvious that an increase in a share's dividend should make the share more attractive to investors and should result in a rise in its price. Indeed, many financial managers and market analysts work on the basis that this is true and markets do often respond to a cut in a firm's dividend by reducing the price of the share. Furthermore, eqn 6.11 clearly says that if the next dividend is set to zero then $P = 0$.

But it is worth considering whether common sense might be leading us astray. Of course, a firm may fail to pay a dividend because it cannot – its earnings are insufficient. This is indeed bad news and it may well be that the share price should be very low or even virtually zero. However, it is quite possible that a firm may reduce its dividend in order to increase retained earnings so that it can expand its investment in a very productive project. After all, if it did not use retained earnings (and maintained its dividend), it would have to raise the funds in some other form, perhaps a new share issue, and thus spread the wealth represented by the firm more thinly among a greater number of shareholders or lenders. Existing shareholders would have their large dividend (adding to their wealth) but there would be more shares in existence (diluting their wealth). By contrast, accepting the lower dividend reduces shareholder wealth but this is offset because the expansion of the firm raises the value of the shares of the existing shareholders.

What we have discovered here is a form of 'trade-off'. Shareholders may add to their wealth by having large dividends and small increases in the capital value of their shares or small dividends and a rapid growth in capital value. Miller and Modigliani (1961) pointed out that under certain assumptions, paying out earnings as dividends or retaining them to finance new investment were strictly equivalent from the point of view of shareholder wealth and therefore shareholders should be indifferent and the market price should not depend upon dividend payments. What determined the value of a share was the value of the firm and this was nothing more than the productivity of its real assets. As far as share values were concerned it was earnings, or profits, that mattered and these in turn depended upon the firm's success in investing in productive assets.

A formal proof of the *dividend irrelevance theorem* is beyond the scope of this book, though it can be found in almost any textbook on financial management. If you look at eqn 6.14, you can see that the return on a share is clearly split into two parts. Thus it is obviously possible for the dividend to be very low indeed and the total return still to be high provided that g offsets the low dividend yield. Formal proofs revolve around showing that reductions in D as a proportion of earnings lead *systematically* to higher values of g.

---

return into these two elements. This disaggregation is crucial to our understanding of the *dividend irrelevance theorem* (see Box 6.4).

Secondly, the value of the future payments has to be discounted because they lie in the future. Here again we are proceeding as we did with bonds, though we shall see that our choice of an appropriate discount rate is different.

Mathematically, we can express the present value of a share as follows:

$$PV = \frac{D_0}{1+K} + \frac{D_1}{(1+K)^2} + \frac{D_2}{(1+K)^3} + \ldots + \frac{D_n}{(1+K)^{n+1}} \tag{6.9}$$

where $D_0 \ldots D_n$ are the dividend payments in each year and K is the chosen rate at which the future payments are discounted. In equilibrium, the price (P) will be equal to the present value of the future income stream. If we rewrite this as

$$P = \sum_{t=1}^{n} D \times \frac{1}{(1+K)^t} \tag{6.10}$$

then the expression is clearly identical to the one that we had for the valuation of coupon payments from a bond (eqn. 6.3), except that D, the dividend, replaces C, the coupon.

However, we cannot realistically act as though D were fixed. In the first of the two expressions above we could imagine the series $D_0 \ldots D_n$ to be a series of variable dividends. The critical question of course is how we estimate their individual likely values. One possibility might be to assume a steady rate of increase of dividends. Doing this the value becomes

$$P = \frac{D_0}{1+K} + \frac{D_0(1+g)}{(1+K)^2} + \frac{D_0(1+g)^2}{(1+K)^3} + \cdots + \frac{D_0(1+g)^{n-1}}{(1+K)^n} \tag{6.11}$$

where g is the growth rate of dividends. Simplifying, this gives

$$P = \frac{D_0(1+g)}{K-g} \tag{6.12}$$

or

$$P = \frac{D_1}{K-g} \tag{6.13}$$

We can rearrange eqn 6.13 to yield some very useful information.

$$K = \frac{D_1}{P} + g \tag{6.14}$$

Equation 6.14 does two things. Firstly, it shows that K, the rate of discount as we have so far called it, is equal to the dividend yield plus the rate of dividend growth. With some additional assumptions and arithmetic, we could show that the rate of dividend growth is equivalent to the rate of growth of the value of the firm. Provided that the quantity of shares is fixed, then the growth in firm value must be matched by the growth in the value of the shares. What all this means is that K, the (total) rate of return on this share, consists of a dividend yield and capital appreciation. We shall see considerable significance in this later.

Concentrating on the pricing of shares for the moment, eqn 6.13 identifies three variables which appear central to the determination of share values.

The first is the dividend payment. This depends upon the size of the firm's earnings and the policy adopted by its directors towards the retention of earnings for further investment and payments to shareholders.

Secondly, there is the term g. Failing any better information this might be taken to approximate the long-run rate of growth of nominal national income, but it will also be influenced by the decisions and characteristics of the firm itself. It might be in a sector of the economy with high or low growth prospects. The firm might be diversifying from a slow-growth into a high-growth market. It might have recently acquired or lost a dynamic chairperson with a reputation for developing successful firms. It might be a drug company rumoured to be about to make an important breakthrough. All of these, and many more circumstances, will have a significant impact on the growth of future dividends.

Such things affect the projected earnings of individual firms and therefore the value of their shares. Many events, however, can affect the projected earnings of companies in general and if this changes the attractiveness of equities relative to other financial assets for which they are close substitutes, then share prices as a whole will change. One obvious source of such circumstances is government policy. If it is expected that in future the government is likely to restrain the growth in demand in the economy, it will generally be expected that earnings will grow more slowly. The precise manner of demand restraint may affect some classes of shares more than others. A rise in direct taxes might cause shares in retail stores to fall more than shares in banks, for example, but the general movement will be downwards. For this reason, a fall in share prices can be sparked off by figures showing a balance of payments deficit. Alternatively, an anticipated increase in the rate of inflation, foreshadowed by falling unemployment and rising imports for example, may cause a fall if it is believed that the government is bound to take deflationary action.

Thirdly, there is the term K. We know that this is both the required rate of return on the share and the rate at which we discount future dividend payments. In eqn 6.13 we can see that a rise in K will lead to a bigger discounting of future earnings and therefore a lower value for the share. A fall in K, conversely, will produce a rise in price.

In Appendix I: Portfolio theory we explain that the capital asset pricing model (CAPM) tells us that:

the required rate of return on an asset is equal to the risk-free rate plus a fraction (or multiple) of the market risk premium where the fraction (or multiple) is represented by the asset's beta coefficient.

For an asset, A, we express this in eqn A1.6 as

$$\bar{K}_A = K_{rf} + \beta(K_m - K_{rf}) \tag{A1.6}$$

If we think of the required rate of return being made up in this way, we can look systematically at some of the circumstances which will cause changes in its composition. Firstly, of course, interest rates, K_{rf}, may rise or fall. K rises or falls accordingly and share prices move inversely, in a way which is similar to that of bonds. Notice that K_{rf} is common to the determination of all share prices and so the change in price will be general. Alternatively, there could be a change in the market's attitude to risk and the market risk premium, $K_m - K_{rf}$, could rise or fall. Again, share prices will move in the opposite direction and since the market price of risk enters into the determination of all share values, the movement will be general.

In addition to both of these, however, circumstances may arise which lead to a change in an individual firm's β-coefficient. For example, a firm's diversification into new activity, as we said earlier, might be successful in raising the growth of dividends.

But at the same time it may increase the *variability* of earnings. In this case both g and K increase and the effect on the market valuation of the share will depend upon the relative strength of the two developments. In a more straightforward case, a firm with a steady record of dividends from activity overseas may find that the country in which it operates is sliding towards civil unrest. Its dividends may remain unchanged but the market valuation will fall because of the increased risk thought to attach to them. Much more commonly, firms will find their share prices fluctuating as a result of changes in exchange rate risk. In the first half of 2006, the US$ started to fall in value against other major currencies and there was a widespread belief that the trend might accelerate. Many large UK companies with interests in the US found their share prices falling because of this possibility.

What can we now say about the demand for a share? According to the CAPM, the demand for a share will be such that its price will produce the required rate of return, which itself is given in Appendix I (eqn A1.6). Thus, in the expression:

$$K = \frac{D_1}{P} + g$$

for given expected values for D and g, P will adjust to yield the appropriate value of K. We can see this more clearly in eqn 6.13, where we can solve for P, given K, D and g.

$$P = \frac{D_1}{K - g}$$

Figure 6.4 shows all of these influences schematically, for a share which we identify as A. Reading from left to right, it says, firstly, that rational investors decide upon the rate of return which they require. To do this, they take into account the rate they could have on risk-free assets, K_{rf}. They then consider the riskiness of investing in this particular company relative to a fully diversified portfolio of risky assets (shown by β_A). Once they know its riskiness relative to the whole market portfolio, they can then calculate the fraction (or multiple) of the whole market risk premium, $\beta_A(K_m - K_{rf})$, to add to the risk-free rate.

Figure 6.4 The capital asset pricing model

Once they know the rate of return they require, investors will then make a decision about the price which they are prepared to pay for the share. Looking at its recent record, they can see its track record of earnings growth and thus its rate of capital appreciation, g. All that is then necessary is to ensure that the price they pay ensures that the dividend yield, D_1/P, is sufficient when added to g to ensure that the *actual* return, K_A, is equal to the return which they require, for this particular share, in these particular circumstances.

Box 6.5 provides a numerical example.

Box 6.5

Imagine you are considering buying shares in XYZ plc. The firm pays out a constant fraction of earnings as dividends and the dividend payment last year was 25p per share. Earnings have grown at a steady 12 per cent for the last ten years and there is every reason to expect this growth to continue. The firm's β-coefficient is 1.1, the market risk premium is 15 per cent and the current risk-free rate is 5 per cent.

1 Find the equilibrium price of shares in XYZ.

Steps:
(a) Find the required rate of return as follows: $K = 0.05 + 1.1(0.15) = 0.215$ or 21.5%.
(b) Find the expected *next* dividend payment: $D_1 = 25p(1 + 0.12) = 28p$.
(c) Use eqn 6.13 to find the price: $P = 28p \div (0.215 - 0.12) = 28p/0.095 = £2.95$.

2 What would be the likely effect on price if the firm issued a warning that future earnings growth was likely to be only 10 per cent p.a.?

Steps:
(a) In eqn 6.13, g will take the value 0.10 instead of 0.12.
(b) However, if the firm continues its policy of paying a constant fraction of earnings as dividends, dividends will grow only at 10 per cent p.a. and thus D_1 will be $25p(1 + 0.10) = 27.5p$.
(c) The new price will therefore be $27.5p \div (0.215 - 0.10) = 27.5/0.115 = £2.39$.
(d) The effect on price will be $£2.95 - £2.39$, a fall of 56p.

Exercise 6.3 **Equity valuation**

(a) Calculate the market price of an ordinary share whose last dividend was 20p and whose earnings are expected to grow by 15 per cent p.a. for the foreseeable future. The current risk-free rate of interest is 8 per cent while the market risk premium is 10 per cent, and the share has a β-coefficient estimated at 1.2.

(b) Calculate the change in price that would result if the rate of interest rose to 9 per cent, everything else remaining as it was.

(c) Keeping the rate of interest at 9 per cent, what would happen to the price of the share if the market risk premium fell to 9 per cent?

Answers at end of chapter

Obviously the market's valuation of a share involves a large amount of judgement: about the future growth of dividends, about the appropriate risk premium and about future interest rates. It is most unlikely that everyone will make exactly the same judgements. Thus at any time, in the population of potential holders of a given share, there will be those who think its current price just right, some who think it too low and some who think it too high. If we vary the price, we shall vary the proportion of potential holders of the share who will fall into these categories. As the price rises, there will be a steady decrease in the number who think it undervalued. If we lower the price, there will be an increase in the number who think it undervalued. If we now add the rather obvious point that a person will buy the share only if he thinks its present value exceeds or is just equal to its market price, we can see that the number of buyers will vary inversely with the actual price. On this basis we can envisage a demand curve for equities which is downward-sloping like those in Figures 6.1 and 6.2.

In the UK, shares are held overwhelmingly by the institutions we looked at in Chapter 4: life assurance companies, pension funds, unit and investment trusts. Until 1984 the personal sector had for many years been a net seller of equities. However, during the 1980s, the government began a series of 'privatisations' – the conversion of public sector organisations to private firms – and worked hard to encourage households to buy the shares issued with their conversions. Between 1984 and 1987 the number of private shareholders rose from four million to nine million. Following the stock market crash of October 1987 many of these shareholders sold out. As a result, the proportion of total equities owned directly by households is very small and the proportion of shares held by institutions has continued to rise.

The important point to remember, therefore, is that when we talk about willing holders of the existing stock of equities, or about traders of marginal quantities of the existing stock, we are talking about decisions being made by large institutions. Indeed, when we talk about movements in the prices of individual shares (though not when we refer to a general movement in share prices), we may be talking about the decisions of a very few large institutions.

In markets as conventionally analysed, the supply and demand curves represent the preferences of a very large number of individual decision makers. A change in the preferences of any one buyer and seller cannot affect the market; only the combined preferences matter. Plainly this is not true for the equities market, where one or two decisions to buy or sell can have a significant effect upon price.

The terms D, g and K are sometimes referred to as the *fundamentals* of a share's value. Accordingly, changes in the values attached to g and K are referred to as changes in a share's fundamentals. Notice though that the fundamentals are not known with certainty. The values of g and K are estimates. Clearly, therefore, it is changes in those estimates which are responsible for changes in the market's valuation of a share. Of course, a change in estimates may turn out, *ex post*, to have been entirely unwarranted, but provided people believe at the time that the event is going to occur and they act upon that belief, prices will change.

This poses an interesting problem for analysts and managers of funds. Imagine yourself for a moment in such a position. The latest consumer credit figures are due to be published tomorrow. To do the best for your clients, you not only have to try to anticipate whether the figures will be large or small but also to anticipate how others will react. This in turn requires that you anticipate how others *think* the central bank thinks about the connection between consumer credit, interest rates and inflation. You may anticipate that the figures will be large. However, you may personally feel that this has little relevance to future inflation and you may even feel that the central bank is likely to agree with you and leave interest rates unchanged. But that is hardly the point. If general opinion disagrees with you and expects the central bank to raise interest rates if consumer credit figures show a large increase, then prices will fall tomorrow (regardless of what the central bank may do later). Unless you sell today, your clients will make a capital loss. It will be no consolation to you, and certainly no comfort to them, if in a few weeks' time your interpretation of consumer credit growth and inflation turns out to have been superior to that of the market.

6.5 The behaviour of security prices

In this section, we summarise what we have said about the theory of asset pricing as it applies to bonds and to company shares. We then look at how the sorts of events that are regularly reported in the media as causing bond and share prices to rise and fall can be fitted into this theoretical framework. We also take a critical look at the theory and consider whether there might be other forces at work.

According to the theory we have developed in this chapter, security prices change largely as a result of shifts in demand. (Remember that in the short term, supply is fixed.) The demand for securities shifts as people change their view of the value of the income stream which the securities promise to deliver.

Consider bonds first. If we assume that the risk associated with any particular bond is fixed, the major source of changes in valuation is changes in interest rates. The value of the income stream from a bond (with fixed coupons remember) falls when interest rates rise because better rates can be earned elsewhere. Its value rises when interest rates fall and the alternatives are less attractive. We also noted in the last section that people would try to profit from a capital gain (and avoid a capital loss) by *anticipating* interest rate changes. Thus any event which might contain information about the next likely change in interest rates will be seized upon. Investors will buy (or sell) and bond prices will change, regardless of whether interest rates do in fact change. With most government bonds, it is generally safe to assume a constant (and low) level of risk, although there have been cases where governments have had to suspend payment of interest and/or apply for the rescheduling of repayment of principal.

Corporate bonds, however, may easily become more or less risky, depending upon the trading performance of the firms which issued them. This creates the opportunity for credit rating agencies to exploit economies of scale and specialist expertise in order to provide assessments of risk. This service is purchased by issuers of bonds who find that a reputable credit rating enables them to borrow on better terms than would be the case if investors had no guidance. The best known agencies are Moody's,

Standard and Poor's, and Fitch (all based in the US), and IBCA, a UK-based organisation which merged with the French firm, Euronotation, in 1992. Box 6.6 shows the basic categories used by Standard and Poor's (S&P). These are sometimes modified by (+) and (–) to produce a finer series of categories. Bonds rated from AAA to BBB (inclusive) on the S&P scale are sometimes referred to as 'investment grade' bonds since it is only these bonds that professional investment managers are normally prepared to hold. But it is only when we get down to grade D that we are dealing with bonds which are either in default or are likely to be in default. It follows from this that the difference in yield required by the market as we move from one grade to another looks comparatively small, usually less than 30 basis points.

Box 6.6

Standard and Poor's bond credit ratings

Investment grade	Speculative grade
AAA	BB
AA	B
A	CCC
BBB	CC
	C
	C1
	D

What events might indicate future changes in interest rates? In Chapter 3 we saw that the immediate cause of changes in the short-term nominal interest rate were the decisions made by the central bank. For this reason, therefore, anticipating interest changes usually involves studying government priorities and guessing what the bank's likely response will be. Since policy changes over time, what might be a good indicator on one occasion may be less effective years later. In the early 1980s, for example, the UK government paid great attention to a monetary growth rule. Annual targets were set for the rate of expansion of the money stock. Thus, whenever actual growth in the money supply showed signs of breaching the target (as it often did), bond holders would sell in order to avoid the capital loss that they expected to occur when the Bank of England raised interest rates. The selling, of course, meant that bond prices *did* fall. Monetary targets were abandoned in 1985 and in the later 1980s monetary policy followed an exchange rate target. In this period, therefore, bond prices became very sensitive to movements in the exchange rate, falling when the exchange rate fell and vice versa. Since 1992, the target has been the rate of inflation itself. In these circumstances, bond prices are sensitive to any news which suggests a change in the rate of inflation which may itself lead the Bank of England to change interest rates. To make it easier for everyone, financial markets included, to anticipate the Bank's response (to understand its 'reaction function' in the jargon), the Bank now publishes a great deal of information which shows how its decisions are reached. The main sources of this information are the quarterly *Inflation Report* and the minutes of the monthly meeting of the Monetary Policy Committee.

Thus, while we can say that bond prices will change in response to changes in risk (for corporate bonds) and interest rates (all bonds), it is difficult to say what actual events will affect bond prices at all times and in all places. Nonetheless, Box 6.7 shows some events typical of those which influence bond prices.

Box 6.7 — Influences on bond prices

Risk
- The state of the economic cycle (corporates)
- Firm-specific events (corporates)
- State of government finances (gilts)

Interest rates
- Inflation
- Monetary growth
- Exchange rate
- Government borrowing
- Overseas interest rates

Box 6.8 contains a report from the *Financial Times* of 18 May 2006 commenting on the general rise in bond yields in the previous few days. It illustrates a number of points which we have made about the bond market in this chapter. Firstly, and most obviously, since the headline refers to a rise in yields, and we know that prices and yields move inversely, we must expect the report to be talking also about a fall in prices. It does this in the third sentence by saying that the UK gilt market was 'hit' (code for an unexpected event which caused prices to fall). The unexpected event turns out to be evidence that inflationary pressures might be greater than markets had thought and therefore that central banks might start raising interest rates. In the UK, the evidence for this appears to be the fact that a member of the Monetary Policy Committee voted in favour of an interest rate rise at the last meeting (when previously all members had voted for a 'hold' or 'cut'). In the eurozone, the evidence came in the form of data which showed core consumer price inflation rising. Notice that the growing fear of an interest rate rise requires market agents to take a view about central bank policy objectives (low inflation) and the instruments at its disposal for achieving them (interest rates).

Turning now to equities, Figure 6.4 tells us that equity prices will respond to any event which causes a change in the required rate of return or in the level of profits and prospective profit growth that contribute to that return. Compared with government bonds, the range of influences is certainly wider. Government bond prices are generally affected only by economy-wide or 'whole-market' events, which foreshadow interest rate changes, and when such events occur, bond prices move pretty much as a whole together. With corporate bonds there is the possibility of firm-specific events affecting some bonds and not others.

Box 6.8   **Inflation data push up yields**

By Richard Beales in New York, Paul J Davies in London and Daniel Turner in Tokyo.

....

The recent bearish trend resumed for US, European and UK government bond markets yesterday, with prices falling and yields rising across the board after two days of price rallies.

US Treasury yields jumped as the latest data suggested inflation was running higher than expected, raising the odds of further rate rises by the Federal Reserve.

. . . In the UK, the gilt market was hit by news that one member of the Bank of England's interest rate setting committee had voted for an immediate rise at its session two weeks ago.

The minutes of the committee's meeting, when it kept rates unchanged at 4.5 per cent, showed David Walton voted for a quarter-point rise in rates while one other member voted for a cut and the others voted for no change. The news surprised markets and suggested UK rates could rise

sooner than expected if other members begin to swing round to Mr Walton's view.

The yield on the two-year gilt rose 2.3bp to 4.756 per cent, while the yield on the 10 year was 2bp higher at 4.636 per cent.

European government bond prices slumped after data showed core consumer price inflation in the Eurozone ticked up in April and an auction of German 10-year bunds met with a lukewarm reception.

Source: Financial Times, 18 May 2006 **FT**

With equities, though, there is wide scope for firm-specific events and economy-wide ones to play a part. Running through the possibilities outlined in Figure 6.4, we can see first of all that equity prices, like the price of all assets, will respond to changes in interest rates. If the central bank raises rates, for example, the rate available on risk-free assets goes up, and if more can be earned on risk-free assets, the holders of risky shares will want a higher return as well. Share prices will also fall if the equity market as a whole becomes more risk averse and demands a higher premium for any level of risk.

Of all the shocks that occur to equity prices, changes in general attitudes to risk ('risk-aversion'), and therefore the price charged for bearing risk, are perhaps the least frequent. In the UK and US the market risk premium has been fairly stable at around 8 per cent for many years. But major upheavals with uncertain outcomes, such as the Iraq War and its threat to oil supplies, have occasionally seen the required return on equities as a whole increase relative to the return on risk-free assets.

Changes in the riskiness of individual shares result from changes in the firm itself. This may happen because of a change in business plans, especially if the plan involves diversification into a new line of activity. More frequently, it happens as a result of changes in the firm's capital structure. As we have seen, increasing the proportion of debt relative to equity means that profits available for distribution, after interest payments to bondholders, become more variable. Changes in capital structure are likely to cause changes in β.

Changes in dividend payments result from either, or both, changes in the level of profits or earnings, or changes in the 'payout ratio', the fraction of earnings paid out as dividends. Many firms operate a dividend policy which features a stable payout ratio.

In this case, fluctuations in earnings will be reflected directly in dividend payments. Fluctuations in earnings will sometimes be the result of firm-specific events, expensive marketing campaigns which fail to generate the hoped-for additional demand, for example. But they can also occur as the result of changes in general trading conditions. In a slump, for example, most firms will find profits at a standstill or even falling, though even in this case some firms are likely to be more affected than others.

Changes in estimates of the future growth of profits will likewise sometimes involve firm-specific events and sometimes economy- or at least industry-wide trends. On 19 May 2006, for example, when stock markets across the world were coming to the end of a week of considerable volatility and when share prices generally had fallen by around 10 per cent, the price of British Airways shares rose by 9 per cent. This followed news that BA had managed to increase its profits by 21 per cent in a period when many airlines were making a loss as a result of a steep rise in fuel prices. It also announced that it expected its profits to rise more rapidly in 2006/07.

Just to make matters a little more complicated still, it will often be the case that single events will have multiple effects. An obvious example is an increase in interest rates. As we saw above, this will cause the risk-free rate and thus the return on all assets to rise. But for firms, it is likely to depress the rate of profit growth, especially if the firm is making goods which are usually bought on credit. If the firm has a large overdraft, which charges a variable rate of interest, this year's profits after interest will be hit; and if it is sufficiently highly geared that extra interest payments may drive it into bankruptcy, its β-coefficient increases too!

Exercise 6.4 invites you to try to design a box similar to Box 6.7, but showing this time the influences on share prices. On the left-hand side of the box, we have put the immediate determinants of share prices. Remember that what will cause people to buy and sell shares, and their prices to move, will be events which lead people to *expect* a change in one or more of these determinants. What you have to do is to make a list on the right-hand side of the box of the types of event that you think cause people to expect changes in risk, profit, interest rates, etc. We have started the list. You will quickly find that you have a spider's web of lines and arrows!

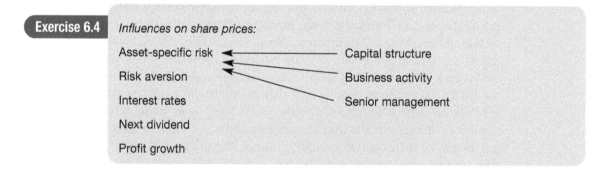

Exercise 6.4

Influences on share prices:

Asset-specific risk   ⟵   Capital structure

Risk aversion   Business activity

Interest rates   Senior management

Next dividend

Profit growth

Valuing shares, or other assets, by discounting their future earnings by a factor which incorporates the current level of interest rates plus a risk premium, may be theoretically correct, but it requires a lot of information and a certain amount of calculation. It could also be said that in many circumstances the effort is unnecessary – we are trying to find out more than we need. The argument here is that the discounting of dividends, using the CAPM, is giving us an *absolute* valuation of an asset. There might be times when this is essential, but what we mainly do with this absolute valuation is to put it alongside other absolute valuations in order to make a comparison. In other words, there are many cases where people have already made the decision to invest in equities (or in bills, gilts, etc. for that matter). The decision that returns are generally satisfactory has already been made. The crucial decision now is whether one should buy shares in *A* or in *B* or in *C*. For this purpose, all one needs is a way of comparing the *relative* values of the shares.

One very common way of making this comparison is to use price-earnings ratios, or *P/E*s. *P* here refers to the price of the share, while *E* stands for earnings (or profit) per share. The logic behind the *P/E* is that the value of any investment (for a given level of risk) lies in its ability to earn 'profits' or 'earnings'. The *P/E* ratio is telling us the price we are being asked to pay for those earnings, and because both numerator and denominator are in 'per-share' terms, we can make instant comparisons across firms of very different size with very different levels of total earnings. In section 6.2.2 we saw that a firm earning profits of 8p per share would have a *P/E* of 50 if the price of its shares was £4. If the share price of another firm with earnings per share of 8p were only £3.20, the *P/E* would be only 40. We would be paying a multiple of only forty times in order to get our earnings of 8p. This applies regardless of the size of firm, number of shares, total profit, etc. In one case we pay £4 for a claim to a stream of payments which at the moment is 8p per year; in the other case we pay only £3.20 for the same claim and this obviously looks a better deal than paying 50.

Clearly, if we are interested only in relative valuations and especially if we restrict our comparisons to, say, one particular industry or type of activity where firms will have similar characteristics, the *P/E* ratio is a quick and simple way of deciding between 'cheap' and 'expensive' firms. On the other hand, the need to restrict comparisons to 'like-for-like' firms is obviously a limitation. In the last section of this chapter we shall see that the *P/E* ratio is part of the standard information about each company share which is published in the financial press. We shall also see that there are substantial variations in *P/E*s, even within one sector of the market where we might expect all firms to have similar characteristics. On the face of it, it appears as though some people are prepared to pay a very high price for earnings per share when they could pay much less for the same earnings per share from similar companies. This is misleading, however, and it raises another limitation of *P/E* ratios. The usual reason for a firm having a high *P/E* ratio, relative to other firms in the same industry, is that the market expects its earnings to grow rapidly in future. Thus, while it might appear that we are paying a very high price for *current* earnings, what we are paying now for the earnings as they might be in two or three years' time might be quite reasonable. To dismiss it as 'too dear' would be a mistake. This complicates the use of *P/E* ratios considerably. If the market is correct in its foresight that high *P/E*s are justified by future rapid growth, there is no obvious reason for preferring high *P/E* shares to low ones (or vice versa), unless we have a special reason for favouring future capital growth over current income. How do we know whether the market is generally correct? The best we can do is probably to look at the recent growth of earnings. If growth has been poor, we might be very careful about buying a share with a high *P/E*, but even then it may be that the market has good grounds for expecting future growth to be rapid. Why else would the market have bid the *P/E* up to high levels?

Before ending our discussion of share price behaviour, it is worth pausing to reflect on the overall picture that we have drawn and to consider how well it reflects the reality which we think we see.

Remember that our theory says that share prices adjust to give the rate of return required by shareholders. The rate of return is central, and determines the price. It is interesting, therefore, that where tradable financial assets are concerned, the dominant discourse concerns *prices* and not rates of return. It is true that newspapers report and commentators discuss deposit accounts and insurance and pension policies in terms of rate of return. But where an asset is tradable, almost all comment relates to its recent, latest and next-most-likely price movement. Rates of return rarely get a mention. Does this signify anything? Maybe not. It may be that everyone discussing asset prices automatically carries the corresponding rate of return in his or her head and talks only of 'price' because it is more convenient than 'rate of return'. On the other hand, it may be that the financial community talks in price terms because they really are more interested in prices than in rates of return. One can see why it could happen. For example, if we go back to our share valuation formula, eqn 6.13, we can see that a price change is part of the rate of return. In the long run, dividends increase (*g* is positive). If dividend yields are not to rise to infinity (i.e. *D/P* is stationary), *P* must also rise. And we all know that investors are in practice very interested in the capital appreciation of shares (eqn 6.14) which may well be a larger part of the total rate of return than the dividend yield.

But we know that prices change because of changes in demand, whatever may be the ultimate cause of the demand shift. A shift in demand causes a change in price just as effectively if it is the outcome of a (false) rumour about a change in interest rates as it does when it is the outcome of an actual change. And once we separate the desire to buy or sell from actual events and link it to *expectations* of events, we open the door to the possibility that demand may shift in response to a wide variety of forces, ranging from those which might be more or less rational in origin to those which have no logical connection with asset values.

Let us think about some possibilities beginning with events which are strictly rational (in the sense we are using here) and then moving towards the more fanciful (but not impossible). An *actual* change in the risk-free rate of interest causes a change in asset prices because it changes the demand for the asset by changing the present value of its future income stream by changing the rate at which we discount that future income stream. Holding the asset when the interest rate changes thus leads to a capital gain (a positive contribution to the overall rate of return) or a capital loss (a negative one). It makes sense, therefore, for investors to try to *anticipate* changes in interest rates. In these circumstances, demand will shift, and prices will change when agents *expect* a change in interest rates. An *expected* event causes an *actual* event. For an individual investor, however, making a capital gain or avoiding a capital loss does not require a belief or expectation that interest rates will change in the very near future. It requires only a belief (or expectation) that other investors believe or expect that interest rates are going to change and that they are going to buy or sell on the strength of that expectation. Indeed, it is not necessary even to believe that other investors believe that interest rates are going to change but only that other investors are going to buy (or sell) *for whatever reason.*

This gives rise to two features of investor behaviour, one of which is certainly observable, while we cannot be sure about the second. The first is the sensitivity of demand (and price) to actual events which might help to predict interest rate changes. This often involves forming an implicit government policy reaction function. For example, if investors know that the government is particularly concerned about the rate of growth of credit and the build-up of inflationary pressures, the announcement of a big rise in bank lending causes asset prices to fall because investors make the connection between an undesirable credit surge and the likelihood of a rise in official interest rates to try to stop it. In small open economies, changes in the balance of trade often cause asset price changes through the same (interest rate) mechanism.

The other feature of investor behaviour which follows from wanting to participate in capital gains and avoid capital losses is the apparent 'herd' behaviour which leads a rising asset price (for example) to go on rising even after any fundamental reason for an increase has ended. A situation where this happens is known as a *bubble.* Sometimes, as with the Big Bull Market in the US, 1928–29, the buying behaviour affects the whole market. The 1987 crash might be an example of herd selling. It is not possible to be absolutely sure whether investor behaviour corresponds to that of a bubble merely by observation. It is always possible to argue that the market's aversion to risk is diminishing or that investors genuinely think that future growth in productivity is going to be much higher than in the past (improvements in the fundamentals). Or, alternatively, that they genuinely think that the fundamentals are getting rapidly worse. The second half of the 1990s saw a steady rise in share prices in the US in particular and in the UK to a lesser extent. Both the Federal Reserve and the Bank of England expressed worries that share prices had risen beyond the level which could be supported by the fundamentals. The reply from the optimists was that economies were entering a phase of low inflation, the like of which had not been seen since before 1939. In these circumstances, firms could expand further and more rapidly than in the past without causing inflation and the rise in interest rates that would cause share prices to fall.

It is hard to believe that fundamentals or even people's perception of the fundamentals of asset values could change so much and so rapidly during some of the great booms and crashes of asset prices. Consider as one example the collapse of share prices by about a third in October 1987. Did the productivity of real capital assets fall by 30 per cent in three days?

A more recent example is the dramatic rise and fall in popularity and value of technology stocks in the course of roughly two years between early 1999 and March 2001 and in particular the group known as the 'dot.coms'. These were firms which, at the time, had earned no profits. There was, strictly speaking, no evidence that they were providing things which people wanted at a price which would justify their production. Nonetheless, these firms attracted large capital flows in the hope that they would eventually meet a genuine demand. Furthermore, as the price of the shares increased, their cost of capital fell. A spectacular example was Lastminute.com which was floated on the London Exchange in March 2000. Its advisers originally expected that each share sold would raise about £2 for the firm. But such was the frenzy of buying of dotcom shares by that stage that, in the few weeks between the issue of the prospectus and the opening of the subscription, the advisers realised that each share could probably be sold for over £3 and raised the price accordingly. Within a year, the shares had lost 80 per cent of their value.

In these circumstances, it is tempting to think that investors are looking after their own short-term self-interest by sticking with the herd. Prices are rising because other people are prepared to pay more. So long as this is the case, we too can increase our wealth by buying. Never mind the fundamentals for the time being. John Maynard Keynes once famously remarked: 'It is not sensible to pay 25 for an investment of which you believe the prospective yield to justify a value of 30, if you also believe that the market will value it at 20 three months hence' (Keynes, 1936, p. 155). Turn this around. There is no sense in avoiding something whose value you think is probably less than £2 if you know that other buyers are going to push the price up to £3 in the very near future. As one fund manager said looking back on the dotcom fiasco: 'You are not paid to sit on your hands while others are making money.' This is the dilemma that faces all fund managers. Their responsibility is to their investing clients and if their investing clients want maximum short-term profit, the manager must follow market sentiment whether or not he or she thinks it soundly based. And the pressures for short-term performance are considerable. Many newspapers run annual league tables of fund performance in which managers are implicitly judged against an index or against other fund managers. If you are a manager, it is no use saying to your clients when you come bottom of the league that your decision not to buy dotcom stocks was correct 'in theory' or 'will be proved right in the long run'. In the long run, your clients will have left and you will have been sacked.

If it *is* true that investors in tradable assets are sometimes buying and selling on the basis of what they expect the price to do in the very near future, rather than on the rate of return offered by the asset, then Figure 6.4 gives a misleading picture. Causalities are reversed. Investors are aiming at a target price for the asset, and the rate of the return becomes the dependent variable. In the world we have just described, buying and selling drives the price, as it always does, to an equilibrium where sell orders match buy orders, but the rate of return, instead of determining this price, is itself determined by it.

Which of the two pictures we have just described is the more accurate is an important issue. The rational determination of prices by the required rate of return is essential if resources are to be allocated efficiently, as we described in section 2.4. We said there that the return to investors was just enough to compensate them for surrendering their ability to purchase real resources plus whatever degree of risk was involved in so doing. The rate of return which they required was the cost of capital. The fact that consumers were ultimately prepared to pay a price for the goods produced by the real capital assets financed by investors indicated that their welfare gain from the goods produced just matched the sacrifice of the providers of finance. No *net* benefits could result to society by changing either the volume of investment or its composition.

This happy situation is not the outcome if people buy assets just because the price is rising (or sell just because the price is falling). In these circumstances the return to investors could settle anywhere, and where it settles the cost of capital also settles. For example, take the case where a company's share price rises on the rumour of some new product development and where, even when the rumour subsides, the price goes on rising because investors are impressed by its recent capital appreciation. Perhaps its price before the rumour was £2 and the dividend payment was 8p per share. The dividend yield was 4 per cent and this was the cost (in terms of dividend per pound raised) of raising new capital by issuing new shares. Suppose that after a few weeks' buying the price settles at £3. If the firm now decides to raise new capital by issuing new shares, the cost (in dividend per pound raised) is now 8/300 or 2.66 per cent. In the circumstances, the firm may be encouraged to expand, though there is no indication that the benefits to society from the output that it produces have increased. Furthermore, the firm's enhanced share price makes it easier for it to make a bid for other firms (by issuing some of its own shares to shareholders of the target firm). There are resource allocation arguments in favour of takeovers. For example, a poorly performing firm, if correctly valued, will have a low share price and will be a target for more efficient firms which will bring their more efficient management to the poorly performing firm. But where a firm is valued as the result of a bubble, its price is no longer an indication of superior performance. We cannot then expect that benefits will follow if it takes over a firm which is priced more cheaply – but correctly.

6.6 Reading the financial press

Bond prices and yields are reported in the *Financial Times* on the page headed 'Market Data'. This page has tables which show current prices and yields and recent price *changes* for UK government bonds, corporate bonds, bonds issued in 'emerging markets', bond futures and options, and 'benchmark bonds' from a variety of countries. Benchmark bonds are bonds of a specified maturity selected from the whole range of government bonds which enable markets to make international comparisons of yields. All developed countries have a ten-year benchmark bond and many also have a five-, fifteen- and twenty-year bond. Commentary on recent developments in bond prices appears on the 'Capital Markets and Commodities' pages. Box 6.8 (earlier) and Box 6.9 contain an example of commentary. Box 6.10 reproduces the table containing a selection of UK government bond data from the *Financial Times* of Thursday 18 May 2006. (On weekdays, the *FT* publishes information for only a subset of bonds; the full list appears on a Saturday.)

Box 6.9   Share prices fall

Interest rate concerns biggest one-day decline for three years

The London market resumed its downward trend yesterday, registering its biggest one-day percentage loss since March 2003, as the spectre of rising interest rates returned to haunt investors.

After a bright opening, leading shares went into reverse following the release of stronger than expected US consumer price data, which stoked fears of further rate rises by the Federal Reserve.

Mining and oil stocks, which have been the best performers in the year to date, took the brunt of yesterday's selling. The FTSE-100 finished down 170.7 points, or 2.9 per cent, at 5,675.5 – the first time it has closed below 5,700 since January and its largest one-day points fall since September 2002. The blue-chip index is now 7.5 per cent below the five-and-a-half year high of 6,132.7 recorded on April 21.

Source: Financial Times, 18 May 2006

Box 6.10   UK government bond prices and yields

UK GILTS – cash market   www.ft.com/gilts

	Price £	Red Yield	.........Change in Yield......... Day	Week	Month	Year	...52 week... High	Low	Amnt £m
Tr 7.5pc '06	101.51	4.70	+0.04	+0.04	+0.21	+0.40	104.77	101.51	12,394
Tr 4.5pc '07	99.84	4.70	+0.05	+0.05	+0.24	+0.42	100.78	99.83	12,071
Tr 5pc '08	100.37	4.78	+0.06	+0.07	+0.27	+0.51	102.49	100.34	14,928
Tr 4pc '09	97.83	4.84	+0.07	+0.06	+0.28	+0.55	99.91	97.78	16,974
Tr 4.75pc '10	99.75	4.82	+0.07	+0.05	+0.27	+0.52	103.05	99.66	12,774
Cn 9pc Ln '11	118.94	4.80	+0.08	+0.04	+0.25	+0.50	125.94	118.82	5,664
Tr 5pc '12	101.11	4.78	+0.08	+0.04	+0.24	+0.45	105.27	100.95	14,009
Tr 8pc '13	119.98	4.75	+0.08	+0.03	+0.21	+0.41	126.66	119.77	6,489
Tr 5pc '14	101.79	4.74	+0.08	+0.02	+0.19	+0.39	107.25	101.54	13,699
Tr 4.75pc '15	100.28	4.71	+0.08	+0.01	+0.19	+0.36	106.18	99.99	0
Tr 4pc '16	94.36	4.70	+0.09	+0.01	+0.18	+0.58	99.16	94.05	3,000
Tr 4.75pc '20	101.16	4.64	+0.09	–	+0.17	+0.26	109.01	100.73	10,743
Tr 8pc '21	136.09	4.64	+0.09	–	+0.15	+0.27	146.62	135.52	17,573
Tr 5pc '25	106.46	4.49	+0.08	−0.03	+0.12	+0.13	115.82	105.71	16,188
Tr 6pc '28	122.65	4.41	+0.09	−0.04	+0.09	+0.08	134.07	121.70	12,340
Tr 4.25pc '32	98.98	4.32	+0.09	−0.06	+0.06	−0.01	109.01	97.49	17,326
Tr 4.25pc '36	99.87	4.26	+0.09	−0.07	+0.04	−0.06	110.42	97.39	15,668
Tr 4.75pc '38	109.14	4.23	+0.09	−0.08	+0.03	−0.08	120.90	106.14	14,958
Tr 4.25pc '55	104.18	4.05	+0.09	−0.09	–	−0.16	116.31	98.89	11,602
War Ln 3.5pc	81.17	4.31	+0.08	−0.07	+0.04	−0.05	93.90	78.63	1,939

xd Ex dividend. Closing mid-prices are shown in pounds per £100 nominal of stock. Red yield: Gross redemption yield. This table shows the gilt benchmarks & the non-rump undated stocks. A longer list appears on Mondays & the full list on Saturdays, and can be found daily on ft.com/bonds&rates.

Source: Debt Management Office (DMO)

Source: Financial Times, 18 May 2006

Notice first of all some of the characteristics of bonds that we referred to earlier in this chapter. The title of each bond contains the coupon rate and the redemption date. The bonds are listed in ascending order of residual maturity. Notice also:

- The first column shows the current price of the bond (this is the mid-point in the spread between the bid and offer prices quoted by market makers). Remember that quoted prices are 'clean' prices – they do not include interest which has accrued on the bond since the last coupon payment. In most cases, buyers will have to hand over more than the price quoted in the table. The difference will be the interest due to the seller for the period during which he held the bond since the last coupon payment.

- The second column shows the redemption yield calculated on the basis of the price shown in the first column. The next four columns show the change in the redemption yield calculated over various periods. If we just look at the change on the day, we can see, for example, that the yield on Treasury 4.75% 2020, has increased by 0.09. In fact, the redemption yield rose on all bonds in the list. From our earlier discussion about the inverse relationship between prices and yields we can use this information to conclude that all bond prices must have fallen in trading on 17 May – and this is entirely consistent with the commentary that we read in Box 6.8.

- The next two columns show the highest and lowest price at which the bond has traded over the last year. This gives us a range against which to judge the present market price.

- The final column is a recent innovation and shows the total market value outstanding of each bond issue. So, for example, we can see that there are £10,743m-worth of Treasury 4.75% 2020 available in the market. (Notice that the units of measurements are £m, so there are over £10.7bn-worth of our stock outstanding.)

Box 6.11 shows similar information for ordinary shares. This is an extract from the pages headed 'London Share Service' and contains details of the shares of companies whose main business is food and drug retailing. The table appeared on 18 May 2006.
Notice:

- The first column shows the current price (as with bonds this is the mid-price from the bid-offer spread).

- The second column shows the change in price that occurred during trading on 17 May.

- The next two columns show the highest and lowest price achieved during the last year.

- The fifth column shows the dividend yield. This is the last dividend payment divided by the current share price.

- The penultimate column shows the *P/E* ratio and confirms what we said in the last section, namely that *P/E* ratios can vary widely even between companies in the same sector.

Box 6.11	**UK retailers' share prices**

FOOD & DRUG RETAILERS

Allnc UniChem	914	−19	944	726.50	2.2	16.4	1,143
Dairy Fm S	187.62xd	−3.18	224.77	147.39	2.4	23.5	397
Euro HomeRetail ...... †	53.50	+2	131	41.50	6.4	6.7	45
Greggs	£34.75xd	−1.13	£49.66	£34.75	3.0	12.1	108
JardnMt S	964.60xd	−15.90	£11.08	874.05	5.0	5.2	137
Morrison .... q	189.25xd	−3	218.35	158.25	1.9	−	24,325
Sainsbry .... ♣q	329.50	−17	360	270	2.3	55.6	41,007
Tesco .... ⊞♣q	318.50xd	−1.25	351	292	2.7	15.8	87,849
Thorntns	114.50	+0.50	177.50	112	6.0	13.4	47
UtdDrug	263.75xd	+3.50	274.86	207.83	1.5	22.1	112

Source: Financial Times, 18 May 2006

- Unlike bonds, the share price tables show the volume (in 000s) of shares actually traded during the previous day's session (see the final column). The entry for Tesco shows a turnover of nearly 88m shares.

The *Financial Times*'s London Share Service provides vital information about the shares of individual companies and also, therefore, about shares as a whole. If we wanted to know about the behaviour of share prices in general, because we were making a choice between investing in shares and investing in bonds, for example, we could scan the columns and see how shares as a whole were performing. However, this is neither convenient nor very accurate. A quick scan might tell us that share prices generally rose yesterday, but how could we tell by how much? In order to provide a general but fairly accurate view of how the market is behaving, the *Financial Times* (often in association with the Institute of Actuaries) publishes a number of share price indices.

The best known index of general share price movements in the UK is the *Financial Times*-Stock Exchange 100 Share Index or 'Footsie' for short. The 100 companies which make up the index are roughly the 100 largest firms, by capitalisation, in the UK. The capitalisation of a company is found by multiplying the number of shares in issue by their market price. We say 'roughly' because a firm will not be included, however large it is, if its shares never change hands or if it is expected that no dividend will be paid. Capitalisation depends partly on the price of shares, and these prices fluctuate: it follows that the 100 largest companies will change from time to time. The constituents of the Footsie are revised every quarter, though to avoid adding and removing the same firms every three months, as they hover around the critical value, the index committee employs a filter. The composition of the index will not normally change until a 'new' firm rises to 90th in the size ranking *and* a firm currently in the index drops to 110th in the list.

The basic principles behind the construction of a share price index are set out in Box 6.12. Obviously, keeping an index up to date involves frequent recalculation, though the effort involved has diminished with computerisation. The FTSE-100 index was established in 1984 because traders wanted a 'real-time' index which could be used for pricing equity-related contracts in futures and options markets. A real-time index is one which is recalculated (and published) *every time* the price of one of its component shares changes. This means, obviously, that the index may change many times during a trading session (even though it may finish at exactly the same level at which it started). Basing the index upon 100 shares was thought to be a reasonable compromise between the demands for the widest coverage and the desire for speed in continuous recalculation. While the FTSE-100 is recalculated every minute of the day, the FT-Actuaries All Share Index (of more than 750 shares) is recalculated only once a day.

Box 6.12

Calculating a share price index

We have firstly to decide whether our index is to be based upon the *population* of all listed firms (as with the FT-Actuaries All Share Index) or upon a *sample* of firms. The latter, being smaller, is quicker to calculate and thus easier to keep up to date. If we decide upon a sample, we have to select a subset whose behaviour we think is likely to be representative of the larger population of firms we are interested in. This might be the 100 largest (as with the FTSE-100).

The next step is to decide upon a *base date* and a *base value* to which all subsequent values of the index can be related. For the FTSE-100 the base date is February 1984 (when the index began) and its base value is 1,000 (chosen in preference to 100 to reduce the need for fractions).

The third step involves calculating the value of shares in the index at the base date and converting that value to 1,000. If we denote each of our 100 firms by i, and let P and N stand for the number and market price of its shares respectively, then we can find the market capitalisation of each firm, at any time, simply as $(P_i \times N_i)$. Letting 0 stand for the values in the base year and remembering that Σ stands for 'sum of', the value of the index in the base year, I_0, will be:

$$I_0 = \frac{\Sigma(P_{i0} \times N_{i0})}{\Sigma(P_{i0} \times N_{i0})} \times 1,000$$

At any future time, 1,2,3 . . . , the value of our companies can be compared with their value in the base period simply by expressing their new value in a ratio to the base value and multiplying by 1,000. If we want a value for the index in period 3, for example, we recalculate as follows:

$$I_3 = \frac{\Sigma(P_{i3} \times N_{i0})}{\Sigma(P_{i0} \times N_{i0})} \times 1,000$$

As we explain in the text, our sample may have to change over time, and we shall also have to make further adjustments if firms in the sample make new share issues after they join the index.

The advantage of an index is that it enables us to make reasonably precise statements about movements in the whole market over a period of time. We need, however, to be careful in the way we interpret movements in an index number. As we have said several times, we would expect share prices to increase over time, and this will be reflected in any index of share prices. During May 2003, for example, the FTSE-100 varied around the 4,000 level. In April 2006 it had risen to over 6,000. Movements in the index are often reported as absolute numbers. In Box 6.9, for example, the market report says that the FTSE-100 fell sharply on 17 May 2006, by over 170 points. But it also converts this to a percentage rate of decline (2.9 per cent) so that we can put the size of the fall into context. This is a reminder that we should always be careful in our interpretation of *absolute* movements in the value of the index. It is not so much the number of points that matters but the number of points as a percentage *of the starting level*. In June 1989 the FTSE-100 stood at 2,147. The same fall of 170 points would then have been equivalent to 8 per cent. Beware of newspaper headlines that scream 'FTSE rises (or falls) by 300 points – largest movement since it began' – 300 on 4,000 is very different from 300 on 10,000.

6.7 Summary

The capital markets are used by both firms and governments to raise funds for long-term use, though most investment by firms is financed by retained profits. Firms can issue corporate bonds and various types of shares, while governments issue bonds. Ordinary company shares entitle their holders to a share of the firm's profits and thus pay variable dividends. They should also experience capital growth over time. Bonds usually pay a fixed rate of interest at pre-determined intervals. Both bonds and shares are traded on a stock exchange and their price fluctuates in response to supply and demand. In the short run the supply of both is fixed and price fluctuations are therefore the result of changes in demand. Our conventional theory says that the price people are willing to pay for such securities reflects the value which they place upon the future income from those securities, given the level of risk associated with them. The value placed upon the future income depends upon what can be earned elsewhere and thus varies with changes in interest rates. In the case of shares, the value placed on the income depends upon the income itself, which can change as a result of the firm's profitability.

In practice, share and bond prices are affected by a wide range of influences whose relevance is that they lead investors to *expect* changes in interest rates, risk or profits.

Questions for discussion

1 What are the advantages to (a) lenders and (b) borrowers of an active 'secondary' market for securities?

2 Why does the calculation of a 'present value' of a security involve discounting?

3 Which of the following would be likely to show the greatest short-run price volatility: a short-dated bond, a long-dated bond, a share in a microelectronics company? Explain your choice.

4 When market interest rates are 10 per cent, what relationship would you expect between the price and redemption yields of two 8 per cent bonds, one maturing in three years, the other maturing in ten years?

5 Give two reasons why institutions like banks prefer to hold short-dated rather than long-dated bonds.

6 Distinguish between a 'quote-driven' market and an 'order-driven' market.

7 You are advising a friend who is considering selling some of her shares in Wyndham Wines plc. Their current price is £2.50. They have a β-coefficient of 1.1 and the firm has shown a steady growth in earnings of 6 per cent p.a. in recent years. The current risk-free rate is 5 per cent p.a. while the market risk premium is 10 per cent. The last dividend payment was 20p. What advice would you give and why?

8 You aim to reduce the *capital* risk of your portfolio by increasing your holdings of government bonds. Given a choice between 'Treasury 5%, 2020' and 'Exchequer 12%, 2007', which would you choose and why?

9 Explain the terms: dirty price, clean price, accrued interest, interest yield, redemption yield.

10 Explain the terms: market capitalisation, dividend yield, P/E ratio.

Further reading

Bank of England, 'Upgrading the Central Gilts Office', *Bank of England Quarterly Bulletin*, 37 (4), February 1998

D Blake, *Financial Market Analysis* (London: McGraw-Hill, 2e, 2000) chs. 5 and 6

M Buckle and J Thompson, *The UK Financial System* (Manchester: Manchester UP, 4e, 2004) chs. 8 and 9

D Cobham (ed) *Markets and Dealers: The Economics of the London Financial Markets* (London: Longman, 1992)

P G A Howells and K Bain, *The Economics of Money, Banking and Finance: A European Text* (Harlow: Financial Times Prentice Hall, 3e, 2005) chs. 16 and 17

J M Keynes, *The General Theory of Employment, Interest and Money* (London: Macmillan, 1936)

M Livingston, *Money and Financial Markets* (Oxford: Blackwell, 3e, 1996) chs. 10 and 19

M H Miller and F Modigliani, 'Dividend policy, growth and the valuation of shares', *Journal of Business*, 34, 1961, pp. 411–33

K Pilbeam, *Finance and Financial Markets* (London: Macmillan, 2e, 2005) chs. 6 and 9

R Vaitilingam, *The Financial Times Guide to Using the Financial Pages* (Harlow: Pearson Education, 4e, 1996)

www.dmo.gov.uk

www.londonstockexchange.com

http://en.wikipedia.org/wiki/Financial_market

Answers to exercises

6.1 (a) £54.35, (b) £156.25.

6.2 (a) £108.47, (b) £96.08.

6.3 (a) £4.60, (b) £3.83, (c) £4.79.

CHAPTER 7

Interest rates

Objectives

What you will learn in this chapter:

- The relationship between nominal and real rates of interest
- The loanable funds theory of real interest rates and its adaptation to deal with nominal interest rates
- The liquidity preference theory of interest rates and how it relates to the loanable funds approach
- How the monetary authorities strongly influence the general level of interest rates in the economy
- The meaning of the term structure of interest rates and the various theories used to explain the term structure

We have seen many times that an interest rate is one form of yield on financial instruments – that is, it is a rate of return paid by a borrower of funds to a lender of them. We can also think of an interest rate as a price paid by a borrower for a service, the right to make use of funds for a specified period. We shall here be looking at two questions:

(a) What determines the average rate of interest in an economy? and

(b) Why do interest rates differ on loans of different types and different lengths – that is, what factors influence the structure of interest rates in an economy?

Of course, interest rates also vary depending on whether you are borrowing or lending. For example, there is a spread between the interest rate at which banks are prepared to lend (the offer rate) and the rate they are willing to pay to attract deposits (the bid rate). There is also a spread between selling and buying rates in international money markets. For example, the *Financial Times* of 25 May 2006 quoted the interest rate on short-term sterling in international currency markets as $4^5/_8$ per cent (the offer rate) to $4^1/_2$ per cent (the bid rate). If we wish to quote a single interest rate in such a case, we can specify that we are referring to the offer rate or the bid rate – as in the distinction between LIBOR (the London Interbank Offered Rate) and LIBID (the London Interbank Bid Rate). Alternatively, we can take the mid-point between the offer and bid rates. Where the *Financial Times* reports a single market interest rate it gives the mid-point between the Offer and Bid rates. In our example above, the mid-point is $4^9/_{16}$ (4.56) per cent.

This spread between offer and bid rates covers the administrative costs of the financial intermediaries and provides profit for them. The spread is itself subject to change and is likely to be smaller the greater the degree of competition among financial institutions. In the UK interest rates example above, the spread is small ($^1/_8$ per cent) because there is considerable competition in short-term international money markets. The spread between the rates at which banks borrow and lend to their retail customers is generally a good deal greater. This spread also reflects the degree of default risk that lenders feel they are facing in making loans since the lending rate (offer rate) will always include a risk *premium*.

> **Risk premium:** An addition to the interest rate demanded by a lender to take into account the risk that the borrower might default on the loan entirely or may not repay on time (default risk).

In this chapter, we look first at another important distinction in the expression of interest rates – that between nominal and real rates of interest. We then go on to consider the principal theories of the determination of the interest rate in an economy. We begin with the well-established loanable funds theory of interest rates. We later introduce Keynes's liquidity preference theory, comparing and contrasting this with the loanable funds approach. The second half of the chapter investigates the structure of interest rates, notably the term structure and the yield curve, which illustrates the term structure. The chapter concludes with an examination of theories seeking to explain the different possible shapes of the yield curve.

> **The interest rate structure:** Describes the relationships between the various rates of interest payable in an economy on loans of different lengths (terms) or of different degrees of risk.

7.1 The rate of interest

Economists talk about *the* rate of interest. This assumes that there is some particular interest rate that can be taken as representative of all interest rates in an economy. The rate chosen as the representative rate will vary depending on the question being considered. Sometimes, for example, the discount rate on treasury bills will be taken as representative. At other times the rate of interest on new local authority debt, the base interest rate of the retail banks, or a short-term money market rate such as LIBOR might be used. No matter which rate is chosen, it is implied that the interest rate structure is stable and that all interest rates in the economy are likely to move in the same direction. If this is true, we should be able to explain what determines interest rates in general. Before going on to look at this question, however, we need to distinguish between nominal and real interest rates.

The rates of interest quoted by financial institutions are nominal rates, allowing calculation of the amounts of money to be received as interest by lenders or paid by borrowers. This is clearly of immediate interest to borrowers and lenders. However, it is equally important to them to know how these amounts relate to their existing or likely future income and to the prices of goods and services. That is, a borrower wishes to know the opportunity cost of borrowing – how many goods and services she must forgo in order to pay the interest on a loan.

Consider the position of someone who takes out a £50,000 mortgage on a house over 25 years at a fixed nominal rate of interest of, say, 6 per cent. Assume further that the annual gross income of the borrower is £20,000. In the first year of the loan, interest on the £50,000 debt will amount to £3,000 – 15 per cent of the borrower's annual gross income. Assume, however, that the economy is experiencing an annual rate of inflation of 2.5 per cent and that the borrower's gross annual income rises in line with inflation. That is, the real value of the borrower's income has not changed – he is able to buy the same quantity of goods and services as before. However, the loan repayments remain the same in money terms and make up a smaller and smaller proportion of the borrower's income. Thus, the real cost of the interest payments declines over time. Therefore we can speak of the *real rate of interest* – the rate of interest adjusted to take into account the rate of inflation.

In this example, the real rate of return to the lender is also falling over time – the interest received would, in each successive year, buy fewer and fewer goods and services because of the existence of inflation. It follows that lenders attempt to set interest rates to take into account the expected rate of inflation over the period of a loan. If lenders cannot be confident about the real rate of return they are likely to receive, they will be willing to lend at fixed rates of interest for short periods only. At the end of the loan period, the borrower might then be able to continue the loan, requiring it to be 'rolled over' at a newly set rate of interest, which can reflect any changes in the expected rate of inflation. Alternatively, lenders can set a floating rate of interest that is automatically adjusted in line with changes in the rate of inflation.

> **Real interest rate:** The nominal rate of interest minus the expected rate of inflation. It is a measure of the anticipated opportunity cost of borrowing in terms of goods and services forgone.

As we have suggested above, it is the expected rate of inflation over the period of a loan that is of particular importance, rather than the present rate of inflation. Consider a simple example. Assume that a bank is willing to make a loan to you of £1,000 for one year at a real rate of interest of 3 per cent. This means that at the end of the year the bank expects to receive back £1,030 of purchasing power at current prices. However, if the bank expects a 10 per cent rate of inflation over the next twelve months, it will want £1,133 back (10 per cent above £1,030). The interest rate required to produce this sum would be 13.3 per cent.

This can be formalised as follows:

$$i = (1 + r)(1 + \dot{P}^e) - 1 \tag{7.1}$$

where i is the nominal rate of interest, r is the real rate of interest and $\dot{P}^e$ is the expected rate of inflation (both expressed in decimals). In our example above, we would have

$$i = (1 + 0.03)(1 + 0.1) - 1$$
$$= (1.03)(1.1) - 1$$
$$= 1.133 - 1$$
$$= 0.133 \text{ or } 13.3 \text{ per cent}$$

For most purposes, we can use the simpler, although less accurate, formula

$$i = r + \dot{P}^e \tag{7.2}$$

In our example, this would give us 3 per cent plus 10 per cent = 13 per cent. Expressed the other way around eqn 7.2 becomes

$$r = i - \dot{P}^e \tag{7.3}$$

If we next assume that r is stable over time, we arrive at what is widely known as the *Fisher effect*, after the American economist Irving Fisher. This suggests that changes in short-term interest rates occur principally because of changes in the expected rate of inflation. If we go further and assume that expectations held by market agents about the rate of inflation are broadly correct, the principal reason for changes in interest rates becomes changes in the current rate of inflation. We could, in that case, write:

$$r = i - \dot{P} \tag{7.4}$$

We are implying here that borrowers and lenders think entirely in real terms.

This leaves us to consider the factors that determine real rates of interest. The central theoretical explanation of real interest rates is known as the loanable funds theory.

7.2 The loanable funds theory of real interest rates

According to the loanable funds theory, economic agents seek to make the best use of the resources available to them over their lifetimes. One way of increasing future real income might be to borrow funds now in order to take advantage of investment opportunities in the economy. This would work only if the rate of return available from investment were greater than the cost of borrowing. Thus, borrowers should not be willing to pay a higher real rate of interest than the real rate of return available on capital. In a perfect market this is equal to the marginal productivity of capital – the addition to output that results from a one-unit addition to capital, on the assumption that nothing else changes. This is influenced by factors such as the rate of invention and innovation of new products and processes, improvements in the quality of the workforce, and the ability to reorganise the economy to make better use of scarce resources.

Savers, on the other hand, are able to increase their future consumption levels by forgoing some consumption in the present and lending funds to investors. We start by assuming that consumers would, other things being equal, prefer to consume all of their income in the present. They are prepared to save and to lend only if there is a promise of a real rate of return on their savings that will allow them to consume more in the future than they would otherwise be able to do. The real rate of return lenders demand thus depends on how much they feel they lose by postponing part of their consumption. Thus, the rate of interest is the reward for waiting – that is, for being willing to delay some of the satisfaction to be obtained from consumption. The extent to which people are willing to postpone consumption depends upon their time preference.

> **Time preference:** Describes the extent to which a person is willing to give up the satisfaction obtained from present consumption in return for increased consumption in the future.

The term 'loanable funds' simply refers to the sums of money offered for lending and demanded by consumers and investors during a given period. The interest rate in the model is determined by the interaction between potential borrowers and potential savers. We need to explain, however, why we might expect the real rate of interest in a country to remain relatively stable over time as Irving Fisher assumed it would.

> **Loanable funds:** The funds borrowed and lent in an economy during a specified period of time – the flow of money from surplus to deficit units in the economy.

The principal demands for loanable funds come from firms undertaking new and replacement investment, including the building up of stocks, and from consumers wishing to spend beyond their current disposable income. The current savings of households (the difference between disposable income and planned current consumption) and the retained profits of firms are the principal sources of supply of loanable funds.

This can all be shown in the conventional way in a supply and demand diagram. Figure 7.1 follows the usual procedure of putting nominal interest rates on the vertical axis. However, we assume for the moment that there is no inflation in the economy and, hence, there is no distinction between nominal and real interest rates. In Figure 7.1, the supply curve slopes up to the right – as interest rates rise, people become more willing to save and to lend because doing so offers increasing levels of future consumption in exchange for the present consumption foregone. That is, *ceteris paribus*, current savings increase as interest rates rise. The demand curve slopes down to the right because it is assumed that additions to capital (net investment),

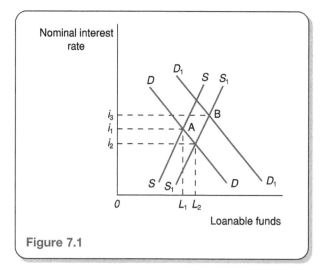

Figure 7.1

with nothing else changing, cause the marginal productivity of capital to fall (there are diminishing returns to capital). Since firms continue to invest only so long as the marginal product of capital is above the interest rate paid on loans, the demand for loanable funds is greater at lower rates of interest. The equilibrium rate of interest is then given by the intersection of the demand and supply curves.

Interest rates are not likely to change frequently in this model because the under-lying influences on the behaviour of borrowers and lenders do not change very often and hence the savings and investment curves do not shift very often. Savings at each interest rate are determined by the average degree of time preference in the economy and by the choices people make over their lifetimes between goods and leisure (that is, by their willingness to engage in market work). These are not subject to frequent change. This is true also of investment. It, remember, depends on the relationship between interest rates and the marginal product of capital. The productivity of capital, in turn, depends on the quantity and quality of a country's factors of production (capital, labour and natural resources). These change but do so, for the most part, fairly slowly and consistently over time.

We can, thus, easily explain the view that real interest rates in a country should not be expected to change greatly over time. We can also easily see why real interest rates might differ from one country to another – differences in time preferences among populations, in real income levels, or in the quantity or quality of factors of production. Of course, if capital were perfectly mobile internationally (it moved freely among countries), differences in real interest rates would not persist since funds would move from those countries where real interest rates were low to high real interest rate countries. As this happened, interest rates would come down in the high interest rate countries and rise in the low interest rate ones. Funds would continue to flow until real interest rates were the same everywhere. In practice, there are many inter-ferences with the mobility of capital and differences in real interest rates persist.

The biggest differences in real interest rates are likely to be between rich and poor countries. In poor countries, real incomes and hence domestic savings are low.

At the same time, the lack of capital in these countries means that the marginal product of capital is likely to be high. Thus, we have a high demand for capital and a low supply of domestic savings. Real interest rates are high. The reverse is true for rich countries.

The differences persist because capital does not flow at all freely from rich to poor countries. Capital is very mobile internationally only among developed countries. There are many barriers to the movement of capital to developing countries, particularly to the poorest of them. These include lack of information and the many risks that investors face. Exchange rate risk is clearly important when we are discussing the movement of capital from one country to another. This is the risk that the value of the currency of the country to which capital is being exported will fall, resulting in a capital loss when the owner of the capital later converts the funds back into his own currency. It follows that interest rates in countries with currencies thought likely to lose value over time include an exchange risk premium.

In addition to facing exchange rate risk, an investor may well fear default risk much more in a foreign country than in his own economy. This may simply reflect a lack of information about the degree of risk in foreign countries. On the other hand, default risk may objectively be much higher in developing countries that are constantly short of foreign currency and have a history of unstable governments. Firms find it harder to plan under such circumstances and may have to deal with frequent changes in regulations and taxes as well as rates of exchange.

Default risk refers specifically to the failure of the borrower to repay a loan. Risk may also arise from the actions of governments. For instance, governments may prevent firms from taking funds out of the country in foreign exchange. There have also been many examples of governments declaring a moratorium on the payment of interest on loans or entering into agreements with creditors to reschedule loans so that they are paid back over a much longer period than in the original agreement. These types of risk are referred to as *sovereign risk* or *country risk*. Whatever the basis for this increased risk, it is easy to see why the risk premium might vary from one country to another. Consequently, real interest rates might vary greatly among countries.

It is even possible that mobile capital moves in the wrong direction – that it moves to countries where rates of return are low but secure, causing differences in real interest rates among countries to widen rather than to narrow as capital becomes more mobile.

7.2.1 Loanable funds and nominal interest rates

Let us next allow for the existence of inflation and the need to distinguish between nominal and real interest rates. Following the loanable funds approach, we continue to assume that people think in real terms. Now, however, the real value of the financial assets they hold changes with the rate of inflation. It becomes important for people to be able to move quickly from one form of asset to another in order to protect the real value of the assets they hold. To do this, they need to hold part of their assets in a liquid form. Thus, some borrowing takes place to allow the building up of liquid reserves.

At first glance, this seems odd since the rate of interest received on such reserves is bound to be less than that paid on loans. It is, however, a common phenomenon. For example, many households with mortgages maintain liquid reserves – liquidity has a value in itself and people are prepared to pay the spread between borrowing and lending rates of interest in order to retain a degree of liquidity (see section 1.3.3). It follows that the supply of loanable funds includes any rundown in existing liquid reserves as well as the current savings of households and the retained profits of firms. We also must now allow for the net creation of new money by banks since the fractional reserve banking system greatly increases the ability of banks to lend.

For the economy as a whole, we can net out some items, leaving us with:

Demand for loanable funds = net investment + net additions to liquid reserves

Supply of loanable funds = net savings + increase in the money supply

We return next to Figure 7.1. Now, however, we allow for the possibility of inflation and so the nominal interest rate shown on the axis might not be the same as the real rate of interest. We assume that the lines *DD* and *SS* are the demand and supply curves when inflation is zero. Consider, then, what happens when the money supply increases, *ceteris paribus*. This adds to the supply of loanable funds, the supply curve moves down to S_1S_1. However, in the set of models of which loanable funds is a part, the increase in the money supply ultimately only causes inflation – it does not cause an increase in output and employment. As prices rise, users of loanable funds need to borrow more to buy the same quantities of capital and consumer goods as before. The demand curve in Figure 7.1 shifts up to the right. We finish at point B, with an equilibrium interest rate at i_3 (equal to i_1 + the rate of inflation). The increase in the money supply causes the nominal interest rate to rise but only because of the inflation it has caused. This is in accordance with the Fisher effect – lenders demand higher nominal rates of interest to preserve the original real rate of interest and to take inflation into account.

The real interest rate does not change. Of course, we may take some time to reach this position and the real rate of interest will be below its original level during the period of adjustment. This persists, however, only to the extent that savers underestimate the true rate of inflation (they suffer from money illusion) or require time to alter the terms of savings contracts into which they have already entered.

> **Money illusion:** A confusion between real and nominal values causing people not to take inflation fully into account. This is assumed to occur only in disequilibrium.

Proponents of this view assume that the monetary authorities have full control over the supply of money (the money supply is exogenous) and so the initial increase in the money supply and the consequent inflation are the responsibility of the central bank. Nominal interest rates are explained by a combination of the loanable funds theory (explaining real interest rates) and a monetary theory of inflation. Real interest rates change only slowly over time. The only significant disturbance to market interest rates comes from the ill-advised activities of the monetary authorities.

7.2.2 Problems with the loanable funds theory

Unsurprisingly, the loanable funds theory has some problems. Firstly, it is clear that people go on saving even when real interest rates become negative and remain so for quite long periods. This can only occur in the model outlined above through the existence of money illusion. It happens only in the short run (when the system is in disequilibrium). In equilibrium, suppliers and demanders of loanable funds are perfectly informed about the real rate of interest. This means, however, that the model does not do very well in explaining changes in interest rates over what economists refer to as the short run, but this can involve quite long periods of actual time.

Secondly, real as well as nominal interest rates are capable of changing rapidly. For example, in the US from December 2004 to December 2005, the Federal Funds rate – the rate of interest controlled by the US central bank – was raised from 2 per cent to 4.25 per cent although the rate of inflation increased only from 2.7 to 3 per cent. Even allowing for the likelihood that expected inflation rates might have been higher, it remains clear that the real interest rate rose significantly during the year.

We can see that the concentration on the long run in the loanable funds approach to interest rates seriously understates the role of the monetary authorities in a modern economy. After all, the Federal Reserve changed interest rates so often in 2005 because it wanted to have an impact on real interest rates, with the aim of preventing the US economy from expanding too rapidly. Equally, when in February 2003 the Bank of England Monetary Policy Committee took everyone by surprise by lowering its repo rate from 4 to 3.75 per cent, it was intending to lower real interest rates because it was worried by the performance of the real economy in the UK. This change is looked at in more detail in Box 7.1.

Box 7.1

The Monetary Policy Committee's interest rate decision – February 2003

In February 2003, the Monetary Policy Committee of the Bank of England surprised financial markets by cutting its repo rate from 4 per cent to 3.75 per cent. Before this decision, the rate had been held steady at 4 per cent since November 2001. Why were the markets surprised by the February decision?

It was widely accepted that the UK economy was going through a period of slow growth and many forecasts suggested that the rate of growth would decline further. Manufacturing industry was doing particularly badly and business organisations had been asking for an interest rate cut for some months. The trade unions, concerned about increasing unemployment, also sought a cut. However, there was considerable concern that the economy was dangerously unbalanced. In particular, house prices were continuing to increase rapidly and mortgage borrowing and household debt had grown to record levels. Some analysts talked of a house price bubble and argued that the longer the bubble persisted, the bigger would be the collapse in prices when it eventually came. An interest rate cut, they thought, would cause house prices and debt to rise even faster in the short run and thus make a large 'correction' more likely.

Such a collapse in house prices would lead to large reductions in consumption as households sought to come to terms with their debt and the lower value of their houses and other assets. A sharp reduction in consumption could tip the UK economy into a full recession. Therefore the financial markets had convinced themselves that the MPC would not cut interest rates.

When it happened, the interest rate cut was praised by the Director General of the Confederation of British Industry (CBI), but the FTSE share index, the value of sterling and gilt prices all fell sharply, providing ample evidence that the markets had been taken by surprise (see Box 7.6 for more information on the impact on gilt prices).

We can interpret the difference in view as a clash between the real and financial economies. The case for an interest rate cut grew easily out of standard economic theory – the economy was growing slowly, inflationary pressures were weak and slow growth was also forecast in the US and Europe, making the prospects for export industries gloomy. There seemed a strong case for cutting the repo rate in order to prompt interest rates generally in the economy to fall. This would push down real interest rates and so encourage firms to invest. The argument against the cut was based on the psychology of markets and consumers and on asset prices and financial ratios.

The MPC surprised the markets by opting for the cut in real interest rates in line with economic theory. This led the markets to wonder whether the Bank of England had information not available to the markets suggesting that the state of the economy was worse than the markets had thought. This turned out not to be the case. In the minutes of the MPC meeting, the seven MPC members who voted for the interest rate cut included in their reasons for doing so worries about weakening demand at home and abroad, dissipating inflationary pressures, weak equity markets and 'geopolitical worries' (which at the time meant uncertainty regarding the likelihood of war in Iraq and its consequences).

Thirdly, there is another problem stemming from the assumption that the rate of inflation or the expected rate of inflation has no long-run impact on the real rate of interest. Unfortunately for the theory, there is no doubt that inflationary expectations do influence the willingness of people to save and of potential investors to borrow. The direction of the impact of inflation on saving is not certain. The existence of, or the threat of, inflation might persuade people to hold their wealth in the form of real rather than financial assets since real assets (on average, over the medium term or long term) maintain their real value during inflations. People thinking in this way would reduce their savings during periods of inflation. However, in some past inflationary periods people have responded to the inflation by saving more rather than less. Why might they have done this?

People hold a considerable part of their wealth in the form of financial assets. With inflation, the real value of these assets falls. It is perfectly logical to respond to this by consuming less now and adding to holdings of financial assets in order to offset in part the impact of inflation on past savings. It follows that the impact of inflation on savers is ambiguous. Clearly, much depends on the rate of inflation and expectations about future inflation rates. When inflation rates are very high, people attempt to convert all of their past savings into goods as quickly as they can as well as refusing to buy financial assets from current income. There is no doubt that in these periods savings fall sharply. However, in periods of relatively low inflation, the overall effect is unclear. Because of the importance of expectations, the level of savings (both in nominal and real terms) might be influenced not just by the rate of inflation but also by the rate at which the rate of inflation is changing (the volatility of inflation).

Changes in the rate of inflation also affect the decisions of potential investors. In deciding whether to borrow in order to invest, potential investors assess the probable rates of return on investment projects and compare these with the cost of borrowing. This is much more difficult to do if there is inflation, particularly if the rate of inflation is volatile. The possibility that the inflation rate might change considerably during the period of a loan introduces an extra element of uncertainty into the investment decision.

The loanable funds model can be modified to take such complaints into account. The problem is that these changes are *ad hoc* and run the risk of destroying the central idea at the heart of loanable funds – that the market economy is stable and has a strong in-built tendency to return to equilibrium. The real rate of interest is a key variable in the explanation of how this might happen. It therefore makes sense to look at a different theory of interest rates – one that is constructed on entirely different assumptions as to how the economy works. This is known as the liquidity preference theory of interest rates. Before explaining the liquidity preference theory, let us look at how the loanable funds approach functions under these different assumptions.

7.3 Loanable funds in an uncertain economy

We saw that the loanable funds theory was based on the idea of people allocating their available resources over their lifetimes. Indeed, to the extent that people save in order to pass on wealth to their children, the analysis can be extended to future generations. Thus, the analysis relates to the very long run. In making their decisions, people are assumed to have full information about future rates of return and inflation and about the effects of their current savings and consumption decisions on their future levels of income. This can be true only if expectations about the future are always correct – there is no possibility here, for instance, of people who wish to work being unemployed.

The difficulty is that in an ever-changing world, we never reach the long-run positions at the heart of loanable funds analysis. The world changes and people begin to adapt to these changes. Before they have fully adapted, more changes occur and so the process continues. We can, of course, look back and see what has happened in an economy over long periods; but each economic agent makes decisions in a series of short runs. In these circumstances, people may have little idea of future interest rates or inflation rates (and hence future real rates of interest). They may be quite unsure of their ability to obtain work in the future or of what they will be paid for their work. If this is true, the notion that the crucial economic decision made by market agents concerns the allocation of consumption across their lifetimes begins to seem far-fetched. They may plan to save a particular proportion of their current incomes, but the absolute level of their savings may change because of unexpected changes in their incomes. Not only incomes change unexpectedly. In recent decades in developed countries people have acquired many more assets than used to be the case (houses, pension entitlements, unit trusts) and have, at the same time, become much more heavily indebted. Changes in house prices, for example, can have dramatic effects on estimates of wealth, as people found out in the early 1990s in the UK when house prices fell so sharply that many people found the current values of their houses were less than the size of their mortgages. Where both future income and estimates of personal wealth are uncertain, the impact of time preference on savings is dominated by events.

Indeed, it is possible that the positive relationship between interest rates and savings in the loanable funds theory is reversed for some people. People unable to think of maximising welfare through the choice between present and future consumption across their lifetimes might well choose to save in order to reach a fixed level of savings by a particular date in the future, for example to allow them to retire. Any increase in the interest rate then allows them to achieve that target by saving *less* in each period. The relationship between savings and interest rates becomes negative for them.

Again, savings decisions may be taken out of the hands of those who are in debt. For many people, a major reason for saving is to allow them to repay their mortgages. Unexpected increases in interest rates cause debt repayments to increase and require reductions in consumption. It can be argued that the great increase in indebtedness has changed the nature of the choice between the present and the future. People are able to consume more in the current period but lose control of their future consumption levels.

What does all this amount to? If we return to our supply of loanable funds diagram, we are suggesting that the slope of the curve is uncertain and that the curve might shift rapidly with unexpected changes in income and asset prices. The interest rate might still be an important *ceteris paribus* influence, but the effect of interest rate changes on savings is difficult to see among all the other changes taking place.

The demand for loanable funds is equally problematic if firms are uncertain of their ability to sell what they produce. The expected rate of return on investment then no longer depends simply on the marginal productivity of capital but will be influenced by factors affecting business confidence. These might include the existing rate of profit, forecasts of the future levels of income and unemployment, expectations regarding future interest and exchange rates, and political factors such as possible changes of government. A project might appear to be very profitable on the assumption of full employment, but firms might not invest if they suspect that the economy is heading into recession. In other words, the demand curve for loanable funds is also subject to shifts that are difficult to forecast.

If both the demand and supply curves are unstable, the loanable funds theory does not help us very much in the explanation of the level of or changes in rates of interest – especially if changes in the rate of interest themselves cause one or both of the curves to shift. The factors underlying these curves – marginal productivity and time preference – remain long-term influences on the rate of interest, but we cannot say much more than that.

The liquidity preference theory of interest rates

In an uncertain world, then, saving and investment may be much more influenced by expectations and by exogenous shocks than by underlying real forces. One possible response of risk-averse savers is to vary the form in which they hold their financial wealth depending on what they think is likely to happen to asset prices – they are likely to vary the average liquidity of their portfolios. In section 1.1.3, we defined a liquid asset as one that can be turned into money quickly, cheaply and for a known monetary value. It is the risk of loss in the value of assets with which we are concerned here. In periods in which people are confident that asset prices will increase, they are encouraged to hold a high proportion of their portfolios in illiquid assets, benefiting from the higher rate of interest that they offer. Increased doubt about future asset prices, on the other hand, encourages people to give up these higher rates of interest in search of the greater security offered by more liquid assets. This happens in financial markets all the time. For example, in the equity market the shares of some companies are likely to fare better than others in a falling market, and investors become more likely to buy these shares if they fear a fall in share prices. Again, bonds with distant maturity dates carry more capital risk than those nearer to maturity and are thus relatively less attractive when the markets turn bearish.

This is not to say that people all have the same expectations regarding future asset prices; that all people with the same expectations behave in the same way; or that everyone is equally risk averse. Nonetheless, there is likely to be a general shift towards greater liquidity whenever confidence in financial markets falls. Even the large pension funds withdraw significant amounts of their funds from the equity and bond markets and hold instead short-term securities and cash during periods of uncertainty. Here we see a quite different role for interest rates than that played in the loanable funds theory. The inverse relationship between interest rates and bond and share prices that we considered in Chapter 6 becomes important. Plainly, an expectation of an increase in interest rates increases the prospect of a fall in financial asset prices generally and of a greater relative fall in the prices of illiquid assets. In other words, an expected increase in interest rates, *ceteris paribus*, increases the preference of asset holders for liquidity.

> **Liquidity preference:** The preference for holding financial wealth in the form of short-term, highly liquid assets rather than long-term illiquid assets, based principally on the fear that long-term assets will lose capital value over time.

This general idea was developed into an economic theory by J M Keynes within a simplified model in which there were only two types of financial asset – money, the liquid asset, and bonds with no maturity date (consols), the illiquid asset. An increased preference for liquidity in this model is equivalent to an increased demand for money. Thus, the demand for money increases whenever more people think interest rates are likely to rise than believe they are likely to fall. This is Keynes's speculative motive for holding money – people hold money instead of less liquid

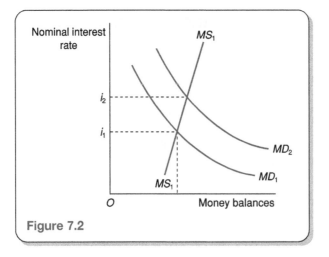

Figure 7.2

assets in order to avoid a capital loss. This, of course, leaves us with the problem of knowing when people are likely to expect interest rates to rise. Keynes's approach to this was very simple. It was to suggest that the lower interest rates currently were, relative to their usual level in the economy, the higher would be the proportion of people who thought that the next interest rate move would be up. Thus, the lower interest rates were, the greater would be the fear of a fall in asset prices and the greater would be the preference for liquidity. The resulting demand for money curve slopes down from left to right as shown in Figure 7.2.

There is very little objection to this negative relationship between interest rates and the demand for money since there are other possible explanations for it. Keynes's theory, however, has two controversial implications. Firstly, the demand for money curve is likely to be less steeply sloped than in most other theories of the demand for money since small changes in interest rates might cause quite large changes in people's expectations about future rates. This is particularly likely at interest rates that are historically very low because at this level the great majority of people are likely to think that interest rates will next rise. This explains the flatter section of the demand for money curves in Figure 7.2.

Secondly, and more importantly, Keynes did not assume that the interest rate was the only factor influencing expectations of future asset prices. Market optimism or pessimism can result from a wide range of economic and political factors, and the views of market agents will be strongly influenced by what they believe other market agents are likely to do. Hence, if we were to believe that there was no objective reason for a fall in bond prices but we thought that other people in the market were likely to sell, we might try to beat the fall by selling bonds and moving to more liquid assets. If enough people behaved in the same way, the price *would* fall. Under these circumstances, the demand for money curve might be highly unstable. It might shift as a result of exogenous shocks that would be difficult to forecast. This has a number of important implications, but before considering them, we need to complete the model by adding a supply of money curve.

The standard model of this kind continues to assume that the monetary authorities are able to control the supply of money. The money supply curve can be drawn as either vertical (as it is in the simplest version of these theories) or, as here, as sloping up steeply to the right. The interaction of the demand for money and supply of money curves then determines the interest rate.

7.5 Loanable funds and liquidity preference

Much effort has been put into trying to show the relationship between the two principal theories of interest rate determination – loanable funds and liquidity preference. It is commonly argued that the two theories are, in fact, complementary, merely looking at two different markets (the market for money and the market for non-money financial assets), both of which have to be in equilibrium if the system as a whole is in equilibrium. Although it is true that, in a technical sense, the two theories can be assimilated, this is done at the cost of losing the spirit of both theories. Let us see why this is so.

Let us assume that there is a sudden, unexplained loss of confidence in financial markets, causing an increase in the demand for liquidity. The demand for money at each level of interest rates increases and the demand for money curve in Figure 7.2 shifts out from MD_1 to MD_2. Interest rates rise from i_1 to i_2. In the nominal interest rate version of the loanable funds theory, this is expressed as an increase in the demand for liquid reserves, and the demand for loanable funds curve shifts up, also causing an increase in nominal interest rates. So far so good, but this sudden change in confidence would be regarded by loanable funds theorists as irrational behaviour. In other words, it would either not occur or would be seen as temporary and unimportant in an explanation of how the economy operated.

Remember that, in our discussion of the loanable funds view, we suggested that any instability in interest rates would be caused by the behaviour of governments or central banks. In liquidity preference theory, on the other hand, instability is inherent in the market economy and there is a possible role for government in stabilising the economy. This argument that the two theories are essentially very different is carried further the next section when we consider the implications of the two theories for monetary policy.

7.6 The monetary authorities and the rate of interest

We saw in Chapter 5 and in Box 7.1 that the general level of interest rates might change in an economy because the monetary authorities change the rate of interest at which they are prepared to operate in the money market. This is usually done in an attempt to influence the level of aggregate demand in the economy (and hence the rate of inflation) or the net inflow of short-term capital into the economy (and hence the exchange rate). Section 5.3 deals in some detail with the operation of monetary policy and with recent changes in the practice of monetary policy in the UK.

In Chapter 5, we pointed out that the ability of the monetary authorities to influence very short-term interest rates in the economy derives from the role of the central bank as the lender of last resort to the commercial banking system. The need for central banks to operate in this way arises from the fractional reserve nature of the banking system (explained fully in Chapter 3) and the desire of banks to keep the average rate of return on their assets as high as possible. Thus, they seek to economise on their holdings of liquid, low-interest assets. However, the fractional reserve system means that banks can easily find themselves short of liquid assets (reserves) as the result of unexpected withdrawals by depositors. The monetary authorities are able to exploit this need of banks to maintain a sufficient stock of reserves by being willing to replenish bank reserves, but only at a price determined by the central bank. Section 5.3 lists the three ways in which central banks might allow banks to achieve the degree of liquidity needed to meet the demands of their depositors while still keeping the average rate of return they receive on their assets high – use of the discount window, open market operations, and repurchase agreements.

Variations by the central bank in the interest (or discount) rate at which it is prepared to lend very short term to the commercial banks influence the form in which banks hold their assets and, in particular, their willingness to make loans to their clients. This then affects longer-term interest rates. This ability of the central bank to influence the general level of interest rates does not, however, mean it fully controls rates of interest. There are several reasons for this.

Firstly, the notion that the central bank can influence the willingness of banks to make loans assumes that banks are profit maximisers and thus that any small change in the costs of a liquidity shortage causes a response from banks. The behaviour of banks certainly shows that they are interested in keeping profits high, but they are also likely to have other objectives. For instance, they may wish to maintain their share of the different markets in which they operate. Banks are in competition with each other for both assets (including competing with each other in the house mortgage market) and liabilities (competition for bank deposits). In order to maintain their spread between borrowing and lending rates, banks that cut their lending rates must also cut their deposit rates. It follows that in a period of intense competition for bank deposits, such as has occurred in the UK in recent years with the establishment of savings banks by supermarket chains and insurance companies and the continued growth of telephone banking, banks might judge that they cannot afford to lower immediately the rates of interest they are offering on deposits. This might cause them not to respond immediately to relatively small changes in the base interest rate of the central bank.

This implies that banks have a choice – to respond or not to the prompting of the central bank. This arises because the larger banks possess a considerable degree of market power. In a perfectly competitive system, all banks would respond to the prompting of the central bank by being more willing to make longer-term loans (including mortgage loans), and this would push down interest rates generally, leading to an increase in borrowing and an increase in the total stock of deposits. However, if the banks are more interested in their share of deposits than in the volume of deposits, they might be unwilling to lower the interest rates they offer to savers, even if that prevents them from lowering mortgage interest rates as well.

In theory, it should be more difficult for banks to resist attempts by the central bank to push up interest rates, as long as the central bank has the power to induce a genuine shortage of liquidity in the economy. If banks hold their assets in a more liquid form than is needed, all they are doing is forgoing potential profits. If they hold their assets in a less liquid form than is needed, they ultimately face the possibility of a loss of confidence by the depositors and hence of collapse. Even here, however, there are limits to the power of the central bank. In developed and sophisticated financial markets, banks have considerable ability to overcome shortages of liquidity without resorting to borrowing from the central bank. In any case, it would be a very risky policy for central banks to squeeze liquidity to such an extent that the banks genuinely feared collapse. Indeed, for such a policy to be effective, the authorities would have to accept reasonably frequent bank collapses. This, in turn, would reduce the confidence of depositors in the banking system – a result that modern governments do not desire.

There is a second quite different difficulty with our analysis. When we described the process above by which banks became more or less willing to make loans, we implied two things: (a) that the demand curve for loans did not shift; and (b) that the market for loans was genuinely competitive – that is, that banks are prepared to lend to anyone prepared to pay the market rate of interest. Let us look at each of these.

We suggested above that the willingness of investors and consumers to borrow depended a good deal on confidence. That is, if firms believe that the economy is heading into a recession, they will not wish to borrow in order to invest because they are worried about their ability to sell their products. Decisions by potential house buyers and purchasers of consumer durables depend a good deal on their current estimates of their net wealth. A major part of the net wealth of many households is the current value of the house in which they live. Any fall in house prices is thus likely to affect consumers' confidence. In addition, estimates of household wealth are now strongly linked to the prices of financial assets. Any sharp fall in the prices of equities or other financial assets or any expectation that such a fall might occur can have a powerful impact on household estimates of wealth and a strong impact on their willingness to go further into debt. It follows that any exogenous influences on the confidence of firms or households might shift the demand curve for new loans.

In Figure 7.3, then, we assume a sharp fall in the demand for new loans. For the moment, we shall assume no change in the willingness of banks to lend. The demand curve shifts down, *and in a competitive market* the interest rate on longer-term loans would fall. As loan rates fall, the cost to banks of holding liquid assets falls and banks hold a higher proportion of their assets in liquid form. The demand for short-term assets rises and short-term interest rates fall. The monetary authorities are not determining interest rates here. This allows us to consider the circumstances in which the authorities might have an influence.

Suppose that the market is not fully competitive and that interest rates do not fall as quickly as they would do in a competitive market. In Figure 7.3, we show the possibility that interest rates do not move at all. We move from point A to point C

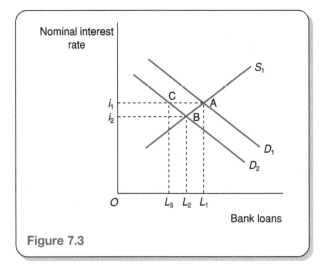

Figure 7.3

rather than to point B. Therefore, the value of loans falls from OL_1 to OL_3. Under these circumstances, the central bank could act at the short end of the market to exert pressure on banks to reduce interest rates in the direction in which they would fall in a competitive system. However, there are clear limits to the influence of the central bank. It could succeed only in pushing interest rates down in the direction dictated by market forces. In general, we can say that in a system that does not have a strong tendency towards equilibrium, the central bank is able to push the rate of interest towards the equilibrium rate. As we shall see later, the job of the central bank is much more difficult than this implies. The point we are making here is that the central bank is not free to push the rate of interest in either direction or by any amount that it chooses.

Let us next return to the question of whether banks are prepared to lend to anyone at the existing rate of interest. This is certainly not so. There is no doubt that there is at least some degree of rationing in the market for bank loans. That is, at least some would-be borrowers are unable to obtain loans even if they are willing to pay the market rate of interest. Some market agents are unable to obtain loans at all; others will be able to obtain loans only at higher rates of interest. One possible explanation for this depends on the presence of asymmetric information (defined in section 4.1). We noted in section 3.1.4 that banks have better knowledge about the risk to which they are going to put funds than do the savers who lend them but we might also argue that banks are less able to know the likely prospects of success of investment projects than are investors. In the case of consumers, banks know less than the would-be borrower about the likelihood that the loan will be repaid. They may respond by imposing additional conditions on borrowers (for example, a stipulation of a certain amount of collateral for the loan) or by including an additional risk premium in the interest rate to take into account their assessment of the risk associated with the loan. Poor people often have no access at all to bank finance and are forced to borrow from pawnbrokers and other informal financial institutions, which charge much higher rates of interest than banks.

This element of rationing in the market for bank loans allows banks to vary the amount of lending they do by changing the percentage of loan applicants they reject. In other words, the supply curve of bank lending may shift because of changes in the assessment made by banks of the future prospects of the economy. We might even think of a kinked supply curve of new loans, indicating the higher risk premium that banks require from customers classified as not such good risks. Such a supply curve could even become vertical, to reflect the fact that some demand for bank loans will not be met at any rate of interest. This approach would allow the position of the kink or the size of the risk premiums demanded to change depending on the assessment made by banks of general economic prospects. This introduces additional exogenous elements into the determination of interest rates.

In different ways and to different degrees both the loanable funds and the liquidity preference theories of interest rates cast doubt on the power of the central bank. According to loanable funds theory, the central bank has no effect on long-run real interest rates. All it can do is to cause (or prevent) inflation and hence influence nominal rates of interest. Monetary changes have no impact on real variables – money is neutral. There may be short-run effects on real variables such as employment and the real interest rate but these occur only to the extent that market agents suffer from money illusion. That is, they confuse real and monetary variables, thinking mistakenly, for example, that an increase in money wages implies an increase in real wages although prices are rising at the same time.

This is not the case in the Keynesian model in which changes in interest rates brought about by the central bank can have an effect on real values – money is not neutral. However, doubts are raised about the size of that effect and about the ability of the central bank to influence the rate of interest. We pointed out above that, in the standard form of Keynesian monetary theory, the money supply is assumed to be exogenous. Assume, then, that the authorities increase the supply of money. This would shift the supply of money curve in Figure 7.2 out to the right. Interest rates would fall, but if this fall persuaded a significant number of people that interest rates were likely soon to go back up again, it might cause a considerable increase in the demand for money. In other words, a large proportion of the increase in the supply of money might be held idly as liquid balances rather than being lent on to firms and consumers wishing to borrow in order to spend. If this is so, increases in the money supply might have a very small impact on interest rates and hence on spending. In the extreme version of this argument, the liquidity trap, liquidity preference is total – any increase in the money supply is matched by an equivalent increase in the demand for money. Monetary policy has no effect on anything.

This does not take us far since we know that central banks cannot and do not try to control the money supply directly but act instead on short-term rates of interest. Supporters of the ideas behind liquidity preference then adopt some of the arguments above, suggesting that the actions of the central bank might not be fully reflected in interest changes throughout the economy. The practice of credit rationing by banks is held to be particularly important in this regard. In addition, if the central bank does succeed in bringing about a change in interest rates, the effects might not be very great since the rate of interest is only one factor influencing investment and consumption. Factors influencing how confident people feel about the future are likely to be more important. All of this is particularly true when economies are in deep recession. The central bank is thought to have more power to help to deflate inflationary economies by pushing up interest rates than to help drag economies out of recession by pushing down interest rates.

We need to add, however, that the very large increase in home ownership and the generally large increase in personal indebtedness in recent years has led to the view that the power of the central bank to affect the economy through its influence on interest rates has increased sharply. Box 7.2 summarises the many factors that we have suggested might have an influence on nominal interest rates.

Box 7.2 **Influences on nominal interest rates**

The following list puts together all of the factors discussed in this chapter which might have an influence on nominal interest rates:

1 The marginal productivity of capital.
2 The average time preference of the population.
3 Business confidence.
4 The economy's wealth.
5 Expectations regarding future changes in asset prices.
6 Expectations regarding the future performance of the economy.
7 Expectations regarding future interest rates.
8 Expectations regarding future exchange rates.
9 The rate of inflation.
10 Expectations of changes in the rate of inflation.
11 The volatility of inflation.
12 The short-term interest rates set by the monetary authorities
13 The degree of competition among financial institutions.
14 The international mobility of capital.
15 Changes in the degree of risk aversion in the economy.

Have we left anything out?

Do you understand where each of these fits into the argument?

Which three factors do you think are most important?

7.7 The structure of interest rates

Let us now drop our assumption that all interest rates in the economy move together. There are, indeed, many interest rates and the structure of interest rates is subject to considerable change. Such changes are important to the operation of monetary policy.

Interest rates vary because of differences in the time period, the degree of risk, and the transactions costs associated with different financial instruments. Let us begin by considering differences in risk. Plainly, the greater the risk of default associated with an asset, the higher must be the interest rate paid upon it as compensation for the risk. This explains why some borrowers pay higher rates of interest than others. The degree of risk associated with a request for a loan may be determined informally, based upon, for example, a company's size, profitability or past performance; or, it may be determined more formally by credit rating agencies.

Borrowers with high credit ratings will be able to have commercial bills accepted by banks, find willing takers for their commercial paper or borrow directly from banks at 'fine' rates of interest. Such borrowers are often referred to as prime borrowers. Those less favoured may have to borrow from other sources at higher rates. Much the same principle applies to the comparison between interest rates on sound risk-free loans (such as government bonds) and expected yields on equities, the factors influencing which were discussed in detail in Chapter 6. There we saw that the more risky a company is thought to be, the lower will be its share price in relation to its expected average dividend payment – that is, the higher will be its dividend yield and the more expensive it will be for the company to raise equity capital. Of course, not everyone is risk averse and shares of companies that have made no profits and paid no dividends for several years continue to be bought and sold and so the loading for risk that must be paid by risky companies need not necessarily be very great.

Interest rates payable on different forms of assets will also vary with transaction costs and these are subject to economies of scale. Thus, other things being equal, we should expect rates of interest to be lower the larger the size of the loan.

7.7.1 The term structure of interest rates

Our principal concern here, however, is with instruments that differ only in their time period – that is, there is an equal risk of default and no difference in transaction costs. The relationship between interest rates on short-term securities and those on long-term ones can be represented on a diagram known as the *yield curve*.

> **Yield curve:** Shows the relationships between the interest rates payable on bonds with different lengths of time to maturity. That is, it shows the term structure of interest rates.

A typical yield curve is shown in Figure 7.4. Here, interest rates rise as the length of time to maturity increases, but the curve gradually flattens out. Yield curves may, however, be of many different shapes. Figure 7.5 illustrates a range of possibilities. To examine the circumstances in which a yield curve might assume a particular shape, we need to consider several theories of the nature of the relationship between long-term and short-term rates.

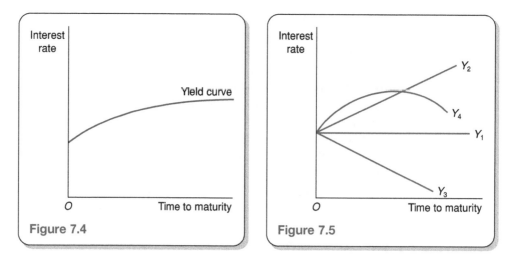

Figure 7.4

Figure 7.5

7.7.2 The pure expectations theory of interest rate structure

This theory assumes that present long-term interest rates depend entirely on future short-term rates. Lenders are taken to be equally happy to hold short-term or long-term securities. Their choice between them will depend only on relative interest rates. It follows that, for instance, a series of five one-year bonds is a perfect substitute for a five-year bond. If this were so, the proceeds from investing say £1,000 for one year and then reinvesting the returns for another year and so on for five years must exactly equal the proceeds from buying a £1,000 five-year bond at the beginning.

Consider what would happen if this were not so. Suppose the proceeds from a long-term bond were greater than from a series of short-term bonds. People would buy long-term bonds, pushing up their price and pushing down the rate of interest on them. This would continue until there was no advantage to be had from holding the long-term bonds. Then people would be indifferent between the two types of bond. Thus, the long-term interest rate would depend entirely on the expected future short-term rates.

The simplest form of this theory assumes that lenders have perfect information and know what is going to happen to short-term interest rates in the future. In this case, the long-term interest rate will be an average of the known future short-term rates. This relationship between long-term and short-term rates can be expressed in the formula

$$(1 + i^*)^n = (1 + i_1)(1 + i_2)(1 + i_3) \ldots (1 + i_n) \tag{7.5}$$

where i^* is the interest rate payable each year on a long-term bond and n is the number of years to maturity of the bond; i_1 is the rate of interest payable now on a one-year bond; i_2 is the rate of interest which will be payable on a one-year bond in a year's time; i_3 is the short-term rate two years into the future, and so on.

It follows that if short-term rates are expected to rise, long-term rates will be higher than the current short-term rates and the yield curve will slope upwards. Box 7.3 provides a numerical illustration of this and Exercise 7.1 gives you some practice with it.

Box 7.3

The pure expectations theory of interest rate structure – a numerical example

Assuming that lenders have perfect information, long-term interest rates will be an average of the known future short-term rates. We assume that lenders know that short-term rates over the next five years will be:

year 1   8 per cent
year 2   10 per cent
year 3   11 per cent
year 4   12 per cent
year 5   9 per cent

Then, £1,000 invested in a one-year bond, with the proceeds being invested in a further one-year bond in the subsequent year, will produce the following results:

	Principal	Interest rate	Interest	Capital + interest
year 1	£1,000	8 per cent	£80	£1,080
year 2	£1,080	10 per cent	£108	£1,188

We can calculate that for a two-year bond taken out at the beginning of year one to produce the same results it would need to pay an interest rate of 9 per cent – the average of the two short-term rates. What does this mean for the yield curve?

We can see that because it is known that short-term interest rates will rise over the following year (from 8 per cent to 10 per cent), the interest payable on the two-year (long-term) bond must be greater than that payable on the one-year (short-term) bond. That is, the yield curve will be sloping upwards.

Let us continue our figures, assuming that our investor continues to re-invest in one-year bonds for each of the following three years. This will give us:

year 3	£1,188	11 per cent	£131	£1,319
year 4	£1,319	12 per cent	£158	£1,477
year 5	£1,477	9 per cent	£133	£1,610

It can be shown that, at the beginning of year one, the interest rate payable on three-year bonds must have been 9.66 per cent (the average of 8, 10 and 11) and on four-year bonds 10.25 per cent. In other words, as long as it is known that short-term interest rates are going to rise, the yield on long-term bonds for the equivalent period must lie above the short-term rate at the beginning of year one and must be rising. The yield curve will be sloping up. However, what about the interest rate at the beginning of year one on a five-year bond? Because it is known that short-term interest rates will begin to fall in year five, so too will the interest rate on a five-year bond. To produce a sum of £1,610 at the end of five years, the interest rate on a five-year bond will need to be only 10 per cent and the yield curve will begin to turn down.

Exercise 7.1

In Box 7.3, assume that it is known that short-term interest rates in years 6, 7 and 8 will be:

year 6	4 per cent
year 7	9 per cent
year 8	13 per cent

What will be the interest rate *at the beginning of year one* on six-year, seven-year and eight-year bonds respectively? Draw the yield curve at the beginning of year one.

7.7.3 Term premiums

However, people do not have perfect information about the future course of short-term interest rates. All they can have are estimates of these rates, which are subject to the risk of error. The further into the future we try to look, the greater is the chance that we shall be wrong. Suppose a lender acquires a long-term bond that pays an interest rate related to expected short-term interest rates but then finds that short-term rates rise above the expected level. As current interest rates rise, the prices of existing bonds fall, and bond holders suffer a capital loss. As we have seen in Chapter 6, the longer the time to maturity of the bond, the greater will be the fall in bond price. It follows that the risk of capital loss associated with any given error in forecasting future interest rates, the *capital risk,* is greater for long-term than for short-term bonds.

People respond to risk in different ways. If they have the same attitude to both the risk of loss and the prospect of gain, the two balance out and they are said to be *risk-neutral.* In this case, the yield curve reflects what investors expect to happen to short-term rates of interest. In equilibrium, the outcome is exactly the same as with perfect certainty. However, now it is possible that investors' expectations will be wrong and thus that the market will not be in equilibrium. This case is set out formally in Box 7.4.

Box 7.4

The expectations view of the term structure of interest rates under uncertainty assuming risk neutrality

Assume that there are two types of bond available to investors. They are identical in all ways but one – one bond is for one year only (short-term bond); the second bond is for two years (long-term bond). A person who wishes to invest for two years has a choice of two strategies.

Strategy A
Buy a one-year bond now and when it matures in one year's time, use the funds to buy a second one-year bond. The investor knows the current rate of interest on one year bonds, i_s, but does not know what the rate of interest on one-year bonds will be in one year's time. However, he holds the same expectation about that rate (which we shall call the expected future short-term rate, i) as everyone else in the market.

Strategy B

Buy a two-year bond now. The investor knows the current rate of interest on a two-year bond (i^*).

Calculations

The investor can thus calculate the certain return to Strategy B and the expected return to Strategy A.

The certain return to strategy B we can write as $(1 + i^*)^2$. All interest rates, remember, are written as decimals. Thus, if i^* were 5 per cent, a £100 bond would return in two years' time: £(100) $(1 + 0.05)^2$ = £100 × 1.1025 = £110.25.

The *expected* return to Strategy A, we can write as: $(1 + i_s)(1 + i)$.

Now we can calculate the value that i would need to be for the two strategies to produce the same return at the end of two years: that is, the value i must take for the investor to be indifferent between the two strategies. We call this value f_2. By definition,

$$(1 + i_s)(1 + f_2) = (1 + i^*)^2$$

and, $(1 + f_2) = (1 + i^*)^2/(1 + i_s)$.

Let i_s be 4 per cent and i^* be 5 per cent. Then, $(1 + f_2)$ = 1.1025/1.04 = 1.06 and f_2 = 0.06 or 6 per cent.

In other words, if investors are to be indifferent between the two strategies, the expected short-term rate of interest in one year's time must be 6 per cent. Then no one would have a reason for changing the balance of their present holdings of one-year and two-year bonds: the market would be in equilibrium.

That is, our equilibrium condition for the market is that i (the expected future short-term rate of interest) be equal to f_2 (the rate of interest that causes the two strategies to produce the same return at the end of two years).

It follows that if people expect the short-run rate in one year's time to be greater than f_2 (i.e. $i > f_2$), they will shift from long to short bonds without limit. In the reverse case ($i < f_2$) they will shift from short to long bonds without limit.

In the latter case, capital risk would increase, but there is both an upside risk (interest rates fall and bond prices rise) and a downside risk (interest rates rise and bond prices fall). Risk-neutral investors will see the upside and downside risk as offsetting each other.

In equilibrium, with $i = f_2$, the term structure indicates what the market expects to happen to short rates, just as under conditions of certainty. Thus, if $i_s < i^*$ and $f_2 > i_s$, then $i > i_s$; people are expecting short-run rates to rise: the yield curve will be rising. Equally, if $i_s > i^*$ but $f_2 < i_s$, then $i < i_s$ and people are expecting short rates to fall: the yield curve will be falling.

If we next assume that people generally do not much like taking risks (they are risk averse), we can argue that lenders will have to be paid a rather higher rate of interest than the average of the expected but uncertain short-term rates to persuade them to buy longer-term bonds. This addition to the interest rate is sometimes known as a risk premium, but is better referred to as a term premium to avoid confusion with the risk premium paid to offset exchange rate risk or default risk. It is also sometimes referred to as a liquidity premium but this, strictly speaking, is incorrect since 'liquidity' refers to the speed and ease with which an asset can be converted into money without risk. A long-term bond can be converted into cash as quickly and as easily as a short-term bond through the secondary market. The term premium is justified by the extra risk of capital loss associated with a long-term bond, not with any greater difficulty involved in converting the bond into cash.

> **Term premium:** The addition to the rate of interest needed to persuade capital risk-averse savers to lend for longer periods.

If we apply this to the example in Box 7.3, the rate of interest on five-year bonds will need to be greater than 10 per cent because, although lenders are as likely to overestimate as to underestimate future short-term rates, since we have assumed them to be risk-averse, they will be more worried by the possibility of underestimating them. (In the jargon we can say that they are more worried by the downside risk than they are attracted by the upside risk.) We can say that interest rates on long-term securities will include a term premium. This provides an extra reason for an upward-sloping yield curve; but yield curves may still slope down, despite the inclusion of a term premium in the long-term rates. For instance, if people expect short-term rates to fall in the future, they have an incentive to buy long-term bonds now to 'lock in' to current rates. However, this increased demand for long bonds will force up their price and force down long interest rates. This effect may be strong enough to outweigh the term premium included in long rates.

Why are borrowers willing to pay this premium? Borrowers raise funds in order to invest – to acquire assets that will produce a profit at a rate higher than they are paying to borrow. However, they do not wish (and may indeed not be able) to repay the loan until they have earned their profits. If their investment projects are long-term ones (as, for example, are most purchases of capital equipment), they will prefer to borrow long (matching long-term liabilities to long-term assets). Thus, we can summarise much of the foregoing by saying that lenders would (other things being equal) rather lend short term whereas borrowers often wish to borrow long. Borrowers may thus be prepared to pay a higher rate of interest on long-term funds than the average of expected short-term rates of interest in order to obtain funds in the form they prefer.

So far, we have been assuming that all lenders have the same attitudes. Specifically, we have been assuming that all risk-averse lenders are worried about capital risk. However, some savers may have no plans to sell their bonds before the maturity date. Since they know that at maturity they will be paid the face value of the bond, such savers have no reason to be worried about capital risk. Rather, their concern might be with the size of interest payments that they receive every six months. For them, long-term bonds provide greater certainty than short-term ones. People buying fifteen-year bonds and intending to hold them until maturity know how much income they will receive for the whole of that period. People buying a series of fifteen one-year bonds do not know this since the income they receive each year will depend on what happens to short-term interest rates in the future. They face the risk that short-term interest rates might fall. In other words, they face an income risk. We have seen in Chapter 4 that some institutions, for example pension funds and life insurance companies, have a good idea of liabilities well into the future and wish to ensure that their future incomes match those future liabilities. They may then be income risk-averse and prefer to lend long rather than short. Box 7.5 treats both risk-aversion cases formally.

Box 7.5 | **The expectations view of the term structure of interest rates assuming risk aversion**

A. Capital risk aversion

Assume that the market is dominated by capital risk averters. Then if $i < f_2$, investors will be deterred from shifting from short to long bonds as in the risk-neutral case discussed in Box 7.4 because of their fear of capital loss (downside risk). This means that in equilibrium, i will be below f_2. That is, investors will accept a lower return on short bonds because going short reduces capital risk. It follows that even when no rise in short rates is expected, f_2 will be greater than i_s and i_s will therefore be less than i^*. The yield curve will slope upwards because of the risk premium attached to long bonds. This is accepted as the 'normal' case.

B. Income risk aversion

Assume that the market is dominated by income risk averters. Now if $i > f_2$, investors will be deterred from shifting from long to short because of their fear of loss of income should interest rates fall. In equilibrium, i will be greater than f_2 and, even with no change in interest rates expected, f_2 will be lower than i_s and i_s will be greater than i^*. The yield curve will slope downwards as a result of the dominance of income risk aversion. This is known as the 'reverse' yield curve.

The existence of inflation complicates things further. We have said above that people who intend to hold bonds until maturity know they will be paid the face value of the bond at maturity and thus face no capital risk. However, they know only the nominal sum they will receive, not what the purchasing power (or real value) of that sum will be. Short-term bonds have an advantage under inflation since their holders have greater flexibility to shift into real assets to maintain the real value of their wealth. Thus, if inflation rates are expected to be high in the future, even those who are capital risk-averse may prefer short to long bonds. It follows that the existence of inflationary expectations should make it more likely that borrowers will have to pay a term premium to enable them to borrow long.

Nonetheless, we can still say that if there are sufficient income risk-averse lenders in the market, it is possible that borrowers may not have to pay such a term premium. Indeed, it is possible that the usual situation may be reversed and that savers wish to lend longer than borrowers wish to borrow. In such a case, the term premium would be negative. Lenders would accept a lower rate of interest on long-term securities than that suggested by the average of expected future short-term rates of interest.

It has been suggested that the attitude to different types of risk varies in different parts of the market – for instance, that income risk averters dominate in long-dated bonds and capital risk averters in short-dated ones. This produced what Bank of England researchers have called the 'walking stick' hypothesis: a yield curve initially sloping upwards as capital risk-averting lenders demand a term premium, but then turning down as income risk-averting lenders accept a negative risk premium.

The term premium approach to the term structure of interest rates proposes, then, that the shape of the yield curve at any time is determined by two factors: (a) expectations regarding future short-term interest rates, and (b) the extent and nature of risk aversion in the market.

7.7.4 Market segmentation

Consider the relationship we have so far proposed between short-term and long-term interest rates. Take our comparison between interest rates on one-year and on five-year bonds. Assume the current one-year bond rate is 8 per cent while 10.5 per cent is payable on a five-year bond indicating:

- that short-term rates are expected to rise in the future;
- that borrowers prefer to borrow long; and
- that lenders require a term premium to persuade them to lend long (that is, they are capital risk averse).

Suppose next that the current one-year rate unexpectedly falls to 7.5 per cent. Five-year bonds at 10.5 per cent will now seem more attractive than before and people will switch towards them, pushing up their price and forcing interest rates on them below 10.5 per cent. The position of the yield curve will change, but there will be no change in its shape. It is often assumed that this will happen very quickly – that is, that short-term and long-term rates are closely linked. In effect, we are assuming that there is a single market for funds and changes in one part of the market are quickly communicated to other parts of it.

Is this necessarily the case? Imagine that people holding short-term bonds so strongly wish to keep their funds in liquid form that the greater relative attractiveness of long-term bonds does not influence them. Perhaps they are strongly capital risk-averse. Alternatively, they may, as with banks and building societies, need to keep a proportion of their assets in very liquid form in order to be able to meet unexpected calls upon them. Again, they may wish to have funds available in case they want to switch from financial assets into goods (increase purchase of consumer durables) or to meet unexpected debts. Further, the transaction costs involved in switching from one type of asset to another may be very high or people may be poorly informed about the different types of asset available and the interest rates payable on them. The market for funds, we are saying, may be *segmented*. Some savers choose short-term securities, others choose long-term ones, irrespective of the difference in interest rates between them. Long-term bonds are not substitutes for short-term ones. Instead of thinking of a continuous yield curve showing the relationship between interest rates on assets of different maturities, we could think of a series of separate markets for assets of different maturities, with the interest rates payable on each type of asset being determined simply by demand and supply for that asset. There would be no link between the different interest rates.

7.7.5 Preferred habitat

It is easy to think of groups of savers that may be strongly attached to particular parts of the market for funds – for instance, small savers who habitually save in National Savings or building society accounts despite changes in interest rate differentials, or those financial institutions which have a definite preference for one part of the market. Nonetheless, the notion that there is no substitutability among assets of different maturities appears extreme.

A compromise position is to accept that people do have attachments to parts of the market (their *preferred habitats*), which are sufficiently strong that they are unlikely to be broken by small changes in interest rates. However, larger changes in interest rates may persuade people to move some (but not all) of their assets of particular maturities to others. That is, assets of different maturities are substitutes for each other, but are imperfect substitutes. In our numerical example, the fall in current one-year interest rates from 8 to 7.5 per cent may have little or no effect on five-year rates; but if one-year rates fell to say 7 per cent, we might expect some switching towards long-term assets and some fall in the five-year rate, although we would also expect the gap between one-year and five-year rates to grow.

7.7.6 A summary of views on maturity substitutability

We thus have a range of views from one extreme to the other. At one extreme we can apply the notion of rational expectations to the expectations theory. This suggests that market agents make efficient use of all available information in order to maximise utility and implies that any small change in interest rate in one part of the market for funds will be instantaneously transmitted to all other parts of the market. All interest rates will move together and differentials between interest rates on assets of different maturities will depend entirely on expectations of future changes in interest rates.

At the other extreme we have the notion of complete market segmentation with its assumption of no transmission between interest rates on assets of different maturities. In between, we have the idea of preferred habitats, with imperfect substitution.

7.8 The significance of term structure theories

The view held about the nature of the term structure of interest rates is important at both a theoretical and a practical policy level. The theoretical issue is the usefulness of monetary policy. The difference of opinion depends on two additional assumptions.

Firstly, Keynesian economists have generally held that monetary policy operates through the effect of interest rates on the level of investment and hence on the level of aggregate demand. Thus, a government wishing to reduce inflationary pressures in the economy will need to raise interest rates in order to reduce investment (and expenditure on consumer durables).

Secondly, it is usually accepted that interest rates on assets of different maturities are important to different groups of economic agents. In particular, much bank borrowing is for short periods and so it (and hence bank lending, bank deposits and the rate of growth of the money supply) will depend on what happens to short-term interest rates. Again, the international flow of short-term funds ('hot money') will depend on what happens to short-term interest rates in different countries. However, the raising of funds for long-term investment projects is held to be related more to long-term rates of interest.

If we accept a strong version of the expectations hypothesis, we shall believe that the monetary authorities need only bring about a small change in interest rates at the short end of the market and this will quickly feed through to other interest rates and have the desired effect on investment. But if we accept something more like the segmented market approach, we shall argue that long-term rates may be affected by government monetary policy only to a very limited extent, and perhaps only very slowly.

Consequently, supporters of the notion of market segmentation are sceptical of the ability of monetary policy to influence the level of aggregate demand and tend instead to be supporters of fiscal policy. Monetarists believe that monetary policy does not only operate through interest rate changes. Nonetheless, they do see the interest rate channel as a powerful one because they argue that small changes in interest rates are rapidly communicated from one part of the market to another.

At a practical level, the notion of market segmentation opens up the possibility that monetary authorities might try deliberately to alter the term structure of interest rates so as to achieve two separate targets although this has not been attempted for many years. The aim was usually to raise short-term rates of interest without causing long-term rates to rise. It was hoped that, by so doing, short-term flows of hot money would enter the economy, temporarily improving the balance of payments and taking downward pressure off the country's exchange rate without causing domestic investment to fall. In other words, the monetary authorities tried to overcome what they saw as temporary balance of payments problems without adjusting their exchange rates and without causing a recession in the domestic economy. Opponents of market segmentation have never believed that such attempts to 'twist' the interest rate structure were sustainable in anything but the shortest of short runs. Market forces, they argued, were much too powerful to allow governments to control the term structure of interest rates. This debate lost a lot of its force when economies moved away from fixed exchange rates and the need to overcome balance of payments deficits by attracting flows of hot money from abroad largely disappeared. It is now widely accepted that changes in short-term rates will feed through into longer-term rates quite rapidly.

The term structure is also used in two distinct areas of forecasting. In international finance, the term structures of interest rates on different currencies imply, in the absence of restrictions on international capital mobility, expected exchange rate changes. The theory underlying this use is explained in Chapter 8.

More recently, great interest has been shown in the use of the term structure as an indicator of the stance of monetary policy. The argument for the use of the term structure in this way rests upon a combination of the pure expectations hypothesis with its assumption of risk-neutrality and the Fisher effect, set out in section 7.1. If the present pattern of interest rates is determined by expected future rates, then today's term structure should be an accurate predictor of future nominal interest rates. Then, if nominal interest rates are made up of a stable real interest rate and expected inflation, forecasts of future nominal interest rates effectively become forecasts of inflation and, if we assume that markets are efficient and expectations are correct, these must in turn be telling us about the current tightness or laxity of monetary policy. That is, a sharply upward sloping yield curve becomes translated into a forecast of sharply rising inflation and a judgement that current monetary policy is too loose. However, this use of the term structure has been subjected to a great deal of testing which has not, in general, been favourable. Its apparent failure has led to a good deal of criticism of the pure expectations approach to explaining the term structure and considerable emphasis on the importance of term premiums. In Box 7.6 we see how easily financial markets can be taken by surprise and how the yield curve can be changed by unexpected monetary policy decisions.

Box 7.6

Monetary policy decisions and the yield curve

We have seen in Box 7.1 that in February 2003, the Monetary Policy Committee of the Bank of England surprised financial markets by cutting the Bank's repo rate from 4 per cent to 3.75 per cent. According to theory, financial markets look well ahead and take into account information about the future prospects of the economy. Thus, financial market prices should provide a good guide to future events. It follows that financial markets should be good at anticipating what the MPC is likely to do at its monthly meetings and asset prices should change before the MPC meetings to reflect any changes in interest rates made in these meetings. This, in turn, should mean that asset prices should not change much immediately after the meeting.

In February 2003, however, the markets had it wrong. The result was that gilt prices (together with equity prices and the value of sterling) fell sharply when the MPC decision was announced. Yields on short-dated gilts fell at the short end of the yield curve (the part of the yield curve most sensitive to interest rate expectations) by up to 20 basis points (0.2 per cent). Two-year yields hit a record low of around 3.35 per cent. The yield curve steepened significantly since yields for ten-year maturity fell only 2 basis points (0.02 per cent) to 4.212 per cent. Gilt futures also rose, with June short-sterling contracts recording a record high of 96.57, implying an interest rate of 3.43 per cent.

According to the *Financial Times*, analysts said that 'the monetary policy committee's decision had dramatically altered the market's perception of MPC's stance. "It electrified the short sterling market – we saw an enormous jump," said Don Smith, bond economist at ICAP. "The interest rate profile priced in has shifted down almost by 25bp for the next 18 months. We pretty much have another cut priced in by June."'*

This episode shows us:

(a) the strength of the impact of monetary policy decisions on interest rates throughout the economy;

(b) the extent to which central bank decisions affect short interest rates more than long rates and thus have an impact on the yield curve;

(c) the importance of expectations in financial markets.

* P Munter, J Wiggins and B Jopson, 'UK interest rate cut surprises gilt traders', FT.com website, 6 February 2003. **FT**

7.9 Summary

This chapter dealt with two questions – what determines the general level of interest rates in the economy and what determines the structure of interest rates, in particular, the term structure. We began by exploring the relationship between real and nominal interest rates, arriving at the conclusion that the real interest rate is equal to the nominal interest rate less the rate of inflation. If the real interest rate were assumed to be stable, nominal interest rates would vary from country to country only because of differences in rates of inflation. This still left us to explain why real interest rates might be stable.

One way of doing this is through the loanable funds theory of interest rates in which the real rate of interest is determined by the interaction of the demand for loans and the supply of savings in a given period. The major determinants of the real interest rate according to this theory are the marginal productivity of capital (demand) and the willingness of people to postpone present consumption (supply). The theory can be used to explain why, in the absence of international capital mobility, real interest rates differ from one country to another. Even with international capital mobility, real interest rates differ largely because of the existence of risk premiums.

The loanable funds theory does not cope very well once the underlying assumption of full information of future income, interest rates and prices is dropped. We thus examined the liquidity preference theory in which interest rates are determined by the interaction of the demand for and supply of money. Attempts are often made to combine the two theories but they are essentially different – the loanable funds theory helps to support the proposition that the market economy is stable; the liquidity preference theory suggests that the market economy might be very unstable and that government may have a role to play in stabilising the economy.

The second part of the chapter dealt with the term structure of interest rates – the relationships among interest rates on bonds with different periods to maturity. We explained the expectations theory in which current interest rates on bonds with longer periods to maturity depend on expectations of future changes in interest rates. We went on to consider term premiums based on aversion to capital and income risk. We looked at the ideas of market segmentation, which raises the possibility that the relationship between short-term and long-term interest rates is not very close, and preferred habitat, which is a compromise between market segmentation and the view that changes in short-term rates lead instantly to changes in long-term rates. The chapter concluded with a consideration of the policy significance of the term structure of interest rates.

Questions for discussion

1 How would you expect an increase in the propensity to save to affect the general level of interest rates in an economy?

2 Explain how an increase in the rate of inflation might affect (a) real interest rates and (b) nominal interest rates.

3 Why are some lenders capital risk averse and others income risk averse? What slope will the yield curve have when the market is dominated by capital risk aversion?

4 Why might interest rates payable on long-term, 'risk-free' government bonds include a term premium?

5 Look at the most recent interest rate change by the MPC of the Bank of England and consider how quickly other interest rates in the economy changed thereafter. Why does the MPC change interest rates each time it acts by only $1/4$ or, at most, $1/2$ a per cent?

6 Could the MPC of the Bank of England raise interest rates when everyone was expecting them to fall?

7 Look at the financial press and find the current interest spread between five-year and ten-year government bonds. Is there a positive term premium?

8 What conclusion might you draw about possible future interest rates if a positive term premium were to increase?

Further reading

A D Bain, *The Financial System* (Oxford: Blackwell, 2e, 1992) chs. 5 and 6

P Howells and K Bain, *The Economics of Money, Banking and Finance. A European Text* (Harlow: Pearson Education, 2005, 3e) chs. 9 and 10

K Pilbeam, *Finance & Financial Markets* (Basingstoke: Macmillan, 2e, 2005) ch. 4

Financial Times (FT.com) website, http://www.ft.com

Answer to exercise

7.1 Six-year bonds: 9 per cent; seven-year bonds: 9 per cent; eight-year bonds: 9.5 per cent.

CHAPTER 8

Foreign exchange markets

The increasing interdependence of countries in recent years has led to a dramatic growth in the proportion of financial transactions that have an international aspect. At the same time, major international imbalances and the volatility of exchange rates have led to the development of new financial instruments and the growth of markets in which they are traded.

As exports and imports have grown as a percentage of the GDP of all developed countries, so too has the proportion of firms earning foreign exchange and/or requiring foreign currencies to purchase intermediate or final goods. Such firms necessarily are exposed to *foreign exchange risk* resulting from variations in exchange rates. Firms have sought both to protect themselves from this risk and to seek profits through speculation on currency markets. The desire to protect against risk has led to the development of markets designed to provide insurance (forward and futures and options markets) and the exploitation of techniques such as currency swaps. At the same time, much attention has been paid to the need to forecast future changes in exchange rates. This has in turn produced a great deal of debate over the nature of foreign exchange markets.

Only a small part of the explosion in foreign exchange transactions can, however, be related in any way to the needs of international trade. A much higher proportion has derived from the great increase in international capital mobility that has characterised the past thirty years. Both large multinational firms and governments have sought to tap international capital markets to widen their access to funds and/or to lower the costs of borrowing. To meet these demands, international banks have grown hugely in size, new markets have opened up and expanded and again new instruments have been developed.

The combination of increasing international interdependence and uncertainty has given governments a greater interest than ever in movements in the international value of their currencies and in the impact of capital mobility on the goals of economic policy and the stability of the international financial system. The post-war world has lurched from a system of fixed exchange rates to floating rates with widely varying degrees of government intervention and, in the case of Europe, back to fixed exchange rates and then to a single currency across much of the European Union (EU).

This world of foreign exchange and international capital markets is the subject of the next three chapters. In this chapter we look at the foreign exchange market itself. We consider both the expression of spot and forward rates of exchange and the market relationships that strongly influence them. In particular, we explain the ideas of interest rate arbitrage – both covered and uncovered – and purchasing power parity. We go on to look at the major arguments for and against fixed rates of exchange and the factors likely to play the major role in the determination of floating exchange rates. This provides the background for us to examine the advantages and disadvantages of monetary union. We conclude the chapter by considering the cases for and against British membership of the euro single currency area.

8.1 The nature of forex markets

Forex markets are deceptively simple. The product (foreign exchange) consists of the currencies of the major developed countries. To the extent that the currencies of developing countries are traded officially, markets are so heavily controlled by governments that often the rates of exchange have little to do with genuine supply and demand.

Prices (the exchange rates) are just the expression of one currency in terms of another. As with all prices, exchange rates can be expressed in two ways – how much of the home currency is required to buy a unit of foreign currency (direct quotation) or how much foreign currency can be obtained for a unit of home currency (indirect quotation). This is no different from the price of anything – one can equally ask how much a dozen eggs costs or how many eggs can be bought for £1. It can be seen from this example that the normal way of thinking of prices is to ask the price of one unit of the object being bought (foreign currency, eggs) in terms of domestic currency. In the currency market, this is direct quotation. The direct quotation of sterling in terms of US dollars gives us how much sterling we need to buy $1.

In the foreign exchange market, however, this approach has one unfortunate consequence. Consider Figure 8.1. To illustrate the direct quotation of sterling, we must draw demand and supply curves for the *foreign currency* (US dollars). The vertical axis

Figure 8.1

then indicates how much sterling is needed to buy $1. Now assume an increase in the demand for US dollars. The demand curve shifts out in the normal way and the price (the exchange rate) rises. But the value of sterling has clearly fallen (it now takes 63 pence to buy $1 rather than 62 pence). Thus, a rise in the exchange rate of a country's currency here means that the home currency has weakened. On the other hand, if we follow the standard British practice of using the indirect quotation (as we shall be doing for the most part in this book), a fall in the value of the home currency is reflected in a fall in the exchange rate. We show this in Figure 8.2.

To show the indirect quotation, we need demand and supply curves for the *domestic currency*. Thus, on the vertical axis in Figure 8.2 we have the amount of foreign currency (US dollars) needed to buy £1. In this diagram, an increase in the demand for dollars is indicated by an increased supply of sterling on to the market. The supply curve moves down to the right and the exchange rate falls (from £1 = $1.61 to £1 = $1.59). Box 8.1 provides additional information on the expression of exchange rates and Exercise 8.1 gives you some practice in the manipulation of rates.

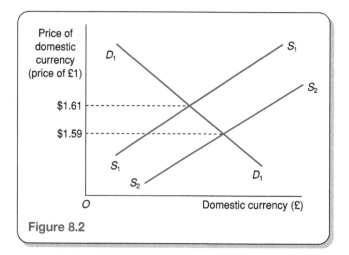

Figure 8.2

| Box 8.1 | **The expression of exchange rates** |

Indirect quotation

The standard British way of expressing the value of sterling is to quote the amount of foreign currency that exchanges for £1 (the indirect quotation of the exchange rate):

£1 = US$1.7343 – 1.7353;   £1 = €1.4321 – 1.4333;   £1 = ¥204.069 – 204.273
    dollars   euros   yen

The first of the two figures in each case is the bid rate – the rate at which market-makers are prepared to buy the home currency (sterling). The second figure is the offer rate – the rate at which they are prepared to sell the home currency. Thus, we have:

bid rates: £1 = US$1.7343   £1 = €1.4321   £1 = ¥204.069
offer rates: £1 = US$1.7353   £1 = €1.4333   £1 = ¥204.273

The difference between the two (the bid–offer or bid–ask spread) covers the market-makers' costs and provides their profits. Thus, the size of the bid–offer spread reflects the degree of risk involved in holding the foreign currency in question. For example, there are many transactions every day between sterling and US dollars (the £/$ market is very deep) and so there is little chance of sudden, large movements in the exchange rate. Consequently, the bid–offer spread represents only a tiny percentage of the value of the currency. For currencies less commonly traded (for example, the New Zealand dollar), we would expect a larger bid–offer spread to reflect the greater risk market-makers face in holding them.

To obtain a single figure for an exchange rate, the mid-point between the bid and offer rates is taken: £1 = $1.7348; £1 = €1.4321; £1 = ¥204.171.

Direct quotation

Given an indirect quotation, the direct quotation can be calculated as its reciprocal. Thus, if we take the reciprocal of the indirect rates above, we obtain the following direct quotations of sterling (the rates at which market-makers are prepared to buy and sell the foreign currency):

£0.5766 – £0.5763 = $1;   £0.6983 – £0.6977 = €1;   Y100 = £0.4900 – £0.4895

Because the unit value of the Japanese currency is so small, it would be inconvenient to express the sterling equivalent of a single yen in direct form (one would need too many decimal places to show the small differences between bid and offer rates). Therefore, it is conventional to express the rate in terms of units of ¥100. Note that, with direct quotation, the first figure is the higher of the two – the market-maker demands more domestic currency in return for a unit of foreign currency than he will offer for a unit of the foreign currency.

Note: On the Currencies & Money page of the *Financial Times*, you are given only the closing mid-point (the mid-point between the bid and offer rates at the close of the market for the day). Separate bid and offer rates are not provided.

Market participants can be split into five groups:

- the end-users of foreign exchange: firms, individuals and governments who need foreign currency in order to acquire goods and services from abroad;
- the market-makers: large international banks which hold stocks of currencies to allow the market to operate and which make their profits through the spread between buying (bid) and selling (offer) rates of exchange;
- speculators: banks, firms and individuals who attempt to profit from outguessing the market;
- arbitrageurs: banks that make profits from buying in one market at the same time as selling in another, taking advantage of small inconsistencies that develop between markets;
- central banks, which enter the market to attempt to influence the international value of their currency – perhaps to protect a fixed rate of exchange or to influence an allegedly market-determined rate.

Exercise 8.1

You are given the following information about exchange rates:

Closing mid-points
£1 = SFr2.2782 (indirect quotation of sterling)
$1 = ¥112.625 (indirect quotation of the US$)
€1 = ¥143.265 (indirect quotation of the euro)
£1 = €1.4583 (indirect quotation of sterling)

(a) Calculate each of these rates in direct terms.

(b) Look in the *Financial Times* and compare the exchange rates reported on the day you read this chapter with the above rates, which were exchange rates at the close of trading on 26 May 2006.

(c) Work out which of the two currencies has weakened and which has strengthened in each case since 26 May 2006.

It is clear from the above list that it is possible for someone to play multiple roles in the market. For instance, international banks may act in up to four capacities, while central banks may be end-users on some occasions, speculators on others.

It appears, then, that the basis of the market must derive from the demand for and supply of currencies originating from end-users. The notion that rational economic motives underpin the behaviour of end-users leads to the view that exchange rates should be determined by the market *fundamentals* – economic factors thought to influence the demand for and supply of currency such as the balance of payments, relative rates of inflation and interest rate differentials across countries. Changes in these basic influences on demand and supply will cause exchange rate adjustments. However, according to holders of this view, exchange rates will always move towards the new equilibrium position, defined as the set of exchange rates that will produce balance in the balance of payments. In the 1950s and 1960s, exchange rate theories concentrated on the current account of the balance of payments, but later theories have placed much greater emphasis on the determinants of the capital account.

One major effect of this was to increase greatly the role of expectations in attempts to forecast likely future exchange rates. Market participants became concerned more with what might happen to interest rates and inflation rates than to their current values. This implied a greater concern with what other people in the market were likely to do and introduced a strong psychological element into decisions as to which currency to buy or sell and when to buy or sell it. Under these circumstances, each piece of economic news that comes to the market needs to be carefully interpreted to try to discover its meaning for the future and the impact it is likely to have on other market agents.

Further, the attempt to outguess the market requires judgements about the future behaviour of policy-makers and the likely impact on economies of political and other news that might influence the composition and/or behaviour of governments.

Any reading of market reports quickly makes it clear how difficult it is, in practice, to interpret news and to decide what information is relevant to the determination of the exchange rate. It is common, for instance, for a market to adjust to 'news' but then to go through a process of reinterpretation, sometimes drawing different inferences from it, other times discarding it altogether as irrelevant. Again, different sets of economic indicators often provide apparently conflicting information about the state of different aspects of the economy and hence of exchange rate fundamentals. There is always a degree of uncertainty as to what is genuine news and what is not. Box 8.2 provides an example of the difficulties of interpreting news in the foreign exchange market.

Box 8.2   **The market interpretation of news**

The following example is taken from the Currencies market report of the *Financial Times*, 25/26 March 2006, p.33

The US dollar this week recovered its losses of the previous five days as traders again revised up expectations for the peak in US interest rates. Ben Bernanke, the chairman of the Federal Reserve, played his part in the dollar's recovery . . . Mr Bernanke delivered a broadly upbeat assessment of the world's largest economy, playing down fears that the flat US yield curve was a portent of doom. Data flow was limited, but the bulk of the economic numbers that did emerge played into the hands of the rate hawks, with core producer price inflation beating expectations and strong existing home sales data attesting to the robustness of the housing sector . . . The dollar wobbled yesterday as data on new home sales came in weaker than expected, allowing dollar bears to revive their view that a slowing housing market would force the Fed to start cutting rates before the year was out, dragging the dollar lower in the process. Such concerns were limited, allowing the dollar to rise 1.3 per cent on the week to $1.2028 to the euro . . .

The usually headline-averse Swiss franc, the Swissie, has fallen 2.2 per cent against the euro since early January, hitting a two-year low of SFr1.5788 yesterday. The Swissie has been undermined by rate expectations, with the market forecasting just two quarter-point rises this year, which would keep its yield well below that of the eurozone where three increases are increasingly being predicted.

Comment

Here we are given reasons for the strengthening of the US dollar and the weakening of the Swiss franc. In both cases, the principal factor was market expectations about future interest rate movements. We have no explanation of those expectations for the Swiss franc, being told only that the market expected Swiss interest rates to rise by less than eurozone interest rates, making eurozone assets more attractive to investors, causing a movement out of Swiss francs.

For the US, however, we are told of a number of influences on interest rate expectations: the generally optimistic view of the US economy given by the chairman of the Federal Reserve, the nature of the US yield curve, and statistics on the inflation rate of producer prices and on house sales. Some of these favoured the view that interest rates would continue to rise (Mr Bernanke's comments, producer price inflation, sales figures for existing houses); others favoured the reverse view (the yield curve – that is, expected future interest rates implied by the interest rates currently available on assets of differ-ent maturities) – and data on new house sales). Over the week, the view that interest rate rises would continue (held by the 'rate hawks') was the stronger and so the dollar strengthened. Yet, there were people in the market who interpreted the news coming to the market differently (the 'dollar bears') and thought interest rates would begin to fall before the end of the year. For a short time during the week (immediately after the release of figures on new house sales) they held sway, causing the dollar to wobble (that is, to fall a little before again starting to rise). Thus, we have here an example of news coming to the market and being interpreted and re-interpreted; and an example of different groups of market agents interpreting the news differently.

Read the following quotation and comment upon it in a similar way to the example above:

> The US dollar fell sharply this week, hitting a seven-week low against the euro yesterday. The dollar's reversal came in the week it emerged that the US current account deficit ballooned to a record 7 per cent of gross domestic product in the fourth quarter of 2005 and that, for the second month running, foreign purchases of US assets, as measured by the US Treasury, failed to cover the burgeoning trade deficit.

Financial Times, March 18/19 2006, p. 33 **FT**

It is hardly surprising that there are difficulties in interpreting news since economists employ a variety of models to explain the formation of prices in any market – and no one model can claim always to produce the best forecast of future market behaviour. Particular problems with the impact of news arise when market participants are using different models or are switching from one model to another. Information that is irrelevant to market price and that succeeds in confusing market participants is called noise, since it interferes with 'price signals'. Some economists who continue to believe in long-run equilibrium acknowledge the existence of 'noise' and thus of short-term disequilibrium.

However, in financial markets in which there are many participants and informa-tion is rapidly transmitted through modern technology, the period of disequilibrium is commonly held to be short. The period may be shortened further by the opera-tion of arbitrageurs and speculators. Firstly, disequilibrium produces inconsistencies in relative prices or in different parts of the market. These give rise to potential arbitrage profits. Actions taken by arbitrageurs to reap these profits act to remove the inconsistencies.

Secondly, speculators who believe that the existing price is, for example, above the equilibrium price will sell the asset or currency in question, helping the price to fall to its equilibrium level. As long as the speculator is correct about the equilibrium position, he will be able to profit by buying in again later at the lower price. Speculation in this case is stabilising.

> **Stabilising speculation:** Speculation is the buying or selling of an asset for the purpose of profiting from changes in the market price of the asset. Speculation is stabilising when it moves the market price towards the equilibrium price and speeds up the process of moving to an equilibrium position.

Although economists employ a variety of approaches to the determination of exchange rates, many depend on one or more of a number of important relationships among interest rates, exchange rates and rates of inflation.

8.2 Interest rate parity

The forex market consists of two distinct markets – the spot and forward markets. In the spot market, currencies are bought and sold for delivery within two working days. In the forward market, exchange rates are agreed for the delivery of currency at some later time. The usual contract periods in the forward market are one month and three months, although longer periods are possible, especially for heavily traded currencies. The forward market allows businesses to insure themselves against exchange rate changes by buying and selling currencies ahead. Forward foreign exchange rates are quoted as being at either a *premium* or *discount* to the spot exchange rate. If a currency is at a forward premium, it is more expensive to buy forward than to buy spot. If it is at a discount, it is less expensive forward than spot. If the spot and forward rates for a currency are equal, the currency is said to be *flat*.

Consider the position of two investors, X and Y. Each of them has €1 million to invest in a secure form for three months (the forex market is a market for large players). X buys German government securities at existing euro interest rates. However, Y notices that interest rates on sterling securities are higher than euro interest rates. She thus decides to sell the €1 million for sterling in the spot forex market and to use the sterling to buy British government securities. At the end of the three months, the British securities mature and Y then sells the sterling for euro in the spot market. Who finishes up with more euro at the end of three months?

Clearly, there are only two factors involved:

- the difference in interest rates on UK and German securities; and
- the difference in the £/euro exchange rate at the beginning and at the end of the three months.

Since interest rates in the UK are higher than in Germany, then, if there were no changes in exchange rates during the period, Y would finish up with more euro. However, X could finish up with more euro if the value of sterling against the euro fell sufficiently during the three months. For example, let the interest rates be 5 per cent on the UK security and 3 per cent on the German security. Assume an initial exchange rate of £1 = €1.50. X buys German securities, obtaining 3 per cent for three months and finishing up at the end of the period with €1,007,500. Y converts her euro into sterling and obtains £666,667, on which she receives 5 per cent interest for three months. Y therefore finishes up with £675,000 and converts this back into euro. We can easily work out that for Y to finish up no worse off than X, she would need an exchange rate of £1 = €1.493. That is, at the beginning of the period Y must have thought that the value of sterling against the euro would not fall lower than €1.493. If it fell to a lower value than that, Y would do worse than X.

The position in which these strategies of X and Y are thought likely to produce the same result is known as *uncovered interest parity*. The word 'uncovered' simply indicates that Y would be taking a risk in following her strategy because she does not know what is going to happen to the exchange rate over the ensuing three months. It is the expected future spot rate of exchange that is crucial to her decision.

Let us consider next how we might arrive at uncovered interest parity. It is clear in our example above that if investors do not switch from euro into sterling and nothing else happens to move the exchange rate away from the £1 = €1.50 rate, they will have missed a profit opportunity. They could have moved their funds into sterling and back and finished up with more euro than they did by keeping their funds at home. Thus, in practice, investors who think that the rate of exchange is unlikely to move will take advantage of the apparent profit opportunity and will follow the strategy proposed for Y above. Think what then happens.

A large amount of euro are sold for sterling at the beginning of the period, increasing the demand for sterling and pushing up the price of sterling. As this happens, the value of sterling rises above €1.50 and later investors receive less sterling in exchange for their euro. At the same time, the increased demand for British securities pushes their price up and pushes the rate of return on them below 5 per cent. The interest rate differential between British and German securities falls below 2 per cent. Clearly, Y's strategy of buying British securities is becoming less attractive for two reasons – British interest rates have fallen and the prospects of investors losing on the currency exchange are increasing. They are now paying more than €1.50 for each pound but have no reason for changing their view that the exchange rate in three months' time will be £1 = €1.50.

As interest rates and exchange rates change, the advantage of Y's strategy over X's is steadily reduced. When the profit opportunity from following Y's strategy has disappeared altogether and there is no longer any incentive to exchange euro for sterling in order to buy British securities, we have *uncovered interest parity*.

Uncovered interest parity: When the gains from investing in a country with a higher interest rate are equal to the expected losses from switching into that country's currency and back into the original currency.

The process described above of moving from one currency to another in order to take advantage of a higher interest rate in another country is known as *uncovered interest rate arbitrage*.

In this discussion, we have made two simplifying assumptions. Firstly, we have ignored transaction costs. As we have seen in our discussion of the expression of exchange rates, there is always a difference between the bid and offer rates of exchange. This difference is a cost to investors engaged in uncovered interest arbitrage and so, in practice, the profit opportunity disappears before we reach full parity. In other words, the expected losses from moving from one currency to another and back include the spread between bid and offer rates of exchange.

Secondly, we have ignored differences in default risk. We have assumed above that the only difference between German and British securities is the difference in interest rates – that is, we have assumed the two types of securities to be perfect substitutes for each other. In practice, there may be a considerable difference in the default risk attached to the two securities. For example, German investors may demand a risk premium before they are willing to hold British securities, not just because of the foreign exchange risk but also because of a difference in default risk. In this case, we certainly do not reach uncovered interest parity. Even if the two securities are objectively very similar, German investors may well feel that they have more information about the risks associated with the German securities and demand a higher interest rate on British securities before they begin to think of buying them.

The existence of forward exchange markets allows a third strategy, one that overcomes the risk associated with uncovered interest arbitrage. A third investor, Z, realises that he can buy sterling securities and, at the same time, sell sterling three months forward at an agreed rate of exchange. This means that he is able to calculate exactly how many euro he will receive when the securities mature in three months' time and so can make a precise comparison between the number of euro he would receive from buying UK securities and from leaving his money invested at home in German securities. This comparison will be influenced by:

- the difference in interest rates on UK and German securities; and
- the difference between the spot and three-month forward exchange rates for sterling against the euro.

Assume that the £ and the euro were trading with no forward premium or discount (spot and forward rates were exactly the same) but that euro interest rates were higher than sterling interest rates. Clearly, then, Z's investment strategy would be better than X's since Z could take advantage of the higher interest rates in the UK without taking on any foreign exchange risk. In the jargon, he would have locked in to the existing spot exchange rate of £1 = €1.50. However, this position would not last for very long. A large number of investors would see the benefits of Z's strategy and would follow suit. In other words, they would *sell German securities* (forcing their price down and pushing the yield on them up); *buy sterling spot* (forcing up the spot exchange rate of sterling above €1.50); *buy UK securities* (forcing their price up and the yield on them down); and to cover their exchange rate risk *sell sterling three months forward* (forcing down the three-month forward exchange rate of sterling below €1.50).

Thus, the interest rate differential between UK and German securities would be reduced and, at the same time, a discount would develop on three-month forward sterling. Both developments would be reducing the profitability of Z's strategy.

This process would continue until the rates of return on the strategies chosen by X and Z came into equality (with some small allowance, as above, for transaction costs and any perceived difference in default risk). We would then have established *covered interest parity*.

> **Covered interest parity:** When the gains from investing in a country with a higher interest rate are equal to the forward discount on that country's currency.

What would be the final outcome? Euro interest rates started below £ interest rates but euro interest rates rose while £ interest rates fell. Thus, the interest rate differential between the two countries would have been reduced. The spot exchange rate of £ rose but the three-month forward rate fell, establishing a discount on three month forward sterling. This establishes a general rule:

The currency of the country in which interest rates are higher will be trading at a forward discount; the currency of the country with the lower interest rates will be at a forward premium.

Box 8.3 provides an illustration of the way in which spot and forward exchange rates are reported in the *Financial Times*.

Box 8.3   **Spot and forward rates of exchange**

At the close of business of the London forex market on 26 May 2006, the spot exchange rate of the US dollar against sterling, as reported in the *Financial Times* of 27/28 May, stood at £1 = $1.8550. The one-month forward exchange rate was £1 = $1.8558. In other words, the dollar was trading one month forward at a discount against sterling (more dollars would be required to buy a given amount of sterling one month forward than spot). Alternatively, we could say that sterling was at a forward premium. We can easily calculate the one-month forward discount on US dollars in percentage per annum terms.

In money terms, the discount was $1.8550 – $1.8558 = –$0.0008. Remember that this was the discount for one month. To convert this into an annual discount we need to multiply by 12, giving us –$0.0096. We then need simply to divide this by the spot exchange rate of $1.8550 and multiply by 100 to obtain a percentage. This gives us –0.5175 per cent per annum.

The general rule stated above suggests that one-month interest rates on US dollars must have been well above those in the UK at the time. A look at the international currency rates on the same date confirms this. At the close of trading on 26 May 2006, the mid-point of one-month interest rates on the US dollar was 5.05 per cent; on sterling it was 4.59 – a difference of 0.46 per cent. Allowing for transaction costs, we can accept that covered interest parity applied, with the interest rate differential between the two currencies being nearly equal to the forward discount on US dollars.

Exercise 8.2 requires you to think about the relationship between spot and forward rates of exchange.

Exercise 8.2 At close of trading on 26 May 2006, the exchange rates for Japanese yen against the US dollar were:

Spot $1 = ¥112.625;   one-month forward $1 = ¥112.15;
three months forward $1 = ¥111.23

(a) Was the yen at a forward premium or discount against the dollar?

(b) What were the annual percentage premiums or discounts for yen one month and three months forward?

(c) Given that US dollar one-month interest rates were 5.05 per cent, approximately what must have yen one-month interest rates been?

Answers at end of chapter

8.3 Other foreign exchange market rules

We have thus established a relationship between spot and forward exchange rates. Several other questions follow, however:

- Why do interest rates differ among countries?
- What determines the existing spot rates of exchange?
- What causes spot rates of exchange to change over time?

Each of these questions may also be approached by a rule based upon arbitrage operations.

8.3.1 Differences in interest rates among countries – the Fisher effect

We saw in section 7.1 that nominal rates of interest consist of two elements: (a) the real rate of interest, and (b) the expected rate of inflation. It follows that differences in expected inflation rates provide *one* cause of differences in international interest rates.

But what about real rates of interest? Ignoring the issue of exchange rate risk discussed above, and assuming perfect markets with perfect capital mobility and perfect information, we saw also in Chapter 7 that market theory tells us that capital should move from capital-rich countries in which the real rate of return on capital is low to capital-scarce countries with high real rates of return on capital, and that this movement should continue until real rates of interest are equal across countries.

We also noted in section 7.2 that this does not happen in practice. There we identified the existence of risk – for example, foreign exchange risk, default risk and sovereign risk – as one reason for the failure of capital to move in the direction suggested by economic theory. *If* all the necessary assumptions did hold, however, and real rates of interest were equal across countries, international interest rates would differ only because of: (a) expected exchange rate changes; (b) differences in expected rates of inflation among countries.

This second point allows the application to the explanation of the differences in interest rates of the Fisher effect, which we introduced in section 7.1 as:

$$r = i - \dot{P}^e \tag{8.1}$$

Applying this to the explanation of differences in interest rates between the US and the UK, we can say that with real interest rates equal across countries and the foreign exchange market in equilibrium, the difference in nominal interest rates on dollars and sterling depends on the difference between the expected inflation rates in the US and the UK.

$$\frac{(i_\$ - i_£)}{(1 + i_£)} = \frac{(\dot{P}_\$^e - \dot{P}_£^e)}{(1 + \dot{P}_£^e)} \tag{8.2}$$

This is sometimes known as the Fisher closed hypothesis.

8.3.2 The determinants of spot exchange rates – purchasing power parity

If real interest rates were equal across all countries, however, and there were no international capital flows, the balance of payments balance would depend solely on international trade in goods and services. If we then ignored differences in quality among goods and services and assumed perfect information, the only reason for preferring foreign goods to home goods or vice versa would be differences in price.

If, at the existing exchange rate, goods were cheaper in the US than in the UK, UK citizens would switch to US goods. To do this they would sell sterling and acquire dollars, forcing down the value of the £ relative to the $. This process of *goods arbitrage* should continue until prices in the two countries expressed in a common currency were equal. This is the essential principle of *purchasing power parity* (PPP). In this form – absolute PPP – spot exchange rates in equilibrium are a reflection of differences in *price levels* in different countries.

Yet people are generally interested not in absolute exchange rates but rather in changes from existing rates. Thus, PPP is usually expressed in relative terms. This suggests that changes in spot exchange rates reflect differences in inflation rates among countries.

$$\frac{(\dot{P}_\$^e - \dot{P}_£^e)}{(1 + \dot{P}_£^e)} = \frac{(S_{t+1}^e - S_{t_0}^e)}{S_{t_0}} \tag{8.3}$$

> **Purchasing power parity (PPP):** The exchange rate between two currencies depends on the purchasing power of each currency in its home country and the exchange rate changes to keep the home purchasing power of the two currencies equal.

But notice that if we were to accept the three rules above, expected inflation rates would be equal to two things: the expected change in spot exchange rates and the difference in interest rates. It follows that in equilibrium, differences in interest rates must equal the expected changes in the spot rates of exchange. This equality is sometimes known as the international Fisher effect or the Fisher open hypothesis.

8.3.3 Equilibrium in the forex markets

Next, we must distinguish between forward rates of exchange and the future spot rate of exchange. The one-month forward rate is a rate agreed now for a delivery of currency in one month's time and thus is known. The future spot rate one month ahead is what the spot rate will be in one month's time and is unknown. However, by assuming perfect markets (implying perfect information about present and future values of variables), we would establish a link between the two.

Covered interest parity establishes, remember, a link between interest rate differentials and forward rates of exchange. But the combination of purchasing power parity and the Fisher effect establishes a link between interest rate differentials and expected future spot rates of exchange. It follows that if people behave rationally and are perfectly informed, and all the other assumptions of perfect markets hold, forward rates of exchange will accurately predict movements in spot rates of exchange.

In other words, in a system of perfect markets, spot and forward exchange rates would adjust immediately to any new information received and the existing forward rates would be a good predictor of future spot rates of exchange. This is because someone needing foreign currency in three months' time could either buy it now three months forward at the existing forward rate or could wait and buy it in three months' time at the spot rate of exchange then ruling. In a perfectly informed market, the cost of these two actions must be equal. If they were not equal, a profitable arbitrage opportunity would exist and the actions of arbitrageurs would bring the two rates into equality.

In practice, the forward rate is not a perfect predictor of the future spot rate. Firstly, some uncertainty attaches to future spot rates of exchange because they might always be affected by unpredictable news reaching the market. But to be genuinely unpredictable, news would need to occur randomly since if there is a pattern to the occurrence of news, well-informed markets would be able to discern it and would be able to predict the news. Random events have an equal chance of being of the type that would cause the exchange rate to rise and of the type that would cause it to fall. This implies that forecasting errors resulting from news should cancel out over time. Nonetheless, market-makers must allow for the possibility of change, and we would thus expect the spread between bid and offer rates to be greater in the forward market than in the spot market. That is, transaction costs should be higher in the forward market.

Secondly, and more importantly than the occurrence of some genuinely unpredictable events, information is neither perfect nor free. There are costs and benefits associated with acquiring additional information, and at some point the costs of doing so outweigh the gains from being able to make an even better forecast of the future spot rate of exchange. Further, the costs of obtaining information are greater for some market participants than others as are the benefits available from making an accurate forecast of future rates. It follows that the costs in money and time of collecting and interpreting information that is relevant to future exchange rates ensures both that market participants will not have full access to all relevant information and that some market participants will have an advantage over others, violating two conditions of perfect markets.

We might accept this but still wish to argue that forward rates better predict future spot rates than do other methods of forecasting exchange rates. In proposing this, we might particularly stress the role of speculators in the market. Speculators might bet on the relationship between, say, the three-month forward rate and the actual spot exchange rate in three months' time. If the forward rate does not *on average* equal the future spot rate, speculators are missing profit opportunities. For example, if the forward price of the euro were typically less than the spot rate when the forward contract matured, one could regularly buy the euro forward and then, on the delivery date, sell the euro spot and make a net profit.

It follows that all one needs to assume is that speculators are abundant and well-informed and dominate the forward market. In this case, speculation is *stabilising* – it pushes the exchange rate back towards its equilibrium rate – and performs the same role as arbitrage does in a case where no risk is involved. This might be sufficient to make forward rates of exchange a fairly reliable guide, on average, to future spot rates of exchange.

8.4 Alternative views of forex markets

Sadly for this view, however, empirical evidence tends to reject all of the international parity conditions with the exception of covered interest rate parity. This leaves open the question of how forex markets do, in practice, operate.

Three broad alternative approaches can be distinguished. The first retains the assumption of rational behaviour but through either assumptions of price rigidities or the incorporation of some non-rational elements within a rational framework produces models in which exchange rates are subject to large swings and considerable volatility. The second goes further and denies entirely the usefulness of economic models in forecasting the behaviour of exchange rates and instead bases predictions on past exchange rate trends and patterns. This is sometimes known as technical analysis. The third approach stresses the psychology of markets and market participants and distinguishes among different types of participant in the market.

One example of attempts to make use of a standard economic model to explain the highly volatile exchange rates observed in practice is overshooting exchange rate models. These continue to assume the existence of long-run equilibrium rates of exchange and incorporate both uncovered interest rate parity and purchasing power parity. These models also typically assume rational expectations. Market participants are assumed to make the best available use of all relevant information and to employ the best available model for forecasting future exchange rates. They are assumed to know what the long-run equilibrium exchange rate is. Nonetheless, exchange rates are held to overshoot their long-run equilibrium positions. That is, when the exchange rate is above its equilibrium, it will fall well below the equilibrium rate before once again rising towards equilibrium. Equally, a rising exchange rate will rise above the equilibrium rate before falling back towards it. This result is achieved by assuming that different elements in the model adjust at different speeds. The best known such model was developed by the American economist Rudiger Dornbusch (in 1976). It assumes that goods market prices adjust only slowly in response to changes in demand and supply conditions (goods prices are said to be sticky) while asset markets adjust instantaneously and can be assumed to be always in equilibrium.

Then the effects of an increase in the domestic money supply can be traced. Everyone knows that in the long run equilibrium prices will be higher and the value of the currency lower, to reflect purchasing power parity. However, initially prices do not adjust and with no price changes, interest rates must fall by a long way to restore equilibrium in the money market. Capital flows out of the country and the exchange rate falls dramatically, well past the long-run equilibrium position. It continues to do so until agents can see that the loss of income from holding funds in the country due to lower interest rates will be offset by a future rise in the exchange rate back to equilibrium. At this point, we reach a temporary equilibrium in which aggregate demand is greater than aggregate supply but in which prices remain flat. The pressure of demand on supply then slowly pushes prices up, the demand for money increases as a result, and both interest rates and the exchange rate are pushed back up towards their long-run equilibrium position. This and other similar models are of interest to economists, but empirical tests do not provide strong support for them. A rather different set of models attempts to account for 'bubbles' – sudden and apparently inexplicable jumps in the value of a currency – while continuing to argue that the market is characterised by rational behaviour.

Yet other models reject the notion of rational behaviour and argue that much trading in forex markets is based on 'noise' and that this results in excessive volatility. Another possibility is to assume that different types of participants behave in different ways. For instance, a model developed by Frankel and Froot (in 1990) divides forecasters into fundamentalists and chartists. Chartists are people who make use of technical analysis – attempting to forecast on the basis of past trends and patterns which they identify in the charts of exchange rate movements that they construct. Box 8.4 indicates some of the features of exchange rate behaviour of interest to chartists and the extent to which market practitioners often combine fundamentalism and chartism.

Another approach divides speculators into those who think short term (which in this context refers to one week or less) and those with long-run horizons (up to three months). It is then suggested that the short-termers hold extrapolative expectations (assuming that an exchange rate will continue in the direction in which it is currently moving) while the long-termers have regressive expectations (assuming that an over-valued/under-valued currency will fall/rise back to its equilibrium level). Much then depends on which group dominates the market at any particular time.

Box 8.4

Forecasting foreign exchange rates with the use of charts

Forecasters who make use of charts of past foreign exchange rates are attempting only to forecast the very short term. This assumes that current demand and supply conditions can best be understood by examining the way exchange rates have been moving. Forecasting is based principally upon three elements in the charts:

(a) Trends

Whether an exchange rate has been rising or falling and the gradient of the trend – relatively flat trends are regarded as being more sustainable, steep trends as more volatile and subject to change. Trends can be established by constructing a channel of two parallel lines which encompass all the exchange rate movements. If an exchange rate then breaks out of its current channel there is a suggestion that the present trend is about to be reversed. Analysis of trends can be supplemented by calculation of moving averages.

(b) Support and resistance levels

A support level is a rate at which the currency appears to be strongly demanded. Thus, it is difficult for the exchange rate to fall below this level. A resistance level is the reverse – a rate that it is difficult for the currency to rise above. Support and resistance levels thus establish the width of the current channel in which the currency is trading. It is usually felt that if support or resistance levels are breached, the currency will fall sharply below the previous support level or rise sharply above the prior resistance level.

(c) Pattern recognition

This is just the recognition of visual patterns in the chart – either continuation patterns (including 'flags' and 'triangles') which suggest that the rate will continue to follow its current overall tendencies, or reversal patterns (such as 'head and shoulders'). In addition, chartists make use of information on *momentum* (the speed at which exchange rates change) and *velocity* (the rate of change of moving averages of exchange rates).

The following examples of financial journalism show how fundamentalism and chartism may be combined:

(i) Marc Chandler at HSBC said technicals[1] supported the dollar's move after the euro closed on Monday below trend-line support drawn through the December and January euro lows. Mr Chandler added that news of Moody's[2] decision to downgrade South Korea's outlook to negative later weighed on the dollar.

Financial Times, 12 February 2003 ▮▮

(ii) The euro saw a flurry of excitement after unexpectedly weak US consumer confidence numbers sent the dollar sharply lower. It reached $1.082 but the rise was brief as comments by Hans Blix, chief United Nations weapons inspector, lifted the dollar once more. The euro stood at $1.078 by midsession in New York, consistent with its levels ahead of the data. Mr Blix allayed fears of imminent war when he said Baghdad was complying with UN requests. However, despite the day's excitement, the pair remained in a range, a trend analysts said was likely to continue.

Financial Times, 26 February 2003 ▮▮

[1] Technicals are those who follow technical analysis.
[2] Moody's is a major risk assessment firm. Here it had changed its rating of investments in South Korea, suggesting that they were riskier than had previously been indicated.

8.5 Fixed exchange rate systems

One way of attempting to overcome the problems associated with volatile exchange rates is for governments to enter into fixed exchange rate systems in which central rates or parities are established for each country's currency and each central bank has an obligation to buy or sell its own currency in order to maintain its exchange rate within a band of agreed width around its central rate. A fixed exchange rate system will normally contain some provision for adjustment of central parities if exchange rates are believed to have moved out of line with economic realities. Clearly, however, exchange rates can be regarded as fixed only if such adjustments of central rates occur relatively infrequently.

Since parities can change, fixed exchange rate systems do not remove the possibility of speculation. Indeed, it is often argued that life is made much easier for speculators since a weak currency can only remain unchanged or be devalued. Speculation against a currency carries little risk of loss. The debate over fixed versus flexible exchange rates has many elements and belongs properly in an international economics textbook. However, Box 8.5 summarises the principal points on both sides.

Box 8.5

Fixed versus floating exchange rates

Points in favour of floating exchange rates

- They allow continuous adjustment to change in the relative real strengths of economies.
- They allow countries to retain control over their own monetary policy.
- Hence, a floating exchange rate system reduces the number of policy targets governments are attempting to achieve and improves the balance between targets and instruments.
- With floating rates, the country is insulated against external shocks of all kinds.
- There will be less need for a country to hold international reserves.
- With fixed exchange rates, there is the problem of the rate at which it is fixed. As with any other form of government intervention, incorrect decisions regarding the exchange rate impose heavy costs on the economy.
- Floating rates will tend towards long-run equilibrium and be relatively stable. Speculation is assumed to be stabilising.
- Fixed exchange rate systems are asymmetrical in the sense that they force action on deficit countries, which are likely to respond with barriers to trade, interfering with comparative advantage as the basis for trade, lowering efficiency of resource use and lowering rates of economic growth.

Points in favour of fixed exchange rates

- Changes in exchange rates are not a good way to overcome balance of payments problems.
- Fixed rates of exchange enforce a discipline on domestic economic policies.

- Floating rate systems have an inflationary bias because there is an asymmetrical effect between countries with depreciating and appreciating currencies.
- Speculation may be destabilising.
- Thus, floating exchange rate systems are likely to be unstable and produce a great deal of uncertainty for traders.
- If falling exchange rates do not work to solve balance of payments problems quickly, reserves will still be needed in a floating system.
- The market exchange rate will be determined by the whole balance of payments (capital and current accounts) but this may not be in the long-term interest of the economy.
- Floating exchange rates allow manipulation of exchange rates in a country's own interests and this leads to competitive devaluations and attempts to export unemployment to other countries.
- Fixed exchange rates lead to reduced uncertainty regarding goods prices and lower risk premiums on interest rates. This, in turn, leads to better investment decisions abroad.

One step beyond a fixed exchange rate system is a monetary union in which a number of independent countries adopt a single currency. Monetary unions have existed in the past and modern examples can be found among former French colonies in Africa. However, by far the most important so far established is the monetary union that began operating among eleven of the fifteen members of the European Union on 1 January 1999, providing the second element of EMU (Economic and Monetary Union) in Europe. Greece became the twelfth member in January 2001.

8.6 Monetary union in Europe

A monetary union consists of a group of politically independent countries with a single currency. It follows from the acceptance of a single currency that the countries must have a joint monetary policy, implying a single base rate of interest. The Treaty on Economic and Monetary Union (the Maastricht treaty), which established the conditions for monetary union in Europe, determined that the single monetary policy in Europe would be operated by a politically independent central bank, the European Central Bank (ECB). The constitution of the ECB followed quite closely that of Germany's Bundesbank, the most successful European central bank in terms of the maintenance of low inflation and the retention of market confidence in the value of its currency. Thus, the principal duty of the ECB is to maintain price stability across the monetary union, although it is meant to do this while supporting the general economic objectives of the EU. That is, the ECB is required to pay some attention to levels of unemployment, rates of economic growth and the competitiveness of EU goods in foreign markets.

The major argument for the establishment of a monetary union in the EU was that it was a necessary adjunct to economic union. The idea behind the Single Market Treaty of 1986 was that the removal of all trade barriers across the EU would play a major role in ensuring that goods and services in Europe would be produced by the most efficient producers. This would allow EU countries to make the best possible use of their economic resources and would help them to remain competitive with other countries, such as the then rapidly expanding Asian economies. The hope was that by encouraging efficient production, Europe could remain competitive without sacrificing the higher wages and better working conditions that had come to be accepted in many EU countries. However, in a world of variable exchange rates, inefficient producers can be protected by the falling value of their domestic currency. In other words, variable exchange rates act as a barrier to trade. In addition, the volatility of floating exchange rates creates uncertainty for producers and traders and may lead to lower investment in the economy.

This establishes only an argument for a tight system of fixed exchange rates, but, as we have seen above, fixed exchange rate systems face many problems, especially when capital is highly mobile internationally as was required by the Single Market Treaty. The further step to a single currency overcomes a number of the problems of fixed exchange rate systems. In particular, it removes the possibility of destabilising speculation within the economic union and removes the possibility of member countries' seeking to devalue their currencies within the fixed exchange rate system for competitive purposes. It removes the foreign exchange risk premiums that continued to be attached to some currencies within the fixed exchange rate European Monetary System. In addition, it removes the costs of currency exchange and it allows EU citizens to compare more easily the prices charged for the same products across the whole of the single market. This *price transparency* is important because it makes it more difficult for firms to deny to consumers the potential benefits of a single market by engaging in anti-competitive and restrictive practices.

There are, however, several problems associated with the establishment of a single currency across the EU, principally because of the wide differences in living standards across the union. If the single market is effective and goods and services are produced by the most efficient producers, it is highly likely that some regions in the EU will prosper while others suffer from the closure of firms and the loss of jobs. It is also probable that the regions that suffer will be concentrated more in some member countries than in others. Thus, the EU as a whole might benefit from the single market while some countries within the union do not. This is more likely to be the case if the countries forming the single market are very different from each other at the outset in terms of productivity, standards of living, levels of unemployment and the provision of infrastructure such as transport and communications networks. We can say, in other words, that the full operation of the single market might produce *real divergence* among member economies, with the gap between richer and poorer member countries growing.

You should note two things about this argument. Firstly, there are a number of 'mights' and 'probables' in the preceding paragraph. It is by no means certain that the formation of a single market produces real divergence among member countries. Economic theory does not help much. Orthodox economic theory is more likely to support the proposition that *real convergence* will result from a single market, but this is based upon a number of dubious assumptions. In any case, even if convergence does occur it is very likely to take a long period of time and may well follow an initial, quite long period of divergence. Spanish workers who become unemployed are not likely to be much comforted by the idea that the same forces that caused them to lose their jobs might produce a higher standard of living for other Spanish citizens in twenty or thirty years' time. Empirical evidence on the issue is also far from clear and will always be difficult to interpret because we shall always be comparing the present state of the world (say, after the formation of the single market) with a hypothetical view of what might have happened under different circumstances (if the single market had not been formed). Such a comparison always requires a number of contestable assumptions to be made.

The second point to note is that we are talking about the *single market* not the *single currency*, and the single market is accepted by all EU members, including those countries that have not joined the single currency. The single currency enters the argument because it removes the last remaining element of protection for those countries that might suffer from the single market by removing the possibility that they can remain competitive through changing exchange rates. In a sense, then, countries that reject the single currency are rejecting the full implications of something they have already accepted. Nonetheless, the argument remains a powerful one in the minds of many people, especially if there is distrust among member countries.

One possible counter argument to the idea that it is desirable for a country to maintain its own currency and, with it, the right to change the rate of exchange between its currency and those of its partners within the union is to point to large countries with a single currency. The US has a single currency in an economy with much the same GDP as the EU and with wide differences in per capita income levels across the country. If a single currency is acceptable for the US, why should it not be so for the EU?

It is usual to point to two differences between the EU and the US in this context. Firstly, as well as having a common monetary policy, the US has a single federal government and a single fiscal policy (although there are variations in local and state taxes). This means that there are automatic transfers through the central budget from rich to poor regions. High-income regions pay more in taxation to the central government and, on balance, are likely to receive less in central government expenditure than do the poorer regions. This is, of course, also true of the UK. It may still be the case that these automatic transfers are insufficient to offset the increase in the differences in standards of living that arise from the existence of a single market. However, a single government is also able relatively easily to support these automatic transfers among regions with a discretionary regional policy to support poorer regions. Naturally, this does not always happen and almost never happens to the extent desired by poorer regions, but it is well within the scope of a national government.

The EU does not have a single fiscal policy and automatic transfers do not occur among EU regions through the normal operation of taxation and government spending. An EU regional policy has existed since 1975, and the Maastricht treaty stressed the importance of cohesion funds to help all countries to benefit from the single market process. However, the central EU budget is small and offers little possibility of meaningful discretionary payments to poorer regions. Experience has shown that it is very difficult to persuade the richer national governments to increase their contributions to the EU budget in order to provide greater assistance to the poorer member countries. It is this argument that leads to the view that for the monetary union to work, it must sooner or later be supported by a single fiscal policy across the union, implying a strong element of political union. Much of the opposition to the single currency stems from a rejection of the idea of political union.

The second relevant difference between the EU and single countries such as the US concerns the mobility of labour. Differences among regions are less serious if unemployed or poorly paid workers are easily able to move to obtain jobs or higher pay. There are many forces operating against labour mobility in single countries – social and family ties, the educational needs of children, lack of information about working and living conditions in other regions and, particularly important in the UK, wide differences in the price of housing and lack of flexibility in the market for rented accommodation. However, it is certainly true that the existence of different languages and the extent of cultural differences together with differences in educational systems and social security and pension regulations cause labour mobility across the EU to be much lower than it is across the UK or the US. This is likely to remain the case for a long time, despite all the efforts of the European Commission to overcome these differences. And yet it is also true that the adoption of the single currency is very likely to contribute to increasing the mobility of labour in Europe. It is also clear that these concerns about growing differences in economic performance among countries essentially stem from the single market, not simply from the single currency.

The argument against the single currency sometimes concentrates on the problems associated with a common monetary policy. This is principally the 'one size does not fit all' argument – that the interest rate chosen by the European Central Bank is unlikely to be suitable for all member countries because different member countries will, at any one time, be at different positions on their business cycles. Since 1999, it has frequently been argued that Germany needed lower interest rates than those set by the ECB because of its slow economic growth and high unemployment, while Spain and Ireland, which were experiencing much faster rates of growth and inflationary pressures, would have appreciated higher rates of interest.

One difficulty with the argument is that it applies at national level as well. When the Monetary Policy Committee of the Bank of England makes its monthly decision about UK interest rates, the interest rate chosen is very likely to suit some regions more than others. It is also likely to suit some sectors of the economy more than others. In recent years, there has often been a conflict between the needs of a booming housing market and those of an export sector suffering from the low level of demand in the world economy. Conditions in the housing market have sometimes appeared to call for no change or for an increase in the rate of interest at the same time as the export sector would clearly have benefited from a significant fall in interest rates.

Obviously, however, a single interest rate is likely to be less satisfactory the greater are the differences across the economy. Looking at the question in this way makes it clear that the underlying issue again concerns the extent to which the single market supported by the single currency is likely to lead to convergence or divergence among members. Certainly, if the single market is a success, business cycles of the different member countries should come into line and the common monetary policy should, over time, cause fewer problems across the monetary union.

8.6.1 The single currency in practice 1999–2006

The single European currency, the euro, came into existence on 1 January 1999. It began trading at a rate against the US\$ of €1 = \$1.1743 and against sterling of €1 = £0.7058. However, it quickly began to fall in value. Despite occasional upward movements, it continued its general slide until October 2000 when it reached €1 = \$0.8273 and €1 = £0.5747, a fall of 30 per cent against the dollar and of 20 per cent against sterling. This was despite the fact that several members, most notably Germany, had wanted the euro to be a strong international currency.

The basic reason given throughout the period for the slide in the value of the euro was the high unemployment rates and low rates of growth in the major EU economies, particularly in Germany. This convinced the markets that the ECB would need to keep interest rates low. The ECB had started with an interest rate of 3 per cent. This was lowered in early April 1999 to $2^{1}/_{2}$ per cent. The ECB gave no indication that it was unduly concerned about the fall in the value of the euro and thus there seemed no immediate prospect of an increase in interest rates to try to stem the fall. In addition, politicians and central bank officials often made conflicting statements concerning the euro, giving the markets the feeling that the ECB would be happy just to let things drift. The markets did not like this apparent lack of leadership. Under these circumstances, other factors, which might normally not have had much impact on the currency, provided additional excuses for selling the euro. These included the resignation of the president and members of the European Commission and the NATO bombing of Serbia and Kosovo. It was suggested that there would need to be genuine news about improved fundamentals underlying the value of the currency to push up the value of the euro, whereas it would fall merely on the basis of rumour and political uncertainty. Nor was the market fully convinced that the ECB would, despite its constitution, be immune from political pressure. This concern was strengthened by the confusion over the length of the term of office of the first president of the ECB, Wim Duisenberg of the Netherlands.

Duisenberg was appointed in 1998 to serve an eight-year term. However, there had been conflict over his appointment because of the fear of some member states, notably France, that Duisenberg's approach to policy would be too conservative and that monetary policy might be deflationary. It was generally accepted that there had been a behind-the-scenes agreement that Duisenberg would serve only half of his full term of office and would then be replaced by a French nominee, although Duisenberg consistently denied this. In the event, he retired from the job on his 68th birthday, on 9 July 2003, having served just over five years of the eight-year term.

In addition to the worry about leadership, because the euro was a new currency there was no firm view as to the long-run exchange rate indicated by economic fundamentals. The starting exchange rate of the euro was simply a weighted average of the values of the eleven participating currencies at the end of December 1998. There was no reason to believe that the new currency would behave in the same way as this weighted average had done before 1999. Indeed, it was likely that recessions in the major economies would have a more depressing impact on expectations about the future of the European economy than was suggested by the weights applied in the old exchange rate mechanism of the European Monetary System.

Thus, the fall in the value of the euro resulted from a mixture of genuine economic news, the existence of uncertainty about the attitudes of the authorities and a variety of short-term political factors. The doubts about when the euro would 'bottom out' encouraged speculators to continue to sell the euro.

By September 2000, the ECB had become concerned about the possible inflationary effects of the weakening currency. After a series of interest rate rises, the ECB joined with the central banks of the US, Japan and the UK to purchase euros in an attempt to prop up the currency. This, together with a further interest rate rise in October, had no immediate effect and the euro reached its low point against the dollar on 26 October 2000. Then, however, the value of the currency did begin, slowly and haltingly, to rise. This was probably largely to do with increasing concerns about the US economy. Having reached $0.9525 in January 2001, the euro began 2002 at $0.9034. From June 2002, it began to climb fairly steadily, finishing the year just below $1.05. Aided by concerns about the impact of the US-led war in Iraq and by regular cuts in US interest rates the euro continued to rise, charging past its starting dollar value to reach $1.36 by the end of 2004. It then steadied and began to fall back towards its starting level, which it again fell below for a time in late 2005. At the end of March 2006 the value of the euro was just over $1.21, only a little different from its value at the beginning of 1999. Much the same applies to the value of the euro in terms of sterling. From a beginning exchange rate at the start of 1999 of €1 = £0.716, the euro had moved to €1 = £0.695 by the end of March 2006, a fall in the value of the euro of approximately 3 per cent over seven years.

The steep fall in the value of the euro in its first two years had led critics to brand the single currency a failure, but recent events confirm that much which happens in the rough and tumble of daily currency trading relates to the market's view of the US economy and to short-term political and economic events rather than to economic fundamentals. The success or otherwise of the European single currency will have to wait until a judgement can be made about its impact on the European economy as a whole and on the economies of member countries, not be made on the basis fluctuations in the market for foreign currency.

8.6.2 The UK and the euro

As part of the negotiations leading up to the signing of the Maastricht treaty in 1991, the UK government had obtained an opt-out, allowing it to choose not to be an initial member of the monetary union. Technically, it was not eligible to join the euro area at the beginning of January 1999 because sterling had not been a member of the exchange rate mechanism of the European Monetary System for at least two years immediately prior to the establishment in 1998 of the membership of the monetary union (sterling had been in the EMS's exchange rate mechanism only from 1990 to 1992). In practice, sterling would almost certainly have been granted membership from January 1999, but the government chose to exercise its opt-out and remain outside, together with Sweden and Denmark. Greece had always wished to join but was not granted membership until January 2001 because of its failure to meet other conditions for membership set out in the Maastricht treaty.

The question was then whether the UK would join in the future and, if so, when. In 1998 the government indicated its willingness to join in principle but said that it would not recommend UK membership until the economic case for doing so was 'clear and unambiguous'. The factors to be taken into account in making that decision were expressed in the 'five economic tests' set out by the Chancellor of the Exchequer, Gordon Brown, in July 1997. The five tests were:

- Are business cycles and economic structures compatible so that we and others could live comfortably with euro interest rates on a permanent basis?
- If problems emerge, is there sufficient flexibility to deal with them?
- Would joining EMU create better conditions for firms making long-term decisions to invest in Britain?
- What impact would entry into EMU have on the competitive position of the UK's financial services industry, particularly the City's wholesale markets?
- In summary, will joining EMU promote higher growth, stability and a lasting increase in jobs?

The Treasury began a detailed study of the five tests, with the Chancellor promising an evaluation of them by June 2003. There was always a problem with the tests since the issues involved were so complex and the uncertainties so great that no one could ever claim that the economic case for joining was 'clear and unambiguous'. Major economic and political decisions never are. Thus, despite the detailed technical work done, there remained great scope for interpretation of the data. In the event, the June evaluation confirmed the general feeling – stemming in part from Gordon Brown's personal scepticism towards euro area membership – that the answer would continue to be 'yes, but not yet and perhaps not for quite a long time'. Nothing has occurred in the intervening three years to bring future British membership any closer. Indeed, the continued poor performance of the economies of some single currency members, notably of France and Italy, relative to the British economy, the possibility of Gordon Brown becoming the next British Prime Minister and the continued opposition to membership of the euro by the principal opposition party have all added to the feeling that British participation in the European single currency is a very distant prospect.

8.7 Summary

An exchange rate expresses the value of one currency in terms of another and can be expressed in either direct form (the domestic currency price of one unit of foreign currency) or indirect form (the foreign currency price of one unit of domestic currency). In addition to the end-users of foreign currency, arbitrageurs, speculators, central banks and market-makers participate in forex markets. Explanations of changes in exchange rates used to start with the demand for and supply of foreign exchange depending on rational economic motives (market fundamentals). However, very little of the currency traded in forex markets is used for international trade in goods and services. Capital movements are now much more important.

To examine the market fundamentals thought likely to affect exchange rates among currencies, we need to look at a number of important relationships. We began with uncovered and covered interest parity. Covered interest parity concerns the relationship between differences in interest rates between countries and the difference between spot and forward rates of exchange. Differences in interest rates can then be related to differences in expected inflation rates (the Fisher effect), which can, in turn, be related to changes in spot exchange rates through purchasing power parity. When we put all this together, we reached the conclusion that, if markets were fully efficient, forward exchange rates would accurately predict future spot exchange rates. We looked at reasons why this is not so and then considered alternative views of exchange rate determination, including the overshooting of exchange rates. This section of the chapter concluded with an account of some of the ideas underlying chartism, which attempts to forecast exchange rates on the basis of past patterns.

We then moved on to look at fixed exchange rate systems and their advantages and disadvantages in comparison with floating exchange rates. The final section of the chapter outlined the arguments for and against monetary union and discussed the issues surrounding the question of the UK's future entry to the EU's monetary union. That is, we were concerned with whether the UK should join and, if so, when it should join.

Questions for discussion

1 List as many items as you can of 'news' which would be likely to cause the value of sterling to fall. Explain why in each case.

2 Under what circumstances might speculation in a market be regarded as a good thing?

3 How might one use the spot markets to obtain protection against foreign exchange risk? What advantages do the forward markets have for this purpose?

4 Under what circumstances might speculators perform the role normally played by arbitrageurs in foreign exchange markets – that of removing inconsistencies among prices? (Note: consider the relationship between forward and future spot rates of exchange.)

5 At the close of trading on 13 June 2006 £1 sterling was worth 394.648 Hungarian forint. Did the fact that £1 was worth so many forint indicate that sterling was then a very much stronger currency than the forint? If not, what did it indicate?

6 In 1970, £1 exchanged for over 8 deutschmarks (DMs). At the time of the formation of the euro in 1999, the exchange rate was £1 = DM2.78. Why do you think this might have been the case? Did this weakening of sterling against the DM mean that in 1999 British goods were very much more competitive with German goods than they had been in 1972? If not, why not?

7 Explain the differences between being a member of the old European Monetary System before 1999 and a member of the euro area from 1999 onwards.

8 Both the UK and Denmark chose to remain outside monetary union when it was set up at the beginning of 1999. Denmark, however, chose to keep its currency within the European exchange rate mechanism while the UK did not. Why do you think the two countries made different decisions in this regard?

9 Examine the following set of exchange rates:

£1 = €1.458; $1 = €0.753; £1 = $1.886

What is wrong with these rates? If these rates did apply, how would it be possible to make a profit by trading in these currencies? Would this be arbitrage or speculation?

Further reading

K Bain and P Howells, *Monetary Economics. Policy and its Theoretical Basis* (Basingstoke: Palgrave, 2003) ch. 14

J A Frankel and K A Froot, 'Chartists, fundamentalists and trading in the forex market', *American Economic Review*, May 1990, pp. 181–5.

P Howells and K Bain, *The Economics of Money, Banking and Finance. A European Text* (Harlow: Pearson Education, 3e, 2005) ch. 18

P Williams, 'The foreign exchange and over-the-counter derivatives markets in the United Kingdom', *Bank of England Quarterly Bulletin*, Winter 2004, pp. 470–84

For current information on foreign exchange markets see the *Financial Times* website, http:/www.ft.com

For historic data on exchange rates see http://pacific.commerce.ubc.ca/xr/

Answers to exercises

8.1 (a) SFr1 = £0.439; ¥100 = $0.888; ¥100 = €0.698; €1 = £0.685.

8.2 (a) Fewer yen were needed to buy one US dollar forward and so the yen was at a forward premium; (b) one month 5.06 per cent; three months 4.95 per cent; (c) Japanese interest rates must have been very close to zero. In fact, they were: one month 0.125 per cent; three months 0.26 per cent.

CHAPTER 9

Exchange rate risk, derivatives markets and speculation

Objectives

What you will learn in this chapter:

- The nature of exchange rate risk
- The meaning of hedging against risk
- A definition of derivatives markets
- The nature of financial futures markets
- How financial futures can be used to hedge against risk
- The different forms of options and their use
- A comparison of the different forms of hedging available in derivative and forward markets
- The problems associated with derivatives markets

We looked in Chapter 8 at problems associated with volatile exchange rates and at attempts to explain this volatility. Whatever the causes are, firms and governments must try in some way to cope with rapidly changing exchange rates. One response, we saw, is to develop fixed exchange rate systems or to take the extra step and move to monetary union. In the absence of any reduction in exchange rate volatility, firms must act individually to protect themselves from the potential losses arising from unexpected changes in exchange rates. In this chapter, we look more closely at the nature of the risk involved and at ways of overcoming exchange rate risk. We shall return briefly to the use of forward forex markets to provide protection and go on to consider other financial markets that have developed and grown rapidly in the past thirty years – markets for derivatives.

> **Derivatives:** A financial instrument based upon the performance of separately traded commodities or financial instruments.

We introduce the major derivatives markets and look at their use both in the protection of end-users from forex risk and in speculation. We conclude the chapter by considering the advantages of derivatives markets and the dangers associated with them.

9.1 Forms of exposure to exchange rate risk

Exchange rate risk takes several forms. The simplest can be appreciated by considering the position of a British exporting company selling in the US market and entering into a contract to supply goods over the next year. Payment is to be made in US dollars within a stated period after the delivery of the goods. The British company bases its sterling prices on its current production costs in the UK, but to convert these into dollar prices must assume an exchange rate for sterling against the dollar. The company is said to be *long* in dollars (it has net assets in dollars in the form of the future payments to be received in dollars). The risk facing a company long in a foreign currency is that the foreign currency will weaken between the signing of the contract and the settlement of the account. A company that owes money in a foreign currency is said to be *short* in that currency (it has net liabilities in the foreign currency). The risk it faces is that the value of the foreign currency will rise before it pays its debts. Market participants who are either long or short in a foreign currency have an *open position* in the market.

> **Open position:** At risk from a change in exchange rates – either *long* (assets in the foreign currency greater than liabilities in it) or *short* (assets in the foreign currency less than liabilities in it).

The form of exchange rate risk faced by the British exporting company above is known as transaction exposure.

> **Transaction exposure:** Exposure to foreign exchange risk deriving from cash flow or current transactions that figure in a company's income statements but not on its balance sheet.

Translation exposure covers the case of a parent company with subsidiaries in other countries, where there is a need to produce a financial statement showing the position of the whole group of companies. If the accounts of the subsidiaries involve foreign currency-denominated assets and liabilities (on balance sheets or in income statements), the translation of these into the group statement may involve foreign exchange exposure.

Economic exposure, like transaction exposure, relates to cash flows but is concerned with the impact on the present value of future cash flows of all changes associated with the depreciation or appreciation of a currency. Consider more closely the British exporter selling its goods in the US. Remember that the risk the firm faces is that the value of the US dollar will fall. Suppose, however, that there is inflation in the US and thus that the firm is able to sell its product for an increasing number of dollars. Suppose further that the fall in the value of the dollar that occurs is just equal to the difference in the rate of inflation in the two countries (relative purchasing power parity holds). In this case, the firm will be no worse off overall. There would be transaction exposure because a fixed quantity of dollars would at a given time exchange for fewer pounds. However, there would be no economic exposure because the firm would have benefited from the difference in inflation rates that had caused the dollar to fall in value. Thus, one way of comparing the two types of exposure is to say that transaction exposure arises from changes in nominal exchange rates while economic exposure derives from changes in real exchange rates (when purchasing power parity does not hold).

However, economic exposure is a rather broader concept than this implies. Consider, for example, the impact on a UK exporting company of a fall in the value of sterling in terms of dollars. The firm could take the benefit of the fall in the value of sterling by increasing its profit margins and leaving the dollar prices of its goods unchanged. Its US dollar profits would convert into more sterling than before, but if UK inflation were higher than US inflation and purchasing power parity held, the firm would not have gained in real terms from the depreciation of sterling. On the other hand, the firm could leave its profit margins unchanged and lower the prices of its goods in dollars, increasing its sales and its market share in the US. In this case, we could not say what the final effect would be without information about the elasticity of demand for the firm's goods in the US.

Again, if the UK exporter used inputs imported from the US, it would face an increase in the sterling price of those inputs. This would increase its costs and reduce the gain made as a result of the sterling depreciation. The firm might also face problems in third markets, for instance if it were in competition in Japan with a German firm. Of course, it might be able to protect itself in a different way by obtaining its inputs from a different source than the US.

A British company competing with US imports in the domestic market would gain from the fall in the value of sterling but the benefit would be reduced by any consequent increase in domestic inflation. The extent of this inflation would depend on supply elasticities in the UK.

These examples of exposure to risk vastly understate the problems caused to individual firms by exchange rate changes. Many firms both sell output and buy inputs in a number of currencies, the relationships between which are constantly changing. They must make investment decisions a long time in advance on assumptions made about the likely profits from different operations. Expected profits in particular markets can quickly be turned into losses by exchange rate changes. Firms may also suffer from the foreign exchange problems of their customers or suppliers. It is no surprise that the breakdown of the IMF fixed exchange rate system in 1972 led to a great demand from firms for means of protection against risk. A major form of protection undertaken by firms was that of hedging foreign exchange risk.

> **Hedging foreign exchange risk:** The act of reducing that risk by undertaking an offsetting transaction in a derivative market. A British firm that is long in dollars and thus risks losing should the value of the dollar fall hedges by taking out a contract in a derivative market that would be profitable should the value of the dollar fall.

9.2 Exchange rate risk management techniques

A variety of techniques have been developed to help firms counter foreign exchange risk (to allow companies to cover themselves against risk, or to move from an open to a closed position in the market). These may be divided into internal techniques, which relate to the accounting systems and the payment and invoicing procedures used by companies, and external techniques, which concern the development of new instruments and markets. We are interested in the market techniques here. They include the use of forward exchange markets, the use of derivatives markets such as those in financial futures and options, swap deals and short-term borrowing in a foreign currency.

Consider, firstly, the use of forward exchange markets. To deal with transactions exposure, a British company selling goods in the US needs to estimate when it will receive the dollars it is expecting in payment for its goods and to sell those dollars forward at an exchange rate agreed now. Equally, an importing company, expecting to have to pay a bill in US dollars at some known time in the future, needs to buy dollars forward to the required amount. By acting in such ways, firms are said to lock in to current exchange rates. They thus obtain a form of insurance against exchange rate change. The cost of this insurance is the premium or discount on forward exchange rates (explained in Chapter 8).

Forward foreign exchange transactions are over-the-counter (OTC) business – that is, they are contracts between a bank and another market agent. The amount of the contract and its terms are determined by the two parties involved. In practice, the period for which insurance is required by firms against exchange rate changes may be longer than the one month or three months most commonly available on the forward market, and is unlikely to be for a precise period. Worse, the date on which the payment might actually be made or required is probably uncertain and subject to change. Because forward deals are individual contracts negotiated with a bank, the amount of the contract is variable, and some flexibility is possible in the time period, although the costs of special arrangements might be quite high.

We have been discussing forward sales and purchases of currency. Another widely used OTC forward instrument is the forward rate agreement (FRA). FRAs were not specifically designed to counter exchange rate risk but rather the risk of loss from changes in interest rates. Thus, FRAs are alternatives to interest rate futures and options and, particularly, to interest rate swaps.

> **Forward rate agreement (FRA):** Interest rate forward contract in which the interest rate to be paid or received on a specific obligation for a set period of time, beginning at some time in the future, is determined when the contract is signed.

9.3 Derivatives markets

Perhaps the major development in financial markets over the past thirty-five years has been the establishment and growth of financial derivatives markets. Derivatives contracts promise to deliver underlying products at some time in the future or give the right to buy or sell them in the future. For example, a contract may promise the delivery of a specified quantity of US dollars. The derivative contract can then be traded in a different market from that in which the underlying product is itself traded (in the case of a derivative contract in US dollars, this would be the foreign exchange market). Markets in which underlying products are traded (such as the forex market) are often referred to as *cash markets* to distinguish them from *derivatives markets*.

Although cash and derivatives markets are separate, the derivatives markets are linked to cash markets through the possibility that a delivery of the underlying product might be required. Consider the following example.

A has some form of derivative contract that requires him to take delivery of a specified quantity of US dollars, say $18,000, in one month's time at a fixed rate of exchange (say, £1 = $1.80) – he is currently long in US dollars. A hopes that the value of the dollar will rise so that as soon as he receives the dollars, he can sell them on the spot market at a profit. With the spot exchange rate at £1 = $1.80, the contract is worth £10,000. If the dollar does start rising in value, in line with A's expectations, clearly the value of A's contract rises above £10,000 (it would now cost more than £10,000 to buy $18,000 on the spot market). In fact, the pricing of derivatives contracts is very complex and we shall have little to say about it here.* Nonetheless, it is clear that there is a close relationship between the prices of derivatives contracts and the prices of the underlying assets they represent, and that the value of a derivative, and hence its price, varies as the price in the cash market fluctuates. We should also add that, in practice, derivatives seldom lead to the exchange of the underlying product. Instead, contracts are *closed out* or allowed to lapse before the delivery date arrives.

Derivatives, then, are instruments that allow market agents to gamble on movements in the prices of other instruments without being required to trade in the instruments themselves. There are three major types of financial derivatives – *futures, options* and *swaps* – and myriad variations upon them. Exchange-traded derivatives (futures and options, which are traded through financial futures exchanges) are dealt with here. They are not OTC business. Contracts differ from those in forward foreign exchange in the form of operation of the market, the terms of the contract, and the likelihood of their leading to delivery of the underlying product. A crucial difference is that a derivatives contract is a tradable instrument and can be sold on to a third party. Swaps, which are quite different in nature and operation, are considered in Chapter 10.

---

* But see section 9.3.2 on the pricing of options and, for more detail, see Howells and Bain, 2005.

Although derivatives trading based upon commodities (agricultural products or minerals) has existed for well over a century, the need for financial derivatives markets was not recognised until the early 1970s. Their development resulted from the globalisation of business, the increased volatility of foreign exchange rates, and increasing and fluctuating rates of inflation.

9.3.1 Financial futures

The most common products underlying futures contracts are foreign currencies (exchange rates), interest rates on notional amounts of capital, and stock exchange indices. The futures contracts are themselves tradable – that is, they can be bought and sold in futures markets. To increase their tradability, futures contracts are standardised in terms of both time period and amount. They specify the quantity and quality of the underlying product, the agreed price and the date of delivery.

> **Futures contracts:** Legally binding agreements to deliver, or take delivery of, a commodity or a financial instrument at some specified future date.

Thus, the Sterling Futures contract (see Box 9.1) offered by the Chicago Metal Exchange (CME) specifies an amount of £62,500, while each Japanese Yen Futures contract offered by CME is for ¥12.5 million. Interest rate futures specify the amount of the notional bond and its interest-rate coupon, for instance, a $100,000 nominal 20-year treasury bond with a 7 per cent coupon. As long as contracts are for relatively small amounts, this standardisation does not much reduce the flexibility of the market since an investor can vary the amount of his exposure by buying or selling a number of contracts on the same underlying product for the same period.

Most financial futures contracts offer a choice of four delivery dates per year. There are a number of delivery details, including lists of eligible assets that satisfy the delivery requirements of a contract, and methods of determining the final settlement price. However, delivery does not usually occur as buyers and sellers of futures contracts are not normally end-users of the underlying product. Traders using futures to hedge against risk to which they are exposed in the cash market are seeking to lock in to existing exchange or interest rates on future transactions. In such cases, the period for which the hedge is needed is unlikely to coincide with the period of the futures contract. Once a firm has traded out of its open position in the cash market, it no longer needs the hedge in the futures market.

Financial futures may also be traded by speculators who wish to profit from the rises or falls they expect to occur in interest rates, exchange rates or stock exchange indices. Through futures, they can take a view about trends in cash markets without having to purchase the underlying product. A speculator who felt that interest rates were likely to rise or a currency's value decline would go short in the relevant asset by selling a futures contract. Traders who are using the futures market to create an open position in this way usually close the position once they have achieved their profit objectives. If it does not seem likely that they will make the hoped-for profit, they will probably cut their losses before delivery is due.

Box 9.1

Exchange rate futures in the *Financial Times*

The following information was provided in the *Financial Times* of 5 April 2006 on the Euro Futures ($/Euro) contract offered by the Chicago Metal Exchange (CME).

Mercantile Euro futures £125,000 per euro

	Open	Sett	Change	High	Low	Est. vol	Open int
Jun.	1.2316	1.2357	+0.0035	1.2364	1.2299	106,590	159,215
Sep.	1.2370	1.2422	+0.0035	1.2425	1.2365	294	2,329

The heading tells us the size of each contract (€125,000) and the form of the exchange rate – 'per £' indicates that exchange rates are being quoted in the form €1 = $1.2316. That is, we have the euro quoted indirectly (the dollar is quoted against the euro).
    The meaning of each of the columns is:

Open   the price of the contract at the beginning of business on the previous trading day (4 April 2006), i.e. the opening price of the contract that promised the delivery of euro at the end of June 2006 was €1 = $1.2316.

Sett   the settlement price – the price at which contracts were settled at the close of the market on 4 April 2006.

Change   the change in the settlement price from the previous day – this is not usually equal to the difference between the first two columns, and where very few contracts have been traded during the day might be significantly different (as with the September contract above).

High   the highest price reached for the contract on the day.

Low   the lowest price reached for the contract on the day.

Est. vol the estimated number of contracts entered into during the day.

Open int open interest – the number of outstanding contracts at the end of the previous trading day.

Note that open interest is much greater for the June contract. This shows the short-term nature of the market. The settlement date of the September contract was still nearly five months into the future and very little interest was being taken in it – only 294 September contracts had been traded on the previous day against the 106,590 June contracts traded.

Source: Financial Times, 5 April 2006

Investors wishing to cancel out the obligation to deliver or to accept delivery of the underlying product do so by entering an offsetting (or reversing) contract. That is, if a market agent has entered a contract to deliver a particular instrument, she can reverse this by taking out another contract that requires her to take delivery of the same amount of the same product on the same date. Her obligations under the two contracts then cancel out. In some cases, such as futures based upon equity market indices or interest rates on short-term deposits, no delivery is possible and traders meet their obligations by making cash payments based upon the changes in the value of the index or interest rate in question.

To reduce default risk and hence to make futures more easily tradable, futures exchanges make use of a *clearing house,* which covers any default arising from a contract. Although all futures contracts involve a buyer and a seller, the obligation of each is to the clearing house, not to each other. That is, after the transaction has been recorded, the clearing house substitutes itself for the counterparty and becomes the seller to every buyer and vice versa. Therefore, the only default risk faced by someone entering a futures contract stems from any doubts about the creditworthiness of the clearing house itself.

This is, in turn, reduced in a number of ways. Firstly, all transactions must take place through members of the exchange who act as brokers for anyone wishing to invest in the market. The number of members (or seats on the exchange) is limited. Seats on an exchange are purchased from existing members but new members must demonstrate their creditworthiness to the exchange. In addition, the members of the exchange must keep with the clearing house special accounts (margin accounts) that are adjusted from day to day to ensure that they are always able to settle their debts to the clearing house. Investors must, in turn, maintain similar accounts with the members of the exchange. This is known as trading on margin. Futures positions are thus said to be 'margined on a *marked-to-market basis'.* These rules should allow the clearing house to guarantee the performance of every contract entered into on the exchange.

> **Trading on margin:** The process of trading in futures markets in which buyers and sellers initially pay only a small percentage of the value of the underlying assets (the margin). Adjustments to this amount are then made daily, depending on whether the value of the underlying assets has risen or fallen.

At the start of the contract period, a member pays into a margin account a small percentage of the value of the contract (the *initial margin*). The size of the initial margin is intended to reflect the maximum daily loss likely to arise on the contract and so is related to the volatility of the price movements of that instrument. Initial margins are generally between 1 and 5 per cent of the value of the contract. Margin accounts are then adjusted daily to reflect gains or losses on a contract over the day.

Consider a contract such as the sterling future offered by the CME. Assume that the contract is for the exchange of £62,500 for dollars in three months' time at an exchange rate of £1 = $1.85 and that this is the current rate of exchange. The contract thus has a commencing value of $115,625 (this is what it would cost at the current exchange rate to buy the sterling promised for delivery). Each counterparty pays an initial margin of $5,000 into their margin accounts with the clearing house. Assume next that during the first day's trading, the spot exchange rate of sterling moves above £1 = $1.85. This increases the contract's value, representing a potential loss for the seller and a potential gain for the buyer. That is, if the contract had to be settled on that day, the seller of the contract (the person who has promised to deliver £62,500 at £1 = $1.85) would need to pay more than $115,625 to obtain the necessary sterling. The buyer of the contract, on the other hand, could take delivery of the sterling at the agreed rate ($1.85) and promptly sell it at the higher price available in the spot forex market.

Let us be more precise. Assume that, at the end of the day, the settlement committee of the exchange declares a settlement price for these contracts of £1 = $1.86. This increases the contract's value to $116,250. Because of the change in the value of the contract, the clearing house transfers $625 from the seller's margin account to that of the buyer. Should the spot exchange rate of sterling rise again the next day, a similar transfer would occur. If the balance in the seller's account fell below a specified level (the *maintenance margin*), he would be required to make additional payments into the account (the *variation margin*) in order to keep the account at or above an acceptable balance. On the other hand, the buyer could, in this case, withdraw his daily profits from his margin account. Some exchanges (for example, Euronext.liffe) set the maintenance margin at the same level as the initial margin.

In our example above, assume that the maintenance margin for buyers and sellers is indeed the same as the initial margin – in this case, $5,000. On the second day of trading, the sterling exchange rate rises to £1 = $1.88, increasing the value of the contract to $117,500 and the potential loss of the seller to $1,875. This amount will have been deducted from the seller's margin account by the clearing house, reducing the balance in that account to $3,125. The seller will then have to pay into the account a minimum additional amount of $1,875 to bring the balance back up to the $5,000 maintenance margin. In other words, the seller will now have deposited a total of $6,875 with the clearing house. The balance in the buyer's margin account meanwhile will have risen to $6,875, allowing the buyer to withdraw $1,875. Alternatively, the buyer might at this stage decide to instruct the exchange to find someone willing to purchase the contract. The price of the contract will have risen to reflect the potential profit that its terms currently imply. If the price of the future has risen exactly in line with the change in the spot exchange rate, the profit from selling the contract would also be $1,875. This amount of profit on capital of only $5,000 in two days gives a very high per annum rate of profit!

Exercise 9.1

(a) Calculate the per annum rate of profit in the example immediately above.

(b) What is left out of this example that would reduce this rate of profit?

(c) Assume that the buyer has withdrawn his profit from his margin account on the first two days so that, at the beginning of Day 3, both margin accounts stand at $5,000. Then, calculate the variation margin on subsequent days should the spot exchange rate change as follows:

Day 3 $1.87; Day 4 $1.855; Day 5 $1.84.

Answers at end of chapter

Of course, should the exchange rate of sterling fall below $1.85, reducing the value of the contract below $115,625, the balance in the buyer's margin account would fall below $5,000 and he would have to make additional payments to the clearing house. Failure to make such payments immediately would lead to the closure of the contract against the defaulting party, who loses any remaining balance in his margin account. This system of marking accounts to market daily prevents losses from accumulating, and the holding by the clearing house of margins removes most default risk.

The settlement price set by the settlement committee of the exchange is normally the closing price for the day (the last price at which the contract has traded). However, if a contract has not traded for some time prior to the market's close, the committee may set a different settlement price in an attempt to reflect accurately the trading conditions at the close of the market. The freedom that the settlement committee has to fix the settlement price also allows it to protect the clearing house from the remaining default risk that might arise from very large daily swings in the price of a contract.

It is not very likely, but suppose sterling were to fall dramatically in one day from £1 = $1.85 to £1 = $1.75. The value of the above contract would fall to $109,375, wiping out all of the initial margin deposited with the clearing house by the buyer. Rather than paying into the exchange an additional $6,250 in what might seem now to be a losing endeavour, the buyer might be tempted to default. To avoid this, the exchange might set price limits – maximum movements up and down from the previous day's settlement price. In our example, we shall assume a price limit of 5 cents per day. Then, if the exchange rate started the day at £1 = $1.85, the limits for that day would be $1.80 and $1.90. If these limits would otherwise be broken, the market would close *limit-up* (£1 = $1.90) or *limit-down* (£1 = $1.80). The hope would be that the temporary closure of the market might lead traders to reassess their positions. However, the system of price limits has its disadvantages. As long as the market remains closed, positions cannot be closed out and contracts become illiquid, destroying one of the major advantages of futures contracts, their tradability. For this reason, many exchanges do not operate price limits during the delivery month of a contract.

We have seen above that the relative smallness of the margin requirements is responsible for another important aspect of futures markets – their high *gearing* (or leverage). If all goes well, the effective rate of profit on a futures contract can be very high. On the other hand, investing in futures markets can be very expensive. In addition to making margin payments, investors must pay brokers a negotiated commission for executing orders. Commission (sometimes referred to as the direct cost of the contract) is charged on both the opening and the closing of a position, and is normally payable either when the position is closed or when delivery takes place. More seriously, the small margin requirement and the high potential profit rate might tempt people to enter contracts beyond their means. Then, if the daily changes in the value of the contract go against the investor and he is required constantly to replenish his margin account, he can quickly run into trouble. Futures contracts, therefore, provide the prospect of high rates of return but involve considerable risks.

Even if a contract turns out to be profitable, the possibility that additional margin payments may have to be made on a daily basis requires an investor to keep a certain proportion of his assets in a liquid form.

Another common type of financial future is the interest rate future. Short-term interest rate futures are contracts on three-month or one-month time deposits in specified currencies. The buyer of such a contract would, on delivery, receive a time deposit at an eligible bank of the amount specified beside the title of the contract. Contracts quoted in the *Financial Times* in April 2006 included a Three Month Sterling Future and a number of contracts on the euro and on eurocurrencies (see Chapter 10) such as a Three Month Euro Swiss Franc Future and a Three Month Euroyen Future. The gamble in such contracts relates to changes in short-term interest rates relative to those rates at the time the contract is negotiated.

The Three Month Sterling Futures contract offered by Euronext-liffe is for £500,000 at points of 100 per cent. That is, the price of the contract is quoted in the form of subtractions from 100 per cent – a price of 94.81 represents an annual interest rate of 5.19 per cent (100–94.81). The minimum price movement (or *tick size*) is one basis point (0.01%). For a £500,000 three-month time deposit, a change in the price of 1 basis point translates into a change in the value of the contract of £12.50 (0.01 per cent per annum interest on £500,000 for three months). This is known as the *tick value* of the contract. The tick value provides a simple way of quoting the profit or loss on a contract – a profit of 10 ticks on the Euronext-liffe Sterling contract is a profit of £125. Box 9.2 provides some more detail.

Long-term interest rate futures are to be found in the Bond Futures section of the *Financial Times*. They are based on notional government bonds. The form of the quotation is given. Interest rates in Europe are all expressed in basis points but for the US are still quoted in 32nds of 1 per cent, with one tick being 1/32 of 1 per cent, as used to be the case in the UK before 1999. In June 2006, the prices of almost all of the contracts quoted in the *Financial Times* were above 100. This might have indicated that interest rates were then lower than the coupon rates on the notional bonds.

However, the fact that long-term bond futures are based on notional bonds introduces an additional complication. In the unlikely event that the contract leads to the delivery of bonds, the seller of the contract is extremely unlikely to be able to deliver a bond with the exact characteristics of the notional bond. Thus, the exchange establishes a list of eligible bonds, any one of which may be used to effect delivery. For example, the notional bond may have a period to maturity of twenty years and a coupon rate of 9 per cent, while the eligible list established by the exchange might include bonds with periods of maturity between fifteen and twenty-five years and coupon rates ranging from 6 to 12 per cent. This causes a complication at the point of delivery because the buyer of the contract must pay for the bond actually delivered whereas the final settlement price of the futures contract will be based on the notional price. To overcome this problem, the exchange publishes a *price factor* or *conversion factor* for each eligible bond that reflects the difference in value between the notional bond and the actual bond delivered. The final settlement price for the notional bond is multiplied by the price factor (which may be either greater than or

Box 9.2

Interest rate futures

In the *Financial Times* of 16 June 2006, the following information was provided for the Three Month Sterling Futures contracts due for delivery at the end of June, September and December 2006 and March and June 2007.

	June 2006	Sept 2006	Dec 2006	March 2007	June 2007
Opening price	95.27	95.17	95.06	94.98	94.92
Settlement price	95.27	95.14	95.01	94.91	94.84

The interest rates implied by the settlement prices were thus:

June 2006	4.73%
September 2006	4.86%
December 2006	4.99%
March 2007	5.09%
June 2007	5.16%

At the time, the repo rate set by the Monetary Policy Committee of the Bank of England was 4.5%, having been unchanged since August 2005 when it had been reduced from 4.75%. At the market close on 15 June 2006, the following interest rates applied to interbank sterling:

Overnight	4.531%	one month	4.612%	three months	4.703%
six months	4.703%	one year	4.953%		

The prices of the futures contracts suggested a market belief that the Bank of England would increase interest rates by 50 basis points in the following nine months, probably in the form of two 25-basis-point increases.

Source: Financial Times, 16 June 2006

Exercise 9.2

Look at the information in Box 9.2 and answer the following questions:

(a) Consult the Bank of England website (http://www.bankofengland.co.uk/monetarypolicy/decisions/). Find the minutes for the MPC's meeting on 8 June 2006 (published on 21 June 2006) and see if there is anything in these minutes to support the views of the markets.

(b) How does the behaviour of interest rates implied by settlements prices of interest rate futures differ from those applying to interbank sterling?

(c) Why does the behaviour of these two sets of rates differ?

Answers at end of chapter

less than one). Thus the settlement prices will also reflect the closeness or otherwise of the terms of the notional bond to those of the bonds eligible for delivery.

Another complication arises because bonds have accrued interest added on whereas futures contracts do not. Consequently, allowance has to be made for interest accrued between the date of the coupon prior to the delivery of the bond and the delivery date. These two modifications mean that the buyer of the contract must pay for the bond delivered to him the final settlement price for the notional bond plus any unpaid interest accrued on the bond. Of the bonds eligible for delivery, the seller always chooses the bond that is cheapest for him to deliver – the cheapest to deliver (CTD) bond. Delivery may take place on any day of the delivery month, although in practice it is always on either the first or the last day of the month. If the current yield on the bond that is to be delivered is greater than the money market interest rate, the seller will retain the bond until the last day of the month before delivering it. On the other hand, if money market interest rates are higher, he will deliver the bond on the first day of the month.

9.3.2 Options

An option gives the right to buy or sell a given amount of a financial instrument or commodity at an agreed price (known as the *exercise price* or *strike price*) within a specified time, but does not oblige investors to do so. Just as with futures, options contracts are drawn up between two counterparties, the purchaser and the writer (seller) of the option, and are registered with and traded through a financial futures exchange. Options contracts are offered both on cash securities (short- and long-term interest rates, exchange rates, equities of individual companies, and stock exchange indices) and on futures contracts. For options on cash securities (*premium paid options*), the buyer pays the full price or premium of the option at the time of purchase. For options on futures contracts (*premium margined options*), buyers and sellers are margined and marked to market in the same way as with futures themselves.

> **Call options:** Options that give the right to buy a given amount of a financial instrument or commodity at an agreed price within a specified time but, like all options, do not oblige investors to do so.

Banks construct non-tradable, custom-made over-the-counter (OTC) options for their customers. These make up a high proportion of the total value of options sold. The average daily turnover in the UK for all OTC currency and interest rate derivatives in April 2004 was $643 billion, comfortably more than double the figure of $275 billion recorded three years earlier. Of this total, 12 per cent were foreign currency options and swaps and 15 per cent interest rate options (up from 5 per cent since 2001). The remaining seventy-three per cent were interest rate swaps (discussed in Chapter 10) and forward rate agreements (FRAs), with interest rate swaps remaining the biggest single category (Williams, 2004). Interest rates clearly remained the dominant underlying asset.

The buyer of a call option acquires the right to buy the specified instrument. For example, an investor who thinks that sterling is likely to rise in value against the US dollar could buy a £/$ option, giving the right to buy sterling at a specified price, say £1 = $1.80. The holder of the option then has the right to acquire sterling at that price at any time during the life of the option and is thus in a position to benefit from a rise in the spot price of sterling. If the spot exchange rate were to rise to £1 = $1.90, the option holder could acquire sterling at $1.80 under the terms of the option and sell it in the spot market at $1.90. The buyer of a call option thus assumes a long position in the underlying product (in this case £). As the price of the underlying product rises, so too will the profit that can be made from exercising the option. Consequently, the premium that must be paid to acquire the option rises and this allows the holder of a call option to realise her profit by selling the option on rather than by exercising it. If the option did not rise as the price of the underlying product rose, there would be a profitable arbitrage opportunity.

> **Put options:** Options that give the right to sell a given amount of a financial instrument or commodity at an agreed price within a specified time, but that do not oblige investors to do so.

The buyer of a put option acquires the right to sell and thus assumes a short position in the specified product. That is, the buyer of a put option stands to gain from a fall in the price of the underlying product. Therefore, someone who buys a put option at £1 = $1.80 hopes that the value of sterling falls below that level. He would be able to buy sterling in the spot forex market at, say, £1 = $1.70 and then exercise the option in order to sell the sterling at $1.80. In this case, as sterling falls, the profitability of a put option in sterling rises and the premium that other investors are prepared to pay in order to acquire such an option increases. As before, the holder of the put option can realise his profit by selling the option on rather than by exercising it.

Just as in the futures market, the holder of an option sells it (closes out her market position) by entering into a reversing contract. That is, in the first case above in which we assumed that sterling was rising in value, a holder of a call option in sterling 'sells' the option by writing (that is, selling) a call option on the same product for the same expiry date, in effect cancelling his right to buy sterling. However, the increase in the price of the sterling will have meant that the premium received for the sale of the call option will be greater than the premium paid to purchase the initial call option.

The example of a call option given above states that the option can be exercised at any time during its life up till (and including) the expiry date. Such an option is known as an American option. There exist also European options, which give holders the right to exercise the option on the expiry date only. Most traded options are American options.

As with futures contracts, few options produce a delivery of the underlying product because profitable market positions are generally closed out before expiry while unprofitable options are left to lapse, with the buyer losing only the premium. Therefore, the profit for most buyers of options is given by the change in the option premium between its purchase and sale. Options, then, like futures, give traders the opportunity to speculate on the likely direction of a market without actually trading in that market.

Consider the case of a firm that is short in the underlying product (say, US dollars). Remember that being short in dollars leaves the firm open to the risk that the dollar will rise. Taking out a call option in dollars provides a hedge against this risk since if the dollar rises in value, a profit can be made on the call option. The hedger can exercise the option at the strike price, which is lower than the rate in the spot market. We can thus say that the call option establishes a maximum price that the firm will have to pay for the underlying product in which it is short. Of course, it might choose not to exercise the option but to sell it on to someone else. It would then pay the higher spot market price for the dollars it needed but would be able to set against this the profit made from the sale of the option.

If the spot market price falls, the hedger has to pay less for the dollars it needs and has only to set against this the premium paid for the option. Thus, an option provides protection against the losses that would occur if the spot price moved in one direction, without removing the profits that might arise if the price moved in the opposite direction. This is not the case in trading in either forward or futures markets.

The reverse arguments hold for hedgers who are long in the underlying product. For them, a put option establishes a minimum price for the underlying product. If the spot price falls, the premium of the put option rises and the holder can exercise the option at the strike price (preventing a loss). Alternatively, he can sell the underlying product at the lower spot price, incurring a loss, but offset this with the profit made from selling the option. If the spot price rises, the holder of the option can benefit from the higher price in the cash market and allow the option to lapse. Thus, holding a long position in the cash market and buying a put option produces the same result as does buying a call option when the trader has no position in the cash market. In both cases, the holder of the option benefits from a rise in the price of the underlying product in the cash market. For this reason the combination of being long in a product and holding a put option is sometimes known as a *synthetic call option*.

Options, like futures, are highly geared (leveraged) because the options price is only a small percentage of the price of the underlying product. Thus, when a profit is made from trading in options, the per annum rate of profit is likely to be high.

A trader may prefer to hedge or speculate by writing options rather than by buying them, although this can be risky. Writing a call option offers protection against a price fall since in this case the option is not exercised and the writer collects the premium on the option. In the same way, writing a put option offers protection against a price rise. Writing options is only effective, however, if the price changes are relatively small, and it carries the risk that if prices go against the writer, the loss may become very large. For example, a trader who writes a call option on the £/$ exchange rate at a strike price of $1.80 agrees to sell sterling at that price. If sterling increases in value and the writer is short in sterling, he will need to acquire it in the spot market at the higher price. The amount he loses will then depend on the size of the contract (for example, £31,250 per contract in the £/$ option offered by the Philadelphia Stock Exchange) and the amount the price rises. If sterling rose to $1.90, the loss would be $3,125 per contract (31,250 × $0.10). Unlike the buyer, the writer cannot abandon a losing option.

The trading of options contracts on organised exchanges guards against the risk that the writer of an option might default on it by not being able to deliver the underlying product to the holder of a call option or to pay the holder of a put option for the delivery. To buy an option, a trader must have an account with a brokerage firm holding a membership on the futures and options exchange. The buyer pays for the option at the time the contract is written and no further payments are required apart from a commission to the broker. However, because the writer of an option enters into an open-ended commitment, he may need large financial reserves to meet his obligations. A writer may write a *covered call* (the writer already owns the underlying product and deposits it with the broker) or a *naked call*. In the latter case, the broker may require substantial deposits of cash or securities to ensure that the writer is able to meet his commitment. As in a futures market, the buyer and writer of an option have no obligations to a specific individual but to the clearing house of the exchange, which manages the exercise process and the standardisation of contract terms.

All currency options are for the US dollar against a non-dollar currency, and a call option gives the right to buy the non-dollar currency. Exercise prices are stated in US cents. The holder of a call option gains if the non-dollar currency rises in value; the holder of a put option gains if the non-dollar currency falls in value. Box 9.3 provides information on $/£ options.

Box 9.3 **Currency options – an example**

On 15 June 2006, the *Financial Times* provided the following information: $/£ options offered by CME

Strike	Calls			Puts		
Price	Sep	Dec	Mar	Sep	Dec	Mar
1.820	4.42	5.64	–	1.88	2.83	–
1.830	3.75	5.05	–	2.20	3.12	–
1.840	3.13	4.5	5.84	2.57	3.55	4.51
1.850	2.99	–	–	2.99	–	–

Previous day's volume: calls 211, puts 46

Previous day's open interest: 9,445

That is, a call option giving the right to buy sterling at a rate of £1 = $1.820 on or before 30 September 2006 would have cost, at the close of trading on 14 June 2006, 4.42 cents per pound. If we assume that each contract had a value of £31,250 as with the Philadelphia Stock Exchange contract, each contract would have cost 31,250 × 4.42 cents = $1381.25. You should note the following points:

● At a strike price of $1.820, the premiums on calls were much higher than those on puts, but at a strike price of $1.850 the premiums on calls and puts for 30 September were the same.

- Both calls and puts are more expensive the further away the exercise date is. This simply reflects the greater risk involved for the writer associated with more distant delivery dates.

- No one was prepared to write call or put options for December at a strike price of $1.850; options were only available for March 2007 (over 8 months ahead) at a strike price of $1.840.

- Premiums were generally high, the lowest being on put options for September at 1.88 cents per pound. This was because the foreign exchange market had been very volatile for some time *and* because the spot exchange rate at the close of the foreign exchange market on that day had been £1 = $1.8464. Thus, someone able to buy dollars at 1.820 would have been able to make an immediate profit of over 2 cents to the dollar (that is, call options at 1.820, 1.830 and 1.840 were all in-the-money).

We can also see that market feeling on balance was that the dollar was likely to stay at around $1.85 in the near future since both calls and puts for September were both priced at 2.99 cents per pound. That is, writers thought that there was an equal chance that calls and puts would be profitable. Given the premium, call options at 1.850 would have become profitable if the dollar were to fall to above £1 = $1.88; puts would have become profitable had the dollar risen to below £1 = $1.82.

Source: Financial Times, 15 June 2006

Intrinsic value of an option: The profit available from immediately exercising an option. Where the value of the right granted by the option is equal to the market value of the underlying instrument (the intrinsic value is zero), the option is said to be *at-the-money*. If the intrinsic value is positive, the option is *in-the-money*. If exercising an option would produce a loss, it is *out-of-the-money*.

The premium of an option consists of two elements: the *intrinsic value* – the profit that would be made by exercising the option on that day – and the *time value* – a measure of the chances that the option will become profitable before the expiry date. One element of the time value of an option is just the length of time that an option has to run to expiry, since the longer that period is, the greater must be the chance that the price of the underlying product will change affecting the profitability of the option. Further, the chances of a change occurring in a price depend not only on the length of time but also on the volatility of the price of the underlying product. Where the price of the underlying product normally changes frequently and by relatively large amounts, the time value of an option will be greater for each period to expiry than where the price of the underlying product is generally stable. It is true that a volatile price may fall sharply as well as rise sharply, but falls in price are relevant only to the extent that they cause the option to be at-the-money at the time of expiry – greater falls in price will simply cause the option to be abandoned. No one would exercise an out-of-the-money option. It follows that sharp price movements up have a much stronger impact on the possible profitability of an option and that volatility will always be positively related to the premium.

Intrinsic value and time value are related. If an option is presently deeply out-of-the-money (it has no intrinsic value), the chances that (for any given time period and volatility of the cash price) a change in price will make the instrument profitable must be less than if the option is only just out-of-the-money or at-the-money. Equally, if an option is deeply in-the-money, the chances that the cash price will go on rising, continuing to increase the profitability of the option, are less than if the intrinsic value of the option is lower.

9.3.3 Exotic options

There are many variations on the simple call and put options dealt with above. They are known as exotic options. They include the following:

● *Barrier options* (knock-in or knock-out) – OTC options that come into being (knock-in) or lapse (knock-out) when specified prices of the underlying product are reached. There are four types of barrier options: calls and puts, each with a knock-out or knock-in feature. A knock-in barrier option pays nothing at expiry unless it is first brought to life as a result of the price of the underlying product reaching a specified level (the barrier). A knock-out option begins life as a standard option but is killed off if the cash price touches the barrier. Because they might never come into existence or might be killed off, they are much cheaper than conventional options. They are often used in the foreign exchange market by chartists who feel strongly that exchange rates will not fall below support levels or rise above resistance levels. *Double no touch* options are killed off if the cash price touches either an upper or a lower barrier.

● *Credit risk derivatives* – such as the credit default option, which protects the buyer against the default of a specific company or country.

● *Lookback options* – these give the right to buy (lookback call) or sell (lookback put) at the lowest price reached by the underlying product during the life of the option.

● *Asian options* – options whose intrinsic value is calculated by comparing the strike price with the average spot price over the period of the option.

● *Options on options* – options that give the right to buy an option.

● *Flex options* – options offered by the Chicago Board Options Exchange (CBOE) that allow an institutional OTC customer to choose any strike price and expiry date up to five years.

9.3.4 Other related products

Other related products include the following:

● *Warrants* – options to purchase or sell an underlying product (company shares) at a given price and time or series of prices and times. A warrant differs from a call or put option by ordinarily being issued for longer than a year. With covered warrants the shares that holders receive, if they exercise their warrants, already exist. Thus, the issuer of covered warrants is usually a bank that has bought up underlying shares. On the other hand, when companies issue warrants, usually in conjunction with bonds, it is generally a means of raising funds by creating new shares if the warrants are exercised.

- *Contracts for difference (CFDs)* – cash-settled futures and options where there is no underlying asset. Contracts for difference are settled on the difference between the purchase or sale price in the case of futures or the difference between the exercise price and the settlement price in the case of options. They involve a swap of cash flows and have been compared to borrowing money and then using this to buy shares.

- *Spread betting* – betting as to whether a market will rise or fall and by how much. The bet can be on a wide range of futures including share price indices, commodities and currencies. Spread betting on financial assets is classified as gambling rather than as investment but is administered by the Financial Services Authority.

9.4 Comparing different types of derivatives

9.4.1 Exchange-traded versus OTC products

Exchange-traded derivatives have three principal advantages over OTC derivatives:

- The existence of the clearing house guarantees all contracts and virtually eliminates the default risk present in OTC trades; thus, exchange-based derivatives are lower in price than OTC derivatives since there will almost always be some residual risk for a bank in writing an OTC contract even though it will attempt to minimise its risks by arranging offsetting contracts with other customers/banks and/or by taking a position in exchange-traded derivatives.

- Markets for exchange-based derivatives are more liquid than bilateral OTC trades since there are many traders dealing in each futures contract.

- Exchange-based futures and options are highly tradable because they are standard-ised whereas OTC options, being non-standard and redeemable only at the bank where they were bought, have a low resale value.

Against these, we must set the fact that OTC options are designed to meet the specific requirements of each customer in terms of size, strike price and expiry.

9.4.2 Forward versus futures contracts

We have seen that forward forex contracts are OTC contracts and so are not tradable in organised markets. On the other hand, they benefit from the additional flexibility of OTC contracts in terms of both the period and the amount of the contract. Forward contracts are available on a much wider range of currencies than are exchange-traded futures and options since futures exchanges are only willing to offer derivatives contracts that are likely to be popular with both buyers and sellers. As with OTC derivatives, specially arranged forward forex contracts involving unpopular currencies are bound to be relatively expensive because of the extra risk that the market-maker (the bank) has to accept. This is made greater by the fact that the spot markets in these currencies are likely to be thin and hence their exchange rates more volatile – a small number of large deals in the same direction might shift the exchange rate by a considerable amount.

There may also be important cash-flow differences between forward forex contracts and futures. Net profits on a futures hedge are accrued on a daily basis whereas the net profits on a forward hedge are realised only on the date of delivery of the currency.

9.4.3 Forward and futures contracts versus options

Forward and futures contracts lock in an investor to a given exchange rate. Thus, the contract provides a hedge if the exchange rate moves in the direction that would have produced a loss in the underlying cash market, but also reduces the profit that would have resulted in the underlying market from a movement of the spot exchange rate in the opposite direction. Consider the following example.

A British firm importing goods from the US in June 2006 has to make a payment of $1 million before the end of September and faces the risk that the dollar will rise against sterling, increasing the sterling cost of the transaction to the firm. The spot exchange rate is £1 = $1.85, but if that were to fall to £1 = $1.80 the goods would cost the firm a little more than £20,000 extra. This could obviously seriously affect the company's profit margin when it sold the goods in Britain. Consequently, it chooses to buy a September sterling future with the Chicago Metal Exchange at a price of £1 = $1.8680. If sterling falls to £1 = $1.80, the value of the futures contract will rise. Thus the company loses on its payment for the imported goods but is able to offset this by reversing its futures contract and making a profit. However, if sterling strengthens, rising say to £1 = $1.90, the firm gains on its import of goods (they now cost less in sterling) but loses on the futures contract because it loses value as sterling rises. That is, the hedge removes both the risk of loss and the possibility of profit. On the other hand, an option allows most of any potential profit to be taken. If the US dollar rose, the option would become out-of-the-money but would simply be abandoned by the firm with the loss only of the premium.

Whether a trader chooses futures or options depends on what she thinks is likely to happen to the price of the underlying product and on her attitude towards risk.

● A trader who has a long position in the underlying market and who is convinced that the price of the instrument in question is not going to fall may choose not to hedge at all and remain in an open position. That is, she will accept the risk of an exchange rate change.

● A trader who is confident that the price will fall may (a) sell the product before the price falls; (b) take an offsetting short position by selling futures contracts; or (c) sell the currency forwards. This eliminates entirely her exposure to the price fall.

● A trader who is uncertain in which direction the price will move may choose options. Even then, if she thinks that the price is more likely to fall than to rise, financial futures are preferable to options because they are likely to offer her cheaper protection. Options are preferable if the trader has no view or thinks that the price is more likely to rise than fall.

Many mixed strategies are also possible. Box 9.4 provides some examples of these.

Box 9.4

Mixed strategies in options trading

Call and put options and the buying and writing of options can be combined to try to profit from expected conditions in the market. Some such strategies are as follows:

A. Cases where a trader either buys or writes options but does not do both

- *Straddle* – a call and a put at the same strike price and expiry date
- *Strangle* – a call and a put for the same expiry date but at different strike prices
- *Strap* – two calls and one put with the same expiry dates; the strike prices might be the same or different
- *Strip* – two puts and one call with the same expiry date; again strike prices might be the same or different

In general, the buyer of these options is hoping for market prices to move sharply but is uncertain whether they will rise or fall. The buyer of a strap gains more from a price rise than from a price fall; the buyer of a strip gains more from a price fall. The writer in all four cases is hoping that the market will remain stable, with little change in price during the life of the option.

B. Spreads: combinations of buying and writing options

- *Butterfly* – buying two call options, one with a low exercise price, the other with a high exercise price, and writing two call options with the same intermediate strike price or the reverse.
- *Condor* – similar to a butterfly except that the call options that are written have different intermediate prices.

Both a butterfly and a condor are vertical spreads – all options bought or sold have the same expiry date but different strike prices. *Horizontal* spreads have the same strike prices but different expiry dates. With diagonal spreads both the strike prices and the expiry dates are different. Other mixed strategies have equally improbable names. They include vertical bull call; vertical bull spread; vertical bear spread; rotated vertical bull spread; rotated vertical bear spread.

9.5 # The use and abuse of derivatives

Derivatives, then, allow firms to hedge against erratic price and interest rate movements while also attracting speculators because of their high gearing. These two aspects of the market have led to conflicting attitudes regarding their overall contribution to financial markets. Supporters of derivatives markets argue that they perform a number of important roles. They are said to:

- facilitate the hedging of risk through sophisticated risk management, and by so doing reduce the cost of protection against risk;

- be quicker to respond to new information than the cash markets, allowing people who do not participate in derivatives trading to forecast more accurately future cash market prices and thus to make better consumption, pricing and investment decisions – this is the 'price discovery' role of derivatives;

- assist in the standardisation of commodity or financial instrument contracts in the cash markets because derivatives contracts are highly standardised themselves;

- contribute to the integration of global capital markets, hence improving the global allocation of savings and fostering higher investment levels;

- help to combat the adverse effects of volatile commodity prices on the economies of developing countries because forward prices tend to be less volatile than spot prices, giving commodity producers an opportunity to reduce the volatility of the price of their output through hedging;

- facilitate speculation, providing liquid markets and enabling hedgers to protect themselves from risk in the most efficient way possible.

Doubts have been expressed about the price discovery role since it assumes that financial markets are efficient – that is, that prices in these markets change immediately to reflect all new information coming to the market and that market agents are able to interpret correctly the implications of this information for future developments. However, the main doubts expressed about the benefits of derivatives have centred on the role of speculation and the difficulties that the increasing complexity of derivatives products have caused for regulators. Support for the attack on derivatives trading has come from problems in markets as a whole and from examples of spectacular losses by individual companies and banks.

For example, derivatives trading was widely held to be partly to blame for a major stock market crash in 1987. The argument was that stock market traders were pessimistic and expected a fall in the price of stocks when the exchanges opened after a weekend. Large orders to sell arrived at brokerage houses prior to opening and, as the market started falling, many traders automatically sold futures in the shares of the major corporations. This destabilised stock markets and contributed to the panic selling of stocks and shares. This view of the crash led to a general concern that the derivatives markets might contribute to the volatility of the cash market. The derivatives markets strenuously deny this, but worries have been expressed at a high level. Towards the end of April 1994 finance ministers from the Group of 10 (G10) leading industrial countries agreed on the need to strengthen co-operation in gathering statistics and assessing the implications for the world financial system of the innovative segments of financial markets. There was also a call for improved disclosure requirements and sufficient capital adequacy standards among financial institutions to underpin their risky activities. Capital adequacy requirements under the Basel Accord (see Chapter 13) were modified to try to take the risks of derivatives trading into account. They became part of the Capital Adequacy Directive, which came into force in the European Union from the beginning of 1996.

Certainly there is some evidence that Wall Street equity prices have been affected by heavy activity in stock index contracts, especially around expiry dates, and there is a possible theoretical argument to support the view that derivatives trading makes the cash markets more volatile and nervy. The argument is that in the past, when people thought prices in a market were becoming too high, they would express their bearish feelings by leaving the market. This would exert downward pressure on prices and help to stabilise them. Now, however, they stay in the market but protect themselves against risk by using the derivatives markets. No sale is made in the cash markets and bearish opinion loses its restraining influence on prices. Thus, although spreading risks through derivatives reduces risks for the individual, it increases risk for the system as a whole (systemic risk). This provides big profit opportunities for the uninsured speculators but increases risks of bankruptcies.

Individual company losses through derivatives have become almost routine in recent years. The most spectacular was the collapse of the British merchant bank Barings in 1995. This was a case where it became clear that the management of the bank did not know what was being done in their name and almost certainly did not understand the complexities of derivatives trading and the extent of the associated risks. Details of the Barings collapse are provided in Box 9.5.

Box 9.5 | **The case of Barings**

The British merchant bank Barings Brothers was bankrupted in 1995, after losses of more than £860 million accrued on the Singapore and Osaka derivatives exchanges. The bank was the victim of its own star trader, Nick Leeson, and the absence of management controls to monitor his activities. Leeson was responsible for both trading and back-office records of his deals at Simex (the Singapore International Monetary Exchange). He had started by running a hedged position in futures on the Japanese Nikkei stock exchange index. The aim was to make money by arbitrage – taking advantage of different prices on the Singapore and Osaka exchanges. However, he soon stopped hedging the purchases made in Singapore and between 1992 and 1995 built up positions in futures and options contracts on the Nikkei 225 (that is, he began speculating). In the early years, this was highly profitable for Barings and the management asked few questions about his activities.

Leeson was gambling that the market would not be volatile – he would make losses if the index either rose or fell by large amounts but would profit from the index remaining stable. During 1994, the index remained within a narrow range and everything was fine. However, in early 1995, the combination of a large earthquake in Kobe in Japan and a turn in investor sentiment against Japanese markets drove the index sharply down. His contracts began to show losses. He faced daily calls for additional margin payments. He assumed that the Nikkei would soon recover and financed these cash calls by writing put options on the contract. If the Nikkei index had risen again, these put options would have been abandoned, leaving Leeson with the options premiums as profit. He sold at least 20,000 contracts expiring in mid-March. Each point of the Nikkei 225 futures contract carries a value of ¥1,000, and so with the Nikkei 225 trading at levels between 18,000 and 20,000 in the first few weeks of the year, each future would have had a value of some ¥18–20 million.

Unfortunately for Leeson and for Barings, the Nikkei index fell over the period from 19,600 to 17,600. The options contracts were exercised and Leeson faced losses of around ¥40 billion on top of the losses from the initial futures contracts. His total losses exceeded the capital of Barings Bank. The bank collapsed. Most of Barings' employees were saved by Internationale Nederlanden Group, which bought Barings and took on its losses for £1. Leeson was later jailed for the falsification of records in an attempt to conceal his activities.

Other well-known problems associated with derivatives trading have included:

- losses in the 1980s by Hammersmith and Fulham local authority in London in the sterling interest rate swaps market (see Box 10.6);
- losses in 1993 by Metallgesellschaft, the fourteenth largest industrial concern in Germany, on futures and OTC swap contracts;
- losses of $102 million on swap transactions by the large American firm, Procter & Gamble, in 1994;
- losses in 1994 by Tokyo Securities of ¥32 billion, one third of the firm's net assets;
- losses of $1.5bn on foreign exchange derivatives trading by Kashima Oil, a Japanese company;
- losses of ¥65bn on foreign currency dealings by Mazda, the Japanese car manufacturer, in 1993/94;
- losses of £15 million on writing currency options by the British company, Allied Lyons;
- losses of £$1.1bn made by Toshihide Iguchi between 1984 and 1995 at the Manhattan Branch of Daiwa Bank on bad trades in the bond market;
- losses of £91 million made by traders in 1995 and 1996 at Natwest Capital Markets, the investment banking arm of the National Westminster Bank in London, on deutschmark and sterling options and swaptions (see section 10.3) and covered up by the mispricing of options on the bank's books;
- losses of $691 million made between 1997 and 2002 by John Rusnak, working for Allfirst Bank in Baltimore, on forward purchases of yen, allegedly hedged by combinations of options and covered up through the development of fictitious options.

Many of these cases have had international implications. However, the most dangerous case from the point of view of world markets in general was the near collapse in September 1998 of the US hedge fund, Long-Term Capital Management (LTCM). Hedge funds were originally US equity funds that hedged against market declines by holding short, as well as long, positions. However, they were using derivatives to take large bets on the direction of markets. Using a very complex system, LTCM risked 40 times its capital, a total exposure of $200 million. Although LTCM's board included Myron Scholes and Robert Merton, who had won the Nobel Prize for Economics for their work on the pricing of options, their system could not cope with the financial crisis that had developed in South East Asia and Russia. As Tracey Corrigan wrote in the *Financial Times* of 26/27 September 1998, 'all the complex formulae and computer models that the best brains had produced simply did not work when financial crisis spilt over from the emerging markets'.

LTCM was, in the event, rescued by the New York Federal Reserve, which recruited fourteen financial groups to help. Prior to the rescue there were genuine fears that LTCM's collapse would have led to the collapse of a large number of major world banks. Even with the rescue, UBS, Europe's largest bank, had to accept a loss of £406 million.

Since 1998, there has been a dramatic increase in the number and size of hedge funds and some concern has been expressed about their role and possible impact on international financial stability. In May 2006, the European Central Bank in its *Financial Stability Review* suggested that hedge funds had created a major risk to global financial stability. The article placed the collapse of a key hedge fund or a cluster of smaller funds in the same category as a possible bird flu pandemic in its ability to trigger widespread disruption in financial markets. The ECB was particularly worried by the herd instinct among hedge funds and their tendency to mimic the strategies followed by others.

9.6 Summary

Exchange rate risk takes several forms and, in the absence of fixed exchange rates or monetary union, firms must take action to protect themselves against that risk. The need for sophisticated risk management in the face of highly volatile exchange rates provides one of the principal reasons for the growth of derivatives markets. These allow firms to hedge risk by taking out contracts in derivatives markets, which carry the opposite risk to that which they face in the underlying markets such as the forex markets. The two principal types of derivatives are futures and options. Both are tradable contracts offered by futures markets. Futures promise the delivery of an underlying asset of a specified kind on a given date, although delivery is seldom made. Options give the right to buy and/or sell an underlying asset, although that right need not be taken up. In order to increase tradability, both futures and options are highly standardised. Both offer the possibility of very high rates of profit. Futures do this through the system of margin payments. In the case of options, this occurs because buyers of options pay only the premium for the right to trade at the specified price.

Financial futures and options contracts are offered in relation to exchange rates, short-term and long-term interest rates and stock exchange indices. They are widely used for speculation as well as for risk management. In recent years, options have become extremely complicated, with new forms of options contracts appearing regularly. The more complex and less common types of options are known as exotic options. Exchange-based options and futures are cheaper and more liquid than OTC products, but OTC products can be designed to meet the specific requirements of each client. Forward contracts are available on a much wider range of currencies than exchange-traded futures and options. There may also be important cash flow differences between forward forex contracts and options. Forward and futures contracts are likely to provide cheaper protection against loss than options, but remove the profit opportunity if prices move in favour of the firm. Thus, options are generally preferable if the hedger is uncertain about the direction the price of the underlying asset is likely to move. A hedger who is confident about the direction in which the price will move is more likely to choose forward or futures contracts or remain in an open position and accept the risk of a price change.

Derivatives markets have been controversial in recent years. Many firms have lost badly in these markets and fears have been expressed that mismanagement in derivatives markets could cause serious problems for the international financial system. This danger must be set against the several advantages offered by derivatives. The question remains as to whether the extra protection provided by the derivatives markets increases the systemic risk.

Questions for discussion

1 Consider the relative advantages and disadvantages of using forward contracts, futures contracts and options as means of speculation.

2 How do futures markets seek to protect themselves and their clients against default risk?

3 Consider the following statement:

> A speculator who felt that interest rates were likely to rise or a currency's value decline would go short in the relevant asset by selling a futures contract.

(a) Why would a speculator go short rather than long in these two cases?

(b) What does going short in interest rates mean?

(c) How does selling a futures contract allow one to go short?

4 The text suggests that it is not very likely that sterling would fall from £1 = $1.80 to £1 = $1.70 in a single day. See if you can find out how much sterling fell against the DM in the week after it was forced out of the exchange rate system of the European Monetary System in 1992 – Wednesday 16 September. (Hint: try http://pacific.commerce.ubc.ca/xr/)

5 Why might the increased protection provided to individual traders by the derivatives markets increase the risk of the whole financial system running into difficulties?

6 Why did the US central bank (the Federal Reserve) feel the need to rescue a privately owned and run hedge fund (LTCM) in late 1998? Should public resources be used in this way?

7 How many ways are there of a British investor going short in US dollars or giving itself the opportunity of going short? Why might a British investor wish to go short in US dollars?

8 Why is it more risky to write (sell) options contracts than to buy them?

Further reading

P Howells and K Bain, *The Economics of Money, Banking and Finance. A European Text* (Harlow: Pearson Education, 3e, 2005) chs. 19 and 20

P Williams, 'The foreign exchange and over-the-counter derivatives markets in the United Kingdom', *Bank of England Quarterly Bulletin*, Winter 2004, 470–84

For stories and latest data on derivatives markets, see the *Financial Times* website, http://www.ft.com

Answers to exercises

9.1 (a) 6,750 per cent (calculation done on the basis of a 360-day year).

(b) Transaction costs, specifically commission to the exchange member who arranged the contract and to the clearing house.

(c) Day 3: buyer pays $625; Day 4: buyer pays $1,250; Day 5: buyer pays $625.

9.2 (b) Both sets of rates rose steadily – the rates implied by futures prices rose from 4.73 for June 2006 contracts to 5.16 for June 2007 contracts. The interbank sterling rates were also higher for longer periods, varying from 4.53% overnight to 4.953% for one year. In all cases, the interbank sterling interest rates were lower than the rates implied by futures prices.

(c) The rates are different in kind. Buyers and sellers of interest rate futures are gambling on changes in the interest rate over the following three, six or twelve months. If the market were fully efficient, the implied rates would indicate what would happen to interest rates in general in the near future. Interbank sterling rates are all current rates for deposits made now of differing periods. That is, interbank interest rates trace out a yield curve. As Chapter 7 explains, a major element in the relationship between shorter and longer-term rates is market expectations about future changes in interest rates, but other factors influence the shape of the yield curve.

CHAPTER 10

International capital markets

Objectives

What you will learn in this chapter:

- the reasons for international capital flows
- what eurocurrencies are
- why eurocurrency markets grew so rapidly
- the characteristics of the eurocurrency and eurobond markets
- the possible connection between eurocurrency markets and inflation
- what interest rate swaps are and how they are used

As we pointed out at the beginning of Chapter 8, the considerable growth in activity on world foreign exchange markets over recent decades has been caused largely by the vast increase in international capital mobility. This has had profound impacts on national economies, on the international monetary system, and on the ability of firms and countries to raise funds abroad. Much of this increase in capital mobility has taken place through international capital markets in which individuals, firms and governments are able to borrow and lend across national boundaries. These markets have both grown massively and changed in form.

Our interests in this chapter lie in the changes which have taken place in the markets and in the way in which financial intermediation has altered as a result of their growth. We begin by looking at the principal types of international capital movements, before moving on to concentrate on eurocurrencies. We explain what eurocurrencies are and how they are created. We look at the major reasons for the rapid growth in eurocurrency markets from the early 1960s on and then consider the impact of this growth on the world economy. We look in particular in this section at the difficulties that the great increase in international capital mobility has caused for governments attempting to control their interest rates and rates of inflation and at the possible impact on the stability of the world economy. We then explain some of the techniques in international capital markets, concentrating on interest rate swaps. The chapter concludes with an examination of the arguments for and against attempting to control international capital flows.

10.1 The world capital market

It is possible to identify a world capital market although it is clearly imperfectly integrated due to the existence of exchange controls, exchange rate risk and sovereign risk (the problem of the creditworthiness of countries). Because of these barriers, the poorer developing countries are, at best, marginal participants in the market, borrowing very largely from other governments or the international agencies such as the International Monetary Fund and the World Bank. Even so, many of them have become heavily indebted, and a high proportion of their annual incomes goes in debt repayments. We return to this issue in Chapter 12. The developed industrial countries participate fully as both providers and users of funds while the better-off developing countries, including most of Latin America, participate as users of funds only. The international capital market may be classified by motives for capital flow, or by types of lender.

International capital flows may be divided into public sector and private sector capital movements. Public sector movements include loans and/or aid by governments and the major international agencies. Private international capital movements can be put into five principal categories:

- those resulting from normal trading relationships;
- foreign direct investment (FDI) of transnational corporations and capital flows resulting from their other activities, including the repatriation of profits and the movement of funds to minimise tax payments;
- flight capital (funk money) which moves to avoid risks of seizure, the blocking of accounts, restrictions on convertibility, taxation, legal requirements for foreign currencies to be converted into domestic currency at unfavourable exchange rates, and so on;
- commercial hot money that moves in order to profit from changes in interest rates in different countries;
- speculation based on expected future changes in exchange rates.

Speculation covers both pure speculation and the leading (payment earlier than needed) and lagging (delaying payment) of bills in foreign currencies in the expectation that the value of the domestic currency will fall or rise in the near future.

A classification of flows by lender would include:

- loans by governments and international agencies such as the World Bank;
- national bank lending in domestic currency to foreign borrowers;
- the euromarkets (offshore markets);
- international bond finance – the flotation of bonds in foreign markets or the purchase of bonds in foreign markets;
- international flows of equity capital (investors entering foreign equity markets);
- export credits (bank loans to exporters who grant extended credit to foreign customers);
- shifting bank deposits by companies with bank accounts in more than one currency.

By far the most attention has been paid to the development and growth of the euromarkets. The euromarkets consist of the eurocurrency, eurobond and euronote markets. The eurocurrency market involves lending by offshore banks through the transfer of bank deposits and is essentially short term. Medium-term bank loans, covering periods of anything from two to seventeen years, are sometimes regarded as part of the eurocredit market. Eurobonds are bonds that are issued on behalf of borrowers in a currency other than that of the country in which it is issued. Banks act not as lenders but as guarantors of loans or as brokers. Lending in the euronote (or europaper) market takes the form of short-term bearer notes that can be re-sold.

10.2 Eurocurrencies

Eurocurrency markets began to develop in the 1950s and grew most spectacularly in the 1960s and 1970s. Since the mid-1960s the growth rate of eurodeposits has been more than double that of the world money supply. According to Podolski (1986, pp. 112–13): 'The development of the eurocurrency system was perhaps the most important financial innovation of the post-war period . . . comparable to that of coke smelting in the development of iron and steel, the steam engine in the development of the railways . . .'

> **Eurocurrency:** A deposit held in a bank outside the country in whose currency the deposit is denominated. For example, eurodollars are US dollar deposits held in banks outside the US – not necessarily in Europe.

A eurodollar deposit, then, is created when a holder of a dollar bank deposit in the US transfers that deposit to a US bank located outside the US (an offshore bank). The depositor then has a dollar claim on the offshore bank and it, in turn, has a dollar claim on the bank in the US. At this stage, a eurodollar is simply an indirect way of holding a dollar deposit with a bank in the US.

However, the offshore bank now has an asset and will lend it on to a borrower outside the US. If we next assume that the borrower spends the borrowed funds and the recipient of those funds re-deposits them with an offshore bank, then eurodollar liabilities outside the US are no longer fully matched by claims within the US and we may say that eurodollars have been created. This process is shown in Box 10.1. It is clear then that there must be dollar deposits within the US at the base of the eurodollar market but these deposits need not be very large for the market to function efficiently. Eurodollars represent by far the most important element in the eurocurrency markets, but euroyen, eurosterling and other eurocurrencies also exist – indeed, the procedure can in theory be applied to any currency in international demand. Now there are even euroeuro.

Box 10.1

The creation of eurodollars

Stage one

Death Mines plc is a British exporter that has earned $1 million on the sale of goods abroad for which it has been paid in US dollars. It has deposited this sum in a US bank. The bank, in the normal way, has used this deposit to make loans within the US. Thus, our starting point is:

Balance sheet of 1st Sunshine Bank in New York

Assets	Liabilities
bank loans to US borrowers	$1 million deposit by Death Mines plc

Stage two

Death Mines plc decides that it wishes to keep its funds in dollars but to shift its deposit to a branch of Lucky Chance Bank, a US bank in London (a eurobank). This has no effect on the US bank in the US since the only change from its point of view has been in the title to the deposit. At this stage the eurodollars are just an indirect way of holding a dollar deposit with a US bank. We now have balance sheets of both the bank in the US and the bank in London:

A. Balance sheet of 1st Sunshine Bank in New York

Assets	Liabilities
bank loans to US borrowers	$1 million deposit by Lucky Chance Bank, London

B. Balance sheet of Lucky Chance Bank, London

Assets	Liabilities
$1 million deposit with 1st Sunshine Bank, New York	$1 million eurodollar deposit by Death Mines plc

Stage three

The Lucky Chance Bank in London now lends to an end-user of funds, say the Frankfurt subsidiary of a US multinational company, Weapons of Mass Destruction Inc. This loan takes the form of a transfer of the title to the original bank deposit in the US. Our set of accounts now reads:

A. Balance sheet of 1st Sunshine Bank in New York

Assets	Liabilities
bank loans to US borrowers	$1 million deposit by Death Mines plc

B. Balance sheet of Lucky Chance Bank, London

Assets	Liabilities
$1 million loan to Weapons of Mass Destruction Inc, Frankfurt	$1 million eurodollar deposit by Death Mines plc

C. Balance sheet of Weapons of Mass Destruction Inc

Assets	Liabilities
$1 million deposit with 1st Sunshine Bank, New York	$1 million loan from Lucky Chance Bank, London

The next stage depends on what Weapons of Mass Destruction Inc does with its loan. It could, for example, use it to buy goods in the US. In this case, the sellers of the goods to Weapons of Mass Destruction may simply re-deposit the funds within the US domestic banking system and the whole process comes to an end. Alternatively, Weapons of Mass Destruction Inc may choose to use its loan in Europe, buying British goods instead of American ones. If we assume that the British firms re-deposit the funds in British banks, and that they convert the dollars into sterling, the title to the dollar deposit will finish up with the Bank of England and the process will come to a halt unless the Bank of England chooses to hold part of its dollar reserves with eurobanks.

Suppose, however, that the British firms that make sales to Weapons of Mass Destruction Inc re-deposit not in domestic British banks but in other eurobanks. Then the process will continue as these eurobanks are able to make further loans to end-users of funds.

Exercise 10.1

In practice, there is a great deal of interbank activity within the eurocurrency market. In other words, the Lucky Chance Bank is not very likely to lend directly to an end-user such as Weapons of Mass Destruction Inc. Rather, assume it lends to another eurobank, the Shanghai and Bristol Bank, and that it on-lends to Weapons of Mass Destruction Inc.

(a) Reconstruct the final set of accounts to include a balance sheet for the Shanghai and Bristol Bank.

(b) Construct the accounts for stage four, assuming that the British firm that sells goods to Weapons of Mass Destruction Inc deposits its receipts with yet another eurobank, All Nippon Bank.

10.2.1 The growth of the eurocurrency markets

A convertible currency: A currency that can be exchanged freely for any other currency in any amount by any holder of the currency. Restrictions on convertibility take many forms – limiting the amount that can be exchanged, the currencies into which exchange is possible, the uses for which foreign exchange can be obtained, or the range of holders who are allowed foreign exchange.

The eurocurrency markets could not develop prior to 1958 since it was only then that the major currencies were made convertible following the Second World War. Even then, they became convertible only for non-residents. Restrictions on resident convertibility of the currency continued in the UK until 1979 and in most of the other major industrial countries into the 1980s or 1990s. Following the introduction of non-resident convertibility, major US and European banks began to open branches outside their country of origin. This was particularly true of US banks because restrictions on branch banking within the US allowed banks to operate only in their home states. Thus the ambitious banks from the major US financial centres sought expansion outside the US.

The opening of bank branches abroad meant that foreign currency earned through ordinary trading transactions could be placed anywhere where there was a demand for such funds, allowing depositors to seek out banks with the highest yields. The growth of the market can then be explained by a variety of supply and demand factors and the interaction between them.

The principal causes of the growth in the supply of funds to the market were:

- regular US balance of payments deficits which produced large dollar holdings by European companies;
- US central bank regulations which (a) established upper limits on the interest rates that could be paid on deposits in US banks and that made it easy for eurobanks to offer more attractive rates; and (b) forbade the payment of any interest on deposits placed for less than thirty days, whereas eurobanks were able to offer interest even on overnight deposits;
- the existence of exchange controls that limited the activities of domestic banks but from which the eurobanks were relatively free;
- the concern of eastern European countries that their dollar deposits in the US might be blocked by the US government for political reasons;
- from 1973 on, the large volume of oil receipts that the OPEC countries wished to deposit on favourable terms, again preferably outside the US for political reasons;
- the dramatic growth of flight capital to Swiss and other banks, encouraged by the development of financial centres such as Luxembourg and Liechtenstein in which regulations ensured the protection of the anonymity of lenders;
- the use by central banks of the market in order to increase returns on their holdings of international reserves.

Thus, the supply of funds to the market increased as a result of a mixture of commercial, economic and political factors. The market would not have grown in the way that it did, however, if there had not also been a large demand from borrowers for eurodollars. Reasons for this included:

- US government discouragement from 1963 of borrowing by foreign companies directly from the US market through the imposition of a tax (the interest equalisation tax) that increased the cost of borrowing in the US for borrowers in most of the industrial nations;

- the fact that the eurobanks were free of the reserve requirements imposed on domestic banks, allowing them to maintain a lower spread between borrowing and lending rates (paying higher rates to depositors and charging lower rates to borrowers);

- the invoicing of a growing proportion of world trade in US dollars, increasing the advantage to firms of holding their working balances for financial and commercial use in dollars in order to avoid exchange rate risk;

- US government limitations on the amount of capital that US transnational corporations could shift out of the US to invest abroad, forcing them to borrow outside the US and providing the market with a major group of very creditworthy borrowers.

The eurocurrency market is largely an interbank or wholesale market with a chain of interbank transactions normally occurring en route to an end-user of funds. It deals only in large amounts, usually of $1 million or more, and loans are made on an unsecured basis. The size of the sums involved means that the fixed costs of transactions can be spread over large quantities of funds, increasing still further the attractiveness of terms the market has been able to offer to both borrowers and lenders. Efficiency has been increased and costs lowered further by rapid improvements in communications and computer technology.

10.2.2 The nature of the market

We have noted the existence of eurocurrencies other than eurodollars. Nonetheless, the market has been dominated by eurodollar deposits. These are typically time deposits for short periods. However, terms tended to lengthen over the years, with an increasing amount of intermediate credit. The existence of differential yields in various financial centres caused arbitrage and interbank activity to be very important within the market.

From the point of view of the domestic economy, the eurocurrency market is a parallel money market serving as a source of funds for the short-term financing of foreign trade, for banks to make window-dressing liquidity adjustments at certain times of the year and, occasionally, as a major source of finance for some borrowers (for example, for local authorities and hire-purchase companies in the UK). The market is outside the control of any single country and is largely unregulated. It would, of course, be possible for individual countries to seek to regulate more thoroughly offshore banks operating from their territories. However, countries in which the market is important fear that such action would cause the market to move elsewhere, resulting in a significant loss of invisible earnings for the country in question. The market is large relative to most domestic European markets and consequently is capable of exerting a considerable impact on domestic short-term interest rates.

Just as most deposits were for very short to short periods, loans initially also tended to be for short periods. However, borrowers' need for loans of longer time periods (eurocredits) was met by the development of *rollover* loans with a floating interest rate. In these cases, the borrower typically receives a six-month credit with a guarantee that it will be renewed (rolled over) every six months for the life of the loan, which may be for ten years or longer. Each rollover is accompanied by adjustment of the interest rate payable to keep it in line with the market interest rates banks are having to pay on their deposits. Such adjustments are made according to a formula such as (LIBOR + spread). Box 10.2 deals with international influences on domestic interest rates. The spread is specific to each loan to cover the administration costs of the bank and its gross profit including lending risk (sovereign risk + default risk). The estimate of the default risk will depend largely on the borrower's credit rating issued by the international credit-rating agencies, principal among which are the US firms Moody's and Standard and Poor's. Because eurocredits tend to be for very large amounts, they are often made by *syndication*, with a lead bank acting to coordinate a loan from many banks (running sometimes, particularly in the case of sovereign lending, into the hundreds).

Box 10.2

International and UK interest rates

In Box 8.5 we stated that, with floating exchange rates, countries retained control over their own monetary policies – that is, over their own interest rates. Sterling has technically been floating against both the US dollar and the euro since the introduction of the euro at the beginning of 1999. It was not a party to any agreement to restrict the range within which sterling could move, although the British government did have a general obligation not to follow an economic policy strongly counter to the interests of other EU members. Thus, in theory, the Bank of England Monetary Policy Committee (MPC) can set its short-term interest rate paying attention only to its domestic target – the achievement of an inflation rate of 2.0 per cent per annum.

Nonetheless, the great increase in international capital mobility had introduced complications even for countries without fixed exchange rates. We know from our discussion of interest rate parity in section 8.3 that, with mobile capital, movements of capital from one country to another are influenced by (a) interest rate differentials among countries, and (b) expectations of changes in exchange rates. We also know that even the governments and the central banks of countries that have not joined fixed exchange rate systems are strongly interested in the value of their currencies. In the UK's case, a high value of sterling against the euro can make it difficult for British firms to compete internationally. In addition, it puts downward pressure on UK inflation rates, possibly causing the inflation rate to fall below the MPC's target. In these circumstances, cuts in European interest rates leading to a movement into sterling and pushing up the value of sterling are likely to put pressure on the MPC to cut its interest rate. Equally, rises in short-term interest rates by the European Central Bank (ECB) may have a powerful impact on the sterling exchange rate and hence on UK competitiveness and inflation. However, the fact that sterling does not need to maintain a fixed relationship with the euro gives the MPC the freedom to allow the spread between its base rate and the ECB's refinancing rate to grow. Thus, since the beginning of 2004 this spread has varied from 1.75 per cent (Bank of England (BOE) 3.75%; ECB 2.0%) to 2.75 per cent (BOE 4.75%; ECB 2.0% – from August 2004 to August 2005). On 8 June 2006 the ECB raised its rate to 2.75 per cent, again narrowing the spread between the BOE and ECB rates to 1.75%.

In contrast, in Denmark, which has maintained a fixed relationship between its currency and the euro despite not joining the euro, the Central Bank needs to change its discount rate in line with the refinancing rate on the euro.

Given the importance of the US dollar in the world economy, US monetary policy has also always been important. Rumours of possible changes in the short-term rates of the US Federal Reserve Board can thus have an effect on the value of sterling – not just against the dollar but also against the euro and other currencies. It is an interesting reflection of the closer integration between the UK and European economies that the Bank of England's repo rate did not respond at all to the steady increase in US short-term rates from 1 per cent at the beginning of 2004 to 4.75 per cent at the end of March 2006.

Of course, it is not only international interest rates that have an impact on UK monetary policy. Any other international change that affects exchange rate expectations will affect the mobility of capital and this will put some pressure on the MPC to change UK interest rates.

10.2.3 Issues relating to eurocurrency markets

There has been a considerable debate over the years concerning the extent to which the development of the eurocurrency market has been a good or a bad thing. The principal argument for the defence is that it has increased the range of opportunities for both borrowers and lenders, has narrowed the spread between lending and borrowing rates of interest, and has provided important hedging facilities for transnational corporations. It has thus greatly increased the international mobility of short-term capital and has been a major force in integrating international capital markets. Supporters also argue that it has played a particularly important role in the recycling of funds from countries with balance of payments surpluses to those in deficit, most notably in the recycling of the surplus of the oil-rich OPEC countries following the large oil price rises of 1973 and 1979.

The case for the prosecution comprises three issues: the contribution of the markets to increased world inflation; their impact on the ability of national governments to control their own economies; and the threat to stability of the international monetary and credit system. These days, the debate over these issues relates to the whole system of international finance, not just to the eurocurrency market. The growth of the offshore markets in the 1960s and 1970s and the consequent ability of financiers to avoid the regulations imposed by national monetary authorities was one of the major factors in the decisions by national monetary authorities in the 1980s to remove restrictions on convertibility. This allowed capital to move much more freely from country to country without the necessary intervention of offshore banking.

The inflation argument rests on the view that the eurocurrency market has acted to increase the stock of international money. The usual form of this argument is through a multiplier model derived from the domestic bank credit multiplier model for domestic economies and can easily be seen from a consideration of Box 10.1. This view is developed in Box 10.3 and is contrasted with the alternative portfolio approach.

Box 10.3 The eurocurrency market and inflation

A. The bank multiplier approach
This can be derived from Box 10.1 by inspection. It is clear that the loans of the 1st Sunshine Bank are unaffected by subsequent eurobank activity. However, on the basis of a single deposit (that of Death Mines plc), the eurobank system generates additional lending to Weapons of Mass Destruction Inc and this in turn leads to extra expenditure. Where the recipients of Weapons of Mass Destruction Inc's expenditure re-deposit in a eurobank, another round of expansion takes place. Thus, it is argued that there is a multiplier in operation and the size of the multiplier will depend on the extent to which the original eurobank loans are re-deposited in eurobanks.

It is usually accepted that most eurobank loans are deposited, rather, in domestic banking systems, bringing the process to a halt. In other words, the re-deposit rate within eurobanks is held to be small and hence the multiplier is thought to be quite small – perhaps around 1.25. Even a small multiplier, however, supports the view that the eurocurrency market has caused a growth in the world money stock and has thus contributed to inflation. Exercise 10.2 relates to the multiplier model.

B. The portfolio approach
Essentially this is based upon the view that eurobanks can lend only if someone wishes to borrow. Borrowers, in turn, will be influenced by prospects of profit on investments undertaken with borrowed funds and the rate of interest payable on loans. Eurobanks will not influence the first of these two. Thus, to the extent that they also do not influence interest rates, any loans made to end-users by eurobanks would have been made in any case. All that has happened is that borrowers have moved from one source of funds to another.

The eurobanks therefore cannot create credit. As long as there is a stable demand for and supply of deposits, expansion within the eurobanks will be balanced by contraction elsewhere. The weakness of this approach as we have suggested is that:

(i) the eurobanks have allowed restrictions elsewhere in the financial system to be avoided, increasing the effective demand for and supply of deposits; and

(ii) by lowering borrowing rates and reducing the spread between lending and borrowing rates, they have encouraged borrowing.

The argument that the eurocurrency market has reduced the power of governments to control their own economies rests on the proposition that the rapid movement of capital from one country to another removes the ability of single countries to determine their own interest rates. Any attempt by governments to control the flow of capital in or out through capital controls can be avoided with increased ease because of the ability of banks and firms to move bank deposits around. In the case of developing countries in particular, the eurocurrency market facilitated capital flight and this put great pressure on many governments, forcing them to operate much more stringent economic policies than would otherwise have been needed.

Exercise 10.2 **The eurocurrency multiplier**

The eurocurrency multiplier may be written as:

$$E = \frac{1}{1 - dep(1 - rve)} \cdot D$$

where E is the total quantity of eurocurrency created, D represents deposits originally transferred from domestic banks to eurobanks, dep is the average propensity to re-deposit with eurobanks, and rve is the minimum reserve ratio held by the eurobanks.

(a) Assuming that $dep = 0.2$ and $rve = 0.01$, calculate the eurocurrency multiplier.

(b) Do the assumed figures seem realistic? What special features of the eurocurrency market might influence the re-deposit rate and reserve ratio?

(c) Using your own words, argue the case against the applicability of the multiplier model.

The instability argument has two facets. Firstly, the free movement of large amounts of capital has increased the ability of speculators to mount attacks on currencies within fixed exchange rate systems such as the attacks launched against sterling and the lira in September 1992. It has also increased the volatility of exchange rates of currencies not within fixed exchange rate systems. Secondly, the fact that the market is largely unregulated and does not have a formal lender of last resort, as in the case of domestic banking systems, is argued to increase greatly the possibility of bank failure. Further, any failure of a single bank is likely to have considerable implications for other banks because of the high number of interbank transactions in the market. In the early years of the international debt crisis of the developing countries after 1982, there were widespread fears of the failure of several major international banks leading to a collapse of a large part of the international banking system. Similar fears were expressed following the problems in the 'newly emerging markets' in 1998 (dealt with in Box 10.4) and the subsequent near-collapse of the US hedge fund, Long-Term Capital Management, in September 1998 (see section 9.5).

Box 10.4 **The rise and fall of the newly emerging markets**

In the late 1970s, Western banks lent large amounts to the more prosperous of the developing countries, particularly in Latin America. These countries built up large amounts of debt, largely denominated in US dollars. The slow-down in growth of the industrial countries following the world oil price rise in 1979, the rise in world interest rates and the strength of the US dollar all helped to make it increasingly difficult for the heavily indebted countries to meet their debt repayments. In 1982, Mexico and Brazil each imposed a moratorium on debt repayments to the international banks and this precipitated what became known as the Third World international debt crisis.

One outcome was that the banks provided no new capital to the countries involved in this crisis for the rest of the 1980s and the early 1990s. International finance sought new markets. This became pressing with the recession in Europe in the early 1990s. The 'newly emerging markets' became very popular. This term described the financial markets of two groups of countries – the rapidly growing Asian economies such as Malaysia, Thailand, Indonesia, South Korea, and more recently, China; and the former Communist countries of Eastern Europe, where fledgling stock and other financial markets were being developed. The newly emerging markets were seen as high risk but potentially highly profitable avenues for financial investment. Speculation increased rapidly on the prospects of these markets.

Problems began in the middle of 1997 with the collapse in the value of the major Asian currencies, the process beginning with the collapse of the Thai baht. Political, economic and social problems had been mounting for a number of years in the Asian 'tiger' economies as they sought to maintain the extraordinarily high growth rates of the 1980s and 1990s. Confidence is very fickle and soon serious doubts began to be expressed about the futures of these economies. A trickle of doubt soon becomes a flood in financial markets and the economies, starting with South Korea, quickly came under pressure. The steep decline in the values of currencies helped to create deep recessions in the Asian countries and these had significant knock-on effects in Western countries as Asian governments cut back on foreign expenditure and Asian imports fell.

Losses in one market frequently cause investors temporarily to become risk-averse, and the long-term doubts about the ability and willingness of Russia to transform itself into a model market economy along Western lines provided the next threat to the international financial markets. Problems spread again to Latin America, with heavy selling of the Brazilian currency. By October 1998, economists and financial journalists were talking openly of a massive worldwide recession. This did not happen, and by June 1999 the financial world was again calm and optimistic.

However, the episode illustrates the fragility of confidence in financial markets. We need also to remember that many people suffered during the financial turmoil. Financial statistics can easily come to be seen as mere numbers that have little contact with the real world – but the impact of financial frenzy on exchange rates and interest rates causes unemployment, hunger, and cutbacks in important areas of social expenditure such as health and education.

On the other hand, it is sometimes argued that the banks know that the governments of the industrial countries cannot afford to let the international banking system collapse and will thus always act to rescue the major banks. This view goes on to suggest that this increases the feeling of security of banks and encourages them to make risky loans with high profit potential. Thus, one side of the debate over the causes of the international debt crisis points to irresponsible behaviour by the banks as a principal factor.

10.3 Techniques and instruments in the eurobond and euronote markets

A eurobond is a debt security handled internationally by syndicates, groups of bankers and/or brokers who underwrite and distribute new issues of securities or large blocks of outstanding issues. It is typically in bearer (non-registered form) and is issued outside the country of the currency in which it is denominated.

Borrowers and lenders are spread around the world, while the intermediaries are spread across Europe, with the majority of business being done from London. The market was founded in the early 1960s and has provided a competitive source of funding for borrowers who can tap discreet but important sources of finance. Japanese banks, pension funds and insurance companies have become important lenders in recent years and there are still plenty of wealthy individuals who prefer the anonymity offered by bearer securities. The eurobond market is the world's second largest securities market after the US bond market in terms of trading volume and the third largest after the US and Japanese bond markets in terms of debt outstanding.

Conventional eurobonds consist of straights and convertibles. Straights are normal bonds that carry unquestioned rights to the repayment of principal at a specified future date and to fixed interest payments on stated dates. They do not carry rights to any additional interest, principal or conversion privilege. *Convertibles* are bonds which can be converted from one form into another. In euromarket usage, the conversion is into ordinary shares at a specified future date and at a pre-determined price set when the bond is issued (usually at a premium to the current share price). Interest rates are usually lower on convertibles because lenders are attracted by the possibility of being able to buy shares at a favourable price.

In recent years, many other forms of securities have developed. These have included floating rate eurobonds and dual currency bonds. *Floating rate eurobonds* are popular with investors seeking the protection of capital. Interest rates are re-fixed every three or six months, removing the threat to capital value posed by very volatile interest rates. Thus, most floating rate eurobonds are bought by banks anxious to lock into assets with a yield greater than, but calculated in the same way as, the cost of their funds in the money markets: as in the case of rollover eurocurrency loans, floating rate eurobonds generally have their coupons set in terms of a percentage margin over LIBOR or another basis rate.

Issues of floating rate eurobonds (floaters) grew greatly during the 1980s, largely due to the increased need for banks to buy assets with low credit risk as other lending, notably sovereign lending to developing countries, became more risky. At the same time, many borrowers have found floaters a much cheaper form of borrowing than syndicated credit and have used them to repay their loans early. This has added to the banks' demand for them by taking other loans off their books. The average life of issues increased from 9.7 years in 1978 to over 12 years by 1984, partly as a result of the issue of perpetuals with no final maturity. Many variations on floating rate eurobonds have developed, including *flip-flop options* which allow the investor to switch from undated perpetuals into a four-year floater paying a lower rate of interest while maintaining the right to switch back again into the perpetual issue.

Dual currency bonds are usually issued in a currency other than US dollars (most commonly Swiss francs), with the coupon denominated in that currency but the bond repayable in dollars. The coupon interest rate is usually greater than it would otherwise be because the lender assumes a forex risk. For example, consider a one-year Australian dollar bond with an option to repay in US dollars. Assume a current exchange rate of $A1 = US$0.74, an exercise price of 76 cents and a coupon rate of 7 per cent against the 4 per cent available on an ordinary one-year bond. If, at the end of the year, the Australian dollar has appreciated, the borrower will repay in US dollars; if it has depreciated, repayment will be in Australian dollars. Reverse dual currency bonds have also been issued, with the bond payable and the coupon rate denominated in US dollars but repayable in other currencies. Sometimes borrowers are given the option to repay in any one of a number of currencies.

Among the great variety of instruments and techniques developed in recent years, perhaps the most interesting has been swaps. These are exchanges of cash flows that originated as attempts by firms to manage their asset/liability structure or to reduce their cost of borrowing. Cash flows generated by many different types of financial instrument may be swapped. Simple swaps such as interest rate and currency swaps are known as plain vanilla swaps. There are many variations on these.

> **Interest rate swap:** An agreement to exchange periodic payments related to fixed interest rates on a notional capital sum with those representing a floating rate on the same sum in the same currency.

Closely related to the interest rate swap is the *basis rate swap*, which involves the exchange of one type of floating rate for another. This can happen because, as we have seen, a floating rate of interest is always expressed in two parts: a general floating rate of interest that reflects the rate at which banks themselves obtain their money (the basis rate) plus a fixed rate spread that is specific to each loan. We have seen that the most commonly used basis rate in the London market is LIBOR (the London Inter Bank Offered Rate). However, other rates may be used as the basis rate of a floating rate loan, notably the US dollar prime rate and now, since the establishment of the European Central Bank, EURIBOR. Thus, a basis rate swap may involve the exchange of LIBOR for the US dollar prime rate in the calculation of the interest rate payable on a loan. Let us take an example of an interest rate swap.

A company wishing to borrow will normally choose to do so in the market in which it can raise funds most easily, perhaps from a bank with which it has done a good deal of business in the past. We shall assume that this is a floating rate loan. However, the funds are being raised to undertake a long-term investment project and the firm, in order to be confident that the project is economically viable, would like to know the interest rate it is going to have to pay. That is, it would prefer a fixed rate loan. Thus, it enters into an agreement to pass the liability (the interest payment) on to another borrower in exchange for the fixed rate structure that best suits it.

Swaps such as these are guaranteed by banks, often referred to as swap or hedging banks. The swap banks do not lend anything in these transactions and so they do not affect the banks' assets and liabilities and thus constitute 'off balance sheet' business. All that the swap bank does is to bear the risk that one of the parties to the deal might default on its payments, leaving the bank partially liable for the interest payments left unpaid by the defaulting borrower. Interest rate swaps work because different intermediaries in the capital market do not always view a borrower in the same way. Thus, our original firm may have been able to obtain a fixed rate loan by issuing a straight eurobond – but, if the firm was not well known to the market, the interest rate may have been higher than it could manage by borrowing on floating rate terms from its own bank and swapping interest rate structures with another firm.

Box 10.5 provides an example of an interest rate swap. This example is one in which payments are swapped, but receipts may also be swapped. Yet again, since the capital sums are only notional, it is possible to speculate on the possibility of an

---

Box 10.5 | **An interest rate swap**

A major defence industry supplier, Death Mines plc, wishes to borrow £1 million for twelve years at a fixed interest rate to finance a new investment project. It could do so by issuing a straight eurobond but, as it is not well known in the market and does not have a high credit risk rating, would have to pay a coupon of 8 per cent which it regards as too high. The firm's own bank is willing to lend Death Mines the required amount via a one-year floating rate note at a rate of 2 per cent over LIBOR, currently at 3.6 per cent.

Clearly, the floating rate loan is much cheaper at the moment, but LIBOR could easily rise over the period of the loan to such a level that Death Mines would finish up losing on the project. Thus, it enters into a contract with a swap bank, Border International, to pay to it 5 per cent on the principal, receiving in exchange LIBOR.

The position of Death Mines now is:

Pays to its own bank	LIBOR + 2 per cent
Pays to Border	5 per cent
Receives from Border	LIBOR
Net position – fixed rate loan at	7 per cent

But what of Border International? It appears to be running a serious risk here. However, it would have entered into the above contract only if it were at the same time entering into another contract with a counterparty which we shall assume to be a large US multinational, GM Foods Inc. GM Foods is a prime borrower and so can borrow on the eurobond market on the finest terms, but prefers a floating rate loan as it is willing to gamble on interest rates falling in the future. Thus, it issues a straight £500,000 eurobond with a coupon of 4.375 per cent. Then it enters into a contract with Border International to pay Border LIBOR in exchange for a fixed return of 4.75 per cent.

The position of GM Foods now is:

Pays on its straight eurobond	4.375 per cent
Receives from Border	4.75 per cent
Pays to Border	LIBOR
Net position – floating rate loan at	LIBOR – 0.375 per cent

Border International's position now is:

Receives from Death Mines	5 per cent
Pays to Death Mines	LIBOR
Receives from GM Foods	LIBOR
Pays to GM Foods	4.75 per cent
Net position – profit of	0.25 per cent

(Interest rate differentials such as this are often referred to in the market in terms of *basis points* where 1 basis point = 0.01 per cent. Thus, 0.25 per cent is 25 basis points.)

interest rate rise or fall through interest rate swaps. For example, a speculator might feel that interest rates are likely to fall and so offer a floating-rate stream (which will fall as market interest rates decline) in exchange for a fixed rate stream which will not. If the speculator is right about the direction of interest rate change he will profit from the swap. Box 10.6 provides an example of a failed interest rate swap.

Box 10.6   **Failed speculation with interest rate swaps**

In the 1980s the Hammersmith and Fulham local authority in London, seeking to max- imise its income to counter the effects of restrictions imposed by the central government, attempted to profit by speculation in interest rate swaps but ran up huge losses instead. It entered the sterling interest rate swaps market on 1 December 1983. Council officers had visited the London International Financial Futures Exchange (LIFFE), where the idea of using swaps to reduce the sensitivity of the council's borrowings to interest rate fluctuations was explained to them. An independent inquiry in 1991, however, showed that such was the level of the user's understanding, that the leader of the council and the finance department were not clear whether they were interested in futures or options transactions. The council's activities in the money markets intensified in May 1987 when it began to become involved in swaptions and other complex transactions, eventually totalling 550 transactions.

At the time, interest rates were falling and the local authorities gambled on their con- tinued fall. Thus, in 1988 when the base rate of interest in the UK was 7.5 per cent, local authorities swapped fixed interest rate for floating interest rate loans of the same value with hedging banks. The only payments made were for the net liabilities on whichever was the higher – the fixed or the floating rate. Thus if interest rates had continued to fall the local authorities would have profited. Their aim was to pick correctly the trough in interest rates and at that stage to reverse the swap, moving back to a fixed interest rate, probably at a lower rate than their original interest payments.

However, the local authorities were taken unawares by the sharp jump in interest rates, which saw the base rate of interest rise to 15 per cent in 1989. They were then, under the terms of the contract, required to pay large amounts to the banks – the difference between the now very high floating rates and the fixed rate on their original loans. Despite the volume of contracts and the size of the risk, there was never any monitoring system established to track the performance and possible dangers of their derivatives business. Happily for them, the ratepayers of the most indebted local authorities were rescued by the courts, which ruled that it had been illegal for the local authorities to use their funds in this way and therefore that the contracts were unenforceable. The banks could be said to have exposed themselves to *legal risk* – the risk of losing through a decision of the courts.

The price of a swap (the charge made by the swap bank for its services) depends on the bank's estimate of the extent of default risk, the ease with which it can obtain a counterparty, and the term structure of interest rates in the bond market.

Currency swap: Contract that commits two counterparties to exchange streams of interest payments in different currencies for an agreed period of time and to exchange principal amounts in different currencies at a pre-agreed exchange rate at maturity.

A currency swap has three stages:

1. An initial exchange of principal: the two counterparties exchange principal amounts at an agreed exchange rate. This can be a notional exchange since its purpose is to establish the principal amounts as a reference point for the calculation of interest payments and the re-exchange of the principal amounts.

2. Exchange of interest payments on agreed dates based on outstanding principal amounts and agreed fixed interest rates.

3. Re-exchange of the principal amounts at a pre-determined exchange rate so the parties end up with their original currencies.

Again this may be done to hedge risk, to speculate on changes in exchange rates, or to attempt to lower the cost of borrowing by borrowing in the currency in which the most favourable interest rates are available and then swapping into the currency that the firm needs to carry out its business. Whether this will be cheaper will depend among other things on the bid–offer spread.

A fixed rate currency swap is the exchange of a fixed interest rate loan in one currency for a fixed rate loan in another currency. This also may be beneficial to all parties because borrowers may have different credit ratings in different parts of the market. For example, a major international borrower, such as the World Bank, may wish to raise funds in Swiss francs but may have a particularly high credit rating in the US dollar market, allowing it to borrow in that market on very good terms. Thus, it may choose to borrow in dollars and swap with, say, a US company with a subsidiary in Switzerland.

A currency coupon swap is a combination of an interest rate swap and a fixed rate currency swap – both the interest rate structure and the currency are exchanged. Other types of swap include *equity swaps*, agreements to exchange the rate of return on an equity or an equity index for a floating or fixed rate of interest. Equity swaps can be used as an alternative to futures and options for hedging but are most attractive to fund managers trying to outperform an index. The fund manager receives a stream of payments replicating the return of a direct investment in an equity index and makes in return a stream of payments usually based on LIBOR. An equity swap may increase a fund manager's ability to increase returns but because swaps, unlike futures, can run for up to ten years, the default risk is greater, although exposure to it is limited by payments normally being made every three months and because there is no exchange of principal.

In a *commodity swap* the counterparties exchange cash flows, at least one of which is based on a commodity price or commodity price index. A high proportion of the market is made up of oil-related transactions. A *diff swap (or quanto swap)* is the exchange of the cash flows on an asset or liability in one currency for those in another. A firm making a diff swap separates foreign exchange and interest rate exposure by paying interest rates based on one currency while taking the foreign exchange risk of another. The swap takes advantage of different-shaped yield curves to create immediate cost savings for the borrower and allows an investor to receive higher interest rates without changing currency exposure. Such an agreement typically runs from three to five years and so the risk for either borrower or investor is that the shape of one or both yield curves will change more quickly than expected, turning expected benefits into losses. Diff swaps became common when US and European interest rates diverged sharply. They involve correlation risk – an assumption that there will be a correlation between an interest rate movement and that of the currency. With a *LIBOR-in-arrears swap*, the borrower essentially takes a bet that implied forward rates are wrong by having LIBOR set, say, six months in arrears.

It is also possible to combine a *zero coupon bond* with an interest rate swap (known as a *zero coupon swap*). Then there are *swaptions* – options that give the right to enter into a swap within a specified period. Because swaps are off-balance-sheet business but carry risks for the swap bank, there was a concern in the past that banks might take on more risk through swaps than was justified by the size of their capital backing. As a consequence, as we shall see in Chapter 13, the rules adopted by a number of countries (known as the Basel rules), which try to ensure that the capital backing of banks is adequate for the type of business in which they are engaged, make allowances for off-balance-sheet business. Because currency swaps involve both default risk and exchange rate risk, they require higher capital backing under the Basel rules and this has slowed down their expansion relative to interest rate swaps.

There are yet other derivatives which do not fit neatly under the futures, options and swaps headings. One such are *equity protected notes* – zero-coupon, index-linked notes that allow investors to protect themselves against potential losses without giving up the possibility of gains. Dynamic hedging involves the buying and selling of forward contracts in the market in order to replicate options. It became popular in foreign exchange markets after the problems in the European Monetary System in 1992, which caused options prices to rise sharply. *Safes* (synthetic agreements for forward foreign exchange) are forward contracts that do not require an exchange of principal. This means that banks need to devote less capital to them and are less exposed to default risk. There are two types of safe: the *Exchange Rate Agreement* (ERA) which protects the purchaser against a change in the forward foreign exchange spread, and the *Forward Exchange Agreement* (FXA) which gives protection against a change in the spot rate as well as the forward spread. *Insurance risk contracts* are futures and options on catastrophe insurance, health, and home-owner's and reinsurance risk.

10.4 Summary

Capital has become much more mobile internationally since the early 1960s. There can now be said to be a world capital market, although barriers to capital mobility still exist, and the poorer countries remain largely excluded from it. International capital flows can be classified by purpose, borrower or lender. A major role in the development of the world capital market was played by the euromarkets or offshore markets – markets conducted outside the country in whose currency the transactions are conducted. The earliest growth was in eurocurrencies, especially in eurodollars

(US dollar bank deposits held outside the US). The market grew rapidly for economic and institutional reasons, including the domestic restrictions on the expansion of US banks at home, the growth of transnational corporations, US government policies to counter pressure on the dollar, and the anonymity offered by many offshore banks as well as political reasons associated with the Cold War. The markets grew particularly rapidly in the 1970s, following the two large world oil price rises.

The operation of the market narrowed the spread between borrowing and lending rates in world markets, provided additional hedging facilities for international companies and played an important role in the recycling of the large balance of payments surpluses of OPEC countries after the oil price rises. On the other hand, it may have added to world inflation, it probably reduced the stability of the world financial system, and it certainly greatly limited the ability of open economies to follow independent macroeconomic policies.

The growth of the market has been associated with the development of a wide range of innovative techniques that have provided additional flexibility for borrowers and lenders and have assisted in the design of complex risk management strategies. However, these techniques have also been much used for speculative purposes, and like the markets in derivatives, have led to many large losses. The most interesting techniques have been the various types of swap that have been practised.

Questions for discussion

1 How is money actually transferred from an account in one country to an account in another?

2 Has the growth of the euromarkets been, on balance, a positive development for the world economy?

3 How many reasons can you think up for preferring fixed to floating rate loans and vice versa?

4 Find out as much as you can about:
   (a) the activities of the international credit rating agencies;
   (b) the role of the international banks in the international debt crisis of the developing countries.

5 What is:
   (a) EURIBOR?
   (b) a euroeuro?
   (c) a swaption?
   (d) a plain vanilla swap?

6 Look in the financial press and find examples of variations on plain vanilla swaps that are not mentioned in the text.

7 If you swapped a floating rate payment for a fixed rate payment, would you gain or lose if interest rates unexpectedly rose? Why?

Further reading

B Eichengreen, J Tobin and C Wyplosz, 'The case for sand in the wheels of international finance', *Economic Journal*, 105, 1995, 162–72

P Howells and K Bain, *The Economics of Money, Banking and Finance: A European Text* (Harlow: Pearson Education, 3e, 2005) chs. 19, 20 and 24

K Pilbeam, *Finance & Financial Markets* (Basingstoke: Macmillan, 1998) chs. 6 and 16

J Podolski, *Financial Innovation and the Money Supply* (Oxford: Blackwell, 1986)

For current stories on international financial markets see the *Financial Times* web site http://www.ft.com

Answers to exercises

10.1 (a) In stage three in Box 10.1, A (the balance sheet of 1st Sunshine Bank) is unchanged. In B (the balance sheet of Lucky Chance Bank), the assets column now reads $1 million loan to Shanghai and Bristol Bank. The liabilities column is unchanged. We now need C (the balance sheet of Shanghai and Bristol Bank) which will have assets of $1 million loan to Weapons of Mass Destruction Inc and liabilities of $1 million loan from Lucky Chance Bank. The liabilities column of the balance sheet of Weapons of Mass Destruction Inc (now D) will be $1 million loan from Shanghai and Bristol Bank.

(b) The German firm that sells goods to Weapons of Mass Destruction Inc will have as an asset a deposit with All Nippon Bank. Its matching liability will be a reduction in the value of its stock of goods. The deposit will feature as a liability in All Nippon's balance sheet but we do not know what All Nippon does with the funds received. It could on-lend to another bank or lend to another end-user of funds.

10.2 (a) 1.247.

(b) Yes, although the re-deposit rate of 0.2 might be a little high. Features of importance include the fact that borrowing is in a currency different from that in use in the country in which the loan is made; euro markets are wholesale markets and are not subject to restrictions from domestic central banks.

(c) See the discussion of the portfolio approach in Box 10.3.

CHAPTER 11

Government borrowing and financial markets

Public sector borrowing has been central to major parts of this book, since the trading of public sector debt instruments in the bond and bills markets is an important element in the activities of financial markets. They also act as the underlying asset in some derivatives markets. The borrowing needs of the public sector are closely scrutinised as analysts attempt to forecast changes in the interest rate policy of the central bank, and these forecasts in turn affect the currency markets. Public sector deficits and debt also played a major part in decisions about the membership of the euro area when it was established in January 1999 and have been much discussed in relation to the terms of the Stability and Growth Pact of the European Union (EU). Thus, we need here to consider some of the important relationships between public sector borrowing and the financial sector of the economy.

This chapter begins by explaining the terms currently used by the Office for National Statistics (ONS) in the UK regarding public debt and discussing the British government's current attitude to public sector borrowing. It then considers the question of the financing of public sector deficits and the relationship between these deficits and interest rates in the economy. There follows a section on the Stability and Growth Pact of the EU and the current debt position of EU members. The last section of the chapter deals with the debate over the impact of large government deficits and high government debt on economic management more generally.

11.1 The measurement of public deficits and debt

Princes, monarchs and elected governments have always needed to spend more in some years than they have received in taxation in those years. In earlier times, these annual deficits largely arose from the desire to fight wars. As we have seen recently, this remains one reason for governments to wish to borrow.

These annual deficits are financed by borrowing from households, firms or banks within the country or from abroad. The accumulation of these annual borrowing requirements constitutes a country's public debt. Before 1939, it was generally held that governments should run annual deficits only in times of national emergencies such as wars. At other times, governments were expected to balance their budgets and, thus, not need to borrow. After 1945, however, governments in many countries took on new responsibilities, notably the achievement of high levels of employment and higher rates of economic growth and the development of a social policy aimed at providing some protection for the poor, ill and old. This was probably the major reason that annual government deficits became a regular feature in developed countries for the rest of the century. Public sector debt grew.

We can distinguish two types of annual deficit – cyclical and structural. Cyclical deficits arise because countries experience fairly regular business or trade cycles – periods of high unemployment and low income followed by periods of prosperity. Naturally, in periods of low income the government's taxation receipts fall and the government's social security expenditure rises, resulting in a budget deficit. However, the reverse should apply in periods of prosperity, producing a budget surplus. Consequently, on this basis, we might expect budgets to balance, when considered over a number of years. Government debt would, in the long run, remain unchanged.

Contrary to this expectation, many countries have run budget deficits even in periods of prosperity. Thus, they have, on average, run budget deficits. This average budget deficit, which appears not to be directly related to a country's position on the business cycle, has been referred to as 'structural' – running a budget deficit, it was argued, had become the normal state of affairs. Attempts have been made to estimate the size of structural deficits by calculating what government debt would have been in different years at some constant level of income or employment. Such measures – the 'cyclically adjusted budget deficit' or the 'constant income budget balance' – make a number of assumptions and are, hence, subjective.

From the late 1970s in the UK, attitudes towards the public sector became more hostile and, along with privatising the great majority of publicly owned corporations, the government began to talk of the need to run balanced budgets. Budgets remained in deficit most years, but the question of the size of these deficits became a major economic policy issue.

We have been talking here of balanced budgets and budget deficits. In the UK, the 'budget' refers to the statement of the planned receipts and expenditure for the coming year of the central government. Financial markets are, however, interested in the finances of the whole of the public sector and that includes any borrowing carried out by public corporations or local authorities. Since the privatisation of almost all the large public corporations, public corporation deficits have ceased to be an issue. Those businesses that remain in the public sector, such as the Royal Mail, are these days required to run at a profit and so are net contributors to the public finances. In addition, since the early 1980s, the ability of local governments to run large deficits has been heavily constrained. In the 1960s and 1970s, public corporation and local authority deficits and debt were significant contributors to the total public sector figures. The changes that have occurred since the early 1980s, however, have meant that central government activities have come again to dominate the public finances.

The central measure of public sector borrowing is the public sector net cash requirement (PSNCR). The PSNCR is a flow – an annual addition to the total stock of public or national debt.

> **Public sector net cash requirement (PSNCR):** The amount that must be borrowed by government in those years in which total public sector receipts from all other sources are less than total public expenditure. It was known until recently as the public sector borrowing requirement (PSBR).

As we shall see in Box 11.1, a number of adjustments have to be made to bring the PSNCR into line with annual changes in total public sector net debt (public debt, for short). The public debt is a stock measured at the end of each financial year. Note that the term 'national debt' refers specifically to the total liabilities of the National Loans Fund. While the national debt is clearly related to the public sector gross debt, it is not identical to it (see Box 11.1, which lists the various components of the public debt). For example, at 31 March 2002, the national debt stood at £434.5bn whereas public sector consolidated gross debt was £372.28bn.

> **Public sector net debt:** The combined debt (gross debt – liquid assets) of the central government, local authorities and public corporations on a given date.

The argument that governments should not run budget deficits is sometimes conducted at a simplistic level through a comparison of government accounts with household budgets. In the 1980s, for example, the British prime minister, Margaret Thatcher, claimed that it was 'bad housekeeping' if the government had to borrow. In fact, the calculation of the PSNCR involves several questions of accounting practice, and its interpretation requires the consideration of a number of important economic issues.

Box 11.1

Measures of the public debt

The overall measure of debt prepared for the UK government by the ONS is:

public sector net debt = public sector consolidated gross debt
− total public sector liquid assets

The principal element of the public sector consolidated gross debt is the **gross debt of the central government**. This in turn consists of the following items:

- **market holdings of national debt** (including holdings of government debt by the Issue and Banking Departments of the Bank of England);
- **national savings**;
- **accrued interest and indexing on National Savings**;
- **coin in circulation**;
- **other** (comprising market holdings of Northern Ireland government debt, bank and building society lending, and balances held by some public corporations with the Paymaster General).

The **market holdings of national debt** make up more than 90 per cent of the total consolidated gross debt and consist of:

- British government securities (sterling, marketable, interest-bearing securities issued by the UK government);
- treasury bills;
- National Savings securities;
- IMF interest-free notes (non-marketable, non-interest-bearing treasury notes at the disposal of the International Monetary Fund as a reciprocal facility for loans received by the UK);
- certificates of tax deposit;
- other sterling debt; and foreign currency debt.

The principal items in public sector liquid assets are:

- the gold and foreign exchange reserves of central government;
- commercial bills and British government stock held by the central government under repo arrangements (see section 5.3);
- the bank and building society deposits of central government, the local authorities and public corporations.

Annual changes in public sector net debt are equal to the PSNCR for the previous year plus certain financial adjustments. For example, foreign currency assets and liabilities have to be revalued to take account of exchange rate changes over the year and the capital value of index-linked debt has to be increased to take account of inflation during the year (this is referred to as capital uplift).

The first problem arises from the division of receipts and expenditure into those on current and capital accounts. Current account expenditure consists largely of consumption of goods and services and interest payments on the existing public debt. Capital account expenditure is, on the other hand, investment, being made up largely of gross domestic fixed capital formation and capital transfers by government to other sectors of the economy. Since the aim of investment is to provide future returns, it can be argued that even 'good housekeeping' on the part of government would permit borrowing to finance capital expenditure. Certainly, most of the corporate sector and a large part of the personal sector borrow for this purpose. Our only concern should be with whether the rate of return on government investment matches the rate of interest payable on borrowed funds. The problem is that much government expenditure produces its returns in the form of social benefits (or the reduction of social costs) and these are not easily measured. For example, how does one estimate the rate of return on the construction of a new prison? It is even difficult to calculate a rate of return on obvious items of government investment such as the construction of new schools and hospitals since the resulting services are not directly sold in the market place.

However, with the election of the Labour government in 1997, the notion that government should be allowed to run deficits in order to invest was re-established. Indeed, it was enshrined in what the Chancellor of the Exchequer, Gordon Brown, referred to as 'the golden rule' of the public finances – that over the economic cycle, the government should borrow only to invest and not to fund current spending. This has led to emphasis, from the point of view of economic policy, being placed on the public sector current balance – the balance between current spending and current receipts – rather than on the PSNCR. Clearly, financial markets also have to pay close attention to the public sector current balance, especially in the run up to the budget (in March each year) and to the government's annual expenditure review (in November) since it might well affect taxation and spending decisions. Nonetheless, the PSNCR remains important to the markets and is the figure more likely to influence the interest rate decisions of the Monetary Policy Committee (MPC) of the Bank of England.

Critics of government deficits argue that taxes must be raised in future to pay the interest on the funds borrowed (which add to the size of the public debt) and that this represents a transfer of income from future generations (who do not have a vote and cannot influence government policy) to the present generation. However, this argument is not a strong one as long as borrowing is undertaken to allow 'wise' investment – that is, investment which contributes considerably to the wealth and social welfare of future generations. The question at issue is not simply one of whether there should be a deficit but the much broader and more difficult one of the use to which the deficit is put and hence of the quality of government investment.

A second issue relates to the possible sale of public sector assets as a method of financing government expenditure. In the calculation of a single figure for the PSNCR, there is no difference between raising revenue through taxation and through selling public sector assets. They are treated differently in government accounts but they lead to the same overall result.

Table 11.1 **The PSNCR and the PSNB**

General government* current receipts

− General government current expenditure

= **Public sector current balance**

+ General government capital receipts

− General government capital expenditure

= **Public sector net borrowing (PSNB)**

+ Net lending by general government to other sectors[†]

= **Public sector net cash requirement (PSNCR)**

---

* General government = central government + local government
[†] Net lending to public corporations and the private sector less net receipts from the sale of public corporations

An increase in income tax, for example, shows up in the accounts as an increase in the current receipts of general government. The sale of government-owned buildings such as a closed National Health Service (NHS) hospital or council houses appears as a reduction in general government capital expenditure. The sale of a public corporation (such as British Telecom (BT) or British Gas) appears as a reduction in the net lending to other sectors by general government (see Table 11.1). Nonetheless, both increasing taxes and selling off public assets lead to a lower PSNCR.

However, the economic effects of these two ways of raising revenue may be quite different. An increase in income tax rates reduces disposable income and people respond by reducing their demand for current goods and services: or, at least, the rate of increase in demand slows down. Consequently, the rate of increase of output in the economy falls. The increase in tax rates acts to contract the economy, having effects on unemployment levels and inflation rates.

By contrast, consider what happened when BT was privatised. Shares in the company were seen as a financial asset by prospective buyers. The decision to buy depended on how attractive the shares seemed as a financial investment compared with other financial assets. Thus, people sold other financial assets to enable them to buy BT shares. In fact, most of the buyers of small packets of shares raised the funds for the purchase by running down their building society balances. Disposable income was not reduced and there was no direct effect on demand for goods and services in the economy. Of course, the very large sales did affect financial markets and may have influenced interest rates on other financial assets. However, the impact, if any, on the real economy was far from clear. The sale of public sector assets may not be contractionary at all. This difference has led to emphasis in the public accounts also being placed on public sector net borrowing (PSNB), formerly known as the public sector financial deficit, and the presentation of statistics on the public finances by the ONS has been changed to make this clear.

> **Public sector net borrowing (PSNB):** Equals the PSNCR plus the net receipts from the sale of public corporations and other financial transactions.

The PSNB is, then, the difference between total general government receipts and expenditure (both current and capital). As can be seen in Table 11.1, it excludes net lending to other sectors and, since the sale of public corporations is treated as a negative item under this heading, it excludes privatisation receipts. Thus, in any year in which the government has significant net privatisation receipts, the PSNB will be greater than the PSNCR. We should note, however, that the PSNB still takes account of revenue raised by the sale of general government assets (assets of the central government or local authorities). For example, net receipts from council house sales reduce both the PSNCR and the PSNB.

An alternative way of classifying the public finances of use in economic analysis involves subtracting interest payments on the public debt from the PSNCR. This gives us the *primary balance*. This, in turn, can be divided into the primary current balance and the primary capital balance. The reason for doing this is to analyse the causes of the growth of public debt. We have seen in Box 11.1 that the public debt has as its principal counterpart market holdings of government securities. As long as these securities continue to be willingly held, the public debt need never be repaid and, indeed, can go on increasing. This is simply a restatement of the proposition above that there is no necessary problem in having a PSNCR each year as long as people are willing to continue purchasing sufficient additional government securities each year.

Nonetheless, the public debt can be argued to constitute a burden on the economy since interest must be paid on it. These interest payments must be met by increased taxation revenue or they will add to the PSNCR and hence to the size of the public debt. A higher public debt in turn increases interest payments on the debt, even if higher government borrowing does not push up interest rates. The size of the problem is, however, reduced to the extent to which an economy is growing. As an economy's real income increases, higher tax revenues are raised without increases in tax rates. That is, the richer a country is, the more easily it can afford to pay the interest on its debt. These points have led to the development of a rule relating to public debt growth – that if public sector deficits are met entirely by public borrowing (generating a PSNCR equal to the deficit), the public debt will continue to grow as long as the real interest rate payable on the debt is greater than the rate of growth of GDP. This, in turn, raised the prospect that the public debt of economies with a high public debt/GDP ratio growing out of control would require them ultimately to renege on their debt repayments. Therefore, the term 'sustainable public debt' came into the vocabulary of economics.

Sustainable public debt: A public debt sufficiently small that it can be financed without adding to inflation and without pushing interest rates above the country's rate of economic growth, which would raise questions about the ability of the country to meet its debt repayments.

Although it is rather odd to express a stock (the public debt) as a percentage of an annual flow (GDP), this ratio has been widely used to provide an indication of a country's ability to afford its public debt. For example, it was used as one of the

Table 11.2 **Estimates and projections of key UK fiscal balances**

Year	Surplus on current budget £ billion	PSNB £ billion	PSNB[d] % of GDP	Public sector net debt % of GDP
2004–5[a]	−19.0	39.7	3.0	35
2005–6[b]	−11.4	37.1	2.4	36.7
2006–7[c]	−7	36	1.9	37.9
2007–8[c]	1	30	1.6	38.4
2008–9[c]	7	25	1.6	38.5
2009–10[c]	10	24	1.6	38.6
2010–11[c]	12	23	1.5	38.6

[a] outturn [b] estimate [c] projection [d] cyclically adjusted

Source: UK Budget Report 2006 Chapter 2. Available on http://www.hm-treasury.gov.uk

indicators of sustainable public finances in the Maastricht treaty convergence conditions for membership of European Monetary Union and remains central to the Stability and Growth Pact. Yet again, the second public finances rule of the Labour government after 1997 – the sustainable investment rule – made use of the ratio. This rule stated that net public sector debt as a proportion of GDP should be held at a 'stable and prudent' level over the business cycle. Box 11.2 considers the current attitude of the UK government towards its public sector deficit and debt. Table 11.2 provides figures for key public sector balances as announced in the UK budget of 2006.

Care needs to be taken with these figures, especially the projections for future years. These are based on a number of assumptions. Important underlying assumptions include the projected rate of growth of the world and UK economies. It is usual for Chancellors of the Exchequer to be optimistic about the future rates of growth of the economy and hence about projections for taxation revenue and social security expenditure in future years. It follows that the projections in Table 11.2 are likely to be revised in the coming years.

Box 11.2   **The fiscal policy of the UK government in 2006**

When the Labour government was elected in 1997, the Chancellor of the Exchequer, Gordon Brown, announced his intention of maintaining sustainable public finances in order to avoid the 'boom and bust' mentality of past British macroeconomic policy. Past Labour governments had had a reputation for high public expenditure and high public sector deficits. Thus, if the financial markets had responded to the new government as in the past, they would have expected higher future inflation and interest rates. They would have sold longer-dated government bonds, lowering their prices and pushing up the yields on them. The yield curve would have become more steeply upward sloping at the long end (see section 7.7). Interest rates would have had to increase on newly issued government debt, increasing the costs of financing future deficits. In his attempt to avoid this, the Chancellor:

(a) made the Bank of England politically independent and gave it control of UK monetary policy, setting it an annual target rate of inflation of 2.5 per cent per annum, changed to 2.0 per cent in December 2003;

(b) set out to persuade the financial markets that the PSNCR/GDP and public debt/GDP ratios would remain low. To achieve (b), he:

    (i) resolved to keep, in the government's first year of office, to the public expenditure limits set by the previous government;

    (ii) adopted the two fiscal rules mentioned in the text – the golden rule of public finances (see section 11.1) and the sustainable investment rule (explained immediately above).

Strategy (a) was clearly successful. In 1997/98, gilt yields fell sharply: at the longer end, they reached their lowest levels since the 1960s. Medium and short yields also fell during the year.

Early budgets also confirmed the determination of the Chancellor to control public sector borrowing. The 1999 budget forecast a surplus (debt repayment) of £1bn and low figures for the PSNCR for the subsequent six years – less than 1 per cent of GDP in each case. The public sector current balance was forecast to be in surplus for each of the following five years.

In recent years, however, government policy has moved partly in the direction of increasing budget deficits in order to increase public expenditure on run-down areas of the public sector, with public expenditure planned particularly on the NHS and in education. This, together with the slowdown of the UK economy, has led again, from 2002–03 onwards, to positive public sector net borrowing figures, despite some increases in tax rates, notably National Insurance contributions. As a result, public sector net debt grew from 30.2 per cent of GDP in 2001–02 to 35 per cent in 2004–05 and is projected to grow to 38.6 per cent in 2009–10. This remains low by world and UK standards. In the UK, net debt fell from 53.9 per cent of GDP in 1975–76 to 26.2 per cent in 1990–91. It rose again to 43.7 per cent in 1996–97 before falling again.

In his 2006 Budget statement, the Chancellor remained confident that he would meet his own rules for fiscal prudence – the golden rule and the rule for sustainable public debt. However, note should be taken of the comments on Table 11.2. Doubts have also been expressed about an alternative method that has been used by the Labour government and by the Conservative government before it to allow increased government investment without adding to public sector debt and endangering the Chancellor's rules. This is known as the Private Finance Initiative (PFI). This is dealt with in Box 11.3.

| Box 11.3 | **The private finance initiative (PFI) and the public finances** |

The Private Finance Initiative (PFI) was first announced by the Conservative government in the autumn of 1992. The Labour Party, then in opposition, objected to the policy but accepted it and expanded its use after it became the government in 1997. The aim was to allow investment in major public sector projects without adding to government borrowing through the involvement of the private sector. Under a PFI contract, a private consortium, usually involving a large construction firm and a bank, design, build, and in some cases manage new projects, say a new NHS hospital. Once the hospital is completed, it is leased by the NHS, typically for a period of 30 years. The payments made by the NHS for the lease provide the private companies with a return on their investment. At the end of the 30 years, ownership of the hospital reverts to the NHS. From the point of view of the public finances, the cost is spread over thirty years rather than the full sum having to be borrowed at the beginning of the project. Clearly, this allows the Chancellor to increase investment in the provision of public services without apparently adding to the public debt. The PFI makes it easier for the Chancellor to keep the public debt/GDP ratio relatively low.

However, there are similarities between government investment financed by increased borrowing and the PFI approach. The PFI commits future generations of taxpayers to meet payments for public expenditure albeit in the form of lease payments rather than as interest on the public debt. The annual payments for the lease come out of the NHS's current budget. The impact on the government budget depends on the extent to which the NHS budget is adjusted to take these payments into account. If we assume that the NHS annual budget is not increased, the budget deficit will be unchanged and no additional debt need be sold. There will be no impact on interest rates or the money supply. This could, of course, make it difficult for the NHS to maintain all of its other services. It remains that, even if the NHS budget and the government's budget deficit are increased by the full amount of the annual lease payments, the government will need to borrow much less in the current year than it would have had to do if the hospital had been built and managed in the public sector. The impact on future borrowings will depend on the relationship between the annual interest payments that would have had to be made and the annual payments for the lease.

Why then the controversy? From a financial point of view, the potential problem is the rate of return the private sector companies will require to persuade them to participate in a PFI contract. Critics of PFI claim that the rate of profit extracted by the private companies is far too high – much higher in the long run than the rate of interest on public debt. It is argued that the PFI allows government finances to look good now but only by transferring large costs to the future. There are many other issues relating to the PFI – over the sharing of the risks involved in the project, the impact on the other services provided by the NHS and other public authorities, the quality of the work and so on. For the government's explanation of and arguments for the policy, see http://www.hm-treasury.gov.uk/documents/public_private_partnerships/ppp_index.cfm or http://www.parliament.uk/commons/lib/research/rp2001/rp01-117.pdf. For criticisms of PFI see the website of UNISON, the public sector trade union, http://www.unison.org.uk/pfi/

11.2 Financing the PSNCR

To understand recent concerns about the size of both public sector deficits and the public debt, we need next to look at the question of the financing of the PSNCR.

Government borrows by selling a variety of types of securities. The most important of these are gilt-edged securities (marketable government bonds), treasury bills, National Savings (which are non-marketable and include National Savings certificates and deposits with the National Savings Bank), and various types of local authority debt instruments. These financial assets are held by: (a) the UK non-bank private sector (M4PS), which consists of the personal sector, non-bank financial institutions and non-financial firms; (b) the UK banking sector; or (c) overseas institutions. The important issues concern:

- what the government needs to do in order to encourage the holding of increased government debt; and
- why it matters to whom the government sells its debt.

11.2.1 The PSNCR and interest rates

Since the second half of the 1970s, the financial markets and hence governments have worried about the interest rate consequences of financing the PSNCR by bond sales that continually add to the stock of bonds. To understand this concern, we begin by assuming that financial markets are in equilibrium and that people are holding just the amounts of the different types of financial assets to maximise utility, given the level of wealth in the economy and the qualities of the various assets (including the time to maturity, associated risk and the present yield). It follows that, if nothing else changes, government will be able to increase its sales of securities (finance a larger PSNCR) only by making them relatively more attractive than other assets. The obvious way to do this is by increasing interest rates payable on them.

Thus, we have the simple idea of a link between the size of the PSNCR and interest rates in the economy. To sell more debt, the Debt Management Office (DMO) – the government office responsible for the management of government debt since 1997 – raises interest rates on new bonds, which now become more attractive than old government securities, leading to increased sales. Prices of old bonds fall, forcing up yields on them until they are again competitive with newly issued bonds. Equally, yields on other financial assets rise. Interest rates are pushed up all round. However, our discussion in Chapter 7 suggested that general interest rates would not be likely to change much through this mechanism in the absence of any change in short-term interest rates by the MPC of the Bank of England. In any case, we have seen (in section 6.2.1) that the DMO sets the coupon rate for new bonds and then accepts the market price for them. Thus, the market sets the yield on new bonds. This approach has applied since 1979 when the sale of bonds by tender was introduced (see below).

Fortunately for the DMO, it may be able to increase its sales of bonds without raising interest rates on bonds relative to those being paid on other financial assets. At the very least, in a growing economy, the level of real wealth and the total holding of all assets steadily increase. With no change in interest rates, we would expect people to be willing to hold more of each type of asset, including more government securities. Thus, as long as there is a positive rate of growth in the economy, real incomes rise, and real savings increase, government should be able to finance a higher PSNCR each year without causing interest rates to rise. We show this effect in Figure 11.1 with the demand curve for bonds shifting outwards with increasing income and wealth, allowing the supply curve of bonds to shift to the right without necessarily inducing any rise in yields (fall in prices).

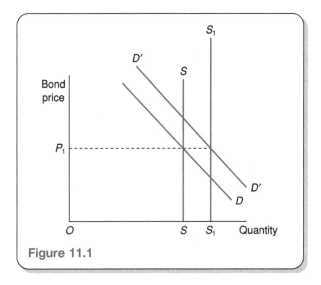

Figure 11.1

We can go further. The ability to purchase financial assets depends on the level of nominal wealth and this in turn depends on what is happening to nominal incomes and nominal savings. Thus, the ability of government to sell securities is influenced by the rate of inflation. If we assume that inflation does not influence the choice between real and financial assets, we can deal with both issues here by looking not at the level of nominal PSNCR but at the ratio of nominal PSNCR to nominal GDP. As nominal GDP rises (either because output increases or because of inflation), government should be able to sell more securities without causing interest rates to rise.

Yet this too rests on an assumption that cannot be sustained. Clearly, inflation does influence the choice people make between financial and real assets. We considered this question in section 7.1 where we calculated real interest rates by subtracting the expected rate of inflation from nominal rates. To keep financial assets (including government securities) competitive with real assets during inflation, nominal interest rates must rise in line with inflation. Nonetheless, it remains that, as nominal incomes rise during inflation, government is able to finance a higher nominal PSNCR without having to force up real interest rates.

We can go further. In section 7.2.1 we argued that as inflation reduces the real value of past savings, people need to save a higher proportion of current income in order to preserve the real value of their assets. This is the idea of inflation acting as a tax. We can apply the notion to the public debt. With inflation, the real value of government securities already held by the public falls (the real value of the public debt falls). In order to maintain the real value of their total holdings of government securities, people need to increase their purchases of new securities. That is, even at unchanged real interest rates people save a higher proportion of current income and buy more government securities.

To sum up, we can say that during inflation, the government may be able to finance a higher PSNCR without causing an increase in real interest rates in the economy for two reasons:

- nominal incomes rise; and
- the real value of financial assets falls, leading to an increase in the propensity to save out of the now higher nominal incomes.

Economists have attempted to capture this second effect in two ways. One has been by calculating the 'real PSNCR'. This adjusts the nominal PSNCR by the amount to which the real value of the existing public debt is reduced by the effect of inflation. A second approach has been to consider what is happening not so much to the ratio of PSNCR/GDP discussed above but to that of the stock of public debt/GDP. It is argued that the PSNCR/GDP ratio may be rising but through a range of values such that, given the rate of growth of nominal GDP, the public debt/GDP ratio may still be falling. In such a case, it is suggested, a rising PSNCR/GDP ratio may be associated with a falling interest rate.

We have already said enough to suggest that the link between the size of the PSNCR and nominal interest rates in the economy is complex and uncertain. Yet there is more. Plainly, government securities can be made more attractive other than through increasing the yield on them. In addition, marketing techniques can be developed to persuade people to hold more bonds at the existing yield. Let us look at these possibilities more closely.

To begin with, the average holding time of long-term bonds in the UK is quite short, suggesting that the market is dominated by people principally interested in capital gains. Such people are more interested in changes in interest rates (and hence bond prices) than in the absolute level of interest rates. We have seen in Chapter 6 that this means that the demand curve for bonds is likely to shift in response to short-term expectations about future interest rates. Indeed, expectations have been so important that the authorities have sought to exploit them in the bond market.

For example, in the 1950s and 1960s it was feared, on the basis of very little evidence, that bond holders held extrapolative expectations – that is, a fall in interest rates led people to believe that they would fall further (and that bond prices would rise).

> **Extrapolative expectations:** The belief that the price of a financial asset would continue to move in the same direction as it was currently moving – extrapolative expectations are major factors in both bull and bear markets and in the development of bubbles and financial panics.

The significance can be seen in Figure 11.2. We begin in equilibrium with bond prices at P. The authorities then sell more bonds to finance a budget deficit. The stock expands, the supply curve shifts to $S'S'$ and the price falls to P_1. The fear was that existing bond holders, having experienced falling prices and capital losses, would fear yet more. Thus they would be less willing to hold bonds at all prices and yields and the demand curve would shift to $D'D'$. As drawn, this pushes the price to a new equilibrium at P_2, but it is obviously possible, if the fear of capital losses is sufficiently strong, for the market to become completely unstable. These anxieties led the authorities to a policy of 'leaning into the wind'. Whenever prices showed signs of changing significantly, the Bank would buy or sell bonds as appropriate to offset the price/interest rate

Figure 11.2

change. This meant a policy of stable interest rates and a level of debt sales that was constrained to whatever the market would bear at prevailing prices. Neither interest rates nor open market operations could be used for monetary control purposes.

In 1974, however, the authorities introduced a more aggressive approach to the selling of gilts, known as the 'Duke of York' tactics. These required interest rates to be raised artificially, leading to a view in the market that they must soon fall again (and hence bond prices must rise). As bond sales increased in the pursuit of capital gains, interest rates did indeed begin to fall. This fall, in turn, persuaded those market participants who still held extrapolative expectations that rates would continue to fall (and prices to rise). The method, practised between 1974 and 1979, enabled the authorities to sell large additional quantities of bonds without any permanent increase in interest rates.

Other new approaches to the marketing of government securities followed. Before 1979, gilts had invariably been marketed using the 'tap system'. Stock was offered for sale at a fixed price (and hence yield), pre-determined to make the stock attractive, given the existing market conditions. When the market was unwilling to purchase the full issue at that price, the unsold stock would be taken up by the Bank of England and subsequently released onto the market as and when conditions suggested that the fixed price would be acceptable. From March 1979, the authorities moved towards a 'partial tender' system in which stock is announced for sale by tender, allowing the market to fix the price which will clear the stock. This is subject to a minimum tender price (hence partial tender) designed to prevent a sudden collapse in stock prices should the authorities miscalculate the timing and attractiveness of the sale. If the minimum price is set realistically, the price is determined by the market and the authorities can be certain of selling given quantities of debt at pre-determined intervals.

In December 1980, the Bank introduced *taplets* (also known as 'tranchettes') – the practice of issuing relatively small amounts of a number of different stocks rather than a single tap stock. For example, in July 1982 eight different long-dated stocks were issued, amounting to a total of £1,200m. In May 1987, following the 1986 reorganisation of the UK gilts market, with the increase in the number of market-makers and the hoped-for increase in the competitiveness of the market (see section 6.2.3), the Bank initiated an experiment with full gilts auctions without a minimum tender price. To the extent that changes in marketing techniques lead to increased gilts sales, the authorities are able to finance a higher PSNCR without causing interest rates to rise.

The 1970s and early 1980s also saw a number of product innovations in both gilts and National Savings, the most important of which was the introduction in 1981–82 of index-linked gilts. These are gilts that pay semi-annual cash flows indexed to the Retail Prices Index (RPI).

We can summarise all this by saying that to the extent that non-price competition is possible in financial markets through product variation, the government is able to finance a higher PSNCR in other ways than by pushing up interest rates on its own products relative to other financial assets.

All of this applies when we begin by assuming equilibrium in the market before the government seeks to finance an increase in government expenditure. It is possible, however, that in periods of budget surpluses or small deficits, the market may become short of government debt. This is because a number of financial institutions are either required or seek to hold a proportion of their financial assets in the form of gilts because of their security and because they are long-term, fixed-interest rate assets. Gilts are particularly useful for life insurance companies and pension funds, which must match expected income from their assets with their expected financial obligations over long periods into the future. Thus, during periods of budget surplus, the supply of new gilts onto the market might not meet the needs of institutions of this kind, pushing bond prices up and yields down.

We have now identified a number of circumstances in which increased government bond sales might be possible without an increase in interest rates. These are summarised in Box 11.4.

Box 11.4 | **Increases in public sector deficits and the rate of interest**

An increase in government expenditure that causes the PSNCR to rise might not influence interest rates under the following circumstances:

- if the additional government expenditure being financed causes an increase in output, employment and real savings such that holdings of all types of financial assets increase;
- if the wealth of the economy is increasing, for whatever reason;
- if inflation reduces the real value of the financial assets of savers, causing them to increase the proportion of income saved;
- if government bonds are sold to the banking sector (monetary or residual financing of the increase in the PSNCR);
- if the managers of the public debt are able to sell more bonds at the existing interest rate by innovative marketing techniques;
- if the development of new or modified products (such as index-linked bonds or strips) succeeds in enlarging the market for public debt.

The sale of bonds to banks

So far we have been assuming that it makes no difference to whom government securities are sold. This is clearly not so in two cases – the sale of bonds (and treasury bills) to the banking sector, and the sale of bonds overseas. Consider firstly the sale of bonds to the banking sector and the ways in which this differs from bond sales to the private sector (M4PS).

Let us assume that there is an increase in government expenditure to pay for increased wages of nurses in the NHS. With no change in taxation revenue, the PSNCR increases. The wage increases are deposited in bank accounts. Bank deposits (bank liabilities) increase. Suppose, however, that the Debt Management Office finances the increased PSNCR by selling bonds to the M4PS, which is willing to purchase additional bonds at the current yield. The M4PS substitutes government bonds for bank deposits (assumed to be non-interest-bearing) and the system returns to equilibrium when bank deposits have fallen by the full amount of the increase in PSNCR. However, this fall is just matched by the increase in deposits resulting from the increase in government expenditure. The net result of the operation – the increased government expenditure financed by the sale of bonds to the M4PS – is an unchanged level of bank deposits, and hence of the money stock.

Consider next what happens if the M4PS is unwilling to purchase more government securities at existing bond yields. Then, the increase in government expenditure will, in effect, be financed by the banking system. Assume the nurses are paid by government cheques. Their now larger cheques are deposited with banks, increasing bank liabilities. But this is matched by increases in the deposits of the monetary sector with the Bank of England. Now, there is no equivalent running down of bank deposits since interest rates do not rise. Banks next realise that their deposits at the Bank of England are higher than they need and run them down by increasing their holdings of all other assets (including government securities). As they increase their loans to the personal and corporate sectors, bank deposits and bank assets rise further. Deposits (and hence the size of the balance sheet of the banking sector) continue to rise, following the familiar money multiplier process, until banks' holdings of government securities have increased by the size of the increase in PSNCR.

> **Residual (monetary) financing of public sector deficits:** The financing of the PSNCR by the sale of government bonds to the banking sector, causing an increase in the money supply.

The net result is an increase in the money supply. This process is known as the residual financing or the monetary financing of the PSNCR. The government is borrowing from the banking sector, and the effect on the money supply is the same as when the M4PS increases its borrowing from banks. This gives rise to the money supply identity

$$\Delta \text{ Money supply} = \text{PSNCR} - \Delta \text{ M4PS lending to the public sector}$$
$$+ \text{D bank lending to M4PS}$$
$$+ \text{overseas impact on money supply}$$

11.2.3 The sale of bonds overseas

This represents a cross between our two cases above. We assume that, in addition to an increase in demand for bonds by the M4PS, bonds are sold abroad. To purchase UK securities, foreigners must exchange foreign currencies for sterling. The foreign exchange reserves of the Bank of England grow, but so too does the money supply. In other words, to the extent that the foreign demand for government securities increases, the system will return to equilibrium before bank deposits fall back to their initial level. Or, to put it another way, the increase in government expenditure causes bank deposits to rise; the sale of additional bonds to the M4PS causes bank deposits to fall; but the inflow of foreign currency counteracts the fall to some extent. The net result is an increase in the money supply, but a smaller increase than if the increase had been residually financed.

Several other possibilities now arise. The increased international demand for sterling may push up the value of the pound and this, in turn, may affect UK exports and imports, as well as expectations about the future value of sterling. Again, once we allow for the possibility that capital is internationally mobile, we need to recognise that the demand for UK government securities will change whenever there is a change in exchange rate expectations or whenever there is a change in foreign interest rates. The relationship between the UK money supply and the size of the PSNCR becomes even more complex and difficult to predict.

11.2.4 PSNCR, interest rates and the money supply – a conclusion

We have seen that the PSNCR may be financed firstly by selling securities to the M4PS. If all of the PSNCR is financed in this way there will be no monetary consequences. We have seen too that, although this may require an increase in interest rates, this is by no means certain. The authorities may be able to sell more bonds without raising interest rates through aggressive selling such as in the Duke of York strategy or by widening the market for bonds. Again, their ability to sell more bonds without interest rate increases will depend on the rate of growth of the economy and on the way in which people respond to inflation.

A second possibility is that the M4PS is willing to fund only part of the PSNCR at existing interest rates and that the rest has to be met by residual or monetary financing through the banking sector. To the extent that this is necessary, there will be an increase in the size of the money stock. Whether this is inflationary will depend on whether the additional government expenditure which has to be financed leads to an increase in the output of the economy.

Thirdly, part of the PSNCR may be financed through the sale of government securities overseas. This too will have monetary consequences through the consequent increases in the UK's holding of foreign exchange reserves. We have also seen that, once we allow for the possibility of international capital movements, the attractiveness of UK securities will depend on exchange rate movements and expectations and on changes in foreign interest rates – factors that are largely or entirely outside the control of the domestic monetary authorities.

Despite all of these possibilities concerning the relationship between the PSNCR, interest rates and the rate of growth of the money supply, one view has dominated the financial world since the 1980s – that increased public sector deficits cause either interest rates to rise or the money supply to grow more rapidly. Higher interest rates were assumed to reduce private sector investment and consumption; a higher rate of growth of the money supply was assumed to increase the rate of inflation. Thus, a low or zero PSNCR became a major aim of economic policy. This was to a significant extent because of the market response to high PSNCR/GDP and high public debt/GDP ratios. We have already seen one example of the effect of this market response in relation to the fiscal policy of the UK government (see Box 11.2).

A major way in which the view of the financial markets is imposed is through the operation of the international credit-rating agencies. Their view of the seriousness of a large public debt has led them consistently to lower the credit ratings of governments with high public debt/GDP ratios. Whether this is justified is irrelevant. The simple fact that the credit rating is lowered increases the interest rate such governments must offer in order to sell their debt on international markets. We shall, however, see an exception to this in Box 11.5, which looks at another problem caused for governments in the sale of their debt by the operation of financial markets. Exercise 11.1 poses some questions on the contents of this box.

Box 11.5	**Liquidity and the sale of government debt**

The following extract comes from 'Small countries pay for lack of liquidity' by Arkady Ostrovsky and Eric Frey on page 45 of the *Financial Times* of 17 June 1999.

Size certainly matters, at least in the euro-zone government bond markets, as small countries have discovered to their misfortune. It is a simple rule: the smaller the country, the higher the premium it has to pay to entice investors to buy its government bonds.

Take Finland, for example, one of the most disciplined members of EMU. Its economy is growing at a healthy 3.8 per cent, its debt to gross domestic product ratio is half that of Italy or Belgium. It has the highest credit rating from two of the three agencies, yet its bond yields are among the highest in the euro-zone. At 24 basis points over the German benchmark, Finland's yield spread is closer to Belgium, which has recently been downgraded because of its massive debts, than to France with whom it shares the same rating.

Observers say small countries get penalised by the markets for the lack of liquidity. Since the launch of the euro, which has eliminated foreign exchange risk, liquidity has become one of the overriding factors in the euro-zone bond markets. Matt King, bond strategist at JP Morgan, says that after the launch of the euro small countries lost some of the domestic investors who swapped their investment into more liquid assets. Meanwhile, the weight of a credit rating in pricing the bond has been significantly reduced since many investors believe euro-zone countries are virtually default-risk free.

According to Satu Huber, director of finance at the Finnish state treasury, only 3 per cent of all international bond issues, excluding domestic issues, were larger than €2bn. Since the launch of the single currency about a quarter of all international bond issues have exceeded that magnitude. 'When we launched our €2bn issue in May last year it was considered a large one, now it is considered average,' says Ms Huber. Last May, Finland was able to launch its 10-year bond at a spread of about 10 basis points over Germany's 10-year benchmark. It is now trading at 24 basis points over Germany.

But Finland is not alone. Austria is also suffering from the lack of liquidity. Austria currently pays a premium of about 20 basis points over the German bund for its 10-year government bond issues solely because of lower liquidity for its debt, says Helmut Eder, director of the Federal Financing Agency. 'Our credit rating is the same as that of Germany, but our liquidity gives us a natural disadvantage,' he says. 'If we were competitive in liquidity, however, we would lose our AAA-rating.' To improve liquidity, the Federal Financing Agency aims to create a certain critical market volume for every maturity. 'When the Republic issues a new bond, the market can be assured that the volume of this maturity will eventually reach €5bn or €6bn,' says Mr Eder . . .

What exactly is the nature of the problem?

Bonds issued for small amounts present two potential problems for their holders:

(a) changes in demand will produce bigger price changes than would occur if the supply were larger – thus, prices and yields are more volatile and the risk associated with holding the bond is greater;

(b) bond holders wishing to sell the bonds at short notice will have less chance of obtaining an acceptable price than if the market were deeper.

It follows that bonds issued in small amounts are less liquid than those issued in large amounts (see the definition of liquidity in Chapter 1), and a premium has to be paid on small issues to persuade the markets to hold them.

Source: Financial Times, 17 June 1999

Exercise 11.1

Answer the following questions on the content of Box 11.5:

(a) Why do many investors feel that eurozone countries are 'virtually default-risk free'?

(b) Convert 24 basis points into a percentage.

(c) What happened between May 1998 and June 1999 to cause the spread over Germany's ten-year benchmark of Finnish ten-year bonds maturing in 2008 to widen from 10 to 24 basis points?

(d) Did the launch of the euro really eliminate foreign exchange risk?

(e) Why do German bonds provide the benchmark?

(f) Why would the Austrian government lose its AAA-credit rating if it became 'competitive in liquidity'?

11.3 Attitudes to public debt in the European Union

Market attitudes also had a good deal to do with the Maastricht convergence conditions for membership of European Monetary Union. Several prospective members, notably Germany, felt the need to convince the financial markets that the single currency would be strong after the establishment of monetary union. This explains the prohibition on the monetary financing of government debt by the European Central Bank (ECB); the requirement for membership of the monetary union of evidence of a sustainable government financial position; and the insistence that any members unable to meet their debt repayments would not be rescued by the ECB. The evidence of a sustainable government financial position according to the Maastricht treaty was that of (a) a general government budget deficit no greater than 3 per cent of GDP at market prices, and (b) a ratio of gross public debt to GDP at market prices no greater than 60 per cent – unless this debt ratio was falling 'at a satisfactory pace'.

This concern was carried into monetary union itself with the Stability and Growth Pact of 1997, which set limits to public sector deficits. This is an agreement among EU members to limit budget deficits under normal circumstances to less than 3 per cent of GDP. The agreement resulted from the fear that countries with past records of high inflation would be tempted, once they were within the monetary union, to operate expansionary fiscal policies with high budget deficits, especially since they would be issuing debt in euro. Euro-denominated debt does not bear the foreign exchange risk premium that had been borne by lira- or drachma-denominated debt before the beginning of the monetary union. Excess borrowing by some governments might increase their total public debt sharply and cause the financial markets to increase their estimate of the default risk attached to the debt of these countries. This might cause the markets to believe that the ECB would need to follow a looser monetary policy to reduce the chance of these countries having to renege on their debt. The fear was that this would lead to a weaker euro, with inflationary consequences for the monetary union as a whole. The Stability and Growth Pact converted the 3 per cent of GDP limit on budget deficits into a permanent ceiling that might be breached only under exceptional circumstances. 'Exceptional circumstances' were defined as a natural disaster or a very severe recession, such that the country's GDP falls by at least 2 per cent over a year. In June 2005, the rule was weakened by redefining 'exceptional circumstances' to include any fall in GDP over a year.

The European Commission may report a member state that does not observe the 3 per cent limit to the European Council and an 'excessive deficit procedure' (EDP) may then be started against the member state. This may lead to policy recommendations that the member state is obliged to follow. A deadline may be set for the member state to bring its deficit down below the 3 per cent limit. Failure to do so may ultimately lead to the imposition of financial sanctions in the form of a non-interest-bearing deposit with the ECB or a fine. However, no one has yet been disciplined in this way although many member states have breached the limit (12 were outside the 3 per cent limit in 2005) and some have regularly done so. For example, Germany's deficit has been above 3 per cent in every year from 2002. It has now been given a deadline of 2007 to conform to the rule and we will need to wait to see what follows if it again fails.

From one point of view, the firm application of the Pact would make little sense since fines levied would make it more difficult for governments to get their borrowing back within the 3 per cent of GDP limit and would lead to the tightening of fiscal policy when economies were at their weakest. The restriction of fiscal policy in this way would remove an element of flexibility in the management of national economies and would increase the costs associated with the loss of freedom to change exchange rates. In late 2002, Romano Prodi, the then President of the European Commission, caused controversy by saying that the Stability and Growth Pact was 'stupid' because it was too inflexible. Various proposals for loosening the terms of the Pact were put forward, including tighter budget limits on countries with a high level of public debt, paying greater attention to structural deficits, and allowing countries to run deficits to finance public sector investment. None of these proposals have been accepted in relation to the 3 per cent limit of the Pact, but in March 2003, the European Council endorsed a report by EU finance ministers on strengthening budgetary co-ordination, which emphasised the importance of taking into account the economic cycle, long-term sustainability and the quality of public investment in assessing the state of public finances in member states. In June 2005 it was agreed that countries would be given longer deadlines to correct their deficits if they were made subject to an EDP.

11.4 The public debt and open market operations

The existence of the public debt introduces the possibility of open market operations – the sale or purchase by the government of securities for monetary purposes.

Suppose first the government wishes to tighten monetary conditions and push up interest rates but that at current rates it can sell to the M4PS all the securities it needs to finance the PSNCR and to refinance maturing securities. It chooses, however, to offer its new securities at a higher interest rate. Members of the M4PS respond by buying more securities than are needed, paying the government by cheque. This causes both bank deposits (bank liabilities) and the banking sector's deposits with the Bank of England (bank assets) to fall. The banking sector will need to replenish its deposits with the central bank and to do so will need to call in loans and sell off other assets, including part of its holdings of government securities. As loans are called in, bank deposits fall further and the process continues. The fall in bank deposits reduces the size (or, at least, the rate of growth) of the money stock; the sale of previously issued government securities by the banking sector forces their prices down and interest rates up in line with the new issues. In turn, interest rates on other assets increase and the interest rate rise sought by the government spreads throughout the economy. At the end of the process, a higher proportion of the public debt will be financed by the M4PS; a lower proportion will be met by residual or monetary financing.

The reverse open market operations case can be outlined easily. Here, the central bank wishes interest rates to fall. It thus reduces the interest rate payable on new securities. The M4PS will be unwilling to purchase at this low rate sufficient new securities to fund the new PSNCR and to refinance maturing issues. Government expenditure thus leads to an increase in bank deposits and in banking sector deposits with the Bank of England. The outcome is the same as in the monetary financing of the PSNCR which we considered in section 11.2.2. Banks acquire more government securities, pushing down interest rates on them and leading to a generalisation throughout the economy of the interest rate cut. This case is often referred to as a 'purchase' of its own securities by the central bank. We see here that instead of directly purchasing its own securities, the authorities may simply determine the interest rate payable on new issues so as to cause fewer such securities to be purchased by the M4PS, leaving a higher proportion of the PSNCR to be financed residually.

11.5 Debt management and interest rate structure

However, the existence of the public debt presents another problem for the authorities. Past issues of government securities (with the exception of a small number of issues of undated stocks) sooner or later mature and must be redeemed. They must then be replaced by new securities in order to refinance the existing public debt. In any financial year, then, the authorities must sell securities equal to the current PSNCR plus the value of old issues of securities maturing in that year. Two things follow. Firstly, other things being equal, the government prefers to sell longer-dated than shorter-dated stocks to reduce the rate at which the existing debt has to be refinanced. Secondly, the authorities need to construct a time profile of the debt that avoids the possibility of too high a proportion of the existing debt maturing at the same time. This is indicated by the long average maturity of the gilt portfolio. At the end of March 2006, this was 13.09 years for all stocks (12.77 years for conventional stocks; 13.95 years for index-linked stocks).

It remains, however, that within this constraint the authorities may choose the profile of government debt. By so doing, they may hope (assuming that there is some degree of segmentation in the market) to influence the relationship between short and long interest rates in the economy.

They may wish to do this to assist them in selling government securities. Gilts are usually issued as longer-term securities and their attractiveness is influenced by the relationship between long and short rates. We have already seen that this played an important part in the Duke of York strategy. Alternatively, as we saw in Chapter 7, the government may wish to 'twist' the interest rate structure – usually, keeping long rates low and pushing short rates up – in pursuit of macroeconomic objectives.

11.6 Summary

All countries have a public debt but there have been frequent changes of attitude towards the public debt and the public sector financial deficits, which add to them. These attitudes have been reflected in alterations in definitions and the ways in which information on the public finances have been presented. The most recent changes in the UK have seen the public sector borrowing requirement (PSBR) replaced by the public sector net cash requirement (PSNCR) and much greater emphasis placed on the public sector current balance than previously. Other calculations such as the PSNCR/GDP ratio, the real value of the PSNCR or the income-adjusted PSNCR can be made to help in interpreting the economic significance of public sector deficits. As long as the bonds sold by government to finance the public debt are willingly held, the debt can go on increasing without causing economic problems. However, in recent years the public debt has been seen increasingly as a burden on the economy and much attention has been paid to the 'sustainability' of the public finances. This has had a strong impact on market attitudes towards highly indebted countries and market responses have in turn influenced government policies.

Much of the debate surrounding the view that high public sector deficits are undesirable concerns the financing of the PSNCR. It has been widely accepted that an increase in the PSNCR either pushes up interest rates (if the deficit is financed by sales to the non-bank private sector) or increases the rate of inflation (if the deficit is residually financed). There are many dubious assumptions underlying this proposition. There are many circumstances in which more government securities can be sold without residual financing and without causing interest rates to rise. For example, the authorities may be able to sell more bonds at existing interest rates through innovative marketing techniques or by improving the non-price charac-teristics of the bonds. Further, the link between the rate of growth in the money supply and the rate of inflation is far from proven. Nonetheless, it remains true that if it is believed in financial markets that high public sector deficits and a high public debt are undesirable, governments have to pay close attention to these views. One way in which financial markets influence governments is through the ratings given to them by international credit-rating agencies.

Although the existence of the public debt poses problems for governments, it also allows them to engage in open market operations. On the other hand, govern-ments must carefully manage their public debt to avoid the possibility of too high a proportion of the debt maturing at the same time. Debt management can have an impact on an economy's interest rate structure.

Questions for discussion

1 Why have governments frequently had difficulty in controlling the size of the PSNCR?

2 Consider the various ways in which the figures for the PSNCR may be interpreted. Why are so many interpretations possible?

3 Explain the theoretical relationship between the PSNCR, the rate of growth of the money stock and interest rates. Why is this relationship unlikely to hold in practice?

4 What was the economic significance of the changes introduced into the gilts market and into National Savings in the 1970s and 1980s?

5 How does the existence of the public debt complicate the funding of the PSNCR?

6 Who are the international credit-rating agencies? Why do they exist?

7 The public debt/GDP ratio is described in the text as 'rather odd'. In what ways is it odd?

8 Find examples in the financial press of:
   (a) government fiscal policy decisions influencing financial markets; and
   (b) the attitudes of financial markets towards public sector deficits and/or public debt influencing economic policy.

9 Explain the differences between each of the following pairs:
   (a) the PSNCR and the public sector current balance;
   (b) the PSNCR and the PSBR;
   (c) the public sector deficit and the public debt;
   (d) the public debt and the national debt.

Further reading

P Howells and K Bain, *The Economics of Money, Banking and Finance: A European Text* (Harlow: Pearson Education, 3e, 2005) ch. 16

J Wormell, *The Gilt-Edge Market* (London: Allen and Unwin, 1985)

Bank of England at http://www.bankofengland.co.uk

Debt Management Office at http://www.dmo.gov.uk

Answers to exercise

11.1 (a) Because they believe that the ECB or other euro-area governments will rescue any member country in danger of defaulting, contrary to the statements in the Maastricht treaty and later.

   (b) 0.24 per cent.

   (c) The average size of bond issues increased dramatically.

   (d) No. It removed foreign exchange risk among euro-area countries, but the risk of the euro changing in value against sterling, the US dollar, the yen and other currencies remained.

   (e) Because Germany has a high credit rating and its bonds are very liquid.

   (f) For the bonds of a small country to become as liquid as German bonds, it would have to issue many more bonds than would be justified by its size. This would imply a high public debt/GDP ratio.

CHAPTER 12

Financial market failure and financial crises

We have seen throughout this book that the efficiency of a modern economy is greatly enhanced by the development of the financial system. It is also true, however, that weaknesses in financial markets can be very costly to individuals, firms and the economy as a whole. As with all other markets, financial markets are subject to market failure – interferences with the market ideal of perfect competition that might arise, for example, from the presence of elements of monopoly or oligopoly, the presence of externalities, the lack of information in general or the existence of asymmetric information. In this chapter, we shall consider problems deriving from the operation of financial institutions and markets. We shall begin by looking at problems relating to the ability of firms and individuals to borrow through the financial system. We shall then consider issues concerning the level of saving in the economy. The chapter continues with sections on complaints about the apparent irrationality and 'exuberance' of financial markets and the possibility of financial market crashes, and on the frequency of financial scandals and fraudulent behaviour in financial markets. It concludes by looking at some international issues.

12.1 Borrowing and lending problems in financial intermediation

We saw in Chapter 2 that financial intermediation should encourage both saving and the borrowing of funds for investment and should channel funds to their best use from the point of view of the overall economy. Over the years, however, there have been many criticisms of the way in which the financial system meets the demands of its many clients. From the point of view of firms, the principal issue has been the extent to which firms wishing to engage in productive activities are able to obtain finance. In relation to households, there has been much discussion of the extent to which people are able to take advantage of the benefits of the financial system. In recent years, worries have been expressed as to whether the system provides sufficient incentives and information to encourage long-term saving. Indeed, it has sometimes been argued that the financial system is in part responsible for the tendency of many households to go deeply into debt, while others do not save enough. We discuss these issues briefly here.

12.1.1 The financing needs of firms and attempted remedies

One major allegation has been that the financial system has sometimes performed less than satisfactorily with respect to those who wish to borrow from it. Until recently, concern has largely centred on the relationship between the financial system and the financing needs of firms. This has long been a matter of controversy.

The Macmillan Committee, for example, with J M Keynes as one of its members, investigated the issue in 1931. More recently, the Wilson Committee (HMSO, 1980) produced a voluminous report (and a dissenting minority report) on the functioning of financial institutions which was for some years a major source of reference on the structure and functioning of the UK financial system.

Three themes run through this recurrent interest in whether the financial system is functioning satisfactorily. The first, important in both the Macmillan and Wilson investigations, is whether the system fails to cater adequately for the financial needs of a particular class of commercial borrower. The 'Macmillan Gap' was the name given to what was seen as the failure of the system to provide funds cheaply and conveniently for 'small' firms. The Macmillan Committee was not persuaded, but the idea that something might be lacking from the spectrum of institutions providing commercial finance has continued and lies behind various government-sponsored initiatives, particularly in the 1960s and 1970s, to make it easier for small firms to raise venture capital. The Wilson Committee recommended public support for a Small Firm Investment Company and a loan guarantee scheme. In the 1980s, the idea that small firms might be at a disadvantage had moved on a stage, with accusations that they were treated less favourably in many ways by their banks, when compared with the services provided to, and the prices faced by large firms.

More recently, venture capital trusts (VCTs) have been established in an attempt to help provide finance for small expanding enterprises. They are companies quoted on the stock exchange which invest mainly in unquoted companies or newly-formed companies. The government's intention was that VCTs would find the successful companies and entrepreneurs of the future and allow them a start they might otherwise have been denied. VCTs were introduced in the Finance Act 1995. They are aimed at medium to large net worth investors who receive tax relief for investing in what are seen as risky enterprises. Investors can put up to £200,000 per annum (increased from £100,000 in 2004) in VCTs, which are required to have 70 per cent of their money in qualifying companies within three years of their launch. Qualifying companies are likely to be UK-based trading companies with gross assets of less than £7m at the time of investment.

VCT shares issued after 5 April 2000 needed only to be held for three years for investors to retain the initial tax reliefs. Beyond that, the benefits become greater the longer the shares are held. In fact, VCTs have proved to be much less risky than was originally thought. All VCTs that have been running for a year or more have paid tax-free dividends. After a fairly slow start, funds invested in VCTs rose to over £400m in the tax year 2000–01 but then fell off sharply. In 2004, the Treasury responded to this by increasing the income tax rebate on funds invested in VCTs from 20 to 40 per cent. This produced a sharp increase in funds flowing into VCTs – to £500 million in 2004–05 and over £700 million in 2005–06. However, the Treasury then decided that the scheme was too expensive in terms of the tax revenue foregone and in the 2006 budget the income tax rebate was cut back to 30 per cent and the minimum holding period required to retain these tax reliefs was increased from three to five years.

A second critical theme is that financial institutions in the UK have been too ready to provide finance to overseas governments and firms at the expense of domestic industry. Certainly, overseas securities form a large part of the existing asset holdings of UK institutions and the flow of funds into overseas securities grew strongly in the 1980s; as we noted in section 4.4, since the ending of exchange control in 1979 the share of overseas assets in institutions' portfolios has grown steadily. The export of capital issue has, however, been a matter of debate since the late nineteenth century. Undoubtedly because of its position as the first industrialised country, the UK financial system has a long tradition of international finance and its institutions are more outward looking in their search for profitable opportunities than are institutions in other, especially mainland European, countries. This has always been a matter of some concern to the left in British politics. Since the principal function of a financial system is to mobilise savings or 'wealth' into productive uses it is clear that it is providing services primarily to those with property. However, in so far as the system is effective in channelling surpluses into productive use in the domestic economy, the propertyless gain some benefit from the resulting output and employment. When surplus funds are directed overseas, the only benefits that accrue in the UK accrue to wealth-holders alone. This criticism is often joined with allegations that UK economic (and especially monetary) policy is too readily aimed at reassuring overseas investors at the expense of production and employment in the UK.

A third but more recent theme is that the structure of the UK (and to some degree the US) financial systems pressurises firms into concentrating upon short-term performance to the detriment of long-run investment, innovation and growth. This is a complex issue on which the evidence is inconclusive. Those who suspect that something is wrong with the service offered to firms by the UK system begin by pointing to some combination of the following, each of which is true as it stands.

Firstly, critics point to the poor investment and growth record of the UK economy over the past 30–40 years, when compared with competitors like Germany and Japan.

Secondly, they can draw quite striking contrasts between the financial systems that operate in Germany (especially) and in the UK. The former is often described as a 'bank-based' system, while the latter (like that of the US) is described as 'market-based'. What this means is that in Germany a comparatively small proportion of firms are quoted on the stock exchange. In Germany, at the end of 2004, there were 764 quoted companies on the Frankfurt Stock Exchange compared with over 2,400 in the UK. This means that banks play a much more central role and since they have both a debt and an equity stake which cannot be readily traded, they take a much closer interest in the operation of the firms which they finance. They generally have representation on company boards and they develop long-term relationships with their clients. By contrast, the debt and equity of UK firms is dispersed in very active financial markets where it can be and is readily traded. A high proportion of it (65 per cent in 1998) is held by non-deposit-taking institutions (NDTIs) such as pension funds and unit and investment trusts that feel no particular long-term commitment and need take no very close interest in firms' decisions since they can sell their interest at any moment.

Thirdly, and reinforcing this perception, is the observation that NDTIs in the UK hold shares for a comparatively short period of time – only two to three years – with investment and unit trusts being the 'worst offenders'. This rapid turnover of stock holding is sometimes referred to disparagingly as 'churning'.

Lastly, this idea of fleeting commitment was reinforced by the merger and take-over booms in the UK and US in the late 1990s. The criticism here was that some large firms, with the support of their banks, were able to grow by acquisition rather than by investing in and developing their core businesses, because they needed only to acquire stakes in the target company from a small number of institutional share-holders. NDTIs, it was argued, could be encouraged to sell their stakes quite easily since they were always more interested in maximising their short-term wealth than in waiting for the value of their shareholdings to increase as a result of the underlying profitability of the firms.

As we said at the outset, each of these observations is broadly true. The big difficulty, however, lies in connecting them with low investment and growth. The argument is, presumably, that in the UK firms are owned ultimately by institutions which want to see share prices rise in the short term. If they do not, the system makes it cheap and easy for institutions to sell the shares, and this puts firms in danger of takeover. Therefore, directors make investment decisions which maximise the short-term share price regardless of the long-term consequences. Specifically, it is argued, they will tend to pay out a high proportion of profits as dividends, instead of reinvesting for the future, and/or where they do reinvest it will be in projects which produce only a short-term profit. Plausible as it may sound, there are some problems with this.

Since the average turnover of shareholdings can be measured and is high, let us accept that institutions concentrate on short-term performance. Does this necessarily affect firm behaviour? Consider a firm whose directors decide on a major investment project whose returns are expected to be substantial but lie a long way in the future. To make matters worse, let us suppose that they even cut this year's dividend in order to finance the project. According to the 'short-termist' argument, institutional shareholders will sell their stakes. The first question is: How does this affect the firm? Firstly, note that the shares must be bought by someone else, probably another institution. The argument must presumably be that if enough shareholders sell, the price must fall and this raises (a) the cost of capital and (b) the likelihood of a takeover when the firm is seen as a 'bargain' by a predator. Unless and until the firm is looking to raise new capital for an investment project, however, the first is irrelevant. The firm may reasonably hope that by the time the raising of new capital becomes an issue, the benefits of its last project will have been recognised and the share price will have recovered. The latter, the takeover threat, *is* relevant. In the event of a takeover, the existing management may be made redundant. At worst, the firm may be closed down. At best, the management will have to adjust to new directors and owners; managers' power will be reduced. In the circumstances, managers may have a good reason for concentrating on keeping the share price high.

The fundamental objection to the 'short-termist' argument that many would make, however, is that it depends upon the equity markets mispricing shares, and this violates both some cherished beliefs and a certain amount of evidence about the way in which equity markets and traders work.

Specifically here, critics would say that the short-termist argument violates both the *dividend irrelevance theorem* (DIT, explained in Chapter 6) and the *efficient markets hypothesis* (EMH). The dividend irrelevance theorem, remember, starts from the idea that the price of an asset represents the present value of its discounted future income stream. For equities, this income stream involves both dividends and capital appreciation. Then, on certain assumptions, a reduction in dividends used to finance new projects is *necessarily* compensated for by an increase in the rate of capital appreciation. (One of the assumptions of course is that the new investment is profitable!) According to the DIT, therefore, dividends and capital growth are interchangeable in the determination of a share's price. It is the future earnings themselves, not just the part paid out as a dividend, that should be discounted in order to arrive at the correct present value. Provided that institutions understand the DIT, dividend policy should not affect the share price and there should be no incentive for firms to 'buy' short-term popularity with high payouts.

The EMH states that financial markets make the best use of all available information in determining a share's price. Thus if a firm cuts its dividend in order to increase retained earnings, the market should know this and it should be able to form its own (reliable) judgement of the likely future profitability of the project and the firm. According to the EMH these long-term earnings will be just as fully reflected in the share's price as its current dividend. If this is true, long-term investment projects should not depress the share price with the risk that the firm becomes a takeover target.

The significance of the EMH is that there are no bargains to be had in the takeover or acquisitions market. That is to say, there will be no firms whose price is depressed by virtue of the failure of the market to recognise the value of future earnings, however far in the future they may lie. There will be companies whose share price is low. But this will be because their underlying assets are unproductive. This may be because of unwise decisions in the past or a change of market circumstances to which the management has failed to react, or the result of any one of countless other causes. With a low share price, such firms will be takeover targets for other firms whose managers think they can do better. But these will not be 'bargains'; they will be correctly priced. And their takeover by superior management is just what one wants in an efficiently functioning capital market. In these circumstances, the takeover is the mechanism for improving the allocation of managerial skill and eventually the allocation of capital resources.

If we were to conclude that the UK's economic performance was poor because of a focus upon short-term investment decisions by firms, a number of potential remedies suggest themselves, though none is without difficulties.

If the problem lies with firms themselves rather than with the financial system, the remedy would seem to lie in either giving managers a different (longer-term) set of incentives or giving more power to groups with longer-term interests. In recent years it has become quite common for senior managers, with large corporations at least, to have their salaries or bonuses linked to the behaviour of the firm's share price. However, the test of success is usually what has happened to the share price in the past year or two. If, by contrast, managerial remuneration were linked to the value of the firm averaged over, say, a five to seven-year period, managers would have more incentive to look to the long-term performance of the firm. More power for non-executive directors, whose remuneration is not linked to the performance of the firm, is another possibility. It does not follow automatically that they would take a longer-term view of investment plans, but it is arguable that they are as interested in long-term performance as in the short term.

Shareholders too might be encouraged to take a more active role in management. In practice, this would require institutions (since they are the major shareholders) to take a more active role. Whether they would wish to do this is another matter. They would need to hire additional staff with appropriate skills who would then be voted onto company boards. This would involve additional expense and it might also cause difficulties under the existing legislation which prohibits 'insider dealing'. As the law stands, an NDTI which had a paid representative on the board of a company could be accused of having inside information about the firm and would then be barred from trading in the shares of the firm. This rather defeats the purpose.

If one thinks that short-termist behaviour is forced upon firms by the financial system, the remedy must lie with innovations which slow down or discourage the frequent trading of shares in a company. This is often described as putting 'sand in the wheels' of the system. Giving the Competition Commission greater powers to prevent takeovers and mergers is one suggestion. At the moment, the Commission is mainly concerned with what a merger will do to competition and consumer choice.

The criteria for making such a judgement are reasonably straightforward: statistical measures of market concentration are available. It is much more difficult to lay down criteria for judging whether a proposed merger is against the long-term interest of innovation and productivity in a firm. Another proposal involves a tax on the trading of shares. This would put up the cost of each transaction and, it is argued, make traders more inclined to hold shares for a longer period. The arguments against this are that if it were imposed in one national market, share dealing would be diverted to centres where the tax was lower or non-existent; reducing the volume of trading reduces the liquidity of shares and may lead shareholders to demand higher returns for holding them; a reduction in the volume of dealing means also that there are fewer buyers and sellers at any particular time and this may mean that prices will fluctuate more than they currently do. Putting sand in the wheels may have some merit, but the benefit seems bound to come only with a reduction in the efficiency of the equity market.

12.1.2 Financial market exclusion

In recent years, the UK government has become concerned about the extent of 'financial exclusion' – the exclusion of significant numbers of people from financial services: from particular sources of credit, insurance, bill-payment services and accessible and appropriate deposit accounts. People may be excluded as a result of the policies and behaviour of the financial services industry or they may be 'self-excluded' because of the type of financial products available or their assumptions about the likely behaviour of financial institutions. That is, they might not apply for financial services because they assume they will be rejected. Poor members of the community, in particular lone parents, people with disabilities, the unemployed and those on low wages, are the most likely to be financially excluded. For them, financial exclusion is one aspect of general deprivation – a major element within 'social exclusion', which implies a lack of economic, political or social citizenship. However, financial exclusion is not limited to the poor. There may be problems also for ethnic minorities as well as for those who do not conform to the standard picture of credit worthy people used by financial institutions in risk assessment. The Family Resources Survey (FRS) for 2002–03 indicates that 1.9 million households covering 2.8 million adults have no bank account of any kind. Approximately 3 million households (12 per cent of the total in the UK) lack a current account. Research carried out by the FSA suggests that 27 per cent of employees do not have an occupational or private pension. Up to a quarter of households have no home contents insurance and 45 per cent have no life insurance cover.

Exclusion from financial services carries a number of costs for those excluded:

- It denies them the ability to borrow and thus to arrange their financial affairs optimally or it forces them to borrow from 'unofficial' sources, possibly at very high interest rates.
- It denies them discounts on many bills available to people able to pay by direct debit.

- It greatly reduces their ability to deal with household and personal emergencies because of their lack of insurance.

- It greatly reduces their ability to plan for the future and to cope with old age and sickness.

Because financial exclusion is concentrated both among particular groups and geographically, whole communities are disadvantaged in these ways.

One of the principal criticisms of the banking system in relation to financial exclusion has been the closure of bank branches, a high proportion of which have been in poorer areas of the country. A Nottingham University study published in early 2006 found that between 1995 and 2003 some 4,041 branches were closed across the UK and only 1,074 new branches were opened. The majority of the branches lost were located in poorer urban, traditional manufacturing areas and in parts with a higher proportion of students. The report said people whose branches closed faced higher transport costs and a feeling of 'abandonment'. Further, the loss of counter services and cash transmission created major problems for local businesses. The report suggested that branch closures threatened to widen the gulf between poorer and more affluent areas.

This pattern of bank closures has arisen because banks do not make significant profits from the provision of current accounts. High profits come from the sale to current account customers of other high-profit-margin services – loans, credit cards, insurance, sale of investment products, etc. In particular, account holders who make frequent use of accounts but save little and who are regarded as high risk from the point of view of potential default on loans are unlikely to be able to afford high-profit-margin services so have little attraction for the banks. One approach to this was the government's requirement that banks offer 'basic bank accounts'. These allow customers to pay in wages or benefits and set up direct debits. They come with a card for use in cash machines, but have no cheque book or overdraft facility, overcoming the problem of default risk for the banks and also reducing the possibility that account holders unable to manage their financial affairs will become heavily indebted. There are seventeen providers of basic bank accounts including all the major high street banks. Since April 2003, 1.3 million of these accounts have been opened but recently there has been a steady decline in the number of new basic bank accounts opened each year. It has been suggested that many providers give little publicity to the possibility of opening such an account.

An alternative to a basic bank account is the Post Office card account, which enables customers who are relying on state benefits and pensions to have payments credited to an account that can be accessed through machines at Post Office branches.

12.1.3 The financial system and long-term saving

A different group of criticisms is that the financial system has failed to provide the products and services that would encourage people to undertake the necessary level of long-term saving. The problem of inadequate saving, together with some suggested innovations, was studied and reported on by Ronald Sandler in 2002. The main conclusion was that the range of products on offer was, if anything, too wide and certainly too complicated. Fearing that they might not make the best choice, Sandler argued, households were not making any choice at all. In an attempt to address this, a range of savings and pension schemes, known as Sandler products, was introduced by the Treasury in April 2005. Details of these are set out in Box 12.1.

Box 12.1 — Stakeholder (Sandler) products

Stakeholder products (also known as Sandler products) are savings and investment products aimed at people on lower incomes who are effectively priced out of the investment market and/or who had found the existing products too complex and the choice among what was available too daunting. They are products that are designed and offered, from April 2005, by approved financial institutions. To be identified as 'stakeholder products' they must meet a number of conditions laid down by the British government. The aim of these conditions is to make the products cheap, easy to understand and use, and transparent, thus encouraging households to save in the medium and long term and to participate more fully in financial markets (to become, in other words, 'stakeholders' in the economy in terms of the ownership of financial assets). The products themselves are not offered or guaranteed in any sense by the government. The label 'stakeholder products' simply provides clear information on what investors can expect from the products and allows a more easy comparison among the wide range of products available. There are four types of stakeholder products:

- stakeholder cash deposit accounts;
- stakeholder child trust funds (CTFs)
- stakeholder pensions;
- stakeholder medium-term investment products. These are sometimes divided into: (i) medium-term investment products (MTIPs); and (ii) smoothed medium-term investment products – investment products are smoothed where some of the return in good years is paid into a 'smoothing account' to be used to top up the return in bad years.

    The principal conditions that must be fulfilled before any of these products may be called 'stakeholder products' relate, in general terms to:

- **cheapness** – charges must be low (no charges in the case of stakeholder cash deposit accounts; in the case of MTIPs, charges must be limited to 1.5 per cent per annum in the first ten years and 1 per cent thereafter);
- **availability to people on low incomes** – the minimum deposit or investment must be low (£10 for deposit accounts; £20 for MTIPs); holders of accounts must be able to make unlimited withdrawals and the sums withdrawn should be paid to them within seven days;
- **value and security** – interest rates on deposit accounts must be reasonable (the minimum rate is 1 per cent below the Bank of England base rate and should respond promptly to increases in that rate); investment products should not be unduly risky (no more than 60 per cent of a fund should be invested in risky assets such as equities);
- **ease of use** – funds can be paid into deposit or investment accounts in a variety of ways (cash, cheque, direct debit, standing order or directly from salaries);

- **transparency** – the prices at which units or shares in a stakeholder MTIP fund are bought and sold must be the same, and the price should be published daily; in the case of smoothing MTIPs, managers must make available information about their policies on smoothing and charging.

This all sounded very good. However, until now at least, the financial services industry has largely ignored these products. Only a year after their launch, the Financial Services Authority (FSA) announced an inquiry into why the products had not taken off. According to the industry, the products were not attractive to providers because of the low limit on the charges that could be levied. The industry association, the Association of Independent Financial Advisers (AIFA), argued that there were high initial costs in the provision of advice on stakeholder products and thus large economies of scale. The provision of advice and the recommendation of stakeholder products would therefore only become worthwhile if financial advisers were convinced that there would be a large take-up of these products. This was not expected because of the lack of financial education among the target groups. The problem then is to decide how to break into this apparently closed circle of lack of knowledge and information, low savings and low take-up of products designed specifically to encourage people to save and invest.

The pensions problem came to a head in a very specific form during the 1980s. As we noted in Chapter 4, pensions can be paid either on a pay as you go (PAYG) system or a funded principle. In the former case, current pensions are paid for by transfers from those currently in work. With an ageing population, and one which was living longer after retirement, the problem for PAYG schemes was that the contributions from those in work (usually in the form of taxes) were becoming unacceptably large. We saw towards the end of section 4.2 that, starting in 1988, legislation was passed to encourage people to take out their own private pension schemes. But this resulted in the sale of many pension products which were unsuitable for savers. Eventually, compensation was agreed but it took a long time for it to be paid (see Chapter 13) and this particular scandal undoubtedly played a part in discouraging people from taking out long-term saving deals.

If the trouble began with PAYG schemes in the 1980s, it spread to funded schemes in the late 1990s. In particular, problems emerged for defined benefit schemes. These, it will be remembered, were schemes which were intended to accumulate a sufficiently large pool of invested funds that they would be able to *guarantee* a pension which was a set proportion of salary at the time of retirement. With the sharp fall in stock markets in 2001 and 2002, however, many pension funds suddenly revealed large 'black holes' – actuarial estimates that suggested that the present value of their assets was far below that of their present commitments and future obligations. Workers and trade unions were angry in cases where firms had, when asset prices were high, reduced or suspended their contributions to their pension funds on the grounds that the funds were in surplus.

In the case of firms, large pension fund deficits frequently had an impact on the firms' equity prices, on the valuation of firms for takeover calculations, and on the ability of firms to raise funds for future developments either through share issues or borrowing. Firms could, of course, attempt to slowly fill the hole by adding to the fund but only at the expense of current profits. As long as the cash flow from the assets in the fund was sufficient to meet current obligations they could also choose to do nothing and hope that the problem would be solved by higher equity prices and interest rates in the future.

However, particular problems arose when firms went out of business. Shortages in the pension funds of these firms meant that full pensions could not be paid and employees could find that their hopes of a comfortable retirement were dashed. The present government came under pressure to provide assistance to pension funds with defined benefit schemes and, under the provisions of the Pension Act 2004, the Pension Protection Fund (PPF) was set up. It is a statutory corporation the main function of which is to provide compensation to members of eligible defined benefit pension schemes when the employer becomes insolvent and where there are insufficient assets in the pension scheme to cover the level of compensation set by the PPF. The PPF became operational on 6 April 2005 and applies only to firms becoming insolvent after that date. The PPF is to be financed principally by compulsory annual levies imposed on all eligible pension schemes. The PPF can also intervene to assist firms to restructure to prevent insolvency being caused by pension scheme shortfalls. Box 12.2 provides an illustration of diverse responses to pension fund problems.

Box 12.2 | **Responses to pension fund problems**

We look here at two different responses to actual or potential difficulties for defined benefit pension schemes.

Restructuring with the help of the Pension Protection Fund
In May 2006, Pittards, a Yeovil tanning firm with 240 employees, became the first company to survive a financial crisis with the help of the Pension Protection Fund. The company had an accounting deficit of £39.2m in its pension scheme, sufficiently large to be regarded as an insurmountable obstacle to future development of the firm. It seemed likely that the firm would be forced into administration and probable closure. However, it chose instead to restructure. The PPF took an equity stake of 18.5 per cent in the company. This allowed the company to raise an additional £2m through a placing of shares with a Swedish investment company. The shareholding of the founding family was diluted from 29 per cent to 3 per cent but the firm was able to continue trading.

For further details see: David Blackwell, 'Protection fund helps Pittards survive crisis', *Financial Times*, 22 May 2006.

Soldiering on in the hope of a brighter future – the USS
An actuarial valuation in March 2005 of the Universities Superannuation Scheme (USS), the UK's second largest pension fund, showed a deficit of £6.6bn (assets of £21.7bn against liabilities of £28.3bn). The large deficit was in part blamed on the fact that the fund held 80 per cent of its assets in equities, going against the standard advice that payments to existing pensioners should be made from income derived from bonds and property since that represents a reasonably close match for outgoings. In the USS's case

this would have implied that holdings of bonds and property should have made up at least 35 per cent of assets. The result meant that the USS was heavily affected by weakness in equity markets. Despite the large deficit, the trustees decided not to raise pension contributions in an attempt to return the fund to balance. They argued that there was no immediate problem of insolvency since income from assets was sufficient to meet current obligations. They chose to put their faith in a recovery of equity prices. Of course, equity prices did rise sharply in the following year and by the end of March 2006, the deficit had been removed. Unfortunately, equity prices again turned downwards soon after. The approach of the trustees caused some controversy and raised doubts about the impact that problems with the USS would have on higher education.

For more information on this controversy see John Plender, 'USS punt could undermine UK universities', *Financial Times*, May 2006 and subsequent correspondence defending the USS position.

Thinking ahead, firms began to close defined benefits (DB) schemes to new employees and even in a few cases to change the scheme to a defined contribution basis, even for existing employees (the shipping firm Maersk was the first example, in 2002). Once again, the credibility of long-term saving was damaged in the eyes of the general public.

The advent of the Pension Protection Fund was of no comfort to contributors to the pension schemes of firms who became insolvent between 2001 and 2005 and were subsequently discovered to have holes in their pension funds. Until now, government has resisted all demands to provide assistance to workers left without a pension in these cases.

A different case entirely, though one which also surfaced as a result of the stock market slump in 2000–02, was the sale of endowment mortgages. Endowment mortgages were long-term loans taken out for the purpose of house purchase. However, instead of making monthly payments consisting largely of interest with a little bit of capital repayment, borrowers paid only the rate of interest. The sum borrowed remained intact for the whole of the loan period. The plan was to repay the whole of the mortgage at the end of the term using the proceeds from a 'with-profits' endowment policy, timed to end at the same time as the mortgage loan. We saw in Chapter 4 that 'with profits' policies offer purchasers a guaranteed minimum plus an entitlement to share in the company's annual profits. This accrues as annual bonuses which are paid with the guaranteed minimum on termination of the policy.

A report submitted by the Financial Services Authority (FSA) in November 2001 to the Economic Secretary to the Treasury outlining the agenda for strengthening insurance regulation identified two issues related to endowment mortgages. The first was that profits (and bonuses) grow over time as a result of the firm's increasing business but *also as a result of inflation* (in other words, the policy accumulates *nominal* amounts). Historically, because the UK had experienced quite high rates of inflation during the 1970s and 1980s, insurance companies and their clients had become used to bonuses growing at a rate which represented a double-digit rate of return year by year. The size of policies (and the accompanying premiums) necessary to produce the desired target amount (the size of the mortgage) had been calculated on that basis. Indeed, in the early 1990s, savers who had taken out endowment mortgages twenty-five years earlier typically found that the endowment policy was worth about twice the value of the mortgage when it matured.

But the past is not necessarily a good guide to the future. With low inflation and low interest rates (after 1995), rates of profit growth came down to around 6 to 7 per cent per annum. By 2001 it was clear that many policies were not going to deliver the target amount and many investors faced a serious shortfall in the funds they would have available to pay off their mortgage. The situation was made worse by the stock market decline in 2001–02 when some life companies earned zero profits. A with-profits endowment policy maturing in late 2002 was worth only about two-thirds of the amount paid on an identical policy in 1999. The consequence was that many savers, in their late to middle age, expecting to pay off their mortgage before retirement, found that after a lifetime of saving they were left with a fraction of the debt still outstanding.

The second issue was the way in which companies calculated the annual bonus. Although 'based on' profits, the connection was not simple; worse, the formulae were not publicly available. Most companies operated a process of 'smoothing'; that is, they held back some of the profits in good years so that they could still pay a bonus in bad years. This was a laudable attempt to reduce the amount of risk faced by investors. But so long as the 'rules' followed by the firm were secret, it was obviously open to abuse. The result was that long-term savings products acquired a bad reputation just at the time when demographic changes meant that the government needed households to commit to more long-term saving.

It might be argued, of course, that financial intermediaries should not be held responsible for the fluctuations in stock prices. Indeed, this was the position that they adopted in the face of much public criticism. But the sensitive issue which lay at the centre of all these problems (and the one that bothered Sandler) was the extent to which people fully understood the products they were buying and the lengths to which intermediaries went in order to point out the risks (or even perhaps to conceal them). Many distressed holders of endowment mortgages claimed that they had no idea that what the endowment policy was buying was an equity-based product which had all the risks of investing in the stock market. Others claimed that they realised this but the insurance company had emphasised the high rates of return which were bound to accrue 'in the long run' by quoting the returns on policies maturing in the 1990s. The response of the FSA to the mis-selling claims is dealt with in Section 13.2.4.

What all these cases illustrate is the importance of financial knowledge and education on the part of buyers. Unfortunately, the public tends to be less informed than the sellers about the nature of many financial products (another example of asymmetric information). In these circumstances people are bound to make unsuitable choices. These will be worse, of course, if sellers try to exploit their information advantage by deliberately selling unsuitable products. But the fact remains that bad decisions, however they are made, could not be made if there was not asymmetry of information in the first place. We return in Chapter 13 to attempts by government to protect savers from their ignorance.

12.1.4 The financial system and household indebtedness

If inadequate saving has been a problem for some households in recent years, for others it has been indebtedness which has increased considerably. Although this indebtedness has largely been in the form of secured debt (largely mortgage borrowing to finance home ownership), there have also been large increases in unsecured debt (personal loans, overdrafts, credit cards, etc.). Nonetheless, the 2005 NMG Research Survey into the state of household finances commissioned by the Bank of England showed that secured debt continued to make up almost 90 per cent of all household debt.

The increases in household debt have led to a widespread perception that a growing proportion of middle-income families has been having trouble meeting debt repayments, once thought to be a problem principally of the poor and unemployed. This view was confirmed in research carried out by the Consumer Credit Counselling Service, a charity set up to provide advice to households with debt problems. (see Box 12.3).

Box 12.3 | **Debt hits more middle-class homes**

A growing proportion of middle-income families is struggling to manage its debts, according to research by the Consumer Credit Counselling Service. The research on unsecured debt . . . shows that households earning a net £30,000 a year and more account for 4.7 per cent of the clients of the debt advice charity, up from 1.4 per cent in 2003. Helen Saxon of the CCCS and the author, said low-income households used credit to pay for essentials but middle-income families resorted to loans and credit cards to fund consumption.

'Accepted wisdom suggests that a take-home income of £30,000 a year should be enough to allow most families to be able to manage the demands on their incomes,' she said. 'But large mortgages, rising school fees, keeping up with the Joneses and the increasing availability of credit have made debt a normal part of life for many of the middle class.' Mark Allen, partner at Grant Thornton, the professional services firm, said the average salary of those going into insolvency had risen to £28,000 a year from £24,000 in the past year. 'The general perception is that personal insolvencies relate to people on relatively low incomes struggling to make ends meet. But we are also seeing greater numbers of individuals earning good salaries but borrowing proportionally more than people on lower incomes,' he said. 'We've even seen stockbrokers earning £100,000 going for insolvency.' . . .

Steve Treharne, head of personal insolvency at KPMG, the professional services firm, said: 'Overborrowing is affecting all income scales, up to a limit. Some people on higher incomes think they can spend with impunity, forgetting they have to pay it back . . .' The CCCS, which advises 1,000 people a week, said its report, based solely on its clients, showed that those earning more than £30,000 ran up an average unsecured debt of £70,000. Households with net income of less than £10,000 a year had an average of £20,000 in unsecured borrowings. Middle-income families were able to run up big debts because credit was more easily available. 'A lender sees less risk in lending to someone with a high income,' according to the report that found that middle-income families had on average 13 credit commitments compared with seven for those with annual earnings of less than £10,000.

Source: Scheherazade Daneshku, 'Debt hits more middle-income homes', *Financial Times*, May 2006

The growth in consumer spending financed by increased debt has played an important part in the relatively high rates of economic growth and low levels of unemployment in the UK economy. This has led some economists and financial journalists to express fears that consumers, worried by their indebtedness, were likely to cut back on consumption and push the economy into recession.

However, this view is not shared by the Bank of England. The 2005 survey of household finances suggests that although total household indebtedness had increased over the previous year, the percentage of households with no debt at all remained at 40 per cent and the increase in debt was not notably in the form of unsecured debt. Indeed, the fraction of households with unsecured debt had fallen from 46 per cent to 41 per cent whereas the fraction with secured debt had risen from 39 per cent to 41 per cent in the year to September 2005. More importantly, from a macroeconomic view, household indebtedness remained heavily skewed towards the poor and the consumption of households with serious debt problems made up only a very small percentage of aggregate consumption. The Bank of England report acknowledges that the sample of households surveyed was quite small and that there are other problems in interpreting the results. Nevertheless, there is no suggestion of a serious immediate problem for the economy as a whole.

This, of course, does not remove household indebtedness as a problem. There clearly is a sufficient number of households finding indebtedness a serious burden for us to take the issue seriously. The next question to address is the extent to which the financial system can be held to be at fault. There are three issues here – whether or not it is too easy for households to go into ill-advised debt, the quality of advice consumers receive from financial institutions and the charges made by banks and other financial institutions on outstanding loans.

The information that, on average, middle-income families seeking advice from the CCCS (see Box 12.3) had thirteen debt commitments provides an indication of the number of opportunities there are in a modern economy for households to borrow. Despite the great amount of information that is now collected on consumers, there still appears to be little indication that new lenders take strongly into consideration the overall position of households seeking to make further borrowings. Rules of thumb followed for agreeing to major loans such as house mortgages have steadily been relaxed and frequently the financial institutions appear to make the most rosy assumptions possible in assessing future ability to pay.

This leads us to the question of consumer education. The principal problems are, as always, inadequate information and lack of foresight. Borrowers might commit themselves on assumptions of unchanging interest and continued employment only to find that they are over-committed when interest rates turn upwards or when the economy turns downwards and unemployment rises. Many poor households also appear to lack information even about the amount they have borrowed and their future liabilities. This can occur particularly when borrowers are offered loans on which no interest is to be paid for the first year or two of a loan – arrangements that are common in the purchase of motor vehicles and household consumer durables. Things are made worse by the extent to which advertising by the financial industry emphasises the ease with which credit can be obtained and encourages people into debt.

The issue of interest rates and other bank charges again came to the fore in the UK at the beginning of April 2006 following a report by the Office of Fair Trading (OFT) which stated that credit card default charges had generally been set at a significantly higher level than was legally fair. The OFT estimated that across the industry this had led to unlawful penalty charges in excess of £300m a year. They argued that such charges should only be made to cover acceptable administration costs to the banks of default and set £12 as the highest possible figure that could be regarded as fair. They threatened to challenge charges above £12 in the courts and gave the industry until the end of May 2006 to respond. As a result, at the end of May, Barclays, Lloyds TSB and HSBC all announced that they were cutting their penalty charges from £20 to £12. It was, however, expected that banks would be likely to raise interest rates to recoup the fall in profits.

This was just another of many skirmishes between the very profitable banking industry and organisations concerned with consumer welfare over the behaviour of banks towards their clients.

12.2 Financial instability: bubbles and crises

There have been many examples of booms and busts in financial markets. Euphoria has accompanied very rapid increases in the prices of financial assets, seemingly driving them well away from any possible assessment of their fundamental values. Under such circumstances, private investors go heavily into debt in order to join the rush into financial markets in the quest for large and easy fortunes. We saw, however, in Chapter 6 that this view of the behaviour of financial markets is rejected by conventional economics which assumes market agents to behave rationally at all times in the sense that they always act to maximise their own individual (or household) utility and ensure that financial asset prices always reflect market fundamentals. On this argument, since asset prices reflect the present value of a future stream of income, the fundamentals always involve an assessment of future conditions and these assessments can change quickly and by large amounts as new information becomes available to the market. Nonetheless, we pointed out in section 6.5 that price changes are sometimes so large and occur so rapidly that it is difficult to believe that individual behaviour is not, on some occasions at least, strongly influenced by what other people in the market are doing. After all, investment in financial markets always involves uncertainty and there are many cases where human beings clearly feel more secure if they are behaving in the same way as everyone else, whether or not we understand the reasons for the general behaviour. Indeed, one can easily see this as maximising behaviour – where information is scarce and choice among conflicting alternatives is difficult, assuming that the majority is correct may, on balance, produce the best results. Thus, we shall here look a little more closely at the notion that market behaviour is, at least on occasions, irrational.

A well-known book written from this point of view by Charles Kindleberger (1996) is entitled *Manias, Panics and Crashes*. Applied to financial markets, a 'mania' is a frenzied burst of buying of a financial asset that causes the price of the asset to rise very sharply. People buy on the assumption that the price will continue to rise and thus they will be able to sell at a higher price later, making a speculative profit. The irrational element in this behaviour is that people appear to forget the possibility that the price might fall and dismiss from their minds potential losses. The use of the words 'craze' and 'frenzied' in descriptions of behaviour in periods of price bubbles suggests that greed and rapaciousness dominate rationality. This, in turn, implies that the big increase in the demand for the asset has little logical basis.

It is also possible that people do not entirely forget the fundamentals underlying the asset price and that they remain aware of the losses they stand to make if the price were to fall. Thus, as they continue to buy at higher and higher prices, they are aware that they are taking ever greater risks. They can only justify these increasing risks by reflecting on the prospects of ever-greater profits. In these circumstances, it can be argued, it is rational to go on buying and, indeed, to buy in ever greater quantities, causing the price to rise even faster. According to this view, the situation has become unreal but people behave rationally within it. Rational individual behaviour produces an irrational market outcome.

Of course, price bubbles, like any other, might easily burst and the price might collapse just as quickly as it rose. This happens as soon as any doubt that price rises will continue causes some people to stop buying. As soon as the rate of increase in demand slows, the price rise slows and people begin to sell to take their profit. The price starts to fall. The mania has ended. This leads people to ask how far the price might fall and to an assessment of the fundamental basis of the value of the asset. People begin to become aware of the extent of the loss they are facing. It becomes imperative to sell before the price falls very far. Many investors rush to sell, the price falls sharply and panic, in which fear becomes contagious, sets in. Even those who have no idea of market fundamentals take part in the frenzied selling. The price might be driven below any possible idea of a fundamental value.

Supporters of this view of behaviour in financial markets see the market as failing because of both lack of information and the irrational behaviour of market participants. They also see many external effects of manias and panics. The sharp rises and falls in the prices of financial assets have effects on the real economy. The sharp financial losses induce cut backs in consumer spending and thus affect aggregate demand, production and employment. Consequently, they see a role for government in overcoming market failure or in correcting the undesirable results of free market behaviour. On the other hand, holders of the view that market agents always behave rationally and market prices always reflect market fundamentals believe that markets should be left to operate freely and that any apparent inadequacies in market outcomes stem from the constraints placed upon markets, notably by governments. For example, it might be argued that sharp price rises are fuelled by easy credit causing low interest rates, and crashes are caused by sudden monetary tightening. That is, governments cause market problems rather than counteracting market failures.

The proposition that markets are subject to manias and panics has largely been supported by the analyses of historical episodes of sharp price rises. The best-known examples from the distant past relate to the tulip market in Holland in the late seventeenth century and the South Sea bubble in England in the eighteenth century.

In section 6.5, we referred to more recent events such as the dot.com bubble of the late 1990s. However, other approaches have been taken. One such approach has been to argue that much trading in financial markets is based upon 'noise' rather than 'news' – where 'noise' indicates irrelevant information coming to the market and 'news' information about market fundamentals. The existence of a great deal of noise in markets results in excessive volatility in prices.

This is the basis of the well-known 'noise trader' model which was first developed in relation to stock markets in an attempt to explain the world-wide bull market in stocks in the 1980s and the subsequent collapse in 1987. The noise-trader model suggests that stock prices result from market psychology unrelated to fundamentals. It follows the form of a number of models that had aimed to explain price bubbles as the outcome of rational behaviour – there are two groups of market agents both of whom act rationally but interaction between them produces bubbles. In noise-trader models, the 'smart money' agents act rationally, basing their actions largely, but not entirely, on fundamentals. The second group, the noise traders, acts irrationally. The interaction of the two groups pushes asset prices far away from their fundamental values.

In section 8.4, for example, we looked briefly at the application of the noise-trader model to foreign exchange rates in which Frankel and Froot (1990) sought to explain the large real appreciation of the US dollar over the period 1981–85 and its subsequent depreciation. They argued that there was evidence that investors had heterogeneous expectations. Surveys of the forecasts of participants in the forex market showed wide dispersion at any point in time. Thus, Frankel and Froot proposed a model of speculative bubbles in which exchange rates were determined by the roles of three groups of actors (fundamentalist forecasters, chartists and portfolio managers). Fundamentalists forecast a depreciation of the dollar which would have been rational if there had been no chartists. Chartists extrapolated recent trends based on an information set that included no fundamentals. Portfolio managers took positions in the market and thus determined the exchange rate based on expectations that were a weighted average of the forecasts of the other two groups. The first stage of the dollar appreciation after 1980 was explained by increases in real interest-rate differentials. The second stage was explained by the endogenous take off of the speculative bubble. As fundamentalists' forecasts of depreciation proved incorrect month after month, the portfolio managers decreased the weight they assigned to those forecasts and increased the weight they assigned to those of the chartists. In doing so, they reduced their weighted-average expectations of depreciation, raised their demands for the dollar and thus brought about the continued appreciation of the dollar. In 1985, the dollar entered a third stage in which an ever-worsening current account deficit reversed the overvaluation caused by the bubble. They thus showed how (non-rational but) *sensible behaviour* could generate not simply short-run volatility in exchange rates but also, and more importantly, large and cumulative exchange rate misalignments.

All of the views we have looked at so far are concerned with particular events or individual behaviour. A different approach, the financial instability hypothesis of the American economist Hyman Minsky, sees excessive market volatility as an inherent part of the capitalist economic system. This begins with a distinction important in many interpretations of the work of J M Keynes – the distinction between risk and uncertainty. Everyone accepts that information about the future is not perfect but it is possible to argue that past experience is a sufficiently good guide to the future that we can specify all potential outcomes and express the likelihood of their occurring in terms of probabilities. For more information on the meaning of risk in financial economics see Appendix I: Portfolio theory where risk is defined as the probability that an outturn differs from what was expected, and is measured by the standard deviation or variance of past returns. This means that decisions can be made mathematically on the same basis as would be the case if there were perfect information. People might, of course, make incorrect assessments of probabilities in the sense that the future may turn out differently from that expected, but if the sample of cases we are dealing with is sufficiently large, decisions will be correct on average. It follows from this that the future can be insured against.

Further, if all the available information relevant to future decisions is available equally to everyone then everyone will make the same assessment of probabilities and will respond rationally to these. This is what is known as 'risk'. If financial decisions were made under risk, there should be no problem of instability. Keynes, however, believed that the uncertainty facing decision makers in financial markets is much more profound than indicated by the notion of 'risk' and that it could neither be treated mathematically nor insured against. In making decisions about the imperfectly known future, market agents need to anticipate how other market agents are going to behave and that, in turn, requires them to know how they are likely to assess future possibilities. We looked at an example of this from Keynes in section 6.5. Any mistakes made in such predictions might lead to a failure of co-ordination and instability. In other words, people face a future that is so uncertain that agents are in no position to attach probabilities to likely future outcomes. They are more likely to make decisions on some conventional basis – some rule of thumb that seems to have worked reasonably well for them in the past. This situation is referred to as 'uncertainty'.

According to Keynes, decision making in financial and investment decisions takes place under uncertainty, leading naturally to instability if shocks cause rapid and fundamental reappraisals of expectations concerning future events. Investment decisions are the key determinant of aggregate economic activity and must be studied within the context of capitalist financial practices. However, disequilibrating forces operate in financial markets where investors must raise finance. These affect the price ratio between capital assets and current output which, along with financial market conditions, determine investment. The two sets of prices in the ratio are determined in separate markets and are influenced by different forces, explaining why the economy is prone to fluctuations. Shocks emanate from financial markets and are spread by way of investment decisions. Because both sets of decisions are made under uncertainty, they can change rapidly, affecting not only the price ratio between capital assets and current output but also the prices of various capital and financial assets.

Minsky accepted the existence of regular financial crises in capitalist economies, but in his later work, argued that they are systemic, endogenously generated events rather than accidents. He focuses on business debts. To service these, firms must maintain sufficient net reserves to meet gross payments due or to permit refinancing, which will only be possible if expected future revenue is thought sufficient. The net revenue depends on investment and thus the ability to finance new investment depends on the expectation that the new investment will generate sufficient cash flows to repay or refinance current debt. An economy with private debt is thus vulnerable to changes in the pace of investment. Instability follows from the subjective nature of expectations about the future level of investment and the returns from it, and the subjective determination by banks and their business clients of the appropriate liability structure for the financing of positions in different types of capital assets. Uncertainty is thus a major determinant of cycles.

Minsky starts with an economy with a memory of recession. In such an economy, acceptable liability structures and contractual debt payments are based on margins that reflect the risk that the economy may not perform as well as expected. As the period in which the economy performs well lengthens and the memory of recession fades, margins for safety decline and investment increases. The period of steady growth is transformed into a speculative boom. This process is reinforced by financial innovation, including the introduction of new financial instruments, which appear when economies are thriving. Speculative economic units expect to fulfil their obligations by raising new debt and are vulnerable on a number of fronts, particularly to rises in nominal interest rates, which increase their cash repayments relative to their expected future receipts. Not everyone engages in speculative finance. The more risk-averse continue to operate with hedge finance, which takes place when cash flows from operations are expected to be large enough to meet debt commitments as they fall due. Speculative finance, on the other hand, anticipates the need for refinancing. In addition to hedge and speculative finance, Minsky refers to 'Ponzi finance', by which he means super-speculative finance that requires payments on debt to be met by further borrowing, thus increasing the total debt outstanding. It is named after Charles Ponzi (1882–1949), an Italian immigrant to the US who became one of the great American swindlers.

High and rising interest rates can convert hedge finance into speculative finance and speculative finance into Ponzi finance. Ponzi finance cannot continue for long because information from the revealed financial weakness of some units affects the willingness of banks and businessmen to debt finance others. The curtailment in investment finance causes investment to fall, leading to a decline in profitability and the ability to sustain debt. Unless this decline in investment is offset by an increase in government spending, a panic can develop quite suddenly as pressure builds to reduce debt ratios. Thus, in Minsky's theory, the normal functioning of the financial system in a recovery period leads to a boom and a financial crisis.

12.3 Fraudulent behaviour and scandals in financial markets

We deal with financial scandals of various sorts in several places in this book. These include problems of: mis-selling (personal pensions, endowment mortgages; split-capital investment funds); misuse of funds (the Maxwell pension fund collapse); and falsification of records (Barings Bank). In Chapter 9, we consider the case of Long-Term Capital Management in which the near collapse of a hedge fund led to problems in many financial markets in different parts of the world. In Chapter 13, we touch upon the problems of the Lloyd's of London insurance market in the 1990s. Many other scandals are given a brief mention and again in Chapter 13, we consider the difficulties in regulating financial markets to try to prevent such problems and thus retain the confidence of investors in these markets.

However, several of the major financial scandals in recent years have involved non-financial firms. Given the nature of modern capitalism, these involve financial institutions – auditors, financial analysts, credit-rating agencies and banks. They also have obvious implications for financial markets – equities markets, bonds markets, and so on. In this section, we look at a couple of these scandals of recent years and consider issues relating to them. Both of the scandals we deal with here were based on deliberate accounting deceptions to misrepresent the financial position of companies. We look at Parmalat of Italy (see Box 12.4) and then Enron in the US.

Box 12.4 **Parmalat**

Parmalat was Italy's best known food company. It had been established by Calisto Tanzi who in 1961, having inherited his father's delicatessen, set up a dairy plant near Parma in northern Italy to challenge a then-existing Italian milk monopoly. Parmalat became Italy's first producer of branded milk and greatly expanded its market through the production of UHT milk. It expanded strongly and by 2002 was the fourth-largest food products group in Europe. It had grown by gradually moving into new product lines and by making a large series of acquisitions, particularly abroad. At the end of 2002, the Parmalat group consisted of 213 companies in fifty countries and had 37,000 employees, of whom about 4,000 were in Italy. The shares of Parmalat Finanziaria, which controlled the industrial firm, were listed on the stock exchange in the 1990s. The company was well-known for sport sponsorships and had bought the Italian Serie A football club, Parma.

Parmalat accompanied its strategy of expansion abroad with a large-scale internationalisation of its financial operations. Acquisitions and investments were financed by entering into debt. Through various group companies Parmalat obtained very substantial financing on the international capital market. Despite the heavy indebtedness of the company, financial institutions and markets seemed happy with the acquisition strategy. At the beginning of 2003 Parmalat's shares were brought into the index of the thirty largest companies listed on the Italian stock exchange. Many international financial analysts continued to advise investors to buy the company's securities. However, by the beginning of the second week in December it had become clear that Parmalat would have difficulty meeting a debt repayment to a group of investors who had bought 18 per cent of Parmalat's large Brazilian subsidiary but who had then exercised an option to sell it back to Parmalat following the failure of the subsidiary to be quoted on the Brazilian stock exchange. Parmalat claimed that it would be able to meet the payment by recovering a €500m ($590m) investment in a mysterious hedge fund in the Cayman Islands tax haven but the fund did not, in fact, exist. The company had been engaged in false accounting, the concealment of liabilities, the inflation of assets and the forging of bank statements. Parmalat had been using Enron-style accounting to hide liabilities and move money around among subsidiaries but the claimed funds sometimes did not exist. The company filed for bankruptcy. Calisto Tanzi was arrested.

In addition, questions were asked about the company's accounting firm, the US-based Grant Thornton, which had audited Parmalat's books until 1999 and had continued to audit the books of Bonlat, the subsidiary with the missing $4.9bn. Grant Thornton claimed that it had been the victim of a fraud but the head of the Italian branch of the company resigned and his partner was suspended after warrants had been issued for their arrest.

As well as the charges in Italy, the SEC in the US charged Parmalat with fraudulently offering $100m of unsecured notes to US investors and of inflating its assets by at least $5bn. In late May 2004, Italian prosecutors sought to have thirty-two Parmalat executives put on trial. Several former executives later pleaded guilty to misleading investors, received jail sentences and testified in the trial of Calisto Tanzi. The trial was still continuing in September 2006.

Parmalat was subsequently rebuilt as a company and again listed on the Italian stock exchange. In 2006, the new management of the company sought to take legal action against banks whom it believed assisted in the fraud.

Enron, a regional natural gas pipeline company, was formed in 1985 through a merger between two other companies, Houston Natural Gas and InterNorth. The chairman and chief executive of the new company, Kenneth Lay, was a long-time friend of George W Bush, who was to become US President in 2000. The US energy market was deregulated in the late 1980s and from 1989 Enron began trading natural gas and electricity allowing users to buy gas or electricity from different producers. It made its breakthrough via contracts to deliver energy products at future dates. It also sold financial instruments designed to protect customers against large swings in energy prices. It thus effectively moved from being a straightforward energy company to a derivatives and financial company. It was frequently recommended by stock market analysts because of its innovative approach to energy trading. In 1999 Enron took advantage of the dot.com boom by launching Enron online, the first global commodity trading web site.

The company had also expanded during the 1990s by takeovers including, in 1998, the British water company, Wessex Water. It became the US's seventh biggest corporation and in 2000 its share price peaked at $90.56. However, Enron had financed its takeovers by going heavily into debt, concealing the extent of that debt by dubious accounting practices including the establishment of complex special partnerships. Thus, their share price was based on misleading information about the state of the company.

By early 2001 things were beginning to go wrong. Within Enron's auditor, Arthur Andersen (itself the US's eighth biggest company), worries were beginning to be expressed about the accounting practices being followed. Nonetheless, it later emerged that the auditor had sought to protect its client from investigation by destroying a number of important documents. Jeffrey Skilling, who had taken over from Kenneth Lay as chief executive in February 2001, resigned from the job in August 2001, the position reverting to Kenneth Lay. Skilling claimed 'personal reasons' for the resignation but it soon became clear that severe difficulties lay ahead. At around this time, the major figures in the corporation began selling their shares in the company while the share price was still high. In October 2001 Enron reported a $618m loss for the previous quarter and disclosed a $1.2bn reduction in shareholder equity, partly in connection with partnerships run by chief financial officer Andrew Fastow, who was sacked by the company. Enron shares lost a fifth of their value and the Securities and Exchange Commission (SEC) began an investigation into the accounting practices. In November 2001 Enron admitted to having greatly overstated its profits over the previous four years. Its credit rating was slashed to junk bond status. This seriously damaged the company because many of Enron's debt agreements were dependent on the retention of its investment grade credit rating – the loss of that rating triggered debt repayments that it could not make.

At the beginning of December 2001 Enron filed for bankruptcy. It was at that time the biggest bankruptcy in US corporate history but was surpassed by the bankruptcy of WorldCom in the summer of 2002. Four thousand Enron employees lost their jobs. The pension plans of many Enron employees lost almost all their value because they held many Enron shares.

In January 2002, the US Justice Department opened a criminal investigation into Enron and, later the same year, charged Arthur Andersen with the obstruction of justice. The accounting company collapsed with the loss of 85,000 jobs. Kenneth Lay resigned as Chairman and Chief Executive and a former deputy chairman committed suicide. In October 2002, Andrew Fastow was indicted on seventy-eight charges including conspiracy, fraud and money laundering. In 2003, Fastow's wife and seven other executives were charged. At the beginning of 2004, Fastow and his wife pleaded guilty. Fastow accepted a ten-year prison sentence and became a prosecution witness. His wife was jailed for one year. Kenneth Lay and Jeffrey Skilling were arrested and their trial began in January 2005.

In May 2006 Lay was convicted on six counts of wire fraud, securities fraud and conspiracy. Skilling was found guilty on nineteen counts of conspiracy, securities fraud, insider trading and making false statements. Sentences were to be announced in September 2006 but Lay who was facing a prison sentence of up to forty-five years died of a heart attack in early July 2006.

We have here added two of the major financial scandals of recent years to the several others dealt with in this book. There have been many others – WorldCom, Allied Irish Banks, the Bank of Commerce and Credit International (BCCI), Daiwa Bank, Hollinger International . . . In scandals such as these, jobs are lost, shareholders lose out, often employees lose savings, high legal costs have to be met and confidence in the equities market and other financial markets are damaged. Two sets of questions arise:

- Are the frauds that often produce these scandals simply the result of a 'small number of bad apples'? Or do they suggest something seriously wrong with the operation of financial markets?
- How do these frauds escape attention for so long? What can be done to reduce their number and importance in the future?

Even if the 'few bad apples' theory were correct, we are still left with the question of why entities are able to hide their frauds for as long as they do. In many cases, in the long period of concealment, companies become much larger and the fall, when it comes, is very much greater.

Among the groups of people charged with ensuring that financial markets and institutions operate honestly and openly, we have:

- the boards of directors of companies including non-executive directors;
- company shareholders;
- company auditors;
- credit-rating agencies;
- other financial analysts;
- financial market regulators.

As both Enron and Parmalat showed, boards of directors can be dominated by a small number of powerful executives who can relatively easily conceal their actions from the board. We saw in the case of Barings (Box 9.5) that the board had little knowledge of what its principal trader was doing on the company's behalf. It is also interesting that the chief executive and other senior executives charged with fraud often claim that they did not know the fraud was being committed.

Non-executive directors may have little knowledge of the operations of the company and frequently hold many positions, making it difficult for them to follow closely what is happening in the company. They seldom appear to ask awkward questions and, at least on occasion, appear interested mainly in collecting their non-executive director's fee.

Given the complexity of modern financial arrangements, small shareholders are seldom able to understand company operations. Where large financial institutions (such as pension funds) are shareholders, there should be scope for the board to keep some sort of check on the actions of company executives and traders. However, shareholders are not likely to ask searching questions while the company is doing well and the share price is rising.

In both the Enron and Parmalat cases, the auditors have been blamed for failing to carry out their task adequately and have been seen as complicit in the fraud. Another example of an auditing failure is provided in Box 13.3 in the Maxwell pension fund case. There is clearly a potential problem when auditing firms themselves are large and are stock-exchange-listed companies needing to keep profits high to keep their own shareholders happy. Auditing companies may have a strong interest in not offending the executives of their clients.

Credit-rating agencies have also been strongly criticised for their failure to notice problems in the Enron and Parmalat cases. In both instances, the credit ratings of the firms were kept high until a few days before the companies were forced to file for bankruptcy. Following the Enron affair, the major credit-rating agencies in the US claimed that they had made changes to their procedures and would be better able to spot the next Enron. They claimed that they had hired accountants and would look much more closely at the published accounts of companies in the future.

They claimed also to have intensified their focus on governance and management at the companies they rate, spending time with board members. However, smaller companies in the industry doubt that much has changed. Large financial scandals are, they say, always followed by confessions of guilt by the big credit-rating agencies and by claims that things would be better next time. The credit-rating market is also dominated by a small number of large companies and there have been complaints of a possible conflict of interest because the large agencies are paid by the issuers of debt, not by investors.

One needs to add to this last comment that financial analysts acting on behalf of investors have not had a particularly good record in spotting financial scandals. We mention above the popularity of Enron with financial analysts during the period when the fraud was being practised. In the Parmalat case, in August 2003 (just over three months before the fraud unravelled), nine out of fourteen international financial analysts advised investors to buy the company's securities and another three recommended holding existing investments. In November, seven out of fourteen analysts still recommended purchase and two continued to favour holding existing investments, and studies by two international banks were released giving positive judgements on the group's prospects and the relative value of its shares. In the early days of December 2003, the rating still reflected a positive opinion of the company's ability to redeem its bonds (Fazio, 2004).

We deal with the issue of financial regulation in Chapter 13. Financial regulators also face difficulty in coping with the complexity of the financial arrangements of firms. Equally importantly, financial irregularities are practised by non-financial firms that are not covered by the remit of financial regulation – Enron, WorldCom and Parmalat were not financial firms. In any case, in any form of regulation, a balance has to be struck between the need to prevent frauds and other types of financial malfeasance and keeping the costs of regulation as low as possible in order not to stifle the activity of the market. In Chapter 13, we look specifically at that issue in relation to the FSA in the UK.

12.4 The damaging effects of international markets?

Towards the end of the twentieth century, attitudes appeared to harden over the effects of the free mobility of international capital. Two issues came to the fore. Firstly, a question initially stated in the late 1970s resurfaced – should an international tax be placed on capital movements to slow them down? The tax proposal was originally made by James Tobin, a Nobel Prize-winning American economist. Tobin (1982) proposed a uniform tax on capital flows, levied by all countries, to make 'hot money' round trips unprofitable and to remove the dominance of capital account movements over exchange rates. Similar proposals were made later for different forms of tax but the idea came to be referred to as the 'Tobin tax', although Tobin later disowned it.

Tobin's particular concern at the time was with the volatility of exchange rates and with the loss of the ability of governments to choose their own macroeconomic policies. The argument gained support, however, following the Asian financial crisis, the financial problems in Russia and Brazil, and the near-collapse of the US hedge fund, Long-Term Capital Management (see section 9.5), all of which occurred between the middle of 1997 and early 1999 and which appeared to threaten the stability of the world financial system.

Naturally, Tobin's proposal had many critics. It was argued that many capital flows were desirable and that there would be a problem in discriminating between speculative capital flows (bad) and those designed for long-term investment (good). Others rejected it on the grounds that it would favour inertia and local asset bias in portfolios and, like any tax, was bound to interfere with the efficient operation of markets. A third argument, from the opposite point of view, was that the usual size proposed for a Tobin tax would be a negligible deterrent to short-term speculation and probably smaller than the deterrent to real trade flows and arbitrage activities, and that something much stronger was needed. The simplest argument was that it would be impracticable. It would be impossible to obtain international agreement on a world-wide tax and, even if agreement were reached, the market would quickly find its way around the tax. Nonetheless, there has been some support for the tax even at a governmental level. For example, a motion was passed in the Canadian House of Commons in 1999 suggesting that the government 'should enact a tax on financial transactions in concert with the international community'. Of course, since there was no prospect of the international community acting in concert on this issue, the motion did not commit the Canadian government to doing anything. This was true also of Belgium where, in 2004, the Commission of Finance and Budget in the Federal Parliament approved the *Spahn tax* (a version of the Tobin tax) which Belgium will introduce if all countries of the eurozone pass a similar bill.

The second issue concerned the heavy indebtedness of the poorer developing countries. It was argued that their large debt repayments (particularly large as a percentage of GDP) were at the expense of essential expenditure on health, education and social welfare; that the need to earn foreign currency to meet the debt repayments distorted their agriculture away from staples for the home population towards producing luxury goods for the markets of the industrial countries; and, above all, that the countries had no prospect of struggling their way out of poverty while they remained burdened with the debt repayments. A campaign for debt forgiveness grew. G8* countries promised limited forms of debt relief but always linked to the countries' following the orthodox economic policies ordained by the IMF. This took the form of the Heavily Indebted Poor Countries Initiative (HIPC) the aim of which was to provide debt relief for the poorest countries while trying to ensure that funds saved from not having to repay loans would be spent on poverty reduction. Opponents of debt forgiveness have always argued that any financial aid provided by the industrial countries would go to corrupt governments rather than filtering down to the poorest people.

---

* G8 = the seven largest industrial countries (US, Japan, Germany, France, Italy, UK and Canada) + Russia.

The HIPC initiative identified 38 countries, mainly in Sub-Saharan Africa, potentially eligible to receive debt relief. At the G8 meeting in July 2005, the Multilateral Debt Relief Initiative (MDRI) was agreed, offering full cancellation of the debts of HIPC countries to the World Bank, the IMF and the African Development Bank. In December 2005, the IMF granted preliminary approval to an initial debt relief measure of US$3.3bn for nineteen of the world's poorest countries and the World Bank began to take action to cancel the debts of seventeen countries in the second half of 2006. For example, at the end of August 2006, the IMF and the World Bank jointly announced a US$2.9bn debt cancellation deal for Malawi, one of the world's poorest countries. The difference between the numbers of HIPC countries potentially eligible to receive relief and those that actually receive help merely reflects the existence of conditions other than poverty that countries must meet.

Any help for the poor countries is welcome even if the amounts ultimately received are almost invariably less than what seems to have been promised initially. However, there is no evidence as yet that sufficient has been done or is likely to be done even to slow down the widening of the gap between rich and poor countries. Yet the rich countries clearly recognise that until this happens they will continue to have problems with migration and 'economic refugees'. This is certainly one example where a financial problem has strong real-life effects.

12.5 Summary

The efficiency of modern economies is greatly enhanced by a well-functioning financial system but failures in financial markets and institutions can cause problems for investors and employees as well as for the markets themselves. Problems arise concerning the ability of firms and individuals to borrow, the extent of savings in the economy, the occurrence of booms and crashes in markets, and the regular occurrence of financial scandals in both financial markets and institutions and in non-financial markets.

One long-running debate has concerned the financing of new and small firms. Governments have, over the years, taken several initiatives to try to improve the position, the most recent example of which has been the tax advantages given to investors in venture capital trusts (VCTs). UK financial institutions have also been criticised for providing finance to overseas governments and firms at the expense of domestic firms and for taking a short-term perspective in the treatment of firms. Evidence relating to this last point is unclear but the issue remains important. A quite different problem concerns the exclusion from financial markets of poor households. This financial exclusion imposes considerable costs upon them and helps to preserve inequalities in society. The government has become particularly interested in this issue in recent years; much research has been done and attempts are being made to improve the position.

There is a strong view that the level of saving in the economy is inadequate. One government response has been to set conditions for a range of simple financial products known as stakeholder products although these do not as yet appear to be having much success. The problem of a lack of saving has come to the fore particularly in relation to the financing of pensions. Problems have arisen with defined benefit pension schemes and many of these have now been withdrawn by firms. A different long-term savings problem emerged in the early years of the decade concerning endowment mortgages.

Another much debated issue has concerned the causes of financial booms and crashes. There has always been a difference of opinion over whether these are caused by irrational behaviour or whether participants in financial markets can always be assumed to act rationally. We need also to consider whether financial instability is an inevitable part of the capital market system. That system also appears to produce regular examples of financial scandals and fraud. Even fraud in non-financial companies has serious implications for the operation of financial markets and institutions.

Finally, there are serious implications of possible international financial instability perhaps associated with the free movement of capital and with the wide gap in wealth and income between rich and poor countries.

Questions for discussion

1 What is meant by 'short-termism'? List and discuss the arguments in support of the view that the UK financial system has been 'short termist'.

2 Why is it a potential problem if long-term savings are too low?

3 Consider the disadvantages in being financially excluded. Are there any advantages?

4 Why are stakeholder financial products so called?

5 Why were stakeholder products not much taken up during the first year in which they were offered?

6 Look up the events of the tulip boom and crash in the Netherlands in the late seventeenth century. Is it possible to see these events as the outcome of rational behaviour?

7 What has happened since this text was written in the Enron and Parmalat cases?

8 The text mentions WorldCom as another major scandal. What was the basis of that fraud?

9 What is a 'Tobin tax'? What prospect is there of its ever being implemented?

Further reading

Bank of England, 'The Distribution of Assets, Income and Liabilities Across UK Households: results from the 2005 NMG Research Survey', *Bank of England Quarterly Bulletin*, Spring 2006, www.bank of endland.co.uk

A Fazio, 'Fact-finding with regard to the relationship between firms, financial markets and the protection of savings', *Economic Bulletin*, 38, March 2004 (Rome: Banca d'Italia)

J A Frankel and K A Froot, 'Chartists, fundamentalists and trading in the forex market', *American Economic Review*, May 1990, pp. 181–5.

HMSO, Report of the Committee to Review the Functioning of Financial Institutions (Wilson Report), Cmnd. 7937 (London: HMSO, June 1980)

HM Treasury, *Promoting Financial Inclusion* (London: HM Treasury, December 2004)

HM Treasury, 'Sandler Report' (2002) at www.hm-treasury.gov.uk/documents/financial_services/savings/fin_sav_sand.cfm

C P Kindleberger, *Manias, Panics and Crashes. A History of Financial Crises* (New York: John Wiley and Sons, 3e, 1996)

Nottingham University, 'Poor and ethnic minority areas bear the brunt of bank branch closures', Nottingham University press release PA31/06, 23 February 2006 http://www.nottingham.ac.uk/public-affairs/press-releases/

M Sullivan, *Understanding Pensions* (London: Routledge, 2004)

J Tobin, 'Money and Finance in the macroeconomic process', *Journal of Money, Credit and Banking*, 14(2), May 1982, 171–204

http://www.pensionprotectionfund.org.uk/www.ceedweb.org

CHAPTER 13

The regulation of financial markets

Objectives

What you will learn in this chapter:

- General reasons for and against regulation
- Specific reasons for the regulation of the financial services industry
- Arguments for and against self-regulation of financial markets
- The major changes that have occurred in the regulation of financial markets in the UK in the 1980s and 1990s
- Details of the principal British Acts of Parliament governing the banking and financial services sectors
- Details of the regulation of banking and financial services across the European Union
- The nature of the problems caused by the globalisation of the financial sector and by the developments in derivatives markets
- Details of the international attempts to deal with regulatory problems

The financial services industry has always been politically sensitive and, consequently, heavily regulated. Such regulation has many aspects. It may be concerned with the degree of competition in a market, the protection of consumers of financial services, the encouragement of small investors, the capital adequacy of financial institutions, the ability of small firms to obtain venture capital, or the preservation of the reputation of the market and the practitioners in it. As well as theoretical arguments for and against regulation in general, there are practical explanations of the regulation of specific segments of the financial sector.

The banking industry, for instance, relies on public confidence. The fractional reserve banking system (see Chapter 3) vastly increases the potential profitability of banks but also leaves them at risk from the loss of public confidence, which may cause a run on their deposits. The risk of collapse is made greater by the contrast between the liquid nature of bank liabilities (deposits) and the illiquid nature of their assets (loans). There are three principal areas of concern in relation to bank collapse.

> **Contagion:** The collapse of one financial institution leading to bad debts and/or a loss of confidence in other financial institutions, possibly causing their collapse – a particular problem for banks.

The first is the prospect of contagion. This, in turn, might have serious consequences for the real economy. Contagion might arise to the extent that a failure of one bank causes a loss of confidence in banking in general. Another possible source of contagion is the very high level of interbank dealings in modern banking – the collapse of one bank creates bad debts for other banks.

The second concern is with consumer protection. The efficiency of a modern economy is greatly enhanced by the development of the financial system and thus it is desirable that as many people as possible participate in that system. It follows that collapse of financial institutions within a sophisticated financial system is bound to affect large numbers of people, small savers as well as large. Further, many people who take part in financial transactions have little knowledge of either the products or the processes of the financial system. In addition, prices in financial markets depend heavily on expectations and can move very sharply as a result of market optimism or pessimism. Large profits (and losses) can be made with great rapidity. It is hardly surprising, then, that greed, chicanery and gullibility are present to a greater extent in financial markets than in many others. Consumer protection becomes a particularly sensitive issue when small savers are threatened with the loss of their life savings. The safest response for politicians is to attempt to regulate the market in the hope of preventing such situations from occurring and/or to provide insurance where they do arise. Box 13.1 considers two contrasting British cases of consumer loss in financial markets.

Box 13.1 **Attitudes towards losers in financial markets**

Lloyd's of London names

Lloyd's of London is an insurance market organised into 400 syndicates supplying a range of insurance services. Syndicates are backed by 'names' who guarantee to meet any syndicate losses from their personal wealth on a basis of unlimited liability. In profitable years, 'names' do not have to provide funds and thus earn a rate of return on money that can also be invested elsewhere. However, in the late 1980s and early 1990s, several syndicates experienced years of large losses and 'names' backing these syndicates were called upon to pay large sums. It was claimed that some losses were the result of manipulation by professionals in the market and the market felt obliged to provide some compensation to losers in order to try to salvage its reputation. Many court actions were undertaken by 'names'. Nonetheless, there was little public sympathy for 'names'. It was widely believed that they were happy to accept the high returns without being prepared fully to accept the accompanying risk.

UK private pensions

In the late 1980s, new legislation opened up the possibility of people taking out private pension plans. Large insurance companies saw this as a major new market and set about persuading large numbers of people to switch from their existing pension schemes operated by their employers to private pension plans or to take out personal pensions rather than joining employers' schemes. Between April 1988 and June 1994, many people were misled by insurance companies into believing they would be better off with a personal pension plan when the reverse was the case. When this became clear, there was widespread public and political anger. The industry regulators imposed fines on the companies involved and required that compensation be paid. However, the form of compensation was not agreed until some years after the problem become known. The mis-selling review was not completed until early 2003. Compensation offered by the insurance companies was over £11.5bn and fines of more than £10m were levied on the companies. The administration costs of the review were £2bn.

Losers and the search for remedy

We have seen in the personal pensions case and shall see again with regard to split investment trusts in Box 13.2 that there is sometimes a case for losers in financial markets to be rescued. On other occasions, as with bank deposit insurance, losers are, up to set limits, insured against loss. In the personal pension example, industry regulators sought recompense for the wronged parties. Mostly, however, losers must seek legal remedy, as with the Lloyd's names above and the Mirror Group pensioners considered in Box 13.3 (later). We mentioned another interesting legal case in Box 10.6, with the ratepayers of Hammersmith and Fulham being rescued by the courts from the folly of their council officials. Other cases abound. All of these cases raise, in different ways, the question of the extent to which people should be held responsible for their actions in complex financial markets.

Box 13.2 ## Consumer protection – split capital investment trusts

Split capital investment trusts are investment trusts – companies listed on the London stock exchange that raise funds to invest in other companies. Investors benefit from both dividend income and capital growth. Split capital trusts typically have two types of shareholders with different investment needs – those interested principally in income who collect dividends and expect their capital returned at the end of the trust's life, and those interested in growth who opt for zero dividend preference shares (zeros), receiving in return for forgoing dividends a share in all the capital growth of the fund at the end of its life.

In the late 1990s, when share prices were booming, split capital trusts were heavily marketed and extravagant promises were made. High annual rates of return were mentioned and the trusts were said to be 'low risk'. Shares in the trusts were bought, in particular, by parents saving for school fees and pensioners wanting income or lump sums.

However, when share prices began to fall sharply in 2000, many trusts did not have enough cash to pay the scale of dividend they had promised. Some trusts borrowed heavily to buy more shares (they became heavily geared) and also invested in each other (crossholdings). One trust lost over 68 per cent of its value in one year. By October 2002, eight split capital trusts had called in the receivers and up to 40 of the 120 trusts were thought to be in serious trouble. Perhaps 50,000 people have lost money in the trusts, some losing heavily. There were stories of pensioners losing their homes.

Initially it was thought that losers had little chance of compensation. The investment industry sought to blame the buyers of zeros. Further, since investment trusts are technically companies rather than regulated funds, the Financial Services Authority (FSA) claimed no responsibility for them and the Financial Ombudsman Service (see Box 13.4) can deal with them only on a voluntary basis.

However, in February 2003, the House of Commons Treasury Select Committee issued a report on the trusts, which accused one of the biggest firms in the sector, Aberdeen Asset Management, of recklessly misleading promotion. More generally, it suggested widespread conflicts of interest and collusive behaviour in the sector, possibly amounting to corruption. This considerably increased the prospects of investors suing companies for mis-selling. The Treasury Committee chair called for compensation, with extra cash where collusion or corruption could be shown. Following an investigation into the selling of splits, the FSA proposed to the firms involved that they take part in collective settlement negotiations leading, where appropriate, to firms compensating investors and taking disciplinary action against staff. This led to the establishment of Fund Distribution Limited (FDL) to administer the payment of compensation to aggrieved investors. FDL made an initial offer of 40 pence for every pound lost, in return for which investors were required to give up the chance of securing potentially higher payouts through the courts or by use of the ombudsman service. The closing date for acceptance of the offer was 15 May 2006. In early June 2006, FDL announced that 96 per cent of the 25,000 eligible investors had accepted the offer and that a second payment would probably bring the total compensation to around 50 pence in the pound.

The split capital investment trusts affair illustrates several points:

- The notion of *moral hazard* – the existence of a powerful regulator and an ombudsman leads small investors to feel their investments are secure. They do not, as a result, always read the small print attached to financial products, even though it could be argued that the high rates of return offered should have alerted investors to the degree of risk they faced.

- The difficulty in determining the extent of consumer responsibility for their loss. Was this really a case of mis-selling, with innocent consumers being misled by dissembling or dishonest professionals? Or were consumers led into the investment partly by greed – the promised high rates of return causing them to act in a foolish way? This raises the question of how much consumer protection should be provided.

- The damage to the industry caused by cases such as these – the Association of Investment Trust Companies felt the need to set up a hardship fund to help out, seeking contributions from fund managers who wanted to restore the battered reputation of the investment trust sector.

The third concern with banks is that their liabilities form the means of payment. Thus, bank regulation aims to guarantee the integrity of the transactions medium and to prevent the process of financial intermediation from failing.

The special features that explain the high level of regulation of the insurance market include the very long term of some contracts, the size of many of the risks being insured relative to policyholders' incomes, and the lack of transparency of many of the products. Until quite recently, in other financial markets – for equities, bonds, bills and derivatives – the funds at risk were largely those of professional investors. Now, however, many people have at least an indirect interest in the performance of such markets through unit trusts, investment trusts, pension funds and endowment mortgages managed for them by professional fund managers. More of us than ever before have a reason for wishing financial markets to be sound.

This chapter outlines the theory of regulation and goes on to consider the changes in the approach to regulation that have occurred in the UK financial sector since the mid-1980s. We then look at the regulation of the financial sector across the European Union. The chapter also examines the problems caused by the globalisation of financial markets and the rapid development of the complex markets in derivatives and swaps. The final section deals with the attempts of governments and central banks to cope with these changes.

13.1 The theory of regulation

The theoretical argument for regulation depends on the notion of market failure – interferences with the market ideal of perfect competition that might arise, for example, from the presence of elements of monopoly or oligopoly, the presence of externalities, the lack of information in general or the existence of asymmetric information. We came across asymmetry of information in section 7.6 in relation to bank managers and their clients. Here we are more likely to be concerned with the ignorance of consumers relative to producers in highly technical markets. This lies at the heart of many consumer protection issues. The possibility of market failure, together with the political sensitivity of financial services, provides firm support for some level and form of the regulation of financial markets.

There are, however, a number of arguments against regulation. These concentrate on four failings of regulation:

● Regulation creates *moral hazard*. That is, it causes people to behave in a counter-productive way. For example, a belief that the government will ensure the safety of deposits with all financial institutions leads savers to deposit their money without giving thought to the behaviour of their bank. This allows organisations that are badly managed or staffed with dishonest people to survive. Equally, if financial institutions believe that they will always be rescued from collapse, they may take greater risks in their lending policies in search of higher returns.

> **Moral hazard:** The notion that people or organisations that feel protected from risk take greater risks than they would otherwise do. The protection of individuals and firms thus makes the system as a whole riskier.

● Regulation results in *agency capture*. In other words, producers often dominate the regulatory process since the activities of regulators are much more important to each of the relatively small number of producers than to each of the much larger number of consumers. Further, the next career move of regulators is often into the industry they have been regulating and so they may not wish to offend producers. Again, regulators may be ex-practitioners who share the judgements and values of the producers.

● Regulation creates compliance costs (the costs of adhering to the regulations) for producers. If producers are able to pass on the costs to consumers, the result is higher prices and lower output.

● The need to comply with regulations increases the costs of entry into and exit from markets. This helps to preserve monopoly positions and make cartels more stable.

Combining the last two arguments produces the proposition that regulation inhibits competition and thus reduces the efficiency with which financial markets help to allocate the economy's scarce resources. However, even if we accept that regulation restricts competition, it is certainly not the only factor in financial markets that does so and there is no guarantee that a reduction in regulation will lead to increased competition. The deregulation argument may work in two ways.

● Regulation keeps out new entrants who, if they could enter, would force existing firms in the market to be more efficient and would compete prices down.

● Regulation prevents mergers and acquisitions and allows small, inefficient firms to remain in business. Thus, deregulation would lead to mergers that would produce economies of scale and scope and the replacement of poor management.

With regard to the first of these, the benefits of lower prices that might arise from deregulation have to be weighed against costs such as possible reductions in the stability of the system and increased risk of loss for consumers. Unfortunately for the second proposition, studies of the considerable merger activity in US banking in the 1980s and 1990s did not produce convincing evidence of increased efficiency or profitability (Rhoades, 1992). On the other hand, if there were significant economies of scale, and mergers occurred to take advantage of them, it would become more difficult for new entrants to come into the market, even in the absence of regulation.

It therefore seems that none of the criticisms of regulation provides sufficient reason in itself to reject all regulation, though the criticisms point to matters that must be taken into account in decisions over the amount and form of regulation.

About the form of regulation, we must ask who should carry out the regulation – the government or a government agency (statutory regulation), or the industry itself (self-regulation). The argument for self-regulation has two elements. Firstly, the industry has a commercial incentive to protect its reputation and members are prepared to pay to achieve this. Secondly, practitioners understand the needs of the industry and are likely to interfere less with its efficient functioning. This refers to a common complaint against statutory regulators that, because they are heavily criticised over the collapse of firms but not praised for actions that lead to lower prices, they tend to impose excessive safety standards, raising the cost of regulation to both producers and consumers.

The assumption then is that self-regulation is almost certain to be lighter than statutory regulation. There is a danger, however, that self-regulation may turn out to be an awkward halfway house. It must be supported by some government regulation at least to the extent that firms are legally required to join the industry regulatory scheme. Otherwise, an incentive would be created for some firms to act as free riders, hoping to benefit from any increase in reputation of the industry resulting from the behaviour of firms within the regulatory organisation without paying the costs of membership.

More importantly, self-regulation creates less moral hazard than statutory regulation only to the extent that it leaves an element of risk for both consumers and producers. Once risk exists, the degree of risk has to be assessed to allow a judgement to be made of the risk/return profile of an investment. This should cause no worries to professionals, but the general public faces two types of difficulty. Firstly, it may be time-consuming and costly to acquire the necessary knowledge to assess risk accurately. Secondly, the ability of non-experts in a field to assess risk is notoriously poor. There is a strong tendency for people to respond to risk by adopting one or other extreme position. They may, as responses to food scares show, eschew a product or activity completely as soon as the existence of risk becomes apparent. Alternatively, they may, as people's behaviour as car drivers or smokers attests, believe that risk exists only for other people. Thus, the possibility of consumers assessing risk at all accurately is remote, especially in markets in which producers have both the incentive and the capacity to mislead consumers.

Further, the existence of consumers who are, in the field of finance, risk-takers or who underestimate the true level of risk ensures that dubious firms continue to survive despite the apparent reduction of moral hazard. On the other hand, those who are risk-averters or who overestimate the true risk may be driven away from products from which they might have benefited. Nor does self-regulation perform particularly well in terms of the other complaints about regulation. By definition, self-regulation places regulation in the hands of the producers. Indeed, it places it in the hands of existing producers and provides an incentive for them to use regulation to increase barriers to entry to the industry. Thus, it may lead to a lowering of some kinds of compliance costs, but not necessarily all.

13.2 Financial regulation in the UK

Financial regulation in the UK went through two major reorganisations in little over a decade. The first set of changes occurred in 1986 and 1987.

Among them we can distinguish three particular landmarks – the 'Big Bang' in equities markets in 1986, with the associated changes in the organisation of the bond market; the Financial Services Act of 1986; and the 1987 Banking Act, following earlier changes in 1979 and 1984. This reorganisation of the practice of regulation followed a series of developments in the financial markets.

Perhaps the single most important of these was the rapid internationalisation of the markets. This had several causes. Firstly, major financial imbalances had developed among countries. These arose initially with the oil price rises of 1973 and 1979 and the consequent need to recycle the surplus funds of oil-producing countries. They continued through the 1980s and into the 1990s with the huge current account deficit of the US and surpluses of West Germany and Japan, and with the growth of the debt crisis of Latin American and other developing countries. Political crises in developing countries led to large movements of 'flight' capital from those countries. The huge growth in sovereign lending required a great increase in international co-ordination among commercial banks, with many loans being syndicated by more than 100 banks from many different countries.

Secondly, transnational corporations continued to grow in importance, contributing substantially to the movement of funds across borders. The sharp movements in exchange rates, which have characterised the past thirty-five years, increased the need for these companies and others engaged in international trade to protect themselves against foreign exchange risk. This, together with the greater availability of funds and the increased international competition and greater freedom in the movement of capital in much of the world, resulted in the continued expansion of world capital markets such as the eurobond, eurocurrency and euronote markets and the development of a range of highly sophisticated financial products to meet the changing needs of companies and governments. Perhaps the most striking change has been the rapid growth of financial derivatives markets, with a vast increase in the number of types of contracts sold. These changes were facilitated by major developments in computerisation and communication that led to twenty-four-hour worldwide markets.

As well, the growth of financial imbalances was associated with the almost constant threat of instability and the fear of collapse of financial institutions, which (because of the huge increase in international interbank transactions) have at times appeared to be a threat to the whole financial system. This concern has caused national monetary authorities to meet to attempt to agree upon rules relating to institutions engaged in offshore financial markets under the auspices of international organisations such as the Bank for International Settlements.

Within the UK system, too, the changes were numerous. The renewed need for the authorities to finance public sector deficits in the 1990s following four years of surpluses emphasised the importance of bond markets. For much of the 1980s and 1990s equities markets flourished, fuelled by the privatisation of large public corporations and by a great deal of takeover activity among companies. New markets developed, for instance the unlisted securities market and the market for commercial paper. Institutions, notably pension funds, grew rapidly. The government sought to encourage small investors into markets and introduced changes such as those in pension arrangements that led to the development of new financial products. The Single European Act 1986 and the steps taken to implement its terms in financial markets added yet another element to the changes occurring.

Among all of these and other changes, supervision of the activities of firms and the operation of markets became, at the same time, increasingly important and increasingly difficult. It is in this light that we need to consider the regulatory changes of recent years.

13.2.1 Regulatory changes in the 1980s

The problem of regulation of the City of London came strongly to public attention as a result of a number of cases in 1986 and 1987 relating to breaches of the City code on takeovers and mergers and of various types of insider dealing (where information gained in one part of a firm's activities is used to advantage in another part of the firm's business). The fear was that such cases, along with other areas of doubtful practice, for example problems experienced over several years in the Lloyd's of London insurance market, would sully the reputation of the City and discourage investors at a time when the government was seeking to encourage investor participation.

As we saw in Chapter 6, the Big Bang reforms in securities markets, most notably the acceptance of the dual capacity system that allowed a firm to act as both broker and market-maker, together with the change in stock exchange rules permitting 100 per cent outside ownership of member firms, led to a series of takeovers among City firms and the growth of large financial conglomerates. To remove the possibility of insider dealing, firms were required to keep their different activities entirely separate from each other. This became known as establishing 'Chinese walls' between the different types of business: for example, between corporate finance and market-making or fund management, or between market-making and stockbroking research.

It became clear fairly rapidly, however, that it was extremely difficult to police all of the Chinese walls and that the costs to large firms of trying to do so were burdensome. In the early years following Big Bang, a number of insider dealing cases arose. The only comfort was that the new computerised dealing services that accompanied Big Bang allowed insider dealing and market manipulation to be tracked down more efficiently. Nonetheless, the problem itself remained and had threatened to damage the reputation of the markets and to undermine investor confidence in them.

In the light of these concerns, the Financial Services Act of 1986, which came into force in April 1988, was seen as crucial for the City as well as for the protection of the investor. The aim of the Act was to create a flexible system of regulation that inspired confidence in both market practitioners and investors based upon the notion that the best form of regulation was self-regulation. It established a new principal regulatory authority to supervise the affairs of the City of London. This body, the Securities and Investments Board (SIB), recognised a number of self-regulatory organisations (SROs), formed of investment practitioners, to supervise their markets. In addition it recognised a group of professional bodies that attempted to maintain the standards of lawyers, accountants, insurance brokers and actuaries who participated in the market and a number of exchanges in which trading occurred.

The SROs, then, were separate from the recognised exchanges in which they operated. Prior to the Act, membership of the Stock Exchange had carried with it the exclusive right to use the trading facilities of the market: the exchange and its regulatory body, in other words, were one and the same, enabling outsiders to be kept out. Members of some SROs now operated in more than one exchange.

The principal arguments made for self-regulation were that:

- a self-regulatory body would be able to react to changing circumstances more quickly than a statutory body;
- the involvement of practitioners in formulating and enforcing rules and in encouraging high standards of conduct would ensure more effective regulation;
- practitioners were better able to spot breaches of rules than a statutory body;
- self-regulatory bodies could be set up more quickly;
- government would be kept at arm's length from the day-to-day regulation of the markets.

This was all very well but problems soon arose. The complexity of the various elements of the industry meant that the regulatory needs of the various activities were different. This was the reason for the establishment of a number of SROs, each dealing with a particular segment of the industry. However, the classification of the industry for the purpose of defining membership of the SROs was far from easy because of the overlapping of activities following the functional integration of financial services firms. This allowed a single firm to be engaged in banking, insurance and securities business. For example, life assurance firms not only provide insurance but also run pension funds, have an interest in housing finance, engage in fund management, provide investment advice, and have entered the world of banking. Under these circumstances, there was bound to be overlap among the SROs, giving firms a choice as to which organisation to join.

This led to the separate SROs competing among themselves for members, introducing the possibility of competitive laxity with the regulating authorities who tried to maintain high standards, losing out to those who chose to lower standards and reduce the burden of regulation on their members.

Competitive laxity: Organisations that are meant to control markets and ensure high standards compete for members among producers by failing to enforce and/or lowering standards.

The SROs were in danger of acting as trade associations, looking after the interests of their members and underplaying the role of consumer protection. Some regulators attempted to maximise membership by keeping subscriptions low, reducing their ability to supervise the behaviour of members. For example, FIMBRA (the Financial Intermediaries, Managers and Brokers Regulatory Association), one of the original SROs set up by the Financial Services Act, kept its subscriptions low and soon ran into financial problems. It then had to be rescued by loans from its larger members, causing it to be heavily dependent on a small number of members who could transfer to other associations if the actions of FIMBRA did not suit them. One of the consequences of this weakening of the regulatory system was the Maxwell pension fund scandal set out in Box 13.3.

Box 13.3

Maxwell and the pension funds

On 31 October 1991 the body of the newspaper tycoon, Robert Maxwell, was discovered floating in the sea off the Canary Islands. During the subsequent unravelling of the affairs of the Maxwell group of companies, including Maxwell Communications Corporation (MCC) and Mirror Group Newspapers (MGN), massive fraud was discovered relating to the pension funds of the Maxwell companies.

Two types of problems were uncovered. The first was the management of the pension funds in the interests of the Maxwell family rather than of the investors in the fund. When Maxwell had taken control of the MGN fund in 1985, investments were largely in UK blue chip equities. By April 1990, more than half of the twenty largest investments in the fund's portfolio were in companies with which Maxwell had a connection or in his own private interests. This was clearly contrary to general trust law, which lays down three obligations for trustees:

- to diversify investments;
- to avoid exposing beneficiaries to undue risk;
- to act reasonably.

However, much worse was to follow. During 1991, Maxwell siphoned off up to £1bn from the pension funds of his companies in the form of unsecured loans for his own use in defending his seriously troubled empire. When the Maxwell companies collapsed, this money was lost, leaving several of the funds unable to meet their obligations to pay pensions to employees and former employees.

How could this have happened?

Pension funds (as mentioned in Chapter 4) are required by law to be kept separate from company accounts. A board of 'independent' trustees is appointed to oversee the running of the fund. However, Maxwell was able to appoint his own trustees and did so to good effect. There was a gradual erosion of representation of employees on the board, and most trustees appeared to know little of what was being done in their name. Maxwell managed the funds through his own private management firm, Bishopgate Investment Management (BIM). It was subject to inspection by auditors and to regulation by one of the SROs, IMRO (the Investment Management Regulatory Organisation).

A report compiled by the House of Commons social security committee later described the events as a 'spectacle to make even Pontius Pilate blush' as everyone in the City seemed mainly concerned to deny blame. The report concluded that if the regulators had 'acted with the proper degree of suspicion . . . and if professional advisers' care had been commensurate with their fees . . . then the Maxwell pension funds would have been secure' (*Financial Times*, 10 March 1992, page 8).

The report particularly criticised the accountancy firm Coopers & Lybrand Deloitte, which had detailed serious shortcomings in the way BIM managed the pension funds as early as February 1991 but had reported this only to the pension fund manager and rarely attended meetings of the trustees of the funds. IMRO was also heavily criticised. It had investigated BIM only five weeks before Maxwell's death but had claimed to find nothing wrong. They had failed, said the select committee, to spot stealing on a massive scale. *Self-regulation*, said the committee, *was little short of tragic comedy*.

For these sorts of reasons, self-regulation is often equated with self-interest. This was particularly true of the City of London system because of the uncovering of a large number of illegal activities and institutional collapses in the late 1980s and 1990s.

Competitive laxity of a rather different kind occurred in the case of the previously unregulated market in eurobonds. The initial intention had been that regulation by the different SROs and the levels of disclosure required by the various exchanges should be compatible. However, fears that placing onerous requirements on the eurobond market in London would drive much of the business abroad quickly led to an easing of its rule book. The self-regulation of the City of London certainly did not overcome the problem of agency capture. The regulators were, in effect, part of the industry – indeed, often they were employees of the producers on secondment from their normal jobs. This led to the concern that they were likely to take too sympathetic a view of the behaviour of the industry and fail to understand the point of view of the consumers.

Another complaint about the operation of the SROs was that retail business was under-regulated, while business carried out for professional customers was over-regulated. The establishment of the Personal Investment Authority (PIA) as an umbrella regulator for retail financial business was a response to the first part of the complaint.

Finally, there was concern over the ability of the regulators to obtain convictions and over the sentences imposed by the courts. Indeed, the Serious Fraud Office (SFO) was set up in 1987 specifically because of the inability of the City of London Fraud Squad to obtain convictions. However, the SFO (which dealt with cases involving more than £1m) itself experienced a number of embarrassing failures. One suggestion was that there were frequently too many agencies engaged in investigations – the SFO, the Metropolitan Police fraud squad, the SIB, the various SROs and the investigation branches of the Department of Trade and Industry – and that their actions lacked co-ordination.

Dissatisfaction with the operation of the system led to the commissioning by the Chancellor of the Exchequer of a report by SIB's chairman, Andrew Large. The report, published in May 1993, listed a number of criticisms of the existing system but still defended the two-tier self-regulatory system and committed SIB to making it work. The report was cautiously welcomed by the SROs but was greeted elsewhere with some scepticism. Many thought it insufficiently radical and as placing too much of a burden on the good intentions of the chairman of SIB. Nonetheless, the system was given the benefit of the doubt for four more years, largely on the grounds that a complex system needed time to settle down. However, by 1997 the industry was still struggling to cope with issues such as the failure of agents to seek the best prices for clients and the giving of unsuitable investment advice. In May 1997, the new Labour government announced major changes to the UK regulatory system. We look at these changes in section 13.2.3.

13.2.2 Supervision of the banking system

We have mentioned two regulatory issues in banking:

- the possibility of contagion as the result of a run on one bank turning into a panic that might lead to a serious reduction in liquidity for the system as a whole; and

- the need for consumer protection, given the nature of the banking industry and the cost and difficulty of acquiring knowledge.

We have added to these the need to cause as little moral hazard as possible, to keep compliance costs low and to interfere as little as possible with competition, either by creating barriers to entry or exit or by favouring some institutions over others within the market. A common approach to ensuring the stability of the banking industry has been to prevent banks from participating in the more risky aspects of finance by limiting them to deposit creation and lending functions. For example, in the US, legislation passed during the 1930s rigidly separated commercial banking from investment banking and other financial activities. Since banks could provide a wider range of financial services not just in their own name but through the acquisition of other companies, this had to be supported by legislation that restricted the ability of banks to acquire non-banking firms and vice versa. In the US, for example, the Bank Holding Act of 1956 sought to prevent companies owning banks from being allied with insurance companies, securities firms and commercial enterprises. Such a separation fitted well with the British and American model of banking in which the various kinds of banking business were undertaken typically by different types of banking organisation. In particular, deposit-taking banks concentrated on short-term lending. This contrasted with the universal banking model common in northern Europe.

Other approaches to ensuring the stability of banks have included guaranteeing the liquidity of the overall banking system by giving the central bank the role of lender of last resort to the system, seeking to prevent runs on individual banks by introducing some form of deposit insurance scheme, placing limitations on interest payments on deposits to prevent competition for deposits, and establishing barriers to entry also with the intention of limiting competition among banks.

All of these restrictions came under challenge in the 1980s and 1990s. High and variable inflation and interest rates put pressure on traditional specialised savings institutions. In the US this was magnified by legal restrictions on rates of interest payable on retail deposits. As financial services became an increasingly international industry, governments became concerned about the competitiveness of their domestic financial industries hobbled by tight regulation. In a world of increasingly mobile capital, firms found their way around existing restrictions and sooner or later forced legislative changes that gave them greater freedom. Diversification of asset bases provided benefits in an increasingly risky environment and firms sought to benefit from economies of both scale and scope. The financial conglomerate was born. All of this was fostered by an anti-government mood in the worlds of both business and finance.

In such a world, fears of instability increased and the issue of bank supervision at both national and international levels grew in importance. In supervising banks, regulatory authorities became concerned particularly with questions of capital adequacy, liquidity, asset quality and the concentration of risks.

Capital adequacy is central because a bank's capital must be sufficient to absorb losses and to finance the operation of its business. The modern approach to the assessment of a bank's capital adequacy is based on a calculation of its risk–asset ratio. This involves a number of steps:

- a definition of the elements of capital for supervisory purposes;
- the allocation of weights to different broad categories of asset (e.g. cash, government securities, loans to banks, loans to firms and households);
- the expression of capital as a percentage of total risk-weighted assets.

The weights applied in the second step reflect the degrees of risk associated with the different categories of assets. More risky assets are given higher weights. Thus, an increase in the proportion of a bank's assets regarded as risky increases the size of its risk-weighted assets and lowers the ratio of capital to risk-weighted assets.

Liquidity relates to the ability of a bank to meet its obligations on time, especially in relation to repayment of interbank borrowings and customer deposits. Since the survival of a bank depends on the retention of the confidence of its depositors, the maintenance of a reputation for trustworthiness is critical. Thus, banks must actively manage liquidity. They seek to do this in three ways. Firstly, they hold a stock of readily marketable liquid assets that can be turned into cash quickly in response to unforeseen needs. Secondly, they identify mismatches between potential receipts and payments in future periods. Thirdly, they respond to potential mismatches by borrowing in the market to smooth out cash flows in particular periods. Regulators may attempt to ensure the continued liquidity of banks by, for example, imposing a required minimum liquidity ratio (a ratio of assets of short maturity to total deposits) and/or by setting limits on mismatches or net positions in particular time bands.

The main issue in relation to the quality of a bank's assets is the ability of its borrowers to service and repay loans. The poor quality of the loans of many banks has been a central element in the problems faced by the Japanese banking system in recent years. The early identification of problem loans is important if remedial action is to succeed. To this end, banks may employ a grading system that classifies loans in a range from trouble-free to non-performing. Some countries require such ratings to be assigned to individual loans in the attempt to evaluate the quality of banks' assets on a consistent basis.

Risk concentration becomes a problem when loans to a small number of large borrowers make up a high proportion of a bank's assets. Then, default by only one or two borrowers can cause serious difficulties for the bank. The usual regulatory response is to limit exposure to single borrowers or groups of borrowers to some proportion of the bank's capital base. Dangers can also arise for banks if deposits come from a narrow range of sources, if individual deposits are large and volatile, if income derives from a small number of transactions or activities, or if a high proportion of loans are made against one particular kind of collateral.

In the UK the Bank of England had, until the 1980s, largely exercised its control of the banking system indirectly through its close relationships with the clearing banks, discount houses and accepting houses. However, banking scandals among secondary banks in the early 1970s, the need for the Bank to rescue the Johnson Matthey Bank in 1984, and concerns about the capital adequacy of the major banks in the wake of the debt crisis of developing countries in the mid-1980s led to a considerable formalisation of the Bank of England's role through the introduction of new banking acts and the issuing by the Bank of prudential rules it expected banks to follow. With the further realisation that the banking industry was changing rapidly with the formation of financial conglomerates associated with Big Bang and with the development of new market places and new financial instruments, the Banking Act of 1987 produced a new framework of supervision for the banking aspects of financial services.

The Act created one class of 'authorised institutions', all subject to the same rules and regulations. It established requirements for banks to report any large individual lending exposure and defined more precisely than previously the circumstances under which the Bank might determine that an individual was not a 'fit and proper' person to run a bank. It also set up a new board of banking supervision to assist the Bank in its supervisory role; gave the Bank power to veto acquisition of a shareholding of more than 15 per cent in an authorised institution; made it a criminal offence to 'knowingly or recklessly' provide false information to the Bank; allowed increased cooperation between supervisors and auditors of banks; and enabled the Bank to seek opinions from reporting accountants on banks' accounting records and internal control systems and to commission reports by accountants or consultants on the information obtained by the Bank. Further, the Act described in general terms the information to be provided to the Bank, defined by circumstances in which an institution might define itself as a bank or as carrying on a banking business, and gave the Bank powers of entry to banking premises where contravention of the Act was suspected.

The Act was supported by a large number of papers setting down prudential rules. These related, among other things, to capital and liquidity ratios which banks were expected to maintain, the measurement of capital, the supervision of the off-balance-sheet business of banks, and the suitability tests the Bank will apply to people wishing to become large shareholders in UK banks. Until 1975, the Bank of England had assessed the capital adequacy of a bank by looking at its gearing ratio: the relationship between the bank's capital and its total public liabilities. From then on, however, it began experimenting with the use of risk–asset ratios (comparing total bank capital with bank assets rather than liabilities). In January 1987, the Bank of England and the Federal Reserve System of the US announced their intention to bring the supervision of banks' balance sheets in the two countries into line on this basis. More detail concerning the calculation of risk–asset ratios is provided in section 13.4 below.

The new system was concerned with the quality of bank assets, not just the quantity. Further, the agreement between the US and Britain allowed the inclusion of off-balance-sheet risk in the calculation. These risks would also be weighted and added to the risk-adjusted balance sheet of banks to arrive at a final estimate of their financial soundness. Again, an increase in off-balance-sheet risk would produce a lower risk–asset ratio.

> **Off-balance-sheet activities:** Activities that earn income for banks in the form of fees without corresponding assets and liabilities appearing on the balance sheet such as the guaranteeing of commercial bills or of swaps or the issuing of commercial paper.

The Financial Services Act also gave to the Bank of England responsibility for regulating UK wholesale markets in sterling, foreign exchange and bullion.

13.2.3 The 1998 reforms

Following the election of the Labour government in 1997, two major regulatory changes were announced. The first was the abandonment of the self-regulatory system for the City of London and the re-establishment of full statutory regulation. This was to be administered by a single regulatory authority, the Financial Services Authority (FSA). This duly came into operation, following the passing of the necessary legislation, on 1 June 1998. The FSA's powers were confirmed by the Financial Services and Markets Act (FSMA), which received royal assent in June 2000. However, the process of taking over regulation from the existing regulatory authorities was not completed until the second half of 2001. Between mid-1998 and 2001, the old authorities had continued to act on behalf of the FSA while it built up its organisation and its handbook of rules and guidance and developed its regulatory philosophy.

The second major change was the transfer from the Bank of England to the FSA of responsibility for the supervision of the banking system and the wholesale money markets. This also occurred on 1 June 1998 under the terms of the Bank of England Act 1998. Although the Bank of England had had severe embarrassments in the 1990s in its role as supervisor of the banking system (notably in the collapse of the BCCI and Barings Bank), it did not lose its supervisory responsibility because of these.

It did so partially because the increasingly blurred boundaries between the different types of financial businesses mentioned above suggested the need to consolidate the supervision of banking together with other financial institutions in a single agency. A more specific reason for the change, however, derived from the other major element in the new Bank of England Act – the granting to the Bank of independent control of British monetary policy. The aim was to avoid a possible conflict between the monetary policy role and the supervisory role. This possibility follows from the argument that, where central banks are involved in bank supervision, financial sector representatives are strongly inclined to lobby central banks for easier monetary policy to reduce the regulatory burden on banks. That is, the supervisory role might compromise the monetary policy of the central bank. There is no strong evidence for this proposition, but many aspects of the movement to independence of central banks were based upon institutional arrangements in Germany. There, and in several other countries, monetary policy and bank supervision were carried out by separate organisations.

Although it lost the responsibility for banking supervision, the Bank of England retained responsibility for the stability of the financial system as a whole. This requires the Bank to work with the FSA. The Memorandum of Understanding, published in October 1997, set out a framework for cooperation between the Bank and the FSA, and for co-ordination between the Bank, the FSA and the Treasury in case of a financial crisis.

The Financial Services Authority (FSA)

The FSMA set the FSA four objectives: market confidence, consumer awareness, consumer protection and fighting financial crime. Each firm now obtains from the FSA a single authorisation to carry out financial business in the UK, with an associated list of permissions setting out what the FSA allows it to do. Under the previous regulatory system, many firms had had a number of authorisations from different regulatory bodies. Single compensation and ombudsman schemes (see Box 13.4) were also developed and from the second half of 2001, all financial firms became subject to a single regime for tackling 'market abuse', a non-criminal offence that was added to the already existing criminal offences of insider trading and market manipulation. Three categories of market abuse were defined: misuse of information, giving false or misleading impressions, and market distortion.

Box 13.4 | **The Financial Ombudsman Service**

As well as setting up the FSA, the Financial Services and Markets Act 2000 established a single financial services ombudsman to help settle disputes between consumers and financial firms. This combined the work of four separate complaints procedures under the previous regulatory system. The introduction of an ombudsman into a regulatory system has two purposes – to increase public confidence in financial markets and thus to encourage consumers to participate in these markets despite the manifest risks of doing so; and to attempt to redress a perceived imbalance in financial markets resulting from consumer ignorance and asymmetric information.

The ombudsman can consider complaints about a wide range of financial matters and the service is free to consumers. The decisions of the ombudsman are binding on firms but not on consumers. Consumers, having first complained to the firm with which they have a grievance, can take their cases to the ombudsman. If the decision there is not to their liking, they retain the ability to go to court. The ombudsman does not, as the FSA can do, either punish or fine firms for breaking rules.

The ombudsman service applies compulsorily to all firms regulated by the FSA for certain types of complaints. In addition, firms not regulated by the FSA can volunteer to participate in the service. Further, firms that are regulated by the FSA can volunteer to have the ombudsman consider types of complaints that are not part of the ombudsman's compulsory jurisdiction. Through consultation, the Financial Ombudsman Service has sought to widen the range of complaints with which it deals.

In the year ended 31 March 2005, 110,963 new cases were referred to the case-handling teams. The number of new cases taken on by the ombudsman service has increased rapidly each year from 25,000 in the year 1999–00. Unsurprisingly, the biggest area for new cases was mortgage endowment cases (63 per cent of the total). The other figures were: other investment-related cases 17 per cent; banking-related cases 9.5 per cent; insurance-related cases 10.5 per cent.

The FSA aims to maintain efficient, orderly and clean financial markets and to help retail consumers achieve a fair deal. However, the FSMA also requires the FSA to be efficient and economic in its use of resources, requiring it to focus its efforts on what it sees as the most significant risks to the achievement of its statutory objectives, while taking into account the principles of good regulation. Good regulation, according to the FSA, should not seek to discourage appropriate risk-taking by regulated firms or by investors. Risk, it accepts, is inherent in financial markets and it is neither practicable nor desirable to try to develop a regime in which no financial firms fail. Attempts to do so produce heavy-handed and expensive regulation that restricts innovation and interferes with competition.

This leaves the FSA with a very fine line to walk and it has been criticised from both directions – as being too large and bureaucratic, and as failing adequately to observe and prevent developing risks facing consumers. Particular problems over which the FSA has been criticised include split capital investment trusts (see Box 13.2), Equitable Life, and endowment mortgages.

Equitable Life is the oldest insurance company in the world, having been established as a mutual society in 1762. Until 1999, it had been regarded as a sound and trustworthy organisation and was the country's second largest insurance company. At the beginning of 1999, however, it announced that it would be unable to meet its commitments to its policyholders and launched court proceedings in order to gain approval for cuts it proposed making in its payments to them.

In the 1950s, Equitable had started selling policies with a guaranteed annuity rate (GAR) that allowed policyholders to opt for minimum pension payouts and a bonus when their policies matured. The guaranteed rates were higher than average and were very attractive. The GARs promised in the 1970s at a time of high inflation came to seem particularly high when inflation rates fell in the 1980s and again in the late 1990s. The society had realised the difficulty by 1988 and stopped selling the guaranteed policies. Nonetheless, it was committed to payments on the policies issued before that date and at the beginning of 1999 it realised it would be unable to meet its commitments of about £1.5bn.

It tried to renege on the guaranteed payouts in an attempt to maintain payments to the majority of its customers who did not hold guarantees but, after several court cases, the House of Lords finally ruled in July 2000 that Equitable had mistreated the 90,000 guaranteed policyholders. Equitable Life, still at this stage a mutual society, sought a buyer who would inject funds into the company, but potential buyers were put off by the society's huge liabilities. In December 2000, it closed its doors to new business. It announced that its with-profits policies would have no growth for the first half of 2000 and increased its penalty fee for withdrawing funds to 10 per cent. At the same time, it tried to come to a compromise with its policyholders. It asked guaranteed policyholders to drop their rights to future guarantees for a one-off increase of 17.5 per cent in the value of their plans. Policyholders who did not have guaranteed rates were offered a 2.5 per cent increase in the value of their policies in return for signing away their rights to any legal claims.

Equitable Life also began to sell off some of its operations in order to raise cash to pay its policyholders. Eventually, the Halifax Bank agreed to pay £1bn to buy the

Equitable's sales force and non-profits policies. In January 2002, policyholders voted in favour of the compromise rescue package and this was approved by the High Court the following month, paving the way for a £250m cash injection from the Halifax. The package was approved at the annual general meeting in May 2002. Members were told that the company was solvent, but increased exit penalties were announced in July 2002 and further cuts in the income to be paid to with-profit annuity holders were made in November 2002.

The FSA was criticised for its failure to spot problems and to follow up issues that had been uncovered, although it was partly excused because the problem had developed during the period in which the FSA was being set up (between January 1999 and December 2000), during most of which regulation was being carried out on the FSA's behalf by its predecessor, the Personal Investment Authority (PIA).

The mis-selling of endowment mortgages also began well before the FSA came into existence. The problems associated with the sale of endowment mortgages have been explained in section 12.1.3. Early in 2000, it became clear that many endowment policies would not meet the mortgage in full at the end of the period. Policyholders were faced with either having to meet the difference at the end of the period or to make top-up payments to the insurance company to ensure that the mortgage would be paid off. Estimates of the number of those facing a shortfall in their policies and of the extra amounts they would need to pay depended on the rate of bonus assumed for the rest of the life of the mortgage. It was clear, however, that the problem was very large.

The FSA required all companies to calculate the position of all policies at assumed rates of 4 per cent, 6 per cent and 8 per cent to maturity and to advise all policyholders of their position during 2000. They also specified that the letters should set out all the available options to policyholders and should not give more weight to the possibility of solving the problem by increasing the premium paid. Companies were only obliged to look at policies taken out from 29 April 1988, the date that the Financial Services Act came into force.

Was this just an unfortunate result of the change in economic conditions and a case of 'let the buyer beware'? After all, people could have opted for straight repayment mortgages but chose the riskier endowment repayment method in the hope of receiving a higher return. Yet things were not as straightforward as this. In October 2000, the FSA admitted that hundreds of thousands of people might have been mis-sold endowment policies. It became clear that many policyholders had not been told that their policies carried any risks. They had been allowed by the insurance companies to understand that their policies would definitely pay off their mortgages.

People who believed they had been mis-sold endowment mortgages were able to apply for redress to the Financial Ombudsman Service or, where the company that sold the policy had gone out of business, to the Financial Services Compensation Scheme. Some insurance companies pledged to make up shortfalls whether or not the policies had been mis-sold. People sold endowment mortgages before 29 April 1988 had little chance of receiving compensation, although some companies agreed to allow the Financial Ombudsman Service to consider on a voluntary basis complaints of mis-selling before that date.

Although mis-selling appeared to have been widespread, the FSA refused to instigate a case-by-case review of the problem, despite criticisms by consumer bodies and the FSA's own Consumer Panel. The FSA argued that such a review was not needed because the vast majority of policyholders were better off than they would have been if they had taken up a simple repayment mortgage. So, even if they could prove that the risks were not explained, they would not be entitled to compensation. However, critics argue that if people, realising that they had been mis-sold an endowment policy, now surrendered the policy and converted to a simple repayment mortgage, they would lose. The chief ombudsman at the Financial Ombudsman Service said that, provided these consumers could show they were mis-advised, they would be entitled to additional compensation for the loss.

On 15 July 2005, the FSA (2005) reported that an independent research report had found that most consumers whose endowment policy was still linked to their mortgage, and who were facing a shortfall, had taken some positive action to deal with it. The 2.2 million households in this position had an average projected shortfall on their mortgage repayment of £7,200 . Sixty-nine per cent of these had taken action to address their situation and a further 14 per cent intended to do so in the future. Just over a million households had restructured their mortgage, savings or endowment; other action taken included seeking advice or pursuing a complaint.

If there remained unhappiness with its behaviour over issues such as these, the FSA could certainly claim in its defence that it had taken advantage of the new provision in the FSMA permitting it to penalise companies for market abuse, giving a clear message to firms in the market that it will not tolerate the mis-selling of products. It has fined several companies for mortgage endowment and other failings. This, the FSA could maintain, will help to overcome problems with the financial services market in the longer term even if all individual problems are not picked up and dealt with as speedily as they might be.

The FSA has also sought to overcome general problems by paying great attention to the objective of consumer awareness. Firms are able to mis-sell products to consumers only because of the high degree of consumer ignorance regarding financial services. Clearly, if the FSA could help to reduce consumer ignorance it would also help to overcome market abuse. Nonetheless, high-profile failures in markets such as the cases dealt with here continue to be a problem for market confidence, the first of the FSA's objectives. See Box 13.5 for a favourable view of the FSA's performance in its first six years expressed in a leading article in the *Financial Times* in June 2006.

Box 13.5 **The regulator judged**

Most employers reward productivity. But it is the curse of regulators that, though they are paid to regulate, the more rules they manufacture or enforce, the more likely they are to be criticised. On the other hand, if a watchdog fails to intervene, it risks being damned for its inaction.

In the six years since it was formally created from a merger of other watchdogs, Britain's Financial Services Authority has largely neutralised this double-edged curse. It has earned a reputation, both at home and abroad, as a successful 'light-touch' authority. Are such accolades well-deserved?

The independent review of the FSA announced this week is unlikely to answer that question directly. The National Audit Office's report will be more of a time-and-motion efficiency study than an attempt to judge the watchdog's overall success in applying its powers. But it is already clear that the FSA has dealt with many of the concerns expressed when it came into being. At the time, the risks of setting up a 'super-regulator' seemed evident. Sceptics warned that the new authority would be too heavy-handed; it would be unable to deal with the differing priorities of wholesale and retail financial services providers and customers; it would hamstring the growth of the City.

There are those who believe the FSA has too frequently succumbed to those risks. Bigger customers of the authority – notably banks and insurers – have a tendency to complain about heavy-handedness. The FSA's consumer panel pointed out earlier this week that the regulator had not championed retail customers' interests sufficiently in five areas of concern.

But critics tend to forget that six years is not a long time for a new regulator to establish a strong and consistent reputation. The FSA has shown enough youthful flexibility to change course if attacks against it are justified – its reform of its enforcement processes last year is one example. Yet it has already demonstrated a maturity that has made it a model for other regulators. Far from diminishing the attractiveness of the UK as a financial centre, the FSA has become an asset, often cited (at least privately) by foreign bankers as a reason for doing business in and with the City.

Credit for the level-headed approach must go to the FSA's leadership, which has avoided the temptation to use the wide powers of the original legislation to create an overbearing regulator. True, the FSA has not yet been tested by a big financial catastrophe or scandal. As Sir Callum McCarthy, its chairman, outlined yesterday, it also faces challenges in reversing the growth of rules and encouraging, in its own staff as well as in those they regulate, greater confidence in a principles-based approach. Vigilance, robust self-criticism and external review will always be necessary. But Sir Callum, Sir Howard Davies, his predecessor, and their management teams have set the FSA on a positive course that even the most incompetent future leaders of the authority will have difficulty reversing.

Source: Leading article, *Financial Times*, 22 June 2006

13.3 The European Union and financial regulation

The 1957 Treaty of Rome, setting up the European Economic Community, set as targets the dismantling of all non-tariff barriers and the free movement of goods and services among members. This included financial services and required the progressive abolition of all restrictions on the freedom to supply services, such as banking, insurance and communications services, across frontiers. It was to be accompanied by the free movement of labour and capital. All discrimination based on nationality was to disappear. However, progress towards these goals was very slow. One major barrier to the achievement of these aims related to the regulation of financial markets. A single financial market across the whole of the European Union clearly required the harmonisation of the regulatory systems of the different countries.

Harmonisation of financial regulations: Requires that all countries agree precisely on a common set of laws.

However, few members were prepared to make concessions regarding their own arrangements. In the absence of harmonisation, great importance was attached to the issue of which regime should apply to a firm when it opened branches in other countries or sold services across borders – the regulations of the home country of the firm or those of the host country in which the firm was locating. The Treaty of Rome had supported host country regulation, and governments and national regulatory authorities clearly preferred this. The political sensitivity of the financial sector meant that national governments wished to oversee the prudential standards of all firms in the domestic market, whatever their country of origin. They were also reluctant to allow national markets in financial services to be dominated by foreign institutions. This led everywhere to action to prevent foreign institutions from competing with domestic financial institutions. Host country regulation made it relatively easy for governments to do this because firms generally need to locate in a country in order to provide financial services within it. Cross-border trade from outside a country, while possible, is much less important in finance than in trade in goods.

To be fair, support for host country regulation did not depend only on fears of foreign competition and on domestic consumer protection issues. In addition, worries existed over competitive distortions resulting from home country regulation, with firms of different nationalities operating in the one country facing regulations of differing degrees of severity and thus with different levels of compliance costs. Yet again, home regulation encourages competitive laxity – in the absence of the harmonisation of regulations, firms are tempted to locate their head offices in the member states with the most producer-friendly regulations.

The early directives on finance from the Council of Ministers were concerned only with the goal of capital mobility and, in particular, with the foreign exchange restrictions on capital movements. The first attack on these restrictions saw the unconditional liberalisation of capital movements associated with foreign trade, foreign direct investment and operations in listed securities. However, governments remained free to impose any restrictions they chose on capital movements related to dealings in money market instruments, short-term financial credits and transactions in bank deposits, while those deriving from the buying and selling of unit trusts and unlisted securities, long-term commercial credits and medium-term financial credits were granted only conditional liberalisation. Even in areas where freedom from restrictions was specified, the directives had little impact. Although they were binding on member governments, the choice of method of achieving the end result was left to individual governments and this allowed scope for many differences in interpretation and practice.

Nonetheless, there was extensive liberalisation of financial markets in the 1960s regarding direct investments, commercial credits and the acquisition of securities on foreign stock exchanges. Yet the 1970s saw this trend reversed in several member states, largely because of the turmoil in international currency markets in the 1970s. Consequently, only a moderate advance towards capital mobility occurred before 1980. In 1979, the UK removed all foreign exchange controls, and in the following few years Germany, the Netherlands and Luxembourg followed suit. Then, as the foreign exchange markets calmed down and, in the middle 1980s, the stability of the European Monetary System increased, exchange controls were eased in other member states.

However, there were barriers to free capital mobility other than foreign exchange controls, and limited capital mobility was only one of many barriers to a single market in financial services. Significant interest rate differentials remained among member states and exchange rate uncertainties returned in the 1990s. The free flow of capital was also hindered by differences in tax regimes among countries, particularly relating to the taxation of profits. The intra-EU mobility of capital was also restricted by differences in capital markets. For example, the takeover of firms was more difficult in Germany than in the Netherlands or the UK, partly because of the role of the major banks as shareholders in Germany. Differences in investor and consumer attitudes may also have been important.

Other important barriers to financial integration in Europe in the 1970s and 1980s were the limitations placed on cross-border trade in financial services and barriers to the free location of financial institutions and other suppliers of financial services. For example, formal authorisation was needed everywhere for the setting up of branches by foreign institutions and, in all countries except the UK, dedicated capital had to be provided. Further, restrictions existed on the acquisition by foreigners of domestic financial firms, especially where major domestic banks were the target of foreign purchase. To this end, most countries required the notification of anything more than minor shareholdings in banks.

The outcome of these various forces was that although competition and integration had become international in some areas of finance such as wholesale banking, other areas such as retail banking and insurance had remained fragmented. Even for corporate business, EU national financial systems were, by the 1980s, far from integrated, with differences remaining between them in regulation, taxation, the competitive environment and the role of the state. Even those firms allowed into the markets of other member states were limited to providing the same range of services that domestic firms were allowed to offer under domestic law. Clearly, host country regulation reinforced other tendencies towards a fragmented and inefficient financial services industry.

Things came to a head in the planning that preceded the Single European Act. The problem of different national regulations had been eased by a European Court case in 1979, which had implied that the Treaty of Rome required the mutual recognition of national laws. This had meant that full harmonisation of national laws was not needed for the movement to a single market. A refusal to recognise the laws of other member states required a demonstration that to do so would cause a threat to public health or the rights of the consumer, or would damage fiscal supervision or the fairness of commercial transactions. Mutual recognition of national laws was much easier to achieve than their harmonisation. The Cockfield Report of 1985 further proposed that, in cases of mutual recognition, regulation would be based on home country requirements. In other words, if two members had different regulations in an area in which the Commission decided that harmonisation was not needed, the regulations of the country in which the financial institution was registered or licensed would apply no matter where it was doing business. This accepted the principle of freedom of establishment and the cross-border provision of services within the EU since an institution authorised in one country would be deemed to be similarly authorised in all other member states.

In areas in which the Commission decided that harmonisation was necessary, it could determine whether national regulations were excessive and constituted a barrier to trade. In the banking sector, for instance, it was agreed that harmonisation of regulation was needed in the following areas: authorisation criteria, minimum capital requirements, the definition of own funds (equity capital), large exposure limits, deposit-protection arrangements, control of the major shareholders in banks, limits on banks' involvement in non-bank sectors, and the quality of accountancy and internal control mechanisms. Everything else was left to mutual recognition.

The Single European Act of 1986 (SEA) set the end of 1992 as the date for removal of all controls, and this was the subject of the Capital Liberalisation Directive, adopted in June 1988. The 1992 Treaty on European Union prohibited all restrictions on the movement of capital and on payments between member states. This does not mean that capital is perfectly mobile. Foreign exchange risk still applies between the eurozone and the EU countries that remain outside it and even within the eurozone small interest rate differentials continue to exist.

13.3.1 Regulation of the banking industry in the EU

The banking industry was one of the most highly regulated industries in the EU and operated with widely varied regulatory practices. In general, barriers to the supply of cross-border services were more of a problem than those related to location. In some countries, laws and regulations restricted the right of non-resident banks and financial institutions to conduct business with residents. Before the SEA, there had been two major directives relating to the banking industry: the First Banking Directive on Co-ordination of Regulations Governing Credit Institutions of 1977; and the 1983 Directive on the Supervision of Credit Institutions on a Consolidated Basis.

The First Banking Directive required member states to establish systems for authorising and supervising banks and other credit institutions that take deposits and lend money. It required such institutions to be licensed. Once licensed, they would be allowed to conduct business in other member countries provided they were authorised to do so by the host government and complied with the conditions and supervision applied to local banks. To be authorised, a credit institution was required to have separate capital from its owners, to meet an initial capital requirement, and to have at least two directors and a reputable and experienced management. However, authorisation could not legally be withheld on the sole ground that the head office was in another member state. As we have seen, the host country principle on which the directive was based meant that a German bank in Spain, for example, could only do what Spanish laws allowed Spanish banks to do in Spain.

The Directive on the Supervision of Credit Institutions on a Consolidated Basis (1983) established the common principle that bank activities were to be supervised, based on their world-wide activities. Thus, capital requirements were to relate to their global balance sheet position, preventing banks from seeking to avoid capital requirements by arranging business through less strictly regulated financial centres. This derived from the growing international concern with the solvency of banks, particularly at the commencement of the international debt crisis of the developing countries.

Since the SEA, there have been a series of directives on the banking industry, most notably the Second Banking Co-ordination Directive of 1989 (SBCD). This was based on the strategy of home country regulation and mutual recognition. It gave the right to banks to establish branches and to trade in financial services throughout the EU based on a single licence obtained from the home country authorities. The directive included some exceptions to home country control. Host countries retained the right to control bank liquidity for monetary policy purposes, and all banks had to comply with host nation consumer protection and similar laws in the public interest. There was some ambiguity in relation to the scope of the consumer protection qualification. However, the directive eliminated the requirement for branches of foreign banks to maintain dedicated capital for their local operations.

The directive covered much else. It set out a detailed list of bank activities to which the directive applied. This was very broad and included much of what is generally included under the heading of securities or investment business in addition to activities more widely considered as banking. This accepted the principle of universal banking on which the German banking industry was organised. The directive established the right of banks with head offices in other EU countries to pursue all the listed activities in a host country, including those that host country laws might forbid to local banks. Essentially, banks were allowed to participate fully in securities business either directly or through subsidiaries. Nonetheless, despite the apparently comprehensive nature of the list, difficulties of interpretation remained.

The directive also included rules regarding the exchange of information between home and host country regulators, and harmonised minimum standards of authorisation and prudential supervision. This included setting minimum requirements for the size of equity capital. The authorities in all countries were given the right to supervise ownership and control to prevent cross-financing and conflicts of interest. Hence, disclosure of the identity of a bank's most important shareholders was required, and limits on banks' shareholdings in other financial and non-financial companies were harmonised.

A number of other directives ancillary to the Second Banking Directive were approved in 1989 and later years in order to meet the harmonisation requirements for banking.

13.3.2 Regulation of the securities markets in the EU

A genuine single financial market across the EU needed to apply much more broadly than to banking. It was accepted that if competition were to be fair for all firms, free access was required to all sources of capital. It was also accepted that if savings were to be utilised as effectively as possible, investors should have free access to all investment products irrespective of their country of origin. With the rapid development of financial markets and the great increase in new financial products from the early 1970s, the securities (or investment) industry (which covers securities trading, unit trusts, broking and market-making, portfolio management, underwriting and investment advice as well as issues related to the access of companies to foreign stock exchanges and the quotation of securities on foreign stock exchanges) was becoming increasingly significant. However, it was also an area in which markets developed much more rapidly in some member states than others. This caused anxiety in some countries that increased competition across the EU would damage, if not destroy, their underdeveloped markets and institutions. Under these circumstances, progress towards a single market was bound to be slow.

Nonetheless, strong efforts were made in some segments of the industry from the late 1970s on, notably in regard to the harmonisation of the different regulations of the member states on the admission of securities to stock exchange listing and the information provided to investors. In 1979, the Directive Co-ordinating the Conditions for the Admission of Securities to Official Stock Exchange Listing set out the minimum conditions to be met by issuers of securities, including minimum issue price, a company's period of existence, free negotiability, sufficient distribution, and the provision of appropriate information to investors. Member states were free to impose stricter requirements. This was the first of four directives (the others followed in 1980 and 1982) that were designed to make it easier for companies to list their shares or raise capital on other EU stock exchanges. Directives concerned with information to investors covered the disclosure of large shareholdings in companies, the provision of information in prospectuses, and insider dealing.

The new principles of minimum harmonisation, mutual recognition, a single passport, and home-country regulation were applied in two directives on the marketing of unit trusts in 1985 and 1988. These allowed a unit trust that had been approved in one member country to be sold anywhere in the EU without further authorisation, provided it met investor protection requirements in force in the host country.

The Investment Services Directive (ISD), which came into force in June 1992, was the first major securities industry directive based on the SEA principles. It extended the single passport principle to non-bank investment firms generally. This extension was essential because the Second Banking Co-ordination Directive had given this right to banks carrying out securities business, but did not grant it to non-banks in this area. There was a particular problem because the banking industry in some member states had traditionally been organised on universal banking principles, whereas in other member states (notably the UK), the two forms of business had been separated. Thus, if the ISD had not been agreed, banks engaged in securities business would have been given a competitive advantage over non-bank firms. The ISD thus provided for the removal of barriers to both the provision of cross-border securities services and the establishment of branches throughout the EU for all firms. It also liberalised the rules governing access to stock exchanges and financial futures and options exchanges.

The difference in the organisation of banking and securities industries among member countries led to problems in relation to capital adequacy. If capital adequacy rules had not been extended to cover non-bank securities firms, they, in their turn, would have been given a competitive advantage over banks engaged in securities business, which were required to meet capital adequacy rules. However, it was widely argued that the same rules should not apply to both forms of business. This ultimately led to the Capital Adequacy Directive (CAD) of 1993 – implemented in January 1996 – which applied both to investment firms and to the securities activities of banks.

One problem with this solution is that the argument for official protection of investment firms is less clear than for banks. A major difference is that the assets of securities houses consist largely of marketable securities, making them much less vulnerable than banks to contagious liquidity and solvency crises. Thus, there is much less chance than in the case of banks that they will cause systemic problems with their associated social costs.

> **Systemic risks:** Risks for the whole of the financial system, probably arising through contagion from problems in individual banks, sectors of the market or countries.

Systemic problems may, of course, arise for banks within a financial market regime characterised by increasing integration of banking and securities business to the extent that banks engage in securities business directly or through a subsidiary, or lend to investment firms. This, however, does not provide a justification for the regulation of separate investment firms. It has been argued that, if both banks and securities houses are to be regulated, different techniques should be applied with the emphasis being on solvency for banks but on liquidity for securities houses.

The Capital Adequacy Directive solution made the securities activities of banks subject to a capital adequacy regime separate from that of their banking business. This approach is known as the *trading book model* since the bank is being required, for the purposes of capital adequacy, to keep its trading business separate from its banking business. The distinction between the *trading book* and the *banking book* of banks is that the trading book covers trading for short-term gain, while the banking book relates to longer-term investment or hedging. Only certain types of instrument can be held in the trading book, but some types of instrument can be held in either the trading book or the banking book depending on the purpose for which it is being held. A single instrument cannot be held simultaneously in both books. Items held in the banking book are subject to the risk-weighting scheme described in section 13.4. Items in the trading book are subject to capital charges. The size of these capital charges varies with the nature of the risk. The capital charges for all trading book items are added together and a measure known as Notional Risk Weighted Assets is produced. This allows the capital adequacy requirement for both the banking and trading books to be expressed as a single unit.

> **Trading book:** The securities and investment activities of banks, until recently not regarded as a normal part of banking business in the UK.

The approach of the Capital Adequacy Directive ensures competitive equality between the securities arms of universal banks and separate investment firms, but in so doing it assumes that banks engaged in securities business can genuinely prevent problems in one part of its activities from spreading to the other. It has been suggested that this approach puts competitive equality before that of the soundness and stability of the system.

13.3.3 Regulation of insurance services in the EU

As with other financial services, the insurance industry has always been highly regulated. The special features of insurance have also, until quite recently, favoured local insurance companies. The combination of these factors ensured the fragmentation of the insurance industry into a number of relatively isolated national markets. With the exception of reinsurance, which deals with very large and often international risks, the insurance industry has, in all EU countries other than the UK, been well protected from foreign competition.

From the beginning, the European Commission acknowledged the additional problems associated with the long average length of contracts in life insurance by the issuing of separate directives for life and non-life insurance. Hence, 1973 saw the promulgation of the First Non-Life Insurance Directive. The First Life Insurance Directive followed in 1979. Both of these directives followed the principle of host country regulation. They established the right for companies to operate in other member states, but harmonisation of regulations across the EU was slow. Several members strongly resisted attempts to open their insurance markets to greater competition. In Germany, for example, non-German firms were required to have a local establishment and were taxed at rates that the European Commission considered discriminatory. In 1986, the European Court of Justice ruled that the restrictions imposed on insurance companies from other member states by Germany, France, Ireland and Denmark were partly illegal. In particular, the Court attacked the practice of requiring establishment and local authorisation before a company could participate in the co-insurance of large risks situated outside its home country.

This court ruling, together with the increased role for qualified majority voting introduced in the Single European Act, encouraged the European Commission to attempt to incorporate the home country regulation principle into insurance directives. It was, however, inhibited from replacing the requirement of full harmonisation of the rules regarding the authorisation of companies by mutual recognition because of the sensitivity of the consumer protection issue in a significant part of the insurance industry.

The Commission tackled the problem by following a 1986 European Court of Justice ruling that had made a distinction between the insurance of large risks (including all marine, transport and aviation risk) and small commercial risks and personal insurance. Whereas host country regulation was preserved for the latter category, the Commission felt able to apply the home country regulation principle to the former category on the grounds that large companies or people responsible for insuring large risks were much better able to collect and assess information about insurance companies than was the average consumer.

Thus, in the Freedom of Services Directive for Non-Life Insurance, the regulations of the country in which the policyholder resides apply for small-risk business, while for large-risk business the regulations of the country in which the company is licensed apply. Large-risk business was defined to cover policies for companies with more than 500 employees or more than £15m turnover. Motor insurance was brought within the scope of the Non-Life Directive by the Motor Insurance Services Directive of 1990.

The distinction between large and small risks could not be made in the Second Life Assurance Directive, so a different distinction was made to allow an element of home country regulation. Host country regulation applied except where the initiative for a cross-border policy came from the policyholder rather than the company – then home country regulation applied. That is, it is assumed that if a consumer seeks a cross-border policy, he is aware of the regulatory differences between his own country and the country that has authorised the company to trade. Host countries also retained responsibility for the regulation of branches of foreign companies, although 'well-established' companies covering large risks were, under the terms of the directive, simply required to notify the host authorities of their intention to provide services in the host country.

Despite continued resistance from some members and problems over the distortion of competition by different tax relief treatment on premiums, the Commission pushed ahead and in July 1994 the Third Non-Life Insurance Directive, the Third Motor Insurance Directive and the Third Life Assurance Directive came into force, introducing the full single passport, home regulation regime to the insurance industry, although derogations giving extra time for implementation were granted to Spain, Portugal and Greece. Although the home country regulation now applies, a role has been retained for host institutions. In practice, most insurance companies will establish a local presence because of the need to provide follow-up customer sales and service. Local rules on sales techniques and advertising apply but cannot be used to discriminate against foreign companies. In certain circumstances, host states can exercise control over particular products, for instance mandatory third-party motor insurance. Finally, policyholders will be protected by the application of domestic contract law.

13.4 The problems of globalisation and the growing complexity of derivatives markets

A major development causing problems for regulators has been the globalisation of financial markets. Since 1980, there has been rapid growth in the stock of cross-border bank assets and cross-border securities transactions. A quarter of stock market trades world-wide involve either a foreign security or a foreign counterparty. Both the size and the interdependence of markets now pose problems. The Bank for International Settlements (BIS) has warned that essentially local events might have disruptive implications for the whole international financial system. The globalisation of the banking industry, for example, led to a great increase in international interbank lending and increased dramatically the possibility that the collapse of a bank in one country could cause serious losses for banks in other countries.

Globalisation has also caused fears of competitive laxity among national regulatory authorities. A national authority may feel that regulation which is too strict would leave its own country's firms at a competitive disadvantage in comparison with firms based in countries with less stringent rules. Since much of the financial services industry is footloose, strict regulation in one country may cause firms to move their operations to other countries, possibly resulting in a considerable loss of income and employment to the country attempting to operate a responsible regulatory regime. To the extent that regulations are loosened everywhere and/or that firms do move to more poorly regulated areas, the level of systemic risk through contagious financial disorders may be increased.

Financial innovation and rapid technological change in the financial services industry have posed yet more problems for regulators. The development of screen-based trading systems, securitisation and the rapid growth in the availability of new, sophisticated derivatives have all complicated the job of the authorities. Particular concern has been expressed over the growth of off-balance-sheet risk and the risk posed by fast-changing on-balance-sheet positions. The traditional regulatory, accounting and legal framework for financial organisations, which depended on the regular scrutiny of balance sheets, has been left behind by such developments.

Securitisation: Transformation of non-marketable assets into marketable instruments.

Because of these various concerns, a standing committee of bank supervisors under the auspices of the BIS was established in December 1974. The committee comprised representatives of the bank supervisors of the eleven Group of Ten (G10) countries* together with Luxembourg. Its formal title was the Committee on Banking Regulation and Supervisory Practices, but it is better known as the Basel Committee. It sought to link together the regulatory regimes in different countries in order to ensure that all banks were supervised according to certain broad principles.

The initial task of the committee was to draw up guidelines for the division of responsibilities among national supervisory authorities. This led to the Basel Concordat of December 1975. The Concordat distinguished between 'host' and 'parent' authorities and between branches and subsidiaries of foreign banks. Under the Concordat, the supervision of foreign banking establishments was to be the joint responsibility of parent and host authorities. Host authorities were to be responsible for the supervision of the liquidity of foreign banks. Solvency was to be the responsibility of the parent authority in the case of foreign branches and of the host authority in the case of foreign subsidiaries. Great stress was laid upon the exchange of information between host and parent authorities.

---

* US, UK, Japan, Germany, France, Italy, Canada, Netherlands, Belgium, Sweden and Switzerland.

The Concordat was voluntary but all countries represented on the committee adopted its rules. There was, however, a good deal of confusion over the interpretation of the rules. The different supervisory standards among countries also led some countries, notably the US, to be more reluctant than others to share or delegate supervisory responsibilities. The collapse of Banco Ambrosiano's Luxembourg subsidiary in the summer of 1982 caused particular concern as neither the Luxembourg nor the Italian authorities would accept responsibility for either supervision or emergency support of the bank.

In an attempt to overcome such problems, the Concordat was revised in 1983, with the revision being based upon the principle of consolidated supervision and provisions designed to ensure adequate supervisory standards. The aim was to encourage national authorities to lock out foreign banks originating from permissive jurisdictions and to prevent their own banks from conducting their international operations from poorly regulated centres. The adoption of the principle of consolidated supervision was intended to make the solvency of foreign subsidiaries a joint responsibility of parent and host authorities. Foreign bank subsidiaries were required to be financially sound in their own right, while also being supervised as integral parts of the group to which they belonged. Responsibility for the supervision of liquidity of both foreign branches and subsidiaries was to remain with host authorities. The new agreement also introduced more precise guidelines for the supervision of holding companies.

Problems remained and these were highlighted by the pressure placed on the international banking system by the debt crisis of the developing countries during the early 1980s. When, early in 1982, the Mexican government declared a moratorium on debt repayments, there was a potential crisis not only for those banks that had lent Mexico vast amounts over the previous eight years but also for the whole international financial system. If Mexico had continued to default on its repayments and if other countries had followed suit, a number of banks would have been wiped out. This possibility raised the spectre of the contagious bankruptcy of many other banks. The IMF, the World Bank and the US combined to help banks out of these particular problems, but the view took hold that a degree of harmonisation of supervisory standards was needed among national regulatory authorities.

The principal outcome of this was the Basel minimum capital adequacy guidelines for international banks approved in July 1988. As mentioned in section 13.2.2, these established common prudential risk-adjusted ratios for banks to apply from the beginning of 1993. In discussing the risk–asset approach above, we mentioned the need to define the elements of capital for supervisory purposes. The Basel agreement initially distinguished between two types of capital:

- *Tier I capital (core capital)* consists principally of shareholders' equity, disclosed reserves and the current year's retained profits, which are readily available to cushion losses.

- *Tier II capital (supplementary capital)* comprises funds available but not fully owned or controlled by the institution, such as 'general' provisions that the bank has set aside against unidentified future losses and medium- or long-term subordinated debt issued by the bank.

Tier II capital cannot be greater than 50 per cent of total Tier I and Tier II capital for the purposes of calculating the risk–asset ratio. A third type of capital (Tier III) was later defined. It consists of:

- subordinated debt of at least two years' maturity that is subject to a 'lock-in' clause (that is, it can only be repaid with the regulatory authority's permission if repayment would cause the bank to breach the required capital ratio); and

- accumulated profit arising from the trading book (that is, securities and invest-ment activities not traditionally regarded in the UK as banking business).

The weights to be attached to bank assets included cash 0; loans to the discount market 0.1; interbank lending 0.2; home mortgage loans 0.5; other commercial loans 1. The Basel Committee proposed a lower limit of 8 per cent for the ratio of total capital to risk-adjusted assets, though national bank supervisors had some dis-cretion in applying this to different types of banks and countries were free to impose a higher minimum requirement on their own banks. In the UK, the FSA sets each UK-incorporated bank a separate target minimum capital adequacy requirement for both its banking and investment business, with an 8 per cent risk–asset ratio being an absolute minimum requirement for all banks.

The Basel Accord also made allowance for off-balance-sheet credit exposures, which are converted into balance sheet equivalent amounts using a formula that takes account of the likely extent of the default risk involved. Box 13.6 provides a simplified example of the calculation of risk–asset ratios.

Box 13.6 | **Risk–asset ratios and off-balance-sheet activities – a simplified example**

A bank had the following set of assets:

Asset	Face value	Risk weighting	Risk-weighted value
Cash	50	0	0
Loans to discount market	150	0.1	15
Interbank loans	300	0.2	60
Home mortgage loans	1,550	0.5	775
Loans to small and medium-sized firms	2,150	1	2,150
Total			3,000

Under the rules of the Basel Accord of 1988, the bank was required to hold a minimum of 8 per cent of its risk-weighted assets as capital for regulatory purposes, 50 per cent of which had to be in the form of Tier I capital. Thus, it was required to hold 8 per cent of 3000 = 240. Tier II capital gives greater flexibility than Tier I capital and the bank chooses to do no more than meet the minimum requirement. Thus, it holds 120 in Tier I capital and 120 in Tier II capital.

The bank then decides to increase its competitiveness by holding less capital and to seek to make up for any lost income through securitisation and acting in the swaps market. It takes two steps:

- It securitises its home mortgage loans, removing them from its balance sheet and increases its loans to firms, which earn a higher rate of interest.
- It acts as a guarantor for swap deals to the value of 500, which also does not appear on the balance sheet.

The bank's risk-weighted balance sheet position now is:

Asset	Face value	Risk weighting	Risk-weighted value
Cash	50	0	0
Loans to discount market	150	0.1	15
Interbank loans	300	0.2	60
Loans to small and medium-sized firms	2,425	1	2,425
Total			2,500

The bank now has to hold only 200 capital and is able to reduce its Tier I capital to 100. Funds that previously had to be kept readily available to cushion possible losses could be used more productively.

When one takes into account the risk associated with the securitised home mortgages and the interest rate swaps together with the increase in loans to firms, it seems clear that the bank now faces more risk than previously. Yet it was required under the Basel Capital Accord of 1988 to hold less capital against the possibility of default. It is easy to see why this type of activity worried the Basel Committee and led to the proposals in the New Basel Capital Accord regarding securitised assets.

The agreement sought both to strengthen the soundness and stability of the international banking system and to ensure competitive equality among international banks. The accord incorporated capital requirements for over-the-counter derivatives (see Chapter 9), with the capital adequacy requirement being determined by estimates of current and potential credit exposure, taking into account the nature of the counterparty.

Other developments followed. In April 1990, an addendum to the Basel Concordat encouraged more regular and structured collaboration between supervisors. In the same year, the Committee tried to deal with the single most important cause of bank failures: excessive concentration of default risk. It did this by recommending common definitions and procedures related to large exposures, recommending maximum limits on single exposures of 25 per cent of the capital base.

That serious problems remained, however, became clear with the forced closure of the Bank of Credit and Commerce International (BCCI) in July 1991. BCCI's corporate structure was based on a non-bank holding company in Luxembourg which owned two separate banking networks incorporated in Luxembourg and the Cayman Islands. The holding company was unregulated and so consolidated supervision of the group was not possible, allowing BCCI to hide its problems by shifting assets between national jurisdictions. The Basel Committee responded to the BCCI affair by issuing a set of minimum standards for the supervision of international banks.

Meanwhile, other problems were coming to the fore, particularly with the rapid growth in derivatives trading world-wide. The speed at which risks of derivatives can be transformed and the complexity of the transformation process results in a loss of transparency. This makes risk assessment much more difficult and weakens both market discipline and regulatory oversight, leading to greatly increased systemic risks. Risk was increased also because end-users frequently did not understand how derivatives worked, and the management of banks and securities houses often did not understand what their dealers were doing. This last problem is magnified to the extent that pay systems reward traders hugely for success in achieving profits and provide them with little incentive to follow cautious strategies. Finally, there were concerns over the concentration of derivatives trading among a few major financial institutions, with the possibility that the failure of a large derivatives dealer could both inflict large losses on counterparties and damage the liquidity of the derivatives market.

One approach to the potential increase in default risk has been to encourage the use of netting agreements, which create a single legal obligation covering multiple transactions between two counterparties, allowing them to reduce both the amount and the number of payments in comparison to settlements on a gross basis. In the US, the International Swap Dealers Association (ISDA) drew up a master agreement that allows an intermediary to reconcile all of its transactions with a defaulted counterparty and come up with a final net payment, permitting the amount of capital set aside to support the business to be reduced by 50 per cent, since the capital adequacy rules have to be applied only to the net value of transactions payments. In line with this, the Basel Committee amended the 1988 Accord by reducing the capital that must be held against those credit exposures subject to bilateral netting, as long as banks are able to demonstrate to their supervisors the legal enforceability of netting arrangements in all relevant jurisdictions. Regulators have also acted to include derivatives transactions in large exposure limits, along with conventional on-balance-sheet exposures.

This still left market risk, not treated at all in the 1988 Accord, to be dealt with. In April 1993 the Basel Committee (1993) published proposals for minimum capital requirements to cover banks' exposure to market fluctuations. Derivatives were to be converted into positions in the relevant underlying asset and become subject to capital requirements designed to capture specific and general market risk. This approach is explained in section 13.3 in relation to the EU's capital adequacy directive. It was criticised on the grounds that static capital adequacy rules could not capture the risk profiles of individual institutions. A more sophisticated approach was proposed, making use of the complex risk management models used by the major derivatives dealers. The role of regulators would be to validate the models and set the risk parameters used in the estimate of the overall value-at-risk against which capital must be held.

In July 1994, the Basel Committee (1994) and the International Organisation of Securities Commissions (IOSCO) produced a joint policy statement on the oversight of the risk management process by senior management; the measurement, control and reporting of risk exposures; and the internal controls and audits re risk management. In April 1995, following the collapse of Barings (see Box 9.5), the Basel Committee agreed to allow banks to use their own computer models to assess the risks arising from market volatility, rather than complying with standardised measures of volatility and risk for particular financial instruments. In addition, for the first time, capital charges were required to cover commodities risks. The Committee later supported a number of steps to improve the quality of risk management. These included stress tests that examine the overall impact of a worse case scenario (such as a repeat of the 1987 stock market crash) on a bank's capital base. In addition, it supported the separation of the trading and settlement arms of banks' trading divisions.

There are still worries about the reliability of the computer models concerning the more complex derivatives products and about the ability of regulators to evaluate the models. It is also feared that the use of the models will greatly reduce the transparency of financial markets because only banks and regulators will know the basis on which risks have been measured.

In June 1999, the Basel Committee issued a proposal for a new, capital adequacy framework that will replace the 1988 accord and be known as the New Basel Capital Accord or Basel II. The original Basel framework is now known as Basel I. Following consultation, a modified proposal was published in January 2001. Yet further consultations were needed with the industry, however, and a third version was published in April 2003. The present plan is for the new accord to go into operation from the end of 2006. Basel II will apply to large complex organisations. In the US, for example, one or two dozen banks are expected to move to Basel II at the end of 2006. Other banks will remain Basel I institutions but amendments are also being made to Basel I to enhance the risk sensitivity of the Basel I rules and to mitigate potential competitive distortions from the introduction of Basel II.

The Basel II rules incorporate the use of internal risk models to assess credit risk, the allowance for market risk and operational risk in the standardised calculation of the risk–asset ratio, and attempts to deal with the greater use of off-balance-sheet asset securitisation by banks.

The new capital framework consists of three pillars:

- Minimum capital requirements, developing and expanding on the standardised rules set forth in the 1988 Accord.
- A supervisory review of an institution's capital adequacy and internal assessment process.
- The effective use of market discipline to strengthen disclosure and encourage safe and sound banking practices.

The three pillars are seen as part of a single package and are to be implemented together. Basel II has been designed to improve the extent to which regulatory capital requirements reflect underlying risks and to address specifically the financial innovation that has occurred in recent years. It also aims to reward the improvements in risk management and control and to provide incentives for these to continue.

Basel II retains the standardised formula for the risk-weighting of assets and makes no changes to the definition of capital. The minimum ratio of capital to risk-weighted assets including operational and market risks will remain at 8 per cent for total capital. Tier II capital will continue to be limited to 50 per cent of total Tier I and Tier II capital. Under the New Basel Accord, the denominator of the ratio will consist of two parts:

● the sum of all risk-weighted assets for credit risk; plus

● 12.5 times the sum of the capital charges for market risk and operational risk.

Assuming that a bank has $875 of risk-weighted assets, a market risk capital charge of $10 and an operational risk capital charge of $20, the denominator of the total capital ratio would equal $875 + [(10 + 20) \times 12.5)]$ or $1250.*

The major difference from the 1988 Accord lies in the adoption of an internal-ratings-based (IRB) approach, which places greater emphasis on banks' own assessment of the risks to which they are exposed. The IRB approach aims to be more sensitive to different kinds and degrees of risk, allowing the incorporation of a much wider range of assets. It is to be introduced at two levels: foundation and advanced. A foundation IRB approach combines a significant external assessment of risk factors with elements of a bank's own risk assessment. Thus, banks that meet robust supervisory standards will make their own assessment of the probability of default associated with assets, but estimates of additional risk factors, such as the expected exposure of the bank if a default occurs, will be made externally through the application of standardised supervisory estimates. The advanced IRB approach will be available to banks that meet even more rigorous supervisory standards and will allow more of the risk components to be estimated internally by the bank. However, the Committee has stopped short of permitting banks to calculate fully their capital requirements on the basis of their own portfolio credit risk models.

The Basel Committee, while acknowledging that asset securitisation can be an efficient way for a bank to redistribute its credit risks to other banks and non-bank investors, has become increasingly worried by the way in which some banks have used it to avoid holding a sufficient level of capital for their risk exposures. Thus, the New Basel Capital Accord develops standardised and IRB approaches for treating the explicit risks that securitisations pose for banks, setting out operational, disclosure and minimum capital requirements for them.

---

* This example is taken from *Overview of the New Basel Capital Accord* published by the Basel Committee on Banking Supervision (Basel: BIS, January 2001).

Basel II does not aim to increase the total amount of regulatory capital required by banks but there are likely to be changes among banks. Big banks with sophisticated risk management systems should be able to hold less capital and therefore strengthen their competitive position. On the other hand, some banks might have to hold more capital than under the old rules to reflect the wider range of risks considered and a more finely tuned assessment of the credit risk associated with different types of asset. The calculation of credit risk will also depend on how exposed a bank is to a single borrower or sector. Further, for the first time, there will be a requirement to hold capital to cover operating risk. Securitised loans will need more capital set aside than in the past unless the risk is completely transferred out of the bank. However, there will be greater allowance for factors that reduce risk, such as collateral or guarantees.

The banking industry has expressed two concerns about the new approach. The first, given the use of IRB approaches, is that the rules should be evenly and consistently applied between different banks and regulatory authorities. To try to ensure this, the new accord includes an extensive auditing system and enhanced requirements for disclosure.

The second concern is that Basel II might increase the pro-cyclical impact inherent in any credit risk approach to capital requirements – encouraging banks to lend when economies are doing well but discouraging loans in recessions, thus making economic cycles more pronounced. Under Basel I, this happened because more loans become problematic during recessions and the valuation of banks' capital falls, requiring banks to set aside more regulatory capital to maintain the minimum capital asset ratio. Under Basel II, this will continue to happen but, in addition, the more sensitive assessment of risk applied to assets will increase the calculation of risk-weighted assets. That is, in a recession, the numerator of the ratio will fall and the denominator will rise, making it more difficult for banks to make new loans. The reverse will happen in booms.

The European Commission has followed developments in the Basel Accord. In May 1996 it proposed the amendment of the First Banking Directive, the Solvency Ratio Directive and the Capital Adequacy Directive (see section 13.3) to change supervisory rules for banks to introduce more sophisticated capital requirements for default risks involved in OTC derivatives in line with the Basel Committee changes. The Solvency Ratio Directive was also amended in 1996 to encourage bilateral netting agreements, allowing the offsetting of mutual claims and liabilities from OTC derivatives contracts.

We can sum up by saying that regulation of financial services faces many serious problems and may, under certain circumstances, make matters worse. We have seen, however, that self-regulation does not provide a simple remedy for such problems. Government regulators have no choice but to work with the industry itself in the operation of regulatory regimes, but a strong case remains for regulatory bodies that are external to the industry. Certainly, the difficulties of regulation do not justify complete deregulation of the industry. It has been frequently argued by those in favour of deregulation that financial markets are not different in kind from other markets but only in degree and so should not be treated differently. However, large differences in degree are equivalent to differences in kind. Financial markets are of great importance to the economy as a whole and to a large number of individual consumers. Views about their regulation cannot satisfactorily be derived from the treatment of non-financial markets.

13.5 Summary

The financial services industry has always been heavily regulated. This has been particularly true of banking because of the vulnerability of banks to a loss of public confidence. The collapse of a single bank arouses fears of contagion, causing problems for the banking industry as a whole and hence for the provision of the economy's medium of exchange. Important consumer protection issues also arise in the failure of banks.

The general case for regulation is based upon the existence of various types of market failure, notably the existence of asymmetric information; while strong arguments against regulation are centred on the ideas of moral hazard, agency capture and compliance costs. Regulation increases the costs of entry and exit for new firms and thus may inhibit competition. In some circumstances, regulation may even increase the instability of an industry. A compromise position is to support regulation but to argue in favour of self-regulation on the grounds that practitioners have an interest in maintaining the reputation of their industry and are in the best position to understand the impact of regulation on the industry. Nonetheless, several problems have emerged in self-regulatory schemes. Self-regulation was tried for the financial services industry in the UK from 1986 to 1997 but did not operate well and the industry was beset by scandals. Consequently, there has been a move back towards statutory regulation, with the establishment in June 1998 of the FSA. From that time, the FSA has also become responsible for the supervision of banking under the Bank of England Act 1998, which gave the Bank full control of UK monetary policy.

The attempt to develop a single financial market across the EU also presented regulatory problems as the different regulatory regimes in member countries were a major obstacle to the integration of the markets. The slow progress in the harmonisation of regulatory procedures led to the acceptance of the mutual recognition and home country regulation principles. Extra problems were caused by the different banking traditions in member countries.

Other serious difficulties have arisen as a result of globalisation and the rapid development of complex derivatives markets. A major outcome of concerns over these issues has been the Basel Accord, which has led to the wide acceptance of capital adequacy rules that at the time of writing are being modified to take account of off-balance-sheet business and market risk.

Questions for discussion

1 What have been the impacts on financial markets of: (a) internationalisation of the markets, and (b) technological change?

2 Consider the arguments for and against self-regulation of financial markets as opposed to statutory regulation.

3 Discuss the extent to which consumers can be held to be responsible for their own difficulties in cases such as split capital investment trusts, endowment mortgages and the Lloyd's of London 'names'.

4 How important is moral hazard as a determinant of people's behaviour? Provide examples of moral hazard related both to everyday life and to the financial services industry.

5 Under what circumstances might regulation decrease rather than increase the stability of an industry?

6 List the arguments in favour of host country regulation and discuss them. Why did the European Commission favour home country regulation?

7 Explain the basis of the distinction between the types of capital in the Basel Concordat.

8 Why is it thought that simple capital adequacy ratios are insufficient as a basis for supervising the activities of firms engaged in securities trading?

9 What aspects of the regulatory problem were highlighted by the collapse of Baring's Bank in 1995?

10 What is meant by systemic risk in connection with the banking industry?

11 Why is consumer protection such an important issue in insurance?

Further reading

Basel Committee on Banking Supervision, *Supervisory Recognition of Netting for Capital Adequacy Purposes*, Consultation Proposal (Geneva: Bank for International Settlements, April 1993)

Basel Committee on Banking Supervision, *Risk Management Guidelines for Derivatives* (Geneva: Bank for International Settlements, July 1994)

R Dale, *Risk and Regulation in Global Securities Markets* (Chichester: John Wiley & Sons, 1996)

FSA, 'Endowments – consumers act but FSA keeps close eye on complaints', FSA Press Release, FSA/PNO8I/2005, 15 July 2005, www.fsa.gov.uk/pages/Library/communication/PR/2005

FSA, 'Mortgage endowments – shortfalls and consumer action', prepared for the FSA by IFF Research Ltd, July 2005, www.fsa.gov.uk/pubs/consumer-research

D Gowland, *The Regulation of Financial Markets in the 1990s* (Aldershot: Edward Elgar, 1990)

H S Houthakker and P J Williamson, *The Economics of Financial Markets* (Oxford: Oxford University Press, 1996) ch. 11

S A Rhoades, 'Banking acquisitions', in P Newman, M Milgate and J Eatwell (eds), *The New Palgrave Dictionary of Money and Finance* (London: Macmillan, 1992)

Financial Services Authority at http://www.fsa.gov.uk

Financial Ombudsman Service at http://www.financial-ombudsman.org.uk

http://www.ex.ac.uk/~Rdavies/arian/scandals for details of past financial scandals

http://www.ft.com for up-to-date information on regulatory practices and problems

Portfolio theory

Objectives

What you will learn in this appendix:

- How to find the present value of a fixed sum of money due for payment at a future date
- How to find the present value of a future stream of payments
- How to make allowance for risk in the valuing of these payments
- How to calculate a price for risky and risk-free assets

In section 1.1.1 we noted that choosing a financial product was rather different from choosing everyday consumer goods because the benefits from a financial product often stretch quite a long way into the future and, since the future is uncertain, those benefits would also have a degree of uncertainty attached to them. In this appendix we set out some rules which enable us to make decisions about the value of assets which yield *future* and *uncertain* benefits.

Because the benefits of most financial assets are uncertain, the assets are said to be risky: the return that we actually get may be different from the return that we expect. In financial analysis we assume that people are rational, risk-averse wealth maximisers. 'Risk-averse' means that they prefer less risk to more. Other things being equal, a high-risk asset is less attractive than a low-risk one. When it comes to pricing assets, therefore, we would expect to find, as a general rule, that in a range of assets *differentiated solely by risk*, the higher the risk associated with an asset, the lower its price is likely to be. This is an important piece of common sense that we should keep close to hand throughout the following discussion.

Risk: The probability that a future outcome will differ from the expected outcome.

Notice that in practice 'time' and 'risk' go together. Outcomes are uncertain (and may therefore differ from the expected) precisely because they lie in the future. However, for the purposes of understanding how to value uncertain future income payments, we shall proceed in a series of steps. In section A1.1 we deal with the valuation of future payments (both lump sum and a series) *as though the payments were known with certainty*. In section A1.2 we look at how risk affects the return that we require from an asset and thus at how risk affects our valuation of assets.

Note that the techniques we are about to discuss can be applied to the valuation of *any* asset generating a future stream of benefits. The finance director of a large corporation, for example, who may be considering a major investment in new plant and equipment, needs to put a value on the likely future earnings from that equipment in order to compare those earnings with the present cost of the project. The following techniques are entirely appropriate for that purpose. There is nothing special about the techniques that restricts their use only to risky financial assets.

A1.1 Discounting future payments

It is a fundamental principle of finance (and economics) that:

Any payment received at some point in the future is worth less than the same payment received today.

A simple way of appreciating this from a personal point of view is to consider the offer of a financial gift from a generous aunt. Would we prefer to receive £1,000 now or wait until next birthday, which might involve waiting for 364 days? Most people would opt for the gift now, but if we think it makes little difference, we have only to think how we would feel if we had to wait five years! If we agree that we would rather have the payment now, we are in effect saying that we value the payment less highly if we have to wait for it. This raises the crucial question of *why* we prefer payment now, and it is crucial because the answer may give us some way of quantifying the amount of 'sacrifice' involved in waiting. What is it about 'waiting' that we do not like?

The fundamental reason is that having the payment *now* gives us the use of it *now*. For example, if we have the payment now, instead of in two years' time, we can buy goods (for example) which will give us two years of their benefits, which we would not otherwise have. The 'sacrifice' involved in waiting is the two years' worth of benefits. If we now think not about goods but about financial assets, we can say that the reason for wanting payment now is that we could use the payment *now* to buy other financial assets which give us their advantages right away. Once again, the sacrifice would be the forgoing of those advantages, for two years in the present example.

If we understand this, we can begin to see how we might put a value upon the cost or sacrifice involved in waiting for further payment and thus how we might adjust our valuation of a future payment to take account of the waiting. Consider again the loss of benefits in not being able to buy our financial assets now if we have to wait for payment in two years' time. What are the benefits forgone? Rather obviously, it depends upon the assets which we would have bought. But let us consider the very least that we would have lost.

If we had the use of the payment now, we could use the payment to buy interest-earning assets. What is forgone, therefore, is the interest on those assets. So far, so good, but there are many rates of interest. High rates are paid on risky assets while lower rates are paid on less risky ones (remember that investors are assumed to be risk-averse and so they need a higher reward to induce them to hold the riskier assets). Which of these many interest rates should we use?

In the present case we are assuming that the future payments are known *with certainty*. In effect, therefore, we are saying that the future payments are risk-free: it is only the delay (not risk) that causes us to adjust their value downwards. If we want to find the cost of waiting for payments from any source, we have to ask what return we could have had from investing the payment (if it were available now) in assets *of similar risk*. In the present case, therefore, the appropriate rate of interest is that which could be earned on some zero-risk asset. (Assets which have strictly zero risk are, in practice, hard to find, but we might take something like a three-month treasury bill. The interest payable on it is fixed, the government is unlikely to default and, if the bill is held to redemption, its maturity value is also certain.) If we are trying to put a price on waiting for risk-free payments it makes no sense to assume that, if we had the payment now, we could invest it at the very high rate of return which might be available on very risky assets. This is just not comparing like with like. Let us assume that the two-year risk-free rate of interest is 5 per cent. Then, if the payment were available to us now, we could have earned 5 per cent on it over the next year and then another 5 per cent on that (already larger) sum.

Notice how the benefits forgone mount up over time. The loss in the second year of waiting is bigger than the loss in the first year because we calculate it not on the original payment but on the original payment already increased by 5 per cent. The effect is to make the losses increase quite sharply as the length of time increases. Remember, though, that we are not concerned to calculate the losses as such; only as a means of making a downward adjustment to our valuation of a payment if we have to wait for it. Put like this, we can say that time and interest rates can have a dramatic (downward) effect on our valuation of a future payment if it lies a long way in the future. When we make this adjustment to the value of a future payment we are said to be calculating its *present value*.

Present value: The value now of a sum of money due for payment at some point in the future.

How do we do it? Remember that the cost of waiting involves two elements: a rate of interest which we could have earned if we had the payment available now *and* the length of time which we have to wait. The simplest adjustment is required when we wish to find the present value of a single payment (a 'lump sum') due for payment at a date in the future. If we let A stand for the amount, i for the rate of interest that could be earned, and n for the number of periods for which we have to wait, the present value of this amount can be found as follows:

$$PV = \frac{A}{(1 + i)^n}$$

(A1.1)

Notice how the rate of interest and the length of waiting combine to reduce the present value of the future payment. Both appear in the denominator so that as they get bigger, the denominator gets larger and present value is reduced. The value of $A \div (1 + i)^n$ can be found from discount tables such as those in Appendix II. The table assumes that $A = £1$. Each row of figures gives us the present value of £1 paid at a given time in future, for different interest rates; reading down a column gives us the present value of £1 at a given rate of interest, but for different periods of waiting. The table clearly shows how the present value diminishes both as interest rates increase and as the waiting term increases. (To see the most dramatic effect, read along a diagonal from top left to bottom right. The present value of £1 diminishes very quickly!) Alternatively, we can find the present value by using a calculator. Exercise A1.1 demonstrates the effect of changing both the rate of interest and the term.

Exercise A1.1

(a) Find the present value of £1,000 to be received in two years' time if the current rate of interest is 5 per cent.

(b) Repeat the calculation for a rate of interest of 6 per cent.

(c) Now calculate the present value if the rate of interest were still 5 per cent but the payment were to be received in four years' time.

Notice the effect of both the level of interest rates and time.

Answers at end of appendix

What we have just seen, then, is that any payment received in future is worth less than the same payment received now. Furthermore, we can place a value on the cost of waiting and we can use this cost to calculate the *present value of the future payment*. This process is known as *discounting* and the rate, i, used in the calculation is known as the *rate of discount* or discount rate. If we ignore any risk that might be attached to the future payments we might discount them simply by using a risk-free rate of interest currently available on assets whose life is similar to the period for which we have to wait. The reason for choosing this rate is that it represents the return that we could have had by investing the payment if it had been available to us now.

Discounting: The process of determining the present value of a sum of money promised at some point in the future.

We have seen that the rate of discount which we use represents the cost of waiting for the payment(s). The rate that we choose must be a reasonable approximation of what we could have earned by investing the payment if it were available now in an asset of similar risk. But consider this: if the discount rate is the rate we could have earned by investing the payment if it were available now, then the discount rate must also be the rate of return which we require from the asset that generates the payment – otherwise we would not hold it. In other words, *the rate at which we discount future earnings from an asset is also the rate of return which we require from that asset to make it worth holding*. Consider Exercise A1.1 again. We assumed there that if the future payment were available to us now, we could earn 5 per cent. The cost to us, in other words, of holding the asset and waiting for payment reduces the present value of the £1,000 payment to £907. In the circumstances, we are saying, we would be happy to pay £907 to acquire an asset which would pay us £1,000 in two years' time (or, alternatively that we would be happy to hold that asset if we had already bought it). This is because the return we could earn on £907 over two years would make its future value equal to £1,000, the sum that we do expect to get in two years. Suppose, however, that it became possible to earn 6 per cent interest on some other asset. Then we could sell (or not buy) the first asset and invest the £907 elsewhere to earn:

$$£907 \times 1.06 \times 1.06 = £907 \times 1.06^2 = £1,019$$

We should be better off in two years' time (by £19) if we were to sell (or not buy) the first asset for £907 and reinvest £907 at 6 per cent. In the circumstances, there would be no demand at £907 for an asset yielding £1,000 in two years' time (and existing holders would want to sell). The consequence would be that the price would fall. To what level would it fall?

The answer is that it would fall to the level such that its future value will be £1,000 when it is invested for two years at 6 per cent. The general formula for finding the future value of a present sum is:

$$FV = A(1 + i)^n \tag{A1.2}$$

where A, i and n all have the same meanings as before. The process of finding the future value of a present sum is known as *compounding*. Exercise A1.2 gives us the answer.

> **Compounding:** The process of finding the future value of a present sum benefiting from regular interest payments.

What we have now established is that we can find the present value of a lump sum payable to us at some time in the future. Furthermore, the present value will always be less than the face value of the payment because if we had the sum available now we could reinvest it. The rate at which we could reinvest is the rate at which we discount the future payment in order to find its present value and because the reinvestment and discount rates are the same thing it follows that the rate *required* to induce us to hold the asset in question is also the rate at which we discount the earnings from the asset.

> **Exercise A1.2** What sum of money, invested now, will yield £1,000 in two years' time if the rate of return is 6 per cent?
>
> *Hint*: Rearrange eqn A1.2, remembering that the future value = £1,000.
>
> *Answer at end of appendix*

This equivalence between the rate of discount and the required rate of return on assets is fundamental to understanding why an asset's present value is also the price which rational investors should be willing to pay for the asset – this is the main theme of section A1.2 below.

> **Required rate of return:** That rate of return on an asset which is just sufficient to persuade investors to hold it.

Finding the present value of a future single payment is fairly straightforward. Finding the present value of a *stream* of payments, made at regular intervals, is a little more awkward since we have to apply the appropriate adjustment to each payment. Such a series of payments is known as an annuity.

> **Annuity:** A series of fixed payments received at set intervals.

Nonetheless, the principle remains the same. Each of the payments has to be adjusted to take account of the level of interest rates and time. Imagine that we are to receive four equal payments at one-yearly intervals. Then each must be adjusted appropriately and the present value of the series of payments will be the sum of the adjusted values. Thus:

$$PV = \frac{A}{(1+i)} + \frac{A}{(1+i)^2} + \frac{A}{(1+i)^3} + \frac{A}{(1+i)^4} \tag{A1.3}$$

Notice again how the effect of higher interest rates would be to bring down the present value and notice too how the more distant payments are more severely affected by the time spent waiting for them. Exercise A1.3 illustrates this.

Exercise A1.3 Find the present value of a series of four annual payments of £1,000, when interest rates are 7 per cent.

Compare the present value of the first and last payments and notice the effect of time.

Answer at end of appendix

With a long series of payments, eqn A1.3 becomes very cumbersome to write out. Thus we often use an abbreviated form:

$$PV = \sum_{t=1}^{n} \frac{A_t}{(1+i)^t} \tag{A1.4}$$

Equation A1.4 says that the present value is the sum of (Σ means 'summation of') *any* series of payments each made at time t (where t takes values from 1 to n), each payment adjusted to take account of the value of t. Writing eqn A1.3 in terms of eqn A1.4 would simply involve changing n to 4.

Unfortunately, whether we use eqn A1.3 or eqn A1.4, finding the present value of a series of payments can be tedious if we are doing it by calculation rather than using discount tables. The first step, dividing A by $(1+i)$, is quick and easy, but next we have to square $(1+i)$ before dividing it into A, and then we have to find $(1+i)^3$ before dividing and so on. Depending upon our calculator and the total number of periods in the series, it could be a very slow job! The good news is that there is an alternative method which enables us to find the value of a series of payments with fewer steps (especially if the series is long). Its disadvantage is that it looks complicated and, except to mathematicians, it does not so obviously describe the adjustments that we are making. In this version we find the *PV* as follows:

$$PV = \frac{A}{i} \times \left(1 - \frac{1}{(1+i)^n}\right) \tag{A1.5}$$

The advantage here is that the term $(1+i)$ has to be calculated only once, though it has to be calculated for n, the total number of periods.

Exercise A1.4 Using a calculator and eqn A1.5, find the present value of a series of four annual payments of £1,000 when the rate of interest is 7 per cent p.a.

(The answer should be the same as in Exercise A1.3!)

A1.2 Allowing for risk

In the last section, we saw that we can assign a present value to future payments (lump sum or periodic) by the process of discounting. Discounting is necessary, we said, because we have to wait for payment and this involves a cost which is the income or benefits that we could have earned from the payment if we had it available now. In all our examples we chose a risk-free interest rate as the rate of discount. We chose this rate because we assumed that the *only* problem associated with future payments was the cost of waiting. We assumed that the payments were known with certainty and thus that the asset producing those payments was a risk-free asset. Since our discount rate has to represent the rate of return which could be earned by having the payments now and investing them in an asset of similar risk, the discount rate in this case must be the risk-free rate.

In practice, however, as we said at the beginning of this appendix, future payments are not likely to be risk-free. On the contrary, the very fact that they lie in the future makes them uncertain and thus risky. This means that they will be subject to a higher rate of discount. (Remember we said that people are risk-averse and therefore the value of a risky asset will be lower, and the return required on it will be higher, than on a risk-free asset.) The question is, how do we find a rate of discount (or required rate of return) which takes account of this risk?

The simple answer is that we add a 'risk premium' to the risk-free rate. In practice, we may not have to do much calculation. We might just look at the return generated in the recent past by an asset of similar characteristics. If we are concerned about the required return on a bond we may find that one of the international risk-rating agencies has placed the bond in one of its many categories, each of which has a risk premium associated with it.

The *theory* behind the risk premium, however, is usually derived from the *capital asset pricing model*. This says:

the required rate of return on a risky asset is equal to the risk-free rate of return plus a fraction (or multiple) of the market risk premium where the fraction (or multiple) is represented by the asset's β-coefficient.

Formally, this is often written as:

$$\bar{K} = K_{rf} + \beta_A(K_m - K_{rf}) \tag{A1.6}$$

where K_A is the required return on asset A, K_{rf} is the risk-free rate of return (what we called i in our discussion above), β_A is the 'beta-coefficient' of asset A, and K_m is the rate of return on a portfolio consisting of all risky assets.

The basic idea is really very simple and quite easy to understand. Notice firstly that the model says that the required return on a risky asset is equal to the risk-free rate (K_{rf}) plus some mark-up. That is exactly what we have been saying all along. The risk-free rate (i or K_{rf}) must set a minimum threshold level of return. Since this can be earned on risk-free assets, it follows that the return on a risky asset must be equal to this plus something further. The expression $\beta_A(K_m - K_{rf})$ is the 'something further'. $K_m - K_{rf}$ is sometimes called the *market risk premium*. This is the difference between the rate of return on a risk-free asset and the return on the 'whole market portfolio', a portfolio consisting of all the risky assets in the market. The return on 'whole market portfolio' is a difficult idea (which we look at in a moment) but it may be taken as representing a 'benchmark' return on risky assets in general. The market risk premium therefore shows the compensation for risk required by the investment community as a whole to persuade it to hold 'representative' risky assets compared with risk-free ones. The market risk premium might therefore be said to measure the investment community's degree of risk aversion. β_A is then an index of the asset's risk compared with that of the whole market portfolio. It enables us to say what premium should be paid on A by comparing its risk with that of a whole market portfolio. Depending on that comparison, the asset may need to earn less, the same, or even more than the market risk premium. If, for example, the asset has the same risk as the whole market portfolio, then $\beta_A = 1$ (and the required return on the asset will be equal to K_m, the return on the whole market portfolio). If asset A is less risky than the whole market portfolio, then $\beta < 1$, and if it is riskier, then $\beta > 1$. Exercise A1.5 provides examples.

Exercise A1.5 Assume that the risk-free rate of interest is 5 per cent p.a. and that the return on a whole market portfolio of risky assets is 15 per cent p.a. Find the required return on three assets whose β-coefficients are 0.8, 1.1 and 1.3 respectively.

Answers in Figure A1.1

The message of the capital asset pricing model can be shown in a simple diagram. Figure A1.1 shows that if we know the risk-free rate and the return on the whole market portfolio, the required return on a risky asset will depend upon its β-coefficient. The security market line (SML) is simply a visual representation of eqn A1.6. Figure A1.1 also shows the answers to Exercise A1.5.

The idea that we should compare the risk of an individual asset with some benchmark and then demand a premium based upon that comparison is sensible enough. But why do we choose the 'whole market portfolio of risky assets' as the benchmark? The answer is that rational risk-averse investors will never hold a risky asset in isolation because they can eliminate a lot of risk by diversification, and the whole market portfolio represents the extreme case of the most fully diversified portfolio. In order to understand this, we need to look in more detail at the benefits of diversification.

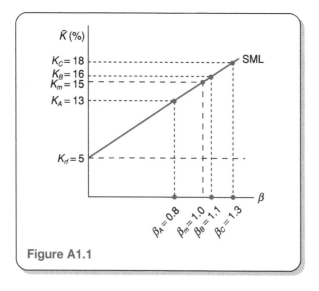

Figure A1.1

Consider an individual risky asset, A. We could take an ordinary company share as an example. The essential characteristics of this asset, from an investor's point of view, can be described by its return and its risk. Unfortunately, we cannot know the return on an asset in advance (if we did, there would be no risk!) and so we have to form a judgement about the return that we expect. We cannot know exactly how people form expectations in practice, but it seems reasonable perhaps to suggest that people are guided by what they have observed to happen in particular circumstances in the past, together with some assessment of the probability of those circumstances occurring again. On this basis, the expected return on an asset, which we write as $\hat{K}$, can be calculated as follows:

$$\hat{K} = \Sigma P_i K_i \tag{A1.7}$$

where P_i is the probability of a particular state of affairs and K_i is the return expected in those circumstances.

To make an estimate of its riskiness, recall how we defined risk above. Risk, we said, is the probability that an outcome (here the return on A) differs from what we might expect. One obvious way of measuring the riskiness of an asset, therefore, is to look at the variance or dispersion of possible returns around the value that we expect. If all the possible outcomes are closely grouped around the expected value, then the probability of being disappointed is low, while if the dispersion is large, the probability of getting a result different from the expected is quite high. The formula for calculating the variance, σ^2, is:

$$\sigma^2 = \Sigma P_i (K_i - \hat{K}_i)^2 \tag{A1.8}$$

Box A1.1 shows how we can use eqn A1.7 and eqn A1.8 to calculate the expected mean return and the variance. In Box A1.1, share A is expected to produce annual returns ranging from 8 to 20 per cent p.a. depending on the state of the economy. The probability of the economy being in a state of 'boom', 'normality' or 'slump' in the next time period varies between 30 per cent, 50 per cent and 20 per cent respectively. The expected return on the share is 14.6 per cent and its variance is 17.64. Sometimes it is convenient to express the risk as the standard deviation rather than the variance of returns. The standard deviation is merely the square root of the variance (here the standard deviation, σ, is 4.2 per cent (= $\sqrt{17.7}$)).

Box A1.1 **Mean and variance**

Share A

State	P_i	$K_i\%$	P_iK_i	$(K_i - \hat{K})$	$P_i(K_i - \hat{K})^2$
Boom	0.3	20.0	6.0	5.4	8.8
Average	0.5	14.0	7.0	-0.6	0.2
Slump	0.2	8.0	1.6	-6.6	8.7
			$\hat{K}_A = 14.6$		$\sigma_A^2 = 17.7$

However, rational investors are not likely to be interested in holding a single risky asset in isolation. This is because they are risk-averse and a great deal of risk can be eliminated, very easily, by holding a diversified portfolio of assets. The risk-reduction effect of diversification can be seen easily if we only diversify from holding one asset to holding two. Imagine that we are presented with the possibility of holding two assets, asset A with the characteristics just described, and asset B, whose characteristics have to be found by completing Exercise A1.6.

Exercise A1.6 **Share B**

State	P_i	$K_i\%$	P_iK_i	$(K_i - \hat{K})$	$P_i(K_i - \hat{K})^2$
Boom	0.3	12.0			
Average	0.5	8.0			
Slump	0.2	8.0			
			$\hat{K}_B = \boxed{}$		$\sigma_B^2 = \boxed{}$

Answers in text below

If we have done the calculations correctly, then $\hat{K}_B$ should be 9.2 per cent, while σ_B^2 should be 3.36. Notice immediately that while asset A has a higher return than B, it is also riskier than B (we should be familiar with this relationship by now). As investors we now have a choice of putting all our wealth into A or, if we feel A is too risky, putting all our wealth into B. But why put all our wealth into either? Clearly we could put any proportion of our wealth into A (call the proportion X) and the balance (1 − X) into B. Suppose we opt for an equal balance of A and B (X = 0.5 and 1 − X = 0.5). What happens to the return and risk that we can expect?

Consider firstly the effect on return. This is simply the weighted average of the two asset returns, where the weights are a proportion of the asset allocated to A and to B. If we let p indicate values for our portfolio, then in general terms:

$$\hat{K}_p = \Sigma w_i K_i \tag{A1.9}$$

where w_i is the 'weight' or proportion of the portfolio allocated to each security and K_i is the return on each asset. In this particular case, where the weight in each case is 0.5, then:

$$\hat{K}_p = 0.5(14.6) + 0.5(9.2) = 11.9\% \tag{A1.10}$$

Consider now the effect upon risk. This is more complicated and is not just the weighted average of the two variances (though the variances of each asset and the weight of each asset do play a part). Why is portfolio risk not just the weighted average of the assets comprising it? We can get a partial answer if we imagine an extreme case of two assets whose returns were variable (and therefore risky) but whose returns varied in exactly the opposite direction. In practice, such an extreme case is impossible, but we might play with the idea that the return on shares in an umbrella company varies in direct opposition to the return on shares in a company making sunglasses. Given such an extreme case, we could put together a portfolio of the two shares in which the portfolio return *never varied*. Movements in the return on umbrella shares would be exactly cancelled by movements in the return on sunglasses shares. Although the individual assets might each have a very large variance, the variance of returns on the portfolio would be zero!

This is an extreme case. A more realistic one might be the returns to shareholders in an oil producing company and the returns to shareholders in an airline company. The dramatic rise in oil prices in 2005 certainly suggested that these could move in opposite directions. However, both the extreme and realistic cases show *why* we cannot just add up the individual variances. In the extreme case, we supposed here that movements in return are perfectly opposed – a movement in one is *exactly* cancelled by the movement in the other. However, a similar, albeit smaller effect will always operate provided only that movements in return are *less than perfectly correlated*. Provided that there is some independence in the movements in returns, there will be some risk-reduction effect from combining risky assets in a portfolio. More formally:

> Provided that the returns on assets are less than perfectly correlated, the risk attaching to a portfolio of risky assets will be less than the weighted average of the risk of the component assets.

Bearing this in mind, we can produce an illustration based on our two assets A and B. Using standard deviation as the measure of risk, the general expression for a two-asset portfolio is:

$$\sigma_p = \sqrt{X_A^2 \cdot \sigma_A^2 + X_B^2 \cdot \sigma_B^2 + 2X_A(X_B) \cdot \mathrm{cov}\, K_A, K_B} \tag{A1.11}$$

The interesting part of eqn A1.11 comes at the end and features the 'covariance of returns' between asset A and asset B. The covariance itself is made up of the individual standard deviations and the correlation coefficient of returns between A and B, ρ_{AB}.

$$\text{cov } K_A, K_B = \sigma_A \cdot \sigma_B \cdot \rho_{AB} \qquad (A1.12)$$

It is this correlation coefficient that plays the crucial role in risk reduction. If this has the value +1, then portfolio risk is simply the weighted average of the risks of component assets. If it has the value −1, then we can construct a two-asset portfolio of zero risk. For any value in between, there will be some risk-reduction effect from diversification. Since the returns on most risky assets move together to some degree, in practice we would expect values for ρ_{AB} ranging from 0 to +1.

Looking at eqn A1.11 we can see that we have most of the information we need in order to illustrate the risk-reduction effect of combining our two assets. What we lack is the covariance of returns, and this we can find as follows:

$$\text{cov } K_A, K_B = \Sigma P_i (K_A - \hat{K}_A)(K_B - \hat{K}_B) \qquad (A1.13)$$

In our case:

$$
\begin{aligned}
\text{Cov } K_A, K_B &= 0.3(20 - 14.6)(12 - 9.2) \\
&\quad +0.5(14 - 14.6)(8 - 9.2) \\
&\quad +0.2(8 - 14.6)(8 - 9.2) \\
&= 4.53 + 0.36 + 1.584 \\
&= 6.47 \approx 6.5
\end{aligned}
$$

Putting everything together (including the variance of share B) we can now solve eqn A1.11 and find the standard deviation of our two-asset portfolio as follows:

$$
\begin{aligned}
\sigma_p &= \sqrt{0.5^2(17.7) + 0.5^2(3.36) + 2(0.5)(0.5)6.5} \\
&= \sqrt{4.43 + 0.84 + 3.25} \\
&= \sqrt{8.52} = 2.92
\end{aligned}
$$

Let us now summarise our three investment possibilities: putting all our funds into A, or all into B, or dividing them equally between A and B in a portfolio, C.

	A	B	C
$\hat{K}$	14.60	9.20	11.90
σ	4.20	1.83	2.92

Investing in A, we can expect a return of 14.6 per cent p.a. if we are prepared to accept a level of risk (shown by standard deviation) of 4.2. If this seems too risky we could opt for asset B and earn 9.2 per cent p.a. for a risk of 1.83. Alternatively we could opt for the portfolio of two assets, C. This would give us a return halfway between A and B. But look at the risk. If combining the two assets A and B equally were to give us half of the risk of each asset, we would expect our portfolio to have a standard deviation of 3.015 (= 0.5(4.2) + 0.5(1.83)). In fact, however, the risk is only 2.92. This is what we promised earlier: provided that the correlation coefficient of returns is less than +1, portfolio risk will be less than the weighted average of the

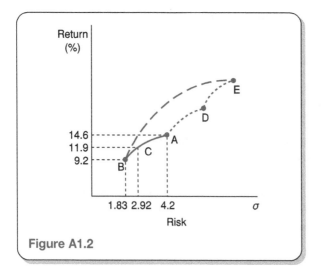

Figure A1.2

risk of the component assets. Out of interest we could use eqn A1.12 to check just what the correlation coefficient of returns is in this case. Since the risk-reduction effect is not especially dramatic, we might anticipate a figure closer to +1 than to 0. Rearranging eqn A1.12 we have:

$$\rho_{AB} = \text{cov } K_A, K_B \div \sigma_A \cdot \sigma_B = 6.5 \div (4.2 \times 1.83) = 6.5 \div 7.7 = 0.84$$

The benefit of diversifying from one to two assets is shown in Figure A1.2. It shows the risk and return available on each of assets A and B, held individually. It also shows that combining the two assets equally gives us a rate of return (shown on the vertical axis) which is halfway between the return on A and the return on B, while the risk (shown on the horizontal axis) is less than halfway between the risk of A and the risk of B. C is a portfolio made up of equal proportions of A and B. But we could, of course, combine A and B in any proportions at all between 0 and 100 per cent. The smooth curve joining A and B in Figure A1.2 shows the risk–return possibilities resulting from all those combinations. Notice that the curve is concave to the horizontal axis, showing that every combination of A and B will produce a return which is the weighted average of the two assets, while the risk is less than the weighted average.

But A and B are not the only assets available. We could combine A with D or D with E. The results of these combinations are also shown – by the dotted curves in the figure.

More importantly, however, the benefits which we can get from combining two assets are even greater if we combine three, and greater still if we combine four assets, and so on. The dashed line, the 'envelope curve', in Figure A1.2 shows the possible risk–return combinations available if we constructed a series of portfolios using different combinations of *all* assets, A to E.

Notice that as we combine increasing numbers of assets, the curve moves up and to the left. What this means is that for any given level of risk, we can increase the available return by diversifying into more assets or, alternatively, for any given level

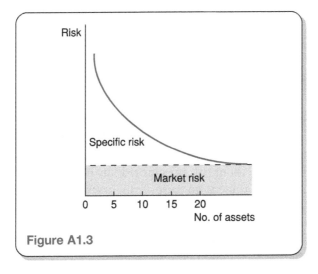

Figure A1.3

of return we can *decrease* the level of risk by adding more assets. This obviously raises the question of whether there is any limit to the benefits of diversification.

There are two answers to this. Firstly, for most investors there is a practical limit since the purchase and sale of each asset involves dealing costs. Although the total benefits of diversification increase with each asset, the increases are very small once a portfolio contains fifteen to twenty assets. This is shown in Figure A1.3. Beyond this point, for most investors the additional benefits do not match the additional dealing costs.

Secondly, even if we ignore dealing costs, there is a theoretical limit which is set by the total number of risky assets available – the whole market portfolio. If we did construct a fully diversified portfolio, we should still find that we had to face some risk. (This can also be seen in Figure A1.3.) To understand why, we need to distinguish between *specific risk and market risk*.

We know that the reason why risk diminishes as we combine risky assets together is that their variations in return are not perfectly correlated: the fluctuations tend to cancel. But the cancelling effect – the imperfect correlation – is due to the fact that each individual asset is subject to events which affect only that asset. If we are thinking of company shares, for example, returns on one company's shares will be affected by the launch of its latest product, while returns on another might be affected by a major strike. These events, which have their effects only on individual assets, are said to be *specific events* and give rise to what is called *specific risk*. It is the effects of specific risks that tend to cancel when we combine assets. However, there are some events which will affect *all* assets to some degree. A rise in interest rates, for example, or the movement of the economy into recession will tend to depress the returns on all assets. Returns will all move in the same direction as a result, albeit to a greater or lesser extent, depending upon the nature of the asset. Such events, affecting all risky assets, are said to be *market events* and give rise to what is called *market risk*. Market risk cannot be eliminated by diversification. Even a fully diversified portfolio will still contain market risk.

> **Specific risk:** The variation in return on an asset which results from events peculiar to that asset alone.
>
> **Market risk:** The variation in return on assets which results from (market-wide) events which affect all assets.

We can now see why the whole market portfolio provides a benchmark return against which we can establish the return required on an individual asset. The reason is that rational risk-averse investors will never hold a risky asset in isolation because they can eliminate a lot of risk (specific risk) by diversification. Since specific risk can be avoided cheaply, there is no reason why investors should be rewarded for experiencing it. The only risk for which people should expect a reward is unavoidable or market risk. A whole market portfolio exposes investors *only* to market risk and thus the return on that portfolio puts a price on the risk for which investors can expect to be rewarded.

Deciding on the return which should be earned on an individual asset is then relatively simple. As we saw above, we look at each asset in order to see how much risk it carries when compared with the whole market portfolio. Since the whole market portfolio is subject only to market risk, looking at how the return on an individual asset moves with the return on the whole market tells us how sensitive the asset is to market risk, the only type of risk that is relevant when it comes to being compensated by a risk premium. It is market risk (and only market risk) for which we can expect to earn a reward.

Figure A1.4 shows how we make the comparison between individual assets and the whole market. The return on the whole market portfolio is shown on the horizontal axis and the return on the individual asset is shown on the vertical axis. The figure contains observations for two assets. The lower group plots the return on asset *B* against the return on the whole market; the upper group does the same for asset *A*. It can readily be seen that when the whole market return increases by one

Figure A1.4

unit, the return on asset B also increases, but by rather less, while for asset A a unit increase in the whole market return produces a larger increase in the return on A. Fitting a line through the observations (either by eye or using standard regression techniques) enables us to find the slope coefficient which relates the change in the market return to the return on the asset. For A, it can be seen that this coefficient exceeds 1, while for B the coefficient is less than 1. The slope coefficient for each asset is its β-coefficient.

In section A1.1, we saw that the present value of the payment(s) produced by an asset could be found by discounting the future payment(s) to take account of the time for which we had to wait and the return which we could have earned had we had use of the payment(s) immediately. We noted that the rate at which we discounted was therefore the rate of return required to persuade us to go on holding the asset. Since we assumed that the payment was due from a risk-free asset, the discount rate which we chose was the risk-free rate of interest. Given that we now know how to calculate a risk premium for the return required on a risky asset, we can go ahead and use the pricing formulae in section A1.1, but using a risk-adjusted rate of discount. Take, for example, eqn A1.1 (the formula for valuing a single, lump-sum payment). Use this in Exercise A1.7 to see how the addition of a risk premium to the discount rate affects the present value of an asset yielding a future lump sum payment of £5,000.

Exercise A1.7

(a) What price would you be prepared to pay today for a non-interest-bearing asset which matures for £5,000 in three years' time if you are assured that the maturity value is guaranteed, and the three-year risk-free interest rate is 7 per cent p.a.?

(b) What price would you be prepared to pay for a similar asset where the payment in three years' time was expected to be £5,000 but where the asset's past behaviour relative to the market suggested a β-coefficient of 0.7? Assume that the risk-free rate remains at 7 per cent p.a. while the return on a whole market portfolio is 17 per cent p.a.

Answers in text below

In the first part of Exercise A1.7, we are simply repeating what we did in Exercise A1.1. We are finding the present value of a risk-free asset by discounting by the risk-free rate of interest. We discount by the risk-free rate because this is the rate of return which we require. And when we calculate the present value (£4,081.63), we are saying that this is the price which we (and other rational investors) would be prepared to pay. In equilibrium the asset will be priced at £4,081.63 in order to yield the required return of 7 per cent p.a.

In the second part, we are doing the same, except that the discount rate incoporates a risk premium. The CAPM tells us that the required return on this (risky) asset is $0.07 + 0.7(0.17 - 0.07) = 0.07 + 0.07 = 0.14$. The rate at which we discount the £5,000 is 14 per cent p.a. which tells us that the present value of this asset is £3,374.96. This is the price which we (and others) would be prepared to pay. In equilibrium, the asset will be priced at £3,467.41 in order to yield 14 per cent p.a. which is the rate of return which we require, given its risk. We can see now that if we are particularly interested in the pricing of assets, we could modify our earlier statement of the CAPM to read:

The market will price risky assets in such a way that the return on a risky asset will be equal to the risk-free rate of return plus a fraction (or multiple) of the whole market risk premium.

Notice the relationship between price and rate of return that is emerging here and remember what we said right at the beginning of this Appendix about investors' attitude to risk and its effect upon price. In Exercise A1.7 we have two assets which are very similar except in their degree of risk. The first (risk-free) asset has a price of £4,081.63. The second, whose earnings are riskier, must yield a higher rate of return. When we discount by this higher rate we find the price is substantially lower at £3,374.96.

Answers to exercises

A1.1 £907.03; (b) £890; (c) £822.71.

A1.2 £890.

A1.3 £934.57; £873.44; £816.33; £763.36.

A1.4 £3,387.70.

Present and future value tables

Appendix II • Present and future value tables

Table 1 Present value of a £1 lump sum, paid in n-years' time, discounted at i. $PV = \dfrac{£1}{(1+i)^n}$

Interest rates ($i\%$)

Periods (n)	1	2	3	4	5	6	7	8	9	10	11	12	13	14	15
1	0.9901	0.9804	0.9709	0.9615	0.9524	0.9434	0.9346	0.9259	0.9174	0.9091	0.9009	0.8929	0.8850	0.8772	0.8696
2	0.9803	0.9612	0.9426	0.9246	0.9070	0.8900	0.8734	0.8573	0.8417	0.8264	0.8116	0.7972	0.7831	0.7695	0.7561
3	0.9706	0.9423	0.9151	0.8890	0.8638	0.8396	0.8163	0.7938	0.7722	0.7513	0.7312	0.7118	0.6931	0.6750	0.6575
4	0.9610	0.9238	0.8885	0.8548	0.8227	0.7921	0.7629	0.7350	0.7084	0.6830	0.6587	0.6355	0.6133	0.5921	0.5718
5	0.9515	0.9057	0.8626	0.8219	0.7835	0.7473	0.7130	0.6806	0.6499	0.6209	0.5935	0.5674	0.5428	0.5194	0.4972
6	0.9420	0.8880	0.8375	0.7903	0.7462	0.7050	0.6663	0.6302	0.5963	0.5645	0.5346	0.5066	0.4803	0.4556	0.4323
7	0.9327	0.8706	0.8131	0.7599	0.7107	0.6651	0.6227	0.5835	0.5470	0.5132	0.4817	0.4523	0.4251	0.3996	0.3759
8	0.9235	0.8535	0.7894	0.7307	0.6768	0.6274	0.5820	0.5403	0.5019	0.4665	0.4339	0.4039	0.3762	0.3506	0.3269
9	0.9143	0.8368	0.7664	0.7026	0.6446	0.5919	0.5439	0.5002	0.4604	0.4241	0.3909	0.3606	0.3329	0.3075	0.2843
10	0.9053	0.8203	0.7441	0.6756	0.6139	0.5584	0.5083	0.4632	0.4224	0.3855	0.3522	0.3220	0.2946	0.2697	0.2472
11	0.8963	0.8043	0.7224	0.6496	0.5847	0.5268	0.4751	0.4289	0.3875	0.3505	0.3173	0.2875	0.2607	0.2366	0.2149
12	0.8874	0.7885	0.7014	0.6246	0.5568	0.4970	0.4440	0.3971	0.3555	0.3186	0.2858	0.2567	0.2307	0.2076	0.1869
13	0.8787	0.7730	0.6810	0.6006	0.5303	0.4688	0.4150	0.3677	0.3262	0.2897	0.2575	0.2292	0.2042	0.1821	0.1625
14	0.8700	0.7579	0.6611	0.5775	0.5051	0.4423	0.3878	0.3405	0.2992	0.2633	0.2320	0.2046	0.1807	0.1597	0.1413
15	0.8613	0.7430	0.6419	0.5553	0.4810	0.4173	0.3624	0.3152	0.2745	0.2394	0.2090	0.1827	0.1599	0.1401	0.1229
16	0.8528	0.7284	0.6232	0.5339	0.4581	0.3936	0.3387	0.2919	0.2519	0.2176	0.1883	0.1631	0.1415	0.1229	0.1069
17	0.8444	0.7142	0.6050	0.5134	0.4363	0.3714	0.3166	0.2703	0.2311	0.1978	0.1696	0.1456	0.1252	0.1078	0.0929
18	0.8360	0.7002	0.5874	0.4936	0.4155	0.3503	0.2959	0.2502	0.2120	0.1799	0.1528	0.1300	0.1108	0.0946	0.0808
19	0.8277	0.6864	0.5703	0.4746	0.3957	0.3305	0.2765	0.2317	0.1945	0.1635	0.1377	0.1161	0.0981	0.0829	0.0703
20	0.8195	0.6730	0.5537	0.4564	0.3769	0.3118	0.2584	0.2145	0.1784	0.1486	0.1240	0.1037	0.0868	0.0728	0.0611
25	0.7798	0.6095	0.4776	0.3751	0.2953	0.2330	0.1842	0.1460	0.1160	0.0923	0.0736	0.0588	0.0471	0.0378	0.0304
30	0.7419	0.5521	0.4120	0.3083	0.2314	0.1741	0.1314	0.0994	0.0754	0.0573	0.0437	0.0334	0.0256	0.0196	0.0151
35	0.7059	0.5000	0.3554	0.2534	0.1813	0.1301	0.0937	0.0676	0.0490	0.0356	0.0259	0.0189	0.0139	0.0102	0.0075
40	0.6717	0.4529	0.3066	0.2083	0.1420	0.0972	0.0668	0.0460	0.0318	0.0221	0.0154	0.0107	0.0075	0.0053	0.0037
45	0.6391	0.4102	0.2644	0.1712	0.1113	0.0727	0.0476	0.0313	0.0207	0.0137	0.0091	0.0061	0.0041	0.0027	0.0019
50	0.6080	0.3715	0.2281	0.1407	0.0872	0.0543	0.0339	0.0213	0.0134	0.0085	0.0054	0.0035	0.0022	0.0014	0.0009

Interest rates ($i\%$)

Periods (n)	16	17	18	19	20	21	22	23	24	25	26	27	28	29	30
1	0.8621	0.8547	0.8475	0.8403	0.8333	0.8264	0.8197	0.8130	0.8065	0.8000	0.7937	0.7874	0.7812	0.7752	0.7692
2	0.7432	0.7305	0.7182	0.7062	0.6944	0.6830	0.6719	0.6610	0.6504	0.6400	0.6299	0.6200	0.6104	0.6009	0.5917
3	0.6407	0.6244	0.6086	0.5934	0.5787	0.5645	0.5507	0.5374	0.5245	0.5120	0.4999	0.4882	0.4768	0.4658	0.4552
4	0.5523	0.5337	0.5158	0.4987	0.4823	0.4665	0.4514	0.4369	0.4230	0.4096	0.3968	0.3844	0.3725	0.3611	0.3501
5	0.4761	0.4561	0.4371	0.4190	0.4019	0.3855	0.3700	0.3552	0.3411	0.3277	0.3149	0.3027	0.2910	0.2799	0.2693
6	0.4104	0.3898	0.3704	0.3521	0.3349	0.3186	0.3033	0.2888	0.2751	0.2621	0.2499	0.2383	0.2274	0.2170	0.2072
7	0.3538	0.3332	0.3139	0.2959	0.2791	0.2633	0.2486	0.2348	0.2218	0.2097	0.1983	0.1877	0.1776	0.1682	0.1594
8	0.3050	0.2848	0.2660	0.2487	0.2326	0.2176	0.2038	0.1909	0.1789	0.1678	0.1574	0.1478	0.1388	0.1304	0.1226
9	0.2630	0.2434	0.2255	0.2090	0.1938	0.1799	0.1670	0.1552	0.1443	0.1342	0.1249	0.1164	0.1084	0.1011	0.0943
10	0.2267	0.2080	0.1911	0.1756	0.1615	0.1486	0.1369	0.1262	0.1164	0.1074	0.0992	0.0916	0.0847	0.0784	0.0725
11	0.1954	0.1778	0.1619	0.1476	0.1346	0.1228	0.1122	0.1026	0.0938	0.0859	0.0787	0.0721	0.0662	0.0607	0.0558
12	0.1685	0.1520	0.1372	0.1240	0.1122	0.1015	0.0920	0.0834	0.0757	0.0687	0.0625	0.0568	0.0517	0.0471	0.0429
13	0.1452	0.1299	0.1163	0.1042	0.0935	0.0839	0.0754	0.0678	0.0610	0.0550	0.0496	0.0447	0.0404	0.0365	0.0330
14	0.1252	0.1110	0.0985	0.0876	0.0779	0.0693	0.0618	0.0551	0.0492	0.0440	0.0393	0.0352	0.0316	0.0283	0.0254
15	0.1079	0.0949	0.0835	0.0736	0.0649	0.0573	0.0507	0.0448	0.0397	0.0352	0.0312	0.0277	0.0247	0.0219	0.0195
16	0.0930	0.0811	0.0708	0.0618	0.0541	0.0474	0.0415	0.0364	0.0320	0.0281	0.0248	0.0218	0.0193	0.0170	0.0150
17	0.0802	0.0693	0.0600	0.0520	0.0451	0.0391	0.0340	0.0296	0.0258	0.0225	0.0197	0.0172	0.0150	0.0132	0.0116
18	0.0691	0.0592	0.0508	0.0437	0.0376	0.0323	0.0279	0.0241	0.0208	0.0180	0.0156	0.0135	0.0118	0.0102	0.0089
19	0.0596	0.0506	0.0431	0.0367	0.0313	0.0267	0.0229	0.0196	0.0168	0.0144	0.0124	0.0107	0.0092	0.0079	0.0068
20	0.0514	0.0433	0.0365	0.0308	0.0261	0.0221	0.0187	0.0159	0.0135	0.0115	0.0098	0.0084	0.0072	0.0061	0.0053
25	0.0245	0.0197	0.0160	0.0129	0.0105	0.0085	0.0069	0.0057	0.0046	0.0038	0.0031	0.0025	0.0021	0.0017	0.0014
30	0.0116	0.0090	0.0070	0.0054	0.0042	0.0033	0.0026	0.0020	0.0016	0.0012	0.0010	0.0008	0.0006	0.0005	0.0004
35	0.0055	0.0041	0.0030	0.0023	0.0017	0.0013	0.0009	0.0007	0.0005	0.0004	0.0003	0.0002	0.0002	0.0001	0.0001
40	0.0026	0.0019	0.0013	0.0010	0.0007	0.0005	0.0004	0.0003	0.0002	0.0001	0.0001	0.0001	0.0001	0.0000	0.0000
45	0.0013	0.0009	0.0006	0.0004	0.0003	0.0002	0.0001	0.0001	0.0001	0.0000	0.0000	0.0000	0.0000	0.0000	0.0000
50	0.0006	0.0004	0.0003	0.0002	0.0001	0.0001	0.0000	0.0000	0.0000	0.0000	0.0000	0.0000	0.0000	0.0000	0.0000

Table 2 Future value of a £1 lump sum in *n*-years' time, compounded at *i*. $FV = £1(1 + i)^n$

Interest rates (%)

Periods (n)	1	2	3	4	5	6	7	8	9	10	11	12	13	14	15
1	1·0100	1·0200	1·0300	1·0400	1·0500	1·0600	1·0700	1·0800	1·0900	1·1000	1·1100	1·1200	1·1300	1·1400	1·1500
2	1·0201	1·0404	1·0609	1·0816	1·1025	1·1236	1·1449	1·1664	1·1881	1·2100	1·2321	1·2544	1·2769	1·2996	1·3225
3	1·0303	1·0612	1·0927	1·1249	1·1576	1·1910	1·2250	1·2597	1·2950	1·3310	1·3676	1·4049	1·4429	1·4815	1·5209
4	1·0406	1·0824	1·1255	1·1699	1·2155	1·2625	1·3108	1·3605	1·4116	1·4641	1·5181	1·5735	1·6305	1·6890	1·7490
5	1·0510	1·1041	1·1593	1·2167	1·2763	1·3382	1·4026	1·4693	1·5386	1·6105	1·6851	1·7623	1·8424	1·9254	2·0114
6	1·0615	1·1262	1·1941	1·2653	1·3401	1·4185	1·5007	1·5869	1·6771	1·7716	1·8704	1·9738	2·0820	2·1950	2·3131
7	1·0721	1·1487	1·2299	1·3159	1·4071	1·5036	1·6058	1·7138	1·8280	1·9487	2·0762	2·2107	2·3526	2·5023	2·6600
8	1·0829	1·1717	1·2668	1·3686	1·4775	1·5938	1·7182	1·8509	1·9926	2·1436	2·3045	2·4760	2·6584	2·8526	3·0590
9	1·0937	1·1951	1·3048	1·4233	1·5513	1·6895	1·8385	1·9990	2·1719	2·3579	2·5580	2·7731	3·0040	3·2519	3·5179
10	1·1046	1·2190	1·3439	1·4802	1·6289	1·7908	1·9672	2·1589	2·3674	2·5937	2·8394	3·1058	3·3946	3·7072	4·0456
11	1·1157	1·2434	1·3842	1·5395	1·7103	1·8983	2·1049	2·3316	2·5804	2·8531	3·1518	3·4785	3·8359	4·2262	4·6524
12	1·1268	1·2682	1·4258	1·6010	1·7959	2·0122	2·2522	2·5182	2·8127	3·1384	3·4985	3·8906	4·3345	4·8179	5·3503
13	1·1381	1·2936	1·4685	1·6651	1·8856	2·1329	2·4098	2·7196	3·0658	3·4523	3·8833	4·3635	4·8980	5·4924	6·1528
14	1·1495	1·3195	1·5126	1·7317	1·9799	2·2609	2·5785	2·9372	3·3417	3·7975	4·3104	4·8871	5·5348	6·2613	7·0757
15	1·1610	1·3459	1·5580	1·8009	2·0789	2·3966	2·7590	3·1722	3·6425	4·1772	4·7846	5·4736	6·2543	7·1379	8·1371
16	1·1726	1·3728	1·6047	1·8730	2·1829	2·5404	2·9522	3·4259	3·9703	4·5950	5·3109	6·1304	7·0673	8·1372	9·3576
17	1·1843	1·4002	1·6528	1·9479	2·2920	2·6928	3·1588	3·7000	4·3276	5·0545	5·8951	6·8660	7·9861	9·2765	10·7613
18	1·1961	1·4282	1·7024	2·0258	2·4066	2·8543	3·3799	3·9960	4·7171	5·5599	6·5436	7·6900	9·0243	10·5752	12·3755
19	1·2081	1·4568	1·7535	2·1068	2·5270	3·0256	3·6165	4·3157	5·1417	6·1159	7·2633	8·6128	10·1974	12·0557	14·2318
20	1·2202	1·4859	1·8061	2·1911	2·6533	3·2071	3·8697	4·6610	5·6044	6·7275	8·0623	9·6463	11·5231	13·7435	16·3665
25	1·2824	1·6406	2·0938	2·6658	3·3864	4·2919	5·4274	6·8485	8·6231	10·8347	13·5855	17·0001	21·2305	26·4619	32·9190

Periods (n)	16	17	18	19	20	21	22	23	24	25	26	27	28	29	30
1	1·1600	1·1700	1·1800	1·1900	1·2000	1·2100	1·2200	1·2300	1·2400	1·2500	1·2600	1·2700	1·2800	1·2900	1·3000
2	1·3456	1·3689	1·3924	1·4161	1·4400	1·4641	1·4884	1·5129	1·5376	1·5625	1·5876	1·6129	1·6384	1·6641	1·6900
3	1·5609	1·6016	1·6430	1·6852	1·7280	1·7716	1·8158	1·8609	1·9066	1·9531	2·0004	2·0484	2·0972	2·1467	2·1970
4	1·8106	1·8739	1·9388	2·0053	2·0736	2·1436	2·2153	2·2889	2·3642	2·4414	2·5205	2·6014	2·6844	2·7692	2·8561
5	2·1003	2·1924	2·2878	2·3864	2·4883	2·5937	2·7027	2·8153	2·9316	3·0518	3·1758	3·3038	3·4360	3·5723	3·7129
6	2·4364	2·5652	2·6996	2·8398	2·9860	3·1384	3·2973	3·4628	3·6352	3·8147	4·0015	4·1959	4·3980	4·6083	4·8268
7	2·8262	3·0012	3·1855	3·3793	3·5832	3·7975	4·0227	4·2593	4·5077	4·7684	5·0419	5·3288	5·6295	5·9447	6·2749
8	3·2784	3·5115	3·7589	4·0214	4·2998	4·5950	4·9077	5·2389	5·5895	5·9605	6·3528	6·7675	7·2058	7·6686	8·1573
9	3·8030	4·1084	4·4355	4·7854	5·1598	5·5599	5·9874	6·4439	6·9310	7·4506	8·0045	8·5946	9·2234	9·8925	10·6045
10	4·4114	4·8068	5·2338	5·6947	6·1917	6·7275	7·3046	7·9259	8·5944	9·3132	10·0857	10·9153	11·8059	12·7614	13·7858
11	5·1173	5·6240	6·1759	6·7767	7·4301	8·1403	8·9117	9·7489	10·6571	11·6415	12·7080	13·8625	15·1116	16·4622	17·9216
12	5·9360	6·5801	7·2876	8·0642	8·9161	9·8497	10·8722	11·9912	13·2148	14·5519	16·0120	17·6053	19·3428	21·2362	23·2981
13	6·8858	7·6987	8·5994	9·5964	10·6993	11·9182	13·2641	14·7491	16·3863	18·1899	20·1752	22·3588	24·7588	27·3947	30·2875
14	7·9875	9·0075	10·1472	11·4198	12·8392	14·4210	16·1822	18·1414	20·3191	22·7374	25·4207	28·3957	31·6913	35·3391	39·3738
15	9·2655	10·5387	11·9737	13·5895	15·4070	17·4494	19·7423	22·3140	25·1956	28·4217	32·0301	36·0625	40·5648	45·5875	51·1859
16	10·7480	12·3303	14·1290	16·1715	18·4884	21·1138	24·0856	27·4462	31·2426	35·5271	40·3579	45·7994	51·9230	58·8079	66·5417
17	12·4677	14·4265	16·6722	19·2441	22·1861	25·5477	29·3844	33·7588	38·7408	44·4089	50·8510	58·1652	66·4614	75·8821	86·5042
18	14·4625	16·8790	19·6733	22·9005	26·6233	30·9127	35·8490	41·5233	48·0386	55·5112	64·0722	73·8698	85·0706	97·8622	112·4554
19	16·7765	19·7484	23·2144	27·2516	31·9480	37·4043	43·7358	51·0737	59·5679	69·3889	80·7310	93·8147	108·8904	126·2422	146·1920
20	19·4608	23·1056	27·3930	32·4294	38·3376	45·2593	53·3576	62·8206	73·8641	86·7362	101·7211	119·1446	139·3797	162·8524	190·0496
25	40·8742	50·6578	62·6686	77·3881	95·3962	117·3909	144·2101	176·8593	216·5420	264·6978	323·0454	393·6344	478·9049	581·7585	705·6410

Table 3 Present value of a £1 annuity, paid for *n*-years, discounted at *i*.

$$PV = \frac{£1}{i}\left[1 - \frac{1}{(1+i)^n}\right]$$

Periods (n)	Interest rates (*i*%) 1	2	3	4	5	6	7	8	9	10	11	12	13	14	15
1	0.9901	0.9804	0.9709	0.9615	0.9524	0.9434	0.9346	0.9259	0.9174	0.9091	0.9009	0.8929	0.8850	0.8772	0.8696
2	1.9704	1.9416	1.9135	1.8861	1.8594	1.8334	1.8080	1.7833	1.7591	1.7355	1.7125	1.6901	1.6681	1.6467	1.6257
3	2.9410	2.8839	2.8286	2.7751	2.7232	2.6730	2.6243	2.5771	2.5313	2.4869	2.4437	2.4018	2.3612	2.3216	2.2832
4	3.9020	3.8077	3.7171	3.6299	3.5460	3.4651	3.3872	3.3121	3.2397	3.1699	3.1024	3.0373	2.9745	2.9137	2.8550
5	4.8534	4.7135	4.5797	4.4518	4.3295	4.2124	4.1002	3.9927	3.8897	3.7908	3.6959	3.6048	3.5172	3.4331	3.3522
6	5.7955	5.6014	5.4172	5.2421	5.0757	4.9173	4.7665	4.6229	4.4859	4.3553	4.2305	4.1114	3.9975	3.8887	3.7845
7	6.7282	6.4720	6.2303	6.0021	5.7864	5.5824	5.3893	5.2064	5.0330	4.8684	4.7122	4.5638	4.4226	4.2883	4.1604
8	7.6517	7.3255	7.0197	6.7327	6.4632	6.2098	5.9713	5.7466	5.5348	5.3349	5.1461	4.9676	4.7988	4.6389	4.4873
9	8.5660	8.1622	7.7861	7.4353	7.1078	6.8017	6.5152	6.2469	5.9952	5.7590	5.5370	5.3282	5.1317	4.9464	4.7716
10	9.4713	8.9826	8.5302	8.1109	7.7217	7.3601	7.0236	6.7101	6.4177	6.1446	5.8892	5.6502	5.4262	5.2161	5.0188
11	10.3676	9.7868	9.2526	8.7605	8.3064	7.8869	7.4987	7.1390	6.8052	6.4951	6.2065	5.9377	5.6869	5.4527	5.2337
12	11.2551	10.5753	9.9540	9.3851	8.8633	8.3838	7.9427	7.5361	7.1607	6.8137	6.4924	6.1944	5.9176	5.6603	5.4206
13	12.1337	11.3484	10.6350	9.9856	9.3936	8.8527	8.3577	7.9038	7.4869	7.1034	6.7499	6.4235	6.1218	5.8424	5.5831
14	13.0037	12.1062	11.2961	10.5631	9.8986	9.2950	8.7455	8.2442	7.7862	7.3667	6.9819	6.6282	6.3025	6.0021	5.7245
15	13.8651	12.8493	11.9379	11.1184	10.3797	9.7122	9.1079	8.5595	8.0607	7.6061	7.1909	6.8109	6.4624	6.1422	5.8474
16	14.7179	13.5777	12.5611	11.6523	10.8378	10.1059	9.4466	8.8514	8.3126	7.8237	7.3792	6.9740	6.6039	6.2651	5.9542
17	15.5623	14.2919	13.1661	12.1657	11.2741	10.4773	9.7632	9.1216	8.5436	8.0216	7.5488	7.1196	6.7291	6.3729	6.0472
18	16.3983	14.9920	13.7535	12.6593	11.6896	10.8276	10.0591	9.3719	8.7556	8.2014	7.7016	7.2497	6.8399	6.4674	6.1280
19	17.2260	15.6785	14.3238	13.1339	12.0853	11.1581	10.3356	9.6036	8.9501	8.3649	7.8393	7.3658	6.9380	6.5504	6.1982
20	18.0456	16.3514	14.8775	13.5903	12.4622	11.4699	10.5940	9.8181	9.1285	8.5136	7.9633	7.4694	7.0248	6.6231	6.2593
25	22.0232	19.5235	17.4131	15.6221	14.0939	12.7834	11.6536	10.6748	9.8226	9.0770	8.4217	7.8431	7.3300	6.8729	6.4641
30	25.8077	22.3965	19.6004	17.2920	15.3725	13.7648	12.4090	11.2578	10.2737	9.4269	8.6938	8.0552	7.4957	7.0027	6.5660
35	29.4086	24.9986	21.4872	18.6646	16.3742	14.4982	12.9477	11.6546	10.5668	9.6442	8.8552	8.1755	7.5856	7.0700	6.6166
40	32.8347	27.3555	23.1148	19.7928	17.1591	15.0463	13.3317	11.9246	10.7574	9.7791	8.9511	8.2438	7.6344	7.1050	6.6418
45	36.0945	29.4902	24.5187	20.7200	17.7741	15.4558	13.6055	12.1084	10.8812	9.8628	9.0079	8.2825	7.6609	7.1232	6.6543
50	39.1961	31.4236	25.7298	21.4822	18.2559	15.7619	13.8007	12.2335	10.9617	9.9148	9.0417	8.3045	7.6752	7.1327	6.6605

Periods (n)	Interest rates (*i*%) 16	17	18	19	20	21	22	23	24	25	26	27	28	29	30
1	0.8621	0.8547	0.8475	0.8403	0.8333	0.8264	0.8197	0.8130	0.8065	0.8000	0.7937	0.7874	0.7812	0.7752	0.7692
2	1.6052	1.5852	1.5656	1.5465	1.5278	1.5095	1.4915	1.4740	1.4568	1.4400	1.4235	1.4074	1.3916	1.3761	1.3609
3	2.2459	2.2096	2.1743	2.1399	2.1065	2.0739	2.0422	2.0114	1.9813	1.9520	1.9234	1.8956	1.8684	1.8420	1.8161
4	2.7982	2.7432	2.6901	2.6386	2.5887	2.5404	2.4936	2.4483	2.4043	2.3616	2.3202	2.2800	2.2410	2.2031	2.1662
5	3.2743	3.1993	3.1272	3.0576	2.9906	2.9260	2.8636	2.8035	2.7454	2.6893	2.6351	2.5827	2.5320	2.4830	2.4356
6	3.6847	3.5892	3.4976	3.4098	3.3255	3.2446	3.1669	3.0923	3.0205	2.9514	2.8850	2.8210	2.7594	2.7000	2.6427
7	4.0386	3.9224	3.8115	3.7057	3.6046	3.5079	3.4155	3.3270	3.2423	3.1611	3.0833	3.0087	2.9370	2.8682	2.8021
8	4.3436	4.2072	4.0776	3.9544	3.8372	3.7256	3.6193	3.5179	3.4212	3.3289	3.2407	3.1564	3.0758	2.9986	2.9247
9	4.6065	4.4506	4.3030	4.1633	4.0310	3.9054	3.7863	3.6731	3.5655	3.4631	3.3657	3.2728	3.1842	3.0997	3.0190
10	4.8332	4.6586	4.4941	4.3389	4.1925	4.0541	3.9232	3.7993	3.6819	3.5705	3.4648	3.3644	3.2689	3.1781	3.0915
11	5.0286	4.8364	4.6560	4.4865	4.3271	4.1769	4.0354	3.9018	3.7757	3.6564	3.5435	3.4365	3.3351	3.2388	3.1473
12	5.1971	4.9884	4.7932	4.6105	4.4392	4.2784	4.1274	3.9852	3.8514	3.7251	3.6059	3.4933	3.3868	3.2859	3.1903
13	5.3423	5.1183	4.9095	4.7147	4.5327	4.3624	4.2028	4.0530	3.9124	3.7801	3.6555	3.5381	3.4272	3.3224	3.2233
14	5.4675	5.2293	5.0081	4.8023	4.6106	4.4317	4.2646	4.1082	3.9616	3.8241	3.6949	3.5733	3.4587	3.3507	3.2487
15	5.5755	5.3242	5.0916	4.8759	4.6755	4.4890	4.3152	4.1530	4.0013	3.8593	3.7261	3.6010	3.4834	3.3726	3.2682
16	5.6685	5.4053	5.1624	4.9377	4.7296	4.5364	4.3567	4.1894	4.0333	3.8874	3.7509	3.6228	3.5026	3.3896	3.2832
17	5.7487	5.4746	5.2223	4.9897	4.7746	4.5755	4.3908	4.2190	4.0591	3.9099	3.7705	3.6400	3.5177	3.4028	3.2948
18	5.8178	5.5339	5.2732	5.0333	4.8122	4.6079	4.4187	4.2431	4.0799	3.9279	3.7861	3.6536	3.5294	3.4130	3.3037
19	5.8775	5.5845	5.3162	5.0700	4.8435	4.6346	4.4415	4.2627	4.0967	3.9424	3.7985	3.6642	3.5386	3.4210	3.3105
20	5.9288	5.6278	5.3527	5.1009	4.8696	4.6567	4.4603	4.2786	4.1103	3.9539	3.8083	3.6726	3.5458	3.4271	3.3158
25	6.0971	5.7662	5.4669	5.1951	4.9476	4.7213	4.5139	4.3232	4.1474	3.9849	3.8342	3.6943	3.5640	3.4423	3.3286
30	6.1772	5.8294	5.5168	5.2347	4.9789	4.7463	4.5338	4.3391	4.1601	3.9950	3.8424	3.7009	3.5693	3.4466	3.3321
35	6.2153	5.8582	5.5386	5.2512	4.9915	4.7559	4.5411	4.3447	4.1644	3.9984	3.8450	3.7028	3.5708	3.4478	3.3330
40	6.2335	5.8713	5.5482	5.2582	4.9966	4.7596	4.5439	4.3467	4.1659	3.9995	3.8458	3.7034	3.5712	3.4481	3.3332
45	6.2421	5.8773	5.5523	5.2611	4.9986	4.7610	4.5449	4.3474	4.1664	3.9998	3.8460	3.7036	3.5714	3.4482	3.3332
50	6.2463	5.8801	5.5541	5.2623	4.9995	4.7616	4.5452	4.3477	4.1666	3.9999	3.8461	3.7037	3.5714	3.4483	3.333

Table 4 Future value of a £1 annuity, accumulated for n-years, compounded at i. $FV = \frac{£1}{i}[(1+i)^n - 1]$

Interest rates (%)

Periods (n)	1	2	3	4	5	6	7	8	9	10	11	12	13	14	15
1	1.0000	1.0000	1.0000	1.0000	1.0000	1.0000	1.0000	1.0000	1.0000	1.0000	1.0000	1.0000	1.0000	1.0000	1.0000
2	2.0100	2.0200	2.0300	2.0400	2.0500	2.0600	2.0700	2.0800	2.0900	2.1000	2.1100	2.1200	2.1300	2.1400	2.1500
3	3.0301	3.0604	3.0909	3.1216	3.1525	3.1836	3.2149	3.2464	3.2781	3.3100	3.3421	3.3744	3.4069	3.4396	3.4725
4	4.0604	4.1216	4.1836	4.2464	4.3101	4.3746	4.4399	4.5061	4.5731	4.6410	4.7097	4.7793	4.8498	4.9211	4.9934
5	5.1010	5.2040	5.3091	5.4163	5.5256	5.6371	5.7507	5.8666	5.9847	6.1051	6.2278	6.3528	6.4803	6.6101	6.7424
6	6.1520	6.3081	6.4684	6.6330	6.8019	6.9753	7.1533	7.3359	7.5233	7.7156	7.9129	8.1152	8.3227	8.5355	8.7537
7	7.2135	7.4343	7.6625	7.8983	8.1420	8.3938	8.6540	8.9228	9.2004	9.4872	9.7833	10.0890	10.4047	10.7305	11.0668
8	8.2857	8.5830	8.8923	9.2142	9.5491	9.8975	10.2598	10.6366	11.0285	11.4359	11.8594	12.2997	12.7573	13.2328	13.7268
9	9.3685	9.7546	10.1591	10.5828	11.0266	11.4913	11.9780	12.4876	13.0210	13.5795	14.1640	14.7757	15.4157	16.0853	16.7858
10	10.4622	10.9497	11.4639	12.0061	12.5779	13.1808	13.8164	14.4866	15.1929	15.9374	16.7220	17.5487	18.4197	19.3373	20.3037
11	11.5668	12.1687	12.8078	13.4864	14.2068	14.9716	15.7836	16.6455	17.5603	18.5312	19.5614	20.6546	21.8143	23.0445	24.3493
12	12.6825	13.4121	14.1920	15.0258	15.9171	16.8699	17.8885	18.9771	20.1407	21.3843	22.7132	24.1331	25.6502	27.2707	29.0017
13	13.8093	14.6803	15.6178	16.6268	17.7130	18.8821	20.1406	21.4953	22.9534	24.5227	26.2116	28.0291	29.9847	32.0887	34.3519
14	14.9474	15.9739	17.0863	18.2919	19.5986	21.0151	22.5505	24.2149	26.0192	27.9750	30.0949	32.3926	34.8827	37.5811	40.5047
15	16.0969	17.2934	18.5989	20.0236	21.5786	23.2760	25.1290	27.1521	29.3609	31.7725	34.4054	37.2797	40.4175	43.8424	47.5804
16	17.2579	18.6393	20.1569	21.8245	23.6575	25.6725	27.8881	30.3243	33.0034	35.9497	39.1899	42.7533	46.6717	50.9804	55.7175
17	18.4304	20.0121	21.7616	23.6975	25.8404	28.2129	30.8402	33.7502	36.9737	40.5447	44.5008	48.8837	53.7391	59.1176	65.0751
18	19.6147	21.4123	23.4144	25.6454	28.1324	30.9057	33.9990	37.4502	41.3013	45.5992	50.3959	55.7497	61.7251	68.3941	75.8364
19	20.8109	22.8406	25.1169	27.6712	30.5390	33.7600	37.3790	41.4463	46.0185	51.1591	56.9395	63.4397	70.7494	78.9692	88.2118
20	22.0190	24.2974	26.8704	29.7781	33.0660	36.7856	40.9955	45.7620	51.1601	57.2750	64.2028	72.0524	80.9468	91.0249	102.4436
25	28.2432	32.0303	36.4593	41.6459	47.7271	54.8645	63.2490	73.1059	84.7009	98.3471	114.4133	133.3339	155.6196	181.8708	212.7930

Periods (n)	16	17	18	19	20	21	22	23	24	25	26	27	28	29	30
1	1.0000	1.0000	1.0000	1.0000	1.0000	1.0000	1.0000	1.0000	1.0000	1.0000	1.0000	1.0000	1.0000	1.0000	1.0000
2	2.1600	2.1700	2.1800	2.1900	2.2000	2.2100	2.2200	2.2300	2.2400	2.2500	2.2600	2.2700	2.2800	2.2900	2.3000
3	3.5056	3.5389	3.5724	3.6061	3.6400	3.6741	3.7084	3.7429	3.7776	3.8125	3.8476	3.8829	3.9184	3.9541	3.9900
4	5.0665	5.1405	5.2154	5.2913	5.3680	5.4457	5.5242	5.6038	5.6842	5.7656	5.8480	5.9313	6.0156	6.1008	6.1870
5	6.8771	7.0144	7.1542	7.2966	7.4416	7.5892	7.7396	7.8926	8.0484	8.2070	8.3684	8.5327	8.6999	8.8700	9.0431
6	8.9775	9.2068	9.4420	9.6830	9.9299	10.1830	10.4423	10.7079	10.9801	11.2588	11.5442	11.8366	12.1359	12.4423	12.7560
7	11.4139	11.7720	12.1415	12.5227	12.9159	13.3214	13.7396	14.1708	14.6153	15.0735	15.5458	16.0324	16.5339	17.0506	17.5828
8	14.2401	14.7733	15.3270	15.9020	16.4991	17.1189	17.7623	18.4300	19.1229	19.8419	20.5876	21.3612	22.1634	22.9953	23.8577
9	17.5185	18.2847	19.0859	19.9234	20.7989	21.7139	22.6700	23.6690	24.7125	25.8023	26.9404	28.1287	29.3692	30.6639	32.0150
10	21.3215	22.3931	23.5213	24.7089	25.9587	27.2738	28.6574	30.1128	31.6434	33.2529	34.9449	36.7235	38.5926	40.5564	42.6195
11	25.7329	27.1999	28.7551	30.4035	32.1504	34.0013	35.9620	38.0388	40.2379	42.5661	45.0306	47.6388	50.3985	53.3178	56.4053
12	30.8502	32.8239	34.9311	37.1802	39.5805	42.1416	44.8737	47.7877	50.8950	54.2077	57.7386	61.5013	65.5100	69.7800	74.3270
13	36.7862	39.4040	42.2187	45.2445	48.4966	51.9913	55.7459	59.7789	64.1097	68.7596	73.7506	79.1066	84.8529	91.0161	97.6250
14	43.6720	47.1027	50.8180	54.8409	59.1959	63.9095	69.0100	74.5280	80.4961	86.9495	93.9258	101.4654	109.6117	118.4108	127.9125
15	51.6595	56.1101	60.9653	66.2607	72.0351	78.3305	85.1922	92.6694	100.8151	109.6868	119.3465	129.8611	141.3029	153.7500	167.2863
16	60.9250	66.6488	72.9390	79.8502	87.4421	95.7799	104.9345	114.9834	126.0108	138.1085	151.3766	165.9236	181.8677	199.3374	218.4722
17	71.6730	78.9792	87.0680	96.0218	105.9306	116.8937	129.0201	142.4295	157.2534	173.6357	191.7345	211.7230	233.7907	258.1453	285.0139
18	84.1407	93.4056	103.7403	115.2659	128.1167	142.4413	158.4045	176.1883	195.9942	218.0446	242.5855	269.8882	300.2521	334.0074	371.5180
19	98.6032	110.2846	123.4135	138.1664	154.7400	173.3540	194.2538	217.7116	244.0328	273.5558	306.6577	343.7580	385.3227	431.8696	483.9734
20	115.3797	130.0329	146.6280	165.4180	186.6880	210.7584	237.9893	268.7853	303.6006	342.9447	387.3887	437.5726	494.2131	558.1118	630.1655
25	249.2140	292.1049	342.6035	402.0425	471.9811	554.2422	650.9551	764.6054	898.0916	1054.7912	1238.6363	1454.2014	1706.8031	2002.6156	2348.8033

Index